Harry T. Burleigh

MUSIC IN AMERICAN LIFE

A list of books in the series appears at the end of this book.

Harry T. Burleigh

From the Spiritual to the Harlem Renaissance

JEAN E. SNYDER

University of Illinois Press

URBANA, CHICAGO, AND SPRINGFIELD

Frontispiece: Harry T. Burleigh, circa 1900.

Publication of this book was supported by grants from the
Lloyd Hibberd Endowment of the American Musicological
Society, funded in part by the National Endowment for the
Humanities and the Andrew W. Mellon Foundation and
from the Henry and Edna Binkele Classical Music Fund.

Library of Congress Cataloging-in-Publication Data
Names: Snyder, Jean E., 1939–
Title: Harry T. Burleigh : from the spiritual to the Harlem
    Renaissance / Jean E. Snyder.
Description: Urbana : University of Illinois Press, [2016] |
    Series: Music in American life | Includes bibliographical
    references and index.
Identifiers: LCCN 2015038368 | ISBN 9780252039942
    (hardcover : alk. paper) | ISBN 9780252098109 (e-book)
Subjects: LCSH: Burleigh, H. T. (Harry Thacker), 1866–1949. |
    Composers—United States—Biography. | African
    American composers—United States—Biography. | LCGFT:
    Biographies.
Classification: LCC ML410.B97 S69 2016 | DDC 780.92—dc23
    LC record available at http://lccn.loc.gov/2015038368

To the Burleigh Family and
Grace Elmendorf Blackwell
without whom this book could not have been written

Contents

Preface

I first became aware of Harry T. Burleigh as an arranger of spirituals in 1977, when my Nairobi, Kenya, friend Cathryn MBathi told me she needed some spirituals, any spirituals, "just so they are arranged by H. T. Burleigh." Cathryn and I sang together in Nairobi while I was on a teaching assignment for the Mennonite Central Committee. A second Africa teaching assignment, at Malcolm Moffat Teachers Training College in Serenje, Zambia, introduced me to ethnomusicology and the study of African story songs. Two years after I returned to the States, I entered the graduate ethnomusicology program at the University of Pittsburgh, expecting to return to Zambia for my dissertation research on Zambian story songs, with Professor J. H. Kwabena Nketia as my adviser. I chose to explore Harry T. Burleigh's work in two graduate seminars, and when personal circumstances made research in Zambia impossible, I turned my focus to Erie, Pennsylvania, several hours north of Pittsburgh, where Burleigh was born.

As a semiprofessional recital, oratorio, and church soloist, I was drawn to Burleigh as a singer. I don't remember when I learned to love African American spirituals; they have always been important to me, especially through the voices of Marian Anderson and Paul Robeson and more recently the voices of friends such as Bessie Sewell, Oral Moses, Bill Brown, Louise Toppin, and many others. When I discovered Burleigh's art songs, I wanted to help twentieth- and twenty-first-century singers reclaim them. As Burleigh's roles as music editor at G. Ricordi Music Publishing Company, recitalist, and mentor began to unfold for me, I determined to carry on the work Anne Key Simpson had begun in her book *Hard Trials: The Life and Work of Harry T. Burleigh.* As she moved on to other projects, Anne shared her Burleigh materials with me and encouraged my ongoing search.

My doctoral dissertation, "Harry T. Burleigh and the Creative Expression of Bi-Musicality: A Study of an African-American Composer and the American Art Song," was the first of several Burleigh projects. Then came two recordings with pianist Ann Sears: *Deep River: Songs and Spirituals of Harry T. Burleigh,* featuring bass-baritone Oral Moses, and *Fi-yer! A Century of African-American Song,* featuring the late tenor William A. Brown. At Edinboro University of Pennsylvania, I worked with colleagues Daniel Burdick and Constance Thompson Ratcliff to plan a series of five events featuring Burleigh's music and that of other African American composers, including the April 2003 national conference, "The Heritage and Legacy of Harry T. Burleigh."

It is gratifying to see greater awareness of Burleigh's accomplishments since the centenary celebrations of Antonín Dvořák's American sojourn, as scholars have examined Burleigh's role in introducing Dvořák to African American music. More singers are searching out Burleigh's art songs in libraries and archives for performance, for recordings, and for doctoral dissertations. It is my hope that this book will help singers, scholars, and general readers who love music to appreciate more fully the breadth and importance of Burleigh's contribution and will be inspired to learn more about this important period of America's cultural history.

* * *

Harry T. Burleigh, African American singer, art song composer, music editor, and pioneering arranger of spirituals, played a leading role in American music and culture throughout the last years of the nineteenth century and the first third of the twentieth century. His gifts as a singer and public speaker won him wide recognition in the Erie, Pennsylvania, community where he was born, and his success as a student and teacher at the National Conservatory of Music in New York City laid the foundation for a career as a singer and composer of art songs that would establish his reputation well beyond the borders of the United States. By the mid-1910s, Burleigh's songs were being performed by a lengthy international roster of opera and recital singers, some of whom considered them among the best American art songs being written.

Today Burleigh is known primarily for introducing Czech composer Antonín Dvořák to the African American oral music tradition and as an arranger of spirituals. Indeed, Burleigh led the way for both black and white composers in his solo and choral arrangements of spirituals in the early part of the twentieth century. His work helped preserve and transform one of America's earliest contributions to the world of music, the songs that arose out of the sufferings of slavery but that give voice to an indomitable human spirit and have engendered some of America's most vibrant musical traditions.

But Burleigh's legacy goes well beyond his songs, though they are central to his work. He was a leader in black New York's cultural and political environment well before what is known as the Harlem Renaissance. As role model, vocal coach, and mentor, his influence on younger African American singers, most of whom today are better known than Burleigh, was profound. As music editor at Ricordi, he not only gained access to publication of his own songs but also facilitated publication of works by other black composers. His office at Ricordi drew younger compos-ers who brought their work for Burleigh's editorial suggestions. The full range of Burleigh's influence requires careful examination, a task this book addresses while blazing paths for others to explore.

Why are Burleigh and his remarkable contemporaries largely forgotten one hundred years later? Part of the answer must lie in the complex and unsettling political and social conditions at the beginning of the twentieth century. Recon-struction offered African Americans a measure of political and economic equality after Emancipation, but a vicious backlash followed in the form of Jim Crow and the rise of the Ku Klux Klan in both the South and the North. Lynchings were frequent and unpredictable. The public stage persona of black Americans, though they sometimes participated in its realization, relied on demeaning stereotypes and caricature. It is an uncomfortable era to consider in depth. But just as African Americans had struggled relentlessly for freedom and individual rights before and during the Civil War, the hard-won twentieth-century civil-rights gains in all aspects of U.S. society and culture were built on the persistence and achieve-ment of African Americans throughout the nation in the late nineteenth and early twentieth centuries. Harry T. Burleigh and his family represent the unwavering determination and remarkable accomplishment that characterized many African Americans in this seminal period.

Harry T. Burleigh's biographer faces significant challenges. Though he was a public figure from his early twenties in Erie, Pennsylvania, and throughout his long career in New York City, relatively few primary documents remain to illu-minate his personal life and his private motivations. The late Josephine Harreld Love, whom Burleigh befriended during her years of study at the Juilliard School of Music, remembered seeing the meticulously kept daybooks in which Burleigh recorded his activities. But the daybooks, along with most of his other personal effects, were lost when the company that stored the contents of his Bronx apart-ment in the late 1940s went out of business. Some items in the possession of James Hall, Burleigh's godson, whose mother was Burleigh's housekeeper for many years, became unavailable in the 1990s after Hall's sudden death.

I have had the help of the Burleigh family, which Simpson did not have in writing *Hard Trials*. Like Simpson, I have relied on newspaper articles, programs, and interviews with people who knew Burleigh. But questions of reliability arise from even a cursory review of articles from the major New York City papers in the last decades of Burleigh's career. Other published accounts, even those by his acquaintances, some of whom he assisted, are often contradictory. It is difficult to know whether in some cases Burleigh gave his interviewers what they wanted, what would enhance the legend, rather than what he knew to be fact. Burleigh was an accomplished performer, and he certainly knew what the Horatio Alger American Dream paradigm demanded. Perhaps he himself relied on accounts that could not be substantiated. At any rate, as is true for any research, the biographer's task requires much careful sifting, corroborating, and cross-checking. I trust that others will build on my work, and there is no doubt that they will find errors of fact, if not of intent, as further research brings new information to the surface.

Burleigh's personality is revealed most clearly through his correspondence, though even here the complex public persona often shades his intensely private life. For example, his relationship with Booker T. Washington is recorded but not fully explained by the letters and telegrams that document their fifteen-year collaboration, during which Burleigh's charismatic singing loosened the purse-strings of the New England donors to Tuskegee Institute on Washington's fund-raising tours. In other letters, Burleigh's advice to younger singers and composers shows his commitment to helping them develop sophisticated professional expertise and win appropriate recognition. And his correspondence with some of the most distinguished critics and performers of his time demonstrates his active participation in the broad spectrum of New York's music world, black and white.

Burleigh's immediate success in New York City was no accident; it was prepared by his family and his early experiences and training. I owe much of my understanding of Burleigh's world during those early years to the indefatigable research on Erie's nineteenth-century black community by local historian Karen James. For fifteen years she searched public and private records, sifting for information that she was assured did not exist, and over and over again, she uncovered what was hidden in plain sight—the story of a vibrant, progressive, and accomplished black community, the social context of Burleigh's formative years. This background lends the record of Burleigh's public singing career in Erie depth and significance.

The Burleigh Society, which was founded in 1991, has been in hiatus since the sudden death in November of 2009 of Rev. Charles Kennedy Jr., its founder and president, and the Burleigh Society website has been taken down. However, Johnny Johnson, a retired teacher and charter member of the Burleigh Society, is the "keeper of the flame" of the Burleigh Society, and Karen James's research materials and the records of the Burleigh Society are in his possession.

I have learned much about the broader historical context of Burleigh's life from my husband, John G. Burt, who taught me that history is stories about people. His research on abolitionists in western Pennsylvania has been invaluable, and his enthusiastic support from the beginning has made this a happily collaborative effort.

*   *   *

A word about the organization of the book: The first seven chapters are chronological, beginning with his family background, and follow his studies at the National Conservatory of Music through the premiere and reception of Antonín Dvořák's Symphony No. 9 in E Minor, "From the New World." Chapters 8 through 18 are topical. Burleigh operated in so many arenas and contexts simultaneously that the topical approach offers a clearer understanding of his involvement and influence in a variety of spheres. This arrangement also makes it easier for readers who wish to focus on a specific aspect of his career.

My website, *Friends of Harry T. Burleigh,* makes some resources available that have not been included in the book: a detailed bibliography, a current discography, Burleigh's recital repertoire, a list of singers who performed his songs during his lifetime, and other resources that may interest those who value Burleigh's work. I intend the website to be a site where Burleigh singers, scholars, and other interested persons can exchange information and continue the search for deeper understanding of Burleigh's work and that of his contemporaries.

Acknowledgments

Many people and numerous libraries, archives, and collections have contributed to this research on the life and work of Harry T. Burleigh. First and foremost, the Burleigh family: Burleigh's grandson, the late Dr. Harry T. Burleigh II and his wife Mary, with their daughter Marie, have made letters, photographs, newspaper clippings, and scrapbooks available to me, helping to fill in many gaps in the story. I owe a profound debt of gratitude to Mrs. Burleigh, who spent countless hours going through the family papers, making photocopies and lists, and sharing invaluable information with me. Though she did not know her husband's grandfather personally, she talked freely and at length with me about what she knew of the family and the context of Burleigh's life. Happily, the family papers include documentation of Burleigh's early recital career; his marriage to Louise Alston, her writing and performance of dialect verse, and the dissolution of their relationship; the life and career of their son Alston; and Burleigh's mentoring of younger musicians. Dr. Burleigh himself answered many questions and shared his memories of his grandfather, and his daughter Marie sent scans of photographs and other materials.

The descendants of Burleigh's stepfather John Elmendorf have also assisted me. Great-granddaughter Monica Marshall Wilson shared family stories and photographs and the family Bible, which lists births, deaths, and marriages. Burleigh's niece, Grace Elmendorf Blackwell, whose father was Burleigh's half-brother Elzie Elmendorf, has shared generously her memories of Burleigh's last years. She has made photographs, letters, and other memorabilia available, and her accounts of her warm relationship with her Uncle Harry reveal a very human person behind the public figure. The extended family's enthusiasm and support of my research have made this a rewarding project.

* * *

I began my Burleigh research in the Carnegie Library of Pittsburgh; thanks to Kathryn Logan and her staff in the Music and Art Department there. The staff of the Baron-Forness Library at Edinboro University of Pennsylvania has always been helpful and supportive; special thanks to Judy Rauenswinter for her persistent help in fulfilling many requests for microfilms and Interlibrary Loan materials. The staff at the Heritage Room of the Erie County Public Library was always helpful. And very special thanks are due Annita Andrick, archivist at the Erie County Historical Society, who with her Library and Archives intern Allyson Hoover provided key locator information for sources in their collection even while they were in the midst of moving their collection to a new location. I found much help from staff and resources in the following archives and libraries: James Weldon Johnson Collection, Beinecke Rare Books and Manuscript Library, Yale University, New Haven, Connecticut; Connecticut Historical Society, Hartford, Connecticut; Library of Congress Music Division and Manuscripts Division and the Moorland-Spingarn Research Center, Howard University, all in Washington, D.C.; Archives of the Robert W. Woodruff Library at Clark Atlanta University, the Manuscript, Archives, and Rare Book Library of Emory University, and the Auburn Avenue Research Library on African American Culture and History, all in Atlanta, Georgia; Burge Plantation, Newton County, Georgia; Bar Harbor Archives, Bar Harbor, Maine; Boston Public Library, Boston, Massachusetts; Roland Hayes Papers, E. Azalia Hackley Collection, Detroit Public Library, Detroit, Michigan; Buffalo and Erie County History Museum, Buffalo, New York; the Morgan Library, the Theater Collection of the Museum of the City of New York, the New York Public Library for the Performing Arts at Lincoln Center, the Schomberg Research Center of the New York Public Library, all in New York, New York; Archives and Special Collections Library, Vassar College, Poughkeepsie, New York; Erie County Historical Society, Erie County Public Library, and Sister Mary Lawrence Franklin Archival Center, Mercyhurst University, Erie, Pennsylvania; the Free Library of Philadelphia, and the Marian Anderson Collection, Annenberg Center for the Performing Arts, University of Pennsylvania, both in Philadelphia, Pennsylvania.

I have been blessed by the friendship and support of a host of singers and scholars too numerous to name here, whose continued interest and encouragement have made the journey endlessly rewarding. Special thanks to Ann Sears for her partnership in numerous Burleigh projects, including two recordings available from Albany Records: *Deep River: Songs and Spirituals of Harry T. Burleigh,* with bassbaritone Oral Moses; and *Fi-yer!: A Century of Songs by African American Composers,* with the late tenor William A. Brown. Ann provided the accompaniment for both recordings and supervised the production. Ann, Sandra Graham, Brian Moon, Marva Carter, and the late Catherine Parsons-Smith have been especially supportive colleagues along the way. Profound thanks to my faithful general readers, Carol Hayes and Richard O'Keefe, who read and commented on every chapter. And thanks to the following, who read and commented on one or more chapters or passages: Luciana Bohne, John Burt, Marva Carter, Dale Cockerell, Catherine Drew, Samuel A. Floyd Jr., Sandra Graham, Maben Herring, Johnny Johnson, Ralph P. Locke, Brian Moon, Rene Lapp Norris, Catherine Parsons-Smith, Willis Patterson, Frank G. Pogue, Thomas Riis, Deane L. Root, Adrienne Rush, Ann Sears, Darryl Taylor, Sarah S. Thompson, LeAnne Wistrom, and Josephine Wright. Thanks also to Jake Gibson and Ronuel Viera, who formatted the music examples, and to Bill Brooks, who corrected and reformatted them. My editor, Laurie Matheson, has been an indispensable guide and supporter throughout the preparation of this biography. Her enthusiasm and encouragement have given me hope when the task seemed interminable. Tad Ringo, who shepherded the manuscript through the production process, deserves special thanks. To my husband John Burt, whose passion for "the nineteenth, greatest of centuries," added depth to my understanding of the world that shaped Burleigh and his family, my love and thanks for your wholehearted and unconditional support.

Chronology of Major Events in the Life of Harry T. Burleigh

1832   Hamilton Waters is granted manumission, with his mother, Lovey Waters, by James Tilghman of Somerset County, Maryland.

1835   Certificate of Freedom is granted for Hamilton Waters and Lovey Waters.

1837   On June 18, Hamilton Waters and Lucinda Duncanson are married in Auburn, New York.

1838   On April 12, Elizabeth Waters born in Lansing, New York. The Waters family moves to Erie, Pennsylvania. Henry Thacker Burley is born in Newburgh, New York.

1855   Elizabeth Waters graduates from Allegheny Institute and Seminary (later known as Avery College) in Allegheny, Pennsylvania, now Pittsburgh's North Side.

1862   On September 17, Elizabeth Waters and Henry Thacker Burley marry.

1863   On September 27, Henry Thacker Burley Jr. is born; he dies three months later.

1864   Henry Thacker Burley joins the Union Navy in September; Reginald Waters Burleigh is born on November 14.

1865   Henry Thacker Burley returns from service in the Union Navy.

1866   On December 12, Henry (Harry) Thacker Burleigh is born.

1867   Lucinda Duncanson Waters dies August 26.

1868   Ada Burleigh [Burley] is born; dies of consumption at age 14.

1869   Hamilton Waters and members of the Henry Thacker Burley family are confirmed at St. Paul's Episcopal Cathedral.

1870   On December 11, Eva Grace Burley is born.

1871   In March, Henry Thacker Burley serves as first the black juror in Erie County.

1873   On February 24, Henry Thacker Burley dies suddenly in Chicago.

1875   On April 15, Elizabeth Burley and John Elmendorf marry.

1877   On February 6, Hamilton Waters dies.

1885   Harry Burleigh's name begins to appear as soloist in public programs of the Erie High School, Clark Business College, YMCA, and church events.

1887   Harry T. Burleigh graduates from Erie High School; gives commencement speech, "How Far Shall We Educate?" reported verbatim in Erie *Morning Dispatch*.

1892   In January, Harry Burleigh leaves for New York City to study at the National Conservatory of Music; John Elmendorf, with his son Elzie, opens a stable for gentlemen's horses. On June 25, Burleigh sings with soprano Sissieretta Jones at Carnegie Recital Hall. In September, Antonín Dvořák arrives to be the director of the conservatory.

1893   Burleigh often sings plantation songs and spirituals for Dvořák. Dvořák completes his Symphony No. 9, "From the New World," in May; premiere performance December 15. On August 25, Burleigh sings at Colored American Day program at the Chicago World's Fair.

1894   Harry Burleigh and Paul Bolin are appointed teachers in "the new department for black students 'of exceptional talent.'" In May, Burleigh is hired as baritone soloist at St. George's Protestant Episcopal Church in Stuyvesant Square.

1896   Burleigh's song "Christmas Bells" is published by St. George's Episcopal Church.

1898   Burleigh serves as conductor for the Williams and Walker *Senegambian Carnival* at Koster and Bial's Music Hall in New York City; Louise Alston joins the company in September. Burleigh's first art songs are published by William Maxwell.

1899   On February 9, Harry T. Burleigh and Louise Alston are married in the home of her mother, Rachel Farley, in Brookland, now part of Washington, D.C.; On August 18, Alston Waters Burleigh is born at Thirty-Third Street and Seventh Avenue, New York City.

1900   On January 23, Burleigh sings two recitals in Albany, New York, one at an afternoon reception at the home of Governor Theodore Roosevelt. Burleigh begins fifteen-year collaboration with Booker T. Washington, singing for Washington's fund-raising tours for Tuskegee Institute. He is hired to sing at Temple Emanu-El.

1903   Burleigh's first commercial success, "Jean," is published.

1908   Burleigh and his wife spend some weeks in London, where he sings for British royalty, partly arranged by contacts from J. P. Morgan and Booker T. Washington.

1909	The Burleighs return to London; Louise places their son Alston in Malden College for Boys and performs as Indian Princess Redfeather in London music halls.
1914	The Burleighs bring Alston home as the war in Europe begins; Alston is placed in Hopkins Grammar School in New Haven, Connecticut.
1915	Harry and Louise separate; Alston is sent to Washington, D.C., where he lives with his grandmother, Rachel Farley.
1917	Burleigh's first arrangements of "Deep River" and several other spirituals sung by Oscar Seagle and many other singers; "Deep River" said to be the song most often performed in the 1916–17 season.
1918	Louise Alston Burleigh leaves New York City to pursue her career as Princess Nadonis Shawa in Wisconsin.
1924	The first Vesper Service of Negro Spirituals, celebrating Burleigh's 30th anniversary as baritone soloist, is held at St. George's Episcopal Church; it becomes an annual event that draws overflow crowds and feature articles in New York City newspapers; the service is broadcast, the first of many radio broadcasts of Burleigh's voice, singing spirituals.
1925	Burleigh resigns his position at Temple Emanu-El.
1944	Burleigh's 50th anniversary at St. George's Episcopal Church.
1946	In November, Burleigh retires as soloist at St. George's.
1947	Alston places his father in a convalescent home in Amityville, Long Island, then at Stamford Hall, in Stamford, Connecticut.
1949	On September 12, Burleigh dies; his body lies in state in St. George's Chapel of Peace for two days before the funeral, mourned by millionaires and "the plain people of Harlem." He is buried in Mt. Hope Cemetery in Hastings-on-Hudson, New York.
1991	The Burleigh Society is founded by Rev. Charles Kennedy Jr. at Mercyhurst College in Erie, Pennsylvania.
1994	The Burleigh Society, with Burleigh's grandson, Dr. Harry T. Burleigh II, bring Burleigh's body back to be reinterred with appropriate ceremony in the Erie Cemetery in Erie, Pennsylvania, on May 29.

PART I

Erie, Pennsylvania:
Foundation for a National Career

1. Hamilton Waters and the Struggle for Freedom and Education

"Originality, versatility, and patient toil"

To understand how a twenty-five-year-old African American man could leave his home town of Erie, Pennsylvania, in January 1892, take the train to the untidy but exhilarating bustle of New York City; win a scholarship for the Artist's Course at the National Conservatory of Music; become Antonín Dvořák's assistant and instructor in the music of the Negro slaves; earn renown as a singer in the homes of the wealthy robber barons of New York City's Gilded Age; make a place for himself in the city's relentlessly white classical music establishment; and represent African Americans as their premiere baritone and leading composer in the first decades of the twentieth century, we must know what shaped him and from what surroundings he came. We must tease out his family history from the few and sometimes unreliable sources available to us, acquaint ourselves with the family and community that nurtured him, tune our ears to the music that surrounded him, and listen to the narratives that encapsulate important themes in the family mythology.

Harry T. Burleigh's family knew their worth as human beings and as American citizens long before the laws of the land defined them as fully human and eligible for the rights of citizenship. To understand who Burleigh was, it is important to know the family who shaped his character and encouraged him to aim for a career that was all but impossible for a black singer of his time. Two generations of Burleigh's family persistently refused to accept the dominant society's definitions, and Burleigh learned from them how to work toward fulfilling his impossible dreams. He would encourage and mentor several generations of African American concert musicians who followed his lead.

* * *

The story of Harry T. Burleigh, as we know it today, begins on March 5, 1832, in Somerset County, Maryland, when his grandfather, Hamilton Elzie Waters, "being of the age of twenty nine years or thereabouts and able to work and gain a sufficient livelihood and maintenance," arranged to purchase his freedom for fifty dollars and that of his mother, Lovey Waters, for five dollars, from slaveholder James Tilghman.[1] The accounts of this transaction and the partial blindness that made it possible leave many questions unanswered but highlight important themes that recur in the family history. The narrative highlights values and attitudes that defined Harry T. Burleigh's character and personality and that ultimately shaped his career. As a young boy who often led his blind grandfather by the hand, Burleigh heard the stories and songs that would become his trademark, but he also absorbed the stalwart sense of self that made it possible for him to function with assurance and dignity as he confronted the barriers that might limit his achievement.

The manumission papers and bill of sale set the price for their freedom, but Waters and his mother would not actually be free until three years later when Waters had earned the money to complete the sale. As Tilghman was a small farmer with assets of no more than $1,000, it is likely that Tilghman allowed Waters to hire himself out to other employers and so fulfill the purchase contract, relieving him of some of the expense of supporting Hamilton and his mother. Other members of the Waters family were held as slaves on farms near the Tilghman farm.[2] On April 13, 1835, the sale process was complete, and Hamilton Waters was issued a Certificate of Freedom that would allow him and his mother (whom he, a "free negro," now owned) to travel out of the state of Maryland. Waters's Certificate of Freedom asserts that he was "the identical person who was manumitted by a certain James Tilghman" and describes him as "five feet eight inches in height and of a bright mulatto complexion." To assure that he could be identified, the description continues, "He has a large scar on the left ankle; a mark on the left wrist & a scar on the under lip—he has a defect in the eyes and is partially blind. He is orderly and intelligent, about thirty two years of age and a native of Somerset County."[3]

It was imperative that Waters and his mother leave the state immediately, as a Maryland law reenacted in 1825 stipulated that "free Blacks who could not give 'security' for proper behavior" would be banished. It was dangerous even to cross Maryland's borders, as "any free Black traveling through the state had to find a job or leave the state within 15 days." The smallest penalty for lingering was a fine of $30 per day; the ultimate penalty was to be sold into slavery.[4] A more oppressive law was passed in 1840 that would have affected other members of the family who were still enslaved.[5] But by 1840, Lovey Waters had died, and Hamilton Waters had settled in Erie, Pennsylvania, with his wife, Lucinda Duncanson Waters, and their first daughter, Elizabeth Lovey Waters, who would be Harry T. Burleigh's mother. They were free and living in the North, but memories of slavery and the knowledge that their freedom was always in jeopardy would persist for nearly thirty years.

His partial blindness was one reason Waters was allowed to purchase his freedom. The cause of his blindness has become part of the Burleigh legend that is now impossible to document conclusively. Burleigh told an interviewer in 1944, "I've been told that my grandfather's owner found a spelling book under his blouse and gave him 70 lashes for it. Slaves were forbidden to study, you know. Perhaps the lash hit the optic nerve. Any how [sic], grandfather went blind. A blind slave wasn't any good, so he was turned out to shift for himself. Somehow he worked his way north from Maryland to Erie, Pa. When I was a little boy I led him around by the hand."[6]

In 1835 Waters was only partially blind, and it was not until 1867 that the *Erie City Directory* described him as blind. Waters's sight seems to have deteriorated gradually, and though visually restricted, he was able to function effectively in supporting his family for a number of years. The account of Waters being whipped for reading corresponds to other narratives of slavery, but in many places the ban against reading did not gain force until after Nat Turner's rebellion in 1831, just a year before Waters purchased his freedom. Whether all the details of Harry Burleigh's account are factual or not, the account demonstrates Waters's thirst for knowledge and explains his determination that his daughters be educated to the highest level possible. The sketchy nature of the account suggests that the story was part of a vague but significant family narrative.

The interplay of myth and reality in this narrative illustrates the difficulty in documenting the lives of African Americans before Emancipation. Even when printed accounts are available, they are often contradictory and details printed as fact may be merely speculative. But several defining characteristics of Hamilton Waters and his family are clear. Waters was determined to win his freedom: freedom to read, to learn, to go beyond the limits imposed by slavery; and freedom from the condition of servitude that bound him and his family. "Orderly and intelligent," he was willing to pursue the legal means available to him, and as he would demonstrate many times, he was quick to assert his rights as a citizen and to support the rights of others. These themes dominate the family history: the importance of family, the refusal to accept racial limitations, the preference for working for change within the social constructs available, and the tenacious pursuit of the highest level of education available.

* * *

In 1835 Hamilton Waters and his mother migrated from Maryland to Ithaca, New York, where his half-brother Henry Johnson was minister of the St. James African Methodist Episcopal Zion (A.M.E.Z.) Church.[7] Ithaca was a transfer point on the Underground Railroad and the St. James Church was an active Underground Railroad station. Waters and his mother settled with the Johnsons in Ithaca until her death two years later.[8] A family trait that raises additional questions about the cause of Hamilton Waters's blindness is that other members of the Johnson family, including a half-brother, William F. Johnson, his son William F. Jr., and his grand-daughter Florence also had eye problems that eventually resulted in blindness.[9]

Waters could purchase only his mother's freedom and his own in 1832, but like many whose families were fractured and scattered during slavery, immediately after Emancipation he attempted to find other members of his family. He advertised in the *Christian Recorder*, the official organ of the African Methodist Episcopal (A.M.E.) church, for word of family members he had left behind: "Information wanted of Matilda Waters, who formerly belonged to a man by the name of Levin Waters, of Princess Ann, Somerset Co., Maryland. She was married to Jeremy Horsey. She had four children when I saw her last, about thirty years ago. Also, of my brother, Simon Cater, or Simon Waters. I should like to hear from him. Also, of Rinaldo Turner, Sandy Anderson and Wm. Handy. Any information of the whereabouts of the said persons can be sent to the Book Store, No. 619 Pine St., Philadelphia—or to HAMILTON E. WATERS, Erie, Pennsylvania."[10] There is no record of whether Waters received a response from this query, but the family stayed in contact with the Johnsons, some of whom later migrated to Brooklyn, New York.

While Hamilton Waters was working toward his emancipation, the life of his future wife was also changing in dramatic ways. In the family narrative, Lucinda Duncanson was the daughter of a Scottish immigrant and an American Indian. She was serving in the household of retired circuit judge Enos Thompson Throop in 1829 when he was elected lieutenant governor of New York. When President Andrew Jackson appointed Governor Martin Van Buren his secretary of state, Throop filled out the term as acting governor of New York.[11] Thus Lucinda Duncanson came to serve in the governor's mansion in Albany, New York, where her grandson would spend the night after singing at a reception there seventy years later.

How and when Lucinda Duncanson left Throop's service is not known, and there is no record of how she and Hamilton Waters met. It has been assumed that she was a free woman, but her status has not been confirmed by documents. The Throop estate was less than fifty miles from Ithaca, and it was not unusual for persons with Native American ancestry to become part of the African American community. The Burleigh Family Bible, now in the hands of Burleigh's great-nephew, John Marshall, a descendant of Burleigh's stepfather, states that Lovey Waters died in Ithaca on May 18, 1837, and several weeks later, on June 10, 1837, Hamilton Waters and Lucinda Duncanson were married in Auburn, New York, near the Throop estate. Their first daughter, Elizabeth Lovie (or Lovy Eliza) was born on April 12, 1838, in Lansing, New York, just outside Ithaca.[12]

* * *

Later in 1838 the Waters family arrived in Erie, Pennsylvania, a small community with a population of less than 3,500.[13] Erie would be the family's home for three generations. There are accounts of freedmen being referred to specific persons in Erie, so no doubt Waters knew he would find a welcoming black community there. The intensity of the Underground Railroad activity in both Ithaca and Erie suggests that the Waters family left Ithaca bound specifically for Erie, and that they were referred to Erie's African American barber, Robert Vosburgh, who became Hamilton Waters's employer and colleague in the Underground Railroad effort.[14]

A half-century later, the Waters family was described in one of the few entries featuring black citizens in the 1896 *Nelson's Biographical Dictionary*. They were an "interesting and unobtrusive family" who came to Erie from Michigan "about the year 1838." Hamilton E. Waters, "the head of the family," was "a person whose originality, versatility and patient toil in all the avenues of life then open to him, made him a favorite with some of our leading citizens, who soon discovered his competency and perfect reliability." Southern whites were known for their "gentility," and Hamilton Waters's "manners and bearing supported his statement of Southern origin." His wife Lucinda Duncanson was from the North, but as she "had been in the household of Governor Throop," her association with society's leaders could explain her admirable character: "Her dialect, conversation and manners revealed the good breeding and polish of the best society, among whom her early life was evidently spent."[15]

A major source for Burleigh's biographers, this account raises several questions. It claims that the Waters family came to Erie from Michigan, and that Elizabeth's birthplace was Lansing, Michigan. Elizabeth Waters Burleigh Elmendorf was still living in 1896; surely she would have known that her birthplace was in New York rather than Michigan, but the author apparently failed to verify the accuracy of his account. Further, what is implied in the description of them as an "interesting and unobtrusive family"? Though laudatory, the description betrays an unconscious paternalism. It also reveals what was important to Erie's white community as they saw free African Americans moving to the area—that their own lives not be disrupted by those who lived on the margins of white society.

Hamilton Waters's "originality, versatility and patient toil in all the avenues of life then open to him" were reflected in the lives of his children and grandchildren, as were the "good breeding and polish of the best society" that characterized his wife's "dialect, conversation and manners."[16] The condescension in these descriptions does not fully credit, however, the active role the Waters family played in Erie's complex society from the time of their arrival in 1838 through Burleigh's early life in the latter part of the century.

In 1841, three years after the Waters family arrived in Erie, their second daughter, Louisa, was born, and in 1846 a third, Jane Simpson (or Sampson) Waters, arrived. Jane died in 1851 just after her fifth birthday.[17] Hamilton and Lucinda Waters and their two surviving daughters established themselves as active members of the small black community in Erie. Unlike Waters's employer, the enterprising barber Robert Vosburgh, and several others who managed to win a measure of financial independence, the Waters were working-class people, but like free blacks throughout the North and the South, their focus on education and on securing a better life for their children built a strong foundation for achievement and upward social mobility in the generations that followed.

The 1896 account and reports of Burleigh's early life suggest that the Waters family was warmly received and their accomplishments affirmed by the broader community. But personal accounts show that most of the white community in Erie did not welcome African Americans in 1838. In Pennsylvania black persons born before 1780 could still be in bondage for life. Erie's black community included some who were born free; others who, like Hamilton Waters, had purchased their freedom; and still others who were fugitives from plantations in the South. Those born after the Gradual Abolition Act instituted on November 1, 1780, were slaves until twenty-eight years of age. The Waters family lived in a community whose members represented various degrees of servitude and freedom. A few of Erie's white citizens supported the abolition of slavery, but this view was not widespread. Diaries and letters describe jeering and rock-throwing incidents that made daily life uncomfortable for Erie's black citizens.[18] The black community was too small to be perceived as a threat to the white majority, but social equality was not easily won. African Americans found their primary support in one another rather than in benevolent white citizens.[19]

* * *

Spreading southward from Presque Isle Bay on Lake Erie, the town of Erie, Pennsylvania, was incorporated in 1795, nine years after the Revolutionary War and forty-three years before the Waters family arrived. In 1799 the first schooner was launched in Erie's harbor. In 1824 the first official survey of Erie's harbor was conducted, and "by 1825, steamships were arriving and leaving daily." Shipbuilder Rufus Reed built the docks at the north end of State Street in 1815 and opened Reed's Wharf at the foot of Sassafras Street. Shipbuilding was a lucrative trade, and cargoes of grain, coal, and iron ore gathered from western Pennsylvania's fields and mines were routed through the Erie docks to many distant points.[20] Hamilton Waters and his family members worked with and for some of Erie's wealthiest citizens, among them the Reed family; William L. Scott, a coal and railroad magnate who later became a member of the U.S. Congress; William Himrod, a partner in Vincent, Himrod & Co., successful iron founders and merchants; William S. Curry, one of the founders of the Second National Bank of Erie; and J. F. Downing, a prominent insurance agent.

By the time the Waters family arrived in Erie, several free black families had established businesses in this growing city. Robert Vosburgh had settled in Erie twenty years earlier, and like black entrepreneurs in many other northern cities, opened a barbershop, one of the few trades readily available to African Americans. By 1838 Vosburgh anchored the black community, providing employment and assistance to other freedmen as they arrived. He invested in land and could provide his family the cultural and educational benefits of middle-class life. His shop offered dry-cleaning services as well as barbering, and he hired Hamilton Waters as a presser and cleaner of clothes.[21]

Waters worked with Vosburgh and others committed to helping fugitive slaves escape to Canada. Vosburgh's shop provided assistance to fugitives grateful for grooming who also might need the disguise a resourceful barber could provide. Escape from and abolition of slavery were not the only challenges to African American citizens. In 1838 when the Waters family arrived in Erie, the Pennsylvania voters ratified a new state constitution barring black citizens from voting, so the struggle for justice needed to be waged on many fronts.[22] During the next thirty years the many changes in U.S. society would be reflected in the lives of Hamilton Waters's children, bringing both hope and disillusionment, and finally causing his grandchildren to leave Erie to find greater opportunities elsewhere.

Details of everyday life for the Waters family are elusive, but public records show that Waters took full advantage of his rights as a citizen. Soon after his arrival in Erie, he testified in a court case on behalf of the daughter of his employer, eleven-year-old Susan Vosburgh, who fifty years later would be Harry Burleigh's piano teacher. While the Vosburghs were picnicking with the family of Oliver Mevis, a white man, the children began to fight. When Susan was insulted by name-calling, she responded with physical force. She was charged with assault and battery, and her father Robert was fined $100 "to secure the peace."[23] Whether or not the judgment was fair in naming Susan the culprit, it is notable that in Erie, the point was settled by rule of law. In many places in the United States black citizens would not have been granted this right, and such a confrontation would have brought serious if not fatal retribution against the Waters family.

In the early 1850s Hamilton Waters purchased property near the docks at the north end of State Street, at 137 Third Street, lot 2679, where he would later build the family home. When his right to own property was challenged, he did not hesitate to defend himself by both physical and legal means. In 1852, James Dutton (presumably white) charged him with assault and battery in an altercation over the property. Ten years later, after Waters had built the house on this site, he was threatened in his home by William Bladen, a former slave and the son of Boe Bladen, the first black man to hold property in Millcreek Township, southwest of the city of Erie. Waters filed charges. He did not tolerate treatment he regarded as unjust from either his white or his black neighbors.[24]

While Waters readily claimed his own legal rights, he spent most of his energy working for education and better conditions for his family and his fellow African Americans. In 1858 he was a founding member of the United Benevolent Equal Rights Society, a mutual aid society to protect and support members of the black community. The society's constitution echoes the Declaration of Independence: "All men are created free and equal and endowed with certain inalienable rights, among which are life, liberty and the pursuit of happiness." Inserting the word *free* underlines the essential injustice of slavery—all persons are created free and are entitled to live as free citizens. A Vigilance Committee would "enquire after the interests of the Society" and "visit the Sick and report their condition to the President, who shall act as circumstances may require." They would also be on the lookout for fugitive slaves who needed assistance while they assured the safety and wellbeing of their members. Initiation fees and monthly membership fees (seventy-five cents and twelve and one-half cents, respectively) formed a fund that might be invested in real estate. Members could borrow from this resource or the money could be used to care for members and their families or their survivors.[25]

* * *

The history of the educational opportunities available to African Americans in nineteenth-century Erie reflects the progressive nature of the abolitionist movement as well as its ironies. One of the most prominent Erie abolitionists, William Himrod Sr., established the first schools for "the colored and destitute"; Hamilton Waters and his family were associated with the Himrods in the abolitionist cause and benefited from his educational leadership for many years. Himrod was a conductor on the Underground Railroad, and both his home and the school offered sanctuary to fugitive slaves. His son later recounted that it "was no uncommon occurrence to find one or more slaves, awaiting transportation, in the kitchen or dining-room" when he came to breakfast. No one in the family questioned who the stranger was. They knew "he was seeking for that which he was unable to obtain in this country, his freedom," and they knew they were "to do all in [their] power to make him comfortable and see that he was unmolested."[26]

Freedom from slavery was not enough. Freedmen needed a basic education to take their place as productive citizens. In 1824 Himrod established a "Colored School" that served both black and white students. Some students are identified on the enrollment lists as "colored" but there is no indication that they were treated differently from their white classmates. In the school's early years, nearly half of the black residents of Erie County, adults and youth, attended, but since the black community numbered only a small percentage of the population, the majority of the students who attended were white. After several years the school closed.[27]

In 1839, in response to a sympathetic white teacher's efforts to accommodate two African American students, Himrod established the French Street Sabbath School for Colored Persons, later known as the Himrod Mission. Hamilton Waters was one of the first students to enroll, and he may have been one of the two who asked to be admitted to the public school. He attended faithfully until he died in 1877. A Sunday-afternoon Sabbath school, Himrod Mission focused on Bible study but also offered instruction in reading, writing, and arithmetic. Many of Erie's black citizens attended the mission, hungry for education as well as spiritual nourishment. Young Harry Burleigh led his blind grandfather to the Himrod Mission on Sunday afternoons, and this was one place in Erie where Negro spirituals were sung.[28]

Waters and his descendants were active members at the Himrod Mission throughout its entire history until it closed in 1912. At the mission's thirty-seventh anniversary in 1876, Hamilton Waters was the only original scholar still living, and he died the following year. Thirteen years later, at the fiftieth anniversary celebration in 1889, singing by Harry Burleigh and other members of his family was "a leading feature of the excellent music provided for the occasion."[29]

* * *

William Himrod's commitment to the abolition of slavery was genuine, but the leadership at the Himrod Mission and all the teachers were white. Himrod, his son William Jr., and his grandson in turn served as its superintendent. Only after his death did black members assume minor leadership roles. Burleigh's aunt, Louisa Waters, served as chorister and occasionally as organist.[30]

Though they appreciated Himrod's work, Hamilton Waters and several other black members were not satisfied with a subservient position. In 1846 Waters helped establish a school that served "all people, sexes, conditions, colors and denominations."[31] The school's founders believed that women as well as men should be educated, and Waters's later choice of a college education for his elder daughter Elizabeth confirmed his commitment to education for women. Elizabeth and her sister Louisa attended the Colored School established by their father and others of the black community as children, and after her graduation from Avery College in 1855, Elizabeth became a teacher there. At its twelfth anniversary celebration in 1858, the enrollment was 300.[32]

A year after founding this Colored School, Waters and four others—William Messick, John Clifford, Amos Burgess, and Luman Harris—formed the Wesleyan Methodist (Colored) Society in the northwest part of Erie known as Jerusalem.[33] Four years earlier, in 1843, Orange Scott and others had gathered in Utica, New York, to found the Wesleyan Methodist Connection of America, to protest the refusal of the Methodist General Conference to take an official stand supporting the abolition of slavery. Wesleyan Methodists were among the most outspoken abolitionists, and their churches in the Erie area were centers of Underground Railroad activity. Not all of the black Himrod members joined the Wesleyan congregation; some were comfortable with Himrod's leadership. Like Robert Vosburgh, Himrod provided employment to a number of black citizens who depended on him for their livelihood as well as their place of worship. But Waters and his collaborators insisted on independence and opportunities for leadership in their school and church affiliations as well as in their employment.[34]

Jerusalem, where the Wesleyan Methodists established their church, was an area in northwest Erie that William Himrod Sr. purchased in 1827 "to offer 'newly freed blacks and destitute whites' an opportunity to purchase a small homestead." "Jerusalem was located on Erie's West Side, from Sixth Street north to the Bay Front and from Sassafras Street west to about Cherry Street. . . . [It was] a remote area and not easily reached from downtown Erie, making the area ideal for anti-slavery action."[35] Because of their abolitionist stance, the Wesleyan Methodist (Colored) Society in Erie was not well received among the majority of the white population, and few records of its activities remain. But surviving records show that the Wesleyans served the black community well. In the 1860s they built a new building, and in 1874 the congregation became the nucleus of the St. James A.M.E. church, which for more than forty years was the only black church in Erie.[36] The congregation has met in several locations but continues in the twenty-first century to be one of the most active black churches in Erie County at its location on East Eleventh Street.

The Himrod Mission and the Wesleyan Methodist (Colored) Society served Erie's black citizens, but segregation in worship in the nineteenth century was not as rigid as it became later, in the twentieth century. Some white churches in Erie (such as the Episcopal Cathedral of St. Paul) that in the twentieth century found it expedient to segregate their black parishioners were less restrictive in the nineteenth century. Some black families joined white churches, and it was not unusual for persons to attend more than one church, regardless of denomination, as was true in Burleigh's family. His grandmother, Lucinda Duncanson Waters, joined the First Presbyterian Church, and later his grandfather Hamilton was baptized in St. Paul's Episcopal Cathedral, as were his daughters and his grandchildren. Burleigh's mother Elizabeth and his Aunt Louisa were active at St. Paul's; Louisa Waters had a pew at the rear of the church, and Elizabeth Waters Elmendorf was active in the cathedral's Women's Friendly Society.

In the twenty-first century both the predominantly white Episcopal Cathedral of St. Paul and the predominantly black St. James A.M.E. Church legitimately claim Harry T. Burleigh and his family in their historical accounts. During the years when St. James did not have a licensed pastor, sacraments such as baptisms, weddings, and funerals were often performed at St. Paul's, and members of the Waters family and their descendants appear in that church's records, as do other black families. But their membership at St. Paul's was to some extent a formality, as most of the family's social activities centered in the St. James A.M.E. congregation.

* * *

Life for the Waters family was "a struggle through many years, especially in consequence of the uneasiness and commotion prevailing among all of their race in the Western States, after the enactment of the Fugitive Slave Law, which made a change of residence essential for so many."[37] Hamilton Waters was not inclined to run from danger, though he must have considered carefully the risk to his family and the relatively short distance from Erie to safety in Canada. But the Waters family remained in Erie, joining with others in both the black and the white communities to assist "the weary travelers" to freedom.

The 1850 Fugitive Slave Act shocked many white Americans who opposed slavery in principle but had been content to accept the status quo. Abolitionists, appalled at the terms of the Fugitive Slave Law, were energized to speak out more decisively for the abolition of slavery and to act more boldly in defense of African Americans, both free citizens and fugitives. Among this group in Erie were Henry Catlin, an outspoken young white abolitionist, and his father-in-law, Jehiel Towner. The Erie *Observer* warned that residents should obey the law, and "not the conscience. . . . What may be deemed a conscientious act by one individual may be held criminal in another."[38] But Henry Catlin was not intimidated.

In 1853 he founded an antislavery and temperance weekly, *The True American,* which he sold for three cents a copy. Catlin billed it as "an uncompromising Political and Reform paper" that solicited "the support and sympathy of all friends of Human Progress." He called it "a medium of free discussion for all manner of men and women, except slaveholders, rumsellers, and codfish aristocrats."[39]

The paper bins in Catlin's printing shop sometimes hid fugitives, and he and his father-in-law worked with others like Frank Henry, another conductor on the Underground Railway. One account documents an instance when Hamilton Waters collaborated with Catlin's father-in-law Jehiel Towner in assisting fugitives. Towner sent a coded message to Frank Henry: "The mirage lifts Long Point [Canada] into view. Come up and see the beautiful sight. I can't promise a view tomorrow."[40] Henry met Towner in Erie and agreed to help three passengers hidden in town to cross the lake into Canada. At dusk the following evening, Hamilton Waters, "a mulatto known to everybody around Erie," with a young boy serving as guide, drove a wagon to the Henry home with the three passengers (actually, three adults and a baby). After a narrow escape, the passengers were smuggled onto a lake steamer for the trip to Canada, where they settled safely.[41] In Severance's story, Waters is mentioned as a minor player, described slightingly as "blind as a bat" and dependent on the help of a young boy, but other sources portray him as a leader whose physical strength and courage made him an invaluable member of the abolitionist team. His apparent helplessness made him the perfect accomplice in such illegal and risky ventures.[42]

Like Hamilton Waters, Henry Catlin acted out his beliefs in an uncompromising manner, despite popular opinion. One Erie historian described him as "a gentleman of many parts. A man of peace, he was nevertheless of leonine courage."[43] Members of the Catlin family were active abolitionists in Sugar Grove and Meadville as well as in Erie. Catlin's views were not generally popular in Erie, and his paper, *The True American,* was the only abolitionist paper in the area.[44]

In 1858, Catlin invited black abolitionist Frederick Douglass to speak in Erie. When his paper announced Douglass's coming, the supporters of slavery threatened his life if he dared to bring Douglass in. "If they had any idea that these threats would intimidate him they little knew Henry Catlin." On the contrary, Catlin met Douglass at the train station, then taking Douglass's bag in his hand, "the editor of the *True American* walked down State street arm in arm with the representative of the despised race, and not a hand was lifted nor a voice of challenge or protest raised. Before this splendid exhibition of courage the very rabble was dumb, and when he introduced the speaker from the stage that evening he was greeted with applause."[45] In 1858 State Street was an unpaved muddy track, but it was Erie's main thoroughfare north to Lake Erie, and Catlin's challenge to his racist opponents was clear. Douglass's appearance would be no clandestine affair but the public display of the strength of the black community and its allies. The Waters family would have been avid listeners to Douglass's oration. Hamilton Waters's grandson Harry T. Burleigh would learn to know Douglass in his last years, after the struggle against slavery had been won, but surely in his childhood he heard the story of this occasion.

With the coming of the Civil War, *The True American* had served its purpose and it merged with the Erie *Dispatch*, the paper that most often reported activities in the black community. But Catlin's leadership in the cultural life of the city extended to music as well as social justice, and his life intersected with the Waters and Burleigh family at significant points for many years.

* * *

Erie's black citizens contributed to the life of the city in a variety of service and working-class occupations in the mid-nineteenth century. Only a few were able to move beyond the role of laborer. In the 1850 U.S. census, Hamilton Waters was listed as the clothes dyer at the Vosburgh dry cleaners, a job that must have required some residual level of eyesight. The other forty-eight black adults are identified in the census as laborers, cooks, sailors, servants, barbers, and a grocer, a lime burner, and a porter. Waters continued working at the dry cleaners until sometime after Robert Vosburgh's death in 1846. The first *Erie City Directory*, published in 1853, listed Waters as city crier, essentially an honorary position, but one that shows the regard of Erie's prominent citizens for his "competency and perfect reliability."[46]

The 1860 census shows a gain of only nine adults among the city's black population, but they were engaged in a wider variety of jobs, some of them reflecting a higher level of education. At this time, in addition to the laborers, waiters, cooks, servants, barbers, and the city crier are whitewashers, draymen, a hackman, a blacksmith, a canaller, a bill poster, a saloonkeeper, a music teacher (Susan Vosburgh), and a school teacher (Elizabeth Waters). At this time Waters's property value was listed as $200 and his personal value as $100. His eyesight was much diminished, but he could still make good use of his voice as he found his way along the streets announcing the news. After his term as city crier ended, he was listed in the city directory as a laborer, or simply as "colored gent."

Another honorary position Hamilton Waters held was that of lamplighter. There is no mention in the public records of his holding this position, but it has become an important symbol in the legends of Harry T. Burleigh's youth. The first gas street lamps in Erie were erected about 1872, just five years before Waters's death. Usually young boys were hired as lamplighters. "They carried a small ladder and a can of kerosene oil. Clinging to the post with their legs, they would trim the wick when needed and fill the cup with oil." If a light went out during the night, the lamp-lighter boys would be called on to relight them.[47] An elderly blind man would have found it difficult to climb up a ladder to tend the lamps, so no doubt Harry and his brother Reggie led him through the streets, as Burleigh later recalled, helping him with this task. After their grandfather died, Harry and Reginald secured the lamplighting contract for themselves.

* * *

To Hamilton Waters, education was of the highest priority for himself and for his daughters. Like free African Americans throughout the United States both before and after Emancipation, he believed that education was the key to full participation in American society. Not satisfied with the education available to them in Erie, he secured places for both Elizabeth and Louisa in institutions that prepared them to move toward more professional or clerical employment, even though they were denied full access to the careers they might have pursued. The Waters family's "sole purpose seemed (aside from their irreproachable daily living), to see in the education of their daughters that place in life for them which circumstances had before that denied to the parents."[48] In the early 1850s Waters's connection to western Pennsylvania's abolitionist community facilitated his sending Elizabeth to the Allegheny Institute and Seminary, later known as Avery College, in Allegheny, Pennsylvania (now Pittsburgh's North Side). Her younger sister Louisa also received a liberal education, at a Presbyterian seminary (or college for women) in Warren County. She worked as a teacher and as a government clerk in Louisiana before returning to Erie at the time of her father's death in 1877.[49]

Hamilton Waters's antislavery network offered a number of choices for Elizabeth's education, but Avery College offered some unusual advantages. Though not the first college chartered for African Americans, it was the first that featured black teachers and administrators. Waters's choice of what might be called a black nationalist college underscores his view that women deserved access to an education equal with men as well as his insistence on equal rights and independence for African Americans.[50]

Avery College was founded in 1849 "for the education of colored Americans, in the various branches of science, literature, and ancient and modern languages."[51] Because she graduated in 1855, Elizabeth probably matriculated in 1851 or 1852, at thirteen or fourteen years of age. As was common in the nineteenth century, students entered Avery College from elementary school, but its classical curriculum offered a more sophisticated education than secondary schools and some undergraduate college programs of the early twenty-first century. Having an eighth-grade education at this time signaled exposure to a far more sophisticated course of study than is typical in the twenty-first century, and nineteenth-century graduates of normal schools and colleges were equipped to teach and to fill other professional positions.[52]

Just as Hamilton Waters was at the center of abolitionist activity in Ithaca and in Erie, so his daughter's schooling in Pittsburgh put her at the heart of the struggle there, though she may not have been directly involved. Avery College was a center of Pittsburgh abolitionist activity. Her years there prepared Elizabeth for a professional career to which she would be denied full access, but her association with Pittsburgh's abolitionist leaders is a part of the pattern of active involvement in the struggle for civil rights that characterized her father, Hamilton Waters, and her two husbands, Henry Thacker Burley and John Elmendorf, and that shaped her son Harry T. Burleigh from his earliest years.

Charles Avery, a wealthy white Pittsburgh philanthropist, made his fortune in textiles and pharmaceuticals. In his travels south to purchase cotton for his mills, his Methodist conscience was seared by the evils of slavery he encountered, and like his friend Orange Scott, founder of the Wesleyan Methodist Church, he became one of the most committed abolitionists of the time. Avery was said to be the most trusted white man in Pittsburgh's "Little Haiti," a black community now known as the Lower Hill District, as well as in black communities in New York and other parts of the country.[53]

Avery worked closely with black Pittsburgh abolitionists Martin R. Delany, John B. and George Vashon, John Peck, and Rev. Lewis Woodson, as well as with white colleagues such as Charles Shiras and Dr. Francis Julius LeMoyne.[54] Dr. LeMoyne conducted his medical practice in his home in Washington, Pennsylvania, twenty-five miles south of Pittsburgh, and he and his wife conducted a safe house for fugitives in their home. He purchased pharmaceuticals from Charles Avery and was a friend and correspondent of other prominent abolitionists, including Quaker poet John Greenleaf Whittier and Charles Francis Adams.[55]

Another Avery associate was white abolitionist and journalist Charles Shiras, close friend of Pittsburgh composer Stephen Collins Foster. Shiras played a major role in sensitizing Foster to the plight of African Americans.[56]

Charles Avery did not do things by halves. He established a college for Pittsburgh's black community that provided an education equal to any available to whites. The Avery College faculty had "the power to grant and confirm such degrees in the arts and sciences . . . as are granted in other colleges in the United States." Avery College "became in all respects as efficient as any of the public schools" of the Pittsburgh vicinity.[57] The college occupied the first and second stories in a three-story building that Charles Avery had built on land near his home. Avery spared no expense in the design of the seventy-five- by fifty-five-foot building. "Elegance and utility [were] everywhere considered." The top floor housed the Avery Memorial African Methodist Episcopal Zion Church. The sanctuary of the church was "finished in an exceedingly chaste and elegant manner; the walls and ceiling ornamented with fresco, skillfully executed by Mr. Mitchell, a German artist."[58] The Avery A.M.E.Z. congregation is still in existence, but this historic building was razed "to make way for the much disputed highway through the East

Street Valley."[59] The congregation now meets on California Avenue some blocks from its original location.

Avery named the college Allegheny Institute and Seminary, but from the first it was referred to popularly as Avery College. After Avery's death it was officially renamed Avery College.[60] In later years the college was reorganized as a vocational school like the numerous other black colleges influenced by Booker T. Washington's philosophy of practical training for African Americans after the Civil War.[61] But the college Elizabeth Waters attended offered a classical curriculum.

The college was coeducational. Like many abolitionists, Avery and his colleagues championed the rights of women to share the same classical education given to men. From a February 1856 article, a few months after Elizabeth's graduation, in the *Provincial Freeman*, a black newspaper from Chatham, Ontario, we can infer that the arts were stressed along with the classical subjects. Chatham's black community, established in 1787, drew fugitive slaves and free blacks throughout its history and in the 1850s welcomed many eager to evade the threat of the Fugitive Slave Act. In the article, former Pittsburgher Martin Delany commended Amelia Freeman, one of Elizabeth's teachers, who had migrated to this community, for her qualifications to give "instruction in painting, drawing, music, writing, etc., . . . which are necessary and useful accomplishments for both ladies and gentlemen."[62]

Men and women shared a curriculum at Avery College, but they did not share classrooms. A lengthwise partition separated the men and women scholars, "each department being subdivided according to convenience. The entrances to these departments are from opposite sides of the house, so that the sexes are kept entirely separate."[63] This division did not mean their coursework was different. The college's students were not to be distracted by adolescent social concerns; they had serious work to do. Avery College offered its women students training in far more than good manners, which many assumed to be sufficient for young women. Martin Freeman, one of the teachers and later the college principal, was renowned for his knowledge of mathematics and science, and later accounts of Elizabeth's teaching Sunday school "with her Greek New Testament at her side" are credible; she had studied Greek, Latin, and French at Avery College.[64] Harry T. Burleigh's mother would set a high standard of educational achievement for her children.

Though their social activities were limited while they pursued their academic work, Avery College students could not have been insulated from the struggle to free enslaved Americans. Like Erie, Pittsburgh was a crossroads of pursuit by slave catchers and a network of refuge for fugitives. The subbasement of the college was a hideout where fugitives fleeing overland and up the Ohio and the Monongahela Rivers "were hidden until they could continue north, to Erie or Buffalo, and then to Canada."[65] Exactly what role the students played is not known, but Elizabeth Waters's graduation speech showed that she was well aware of the urgency of the cause.

Accounts of the commencement exercises on July 11, 1855, demonstrated her educational achievements and her desire for the abolition of slavery. Two of her fellow graduates were daughters of abolitionist Rev. Lewis Woodson, Martin Delany's teacher and mentor. Another classmate was Benjamin Tucker Tanner, who was to be a bishop of the African Methodist Episcopal church and father of artist Henry Tanner. The newspaper reported, "M'lle Waters delivered an address—"La Salutation"—in the French." She was "a very intelligent young lady in appearance," whose "pronunciation of the French language was correct and indicated an excellent knowledge of the tongue." Later in the ceremony she gave "a very neat essay on 'American Institutions,' in the course of which she adverted in terms of sorrow to the enslaved condition of so large a portion of her race. She thought slavery the only stain upon our country's fair name."[66]

The Erie press also noted Elizabeth Waters's graduation from Avery College. The Erie *Weekly Gazette* picked up the Pittsburgh announcement, creating several levels of unintentional irony in its praise of Miss Waters: "The first-named of these graduates is the eldest daughter of Mr. H. E. Waters, of this city—a colored man of unusual intelligence. Superadded to her well-known natural talents, she has now an education qualifying her for the position of a Teacher in the first Seminary in the land. We are happy to have it in our power to record the fact. It is a glorious commentary on the progressive tendencies of the age."[67]

The reference to Hamilton Waters as "a colored man of unusual intelligence" reflects the assumption of even liberal white Americans that most black Americans were intellectually inferior to whites. The Waters family was seen to be exceptional. But for all the public recognition of Elizabeth Waters's achievement, she was not to benefit from "the progressive tendencies of the age" in her teaching career. She might be qualified to teach in "the first [women's] seminary in the land," but Erie's public schools were not yet open to black teachers. In a 1924 interview Burleigh said that his mother had applied for a public school position, "but race prejudice was so rife at the time she was unsuccessful."[68] Provision was made later for separate schools for minority students, but the hiring of African American teachers would not come till some forty years later, in the 1890s.

Elizabeth Waters taught at the Colored School founded by her father and his Wesleyan Methodist associates rather than at a public school. Eighteen years later, in 1873, after her first husband died, when she applied for a teaching position in Erie Public School No. 1, she was offered not a classroom but the entire school—to clean.[69] But the story does not end there. Two of her daughters did accomplish what she was denied: after her graduation from Erie High School in 1890 Burleigh's sister Eva Grace entered the normal training school and in 1892 was one of two black public school teachers hired to teach in the Erie Public Schools. She was listed in the Erie city directories as a music teacher for a number of years. And in 1899 Burleigh's half-sister Bessie Elmendorf brought a kind of poetic justice to the saga: she was hired to teach second grade at P.S. No. 1 at a salary of $37 per month, the school where her mother had served as "janitress."[70]

Historical memory of these Reconstruction-era black teachers in Erie's public schools has faded. Late-twentieth-century and early-twenty-first-century Erie newspapers frequently refer to Miss Ada Lawrence, who was hired in the 1940s, as the "first black teacher in Erie public schools." Lawrence's family were close friends of the Burleighs; the Fisher and Lawrence families who were her ancestors arrived in Erie somewhat later than the Waters family, but their names appear frequently along with those of Burleigh's family. Ada Lawrence (who died in March 2014) had vivid memories of Harry T. Burleigh, who often stayed in their home when he returned to Erie. Her father, Earl Lawrence, taught music in the Fairview schools near Erie, and his students still remember him well. Clearly, the post–Civil War openness to African Americans' contributions in education waned during the early to mid-twentieth century, and it would be several generations before Erie public schools again employed black teachers such as Ada Lawrence.

Even without the distinction later won by his grandson, Hamilton Waters accomplished much through his "originality, versatility and patient toil" in his forty-five years as a free man. Like many other free African Americans throughout the country before the Civil War and President Abraham Lincoln's official Emancipation Proclamation, Waters and his family were building a firm foundation for the enhanced opportunities that would emerge, though painfully and in the face of constant obstacles, throughout the last half of the nineteenth century. Education led to frustrated ambition for Elizabeth Waters, but she would instill in her son the belief that no dream of achievement was unattainable. And through his early relationship with his grandfather, young Harry Burleigh absorbed Hamilton Waters's belief in his entitlement to full citizenship as well as a knowledge of the distinctive cultural heritage through which those who were enslaved transcended the pain and the limitations of their captivity. Other musicians of his generation might have had deeper personal knowledge of that cultural heritage, but Burleigh's ability to move with dignity and integrity both among the leaders of the black elite and among wealthy and influential whites empowered him to be in the vanguard of musicians making their African American music heritage an inextricable part of American music culture.

2. The Family and Community That Shaped Burleigh's Youth

"A fixity of purpose"

In the early 1860s, as the country moved toward Civil War, energetic young Henry Thacker Burley settled in Erie. (The family used the "Burley" spelling during his lifetime but eventually changed to the English spelling, "Burleigh," though the shift was not consistent in the public records). Census records name Boston, Massachusetts, as his birthplace,[1] but he may have come to Erie from Newburgh, New York, where his parents were living at the time. Burley threw himself into the struggle against slavery and for equal rights, and he soon found the Waters family and the Vosburghs to be kindred spirits. He gave leadership and new direction to Erie's abolition and civil-rights movement. He worked with Charles Vosburgh, son of Robert and Abigail, to develop the Colored School and became its superintendent. Elizabeth Waters was among the seven teachers, and their relationship developed into courtship.[2]

In fall 1862 the Erie papers were full of reports from the Civil War battlefields: the injuries and deaths of area soldiers; the likelihood of a draft; the threat of an invasion of Pennsylvania; the gathering of clothing, bedding, bandages, jelly, fruit, and tea for the troops by ladies aid societies; and rumors of President Abraham Lincoln's intent to declare the emancipation of slaves in Confederate states. On August 28 Erie's Republican paper carried the full text of President Lincoln's response to Horace Greeley stating that his primary goal was to save the Union, whether that meant freeing all of the slaves, some of the slaves, or none of the slaves. It had become apparent to Lincoln that the Union could not be saved without emancipation, and he was meeting with Union leaders to map out the most effective strategy for doing so.[3] The anticipation of African Americans throughout the North and the South—and in Erie—as word of these developments spread was intense.

On September 17, 1862, the day of the Battle of Antietam, the bloodiest battle of the Civil War, Henry Thacker Burley and Elizabeth Lovey Waters were married. They could not have known how decisive this battle would be or that five days later

Henry Thacker Burley. (Photo from Dr. James Hall, Jr., *Hard Trials: The Life and Music of Harry T. Burleigh,* Anne Key Simpson, 1990.)

President Lincoln would present to his cabinet the Emancipation Proclamation, freeing the slaves in the Confederate states. It was announced to the public the following day, on September 23, 1862, though it took effect several months later, on January 1, 1863.[4] But the auspicious timing of their wedding would not have been lost on them. Many more battles would be fought, thousands more lives would be lost, and the war would come much closer to the Burley family before General Robert E. Lee surrendered at Appomattox in April 1865, but the early days of their marriage must have filled them with hope for an imminent end to the conflict.

A year later, on September 27, 1863, their first child, Henry Thacker Burley Jr., was born. This child, his father's namesake, lived just over three months. He died on January 8, 1864.[5]

By this time, hundreds of black men in the North were volunteering to join the U.S. Colored Troops, and a dozen or so left Erie to join the Union Army. Burley did not follow immediately, but in September 1864, two months before their second child, Reginald Waters Burley, was born, he enlisted at St. Vincent Post No. 67 and joined the U.S. Navy as landsman on the steamer *General Burnside.* He later served on the *Moose,* a wooden sternwheeler gunboat.[6]

For Burley, Lee's surrender in April 1865, like Lincoln's Emancipation Proclamation, was a milepost, not a final destination. Upon his release from service in June 1865, he returned to the peacetime war for civil rights in Erie. He joined Charles Vosburgh, John Clifford, and Washington Williams to form the Equal Rights League, which lobbied for full citizenship for African Americans. They supported the new definition of citizenship guaranteed by the Fourteenth Amendment to the Constitution proposed by Congress in April 1866, and they pushed further for full voting rights for African American men—and women. They petitioned to "remove both race and gender barriers from all state elections." Again the Wesleyan Methodist Church in Jerusalem provided a meeting place for civil action. John Clifford was the first president of the Equal Rights League and Henry T. Burley its secretary.[7]

The following year, on December 12, 1866, Elizabeth and Henry Burley ensured that Henry's name would survive by naming their third son for his father, as they had their first. Indeed, it was this third son, Henry Thacker Burleigh, who would keep the family's name alive into succeeding generations. Harry, as the family called him, would absorb by both inheritance and nurture his family's commitment to bringing social change.

Harry's mother Elizabeth continued teaching for some time after his birth; in 1867 she had nineteen pupils at the Colored Church on Fourth Street between Chestnut and Walnut Streets.[8] Even when family responsibilities limited her work outside the home, her love for music is evident in reports of her singing in musicales

Harry T. Burleigh as an infant. (Courtesy of the Burleigh Family)

and in family quartets, and she gave unwavering support of Harry's ambition to become a concert singer, despite the obvious obstacles to such a career in the late nineteenth century.[9]

In 1868 the Burleys' first daughter, Ada, was born. Like her brothers, she enjoyed singing, but she lived only fourteen years. In April 1883 she died of consumption (tuberculosis).

* * *

Most of the Burley family's activities centered in the black community, but in their employment and their church affiliations they established important connections among Erie's wealthy white citizens. The Episcopal Cathedral of St. Paul was a congregation of Erie's financial and social elite. Shipbuilder Charles Reed, son of Erie's founding shipbuilder Rufus Reed, built the bell tower, and among the members was the prominent Vincent family. In 2002 the congregation would honor Bishop Boyd Vincent, General Strong Vincent, and African American composer Harry T. Burleigh with a stained-glass window commemorating their lives and their contributions to the Episcopal church.

As elsewhere, Erie's antebellum Episcopalians were more likely to be slaveholders than abolitionists. One of the founding members of St. Paul's, P. S. V. Hamot, advertised the loss of a runaway slave in 1825, just two years before he gathered "a

Hamilton Waters with Harry (circa 2 years old) and Reginald (circa 4 years old). (Courtesy of the Burleigh Family)

group of prominent Erie men" in his home to form the St. Paul congregation.[10] In 1862, the year Henry and Elizabeth Burley married, Rev. John Franklin Spaulding, a new rector with abolitionist leanings, determined to energize the congregation and extend its outreach throughout the community. At the St. Paul's centennial in 1927, Sarah Reed, daughter of General Charles Reed, recalled some of the changes Spaulding initiated: "When the first Bishop Spaulding came to St. Paul's in 1862 it was a sleepy congregation. If they got up in the morning and went to church they had done a great deal and especially if they took their children. I remember his first text—'To what intent have you sent for me.' And he soon found out, and nobody went to sleep any more." He mobilized the women of the congregation, challenging them to bring children into the Sunday school from the outlying districts. Two years later the Sunday school had grown from seventy-five to "more than one hundred fifty children, and there were four missions."[11]

In 1869, Rev. Spaulding welcomed Hamilton Waters and his family into membership at St. Paul's. He and his daughter Elizabeth Burley were confirmed on April 25, and a month later, on May 27, Waters sponsored the confirmation of his son-in-law, Henry T. Burley, and his grandchildren, Reginald, Harry, and Ada.

Harry Burleigh, age 7. (Photo from Dr. James Hall, Jr., *Hard Trials: The Life and Music of Harry T. Burleigh,* Anne Key Simpson, 1991.)

The other sponsors were Boyd Vincent and Clara Austin, the director of the Lady's Parochial Society.[12]

Burleigh's mother and her family did not experience the blatant discrimination in the 1870s and 1880s that black members of St. Paul's experienced in the twentieth century (when they worshiped separately for some years), but it is unclear to what extent they were fully involved in the life of the congregation. A 1944 article published in an Episcopal church magazine reported that Mrs. Burleigh found "sympathy and freedom from bigotry" at St. Paul's,[13] but she would not have had the financial resources to participate in the Chautauqua and Niagara excursions, the dramatic tableaus, the Dime Socials, and cake sales of the St. Paul's Ladies' Circles. She was not listed as a member of the Ladies' Parochial Society, the St. Agnes Guild, or the Women's Missionary Association, but in 1900 she served as secretary of the Women's Friendly Society. Several other black families joined St. Paul's in the 1870s and 1880s, and women from these families were also active in this group. The Girls' Friendly Society was closely related to the Women's Friendly Society in purpose: "to bind together . . . church women as Associates and girls and young women as Members, for mutual help (religious and secular), for sympathy and prayer," and to "encourage purity of life, dutifulness to parents, faithfulness to employers, and thrift."[14] Burleigh's half-sister Bessie Elmendorf was a member of the Girls' Friendly Society in 1900.

After the founding of the St. James African Methodist Episcopal Church in 1874, most of the family's church and social activities revolved around this congregation, but young Harry often accompanied his mother to Sunday morning services at St. Paul's. The strong music tradition there nourished his lifelong commitment to church music in general and to the Episcopal Church in particular. During his childhood, the annual Easter festivals brought more than six hundred children marching in procession with banners and carols.[15]

* * *

Meanwhile, Elizabeth and Henry Burley's family grew. Henry's position as messenger at the Second National Bank was limited but not menial, and the family's continuing relationship with the family of bank founder William S. Curry, even after Curry's death, suggests that he and his wife were well regarded. Burley also worked as janitor of the First Universalist Church.[16]

Burleigh's sister Eva Grace was born on December 11, 1870, the day before his birthday. Of his siblings, Eva was closest to him in interests and in accomplishment. She often appeared in notes of musical performances in Erie as accompanist to singers or as song leader, and after some years of teaching in the Erie public schools and in Lawrenceville, Virginia, she followed her brother to New York City.[17]

Five-year-old Harry was too young to appreciate fully an event in his father's life in 1871 that confirmed the respect he had won in the broader Erie community despite—or perhaps because of—his civil-rights activism. Henry T. Burley was chosen to serve as the first black juror in Erie County courts. The jury found the defendant, a white man named John Stohl, guilty. He was fined $50 and costs and sentenced to serve four months in the county jail.[18] That a black man could serve as juror in the trial of a white man just thirty-three years after Pennsylvania had passed a law barring black persons from voting illustrates the profound changes that followed the Civil War and the Emancipation Proclamation. But as elsewhere, the history of Erie's race relations is complex, and this step forward was one along a path that included obstacles and detours for Burleigh's family as well as remarkable progress and advancement. Reconstruction may have faded more slowly in Erie than in the Deep South, but in the early twentieth century, hard-won progress faded for Erie's black citizens just as inexorably.

Like his father-in-law Hamilton Waters, Henry Thacker Burley assumed full rights of citizenship for himself, and he was quick to support the claims of others as well. Though most Grand Army of the Republic units were segregated at this time, a month after the trial at which he was a juror, Burley was mustered into the Strong Vincent Post No. 67, "the first and only African American man to be mustered into the post at that time."[19] That same year, he signed the Declaration of a Widow for Pension on behalf of Catherine Fleming, the widow of Benjamin Fleming, a veteran of the War of 1812, one of the black sailors who had helped Commandant Oliver Hazard Perry defeat the British forces on Lake Erie.[20]

The Burley family's fortunes changed abruptly when banker William S. Curry died in an accident on the Hudson River Railroad in February 1871, though the connection between the two families continued. After Curry's death, Henry Burley left his position as messenger at the Second National Bank to take a job as conductor of a sleeping car on the Lake Shore Railway and Michigan Southern Railway. In 1869 the Lake Shore Railway running from Toledo, Ohio, to Erie was consolidated with the Michigan Southern and Northern Indiana Railroad Company and the Buffalo and Erie Railroad Company, so Burley's run stretched from Buffalo, through Erie, to Chicago.[21] This was a significant position commonly open to African American men at this time. Despite low wages and the necessity of being absent from their families for long periods of time, railroad workers, like sailors and roustabouts along the seacoasts and rivers, formed an important cross-country network of communication among black communities.

We know little about the connections Henry Thacker Burley established during his months on the railroad. But we do know that he gravitated to a church community, one of the surest centers of contact wherever one might travel. On a run to Chicago in February 1873, he attended a black Baptist church on a Sunday night. There is no indication that he had any warning of illness or impending death, but the next morning on his way to breakfast, thirty-five-year-old Burley fell dead on the Chicago street, the victim of heart disease.[22] The news of his death shocked Erie's black community and was noted in the broader community as well. Erie papers featured brief articles in addition to the ordinary obituary, saying he was "well known in this city." A note printed next to his obituary in the Erie *Weekly Gazette* shows how closely Burley's name was associated with the struggle for the abolition of slavery in the minds of his Erie friends and acquaintances: "To the survivors of the original Abolitionist, who first organized the party amid taunts, persecution and division on all sides, they have lived to see their own government take the abolition society into their hands, carry it out, and give the black man not only freedom, but his elective franchise and equal rights. They stood then alone; now the Government and nearly the whole world is with them. They have lived to see their wishes carried out, and will receive their rewards."[23]

This oblique reference to the involvement of Hamilton Waters and his son-in-law in the struggle for basic freedom and citizen's rights honored Burley's memory, but the assurance of equal rights was deceptive, and financial rewards were hard won. For Elizabeth Waters Burley, her husband's death increased the burden of care for her family. Her sister Louisa was still working in Louisiana, so the responsibility for the support of the Burley children and her aging father was Elizabeth's. It was at this point that she applied for a teaching position at Public School No. 1; she was offered instead the position of janitress. She was listed in the 1873–1874 *Erie City Directory* as Mrs. H. T. Burley and in 1874–1875 as Mrs. Lizzie Burley, janitress.[24]

* * *

Three years before Henry Burley's death, another Civil War veteran, John Edgar Elmendorf, moved to Erie from Kingston, New York. Like Burley, he had served in the U.S. Navy.[25] In Erie he worked first as a coachman for coal merchant, business tycoon, railroad baron and later congressman William L. Scott.[26] After several years he began working for the widow of millionaire shipbuilder Charles Reed, whose mansion stood at the corner of Peach and Sixth Streets.[27] Her trusted coachman and steward, he handled her affairs until 1892, when he and his son Elzie set up a livery stable business. Like Hamilton Waters and Henry Burley, John Elmendorf demonstrated the strength of character and commitment to justice that earned him the respect and sometimes the resentment of his white fellow citizens.

John Elmendorf and Elizabeth Waters Burley were married on April 15, 1875. In later years when Burleigh spoke to journalists about his family, it was to John Elmendorf that he referred when he described singing harmony with his father and his older brother Reggie as they helped his mother clean the desks at P. S. No. 1.[28] His inscription, "To my dear father," on the photograph in his choir robes that he sent home when he was hired as baritone soloist at St. George's Episcopal Church in New York City in 1894, shows the warmth of Burleigh's relationship with his stepfather.[29]

* * *

With his mother's marriage to John Elmendorf, the third of the men who would shape young Harry T. Burleigh's sense of self and his understanding of his place as an African American man entered his life. From each of these men he learned how to live in a society dominated by the majority white American culture of a Northern city sometimes tolerant and even admiring of his achievement, but often reluctant to grant him full rights of citizenship. Burleigh never spoke publicly of his memories of his father, Henry Thacker Burley. Of the women in the family, he would have known his grandmother Lucinda only through family accounts, as she died in 1867 before his first birthday. His mother Elizabeth and his aunt, Louisa Waters, encouraged him to develop his music ability beyond anything either of them could achieve.[30] But his grandfather Hamilton Waters was an especially important model for the young Harry in his first eleven years, defining the stalwart self-assurance that shaped his character and imparting his most immediate knowledge of slavery times and of the songs that were to become his trademark. Burleigh spent a good deal of time with his grandfather, leading him through the streets and taking him to the Himrod Mission on Sunday afternoons, so it is likely that, as Henry Burley died when the boy was only six, his relationship with his grandfather was more formative.

When Hamilton Waters died in 1877, his obituary reflected the importance of personal freedom and faith to him and his family: "Many years of his early life was [sic] spent in slavery. Now he has gone to the land where there is no oppression and the bondsman is free. A few hours before he passed away, he said to a friend, 'I have my trunk packed—been packed a good while—and am waiting for the boat to round the curve.'"[31]

Hamilton Waters, the family patriarch, demonstrated the importance of education through his own pursuit of literacy and through providing his daughters a level of training not readily available to women in the mid-nineteenth century. He had legally purchased freedom from slavery for himself and his mother a generation before the Emancipation Proclamation, and he was not a passive citizen. He assumed full rights of citizenship for himself, and he actively worked to assist others to freedom. Beyond the strength of character he demonstrated, he also passed on to his children and grandchildren the musical heritage that helped sustain the slaves and that would enrich America and the world through his grandson's transformation of that legacy. His influence on young Harry is evident in the frequent references Burleigh made to him in interviews throughout his life. At the end of his fifty-year career as baritone soloist at St. George's Episcopal Church in New York City, Burleigh commented that his grandfather would have been proud of his many years of singing in a white church. From what we know of Hamilton Waters, it is clear that he would have expected his grandson to serve as a conscience, not as a servant, to St. George's wealthy white parishioners.[32]

* * *

Shortly after Hamilton Waters died, John and Elizabeth Elmendorf's first child was born. They named him after his father and his grandfather, John Hamilton Elzie

Elmendorf; he was known as Elzie. Burleigh grew closer in his relationship to his half-brother Elzie than to his older brother Reginald. Elzie's daughter Mrs. Grace Blackwell reported that their bond was closer than that of many full blood brothers.[33] The Elmendorfs' second child, born October 6, 1878, was a daughter, Bessie, named for her mother and her step-grandmother: Bessie Duncanson Elmendorf. Elzie inherited his father's business acumen and Bessie the family's musical gifts.[34]

* * *

Burleigh's most profound influence in his formative years was this strong family, for whom education was a primary value, and through his public and business education in Erie, he developed the skills and the confidence that facilitated his entrée into New York City's broader public arena. Both his grandfather and his mother demonstrated the importance of education in their own lives. His mother, in particular, modeled her determination for educational excellence, for example, in making use of her Avery College study of Greek in teaching Bible classes. It is not surprising to find Burleigh and his siblings among the first black students in Erie's public schools. Their earliest education was in the home, at the Colored School, and at the Himrod Mission. Burleigh appeared in an 1881 eighth-grade graduation picture from Public School No. 11, but it is likely that the black students studied separately and Burleigh was simply allowed to have his picture taken with the other students graduating in that year. All the students portray the proper Victorian gravitas in the photograph, but the sadness in young Burleigh's eyes suggests the price he had to pay for even this modicum of equality.[35]

Burleigh attended Erie High School, and he is thought to have been the first black graduate. His high school records show above-average performance, even though he was carrying a heavier load of studies than most of his classmates. He was simultaneously taking business courses at Clark's Commercial College. The Erie newspaper reports of the semiannual examinations show Burleigh scoring near the top of his class. In the spring of his junior year he scored 83.6 among the students testing in three subjects; the highest score in that category was 93.2. In December of his senior year his score in four subjects was 78.2. Among his classmates in that group the highest score was 86.8 and the lowest was 48.9.[36]

During his high school years Burleigh began to gain public notice outside the classroom. On several occasions he sang solos on public programs such as the High School Literary Society. He also began to make his mark as a public speaker. In October 1885, he spoke on "the influence of music on the circulation of the blood" at a literary program at Clark's Commercial College.[37] The next year, in February of his junior year, for the high school's Washington's Birthday celebration, Burleigh gave "the declamation of the day, considered either in its own significance or the remarkably fine oratorical display in its delivery." His speech, "Washington as a Politician," indicates that students were exposed to a serious study of U.S. history and political development, and the reviews emphasized Burleigh's oratorical skill. Elocution and public speaking and debate skills were an important part of the curriculum, and in the "significance" of its content and the "remarkably fine oratorical display," Burleigh demonstrated his grasp of the historical issues and his emerging capacity for public presentation that he would put to such good use as a singer. "The young man's effort would not have discredited many a public speaker of acknowledged recognition, and suggested the future possibilities which lie before the proper development and use of his undeniable gifts."[38]

Professor H. C. Clark had founded Clark's Commercial College in 1883. He espoused a liberal view of commercial education that reinforced Burleigh's public school studies. In addition to their standard business courses, the students put on regular literary entertainments that featured vocal and instrumental music, debates, readings, and orations. Sometimes Clark lectured on business success or engaged attorney and insurance agent J. F. Downing (Louisa Waters's and Henry Catlin's employer) to lecture on standards of conduct in business. At the business college Burleigh developed the fine penmanship that would make him such a valuable assistant to Antonín Dvořák at the National Conservatory of Music.[39]

Burleigh appeared frequently on programs given by Clark's Business College students as well as on high school literary programs. The evening after his declamation at the high school, Burleigh delivered a tribute to Washington at the Clark College Washington celebration that "was unanimously voted the best thing of the evening." The reviewer emphasized that Burleigh had written the speech himself, and it was "a remarkable production."[40]

In addition to intellectual challenges, Professor Clark also planned social events such as picnics or an excursion to Niagara Falls for his students, accompanied by Erie's finest instrumental ensemble, the Knoll Family Band. He even enlisted the services of a doctor to test the eyesight of his students and found that 15 percent of his students had defective eyes, most of them being nearsighted.[41] On at least one occasion Clark invited students to his home, where Burleigh was a soloist on the program.[42]

Late-nineteenth-century Erie society offered many opportunities for an ambitious young man to develop the skills and deportment for a life in the public arena. Burleigh's high school courses, supplemented by the accounting and stenographic skills he developed at Clark's Commercial College and the experience in public speaking offered by both institutions, were important preparation for a professional career. Burleigh also took advantage of educational opportunities offered by the YMCA. In 1886 Burleigh was chosen as a delegate to the regional YMCA convention that met at Titusville with representatives from Erie, Corry, Warren, Oil City, and Meadville, Pennsylvania.[43] He often performed vocal or instrumental music selections on YMCA programs, and occasionally he was featured as a speaker or reciting a selection from a Shakespeare play.[44]

Burleigh's preparation for a public career was moving onto the fast track, and notices of his activities began to appear more and more frequently in Erie papers and in the Cleveland *Gazette* (a black newspaper founded in 1883). In addition to the educational and civic venues where Burleigh honed his skills, church literary and benefit programs offered additional experience. He was one of the graduates chosen to speak in the Erie High School commencement exercises in June 1887. The Erie *Morning Dispatch* published the full text of the commencement orations; Burleigh's was titled "How Far Shall We Educate?"[45] In this speech the twenty-year-old stressed themes reflecting the environment that nurtured him. Education is important for advancement, he asserted, for improving one's life condition. "Everybody in this world wants to make the best of life; nobody wants to work beyond what is essential, everybody wants to 'lay up enough treasure upon earth' to make him comfortable, not rich necessarily, but enough to secure his welfare and happiness." Intellectual growth would help one advance, each new achievement preparing the way for the next. "Just in proportion to the power devoted to the extension of knowledge and the broadening of our capacities we better our conditions and lessen the burdens and difficulties of life."[46]

Material benefits were not enough, however: "That scheme of education which gives a man just enough to carry him through life is selfish and short-sighted. . . . The bread and butter education is good enough for bread and butter, but it is soon exhausted. The truly successful man has more power than will carry him through a difficulty; he always has a surplus. A merely practical education is a preparation for the work we have to do now. It is not a preparation for the unknown work of the future."

Burleigh refuted arguments against providing higher education to the masses. By its nature, education does create a desire for something better, he acknowledged, but this discontent is healthy: "Contentment with present place and position is the enemy of progress and makes of life a stagnant pool fit only for the lower orders of existence. Such doctrine may do well enough for Russia or Turkey. . . . The true prop of government is an intelligent public opinion, and there can be no intelligent public opinion without intelligent public education." After "a sound foundation in the first six or seven years of schooling," should come "the studies that broaden and strengthen. 'First the blade, then the ear, then the full corn in the ear.' Equipped in mind, strengthened in body, firm of purpose, these are the results of true education." In his conclusion Burleigh drew on a Latin phrase: "'*Quisque suae fortunae faber*'—'Every man is the maker of his own fortune,'" a phrase that he believed still held true. "Tell a man to stay where he is and we will have no excellence, for we will have no incentive; and where there's no incentive you cannot expect progress."[47]

In its echoes of sociologist W. E. B. Du Bois and his emphasis on training an intellectual elite, or the "Talented Tenth," this oration is interesting for its apparent contrast to views Burleigh later expressed supporting educator Booker T. Washington's promotion of industrial education. Burleigh's training and career path secured his place among the Talented Tenth, and in his speech, Burleigh clearly articulated his own intention to progress beyond a merely practical education, to prepare for the unknown work of a brighter future.

* * *

In the several years after Burleigh's high school graduation, his stepfather extended his own education and modeled active participation in political and community affairs, despite opposition by white Republicans. Like the majority of African Americans, John Elmendorf supported the party of Lincoln. In an 1889 incident he carried on the family tradition of political activism and resistance to injustice. Elmendorf's "zealous efforts and weighty shoulder to the wheel helped *materially* in electing the Republican candidate" in the 1888 congressional election. After the election, he applied for a political appointment, that of janitor in a government building. He secured the signatures of prominent men in the community supporting his appointment, and when he presented them to the congressman-elect, he was assured that the position was his.[48]

However, opposition arose among the Republican ranks charging that Elmendorf had "never served his country as a soldier" and had no right to claim "soldier's rights" to a political appointment. An Erie paper adamantly refuted this accusation: "Now, for the information of *those* who *do not know,* we will state that Mr. J. C. Elmendorf entered the United States Navy on May 3d, 1863, as landsman and worked his way up to an able seaman, serving in many tight conflicts with the rebel forces. He was one of the crew of the United States man-of-war Louisiana who loaded the guns with an intent to blow up Fort Fisher, in which they were not successful. He was finally discharged with honor as coxswain of Captain Sam Swain's gig."[49]

This record of service proved Elmendorf's right to be awarded the position, and his exemplary character strengthened his case. "He is temperate, industrious, and gentlemanly, not acquired, but instinctively so. We trust he'll be granted his request without further question."[50]

When Elmendorf resubmitted his request, again he was assured that the job was his. Prominent Republicans spoke "in gratifying words of his worth and unquestioned fidelity to the party." But these same men were spreading the rumor that Elmendorf was illiterate and that his honesty and reliability were questionable. The Cleveland *Gazette* refuted this charge also, pointing out that "It is well known in Erie that for nearly nineteen years Mr. Elmendorf has acted in the capacity of steward for Mrs. General C. M. Reed, doing all her buying and expending, and other responsible things requiring intelligence and truth," so no honest person could question his qualifications or his integrity.[51]

When Elmendorf realized that the Republican leaders had no intention of rewarding him and would also renege on other promises to black voters, he took his protest to the Republican headquarters. He "told the leaders there what he thought of them and what he intended to do in the future." Knowing that he wielded strong political influence among Erie's black citizens, they attempted to placate him by making him assistant to the white man they intended to appoint. Elmendorf rejected this insulting proposal. The lesson for black voters was clear: Rather than continue their "blind allegiance to the Republican party . . . they should form an Afro-American League," demonstrating the importance of the black vote. This organization would bring more effective pressure on the white Republicans to reward their loyalty by granting such patronage positions, however minor.[52]

Twenty-three-year-old Harry T. Burleigh could not have been more effectively taught to recognize his own rights as a citizen and as a human being. In his later years some thought he had sold out to the white music establishment, but careful study of the facts suggests otherwise. From his grandfather, his mother, his father, and his stepfather Burleigh inherited a strong sense of self, and like them he refused to accept demeaning treatment, often refusing to put himself in situations where overt discrimination was to be expected.

* * *

In Harry T. Burleigh's early years several black Erie entrepreneurs built flourishing business as barbers, ice cream manufacturers, waiters, and other trades, sometimes leading their white colleagues and competitors in modeling effective business practices. James Franklin was one of a number who worked as waiters, a position that at this time involved more than simply waiting tables. They functioned as caterers, supplying table linens and appointments as well as food.[53] As a waiter, Franklin saved enough money to invest in an ice cream business, which he built into a successful enterprise. In 1915 when Burleigh's half-brother Elzie Elmendorf resigned from his position as assistant secretary of the YMCA in Harlem, he went into business in New Rochelle, New York, with Charles Franklin, a junior member of the Franklin Ice Cream Company of Erie.[54]

A prime example of a black businessman who modeled progressive business practices was ice cream manufacturer John S. Hicks, who in 1872 built the first steel-frame brick building in the city and laid the first cement sidewalks on State Street.[55] Hicks fitted up the Undine Boat House at the north end of State Street (now Dobbins Landing) to furnish excursion parties with "the best luncheon at reasonable prices; fine stock of tropical fruits—bananas, oranges, etc.,—on hand; also ice cream, soda water and confectionery of the best kind. Smokers furnished with the best of cigars."[56] In 1889 he purchased additional property at the corner of State Street and Twelfth so that he could move his manufactory to a building separated from his retail store.[57] A leading black Mason, in 1887 he was appointed deputy grandmaster "for the 7th district by the Grand Lodge of Colored Masons," which covered Erie, Crawford, and Mercer counties.[58]

In this Great Lakes town, where black businessmen served the entire community and exerted leadership in the black community, earning financial stability and the respect of their neighbors in Erie's diverse and expanding economic community, young Harry T. Burleigh learned to move with confidence in the several worlds that surrounded him and his family.

* * *

If the men in his family taught Burleigh to be a responsible citizen, it was the women, his mother Elizabeth, and his aunt Louisa, who nurtured his artistic and professional ambitions. In proper Victorian mode, Burleigh spoke more often of his mother's influence, but one source suggests that his aunt Louisa played as significant a role in his music development and in providing emotional support during his adolescence.[59] After working for a number of years filling "an important clerkship under the State Government of Louisiana," Louisa Waters returned to Erie shortly before her father's death in 1877 and remained in the household most of the time until her death in 1914. For many years she worked as a clerk and type writer at J. F. Downing's insurance agency, where Henry Catlin worked as correspondence clerk.[60]

An article in the 1930s *New Deal* newspaper described Burleigh's relationship with his aunt. He spoke "with reverence and affection of his now long deceased parents," but it was "only when he speaks of Aunt Louise, . . . that his voice breaks with sorrow and his eyes fill with tears." She arranged for his first piano and vocal lessons, and it was she who provided emotional support "when the white boys' stings about his color made him feel that life was just absolutely unbearable." "It was to Aunt Louise that he also ran when as he grew to early manhood he began to cherish the hope that he might by some happy chance become a great singer. . . . He had, even [then], a voice that had much of future promise and she encouraged . . . in every way possible this then secret ambition."[61]

Louisa Waters was active in black Erie's social scene. She shared the family's musical gifts and was often cited as a singer, choir director, or director of children's performances at St. James A.M.E. Church. On one special occasion, a grand celebration of the Emancipation Proclamation in August 1891 at which the Honorable John M. Langston was the orator, she was among those ladies whose dresses received honorable mention: she wore black lace with roses.[62]

Burleigh remained close to his aunt Louisa after he left for New York City, assisting her financially from time to time. She married Thomas E. Williamson at age sixty-one in 1902 and was widowed less than two years later, not long after her sister Elizabeth died.[63] Burleigh's recital and composing career was in its early stages when his mother died in 1903, but his aunt Louisa, who died in 1914, lived to see him rise toward the peak of his success as an art song composer.[64]

* * *

The Hamilton Waters family had arrived in Erie with few material assets, but their personal integrity, religious faith, persistent struggle for equal rights, and commitment to education won them a position of respect throughout the Erie community. Waters was a laborer, but his younger daughter Louisa moved into the ranks of white-collar employees. His older daughter Elizabeth, despite her superior educational background, could work as a teacher only in the black community and later in the white community as a janitress and sometime maid for the daughter of her first husband's employer, but in her church affiliation at the Episcopal Cathedral of St. Paul, she related at least to some extent to members of Erie's social and political elite. Waters's sons-in-law both worked for some of Erie's wealthiest citizens, and eventually John Elmendorf was able to establish an independent business, his stable that served the white community's affluent citizens.

Clearly, the family pursued a path of upward social mobility, preparing the way for Harry T. Burleigh's generation to move comfortably among "the best" of both black and white society. After completing his high school and business college studies, young Harry Burleigh readily found his place as a white-collar worker, while developing a significant public singing career in his personal time. His mother lived to see him move purposefully toward his ultimate goal of becoming a concert singer.

A portrait of Elizabeth Elmendorf found among the glass negatives at the Erie County Historical Society shows a woman of great determination.[65]

Unlike the background setting in similar portraits of the time, Elizabeth has chosen props that emphasize her love for learning. She holds a book, and several books lie on the table beside her. She was drawn to a way of life that could not be fully supported by her family's financial situation, but she pointed the way for

Elizabeth Waters Burleigh Elmendorf. (F. J. Bassett Glassplate Negatives Collection, Erie County Historical Society)

her children. She involved herself more fully at St. Paul's Episcopal Cathedral than most members of the family, a setting that heightened the contrast between her artistic and social values and her personal circumstances.[66] Other African American women in the community who shared her sophistication and educational background tended to be from affluent families like the Vosburghs, who could afford to support their children's intellectual and artistic intentions. Elizabeth was determined to see her son benefit from his education more fully than she could ever hope to, and like her, Burleigh accomplished more in his professional career than many other black musicians whose family's affluence supported their ambition.

A telling footnote to the family history is evidence that Burleigh's mother suffered from mental and emotional distress that could not be publicly acknowledged in a late-nineteenth-century family with social ambitions. Though Lizzie Elmendorf kept an active schedule of church activities and often entertained guests in her home, she suffered from frequent illness. Some was physical, such as the bout with breast cancer several years after Harry had left for New York City.[67] But both Elizabeth and her daughter Bessie Elmendorf were afflicted with emotional difficulties occasionally requiring hospitalization. That some of Burleigh's descendants seem to have been unaware of these problems is not surprising, given the lengths to which families often went to hide or explain away traces of mental illness or emotional instability. An Elmendorf descendent reports that the family of Bessie Elmendorf's first husband had her marriage annulled when they learned that she and her mother had been hospitalized in an asylum. In a family such as Burleigh's, the determination to overcome all obstacles to upward mobility would have made such episodes especially painful.[68] One must wonder whether the struggle to achieve her ideals for herself and her family and the dissonance between those ideals and her lived reality sometimes became unbearable. Depression or another condition that could be successfully treated today was difficult to treat at this time, and any mental illness carried significant social stigma. The notices of Mrs. Elmendorf's frequent illness reported in the Cleveland *Gazette* may in some cases have been coded references to her bouts of emotional distress that would have been clear to those who knew the family well.

When Burleigh's career in New York City was established, he bought a more substantial house for his mother and stepfather on the property on East Third Street. A photograph shows Burleigh's mother standing on the porch of a two-story house with a white picket fence surrounding the yard, and another shows her, now more frail, seated in the parlor. That home is still remembered today by some in Erie, but unfortunately, it was demolished in 1969.[69]

* * *

In 1892, the year Burleigh left to study in New York City and his half-brother Elzie Elmendorf passed the high school entrance examination, John Elmendorf left his longstanding position with Mrs. Charles Reed to open a livery stable for gentlemen's horses. The City Directory carried a bold-type ad for the business, with a telephone number, listing both John E. Elmendorf and his son, John H. E. Elmendorf. At various times after Elzie left for New York City in 1903 or 1904, Reginald Burleigh and Elmendorf's son-in-law, Richard Marshall (Bessie Elmendorf's second husband), worked with him in the livery business. In March 1892 Elmendorf's leaving his service to Mrs. Reed was reported in Erie and Cleveland: "Mr. John Elmendorf, who has been in the employ of the Reed estate for twenty-two or twenty-three years as coachman and custodian of the homestead and grounds, has resigned the trust which he has filled with recognized fidelity." He had "leased the Spencer barns on Eighth street, between Peach and Sassafras," and would open a boarding stable for gentlemen's horses. Though Elmendorf felt a sense of personal loyalty to his longtime employer, he had decided "to provide a business for himself," an enterprise "which from the very fact that of his honesty and trustworthiness, can not prove otherwise than successful." Indeed, several months later, Elmendorf and his son were "succeeding in their business venture beyond their most sanguine expectations."[70]

Progress, achievement, and excellence are themes that resonate in Burleigh's family history. In every generation, they refused to accept the status quo. They worked, sometimes within the system, sometimes by going outside the system or by creating alternative structures, to bring change that would allow genuine progress. For the most part Burleigh worked within established structures, but always his goal was to bring change.

* * *

Erie's black community provided its youth with a variety of social activities. The family's social life centered in the St. James A.M.E. church and activities in the black communities in nearby towns. It was a lively scene. In addition to Sunday school programs and fairs to benefit the church, there were picnics by Lake Erie, calico hops, necktie socials, crazy quilt socials, Mother Hubbard suppers, sails on lake steamers, a letter-carrier's ball, egg socials, nut-cracking socials, washerwoman's socials, sleigh rides, old-fashioned tea parties, strawberry socials, dime socials, dancing classes, and masquerade balls.[71] Some seasonal activities marked the coming and going of the young men like Burleigh's older brother Reginald, who worked at resorts and on the Great Lakes steamers. When the resorts closed and the lakes froze over, their homecoming for the winter was cause for celebration.[72]

Dancing could be controversial entertainment. In November 1891, Eva Burleigh and three other young women formed a dancing class so "the young men need have no excuse . . . for not knowing how to trip the light fantastic." Herbert Jackson was to be the dancing master and H. T. Burleigh, the musical director.[73] One of the four young women reported to be the instigators of the dancing class was a Miss Baxter. Two weeks later, Maggie and Eva Baxter published a retraction. They claimed that "an item stating that the Misses Baxter, in company with other ladies and gentlemen, had started a dancing class" was false, as they were "in no way connected with any dancing"; they did "not even favor such."[74] Burleigh had no such compunctions. One of the early reports in 1892 from New York City commented that he was one of those artists "who are able to combine their love for art with a liking for social diversions."[75]

There were also literary clubs, lodges, and a temperance society. African Americans were not allowed to form secret organizations until after the Civil War, but the leaders in Erie's black community established their Masonic post in 1883, "the only colored lodge in Northwestern Pennsylvania" and the second lodge in Erie.[76] The washerwomen and the letter carriers, the waiters, and the railway workers formed social clubs that planned lively community affairs. The waiters put on splendid catered events. And in December 1891 the Order of Railway Conductors, which included "all the conductors running into this city," celebrated their fifth anniversary by giving an entertainment and ball in Maennerchor Hall. Burleigh was one of the featured singers.[77]

Several social clubs catered to Erie's young black men. In March 1891, The Entre Nous Society, "an organization of Erie people of African descent, whose object it is to cultivate literary and musical tastes," announced their Friday evening meetings "at the residences of the members." These meetings were reported to be "highly beneficial, evidently promotive of taste and culture and the development of local talent." Their grand ball and supper in May 1888 drew "many strangers from the surrounding cities." A similar club was "The Upper Ten, . . . an organization of gentlemen of [Erie] for social purposes." No documentation of Burleigh's membership in either society has been found, but as he joined similar societies in New York City soon after his arrival, it is likely that he was a member.[78]

In October 1891 Austin Mount, a young African American who defied the exclusion of black bikers from the Erie Bikers' Club by setting his own cycling records, established the Union Club, which was expected to "make things lively" through the winter. Mount was its president; Archie Thomas, vice president; H. T. Burleigh, secretary; and John Purdy, treasurer. The organization was "in a certain sense exclusive"; though its exclusivity was not defined, the implication is that it catered to black Erie's "best" young men. The club would rent rooms and hoped to "do a great deal toward the betterment of the young men socially and intellectually." In a social context where membership in white social clubs was not possible for these young men, they created their own alternative venues and constructive social activities. That Burleigh was a founding member of an exclusive club indicates that although he and his family would always work for their living, at least in the black community he had earned an elevated place among his peers.[79] Burleigh and his sister Eva Grace were frequently mentioned in reports of gatherings of their generation's social elite in Erie and Cleveland; they were on their way to fulfilling their family's aspirations for them.

Social organizations provided a core of community leadership that could be rallied for public events that reached well beyond the city. Burleigh's clerical and leadership skills were called on as secretary of the local executive committee that planned a grand Emancipation Celebration held on August 15, 1891. Erie was "resplendent with flags and bunting in honor of emancipation day." Trains brought people from surrounding cities and small towns. Burleigh and the other members of the local committee, including prominent businessman John S. Hicks, led the parade from Seventeenth and State Streets. Cleveland's Excelsior Cornet Band, directed by Burleigh's friend, H. C. Smith, editor of the Cleveland *Gazette,* and two local bands, the Marshall Band and the Massassauga Band, provided the music. The Massassauga Band also played an open-air concert for afternoon and evening dancing at the Pavilion at The Head (now Presque Isle) after the oration by the Honorable John M. Langston and other addresses by H. C. Smith and ministers from Pittsburgh, Allegheny, Franklin, and New Brighton, Pennsylvania.[80]

* * *

Burleigh's friendship with Cleveland *Gazette* editor H. C. Smith reveals an important but little-known aspect of Burleigh's life at this time. Both editor Smith and publisher Ernest Orsburn were musicians. But the political and social activism Burleigh's family espoused forged a natural bond with Smith as well. An outspoken crusader for civil rights, he used his paper to champion the rights of African Americans and to protest the increasingly oppressive events in the South that were destroying the gains so precariously won during Reconstruction.

Smith's speech at the Emancipation celebration in Erie illustrates the vigor with which he expressed his views, as reported (probably by Smith himself) in the August 7, 1891, *Gazette.* He described emancipation movements in America's history and the progress made by African Americans in the years since Lincoln's proclamation. Citing a reactionary bill by a Georgia legislator intended to prohibit racially integrated education in Georgia, Smith proposed that those most in need of emancipation in 1891 were the majority of Southern whites, and that they needed to be civilized as well as emancipated. Their efforts to dismantle Reconstruction in the South and impose Jim Crow laws nationwide were meeting with apathy rather than resistance. According to the reviewer, Smith's speech was well received by both the white and the black citizens at the celebration.

Smith's stance in the 1890s echoes themes seen earlier in Burleigh's grandfather, Hamilton Waters, his father Henry Thacker Burley, and his stepfather, John Elmendorf. In June 1895, between his third and fourth years at the National Conservatory and three months before Booker T. Washington's famous Atlanta Address, Burleigh stayed with Smith and his mother when he went to Cleveland at Smith's invitation to serve as an alternate delegate at the National Republican league convention.[81] Smith attacked Washington's accommodationist "doctrine of surrender" and was among the first to criticize his Atlanta Address in September 1895. In 1905 Smith was one of the militant black leaders who joined the Niagara Movement in opposition to Washington's leadership. By this time Burleigh was closely allied with Washington, at least in his public appearances. In 1910 Smith joined the National Association for the Advancement of Colored People (NAACP) and became a member of its select "Committee of One Hundred."[82] Though Burleigh would address the NAACP on several occasions, as we will see, the focus of his efforts to bring change shifted away from overt activism.

In the first year or two that Burleigh was in New York City, Smith published detailed reports of Burleigh's activities in the black community. Perhaps his silence in later years is a measure of the distance by which their political views had diverged. But in the early 1890s, at this critical transition in Burleigh's career, Smith's friendship may have reinforced Burleigh's initial willingness to resort to direct political action in protesting the discrimination he faced in New York City.

* * *

Harry T. Burleigh's first twenty-five years of life in Erie, Pennsylvania, equipped him to make his mark in a wider world, giving him several options for a successful adult career. He was a skilled stenographer and had worked as an accountant. But his primary goal was to build a public career as a classically trained singer, and all of his other gifts were focused on bringing that goal within reach. "Equipped in mind, strengthened in body, firm of purpose," Harry T. Burleigh was first and foremost a singer. With the musical ability he inherited and his family nurtured, Erie offered a worthy proving ground to advance his nascent singing career.

3. Burleigh's Music Experience and Training in Erie

"He was always singing"

Harry T. Burleigh demonstrated his love for music and his gifts as a singer long before he left Erie to study at the National Conservatory of Music in New York City. His family was recognized in Erie for their singing, and the soundscape of his early years was diverse: He heard songs of stevedores on docks and piers along the shores of Lake Erie, bands that paraded the streets, choirs of Episcopal and Presbyterian churches and the Hebrew temple, and parlors where musicales featured local talent and touring artists. Music education at home and in studios opened doors for Burleigh to a variety of performance venues that prepared him for his successful audition at the National Conservatory and the rigorous course of study he would pursue there. Along the way he earned the support of many of Erie's prominent citizens, who would contribute to a fund supporting the early months of his training in New York City.

Some echoes from that Erie soundscape can be heard in interviews years later. Other themes emerge in a survey of Erie's musical environment during his early life there. That Burleigh's ears were attuned to the whole range of sounds in his world is suggested by his comment in an interview that "the first music he ever heard was the rumble of trains and the songs of stevedores."[1] It was a short walk from his home on Third Street to the docks at the north end of State Street and the train tracks that ran alongside the bayfront. Many African American dockworkers and stevedores were from the South, and Burleigh may have learned work songs and jubilees (now known as spirituals) from them as well as from his family.

Other ambient strains of music were the insistent medleys of Erie's brass bands. Burleigh preferred the music of salon and recital hall to that of city parks and hotel ballrooms, but he demonstrated in the orchestra pit of Williams and Walker's *Senegambian Carnival* that he could function successfully in more informal, popular, and semiclassical settings as well. His exposure to the fine bands in Erie was a part of his preparation for New York's varied music scene. German workers who migrated to Erie in the 1840s and 1850s included many skilled musicians. They formed bands such as the Elks Sympathy Band, rated "most grotesque and funniest," the "snappy" Elks White Squadron Band in their spotless white uniforms (called the "Bean Soup Brigade" by their friends),[2] and the Knoll Family Band (with whom Burleigh performed on at least one occasion), "considered the best in the country from 1870 to 1880."[3] There were also Mehl's Band, the Tenth Street Orchestra, and the Juvenile Band, all conducted by perfectionist Anton Kohler. Kohler came to Erie with the Dan Rice Circus Band. He directed some of Erie's best orchestras and bands at social events and theaters and was notorious for his sarcasm directed at musicians who failed to meet his standard of excellence: "Woe unto them if they struck a sour note."[4]

Burleigh would not have been a guest at the social events where these bands played, but he could hear them perform in the streets. During his leisure time he could hear some of the outdoor concerts or the hotel performances while working as elevator operator at the Reed House Hotel. When Anton Knoll's Family Band conducted concerts at Perry Square Park on summer evenings, people from the surrounding countryside drove in to listen. Burleigh could hear them even without walking the few short blocks from his home. Perhaps he fine-tuned his own standards of excellence listening to Anton Kohler's bands and the virtuosic cornetists of the Knoll Family band.[5]

His home was filled with singing. "I don't recall when I started singing, it seems I have been doing so since infancy," he later recalled.[6] His was a working family, and they sang at their work. His blind grandfather was remembered for his "exceptionally melodious voice";[7] Burleigh said that he learned plantation songs and stories from him as he and his brother Reginald led him through the streets, assisting him as gas lamplighter and town crier. His mother sang at her work at home, and the rest of the family joined in.[8] Like his coachman stepfather, Burleigh worked as a carriage driver for the Carroll family, who lived at the corner of Fourth and Peach streets. According to family stories recalled by Virginia S. Reitzell, a granddaughter of the Carrolls, Burleigh "was always singing."[9] His stepfather's connection with the Reed family, shipbuilders and owners of lake steamers and freight vessels, helped Burleigh secure jobs loading freight on the docks and working as a pantry man on lake steamers sailing out of Buffalo, New York. And always, Burleigh listened and sang.

Burleigh described his mother as a fine natural singer. He said the "whole family was very musical and they often had family concerts in their home."[10] These family concerts would have occurred more frequently after his mother's marriage to John Elmendorf, as the children grew older and their economic situation was, if not easy, somewhat less precarious.

Burleigh credited his mother as his first music teacher, and he learned spirituals from her as well as from his grandfather. In her Burleigh saw a love for art music combined with an appreciation for his African American oral music heritage. The middle-class social and cultural values Burleigh's family shared with many free African Americans did not include the reluctance to sing spirituals that was common at this time among the well-educated children of former slaves.[11]

Given Burleigh's later renown as an arranger and interpreter of spirituals, it is important to note when and where he heard and sang these songs and what exposure he had to black musicians who toured the country. The first important collection of African American folksong transcriptions, *Slave Songs of the United States,* was published in 1867, the year after Burleigh's birth. This volume did not become well known to the general public, so Burleigh may not have had access to it in Erie, but he would certainly have been familiar with the collections of spirituals sung by the Fisk and the Hampton Jubilee Singers that appeared in the early 1870s. Both the Fisk and the Hampton singers performed in Erie, as did other jubilee groups.

Burleigh's family would also have known of James Monroe Trotter's 1878 *Music and Some Highly Musical People,* the first music history by a black music historian, which recorded the achievements of classically trained African American musicians who established themselves earlier in the nineteenth century. Some of these performers were still touring during Burleigh's youth, and Erie was a stop on their itineraries. Trotter himself, whom President Cleveland appointed recorder of deeds for the District of Columbia in 1887, was often mentioned in the Cleveland *Gazette,* which the family read and to which they contributed correspondence from Erie.[12]

Erie's newspapers seldom recorded performances of jubilees or spirituals by black citizens, though this may mean that they rarely performed them publicly rather than that they didn't sing them. The early leaders of the A.M.E. church, who were interested in seeing African Americans demonstrate their ability to move into more "enlightened" American culture, did not encourage use of the songs created by their unschooled ancestors. Bishop Daniel Payne and others emphasized choral and instrumental music in worship, rather than the "corn-field ditties" or "spiritual songs" of the plantation.[13] It is likely that at St. James A.M.E. the congregation sang the Isaac Watts and other gospel hymns commonly sung in Methodist churches. But spirituals did appear on programs when St. James held fundraising entertainment for the larger community. Burleigh's friend John Diehl recalled singing "many of the Negro spirituals which he arranged with such good effect in later years" with him on Sunday afternoons at the Himrod Mission, led by "the long-bearded song leader, P. G. Finn."[14] Jubilee songs and spirituals were a common feature of outdoor camp meetings. Some white people in the community enjoyed hearing them and knew that their black neighbors could sing them. On one occasion, at the request of a bereaved family, Burleigh organized a "colored quartette" for a concert in their benefit.[15]

Burleigh also had opportunities to hear several of the touring troupes of jubilee singers that proliferated from the 1870s on. The success of the Fisk Jubilee Singers in raising money for their Nashville college, Fisk University, in the early 1870s inspired many imitators who raised money for their black schools in the South. Jubilee performances were announced in the Erie newspapers along with the vaudeville, minstrel, popular theater, and opera troupes coming to town. In addition to singers from Hampton Institute in Hampton, Virginia, the Fisk Jubilee Singers performed in Erie on a number of occasions, as did the New Orleans University Jubilee Singers. In fact, the Hampton Singers appeared in Erie the week Burleigh's mother married John Elmendorf in 1875.[16]

Erie audiences might be integrated or segregated. Erie's black population was small, so the impulse to exclude them was less compelling than in centers where a larger proportion of the population was black. Even if black citizens were not welcome at the main concert, Burleigh would have had occasion to hear them sing in informal settings. Black performers were not allowed to stay in local hotels, so black families provided hospitality for them, and it was common for traveling musicians to perform at a reception or gathering after the concert.[17] Many of the minstrel troupes featured classically trained black singers, so he was exposed to a significant number of distinguished black musicians before he left for New York City. There were appearances by blind pianist Thomas Wiggins (also known as Thomas Greene Bethune), as well as the famed Hyers Sisters, "silver-voiced" tenor Wallace King, and baritone John Luca. Madah and Louise Hyers came to Erie on several occasions with the Callender Minstrel Troupe, and the papers reported enthusiastically on their performances.[18]

From the time of their emergence in the 1830s, minstrel shows became America's favorite public entertainment. Immigrant groups such as the Irish and the Germans were also targets of satirical stereotyping on the minstrel stage, but the complexity of racial relationships embedded in chattel slavery in the United States made the public representation of African Americans on the minstrel stage peculiarly poignant. Given the pervasive racist stereotyping of African Americans in minstrel shows and the relatively recent appearance of black musicians in a performance tradition largely dominated by white performers in blackface, black minstrel and jubilee troupes often needed to validate their authenticity as black performers, their music training beyond their "natural musical gifts," and their gentility, to counter the shuffling lowbrow stereotype.

One might wonder why any black American would stoop, much less aspire, to a career in minstrelsy or vaudeville. But for talented black musicians, comedians, or actors, few other options for public performance could be found in the nineteenth century. And the impulse to create a more authentic, dignified and nuanced representation of African American life, whether on the plantation or in the urban North, was irresistible to many, in addition to the attractive prospect of a lucrative stage career.[19] Why shouldn't black performers share in the financial rewards and the public recognition accruing from a performative tradition supposedly steeped in their own cultural heritage? A few black performers could be found in white minstrel troupes before the Civil War, but their numbers increased dramatically after Emancipation, and white-managed black troupes were soon competing with troupes fully cast by black performers, managed by black entrepreneurs.[20] Well into the twentieth century audience expectations limited the changes black performers could incorporate in their shows, but the black troupes capitalized on their innate authenticity at the same time that they attempted to counteract the derogatory images of African Americans as ignorant, uneducated, musically unsophisticated, subhuman beings.[21] Some of the performers who found their greatest public and financial success on the minstrel and vaudeville stages could have developed fine careers in mainline opera or theater houses had they been allowed to participate. Burleigh himself would be caught up in the tension between these competing performance traditions, to all of which he was introduced in Erie.[22]

In January 1884 Donavin's Famous Company of Tennesseeans came to Erie's Park Opera House under the auspices of the Women's Christian Temperance Union. At this time the Hyers sisters, Wallace King, and John Luca comprised the nucleus of the troupe, and the Erie response was consistent with reviews of their performances across the country. Advance notices stressed the authenticity of their performance, their commendable music accomplishment, and their dignity and moral character. Each of the singers was described in glowing terms: soprano Anna Madah Hyers, for the flexibility, range, and power of her voice; her sister Emma Hyers, for her deep contralto voice, "of sympathetic quality and great range"; Wallace King, for his tenor voice, which he used with "great feeling," taking the tenor's obligatory high C "with ease and accuracy"; and baritone John Luca, who sang "with fine effect." Each of the four displayed ability primarily in solos, but their ensemble singing was also praised for the harmonious vocal blend. In musical terms, their rhythmic precision, their interpretation, and their pitch intonation, were "as near perfection as seems possible to attain." The W.C.T.U. took pains to "fit up quarters" for them, doubtless in African American homes. The group was billed as "thorough vocalists" who "give a legitimate and varied concert programme." Testimonials vouched for their "high character" and "genuineness."[23] An enthusiastic reviewer lauded them: "A richer musical treat . . . has not been had in Erie for many a long day." Local newspapers occasionally lamented that even the "world's best singers" might draw small audiences in Erie. But on this occasion the Tennesseeans drew "a splendid audience," and the reviewer assured his readers that the performers met the necessary criteria: they were "all refined people, ladies and gentlemen in appearance as well as fact."[24]

In March and in November of the same year, the Hyers Sisters were featured stars of the fifty-member Callender's Consolidated Spectacular Minstrel Company. In March the troupe held a street parade to publicize their program on the day of their performance. Newspaper reviews said that both the novelty acts—the Zouave drill, the lightning expert, and the contortionist—and the singing were excellent. But there was one complaint: the Hyers Sisters, who were "greatly admired in Erie," limited their appearance to one operatic duet. After their duet from Verdi's opera *La Traviata,* the audience clamored for more. The sisters "appeared, bowed and retired," but the applause continued even after the next performer appeared: "The cheering went on for fully five minutes, to the great embarrassment of the person who had come on the stage."[25]

These appearances featured the Hyers Sisters and other star singers in one or two special selections on a program presenting numerous other performers. On other occasions the sisters gave full concerts of operatic arias, art songs, and ballads. Most of their repertoire consisted of secular songs, with a few religious songs and hymns. But as the jubilee troupes proved the drawing power of the spirituals, other singers followed their lead. In early 1876, the Hyers Sisters added jubilee songs to their usual programs.[26] So Burleigh's practice of including a set of plantation songs and spirituals alongside opera arias, German lieder, and American art songs in his recitals was not unique; this pattern had been modeled by the Hyers Sisters and other black vaudeville performers.

* * *

Burleigh learned from these troupes of talented musicians what performance opportunities were available to a trained African American singer. He set his sights on joining their ranks and extending the scope of his performance beyond the minstrel and vaudeville stage. Burleigh's fine voice had been discovered in elementary school, and during his high school years (in his late teens), he was increasingly in demand for solos and ensembles at churches and various community events. In a 1956 letter to music critic W. J. Henderson, Sarah B. Ball, who grew up in Erie, recalled that her brother had brought Burleigh home from high school one day to sing for her family. "I remember standing in the doorway of the living room listening to him sing." She reported that at that time he was singing in a church choir.[27]

From his high school years in his late teens until he left Erie, Burleigh's name appeared with increasing frequency in Erie papers and the Cleveland *Gazette,* as a soloist on programs in a wide variety of church and community venues. His immediate success at the National Conservatory of Music was simply the next step in a career that was well on its way before he left his hometown. A 1961 Erie *News* article quoted family friend Earl Lawrence as saying that Burleigh's musical talent was not widely recognized in Erie: "He sang in the St. Paul Choir, but that's all anyone heard of him."[28] But the public record shows that from 1885 to 1892 Burleigh won his way to the top ranks of Erie's classical singers and achieved wide recognition for his singing in Erie's broader community as well as in Cleveland and Buffalo.

In the earliest newspaper reports, Burleigh sang baritone in a family quartet. On June 9, 1881, the choir of Grace Mission (an outreach congregation of the Episcopal Cathedral of St. Paul) "gave a pleasant entertainment at the church, at which there was a very large audience present."[29] The program featured Burleigh, his older brother Reggie, and his younger sisters Ada and Eva Grace, singing "Beautiful Sunset." The next account of a Burleigh family ensemble appeared in November 1883, when the ladies of St. James A.M.E. Church gave a supper and concert at Grand Army Hall. The music was under the direction of Professor Lawrence (a great-uncle of Ada Lawrence). The quartet—Burleigh's mother, now Elizabeth Elmendorf; his sister, Eva; Burleigh; and Mr. Lawrence—sang "Sweet and Low," in a rendition that was pronounced "especially fine."[30]

By 1884 the eighteen-year-old Burleigh had begun his high school studies. Principal H. C. Missimer reported the array of subjects students could choose in 1885–86, and the number of students enrolled in each option. Burleigh could choose among a wide range of academic subjects. Though we do not have documentation of the specific courses he chose, one can be sure he was among the 229 music students. He probably studied German, and declamation seems to have been required, along with English composition and the General Information course.[31]

From this point on, Burleigh's singing was not limited to private homes. He appeared in public performances such as the high school's February 1885 Washington's Birthday celebration."[32] He was hired as a chorister and soloist in several churches. In fall 1885 the Episcopal Cathedral of St. Paul established its first Men and Boys Choir. Burleigh sang baritone, and two younger African Americans, Charles Fisher (an uncle of Ada Lawrence) and Charles Franklin sang soprano.

Their first performance was deemed a great success. Burleigh's lifelong commitment to church music and to an Episcopal mode of worship was nurtured here. The hymns, anthems, and liturgical responses chosen by the organist and choir director with whom Burleigh sang at St. Paul's familiarized him with many European and American composers of church music in Episcopalian services: Giovanni Pierluigi da Palestrina, Thomas Tallis, Franz Joseph Haydn, Ludwig van Beethoven, Hans

Men & Boys Choir, Episcopal Cathedral of St. Paul, 1885. (Courtesy of the Burleigh Family)

Leo Hassler, Gabriel Fauré, Carl Maria von Weber, Ignaz Pleyel, John Barnby, J. B. Dykes, Lowell Mason, John Stainer, and Arthur S. Sullivan.[33]

An 1873 article by Bishop J. F. Spaulding, who had welcomed Burleigh's family into the congregation a decade earlier, described the ideal church musician: fine musicianship was expected, but the musician's art was always to be subservient to the purpose of worship. Spaulding proposed a "test of good taste in Church Music (and of good churchmanship also)": to request the singing of a long hymn of six or seven verses or "any long psalm to a *single chant,* which is purely melodious and devotional." If the singer objected "on artistic grounds" to singing all the verses of a hymn, no further evidence was needed "of a defective and spurious taste."[34] Six-year-old Burleigh would not have understood the argument, but attending Sunday morning services with his mother from childhood and singing in the Men and Boys Choir as an eighteen-year-old, he would certainly have absorbed its reverberations. His habit of coming into the sanctuary at St. George's Episcopal Church to "get the feel of the place" and his comments about the importance of music in worship show that the seeds planted at the Cathedral of St. Paul took deep root. His protests against the misuse of spirituals in secular settings and in jazz arrangements also arose from an aesthetic grounded in his sense of the sacred and what was appropriate in Christian worship.

The same year the Men and Boys Choir was formed at St. Paul's, Burleigh also began singing at Park Presbyterian Church, where the Himrods and Elizabeth Russell and her family attended and where his grandmother Lucinda Duncanson Waters had been a member; at the First Presbyterian Church; and at the Reform Jewish Temple, where Isador Sobel, a Jewish attorney who took an interest in Burleigh, was a member. These choirs did not sing every week, and their responsibilities varied with the seasons of the church year, so Burleigh could participate in more than one congregation's music program. Because his responsibilities at the Jewish Temple would have required his presence on Friday and Saturday rather than Sunday, like professional church singers today, he could easily accommodate them in addition to the services in Christian churches. These paid positions allowed Burleigh to contribute to the family's income, and they prepared him to serve at St. George's Episcopal Church and Temple Emanu-El in New York City.[35]

* * *

It is not surprising that Burleigh's name appeared in programs presented by high school students, but we might not expect to see him featured on programs sponsored by a business college. Burleigh took business courses in addition to his regular high school classes and his work at various jobs. Bookkeeping was offered at the high school, but Burleigh attended Clark's Commercial College for a more comprehensive business program. There he gained the stenographic skills that later secured his positions as assistant to the registrar at the National Conservatory of Music and as music copyist for Antonín Dvořák. Advertisements for the college displayed the ornate style of penmanship that good businessmen and secretaries (often male) were expected to master. H. C. Clark, the college's founder and director, promoted an active literary society that presented frequent public programs. Knowledge of poetry was expected of the educated person, including those pursuing a commercial career. In March 1885, Burleigh was featured on Longfellow Day at the Clark College literary society meeting, where members "responded to the roll call by sentiments from the writings of the poet."[36]

We know Burleigh as a singer, but he gained proficiency on several string instruments as well. On this occasion he played guitar in a duet with George Dinkey. "The programme proved to be a highly seasoned intellectual fest, and those who braved the storm in order to be present were rewarded."[37] Several years later, in February 1888, he entertained the YMCA Quarterly meeting with a violin solo.[38] The tribute heading the subscription lists as he left Erie in 1892 referred to his bass viol, which he later played along with the timpani in the National Conservatory orchestra.[39] But as his competence grew, his singing assumed greater importance than his instrumental playing. He may have seen in the troupes of black performers that there were more opportunities for singers than for classical instrumentalists at this time, so his voice gave him his most realistic chance for success as a professional musician.

Burleigh's first piano teacher was Susan Vosburgh Dickson, the daughter of his grandfather's employer. He became a competent pianist, often accompanying himself on his early recitals and when he gave lecture recitals on the spiritual genre. But his dream of becoming a concert pianist could not be fulfilled; the fourth finger of both hands was the same length as his little finger, a congenital shortening that made a professional piano career impractical.[40]

Burleigh's most important music teacher in Erie was George F. Brierly. English by birth, Brierly trained as a Worchester Cathedral chorister. On migrating to the United States, he worked as an organ tuner for the Burdett Organ Company in Chicago. After the Great Chicago Fire in 1871, several organ companies such as the Felgemaker and the Burdett Organ Companies relocated from Chicago to Erie, and Brierly came to Erie with the Burdett Company. He took the position of music director for the Central Presbyterian Church and became a prominent singer, choir director, and teacher in the Erie art music scene.[41]

Erie boasted several choral groups such as the Erie Liedertafel, the Erie Sängerbund and the Erie Maennerchor, whose names reflected their predominantly German membership. The Union Musical Association was formed in 1868, with a broader membership drawn from the church choirs of the city; former abolitionist and Oberlin College graduate Henry Catlin served as president. The membership of the association grew to 250, but when the group disbanded, Catlin and George Brierly established the Orpheus Society, with Catlin again serving as president. By the mid-1880s the Orpheus Society was considered the finest community choir in Erie. Membership was by audition and was not limited to members of church choirs.[42]

In 1884 George Brierly resigned his positions at the Burdett Organ Company and Central Presbyterian to take charge of the music program at the First Methodist Church, where Burleigh's mother was a Sunday school teacher. Here his public concerts showcased the church's fine choir and professional soloists. In January 1885 the Orpheus Society offered a singing class under Brierly's direction. In March 1886 the Erie Conservatory of Music advertised a series of twenty voice lessons for $15 or for a class of two ($7.50 each) taught by George F. Brierly.[43]

One musical milestone in Burleigh's Erie singing career came a few months after his high school graduation, in fall 1887, when Burleigh, his mother, and his sister Eva Grace were invited to join the Orpheus Society.[44] This was significant recognition of their musicianship, and they likely integrated the choir. Henry Catlin's interest in music and his commitment to racial equality were both in play in opening the door for the Burleighs to participate, but Burleigh also won his place by demonstrating his aptitude to his voice teacher, George Brierly.

* * *

Burleigh understood the importance of hearing professional singers. An intriguing example of his determination to hear visiting artists had far-reaching implications for Burleigh's career at the National Conservatory of Music. The daughter of William C. Curry, his father's former employer, married Robert W. Russell. Originally a clerk at his father-in-law's bank, Russell became a successful wood and coal merchant and was now a bank director and attorney. Both R. W. and Elizabeth Russell were sophisticated lovers of music. Elizabeth was a sensitive and accomplished pianist, and in 1880 she and her husband purchased a fine Steinway grand piano. The Erie audience for fine music was sometimes quite small, and the elegant parlors of the Russell home became an important recital venue.[45]

Burleigh said that from time to time his mother assisted Mrs. Russell as maid at these musicales. Thirty years later, he described one particularly stormy winter night when the famous Hungarian pianist Rafael Joseffy, a friend of Franz Liszt, was the featured soloist. When Joseffy had performed at the Park Opera House several years earlier, the audience was sparse, and he vowed never to return for such a small audience. In comparing Joseffy's listeners to the full house that greeted Buffalo Bill the following day, the Erie *Morning Dispatch* reported ruefully, "Joseffy has slain his tens and Buffalo Bill his thousands."[46] But Mrs. Russell lured Joseffy back to Erie by providing a setting more congenial to his artistry, a musicale in her beautiful home, with an enthusiastic audience of music lovers.[47] As Burleigh told the story, he was determined to hear the recital "at any cost," and stood in snow drifted up to his knees outside the drawing-room window to hear "the great Joseffy in his fullest powers."[48] But the price of his admission to the recital was dear. When he nearly developed pneumonia, his mother insisted on knowing the truth. Alarmed at his answer, she asked Mrs. Russell if he could perform duties in the house for future musicales so he could hear the performances without endangering his health. Mrs. Russell agreed that he could serve as doorman.

In Burleigh's account, the next musicale featured the young Venezuelan pianist Teresa Carreño, Edward MacDowell's teacher. Her traveling companion was MacDowell's mother, Frances Knapp MacDowell, whom Burleigh would meet again as the registrar at the National Conservatory of Music.[49]

Rafael Joseffy appeared in Erie several times, at the Park Opera House, with Theodore Thomas's orchestra, and in the Russell home. Teresa Carreño also performed in the Russell home on several occasions, including on May 6, 1885, when she provided "the grandest musical entertainment" heard in Erie for some time.[50]

These were only two of numerous musicales in the Russell home featuring internationally recognized artists and these two artists in particular. Erie was a major inland port and a crossroads of traffic between Buffalo and Cleveland, making it a convenient stopping place for artists who had connections to music-loving families like the Russells.

No evidence has been found that Burleigh ever appeared in a concert with Mrs. Russell, but he often performed with musicians who played with her on other occasions. Despite the two families' long association, in their relationship to the Russells the Burleighs were members of the servant class rather than social equals. R. W. Russell achieved his social status largely from his wife's family, but the Russells were eligible to attend a grand ball put on by "the Queen" of Erie society, Mrs. Charles Reed (John Elmendorf's employer);[51] the Burleighs, if present at all, would have been among the downstairs staff, no matter their intellectual and cultural accomplishments. If it is true that Mrs. Russell felt it to be inappropriate to perform publicly with the son of her father's bank messenger, it should not surprise us. It may have been easier for musicians who had not been Burleigh's employers to accept this rising young artist as an equal—or nearly so.

* * *

Burleigh's job history is inseparable from his music experience. Not only did he sing at his work, but he took advantage of any job-related opportunity to further his music study. He worked in the warehouse at the Colby Piano Company, and after hours he was allowed to practice piano there.[52] On several occasions, Mrs. Colby accompanied him in recital.[53]

The early notices in Erie newspapers of Burleigh's singing were simple announcements or programs of events. But in August 1886 the first complimentary reviews of Burleigh as soloist appeared. One reported a full house and an appreciative audience. Like many of Burleigh's appearances, it was a benefit, this one in support of the Cross and Crown church, one of the outreach congregations of St. Paul's Episcopal Church. Burleigh's singing of Dudley Buck's "Come Where the Lindens Bloom" was enthusiastically encored, and he followed with "When the Flowing Tide Comes In."[54]

Burleigh was now singing in a broader range of civic and church circles such as the Loyal Ladies' League of the U.S. Grant Circle of the Grand Army of the Republic, the Select Knights of the Ancient Order of the United Works, and the First Baptist

Church. Some of these organizations were based in the black community, and some were segregated, but as time went on, more of his audiences were predominantly or exclusively white. The review of his performance with other singers at the Baptist Church in April 1887 commented that despite bad weather, the church was "filled to overflowing, aisles and all." Burleigh's solo "displayed his really good bass voice to fine advantage," and, as usual, his audience demanded an encore.[55]

During his senior year of high school, Burleigh moved into a more sophisticated stratum of Erie's singers. In January 1887 he was a soloist on a program with Mrs. Minnie Eggleston, George Brierly's soprano soloist at First Methodist Church.[56] Two days after his eloquent address at his graduation from Erie High School in June 1887, Burleigh sang at the Young Men's Debating Society of the YMCA. He often performed in programs for the Y, but "his solo on this occasion was above his usual standard." In tribute to his accomplishment, Burleigh was presented with a set of Shakespeare works.[57]

While he was gaining recognition as a singer for church and social events in the broader community, Burleigh continued to participate in programs to benefit St. James A.M.E. Church. In mid-October, the Grand Army of the Republic Hall was "crowded to suffocation" for a program of "songs, readings and tableaux offered by members of St. James A.M.E. Church." Burleigh sang "The Vagabond" by Molloy and gave his "Spartacus to the Gladiators" declamation.[58]

* * *

Burleigh appeared as a soloist more frequently in the last months of 1887 and early 1888 until the New Orleans University Jubilee Singers came to town in May 1888. This group of Jubilee Singers had come to Erie earlier in the 1880s on their tours through Pennsylvania and Ohio. Their 1888 appearance was sponsored by the Sons of Veterans and held in the Grand Army of the Republic Hall. "Everybody was pleased and went away asking when they could hear them again."[59]

The May 10, 1888, Erie *Morning Dispatch* review gives more information than most, and as Burleigh traveled with the group for the next eight months, the program details are instructive. Stephen Foster's songs were represented by "Swanee River," which their prima donna soprano Tillie Jones Thomas sang with "great expression." She also sang "Polly, the Cows are in the Corn" with a voice of "unusual power." The basso, a Mr. Johnson, "astonished the audience" with the flexibility of his deep bass voice when he sang "The Gravedigger." The group sang jubilee songs, but for comic effect rather than pathos: "Who Build de Ark" and "Didn't Ole Pharaoh Git Los." Their audience responded with "a continual laughter." The concert was a financial success, and so many in the audience wished to hear them again that the Women's Relief Corps arranged for a second concert the following evening at the Grand Army of the Republic Hall. This time local talent would be featured with them, in a program that may have served as Burleigh's audition for membership in the group.[60]

His tour with the New Orleans Jubilee Singers gave Burleigh the opportunity to experience personally what the minstrel and jubilee troupes he'd been hearing went through to raise money for their institutions or to build independent performing careers. Like many jubilee ensembles, the New Orleans University Jubilee Singers originated to raise funds for their school, a freedman's school founded by the Methodists. They were sent on the road in 1877 to raise funds to save the Colored Orphans' Home on Bayou Teche. Their prima donna soprano, Mathilda (Tillie) Jones (sometimes confused with "the Black Patti," Matilda Sissieretta Jones), was a member of the original group, and her husband, F. S. Thomas, managed the company. They completed their fundraising commitment in 1881 and then continued to tour as an independent group, retaining their original name.[61] Before coming to Erie, they sang in Sandusky, Ohio. Information on the itinerary while Burleigh was a member is incomplete, but in January they appeared in Galion, Ohio; in April at Union Chapel in Painesville, Ohio; and in October for a month in Williamsport, Pennsylvania, before returning to Erie in December, with Burleigh in the company. The *Dispatch* suggested that he intended to continue touring with the group, and that he "was in the city visiting his family," but he remained in Erie when the troupe departed.[62]

A few days after Burleigh returned to Erie, a company of Fisk Jubilee Singers came to town, under the auspices of the Women's Relief Corps of the Strong Vincent Post. The advertisements emphasized that this was indeed "The Original Company," though now two groups claimed that heritage, with equal credibility (though they were by no means the only "Fisk Jubilee Singers" on the road).[63] Having so recently heard the New Orleans University Jubilee Singers, Erie did not turn out for the Fisk Jubilee Singers. Ticket prices were reasonable—25, 35, and 50 cents—but the audience was disappointingly small. "Those present, however, had the pleasure of listening to an excellent concert" notable for the singers' "remarkably sweet harmony." The review added typical descriptions of plantation or jubilee music: "Their songs are of that wild, weird music, the distinguishing feature of southern plantation Negro songs, and reaches the sensibilities of the listener with great force."[64]

We see that Burleigh was familiar with the diverse repertoire presented by the touring jubilee groups: jubilee songs, sacred songs, and secular plantation songs alongside ballads and parlor songs. One can only speculate on his progress from familiarity with the repertoire to his strong advocacy of the spirituals as a treasured heritage that must be presented with dignity. Was he comfortable in 1888 using the jubilees primarily as comic interludes? Or did he leave the New Orleans University Jubilee Singers partly to distance himself from that kind of presentation?

Ten years later he demonstrated his own comic flair on the *Senegambian Carnival* stage, and reviews of his solo recitals reveal a warm and engaging stage presence. But the solo repertoire he was developing in his formal voice training was oriented toward European and American classical works. In 1917 when the G. Ricordi Music Publishing Company began issuing the spirituals that he had been singing in his own recitals for more than ten years, he forcefully rejected superficial and frivolous interpretations of the spirituals and challenged singers to treat them with dignity. He had learned to appreciate both the humor and the spiritual depth in these orally transmitted, improvisatory songs in his home. All these songs, both wry and sacred, belonged to the African American musical treasury, and it would take little urging from his mentor Antonín Dvořák and his friend Samuel Coleridge-Taylor to convince him that they should be given to the world.

* * *

In September 1891, a few months before he left for New York City, Burleigh again left Erie to join a jubilee troupe. He stopped in Cleveland to visit Cleveland *Gazette* editor H. C. Smith, on his way to Ravenna, Ohio, to join Frederick Loudin's Fisk Jubilee Singers. Loudin had emerged as one of George White's most impressive soloists in the Jubilee Singers from Fisk. In 1882 he assumed the management of the Fisk singers when George White withdrew from touring, and his career as a "globe-trotting jubilee singer-manager" steamed ahead. He understood marketing and publicity, and he also understood the power of the jubilee stage for civil-rights advocacy. He frequently challenged audiences to go beyond nostalgic listening, to work actively for change. Recent scholars term him "the most politically outspoken black entertainer of the nineteenth century." Under his leadership the Fisk Jubilee Singers brought accounts of the discrimination they suffered to public notice nationwide. They also campaigned, unsuccessfully, for the Civil Rights Bill of 1875.[65]

Loudin's Fisk Jubilee Singers had just returned from their six-year tour abroad when he recruited Burleigh in September 1891. Burleigh's civil-rights sentiments were in tune with Loudin's, and both were frequent associates of the Cleveland *Gazette's* fiery editor, H. C. Smith.[66] But Burleigh's Erie fans were reluctant to release him, and they persuaded him to decline "the flattering offer" to join the Fisk tour.[67] To his astonishment, the pastor and congregation at the First Presbyterian Church urged him by telegram not to leave and made their plea irresistible by raising his salary. He aborted his trip to Ravenna, and Erie's music lovers were assured that they would continue to hear him sing. He appeared in a concert of the First Methodist Episcopal Church and other community events in quick succession, though, as it happened, he would stay in Erie for only a few more months. The opportunity to audition at the National Conservatory of Music in New York City proved even more compelling, and no offer from the Erie Presbyterians could hold him back.[68]

* * *

When Burleigh graduated from high school in 1887, he moved into full-time employment as a stenographer at the Brown Folding Machine Company, owned by J. F. Downing. This was long before labor unions set the standard for an eight-hour day and a forty-hour work week, and Burleigh's evening singing engagements often followed a ten-hour work day. In June 1890 Burleigh was promoted from stenographer to bookkeeper.[69]

Six months later the Erie *Morning Dispatch* reported that the owner's son, Wellington Downing, who managed the plant, announced that the company, without agitation from the workers, would reduce the workday from ten to nine hours, recognizing "the justice of labor's claim that nine hours were enough" for an employer to ask. These far-sighted and liberal employers argued that working men needed more leisure time "to devote to their families, to the pursuit of knowledge, and in rational pleasures." Furthermore, the men would receive the same wages for working nine hours as they had for ten. The challenge to the workers was to "so use their extra time as to make converts even among employers to the nine hour theory" and "by increased diligence, prove, in the coming year, that the longest hours do not always produce the largest quantity nor the best quality of finished product."[70]

The demands of Burleigh's evening performances made this an especially welcome change and like his coworkers he would celebrate the New Year with enthusiasm. "To say that the men were pleased, hardly expresses their feelings, for they have all along been paid the highest wages paid in the city in their line of work, and good feeling has always existed between employers and employees."[71] Burleigh, avid in his "pursuit of knowledge" and the "rational pleasures" of music, would have needed no urging to make effective use of his extended leisure time.

* * *

In 1889 the benefits of George Brierly's vocal instruction become apparent in a more challenging solo repertoire and in the growing competence reflected in the reviews of Burleigh's singing. His repertoire was more sophisticated, now including opera ensembles and arias as well as German lieder, and ballads and art songs by American composers.[72] He was reaching a wider audience and was appearing in concerts with Erie's most distinguished singers—all of them white. Some of their audiences were racially mixed, but in venues such as the Park Opera House, neither Burleigh nor his family would have been welcome in the audience. Burleigh was a soloist at an entertainment for two hundred Clark College students at the Clark home (an integrated group), a musical soiree at the home of Mr. T. P. Barton on Twenty-Third Street (probably not integrated), the Solders' and Sailors' home with the St. Paul Episcopal Choir (both choir and audience were diverse), and a concert to benefit the victims of the Johnstown Flood, at which Burleigh sang in a duet from Bellini's *Il Puritani* (probably segregated). At the closing concert of the Orpheus Society's season, Burleigh was a featured soloist—he sang the Toreador Song from Bizet's *Carmen*—and two selections in a quartet with his voice teacher and conductor, George Brierly, and his good friend, tenor John Diehl. The Toreador Song became a regular feature of Burleigh's repertoire.[73]

The newspaper reviews of Burleigh's singing were becoming more detailed, demonstrating a growing public reputation, and he sang more frequently in the company of George Brierly, Minnie Eggleston, John Diehl, and Turner W. Shacklett, the premiere classical singers in the city. He sang works by Charles Gounod, Luigi

Denza, and Robert Schumann, including Schumann's "Two Grenadiers," which also settled into his recital repertoire.[74] At St. Paul's Episcopal Cathedral Burleigh was a featured soloist as well as a chorister. On October 4, 1889, he sang the offertory "One Sweetly Solemn Thought" by Robert Steele Ambrose, a number described as "very exacting and difficult to render, though the theme is delightful in senti-ment." He was developing consistency of tone quality throughout his vocal range, every singer's challenge, and there was evident improvement in his "clearness of enunciation, purity of tone" and expressive feeling.[75]

* * *

Years later Burleigh told another story of the lengths to which he would go to hear a visiting professional singer. On September 30, 1889, he slipped past the Park Opera House staff to hide in the balcony to hear the famous Italian tenor Italo Campanini and his company. Burleigh's feat was risky; several years before two young boys had been arrested for trespassing on the Park Opera House property. But Burleigh knew the importance of learning from one of the most famous singers of his time, and he was determined not to miss the opportunity. He would have been able to pay the fifty-cent charge for a gallery seat, but Erie audiences at such events were not integrated. Burleigh had forgotten that the performance was in the evening, not in the afternoon. It was dark in the balcony, and the afternoon was long. "I did not stir, so fearful was I of detection. But I heard Campanini and his fellow-artists and enjoyed the concert immensely." Burleigh himself had spoken from and would sing on that stage before he left Erie, but as was often the case, African Americans could perform on stages where they could not join the audience.[76]

* * *

By 1890 Burleigh had become a star in Erie's classical music constellation and in three out-of-state venues. In addition to the thirty-six solo performances reported in Erie, he was a featured soloist in Cleveland and Austinburg, Ohio, as well as Buf-falo, New York. Reviews of programs often specifically mentioned his singing and indicate that his audience now anticipated an especially fine performance when he appeared. In February 1890 the kind of winter storm that often visits the Lake Erie shoreline threatened to sabotage an evening of dramatic reading interspersed with vocal selections for the Young People's Society of the First Presbyterian Church. "The night was wild; the boisterous gale was laden with snow, sleet and rain mixed; just the kind of a weather combination that is the meanest of all." The small but hardy group of listeners was not disappointed: "At intervals in the programme there were vocal selections by Miss Sadie Kinnear and Mr. Harry Burleigh, selections that it is needless to say were excellently sung."[77] The themes of anticipation and satisfaction run through reports of Burleigh's singing. In March he appeared with the celebrated Knoll's Band in a concert at Riblet Hall, and in April when he sang for the Veterans at the Soldier's Home, the reviewer said, "Mr. Burleigh gave some of his delightful solos, which are always well received."[78] In June the announcement of a program given at the Tabernacle to raise money for the gymnasium fund listed Burleigh among a "list of well-known artists [that] bespeaks a most delightful evening for those who will attend." Mrs. Charles Colby of the Colby Piano Company, where Burleigh had practiced piano in the warehouse, served as accompanist for this event. The Burleigh family was still occasionally called on for musical selections. At the 50th anniversary celebration of the Himrod Mission and School, where Burleigh's grandfather, Hamilton Waters, had been active, they provided "a leading feature of the excellent music provided for the occasion." Burleigh also sang a solo.[79]

Burleigh's performances were spreading in the tristate area, but they were also increasing in Erie. During 1890 Burleigh appeared as a soloist in Presbyterian, Methodist, and Episcopal churches as well as at St. James and in various community events: at First Presbyterian Church, Park Presbyterian Church Mission, St. Paul's Episcopal Cathedral, the First Christian Church, the Simpson Methodist Episcopal Church, and at the Tenth Street Methodist Episcopal Church. He also was a member of the Madrigal Club (though they didn't sing madrigals, at least in public), which gave a benefit concert for the Central Presbyterian Church organ fund. When the Pythagoras Commandery gave an entertainment at Liedertafel Hall, Burleigh sang a solo and joined a Burleigh family quartet with his mother, his Aunt Louisa, and his sister Eva.[80]

In 1891, the last year before Burleigh left for New York City, he was on the go in Erie and the surrounding area as well as Cleveland and Buffalo. May found him performing with the Excelsior Cornet Band in Cleveland and at St. Philip's Episcopal Church in Buffalo, an appearance which "was highly appreciated." His "many warm friends" in Buffalo wished him "the greatest success."[81] He also sang at the commencement exercises in Girard, Pennsylvania, where he was the guest of the school principal and "was presented with a floral tribute."[82]

Burleigh's usual appearances at church and community events continued. He sang at a memorial service at the First Presbyterian Church.[83] He entertained a group of his friends at "an evening of recitation and song," where he sang "I Fear No Foe" "in his usual happy manner."[84] And he was among the musicians who entertained at the ball in honor of the fifth anniversary of the Order of Railway Conductors.[85]

* * *

Burleigh's connections in Cleveland, Ohio, and Buffalo, New York, were preparing him for the new stage of his career in New York City. Both cities were easily accessible by train, and from 1889 on the Cleveland *Gazette* reported that Burleigh and his sister Eva were frequent visitors in that city.[86] The Burleigh-Elmendorfs had family and friends in Cleveland, and Burleigh's usual hosts were Ernest O. Orsburn and H. C. Smith, the editor and the publisher, respectively, of the *Gazette.*

These two men shared Burleigh's music interests; Orsburn had a fine baritone voice and H. C. Smith played cornet, led the Excelsior Cornet Band, and wrote songs in addition to his editorial duties.[87] Both Orsburn and Smith often visited Burleigh in Erie, and Burleigh and Orsburn frequently appeared on the same programs.[88]

* * *

Burleigh's family also had connections in Buffalo, New York. His father established contacts there during his brief service on the Buffalo–Chicago run on the Lake Shore Railroad, and Burleigh himself served as a pantry man on lake steamers out of Buffalo. Among Burleigh's "many warm friends" in Buffalo were the Talbert family, who also had ties to Cleveland.[89] Robert Talbert (sometimes spelled Tolbert), the patriarch of the Talbert family, amassed his fortune in the California gold rush and married the daughter of the richest man in Buffalo, "who was extensively engaged in the shipping and passenger traffic between here and New York City via the Erie canal." When he died in December 1892 he was considered "the wealthiest colored man in Western New York."[90]

His younger son, sixteen-year-old Walter T., or Thaddeus (Thad), excited comment in 1887 as a fine pianist after only two years of study. In May a traveling agent for the Cleveland *Gazette* heard him play. "Two years ago he was entirely ignorant of the piano; could not strike a chord. Today he can play the most difficult music from the compositions of our most celebrated composers."[91] In February 1891 Thad Talbert was admitted to the National Conservatory of Music in New York City, to study harmony and organ. He set up a studio on Thirty-Seventh Street near Broadway and soon had a number of students. He reported playing "at several of the largest churches" in New York City, undoubtedly black churches. When Talbert returned to Buffalo for the summer, his Buffalo friends heard "marked improvement" in his playing.[92]

On September 8, 1891, Burleigh was best man at the wedding of Thad's older brother William to Mary Burnett. Mary Burnett Talbert, also a musician, had trained at Oberlin College.[93] Burleigh and the Talberts shared a concern for social justice. A strong advocate for civil rights and a nationally recognized leader in black women's groups, in a few years Mary Talbert would be working with Ida Wells-Barnett in her position as leader in the National Association of Colored Women. One of Talbert's accomplishments was the dedication of the Frederick Douglass Memorial Home in Anacostia, Maryland. When she died in 1922, she was regarded as one of a group of women who sacrificed their very lives for the race.[94]

With Burleigh's Johnson cousins in Brooklyn and the Talbert family in Buffalo, Burleigh's knowledge of the scholarship competition at the National Conservatory of Music in January 1892 is no mystery. Thad Talbert's experience at the National Conservatory was less happy than Burleigh's, but during Burleigh's first year in New

York City, he and Talbert collaborated on several concerts. The year after Burleigh joined him there, Talbert transferred to Oberlin College.[95]

* * *

During the last two months before Burleigh left Erie to audition at the National Conservatory, John and Elizabeth Elmendorf spent a month visiting family and friends in Kingston and Brooklyn, New York. Reverend W. F. Johnson, one of the Johnson cousins from Ithaca, New York, held a wedding anniversary celebration for them. Though legally blind, Johnson was the superintendent of the Howard Orphan's Asylum in Brooklyn, which provided a strong education program for its 120 children. He was an active leader in the church and social affairs in Brooklyn, and his name appeared frequently in the New York *Age*. Among the guests at the anniversary dinner were other family members, including Burleigh's older brother Reginald and such luminaries as T. Thomas Fortune, editor of the *Age*. Thad Talbert played the piano, and "at a late hour goodbyes were said and all returned to their homes."[96]

The timing of this trip is significant. The Elmendorfs would soon send their son Harry to New York City to audition for a scholarship at the National Conservatory of Music. Thad Talbert could introduce them to the school. When Burleigh's family sent him off to New York City, they did not release him into a Great Unknown. Their own circles stretched far beyond Erie, Pennsylvania. They knew he was going to a school that would help him achieve his dream of becoming a professional singer, and there were trusted family and friends who would interest themselves in his progress.

* * *

In December 1891, just two weeks before he left for New York City, Burleigh was a featured soloist at a historic event that confirmed his place among "the finest vocal talent in the city."[97] Erie's new St. Peter's Roman Catholic Cathedral had been completed but not yet consecrated, and a gala concert would inaugurate it on Tuesday, December 15. The papers announced the program several days in advance and all the papers carried reviews the day after the event.[98]

Burleigh sang Mattei's "O Patria" or "My Native Land," one of his signature songs. The reviews in three Erie papers the following day lauded Burleigh's performance. The *Morning Dispatch* described the anticipation that his singing aroused: "That Mr. Harry Burleigh has the same power as of old over Erie hearts was evinced by the tremendous applause that greeted him as he stepped forward to sing Mattei's 'Native Land.'"[99] The *Daily Times* said he "threw much dramatic feeling into its execution."[100] And the *Evening Herald* reported that he "had an opportunity to use his well-cultivated voice with all its fullness, and the hearty applause that followed was well merited."[101] The final number on the program called on Burleigh's comedic gifts: "A Catastrophe" by N. B. Sprague, "which recounted the mishaps of a tack, a boy and a school master." It was sung by a male quartet, with Burleigh singing baritone and Turner (T. W.) Shacklett, a warden of the St. Paul Episcopal Cathedral, singing bass, "in magnificent style."[102]

The Christmas Mass ten days later would be celebrated at the old St. Patrick's Cathedral, now designated the Pro-Cathedral, and Carl Maria von Weber's *Jubilee Mass* was featured in this last "most important event of the Catholic church" to be celebrated there. The Massassauga Orchestra accompanied, and Burleigh, John C. Diehl, and T. W. Shacklett were among the distinguished singers assisting the choir.[103] Burleigh's singing had always served a broadly ecumenical audience, but these gala events just preceding his departure for New York carried him into new ecclesiastical territory. St. Paul's Episcopal Cathedral was a high-church congregation, so the Roman Catholic liturgy was not foreign to him. The twenty-five-year-old Burleigh had achieved all that was possible for a classically trained singer in Erie. He was ready for new challenges in America's musical mecca: New York City.

* * *

It is not clear whether Burleigh's Erie friends knew of his plans to leave for New York City, though the especially warm praise for his singing in the previous months may have arisen partly from anticipation of his prospects. Burleigh's social calendar was full in his last few days in Erie. On Sunday, December 24, the St. Paul's Choir sang for prisoners at the jail and Burleigh sang at the Pro-Cathedral. Cleveland friends were visiting on Christmas Day, including Lillian Chesnutt, daughter of writer Charles Chesnutt. She and a friend were guests of Mattie and Nettie Dickson. In the evening, Harry and his sister Eva joined them, and "a pleasant theater party was enjoyed."[104] The Cleveland *Gazette* reported simply, "Mr. Harry T. Burleigh left for New York Sunday night [January 3]."[105]

But when Burleigh returned to Erie after winning a full scholarship for four years of tuition at the National Conservatory of Music, several Erie papers were happy to report.[106] A January 15 article entitled "Merited Success" announced Burleigh's return from New York City. In his audition, "an exhaustive competitive examination," he had to demonstrate proficiency "in writing, music, solfeggio or scale sing[ing], songs, ballads, oratorio, etc." Burleigh would return to New York City the following week to begin his studies.[107]

This was the first of a flurry of articles in the Erie papers commenting on Burleigh's deserved success in the audition and proposing a fund-raiser to assist him in his early months at the conservatory. Two columns "From Bystander" in the Erie *Evening Herald* asserted that Burleigh had earned the community's support through his own generosity in assisting charitable causes. The first drew an analogy to the biblical promise, "Cast thy bread upon the waters, and it will return to thee after many days." Gifted young men and women should be given generous support, and Burleigh was "a case in point." Burleigh shared his musical talent freely: "People liked to hear him sing, and whenever he was called upon to assist in church or charity work he never said no." He sang his way "into the hearts of all who listened to him," with no expectation of a reward. People in Erie who loved hearing him sing and appreciated his generosity in using his voice to assist others said, "Now is our time to assist Mr. Burleigh." He will need money to live in New York, "and we must help him now in return for the oft-repeated assistance given to enterprises in which we have been interested." He had "cast his bread upon the waters," and no one would "question that the fruits of the good done by Mr. Harry Burleigh have returned to him after many days. This is the rule. It always has been; it always will be."[108]

It quickly became apparent that there was not time to organize a benefit concert. To keep his scholarship Burleigh needed to be back in New York City by January 20 to begin his studies, so it was decided to collect subscriptions for a fund to be given to him directly. "It is not the intention to ask anyone for large amounts, but persons who desire are requested to contribute the amount they would have cheerfully expended for tickets to a benefit concert."[109] By January 18 subscription lists were posted at the city drugstores. In the next few days lists were added at City Treasurer Hanley's office, the Strong Vincent Veterans Post, and the office of the Brown Folding Machine Works, where Burleigh had worked as a clerk and accountant.[110]

Meanwhile, Burleigh brought back a critique of the New York music scene. While in New York City he had heard Adelina Patti, the famous soprano against whom other singers were often measured. Burleigh found her performance less impressive than that of "the American nightingale," Annie Louise Tanzer-Musin, who was to appear at the Tabernacle in Erie the following week. He reported that her "wonderful range of voice exceeds that of Patti by several notes," and in his opinion her "execution is not excelled by any singer in the world." Burleigh even delayed his departure for New York in order to hear Tanzer-Musin in Erie before he left.[111] The *Dispatch* had carried more frequent reports of Burleigh's music activities than the other newspapers, but publishing the young singer's concert review as a newsworthy item confirms his place among the city's musical elite.

This was Burleigh's time in Erie. The subscription lists now held at the Erie County Historical Society tell the story. Several of Burleigh's musician friends—Charles F. Allis, Turner W. Shacklett, and John W. Little—pitched in to help. Allis was a cashier at the Second National Bank and the organist at First Presbyterian Church, the congregation that had been so reluctant to see Burleigh leave. Shacklett, a city councilman and a vestryman at St. Paul's Episcopal Cathedral, was in constant demand as a bass soloist, dramatic reader, and actor. Burleigh had often sung with him. Little was the choir director at the First Methodist Episcopal Church before George F. Brierly took the position, and he served as librarian for the Orpheus Society. These three each carried lists and collected donations. Shacklett and Little collected the largest amounts and collected the largest individual donations. Both collected numerous donations of $5, some of $10, and even a couple of $25. Burleigh's stepfather John Elmendorf collected by far the largest number of donations, but most of his donations were smaller. He did, however, collect one anonymous donation of $25 (perhaps from Elizabeth Russell?). Most of the pledges were for $1, some for fifty or seventy-five cents.

Names of long-time friends appear as well as names of those who would have known Burleigh only as a singer or as a member of the Waters-Burleigh-Elmendorf family. J. F. Downing pledged $10, as did Mrs. W. L. Scott. Henry Catlin and Burleigh's high school principal, H. C. Missimer, each pledged $3. Reverend John Huske, rector at St. Paul's, contributed $5, and John Depinet, a tenor who sang with Burleigh at the St. Patrick's Cathedral concert, also donated $5. Some donations were made anonymously, and some women contributed, whether their husbands did or not. But the outpouring of support for Burleigh was remarkable, both in the number of donations and in their total: $466.50, a substantial amount in 1892.

The paragraphs typed at the top of Charles Allis's subscription list give the rationale for the support of Burleigh's friends and why Erie's citizens, white and black, showed such generosity to this young black singer:

> We, the undersigned, hereby subscribe and pay the amounts set opposite our names respectively, towards a fund now being raised for Mr. HARRY T. BURLEIGH of this city, as a testimonial of appreciation from his friends and acquaintances for the many favors gratuitously conferred by him in singing at funerals, entertainments, and concerts, etc. etc., and for the benefit of churches, societies and other associations in the city.
>
> While Harry could get a living as a book-keeper, stenographer and typewriter no one will question his commendable ambition to continue the study of music and under the best masters to train a voice so seldom equaled in this country.
>
> Out of some 250 applications he was one of four who have been given free scholarships, (tuition only) during a term of five years if desired at the National Conservatory of Music, 126 and 128 East 17th St. New York City. During his musical studies he will only have occasional opportunities to earn money for his own support and a little assistance now from his Erie friends will do him more good than many times the amount later on. With his clerical education, his bass viol and a well trained voice he will be well equipped for life.[112]

The number of Burleigh's competitors for a tuition scholarship had grown in the public report from two hundred to two hundred fifty,[113] and Erie was sending a favored native son off to seek his fortune. Burleigh had attained a local celebrity even his mother and his Aunt Louisa could not have anticipated. They and his stepfather John Elmendorf must have shared a great sense of satisfaction and excitement as they saw Burleigh off on the train for New York City, where he would establish his multifaceted career as a professional musician.

PART II

To New York City and Beyond

4. Burleigh at the National Conservatory of Music

"In the center of American musical activity"

In September 1885 when music philanthropist Jeannette Thurber secured the Certificate of Incorporation from the State of New York for the National Conservatory of Music, to be located at 126 and 128 East Seventeenth Street in New York City, eighteen-year-old Harry T. Burleigh was busy with his high school and business college studies in Erie. He was finding expanded opportunities to sing publicly and he had begun to study voice with George F. Brierly. He could not have been aware that a new era in music studies for American students was beginning, and certainly he could not have anticipated that more than one hundred years later his name would be inextricably linked with the National Conservatory of Music.

He may have been aware of the American Opera Company, a related project the indefatigable Mrs. Thurber was launching simultaneously. In May 1885, the Erie *Morning Dispatch* reported the founding of the American Opera Company, which would tour the United States, presenting opera in English in places far from New York City, performed by well-trained young American singers.[1] Both the Metropolitan Opera Company founded in 1883 and the older Academy of Music in New York City operated on the star system—presenting Italian, French, and German opera in the original languages and relying on highly paid European singers in the lead roles to draw elite, wealthy audiences. Jeannette Thurber had a different vision. Her father had sent her to Paris as a teenager to study music at the Paris Conservatory.[2] She became convinced that art music should be accessible to Americans throughout the country, not just to those clustered around New York, Boston, and other metropolitan areas. The best music education should be available to any talented student, regardless of ability to pay, a policy she had observed at the Paris Conservatory. Thurber's plan included something new. At the same time that the American Opera Company would make opera accessible to ordinary Americans in their own language at affordable prices, she would show the country and the world that America had a wealth of talented young musicians who, given a rigorous and comprehensive education, could compete with the best of Europe's stars.

In its brief existence, the American Opera Company produced twenty operas, including Richard Wagner's *Lohengrin,* Wolfgang Amadeus Mozart's *Magic Flute,* Charles Gounod's *Faust,* Giuseppe Verdi's *Aida,* Giacomo Meyerbeer's *Les Hugue-nots,* and Friedrich von Flotow's *Martha.*[3] The foundation for the opera company was to be the National Conservatory of Music (initially named the American Opera School), which would provide the best possible music education to gifted American students, primarily singers. Their training at the conservatory would prepare them to compete for positions on the roster of the opera company, where they might be considered for lead roles rather than being limited to the role of permanent understudies to second-rank European singers.

After an artistically successful but financially depleting first season, the second ended midseason in bankruptcy. Mrs. Thurber's critics, one of whom later compared her publicity tactics to those of P. T. Barnum, exulted in her defeat, but they underestimated her persistence and the breadth of her vision. As James Gibbons Huneker, who worked closely with Mrs. Thurber, observed, she "achieved more by her failures than others do by their successes."[4]

* * *

Thurber's dream of a traveling American opera company failed, but the conservatory she founded became a magnet for talented music students from across the nation. Its faculty included some of the most renowned musicians in the United States and Europe, and it modeled principles for postsecondary music education that are now taken for granted. For Harry T. Burleigh, the most important principles were the openness to African Americans as well as women and handicapped students, particularly the blind, and the opportunity to compete for a tuition scholarship. A significant number of black musicians whose families had sufficient financial means had studied at the New England Conservatory, at Oberlin Conservatory, or in Europe, but Thurber's stipulation that talented students could compete for tuition scholarships offered hope to Burleigh, whose family could not finance his music education.

By the time Burleigh matriculated in January 1892, the National Conservatory curriculum had broadened from training singers for operatic careers to a comprehensive program that included "every branch of musical practice or adjunct then conceivable, even fencing," and the enrollment had grown from sixty students to six hundred.[5] There were major departments in piano, organ, violin, and cello as well as comprehensive vocal training.[6] Mrs. Thurber had gathered a stellar faculty. Rafael Joseffy, the virtuosic Hungarian pianist whom Burleigh had stood outside the window in Erie to hear, headed the piano department. He did not give private lessons but conducted piano classes in which, as one student played on a Steinway grand piano (supplied by William Steinway, whose establishment was nearby),

Joseffy sat at another, carefully demonstrating "by practical illustration how each imperfectly played bar [could] be improved."[7] Operatic conductors Frank Van der Stucken and Gustav Heinrichs taught orchestral classes that gave students ensemble experience. Victor Herbert, having returned to the United States from Germany in 1886 to fill the principal cellist's chair in the Metropolitan Opera Orchestra, headed the cello department; the vocal department to which Burleigh applied was headed by Romualdo Sapio, "an Italian of the modern school, . . . who [tried] in a cosmopolitan way to unite what is best in modern French and German methods with what is best in Italian methods." His students learned "dramatic expression and distinct enunciation of words," which some felt was often lacking in vocal instruction. Sapio's faculty included Burleigh's voice teacher, Christian Fritsch, one of the founding vocal instructors. In addition, Mrs. Thurber had hired "an expert in diction," who attended all vocal lessons and was quick to interrupt students who mispronounced or slurred their words.[8]

Thurber introduced several innovations that became standard practice in music schools. Her students were not only to be facile in their technical skills but also to understand how Western European art music had developed. All students were required to take music history, taught by Henry Theophilus Finck, music editor of the New York *Evening Post*. And to ensure that her graduates were not narrowly focused only on a particular instrument, all students learned sight-reading and ear training using solfeggio."[9] The study of music history anchored the technical studies in a broader humanistic framework. The solfeggio requirement was common in European schools such as the Paris Conservatory, but Thurber's conservatory was the first in the United States to require it of all students. The validity of this requirement was confirmed when music educators such as Frank Damrosch recognized its value and made solfeggio a standard part of his Institute of Musical Art curriculum.[10]

By 1890 each department in the conservatory offered a preparatory and an advanced course, but the vocal department offered four courses: The Preparatory Course offered singing, solfeggio, elocution, Italian, history of music, and chorus. The Concert and Oratorio Course consisted of singing, solfeggio, elocution, Italian, the history of music, and chorus. The Artist's Course, to which Burleigh was admitted, required courses in "Singing, Solfeggio, Deportment, Opera Repertory, Fencing, Italian, Elocution, and the History of Music and Chorus." This was the program to train singers for professional careers.[11]

The conservatory also offered the Amateur Course for those who would not make their living as musicians but would be active as music lovers—literally, amateurs. Their course would develop skilled church and community chorus members, sophisticated parlor performers, and, what every arts community needs, an educated, supportive, and appreciative audience. They studied "Singing, Solfeggio, and Theory of Music, Italian, Elocution, History of Music, Deportment, Fencing and Chorus."[12]

General tuition in 1892 was $100 per semester. There seems to have been some flexibility for students who had difficulty paying, but it was only applicants for the Artist's Course who could compete for a full tuition scholarship.[13] The scholarship was not intended as a grant; it was given "on the condition that, having completed their education, [recipients would] aid others as they were themselves assisted." Those receiving scholarships committed themselves to contribute to the conservatory a quarter of their income above one thousand dollars a year for the first five years of their career after graduation. In addition, "specially gifted students" could serve as assistant teachers in the later years of their study and begin to meet this obligation.[14] Harry Burleigh benefited from both the tuition scholarship and the opportunity to teach while still a student. Mrs. Thurber's dream of a network of branches in cities across the country that would send their advanced students "to receive their 'finishing touches' in the centre of American musical activity" did not materialize in a formal way, but in the 1890 examinations, applicants came from thirty-nine of the forty-four states then a part of the Union.[15]

Another of Jeannette Thurber's unrealized dreams was to secure government funding for the conservatory, thus validating the conservatory's program and moving American music education closer to the state-supported European model. She argued that "America has, so far, done nothing in a National way either to promote the musical education of its people or to develop any musical genius they possess, and that in this, she stands alone among the civilized nations of the world."[16] With typical political acuteness, in her petition to Congress for an annual grant of $200,000 Mrs. Thurber buried a plum: should Congress approve the grant, "every Senator and every member of the House of Representatives would be given the right to send any deserving young musician of his State to the National Conservatory free of charge."[17]

But America was not ready for state-supported arts education. When news of her petition reached the press in February 1888, newspapers heaped scorn on the idea. One argued that music was for the elite, another that it was a frill. "Music is a luxury for the wealthy, and it would seem that Mrs. Thurber should take from her own well-filled pocket all she can afford in the shape of assistance to her pet conservatory," retorted the Boston *Gazette* of February 25, 1888. The Indianapolis *Journal* scoffed, "Imagine a member of Congress facing his constituents after voting to appropriate $200,000 to teach young people how to execute vocal gymnastics, or play on the fiddle. We are not as esthetic as that."[18] Even though Congress was looking for "a politically expeditious" way to spend a large tax surplus, Thurber's request for a line item to fund the conservatory was denied.[19]

Thurber was undeterred. This was not the first time her endeavors had brought jeers from the (predominantly male) news media and the conservative music establishment, and it would not be the last.[20] She simply modified her approach. In 1890 she campaigned successfully for a congressional charter, intending to move the conservatory to Washington, D.C., where its standing as the National Conservatory of Music might be taken more seriously by the legislators. The bill to charter the conservatory passed in both the House and the Senate in March 1891. For a variety of reasons, the effort to move the conservatory to Washington died, but no other American school of music before or since has been granted the official recognition that Mrs. Thurber won for the National Conservatory: the prestige and affirmation of a congressional charter.[21]

In 1892 Thurber managed a coup that even her harshest critics had to acknowledge. She persuaded the famous Czech composer Antonín Dvořák to serve as the conservatory's director. He would arrive in the fall of the new academic year after Harry Burleigh began his Artist's Course at the National Conservatory. Dvořák's three-year tenure as director of the conservatory covered much of Burleigh's time there, and their relationship would dramatically affect the course of Burleigh's career and would challenge the direction and definition of American music.[22]

* * *

The January 1892 reports in the Erie papers of Burleigh's successful audition for the tuition scholarship gave no hint of the difficulty he experienced in the process. Burleigh gave the most detailed account in a 1924 interview. The audition for the tuition scholarship for the Artist's Course stretched over four days.[23] It required him to sing for the jury and demonstrate his ability in basic music skills such as sight-reading. Pianist Rafael Joseffy headed the audition jury. To be judged by the famous pianist whom he had heard from such an impossible social and artistic distance several years earlier would have daunted a singer with far more extensive professional experience. Burleigh was a veteran of many performances before Erie audiences, but this audition was the ultimate test—how would he measure against the rigorous artistic standards set for the National Conservatory?[24]

Initially, he failed. When he went to the registrar to get his results, he found he had come up short: "I think I was given ABA for reading and B for voice. I was told that AA was the required mark, below which I had fallen a little."[25] But he recognized the "kindly lady" whom he had seen when he served as doorman in the Russell home in Erie when Venezuelan pianist Teresa Carreño played, and now he learned that the registrar was Frances Knapp MacDowell, the mother of the composer Edward MacDowell. "When I learned from her of my failure I told her my cherished longings, and she sympathized with me." He told her that he was from Erie and showed her a letter of recommendation from Mrs. Russell, who had been her hostess in Erie. Mrs. MacDowell arranged another hearing for him, and this time he was awarded a scholarship.[26] Burleigh amply rewarded their trust, soon earning a reputation as one of the conservatory's most apt pupils.

Years later Burleigh gave a hint of how he spent the days after he learned of his failure and before his second meeting with Mrs. MacDowell. In 1892, nearly every issue of the black newspapers reported on the trials and success of the traveling black minstrel and vaudeville troupes. In his discouragement, Burleigh "was tempted to sacrifice a serious career and join the chorus of a traveling minstrel show. But remembering his mother, he decided to try again."[27] When Lizzie Elmendorf and her sister Louisa Waters encouraged Burleigh's ambitions for a professional singing career, the minstrel stage was not what they had in mind.

Now he had his opportunity to study with some of the finest musicians in New York City. But in the immediate days and months, Burleigh needed to find work to pay his living expenses. If the subscribed funds in Erie had all been collected, Burleigh should have been able to live comfortably for some time. Perhaps, as Maurice Peress suggests, he lived in one of the apartments owned and managed by St. Philip's Episcopal Church, a historic black church then located in the Tenderloin district "less than a mile from Dvořák's house on East Seventeenth Street."[28] (Many black citizens migrated to the Tenderloin District before the majority of the black community and the church moved north to Harlem.)

It is possible that the Erie subscription lists demonstrated more goodwill than they generated in actual cash. Burleigh kept careful records of his expenditures and reported back to his Erie supporters: 10 weeks' board, $52.50; rented a piano, $10.00; 10 weeks' room, $20.00; pair pants, $8.00; shoes, $3.75; dress suit (rented three times), $15.00.[29] He was accustomed to living frugally and finding a variety of jobs to support himself. Showing the same determination and ingenuity as he had in Erie, he washed dishes in the neighboring brownstone houses and worked as janitor in the conservatory. A later interviewer reported that "the Conservatory let him sleep in its big, cold building," in a room on one of the upper floors, but since his expense lists payment for board and room, this must have been a very temporary arrangement.[30] Drawing on his stenographic experience, Burleigh became Mrs. MacDowell's assistant, his fine penmanship a valuable asset in "the writing of class books, addressing letters and sending out circulars." Charlotte Wallace Murray, a singer who knew Burleigh well, reported that he "trained several small choirs in New York and the vicinity but the pay was very meagre."[31]

In 1892 "coal was $3.94 a ton, bacon 11 cents a pound, eggs 22 cents a dozen, and sugar 44 cents a pound."[32] But even at these prices, in the first year or two of his study there were times when his budget was stretched thin. In 1934 Burleigh recalled, "I used to stand hungry in front of one of Bennett's downtown restaurants and watch the man in the window cook griddle cakes. Sometimes I would take a toothpick from my pocket, pretend I had just eaten, and walk down the street singing to myself. That happened more than once or twice."[33]

This story, which Burleigh recounted on a number of occasions, raises a question that surfaces several times in the story of Burleigh's life. Did Burleigh, knowing that his audience preferred the Horatio Alger rags-to-riches story to one of a successful young black man coming to the city, exaggerate his hard times? If all the funds detailed on the subscription lists were collected, his $7.25 per week's boarding and room cost would have been covered for quite some time. However, his financial need certainly figured into the formula that made him eligible for a tuition scholarship. The truth is likely somewhere between the story of a penniless young man coming to New York City in a shabby mended suit and that of a favored son of Erie generously supported by the contributions of his admirers through his first months as a student. His suit may have been mended, but Burleigh was not the naïve boy from the hinterland that some accounts suggest. However, by fall 1892 Burleigh was moving into the upper echelons of New York's black community, singing and taking part in various social activities, even before he secured his coveted position as baritone soloist at St. George's Episcopal Church in May 1894.

Whatever the immediate personal cost and stringent economies he endured, twenty-five-year-old Harry T. Burleigh was ready for the intense discipline of the conservatory's requirements. He later reported on the outstanding teachers he worked with in his courses: "I studied voice with Christian Fritsch, harmony with Rubin Goldmark, counterpoint with John White and Max Spicker. Later I played double bass and subsequently tympani in the Conservatory Orchestra under Frank Van der Stucken and Gustav Heinrichs and was librarian of the Orchestra."[34] By all accounts Burleigh impressed his teachers from the outset, and the respect he earned, even from members of the faculty who did not teach him directly, opened doors for him throughout his New York career.

An undated postcard in Burleigh's personal papers is a "Happy New Year!" greeting from his voice teacher, Christian Fritsch. "With best wishes for your health and happiness! To You and Yours, Yours sincerely, Christ. Fritsch."[35] Whether this was sent while Burleigh was his student or years later after Burleigh had become well known, the card shows that Burleigh had established a warm relationship with Fritsch and valued this keepsake. His music history teacher, Henry T. Finck, reported that Burleigh was the best student in music history he ever had—Burleigh the trained stenographer wrote down all his lectures verbatim, in shorthand.[36]

His counterpoint teacher Max Spicker was instrumental in securing Burleigh's second long-term paid position in 1900, at Temple Emanu-El, the wealthiest synagogue in the United States. Spicker was organist and choir director from 1891 to 1902.[37] Burleigh also became personally acquainted with another teacher, cello instructor Victor Herbert, who remained a lifelong friend. In 1914 he invited Burleigh to be a charter member of the music union ASCAP, the American Society for Composers and Performers.[38] Horatio W. Parker, who taught organ, is not known to have taught Burleigh, but he later hired him as occasional soloist at Holy Trinity Episcopal Church, and the Parkers were among the honored guests at Burleigh's Fiftieth Anniversary Reception at St. George's Episcopal Church in 1944.[39]

Burleigh is not likely to have studied harmony or counterpoint in his first year at the conservatory. All instrumental students and some vocal students studied harmony, but only after they had passed "a thorough examination" showing their mastery of solfeggio.[40] Despite the erroneous report of two of the conservatory teachers, Burleigh was not among Dvořák's composition students, but he studied under one of Dvořák's advanced composition students, Rubin Goldmark.[41] Two of Goldmark's later students achieved greater fame: George Gershwin and Aaron Copland.

But all this came later. As he settled into his studies in winter 1892, Burleigh kept his family informed. A few weeks into the term, the Erie correspondent for the Cleveland *Gazette* reported, "Frequent letters from H. T. Burleigh, speak of his close application to his musical studies and give assurance of the progress he is making."[42]

* * *

By the time Harry Burleigh arrived in New York, his friend Thad Talbert from Buffalo had already been studying at the National Conservatory for a year, and he was not the only black student. Harry P. Guy, an African American from Ohio, was on the conservatory staff as a tutor in one of the departments.[43] James Huneker, one of the piano teachers, wrote that Guy was "an especially talented" student in his all–African American piano class.[44] He was one of the advanced students who became part of the conservatory's teaching staff, thus defraying part of his tuition costs.

Burleigh spent the summer of 1892 working as wine steward at the sumptuous Grand Union Hotel in Saratoga Springs. Though socially on the periphery, he was close to the center of music events related to his study at the National Conservatory of Music. He witnessed an early triumph of African American soprano Sissieretta Jones, with whom he had sung at Carnegie Hall in New York City earlier in the summer.[45] A few weeks later he appeared in concert with her again in Washington, D.C.

It is not known whether Burleigh's personal friendship with Victor Herbert may have grown in Saratoga Springs, or whether Herbert, the cello instructor at the conservatory, helped him secure his position at the Grand Union.[46] As was true in many resort areas, there was an established black community in Saratoga Springs. Some residents worked in the hotels and on the racecourse. Young men like Burleigh's brother Reginald often spent their summers working these vacation spots, and Burleigh may have had prior connections in Saratoga's black community.

The Grand Union Hotel was "a miracle of spacious luxury," and Burleigh's job as wine steward was a coveted position among the service staff. Herbert, an indefatigable performer, often directed the hotel orchestra that summer for his friend John Lund, whose alcohol consumption frequently rendered him unfit for his duties. Herbert's consumption was more measured, but Burleigh's son Alston reported that his father the wine steward "could never get the wine cold enough to suit the maestro!"[47] Some sources report that Burleigh sang with Herbert's orchestra at the Grand Union.[48]

Burleigh's position at the hotel allowed him to take in some of the scheduled events at the resort in his time off. He was especially interested in a conference of educators, which featured a particularly controversial presentation by George

E. Hardy of New York, who argued that African Americans tended to display higher moral values than educated whites. He "made a comparison of the morality of blacks and whites, and from the statistics presented proved that the greatest amount of immorality obtained among the educated whites and the least among "the Negroes." It is not surprising that Hardy's argument "created a profound sensation."[49] Hardy's paper was published as part of the conference proceedings but not publicly discussed at the conference. As the Republican party was more supportive of African American civil rights than Democrats, Hardy's assertion was all the more startling—he was a Democrat. How could a Democrat have "instituted such a comparison"? No wonder Harry T. Burleigh wrote of having "a very enjoyable time at the education convention and at the lake." Discussions of racial disparity and comparisons of achievement between newly emancipated black Americans and the white citizens who squandered their historic rights as free citizens in dilatory behavior were common in the black press; no doubt they enlivened many a conversation among Burleigh and his friends.

The triumphant appearance of Sissieretta Jones, would have been a momentous event for Burleigh. Some weeks earlier Jones had signed a contract with "Major James B. Pond, the white proprietor and manager of the American Lecture and Musical Agency,"[50] who had been the agent for such luminaries as Charles Dickens, John Greenleaf Whittier, and Mark Twain.[51] Jones had sung for President Benjamin Harrison, but up to this time she had appeared primarily in African American venues. Her audiences included a sprinkling of white listeners, and her singing was so extraordinary that she was attracting significant notice in the white press throughout the country. Pond quickly booked her for a series of concerts before large white audiences, where her appearances would be covered by the white press. This proved a shrewd move. He programmed "the Black Patti" as the star of a small ensemble of white musicians, and on August 5, she made her first appearance in Saratoga Springs. She "drew such large audiences that, to meet the public's demand, she was invited back twice more during the month, for a three-performance stint on August 15, 19, and 20, and for another two-day engagement beginning on August 27."[52]

The new academic year at the National Conservatory of Music opened in October, and Burleigh's job at the Grand Union Hotel probably lasted through August. As Sissieretta Jones would not have been welcome to stay at the Grand Union Hotel, she most likely found housing in the black community, as many touring black musicians did. The following month Burleigh appeared in a concert in Washington, D.C., with Sissieretta Jones and Florence Batson-Bergen, two of the reigning black sopranos.[53]

Except for several years in the 1890s, the opportunities available to Sissieretta Jones were to provide the operatic scenes in vaudeville shows and to appear in Star Concerts in the black community. She preferred to sing arias from classical opera, art songs, and ballads, and for several years her association with Major Pond and other white impresarios made this possible. Her preferences as a singer matched Burleigh's, and though ultimately their careers would diverge, his appearances with Sissieretta Jones facilitated his early recital career.

Despite the ripples the educator's convention stirred, Saratoga Springs was far removed from one of the most urgent concerns to all African Americans and the white citizens who supported their cause. Just as the Cleveland *Gazette* reported Burleigh's progress at the National Conservatory and his summer work in Saratoga Springs, it also informed its readers of events affecting African Americans nationwide—most notably the rising tide of lynchings. The paper reported that in July the *North American Review* featured a "pertinent and well-directed article" by elder statesman Frederick Douglass, protesting the outrage of "Lynch Law in the South."[54]

Thirty-four years before, Burleigh's family had heard Douglass speak in Erie, and the following summer Burleigh would share the platform with Douglass at the World's Fair as he inveighed against racial discrimination. Burleigh had been reared in a family that took an active interest in bringing change, so even though his personal situation was relatively privileged, he was aware of the disintegration of Reconstruction and the rise of Jim Crow laws and the Ku Klux Klan. Two months before, the Virginia Baptist convention had met in Washington, D.C., and during their meeting had presented a special petition to President Harrison protesting "crimes against citizenship, against law, against humanity, against God, which are so common in certain sections in the south" and imploring him to do all he could to stop them. President Harrison promised "strenuous endeavors," but lynching continued in both the South and the North for many years.[55]

Throughout Burleigh's career, the contrast between his growing success in an ever-broadening arena of American public life and the plight of the majority of African Americans, particularly in the southern United States, was emblematic of an irony that persists more than a century later. Burleigh and other successful musicians, artists, teachers, doctors, lawyers, and businessmen persistently and convincingly gave the lie to racist portrayals of African Americans as an inferior, childlike group, barely human, who were incapable of achieving excellence in any sphere of human endeavor. At the same time the fevered determination to destroy the gains of Reconstruction in the South, tacitly supported by the federal government and the North, resulted in frequent and violent retribution against those who, like Burleigh, refused to be defined by their detractors. For a number of years Burleigh followed the example set by the older men in his family, confronting injustice with direct though nonviolent action. In his later career he chose different weapons, but he never stopped believing that as he pursued the various paths in his music career, he was helping to bring social change.

5. Introducing Antonín Dvořák to African American Music

"All that is needed for a great and noble school of American music"

Burleigh acquitted himself with distinction in the first four months of his study at the National Conservatory of Music. After his summer in Saratoga Springs, it was time to begin his second year—and he was ready. Eligibility for the year depended on results in examinations at the beginning of the new academic year. Burleigh had not forgotten all he had learned while he was working out of the city: He "passed his examination last week, making 100 per cent. He has a four-year scholarship, but at the present rapid rate of progress will finish his course in three years."[1]

Burleigh's second year at the National Conservatory would be a momentous one, for him, for the conservatory, and for American music. Czech composer Antonín Dvořák would come to be the director, and during the year Burleigh would learn to know him well. Burleigh would be Dvořák's most direct link to the African American music traditions in which he was keenly interested. And by the end of the academic year, Dvořák would complete the composition of his most famous American work, his Symphony No. 9 in E Minor, "From the New World." Burleigh would be intimately involved in the process of its creation.

The conservatory had been without a director after its first director, baritone Jacques Bouhy (who had created the role of Escamillo in Bizet's opera *Carmen*) resigned to return to France in 1889.[2] Jeannette Thurber's efforts to make her conservatory the official conservatory of the United States had failed, though it had grown in enrollment and prestige because of the eminence of the faculty she had drawn to it. To entice one of the most distinguished European composers to be its director brought unquestionable distinction, and perhaps Congress would reconsider its refusal to subsidize the conservatory. But there was more.

Mrs. Thurber had sharpened her focus on bringing fundamental change to the way American musicians, composers in particular, would be trained. Just as American singers and other musicians should not need to travel to Europe to receive the best music education and to validate their competence before European audiences, so American composers should free themselves from relying on European, particularly German, formulae and standards of composition.

It was not unusual for European or American composers to flavor their compositions with folk melodies and rhythms. From Haydn and Mozart to Beethoven, Chopin, Liszt, and Brahms, composers made use of "simple material evocative of distinct nations and races,"[3] and Haydn, Mozart, Beethoven, and Brahms had written art song arrangements of folksongs. American composers also flavored their compositions with sprinklings of the music of African Americans and Native Americans or with folk themes from European traditions, long before Dvořák's arrival. More than forty years earlier, Louis Moreau Gottschalk introduced American and European audiences to African American rhythms and melodic patterns in his "Bamboula" and "Danse de Nègres." Several composers of Burleigh's time drew on what they knew of black rhythms. Even Edward MacDowell, who objected strenuously to the notion that American composers should try to produce music that sounded "American," composed his famous *Indian Suite* as well as several works with Negro themes. But American composers were still making their sojourns to Europe to study composition with masters of the German tradition, and their music was more Germanic in sound and effect than American. It was not intended to sound American, whatever that might mean in a country swelling with immigrants. If their music should eventually develop a distinctly American character, the last source most of them would choose was the music of America's "primitive" races, Native Americans and African Americans.[4]

For Antonín Dvořák, the use of traditional Bohemian songs and dances in his compositions arose partly from his belief in the intrinsic value of the music of ordinary Czech people. Bohemia had for more than two hundred years been under the control of the Austro-Hungarian Empire. German rather than Czech was the language taught in schools. German was also the language of the government, and Czech-speaking nationals lost their positions to German politicos. Even in the National Opera and Orchestra, Czech musicians were replaced by German, Austrian, and Hungarian musicians.[5] Born in 1841, Dvořák saw many changes come to Bohemia in his early years. The peasants, having retained their language, their music, and their customs, revolted, and in 1848 the emperor abolished the hated feudal laws. Scholars and artists demanded the right to reclaim their culture in all its expressions.[6]

Dvořák's father was a butcher and an innkeeper, but skill in playing musical instruments was not unusual in the family, "a normal enough accomplishment in Bohemian villages and towns during those times." Dvořák's father played and composed for the zither, though his creations were not distinguished. The ordinary musical gifts in his family heritage gave "no hint that the family would one day produce a musical genius."[7] Despite his father's initial resistance (partly because of financial constraints), Dvořák was eventually allowed to go to Prague to study music and work his way toward a career as a violist and composer. There he was introduced to the innovative music of Richard Wagner by playing it under the baton of the composer himself.[8]

More significant was his involvement in the emergence of "music that was essentially Czech." In 1863, he participated in "the historic series of first performances of operas" by Bedřich Smetana, the pioneer composer of Czech nationalism.[9] Smetana, Dvořák's mentor, was greatly influenced by Wagner's revolutionary music drama, but he eventually devoted himself to writing operas and orchestral music that celebrated the stories and the countryside of his native land.[10] Like Smetana, Dvořák was fascinated by Wagner's music dramas. But also like Smetana, he reclaimed the energy and joy of the Czech peasant culture that had surrounded him in his early years, and his compositions reflected a deep nationalistic pride.

In the early 1890s Jeannette Thurber saw Antonín Dvořák as the ideal role model for young American musicians and composers. Just as he had created music universally admired throughout Europe, England, and America that echoed the distinctive sounds of Czech songs and dances, he could help American composers to transcend their reliance on European models and fully embrace the indigenous music of America's "peasant" classes—Americans of African and Native American descent.

The perceived ironies inherent in this claim—that classical musicians of a refined, cultivated class should draw on the music of people and cultures they regarded as primitive—led to fierce controversy. But for some conservatory students, and for Harry T. Burleigh in particular, Dvořák's call to value and to make use of the oral traditions in his own music heritage to create art music rang with transforming force. Like the Czechs of Bohemia, the former African slaves of America and their descendants needed to reclaim their music heritage and demonstrate its inherent artistic value; Burleigh would be at the forefront of this movement.

As John C. Tibbetts observed in his 1998 essay, "The Missing Title Page: Dvořák and the American National Song,"

> Dvořák's American adventure [was] fraught with significance and controversy. The most modest of men, he himself was a creature of contradictions: Born a Czech villager, a minority figure in a German-dominated musical establishment, Dvořák became a cosmopolitan artist feted in all the musical capitals of Europe, Russia, and America. Many of his countrymen accused him of turning his back on his own roots; and, conversely, the German musical establishment criticized him for his inordinate employment of folk idioms in his music. The truth is, he lived in both worlds, exploiting the idioms of his own culture in a vocabulary befitting the academic, or classical style. He was precisely the right person to assume the leadership of the National Conservatory.[11]

And, we might add, precisely the right mentor for Harry T. Burleigh. Dvořák modeled a way to live in two worlds, how to succeed in the world of Western European–influenced art music while introducing his own African-derived musical heritage into that world. He would "ever feel [his] twoness," in W. E. B. Du Bois's memorable phrase.[12] Even though in much of his career Burleigh worked within the white music establishment, his goal was always to be a worthy representative of his race. Black Americans lived in at least two worlds, the sometimes insular but never uncomplicated world of African American life and the world of the European American culture, which was increasingly assigning value rankings to musical styles. Especially for musicians, those worlds overlapped in complex ways. In experience parallel to Dvořák's, Burleigh would be criticized by educated African Americans for singing and arranging the music created by unsophisticated, unlettered Americans of African descent, and later he would be accused by younger black artists and their white supporters of betraying his roots by adopting and adapting the musical language of the dominant Euro-American culture. But Burleigh's friendship with Dvořák had a profound effect on them both, finding eloquent expression through their music. The parallels in their family backgrounds deepened their musical affinity.

Dvořák, his wife, and two of his six children arrived by ship in the harbor at Hoboken, New Jersey, on Tuesday, September 27, 1892, a few days before the start of the new academic year. A delegation from the National Conservatory and a group of Czech citizens met the family and took them by carriage to Hotel Clarendon, near the conservatory at East Eighteenth Street and Fourth Avenue, overlooking Union Square. Dvořák's salary was generous—$15,000 for the year, one-third more than the salary of the mayor of New York[13]—but the Dvořáks soon decided the hotel was too expensive and too noisy. Two weeks later they moved to an apartment in a brick row house at 327 East Seventeenth Street, where Burleigh would often visit.[14]

It is not known exactly when Burleigh met the new director, but working in the conservatory office with Mrs. MacDowell could have given him his first unofficial view of the composer. New York City was in the midst of exuberant celebration of the four hundredth anniversary of Columbus's discovery of America, and on September 28 when Dvořák visited the conservatory offices, he looked down from the windows on the parades on Third Avenue celebrating the Columbus Quadricentennial.[15] Thanks to earlier publicity generated by editors such as the *Tribune's* Henry E. Krehbiel, the newspapers followed Dvořák's every move and reported his every pronouncement. They described his unusual attire, an "emerald-green necktie, silk vest, ulster coat, and homburg hat, which he wore at a rakish angle," but acknowledged that he was a man "of great natural dignity, a man of character," with "so much emotional life in the fiery eyes and lined face, that when he lightens up in conversation, his face is not easily forgotten."[16]

Krehbiel and several conservatory teachers lost no time in introducing Dvořák to the restaurants and bars in the area where musicians gathered. Many of their discussions centered on the music of Wagner, whose music dramas were challenging the star-centered conventions of Italian opera. Piano instructor and newspaper critic James Gibbons Huneker, press agent for the National Conservatory, vividly recalled Dvořák's capacity for liquor as well as lively conversations about Wagner.[17] Music history instructor Henry T. Finck was "a pronounced disciple of the Wagner school."[18] Metropolitan Opera director and former Wagner associate at Bayreuth Anton Seidl would conduct the first performance of Dvořák's Symphony No. 9 in E Minor, "From the New World." Cello instructor Victor Herbert, whose cello concerto may have inspired Dvořák's own cello concerto, later described a warm friendship with Dvořák in a 1922 letter to German critic Hans Schnoor.[19] All these colleagues enjoyed lively discussions or (in the case of Seidl) companionable silence with Dvořák.

Victor Herbert wrote, "We all loved him, for he was so kind and affable—his great big beautiful eyes radiated warmth—and of such childlike simplicity and natural-ness—and when he left us, we lost not only a master-musician, whose presence had had a marked influence on musical activities in N. Y. but a most admirable, lovable friend."[20]

Knowing Dvořák's eagerness to learn more about African American music, James Huneker brought him an article entitled "Negro Music" by Johann Tonsor of Louisville, Kentucky, from the December 1892 issue of *Music,* a Chicago journal. The article included notations of excerpts of several songs, including "Swing Low, Sweet Chariot," a brief echo of which would appear in his "New World Symphony" less than a year later.[21] Huneker was skeptical of Dvořák's view that the unique voice of American music would be found in the music of "native" Americans, the Negro and the Indian. In fact, there was more than a touch of condescension and racism in his view of Dvořák and of his interest in folk music. He preferred Dvořák's earlier works, which he believed were more influenced by Franz Schubert and Richard Wagner. Dvořák's "American theory of native music never appealed to me," Huneker wrote. "He did, and dexterously, use some negro, or alleged negro, tunes in his 'New World Symphony,' and in one of his string quartets; but if we are to have true American music it will not stem from 'darky' roots, especially as the most original music of that kind thus far written is by Stephen Foster, a white man."[22]

The irony of characterizing Stephen Foster's music as the "most original" African American music is painfully obvious to twenty-first century ears, but Huneker was not unique in his ignorance of the power of Negro music. It was the prevalence of this attitude that made Dvořák's views and the authority with which he expressed them so dramatically controversial.

Dvořák was not totally uninformed about the music of African Americans when he arrived in New York City. It is possible that on one of his nine trips to England between fall 1884 and spring 1891, he heard one of the Fisk Jubilee groups perform.[23] He may also have seen their printed collections of spirituals. But it was Harry T. Burleigh who brought this music to life for him in the most personal way. James Huneker would have had contact with Burleigh at his office duties, and he later claimed to have introduced Burleigh to Dvořák. It is also possible that Jeannette Thurber introduced Dvořák to this gifted young student rather than Huneker. In either case, the introduction was made early in the fall term, because in November when Cleveland *Gazette* editor H. C. Smith visited Burleigh in New York, he met both Mrs. Thurber and Dvořák at the conservatory. He reported that Burleigh's standing was "most creditable indeed—at the head of his classes. The faculty, headed by the famous foreigner and finished musician and author, Dvořák, and the presiding genius of the conservatory, Mrs. H. K. Thurber, are both pleased to note my friend's splendid progress."[24]

When he heard Burleigh sing, Dvořák invited him to his apartment to sing the songs he had learned from his grandfather and his mother, and Burleigh became a frequent visitor. He often accompanied Dvořák on his walks through the streets of the city, as Dvořák did not like to walk alone.[25]

Another source confirms that Burleigh's relationship with Dvořák began early in the fall term. Milos Šafránek, a Czech scholar and diplomat, who met Burleigh in Dvořák's apartment, reported that "immediately after Dvořák's arrival," Burleigh "established an animated, cordial, and permanent relationship" with him. Šafránek "learned that Burleigh visited Dvořák quite often, perhaps daily, and sometimes the composer took him to see a new [train] engine or to watch the departure of a steamship from New York." Several witnesses remembered Burleigh singing spirituals for Dvořák early in his New York tenure, "and definitely before the Symphony from the New World was written."[26]

In an interview in 1941, the centenary of Dvořák's birth, Burleigh described his evenings with the Dvořák family. After supper, Burleigh would sit down at the grand piano (loaned free of charge to Dvořák by William Steinway). "He was in his shirtsleeves, with all his kids around him," Burleigh recalled. As only two of the Dvořák children were with him the first year, Burleigh's memories indicate that his visits to the Dvořák apartment continued in the second year, after all six children were with their parents in New York. Dvořák loved birds, and missing the pigeons he had left behind in Bohemia, "he had bird cages all over the house with thrushes in them. He kept the cagedoors open so the thrushes flew about freely and joined in the singing." Burleigh accompanied himself, and as he sang, Dvořák listened intently, analyzing and immersing himself in the spirit of the music, just as he had absorbed the folk music of his Czech heritage. When struck by a distinctive note, Dvořák "would jump up and ask: 'Did they really sing it that way?'" But Dvořák was not interested only in the sound of the music; he wanted to know about the lives of the people who had created it. "He asked hundreds of questions about Negro life."[27] Dvořák did not intend simply to apply quotations of specific songs to the surface of his work—that was not his way of using folk music in either Bohemia or America. Employing the sophisticated craftsmanship of the skilled composer, he incorporated the distinctive elements of the music into his own musical vocabulary.[28]

Knowing of Burleigh's friendship with Dvořák and respecting Burleigh's accomplishments as a composer, at least two of the conservatory faculty who knew Burleigh later contributed to a misunderstanding of his relationship to Dvořák. In his 1922 letter, Victor Herbert wrote of "the very talented Harry Burleigh" as "one of Dr. Dvořák's best pupils in composition."[29] Likewise, Henry T. Finck, Burleigh's music history teacher, named Burleigh in a list of composers—others being Rubin Goldmark, Harvey Worthington Loomis, William Arms Fisher, Harry Rowe Shelley, and Will Marion Cook—who had studied with Dvořák, "all of whom soon achieved national distinction."[30] Though Burleigh did not formally study composition with Dvořák, these erroneous statements confirm Burleigh's reputation as one of the conservatory's outstanding pupils. Dvořák took only advanced composition students, and the tuition charge for Dvořák's Advanced Class in Composition was $300.[31] The tuition fee might have been waived for Burleigh, but as he explained on several occasions, he was not eligible for Dvořák's class at that point in his studies, and his career aims were more modest. "I didn't even dream of being a composer—at least not out loud. I was going to be a singer and I am."[32]

Burleigh may have absorbed aspects of Dvořák's teaching through his study with Rubin Goldmark, who was in Dvořák's advanced composition class, but the time he spent with Dvořák would have a more direct influence. Dvořák and Burleigh came from similar backgrounds. As Dvořák told an interviewer in May 1893, "If in my own career I have achieved a measure of success and reward it is to some extent due to the fact that I was the son of poor parents and was reared in an atmosphere of struggle and endeavor."[33] Those words could have been said by Burleigh thirty years later. A warm friendship developed between the two. As Victor Herbert recalled, Dvořák was "kind and totally unaffected," and Burleigh was one of the students in whom he "took great interest."[34]

Burleigh brought the skill he had developed on the double bass to the student orchestra, and his clerical skills made him a natural for orchestra librarian. He listened carefully to Dvořák's strong opinions about and insights into the music the orchestra played, however inexpertly (Victor Herbert referred to the student orchestra as the conservatory's *"enfant terrible,"* and resisted having his cello students join).[35] Burleigh's music manuscript writing, like his fine penmanship, was done "with an engraver's precision,"[36] and soon he was copying scores for the orchestra and for Dvořák's compositions. Maurice Peress describes the unique relationship of an orchestra librarian with the conductor: "Dvořák led the Conservatory orchestra, which met twice a week. Burleigh served as the orchestra's librarian and copyist and filled in on double-bass and timpani. I can attest that the conductor's lot is a lonely one. The orchestra librarian is among the few orchestral musicians we get to talk with off the podium, and the one we depend upon for a myriad of editorial details and drudge jobs."[37]

Working closely with Dvořák at the conservatory and sharing his music with the family in the home, Burleigh learned to know the Dvořák children. During Dvořák's second year, when all his children had joined him (and as Burleigh reported, "There were a lot of them"), nine-year-old Otakar would on occasion come to the orchestra rehearsal with his father. In a letter to the family back in Prague, Dvořák reported that Otakar "sat on Burleigh's lap during the Orchestra's rehearsals and played the tympani."[38] But Otakar was not always on the beat, and when Dvořák heard some stray beats, he growled, "Push him out!"[39]

On May 9, 1893, the conservatory held a concert of music by Dvořák's composition students. Though Burleigh was not among the students in the master's composition class, the program included some of his songs, along with songs by Edward H. Kinney, who was in the class. Kinney was the organist and choir director of St. Philips African Episcopal Church, where Burleigh was singing at the time. Including Burleigh's compositions on a program of works by Dvořák's composition students strengthened the general perception that Burleigh studied composition with Dvořák.[40] And like many other composers, he learned much about the art of composition by copying the manuscripts of the master.

* * *

During late winter and early spring 1893, Dvořák was busy composing his Symphony No. 9 in E Minor, "From the New World." Much has been written about this symphony, its impact on the course of American music, and the controversial views Dvořák expressed about the value of African American music just as he was completing the work. Many people who know nothing else about Harry T. Burleigh are aware that he sang plantation songs and spirituals to Dvořák during the time he was composing it and that to some extent the symphony reflects the influence of those songs. It is important to note what Burleigh himself said about his involvement in the writing of the symphony as well as what others said, and also to hear Burleigh's testimony as to how his work with Dvořák affected his own composition.

Many of those evenings would have occurred during late winter and spring 1893 when Dvořák was composing the symphony. Even before Dvořák's public statements about the value of African American music, he helped Burleigh understand the artistic worth of his heritage. Though Burleigh enjoyed singing the plantation songs and spirituals (and the songs of Stephen Foster), we cannot be sure that without Dvořák's help he would have seen them as inherently worthy as art and as important for a classical recitalist as the Ludwig van Beethoven, Franz Schubert, and Robert Schumann songs he was studying. But when Burleigh sang "Go Down, Moses" for him, Dvořák exclaimed, "Burleigh, that is as great as a Beethoven theme!"[41]

This was highest praise from Dvořák. Paul Stefan wrote in 1941 that Dvořák made music "in the same joyous spirit" as did Joseph Haydn and Wolfgang Amadeus Mozart, but "in the realm of the symphony and of chamber-music writing, his spiritual guide was Beethoven. He never spoke of Beethoven except with awe," and he expected the same of his students. "'Why don't you kneel?' he would cry out in his explosive manner to the class" when they played a Beethoven sonata.[42] In his composition classes, when his students had, after many tries, come up with a melody or theme that was their own and strong enough to develop, he might insist that they "wrap the theme around an existing Beethoven sonata, imitating, measure by measure, the modulations and key relationships."[43]

But Dvořák went further than simply affirming the artistic value of the songs Burleigh sang. He urged Burleigh to actively preserve and promote them. "Give those melodies to the world," Dvořák said, a mandate that would eventually become a primary mission for Burleigh. As he said in the 1941 interview at the centenary of Dvořák's birth and just after his own seventy-fifth birthday, "Dvořák, a Czech with a great love for the common people of all lands, pointed the way."[44]

The famous Largo theme in the second movement has entered American musical culture so deeply that many believe it was originally a spiritual. Given words and arranged for solo voice and chorus in Dvořák's centennial year (1941) by William Arms Fisher, another of Dvořák's students, "Goin' Home" is known to many who have never heard of either Dvořák or Burleigh.[45] Camille Zeckwer, one of Dvořák's composition students, reported that his teacher played through the entire symphony for him "as he composed it," and Dvořák's own response to the Largo theme is instructive: "He played the theme of the Largo of the 'New World Symphony' twenty minutes after he had written it, singing the immortal theme with great passion and fervor, . . . his whole body vibrating as he played this music to his first listener, saying, 'Is it not beautiful music? It is for my symphony; but—it is not symphonic music.'"[46] The Largo theme did not originate in the composer's garret—it was inspired by the lives and the songs of a people with whom Dvořák felt great empathy, and whose voice he felt should be heard in the same concert halls where his Stabat Mater, his Requiem, his operas, and his symphonies were performed.

Victor Herbert wrote in a similar vein of Burleigh's influence on the "New World Symphony": "[T]he very talented Harry Burleigh, had the privilege of giving the Dr. some of the thematic material for his Symphony—'From the New World.' I have seen this denied, but it is true. Naturally I knew a good deal about this Symphony—as I saw the Dr. two or three times a week—and knew he was at work on it."[47]

It is not only the voice of the Negro, as mediated by Harry T. Burleigh, that can be heard in the Largo movement. Another indigenous American influence is that of the American Indian as Dvořák heard it through Henry Wadsworth Longfellow's *Song of Hiawatha,* which he had first read in a Czech translation thirty years earlier.[48] Burleigh acknowledged this in a letter to the editor of *Musical America* in 1924. Dvořák wrote the Largo "after he had read the famine scene in Longfellow's *Hiawatha.* It had great effect on him and he wanted to interpret it musically."[49]

On May 24, 1893, Dvořák completed the symphony, inscribing the last page, as he usually did, "Thank God!" But he added another jubilant note. Having decided

to spend the summer with his family in Spillville, Iowa, where there was a community of Czech immigrants, he had sent for the four children still in Prague,
accompanied by his wife's sister, Terezie Koutecká. The second note on the final
page of his symphony manuscript read, "The children have arrived in Southampton.
We received a cable at 1:33 in the afternoon."[50]

* * *

A few days before Dvořák inscribed the last page of his symphony, he granted an
interview, published in the New York *Herald,* May 21, 1893, that hit the music world
with percussive force. The Czech composer now publicly proclaimed his belief that
American composers should take the music of African Americans seriously and
use it to create a distinctively American music: "I am now satisfied," he said, "that
the future music of this country must be founded upon what are called the negro
melodies. This must be the real foundation of any serious and original school of
composition to be developed in the United States. When I first came here last year
I was impressed with this idea and it has developed into a settled conviction. These
beautiful and varied themes are the product of the soil. They are American."[51] Listening to and talking with Burleigh surely contributed to his conviction. We now
know that this article was substantially influenced by journalist James Creelman,
so the extent to which it recorded Dvořák's exact words must be questioned. At
the time, however, this publication and those that followed were taken to be the
composer's verbatim pronouncements, and the ensuing controversy arose from
that assumption.[52]

The end of the article announced that the conservatory would add a new department "for the instruction in music of colored pupils of merit." The institution
had always been open to black students, but now it would actively recruit them,
"largely with the view of forming colored professors of merit." Tuition would be
free of charge for "students of exceptional talent," and two "young but efficient"
conservatory students had been appointed as teachers.[53] Burleigh was one of the
two teachers of the proposed class. Paul Bolin (or Bohlen) was the other.

Bolstered by the support of several of her trustees, Mrs. Thurber's official
announcement stated that "The National Conservatory of Music of America proposes to enlarge its sphere of usefulness by adding to its departments a branch for
the instruction in music of colored pupils of talent, largely with the view of forming colored professors of merit. The aptitude of the colored race for music, vocal
and instrumental, has long been recognized, but no definite steps have hitherto
been taken to develop it, and it is believed that the decision of the Conservatory
to move in this new direction will meet with general approval and be productive
of prompt and encouraging results."[54] This did not mean that every Negro student
who applied would be admitted to the program; as always, the offer of free tuition
was for "students of exceptional talent." Additional teachers would be hired as
needed. The new department soon added one hundred fifty black students to the
six hundred white students enrolled.[55]

Dvořák's validation of the artistic value of their folk music has been noted by African Americans many times throughout the century that followed, but immediately, this announcement evoked "a chorus of gratitude" from Poughkeepsie, the home of Paul C. Bolin. In a letter to Mrs. Jeannette Thurber, Bolin's brother Gaius wrote, "Amid the many discouragements which come to the colored people of this country in this fierce struggle for existence," Dvořák's words offered "a ray of hope and encouragement"; the director and Mrs. Thurber were "broad minded, liberal viewed and humane enough to consider and truly feel that no matter what the color of a man's skin, no matter what the place or condition of his birth, he is a man, endowed with all the attributes of man, and that he stands before the just law and before his Maker as significant and as precious as any other human being." It was not simply a matter of admitting black students; that their teachers would also be African Americans was significant: "The fact that in your latest project in connection with your institution you have decided to employ colored teachers and to give them a chance to develop themselves while endeavoring to direct the effort of others is a source of grateful appreciation to every black person in America." He admitted that "perhaps my own elation is somewhat colored by the fact that my own young brother, Paul C. Bolin, is one of the lucky chosen ones."[56]

Maurice Peress traces the flurry of articles that followed throughout the week following the Dvořák pronouncement, in the *Herald* and in its sister paper in Paris by way of their new Atlantic cable, the English-language Paris *Herald*. The Paris paper immediately sent stringers "to Vienna and Berlin to interview famous musicians about Dvořák's curious theory. So strong was the notion of German musical authority that French musicians of note, such as Camille Saint-Saëns, conveniently nearby in Paris, were not consulted."[57]

As could be expected, the responses varied. One of the most positive came from violinist and teacher Joseph Joachim, who had worked with another young African American several years earlier. In 1889 Will Marion Cook, whom Burleigh would introduce to Dvořák a few months after the May 1893 furor, was said to have made "rapid and exceptional progress with his studies with the master and virtuoso, Joachim, in Berlin, Germany."[58] Whether or not Cook had introduced Joachim to black music, Joachim's respect for him may have influenced his response to Dvořák's words. He agreed that "It may be a very good idea to try and merge American Negro melodies into an ideal form, and that these melodies would then give the tint to the National American Music."[59]

Pianist Anton Rubinstein and Arthur Bird, an American composer, responded similarly with "thoughtful and respectfully curious" comments, while Viennese organist and composer Anton Bruckner flatly rejected the value of a music known only orally: "German musical literature," he declared, "contained no written text emanating from the Negro race, and however sweet the Negro melodies might be, they could never form the groundwork of the future music of America."[60] To argue that only music that had been transcribed in written form (and in German musical literature at that) could be resources for composers seems odd, in that a large number of composers throughout the history of European art music had organized their work around folk melodies from oral traditions. But Bruckner's words still find a familiar resonance in some hallowed musical halls more than a century later.

Bruckner's dismissal of Dvořák's views was countered by F. G. Rathbun, music and choral director at Hampton Institute. Rathbun believed Hampton was the only school in America "where this plantation and slave music is taught regularly and systematically to its students," so his comments might interest the *Herald*'s readers. He described the songs as "strikingly original, quaint, pathetic," and, betraying a view less open than Dvořák's, "in some cases . . . even artistic in their beauty." He went on to analyze the "utter simplicity" of their three-chord harmony and lack of modulation. A Hampton volume featured more than one hundred of the slave songs, and he had transcribed many additional manuscripts "from the lips of our students from various parts of the South year after year, making a valuable legacy to the 'future music' of America."[61]

Rathbun commented on the effect of such transformation: "But whether these songs will retain their beauty and effectiveness when rendered into instrumental form I seriously doubt, for it is now a difficult matter to make them 'sound right' to the 'old slaves' even when the slight alterations of adding simple harmonies here and there are made, and I often hear expression after one of our concerts, 'Dose are de same old tunes, but some way dey do'n sound right.'"[62]

Rathbun commented on how quickly his students changed their renditions after exposure to "civilized" ways of communicating: "After a contact with our sight singing teacher, our English teacher and teacher of elocution, something is missing from the songs, and this goes on as long as the student remains here." Educated black people could scarcely learn to sing them "in the old time way." Regardless of their music training, white singers were sure to "make absolute failures of them. How to sing them cannot be explained in words. Study all the rules you please and then go listen to a native."[63]

By Rathbun's definition, Dvořák had not listened to a "native." Burleigh had sung Negro spirituals at the Himrod Mission in Erie and had toured with the New Orleans University Jubilee Singers, but he was educated in the North and trained by white teachers steeped in the European tradition. Rathbun continued, "If these tunes are to form the basis of our future symphonies, &c., they must be taught right and by those who thoroughly understand their characteristics." Without such care, it would be very easy to veer into minstrelsy, a distinction that only those with personal experience of the genuine slave songs could detect.[64]

As deeply as Dvořák was moved by the songs of African Americans and by what Burleigh told him of their lives, the model he demonstrated for giving them to the world certainly altered both their form and their function so as to be unrecognizable to their original creators. Much of the criticism of Burleigh's work that arose thirty years later centered on the fact that for Burleigh, the essence of the spirituals was melody, while for some of his critics the communal, interactive, and improvisatory way they were sung and the manner in which the songs emerged from and were transformed by life experience was more important. But for Burleigh the singer, schooled and affirmed in the art of solo performance and nurtured in an urban environment in the North, it was only natural to focus on the melody, fusing it with the harmonic language of late romanticism (while retaining subtle gestures of oral performance in his accompaniments), and present them to the world as solo and choral songs for the concert stage, church, and parlor.

* * *

Now Burleigh stood at the center of a maelstrom of controversy, only intensified by two items in the May 28 edition of the New York *Herald*. The first was Dvořák's letter to the editor, in which he reiterated that he found "a sure foundation in the Negro melodies for a new national school of music," and that the National Conservatory was leading the way in developing that distinctive voice. "The new American school of music must strike its roots deeply into its own soil. There is no longer any reason why young Americans who have talent should go to Europe for their education. It is a waste of money and puts off the coming day when the Western world will be in music, as in many others, independent of other lands."[65]

Dvořák stressed the importance of hearing the music of the peasant classes. "It is to the poor that I turn for musical greatness. The poor work hard; they study seriously" (as Dvořák himself and Burleigh both exemplified). "Rich people are apt to apply themselves lightly to music, and to abandon the painful toil to which every strong musician must submit without complaint and without a rest. Poverty is no barrier to one endowed by nature with musical talent. It is a spur. It keeps the mind loyal to the end. It stimulates the student to great efforts."[66]

The second item, "Antonín Dvořák on Negro Melodies," was subtitled "The Bohemian Composer Employs Their Theme and Sentiments in a New Symphony." This article "exploded the time bomb that had been ticking all week." Dvořák was not only offering advice that might be dismissed as presumptuous coming from a foreigner—he himself had written a symphony that "reflect[ed] the Negro melodies, upon which . . . the coming American school must be based."[67]

Having detonated a charge that would echo across the American musical landscape for more than a century, Dvořák gathered his wife, his six children, and his Czech assistant and boarded the train for Spillville, Iowa, where they would spend the summer. En route they stopped briefly in Chicago to take in the sights at the World's Fair or Columbian Exposition, which had opened officially in May. Dvořák returned to Chicago to conduct his G Major Symphony and some Slavonic Dances on Bohemian Day for an audience that included some thirty thousand Czechs and Moravians. He also traveled to Omaha, Nebraska, and St. Paul, Minnesota, to visit the Minnehaha Falls in memory of *Hiawatha*, where he scratched down a melody on his shirt cuff that became the theme for the Larghetto of his Sonatina, Op. 100.[68]

But for most of the summer he would be almost at home, in Spillville, his "sum-mer Vysoka" with his family, enjoying the country sights and sounds in the quiet countryside so like his country home in Bohemia.[69] He completed the orchestra-tion of his symphony and continued composing with a facility that had escaped him in the busy metropolis of New York City. In only four days he composed the String Quartet in F major, Op. 96, now known as his *American Quartet*.[70] The second movement of this quartet reflected the sound of the spirituals so strongly that when a younger black composer, R. Nathaniel Dett, heard it performed at Oberlin College, he decided to dedicate himself to preserving the spirituals and basing his own compositions on them.[71]

* * *

As Dvořák was composing his Ninth Symphony, Burleigh was involved in some ambitious plans for representing African American music at the World's Fair, which will be described in chapter 6. But he also appeared in public performances at the conservatory and strengthened his connections with leaders in the black com-munity. In February he took part in "the grand success of the opera 'Faust,'" pro-duced by the conservatory.[72] And he remembered a special birthday—that of his mother (the Erie correspondent for the Cleveland *Gazette*)—with a special gift: "an exquisite bunch of violets, 'the dark blue eyes of springtime,' . . . breathing with fragrance and affection." Burleigh came honestly by his way with words.[73]

Along with the violets came the assurance that Burleigh had not forgotten the importance of continuing the struggle for justice. He had gone "down to the North Star Line to see Miss Ida B. Wells off to Scotland, and bade her 'bon voyage.'" Wells was a journalist who, after the lynching of three young black businessmen who were her friends, launched a vigorous investigation into the stories behind the frequent lynchings of African Americans. She found that despite the alleged sexual misconduct of the victims, most had actually been killed because their enterprise and financial success were perceived as a threat to their white neighbors. These men refused to conform to the racial stereotypes or to stay in "their place." As Frederick Douglass and other abolitionists had done before, Wells was going to England and Scotland to present the case for justice for African Americans to the British public. Here again Burleigh was close to the action, aware and supportive of aggressive political efforts to bring change. In the following months, black newspapers carried many reports of Wells's activities in England and the warm reception her speeches received. As had been true earlier in the century, raising awareness in England could bring positive pressure on American leaders, increasing the momentum for change.[74]

At the end of the conservatory's academic year, the Cleveland *Gazette* featured an article reporting Dvořák's views of the importance of African American music. The headline read ""Negro Melodies"—"Must be the Foundation of Any Serious and Original School of Composition"—"To be Developed in the United States, Says

Dr. Antonín Dvořák, the Eminent Musician—His Radical Opinions Endorsed by a Majority of Eastern Musicians—To Aid Our Students."[75]

With classes over for the year, Burleigh again left New York City for the summer. Some sources say that Burleigh returned to Saratoga Springs, where he sang in Victor Herbert's orchestra at the Grand Union Hotel and served as baritone soloist at the Bethesda A.M.E. Church. But the Cleveland *Gazette* and the Erie *Morning Dispatch* tell a different story. In mid-May Erie had suffered a devastating flood that took the homes of hundreds of Erie families and severely damaged the St. James A.M.E. Church, then located on East Sixth Street. Because one side wall and the back wall of the building were lost, the congregation held their services in the Grand Army of the Republic Hall for some months.[76] Burleigh's family home had not been affected, but he felt his place was in Erie. He would be closer to Chicago, where he would spend much of August preparing for Colored American Day at the World's Fair. He took up his previous position in the choir of the First Presbyterian Church,[77] and he had scarcely unpacked his bags before he was swept up in performances around the city. The Presbyterians were glad to have their favorite soloist back. The first Sunday he sang a solo after the sermon for the special Children's Day services, and in the evening praise service, he sang "Save Me, O God."[78]

The grandest musical events of the summer were those connected with the dedication of the Columbia Grand Organ at the new St. Peter's Roman Catholic Cathedral, followed by a twenty-fifth anniversary celebration for the bishop and the consecration of the new cathedral. Burleigh had been a featured soloist at the gala concert celebrating the completion of the new cathedral just before he left for New York City in December 1891. Now, eighteen months later, his Erie admirers could assess the progress he had made in his New York City studies. On July 11 he sang in the inaugural concert on the Columbia organ, "a grand success, financially and artistically." Burleigh's solo demonstrated that he had "applied himself in his studies in New York and achieved very marked success." His Erie admirers were confident that as he completed his musical studies he would continue to "cultivate a voice of great compass, rare quality and flexibility."[79]

On July 17 he was one of the soloists featured at a benefit concert for the St. Paul's Church Choir that included soloists from Brooklyn and New York City as well as contralto Winnie Eggleston and violinist Otto Malms. Burleigh sang "Visions Fair, Herodiade," by Massenet. That day's announcement said, "It is only necessary to give the names of those who are to appear upon the programme to intimate what is in store for the large audience which will undoubtedly be present."[80] The review the following day confirmed the prediction: "Although the evening was warm the audience never tired of the music and was loath to leave as the last notes of Mr. Burleigh's sweet German song died away and the programme was ended." The reviewer was generous in his praise: "Mr. Harry Thacker Burleigh sings because he can't help it and it is as easy and natural to him as breathing. One notices no effort in his singing, and with a fine voice under excellent cultivation his work is always received with enthusiasm by Erie audiences. He was heard at his best last night in DeKoven's 'Where the Ripples Flow' and Godard's 'Arabian Song' and kindly responded when the audience insisted upon a recall."[81] While the first sentence seems to reflect the stereotype that "all negroes are natural singers and have rhythm," the review also acknowledged his advanced training—a natural gift enhanced by discipline.

Meanwhile repairs to St. James A.M.E. Church were nearing completion, and an elaborate program was held for its opening on Sunday afternoon, July 30. Burleigh was in charge of the music, and he brought to the celebration some of the "leading white singers" with whom he often performed. The music was "excellent. The affair was a financial success, the collection for the day being $146." It was a busy day for Burleigh; in the evening after the St. James program he was a featured soloist at the First Methodist Church, singing Dudley Buck's "Judge Me, O God."[82]

August was an extremely busy month, starting with the celebrations at St. Peter's "Grand Cathedral." The Erie *Dispatch* outdid itself in describing this "Occasion of Distinguished Pomp and Ceremony." On August 1, the first event commemorated the twenty-fifth anniversary of the ordination of the bishop of Erie, the Right Reverend Tobias Mullen. The second was the dedication of the cathedral itself, "one of the sublimest pieces of sacred architecture in the state and equal in symmetry and impressiveness to many of the most famous cathedrals in this country." The new Columbus organ furnished appropriate music, led by organist and director Alois F. Lejeal of Los Angeles, California. A fifty-cent admission fee was charged at each service during the two days of pageantry, and the soloists assisting the choir included Mrs. Eggleston, H. T. Burleigh, and T. W. Shacklett.[83]

For the rest of the month, Burleigh's attention turned to Chicago and the World's Fair, where he and Will Marion Cook were arranging the program for Colored American Day, August 25. He stayed in Chicago until early September. In mid-September he departed for New York City and his third year at the National Conservatory of Music, continuing his studies and taking up his role as teacher in the conservatory's new branch for colored students.[84]

The fall term brought even more controversy with the first performance of Dvořák's *New World* Symphony, and in the course of the year the New York newspapers carried some of the first notices of a young African American singer who was a student at the conservatory. Twenty-five years later this student's performances would be frequent newsworthy events, with feature articles appearing in New York City papers to mark his singing on Palm Sunday and the annual Vesper Service of Negro spirituals as well as other occasional appearances. But in fall 1893, Burleigh's growing stature was noted for his academic aptitude and for his personal assistance to Dvořák in preparing for the first performance of his "New World Symphony."

6. The Columbian Exposition— The Chicago World's Fair

"A World's Fair for the World's Fair"

The 1893 World's Columbian Exposition, also known as the Chicago World's Fair, brought the American nation together in unprecedented ways. Some estimated that more than 300,000 people gathered for the opening celebration on May 1, 1893, the largest crowd "ever assembled in one place in the United States."[1] The Burleigh family was not part of the crowd on opening day, but Harry and his half-brother Elzie Elmendorf visited the fair later in the summer. For both, this time at the fair was a measure of their individual accomplishments. Both enjoyed sharing their memories of the fair with their families. But Harry Burleigh found himself at the side of an aging and disheartened Frederick Douglass, embroiled in fierce debate over how—or whether—African Americans should participate in this historic event. And he would be caught up in a swirl of unrealistic plans and expectations conceived by his friend Will Marion Cook.

The exposition was designed to celebrate four hundred years of progress toward building a lively industrial nation, which Chicago, "the City of the Big Shoulders," in Carl Sandburg's later metaphor, seemed to symbolize.[2] It drew Americans from across the country, in company with Europeans, royals as well as commoners, to see whether the Americans might very literally be able to outshine the Paris Exposition of 1889.

They could.

New York, the city of immigrants, had lost its bid to host the exposition, and Chicago had accomplished the impossible—building a gleaming White City seven miles from downtown, on a drained swamp near Lake Michigan, demonstrating through feats of daring and imaginative engineering—and landscape artistry—the irrepressible energy and bold economic strength of this young nation. Not only did the exposition display abundant evidence of America's leadership in industry and manufacturing, but the electric lights in the glistening white buildings of the Court of Honor and throughout the fairgrounds dramatically extended the summer's natural daylight into dazzling night. In the words of President Grover Cleveland at the official opening of the fair, just before he tapped the telegraph key that switched on this unprecedented light display, the fair would "show the world the glorious story of the United States of America, the amazing progress of the New World, the unparalleled advancement and wonderful accomplishments of a young nation; the triumphs of a vigorous, self-reliant, and independent people." He concluded, "We and our guests from other nations cooperate in the inauguration of an enterprise devoted to human enlightenment in the noblest sense, the brotherhood of nations."[3]

The United States, only one hundred seventeen years old, was celebrating a coming of age among nations. But in addition to showing the whole world, and particularly the Old World, what the New World was becoming, the fair dramatized through exotic ethnography exhibits on the Midway Plaisance that America represented the apex of human evolution. President Cleveland's "brotherhood of nations" claimed only the "civilized" branches of the family of humankind. Though modified to maximize profits, Harvard anthropologist Frederick Ward Putnam "envisioned the Midway as a living outdoor museum of 'primitive' human beings that would afford visitors the opportunity to measure the progress of humanity toward the ideal of civilization presented in the White City."[4] This march through Social Darwinism was to demonstrate how human society had been evolving through the millennia; the United States represented the highest, and doubtless the ultimate, in human evolution and achievement. That African Americans were systematically excluded from the paths to achievement was not to be acknowledged, and their remarkable economic and educational progress in the preceding quarter-century after the Civil War and the end of slavery was not to be displayed. Further, that there had been "550 lynchings and 332 'legal' executions in the years 1890–1892,"[5] and that more than 160 lynchings both the year before and the year of the fair was not to be considered. Like the swamp on which the fair was built, the darkening tide of injustice barely beneath the glittering surface of the White City was to be resolutely concealed.

If the United States represented the zenith of human evolution, the Midway also offered a glimpse of what was assumed to be the nadir, the least advanced on the human evolutionary scale. The Dahomey Village, where Africans recently colonized by the French could be seen and heard, drew thousands of visitors. Other exhibits on the Midway might display the exotic and the vulgar, wandering musicians might play what was described as "hideous music, squeaking along the thoroughfare."[6] But these alien cultures fell along the intermediate steps of the developmental scale between savage Africa and America's superior civilization. Dahomey Village, personifying Africa, represented the antithesis of American achievement. By extension, Americans of African descent were seen in this paradigm to inhabit a space closer to the nadir than to the zenith.[7]

His excursions along the Midway Plaisance may have been a source of Burleigh's later reluctance to credit the African roots of the spirituals. Like Frederick Douglass, who railed against the "sound of the barbaric music" and the "sights of barbaric rites,"[8] at the Dahomey Village, Burleigh could not allow himself to hear the aural kinship that Paul Laurence Dunbar recognized between the music of the Dahomeyans and the music of black Americans. In Dunbar's words, "The strange, fantastic melody of the old plantation has always possessed a deep fascination for me. . . . But question as I might, I could never find out its source until passing through Midway Plaisance I heard the Dahomeyans singing. Instantly the idea flashed into my mind: 'It is a heritage.' . . . I heard in the Dahomeyans the same rich melody, the same mournful minor cadences, that have touched the heart of the world through negro music."[9]

Burleigh's response also differed from that of music critic Henry Krehbiel, who watched and listened carefully to the Dahomeyan musicians, just as Dvořák had listened to Burleigh's singing. Krehbiel reported his observations in a series of articles in the New York *Tribune* and later in his 1914 book *Afro-American Folk Songs,* for which Burleigh provided a number of arrangements. Social Darwinism also determined the status of various styles of music, with the "serious music" of the orchestra and recital hall representing the apex, popular music styles ranging lower, and the music of "primitive people" at the lowest level. Perhaps this child of the Reconstruction, the rising classical singer and future composer, was too focused on his struggle to win recognition from the musical elite, black and white, to acknowledge a cultural debt to the "savages" at the wrong end of the Midway Plaisance.

The Chicago World's Fair was meant to demonstrate four hundred years of progress for America. Even more urgently, America's citizens of African descent, only thirty years released from their two hundred and fifty years of involuntary servitude, hoped for a platform on which to demonstrate the enormous strides they had made in the tumultuous years since the Emancipation Proclamation and the end of the Civil War. When the fair commission designated August 25 as Colored American Day, some welcomed this opportunity to counteract the demeaning caricatures that the press and the underlying philosophy of the fair presented. In February 1893 a committee from Worcester, Massachusetts, proposed that it be a "most comfortable day of praise and thanksgiving" for God's care throughout the troubled history of Africans in America, asserting that "there is in the record of history no people that have made the progress that we have in the same space of time."[10] They envisioned a gathering of 100,000, with a chorus of 500 schoolchildren, an adult chorus of 3,000, and an orchestra of 100, performing selections by Johann Sebastian Bach, Felix Mendelssohn, Camille Saint-Saens, and Ludwig van Beethoven.

But to those not part of Massachusetts's elite black communities, this plan reflected the committee's privileged status, not the reality of life for ordinary black

Americans. Leading the protest, the Indianapolis *Freeman* retorted, "There is no accounting for taste, however, and if the colored people of the 'Old Bay State,' backed by one or two Negro Bishops with time on their hands, desire to have such a distinction, may the Lord have mercy on their foolish souls, for they know [not] what they do, but let it be distinctly confined to Massachusetts, and the race in general be spared the humiliation of the thing."[11]

Indeed, the achievement of African Americans was extraordinary, even in a society driven toward progress, though it was based on a foundation of unremitting struggle throughout their previous enslavement. If the fair's commission wished to show the apex of civilization, they had only to look to black Americans. The American Negro should be commended "as a man and as an American" whose progress "since emancipation, in knowledge, in professional skill, in material acquirement, and in literary achievement [was] the most marvelous work of civilization."[12]

Twelve years later, Burleigh would applaud the analysis of Archibald Grimke, then ex-consul of Santo Domingo, that in the South the accomplishments of black people far exceeded those of white southerners, their former masters, who were "sunk in mediocrity."[13] Now he joined his friend Will Marion Cook, Frederick Douglass, and others in planning the program that would demonstrate African American progress in music—thus symbolizing the whole range of economic, educational, and cultural advancement of a people.

Despite resistance by the commission, there was some official representation of African Americans. Frederick Douglass, U.S. ambassador to Haiti from 1888 to 1891, presided over the Haiti exhibit at the invitation of Haiti's president and was conspicuously present every day. The Haiti Pavilion became a gathering place for black visitors to the fair, as well as white Americans and foreign dignitaries who came to greet the famous abolitionist and orator.[14] In addition to his colleague Will Marion Cook, among those who gathered at the Haiti Pavilion were two others who became significant Burleigh friends and colleagues. The young poet Paul Laurence Dunbar assisted Douglass in meeting visitors and the press at the Haiti exhibit. And poet and future diplomat James Weldon Johnson, with twenty-five of his Atlanta University classmates spent the summer among the one-thousand-plus "chair boys" propelling wheel chairs in which, for seventy-five cents an hour, visitors could explore the exposition "with a minimum of effort."[15]

But in the months before the fair opened and throughout the summer, many African Americans argued that they should boycott the fair to protest their official exclusion from the program and the increasing betrayal of their civil rights. They especially opposed a Colored American Day similar to days set aside for other nationalities. Why should African Americans be treated as foreigners in the nation that their labor had built, and for which they had fought and died? Even more, why should the nation that had enslaved them now fail to honor their hard-won freedom and achievements?

In strong, often vitriolic language, black newspaper editors featured the debate with Frederick Douglass, who argued that African Americans should participate as actively as possible. At the same time as they voiced their opposition to a "Nigger Day," fearing that it would give license to even more discrimination and mockery,[16] the black newspapers reported on African Americans who would be represented in state exhibits or as artists, on black musicians who would perform, and on individuals and groups who would attend the fair. The Washington *Bee* even described in detail the outfit one stylish young woman would wear on her two weeks' visit to the fair.[17]

Many feared that Colored American Day would degenerate into a day of watermelons, fried chicken, and cakewalks, reinforcing stereotypes that they were eager to prove false.[18] These were not idle concerns. Any program showcasing African American progress would need to contend with the many expressions of antipathy toward blacks that permeated the fair. A glaring example was a two-page color cartoon published in *World's Fair Puck* depicting a procession of Africans and African Americans, "thus amalgamating the two stereotypes." The caption asserted that they had been "diverted from the grand parade by a discontented African American who distracted them with watermelons which they gobble up without paying him."[19]

In an April 1893 letter to the Indianapolis *Freeman*, Douglass answered his critics, deploring the persistent efforts of the black press "to misrepresent and disparage the proposal to set apart one day of the World's Columbian Exposition for the exhibition of the musical attainments of our people." He argued, "The fact that we are but meagerly represented in the management of the great Exposition should not in a spirit of petulance be resented by a spirit of refusal to avail ourselves of any advantage to our people, however small that advantage may be. All that we have ever received has come to us in small concessions and it is not the part of wisdom to despise the day of small things."[20]

Furthermore, he argued, African Americans must distance themselves from the inhabitants of the Dahomey Village on the Midway Plaisance, "to counteract the baneful influence of those West African savages who have been brought here to act the monkey." In contrast to these uncivilized black persons, African Americans "ought to show the progress, achievements, culture, musical genius and real position of the American Negro."[21] Unfortunately, Douglass essentially undermined his own argument by drawing on the basic tenets of social Darwinism so often used by white cartoonists and others to perpetrate racist stereotypes. But the White City was indeed all too white, Douglass said, as the Negro had "no part nor lot in it; a World's Fair for the World's Fair. We owe it to ourselves to take vigorous hold and make it a magnificent success."[22] The White City needed some color, but it must be the right color. Judging from his lifelong advocacy of high culture, one senses that young Burleigh agreed.

To counteract the underlying racism and the refusal to acknowledge African American progress officially, Douglass planned with Ida B. Wells to prepare a pamphlet, "The Reason Why the Afro-American Is Not in the World's Columbian Exposition." It would highlight the accomplishments of black Americans and refute the slanders of their detractors. They intended to pass it out to all of the thousands who attended the fair. But when Wells returned from her antilynching lecture tour of England shortly before Colored American Day, she found Douglass discouraged by the constant barrage of criticism and ready to abandon the pamphlet. He would concentrate his waning energy on the preparation for August 25, which he termed Jubilee Day, celebrating freedom and African American achievement. Wells persuaded him to continue working with her on the pamphlet, though it would not be ready for August 25. She boycotted Colored American Day, but Douglass held out for the chance to highlight the musical accomplishments of the race, and Burleigh would play an important role in the performance.

* * *

Frederick Douglass, himself a violinist, took special interest in young violinist Will Marion Cook, from Douglass's hometown of Washington, D.C. After studying at Oberlin College in his early teens, Cook had gone to Germany to study with the great violinist Joseph Joachim. Douglass scheduled a benefit concert to contribute toward the cost of Cook's European study. After a year in Berlin, Cook returned to his home in Washington, D.C.,[23] where he joined Christian A. Fleetwood in forming an orchestra, which Cook conducted. Douglass served as president of the orchestra, and his patronage supported local concerts by the orchestra as well as performances in other cities in the East.[24]

Cook promised Douglass that he would write an operatic version of *Uncle Tom's Cabin* for Colored American Day. In 1851 the serialized version of Harriet Beecher Stowe's novel about the evils of slavery sold more copies than any previous work by an American author, and in 1852 when the book was published it quickly became a worldwide phenomenon, translated into thirty-seven languages, and inspiring innumerable "dramatizations, musicals, songs, figurines, cartoons, and eventually film versions."[25] The novel's political and social impact could not have been anticipated: it would "galvanize the country's opposition to slavery, become a global pop-culture phenomenon . . . and would, to some minds, spark a civil war."[26] By 1893 performances by traveling troupes and local theater companies proliferated, offering many black performers their stage debuts. Cook was building on a forty-year heritage of stage plays in creating his opera. Judging by his later Broadway productions, he would bring an unconventional voice to the tradition.

Frederick Douglass had campaigned for President Benjamin Harrison, and displaying great confidence in Cook (perhaps more than later events would justify), he arranged for Cook to meet with the president. As a result, Harrison intervened, persuading the World's Fair commission to permit an "exhibition of the progress made by [the Negro] race in music."[27] The opera performance on Colored American Day was to feature some of the most distinguished black artists, Burleigh among them.

There were many changes in the program and personnel in the months before August 25. A January 1893 article in the New York *Times* listed a stellar cast: tenor Harry A. Williams, a native of Cleveland, now a voice teacher at the London Conservatory of Music; soprano Sissieretta Jones, at the peak of her international fame; contralto Mrs. Waring, who was studying at La Scala in Milan, Italy; Jennie Jackson De Hart, a former member of the Fisk Jubilee Singers; Mumford's Fisk Jubilee Singers; and baritone Harry Burleigh, who with his "splendid baritone voice," would assist Cook and would take the part of Simon Legree in the opera.[28]

The Theodore Thomas Exposition Orchestra, conducted for this occasion by Will Marion Cook, would play a suite of Negro dances by Maurice Strothotte, an African American composition student of Dvořák's.[29] Douglass would be the featured orator, and other dignitaries would attend. Jeannette Thurber, "who so generously planned to foster and develop" the "musical genius" of African Americans, was expected.[30] Other invited guests included Colonel Robert Ingersoll, Judge Albion W. Tourgee, Carter Harrison, Susan B. Anthony, outgoing U.S. President Benjamin Harrison, and the newly elected President Grover Cleveland.[31] This list may be an example of Cook's typically grandiose ideas, but perhaps in January Douglass and Cook could hope to realize these plans. Burleigh left for Chicago a few days after the January *New York Times* report, presumably to help Cook to recruit the "trained chorus of 100 voices" drawn from the various jubilee choirs.[32] But as Chicago's summer heat intensified, so did the opposition to the plans for Jubilee Day, and the actual event would barely cast a shadow on the White City.

* * *

A number of Erie citizens visited the fair that summer, including Albert Vosburg and his daughter Florence and Burleigh's friend John Diehl. Lizzie and John Elmendorf experienced the fair vicariously, through their sons Elzie and Harry. Early in 1893 the Erie *Morning Dispatch* announced a plan to sponsor a tour to the World's Fair for high school students and teachers. Students with the largest number of votes would earn a week at the fair at the newspaper's expense. By July Elzie had taken the lead and "kept it to the end."[33] A special train of two sleepers, a day car, and a baggage car was reserved for the party, along with others who wished to accompany the *Dispatch* guests.[34]

When the *Dispatch* party arrived back in Erie a week later, Elzie reported "the wonders he saw and heard": he "visited all the buildings [a feat in itself], rode on the Ferris wheel, saw the Krupp gun, Midway Plaisance, visited Washington park and Lincoln park, the auditorium, heard [Chicago evangelist Dwight L.] Moody preach."[35] His brother Harry surely enjoyed the stories, though his music respon-sibilities probably limited his time for cruising the Midway and riding the Ferris wheel.

* * *

After his busy summer in Erie, Harry Burleigh again left for Chicago on August 9 to help train the choir. The Dvořák family was enjoying the second of their three visits to the fair, from August 8 to 18,[36] as they made their way back to New York City from their summer in Spillville, Iowa. A highlight of this visit for Dvořák was August 12, Bohemian Day, when he conducted several of his works in "a gala concert." The following day, Burleigh stopped by Dvořák's hotel to introduce Will Marion Cook, who was hoping to be admitted to the National Conservatory of Music. With typical modesty, rather than disturb the composer,[37] Burleigh left Dvořák a three-page handwritten letter:

> Dear Doctor,
>
> I want to introduce to your consideration Mr. Will M. Cook, a former pupil of the great Joachim. Mr. Cook has marked ability in the line of composition and desires very greatly to meet you and speak with you about his work. He has composed an opera the principal role of which I will sing. . . .
>
> I am going away from Chicago to-day but will leave this note for you, and Mr. Cook will call and see you. . . .
>
> I sincerely trust you will listen to his work and give him your opinion.
>
> Hoping you will be blessed with continued good health and success and that I will see you in the Conservatory next September I have the privilege to remain
>
> Yours very truly,
>
> Harry T. Burleigh[38]

Cook took the opportunity to meet Dvořák, and the following month he joined Dvořák's composition class.[39]

The fair offered many opportunities to hear music by American composers, and some reflected an interest in the music of African Americans. Their inclusion by Exposition Orchestra leader Theodore Thomas in the fair's music program shows his willingness to grant air time to composers who explored Dvořák's nationalistic territory. But Cook, Burleigh, and Douglass intended Colored American Day to demonstrate "real" black music, composed, arranged, and performed entirely by African Americans, in addition to showcasing their mastery of European classics.

The *Daily Columbian*, the fair's daily newspaper, announced the plans, con-siderably modified since the January announcement: "At 2:30 in Festival Hall the Honorable Frederick Douglass will deliver an oration 'Race Problem in America.' Mme. S. Jones, the famous 'Patti,' Mr. Sidney Woodward of Boston, and Mr. Harry Burleigh of the National Conservatory of Music of America, will sing selections from the famous opera Uncle Tom's Cabin, written by Mr. Will M. Cook."[40]

It is surely Cook's voice that we hear in the advertisement: the "famous opera" had not yet premiered. The announcement continued, "Miss Hallie Q. Brown, the distinguished elocutionist, will recite stirring and patriotic selections. The famous Jubilee Singers will render their quaint and plaintive plantation melodies." And several violin selections would be played by Douglass's grandson Joseph Douglass.

It is difficult, among the conflicting reports, to document the full details of the Jubilee Day program. The next day's review in the *Daily Columbian* did not mention the chorus of Jubilee singers. Dvořák's student Maurice Strothotte performed, but rather than hearing his Negro dance suite played by the Exposition Orchestra under Cook's direction, he played it himself on the piano, and he accompanied the other performers.[41]

The reality of that day must have been painfully anticlimactic to Burleigh, Cook, and Douglass for many reasons. Sissieretta Jones did sing at the fair, but not on the platform with Cook and Burleigh.[42] She appeared a month later, on September 25, at the Women's Building, to an audience that packed the large building. She declined to sing for Cook's production, ostensibly because her advance payment failed to reach her in time. Douglass knew that she had joined the boycott; her agent, Major Pond, had scheduled her to sing at Asbury Park, New Jersey, on that day.[43]

Only a duet from Cook's "famous opera" was performed, by Sidney Woodward and Burleigh. No explanation was given for the truncated performance. Scholars have been unable to find any trace of the *Uncle Tom's Cabin* opera, though two songs, "He Shall Burn" (Simon Legree's song) and "Thou Art Gone Forever," were listed on an advance program.[44] The opera may never have been finished, or perhaps in his frustration over the mounting difficulties Cook destroyed it. He may have incorporated some of the music into his later productions, but the opera remains a mystery.

One thing is certain: There was no ragtime on this program. Music historians trace the launching of ragtime into national prominence in the fecund interaction of musicians who flocked to Chicago's bars and music halls during the World's Fair.[45] Judging from remarks he made later about ragtime and the World's Fair, Cook frequented such venues,[46] but it is unlikely that Burleigh joined him. Such music did not fit into Douglass's plan to represent "the highest musical achievements of the race." Nine years later, Will Marion Cook produced "an ironic postscript" in his "Negro Musical Comedy," *In Dahomey,* with its "masterful score . . . chock full of ragtime," a tribute to his fascination with the sounds of the Dahomey Village as well as his emersion in ragtime.[47]

Despite the calls for a boycott, there was a substantial African American presence in Festival Hall for the 2:30 p.m. program. The "few" in later reports were in fact "a throng of sober black citizens, ringed by some white spectators,"[48] said to number between 1,000 and 2,500.[49] This was far fewer than the 100,000 the Massachusetts Committee predicted, but not an insignificant number. Burleigh had sung for larger audiences, but this was certainly his first appearance before a national gathering.

Perhaps in expectation of the *Uncle Tom's Cabin* opera, but also "to remind [his audience] of a time, not that long ago, when a significant number of whites had worked with black abolitionists to hasten the end of slavery,"[50] Harriet Beecher-Stowe's sister, Isabella Beecher-Hooker, arrived with Douglass. They were greeted with deafening applause.[51] As Douglass began his speech, "The Race Problem in America," "several white hecklers disrupted his remarks with 'jeers and catcalls.'" For a moment, the elderly Douglass faltered. In dismay, Paul Laurence Dunbar, sitting on the platform near Douglass, saw his hand shake and heard his voice falter. But Douglass had faced hostile audiences before. "Then, to the young poet's surprise and delight, the old abolitionist threw his papers down, parked his glasses on them, and eyes flashing, pushed his hand through his great mane of white hair," and spoke, his voice "full, rich and deep . . . , compelling attention, drowning out the catcalls as an organ would a pennywhistle."[52] Burleigh, also on the platform, was in familiar territory, at the center of a struggle for the rights of his people.

Douglass, the old lion, could still roar. "Men talk of the Negro problem. There is no Negro problem. The problem is whether the American people have loyalty enough, honor enough, patriotism enough, to live up to their own Constitution." He spoke for an hour, stressing that "We Negroes love our country. We fought for it. We ask only that we be treated as well as those who fought against it."[53]

After Douglass's speech, Isabella Beecher-Hooker presented him with a copy of the latest edition of *Uncle Tom's Cabin*, "together with the photograph and autograph of the author."[54] Then Douglass yielded the platform to his grandsons' generation: violinist Joseph Douglass, tenor Sidney Woodward, baritone Harry T. Burleigh, and pianist and composer Maurice Strothotte. Deseria Plato, a mezzo contralto from New York, was "well received." Paul Laurence Dunbar, Douglass's assistant at the Haiti Pavilion, read his poem "The Colored American," written for the occasion.[55] The audience responded enthusiastically to this part of the program; "Harry T. Burleigh's baritone solo brought him encore after encore."[56]

Cook himself did not appear on the program and apparently had left the fair-grounds. Those in the audience who wanted to congratulate him on the songs Burleigh and Woodward sang from his opera could not find him. Whether unwilling to face questions about the discrepancies between his advertised program and what was actually presented, frustrated with the barrage of criticism of his plans, or for other reasons, he absented himself.[57] One can only imagine how Cook, ever the visionary but always volatile, must have felt about the dramatic diminution of the program he had envisioned. Burleigh left us no record of the day, but he and Cook's other colleagues carried the day without him.

Some bias in the reports of the black press could be expected from their intense opposition to the celebration, but their first reports focused on Douglass's oration and reported that few had attended. The Cleveland *Gazette*'s article was erroneously entitled "The Watermelons Absent": "Colored Folks' Day" (yesterday, August 25) at the world's fair was a farce. Few of the prominent persons expected to participate—to speak, sing and play—were present. Even the promised watermelons were conspicuously absent."[58] In fact, watermelons did appear; Douglass found the vendors setting up their stalls when he came onto the grounds that morning. Surely those who planned the event must have expected to profit financially, the *Gazette* sniffed, especially Will Marion Cook and Charles Morris (who was married to Douglass's granddaughter).[59]

Similarly, the Indianapolis *Freeman* reported in early September that Colored American Day had been "Minus the Negro," though it quoted extensively from Douglass's impassioned speech, and it praised the musical performances. "As 'Colored American Day,' supposing to represent the growth of the Negro race during the last twenty-seven years, it was a dismal failure. As a concert of a very high order, it was a glittering success."[60] The *Freeman* exulted with questionable accuracy over the success of the opposition to the day: "Those who opposed the affair are jubilant. With a population of more than 30,000 Negroes in Chicago and visitors several thousand strong, it is a fact that less than 1,000 attended the jubilee. . . . The day, on a whole, was a failure and the managers tacitly admit as much. The 'Negro Jubilee Day' has gone glimmering."[61]

The local boycott may have been effective, expressing the disapproval of many in Chicago's black community, but Ida B. Wells disagreed with the *Freeman*'s conclusion. When she read the newspaper accounts of Douglass's speech, she "so swelled with pride over his masterly presentation of our case that I went straight out to the fair and begged his pardon for presuming in my youth and inexperience to criticize him for an effort which had done so much more to bring our cause to the attention of the American people than anything else which had happened during the fair."[62] The Douglass-Wells pamphlet did reach many fairgoers, if not the thousands they had hoped for. After August 30, when the pamphlet was ready, Wells herself handed out hundreds of them to visitors to the Haiti Pavilion.[63]

The editor of the Chicago *Conservator*, a black newspaper, also commented caustically on the role of Will Marion Cook and Charles Morris in planning for Jubilee Day. They were "a precious pair of straw colored pets, . . . who blarneyed a confiding people by one of the boldest confidence games ever seen in Chicago." He claimed that Cook had forced out another manager "who had already planned the musical celebration," but this is doubtful, since Cook had been working with Douglass and Burleigh for months. This critic alleged further that Cook and Morris "first fastened on two good singers, Burleigh and Woodward who were in town and hence didn't cost very much."[64] In fact, Woodward reported in November 1892 that Cook had asked him to sing in the opera,[65] and Burleigh worked with Cook in the planning from January of that year; neither of them "just happened" to be visiting the fair.

However, the charge that their intent was to draw people to the event by announcing the appearance of Sissieretta Jones is credible. She had sung in the January Carnegie Hall concert to raise money for the occasion, so at that time she apparently intended to participate, but to appear under the auspices of what many believed to be the losing side of the controversy over Jubilee Day would not have helped her growing celebrity; she and Major Pond made other plans.

* * *

An important adjunct to the Chicago World's Fair was the convergence of black musicians on Chicago churches and concert halls as well as on the bars and saloons where ragtime was evolving. Burleigh was among the singers invited to perform in the city on several occasions. Near the end of October, Washington, D.C., black music critic Walt B. Hayson wrote his critique of the black singers who were featured in the Windy City during the World's Fair. His two articles covered performances during the World's Fair and in the months after the exposition. The musicians appeared at numerous venues, "the various congresses, churches and in the world's fair ground."[66]

In his second article, Hayson commented that Burleigh's reputation had preceded him to Chicago, "and when he appeared in our midst as a concert singer, much was expected from him." However, Burleigh did not entirely measure up to Hayson's standards. "His stage presence somewhat cooled the ardor of our expectations, for the *nonchalance* of his bearing is quite distracting." Without other contemporaneous descriptions, it is difficult to interpret this comment. Burleigh was an experienced performer, and he had been exposed to rigorous training in stage deportment. One wonders whether his reception was affected by the Colored American Day controversy that surrounded his Chicago appearances. Or perhaps his vocal presentation was more relaxed, less stilted than that of his colleagues.

Hayson was better impressed by Burleigh's voice. His "careful vocal training . . . is established at once by the manner in which he treats such songs as Massenet's Vision Fair and *The Toreador's Song* by Bizet." Burleigh had been singing the Toreador Song for a number of years. Though it was written for a tenor, Burleigh's voice extended into the tenor range and was sometimes described as a high baritone. Hayson commented, "Mr. Burleigh has a robust baritone voice of wide range, and a good quality, especially in the middle register." Hayson's critique closed with "the best wishes of us all" in Burleigh's new work, an apparent reference to his appointment as a teacher at the National Conservatory.[67]

His experiences at the Chicago World's Fair and in Chicago's black community profoundly affected Burleigh the singer, Burleigh the rising public figure, and Burleigh the activist. Having risen to the top echelon of classical singers in Erie, all of them white, he was now finding his place at a national level among black classical singers. In Chicago he mingled with several of the most distinguished black singers of his time. He worked closely, if not easily, with the brilliant but unpredictable

Will Marion Cook. He sang before a national audience, in the midst of conflicting expectations, in an attempt to represent African Americans as accomplished and worthy citizens.

But beyond the music itself, the Chicago World's Fair took Burleigh into the arena where black journalists and political leaders struggled to find the most effective means to stem the rising tide of injustice. Though they might disagree as to the most effective weapons, as did Frederick Douglass and Ida B. Wells, their common goal was to benefit the race and to disprove by their own persistent example that the dominant white society was wrong in demeaning them and in underestimating their capacity for achievement. With them, he struggled with issues of representation and the ambiguous role that music and public performance could play in confronting discrimination and racist stereotyping. And he saw firsthand how vicious racist stereotyping could be. Burleigh had learned from his family that injustice could be confronted directly and with good effect. On Jubilee Day he saw Frederick Douglass, one of the race's most ardent and effective activists, meet racist hostility head-on, overwhelming it with his legendary eloquence. He renewed contact with Ida B. Wells, who could match Douglass's forcefulness in protesting the evils of Lynch Law.

Burleigh left Chicago before the international Labor Congress, where Booker T. Washington, the "young and relatively unknown principal of the Tuskegee Institute," challenged Wells and Douglass with his argument that skilled labor was more important to African Americans in the South than political activism for civil rights and social equality. Washington's remarks caught the attention of a group of businessmen from Atlanta who were planning a fair in their city. They asked Washington's help in persuading Congress to support their plan and invited him to deliver an address on opening day.[68] Washington's "Atlanta Exposition Address," a watershed in African American political thought, provoked even greater divisions and controversy than had Colored American Day at the World's Columbian Exposition in Chicago. And a few years later, after Frederick Douglass's death, Burleigh began a fifteen-year association with Washington, facilitating Washington's fundraising in the North.

It is simplistic—and, as we shall see, inaccurate—to suggest that Burleigh's own political alliance shifted immediately from Douglass's and Wells's preference for direct confrontation to Washington's tactic of strategic accommodation. With the history of activism in his family and his own increasing public stature, he would need to find his own way between these contrasting paths. As W. E. B. Du Bois mounted a serious challenge to Washington's influence in the early 1900s, Burleigh would find himself on the front lines of the controversy, just as he had been throughout the summer of 1893.

7. The Symphony "From the New World"

"He loved to hear me sing the old melodies"

After the grandeur and controversy of the Chicago World's Fair and his return to Erie as a favorite son, Burleigh arrived in New York City in late September 1893 to continue his studies, now joined by his friend Will Marion Cook. Cook was impressed by Jeannette Thurber's genuinely inclusive approach in recruiting students. "She made no distinction of color, creed or state of good looks. She didn't even care much about the money. . . . Fact was a little bit of everything and every body was in the musical melting pot. All she and Dr. Dvořák asked was talent—heaps of it—and the power of concentration on the subject at hand."[1]

It may be that Burleigh was more prepared to concentrate "on the subject at hand" than Cook, but the two of them relished opportunities to enjoy the abundance of fine music the city had to offer. Together they bartered their skill as a music copyists for free tickets to concerts, spending many evenings at the New York Academy of Music listening to orchestras of eighty to one hundred players led by Emil Paur and Hans von Bülow and others bring the music of Richard Wagner and Carl Maria von Weber to life—thrilling to the "tempestuous, langorous [sic], voluptuous, tumultuous, dynamic music, expressing every human and sometimes unearthly emotion," studying orchestration, sleeping "with petite editions of Beethoven symphonies and overtures," and pondering how African American music should find its place in such settings.[2]

Cook, whose métier would be black musical theater, found his concert experiences and his orchestration lessons of little help in setting a dance or a song "for five, six, seven at most, which one had to do as music director at Worth's museum," his first show business job, with Bob Cole.[3] Characteristically, he found "the kindly martinet" Dvořák's demanding style of pedagogy difficult to tolerate.[4] He refused to play violin in the conservatory orchestra, claiming that he "had forgotten how to play [his] fiddle." He had pawned it and neglected to redeem it; surely no one would expect him to starve! "'Twas tough going those blessed years." He claimed somewhat peevishly that Burleigh was "Dvořák's pet." In contrast to Burleigh, he saw himself to be "the outcast of the whole school," while Burleigh "ran errands, played the tympani (extremely well) in the school orchestra, sang baritone and bass in [the] school Negro chorus. And smiled his way into the hearts of all."[5] Characteristically, Burleigh's dignity and sense of self, his good-humored personal diplomacy and academic excellence set the pattern for his success at the conservatory, just as he would later secure and maintain his long tenure in his positions at St. George's Episcopal Church and the Ricordi Music Publishing Company. For all his brilliance, Cook's volatility repeatedly threatened his professional achievements, but Burleigh and Cook's mutual respect sustained a lifelong friendship, and they would collaborate on many projects in the years ahead.

At the premiere of Symphony No. 9 in E Minor, "From the New World," Cook had been in Dvořák's composition class only a few months, but the composer apparently recognized his ability, despite his intransigence. In a 1908 feature article on Cook, New York *Age* music critic Lester A. Walton quoted "no less notable an authority than Dvořák" in asserting Cook's brilliance: "Plantation melodies constitute the soul of American music, and this boy may some day be the greatest American composer."[6] Taking Cook's penchant for self-promotion and exaggeration into consideration, one must be somewhat wary of this claim, as it seems not to be confirmed in any other source, but Dvořák would certainly have recognized his student's genius if he could not applaud his self-discipline.

Cook did not complete his course at the conservatory, but Burleigh's place there was secure. In addition to his coursework, as had been announced in the spring, he and Paul Bolin served as the staff of the new department for black students of exceptional talent who had been recruited to join the student body at no tuition cost. Burleigh taught singing and solfeggio. One of his voice students, a Mrs. Tadlock from Cincinnati, Ohio, spoke warmly at the end of the year of her progress under Burleigh's tutelage, describing him, not surprisingly, as "a thorough teacher."[7]

* * *

In December 1893 Burleigh and Will Marion Cook were working "under the direction of" Jeannette Thurber to "annex a normal school of music to Howard University, Washington, D.C."[8] Cook's biographer, Marva Carter, suspects that this report was based primarily on Cook's wishful thinking, as he was notorious for feeding misinformation to the press,[9] but if based on fact, it was one of many plans that did not materialize. A possible alternative to Thurber's earlier plan for the National Conservatory to be moved to the nation's capital and supported by federal funds, it went the way of her previous plans for expansion. Collaboration between Howard University and the National Conservatory would have provided a fertile environment in which to nurture composers who would create the American school of music that Dvořák and Thurber envisioned. But this dream was not to be fulfilled.

* * *

Burleigh's evenings with the Dvořák family continued through the fall, and with all six children now sharing the apartment with their parents and their Aunt Terezie, it was a lively scene. Dvořák expressed his delight in having all his family with him in November by composing his Sonatina, Opus 100, for his children. He dedicated it to them, and at its completion in early December, the children performed it in their home, their proud father's "favorite premiere."[10] Whether Burleigh was present on this occasion we do not know, but on December 4, the day after Dvořák finished the Sonatina, Burleigh, Cook, and Maurice Arnold were among the students who performed at the Scottish Rite Hall in Madison Square Garden, with Dvořák as conductor.[11]

In mid-November, when Anton Seidl broke one of their companionable silences at a neighborhood cafe to ask Dvořák's permission to premiere his new symphony, Dvořák did not give an immediate reply. But that evening he sent his assistant, Josef Kovarik, to deliver the score, which "at the last minute" he had dubbed *Z Noveho sveta* (*From the New World*). In his *Reminiscences,* Kovarik commented on the "much confusion and division of opinion" the title caused, particularly in the United States, for those who understood the title to indicate that it was an "American" symphony, or "a symphony with American music." "Quite the wrong idea!" Kovarik countered. "This title means nothing more than 'Impressions and Greetings from the New World.'" Dvořák himself smilingly acknowledged the controversy saying, "It seems that I have got them all confused."[12] But many of Dvořák's American listeners, including the most musically erudite among them, would hear familiar echoes in this most American of symphonies, and it would be for African Americans the touchstone of a new pride in their own distinctive musical heritage.

As the manuscript had not yet been sent to Simrock, Dvořák's European publisher, his copyist Harry Burleigh and his assistant Josef Kovarik were very busy in the weeks before the December 15 premiere (performed in manuscript), preparing the orchestral parts from the "original *partitur* [score]."[13] Will Marion Cook may have worked with them, as five days after the premiere, Dvořák wrote his publisher Fritz Simrock in a letter accompanying the score that he had four copyists "sitting next to [him] copying parts."[14]

New York *Tribune* music critic Henry E. Krehbiel, who had greeted Dvořák's coming to America the previous fall with an article in *Century* magazine and several extensive articles in the *Daily Tribune*, wrote Dvořák three days before the December 15 premiere to say he had heard the symphony in rehearsal and had read the score. "I am delighted with it and intend to print an article to help people to understand and enjoy it on Friday." He asked to meet the composer to show him the excerpts from the score that would accompany the article. Dvořák responded by sending his notes on the music, giving Krehbiel's explanatory introduction special authority. The first public hearing of the music was an open rehearsal on Saturday afternoon before the evening premiere.[15]

As Krehbiel pointed out, this new symphony had "unique and special value" because in it Dvořák "exemplified his theories touching the possibility of founding a National school of composition on the folk-song of America." Dvořák's views "put forth in an incomplete and bungling manner" in the articles of the previous spring had caused "a great deal of comment at the time, the bulk of which was distinguished by flippancy and a misconception of the composer's meaning and purposes." Krehbiel attributed much of the misunderstanding on the part of Dvořák's American critics to their assumption that he was referring to "the songs of Stephen C. Foster and other contributors to old time negro minstrelsy, and that the school of which he dreamed was to devote himself to the writing of variations on 'The Old Folks at Home' and tunes of its class." Class consciousness as well as a barely disguised racism resounded in some of the most vociferous objections to Dvořák's promotion of American Negro and American Indian folk music.[16]

In his nearly full-page article on the new symphony, illustrated with nine music examples, Krehbiel argued that African American folksong was the "most characteristic, most beautiful and most vital" folk music of America. Dvořák, "whose music is a language, was able quickly to discern the characteristics" of this music and "to recognize its availability and value." Krehbiel's purpose in the article was to help the listeners "to appreciate wherein its American character consists"; he would discuss its artistic merits in another article after the performance.[17]

Krehbiel noted that though Dvořák was "unquestionably the most ingenious orchestral colorist among living composers" (a worthy successor to Hector Berlioz and other midcentury Romantic composers), this symphony followed classical forms more conventionally than some of his earlier compositions. As to the orchestration, it was, as W. J. Henderson, the New York *Sun* critic, observed, "the classic symphony of Beethoven with the addition of the English horn." Its American character, Krehbiel said, consisted in "the melodic ideas and the spirit of the work." After the "long, beautiful, and impressive introduction," the first main theme of the allegro movement had "two elements that stamp it with nationality." The first was syncopation, "the effect of the short note on the accented part of the measure followed by a long note which takes the greater part of the stress which ordinarily belongs to the first beat." Krehbiel discussed the use of this syncopation in Scottish, English, and Hungarian music but more to the point, asserted its pervasiveness in African music," probably arising from "the structural peculiarity of some African languages." Krehbiel included references to Native American music as well throughout the article, though Dvořák had had far less exposure to these traditions: He noted that a similar syncopation was also prominent in the music of the Plains Indians.[18]

The second "national characteristic" was the pentatonic scale (do, re, mi, sol, la, omitting the half-step intervals). This scale also was not limited to African or African American music, but it helped to "give expression to American feeling" because it was familiar to Americans, especially in the black music they knew. Further, in the "subsidiary melody" (the first phrase of which has often been identified as a brief quotation from the Negro spiritual "Swing Low, Sweet Chariot"), Krehbiel noted the flat seventh, giving it "a somewhat Oriental tinge," as well as the rhythmic motif of the first four notes, an important source of unity in the development of the entire symphony (♩.♪♪♪), which Dr. Dvořák used "with great ingenuity and effect in the development of the music."[19]

Krehbiel waxed eloquent in describing the principal theme of the second movement, the Larghetto, which we now know as the Largo. In rehearsal for the premiere, conductor Anton Seidl convinced the composer that the tempo of this movement should be somewhat slower than Dvořák originally intended, to bring out the national character of the music, giving "the full exotic effect of the so-called negro tunes."[20] This was the melody, Krehbiel predicted, that would "cling most pertinaciously to the memory of those who hear the symphony, and which they will most quickly recognize as containing the spirit of the music which the people, as a whole, like best. It is Irish, it is Scotch, it is American. It has the rhythm of the principal subject, and it has the feeling of a pentatonic melody," though slightly modified. "In the larghetto we are stopped from seeking forms that are native and thrown wholly upon a study of the spirit."[21]

Many Americans who have never heard this symphony will recognize the truth of Krehbiel's prophecy: the melody of the Largo, to which William Arms Fisher, one of Dvořák's composition students, supplied words in 1941, has become engrained in American musical memory as "Goin' Home." And it is this melody that has become permanently associated with Harry T. Burleigh. For some, its character so closely resembles the Negro spirituals Burleigh sang to Dvořák that they believe it was a spiritual that Dvořák quoted.

This belief simply confirms that Dvořák had immersed himself so completely in the style of the songs Burleigh sang that he could write in the style of the spirituals. The Largo melody has in fact become a spiritual, now with religious words, thus completing the circle: Burleigh sang the folksongs, including spirituals, to Dvořák, who "saturated himself" in them, then wrote so successfully in the style of this music that the melody, with its added words and its mood of longing, has in turn (re)entered the realm of American folk music as a "spiritual." The Largo melody, or "Goin' Home," has become so deeply embedded in the American psyche that it has become an icon, a trope of Americanness, used by filmmakers, dramatists, and composers, to say nothing of the creators of television commercials, to symbolize the spirit of America. This melody "has thus gone out to the people, been absorbed, 'lost its title page' (as it were), and returned bearing the marks of its new owners."[22]

The one departure from traditional classical orchestration was Dvořák's use of the English horn to introduce the Largo melody. After British music critic H. C. Colles, an early Dvořák biographer, asked Burleigh to sing "many of the songs that Dvořák heard from his lips." Colles wrote that Dvořák had originally given the melody to the flute but changed it to the English horn, adding that instrument to the orchestra specifically for the purpose. Colles believed that "the sound of an English horn resembled quite closely the quality of Burleigh's voice, and that Dvořák may have chosen it for that reason."[23] Though it must remain speculative since we have neither Dvořák's nor Burleigh's word on it, Colles's belief has added to the sense that Burleigh, his voice, and his African American folksongs were deeply resonant in Dvořák's mind as he wrote the symphony.

Whether this and other melodies in the symphony "From the New World" reflect the spirit of African American or Native American music—or the spirit of a homesick Bohemian or all of the above—was a source of intense debate for years after its premiere. In his explication of the symphony, Krehbiel said, "It is Dr. Dvořák's proclamation of the mood that he found in the story of Hiawatha's wooing, as set forth in Longfellow's poem. In its principal melody, which is sung with exquisite effect by the English horn over a soft accompaniment by the divided strings, there is a world of imagination."[24] Though he confirmed the influence of African American music in the work, Burleigh also acknowledged that Dvořák had read the famine scene in Henry Wadsworth Longfellow's *Hiawatha*. "It had a great effect on him, and he wanted to express it musically" in the Largo.[25]

Much ink has been spilt and many words pitched in the century since its premiere, arguing Dvořák's intent, whether the musical sources of the symphony were primarily African American or Native American or Bohemian, and what was the ultimate effect of the melodies, harmonies, rhythms, and formal organization of the symphony "From the New World." But more important for our understanding of Burleigh and his relationship to Dvořák, and for an exploration of the meanings of the symphony to Americans and to American music, are Burleigh's own comments about it. Beyond his words we need also to see how Dvořák's words and his music, especially this symphony, have been heard, interpreted, and used, since for most Americans this Largo melody may be their only sampling of Dvořák's music. More specifically, the meanings of this symphony to African Americans and the close association of the Largo melody with Harry T. Burleigh and his arrangements of spirituals tell us much about the profound effect of Dvořák's American sojourn.

Burleigh's most extensive discussion of the symphony was published eighteen years later, in the program notes for the Philadelphia Orchestra performance of the symphony on February 24 and 25, 1911. Burleigh and Dvořák's composition student Camille W. Zeckwer were asked to comment on the symphony's origins and Dvořák's intentions. By this time some of the vitriol had faded from the debate, and H. M. W., the program annotator, asked these two musicians, who had both been close to Dvořák at the time he composed the symphony, to offer their insights.

Burleigh pointed out that by 1911 there was "a tendency . . . to ignore the negro elements in the 'New World' Symphony." Even critics who saw and heard "traces of negro musical color all through the Symphony" in 1893 could now "not find anything in the whole four movements that suggests any local or negro influence."

Recalling that he had often sung "the old Plantation songs" for Dvořák in his home on East 17th Street, he said that "one in particular, 'Swing Low, Sweet Chariot,'" greatly pleased him. Using notation to show the similarity of "the old melody as the slaves sang it" and the second theme of the first movement, Burleigh remarked, "The similarity is so evident that it doesn't even need to be heard; the eye can see it." He commented on the flat seventh in the subsidiary theme of the first movement, "I feel sure the Doctor caught this peculiarity of the most of the slave songs from some that I sang to him;—for he used to stop me and ask if that was the way the slaves sang."[26]

Burleigh continued: "I have never publicly been credited with exerting any influence upon Dr. Dvořák, although it is tacitly believed that there isn't much doubt about it, for I was with him almost constantly, and he loved to hear me sing the old melodies." Walter Damrosch had spoken of Burleigh's "having brought these songs to Dvořák's attention," but in the wrangling over whether the basis for a national school of music could lie in Negro songs, "all reference to the real source of his information was lost sight of."[27]

Significantly, Dvořák was interested in the life experience of the slaves who had created this music as well as in the musical sounds—the melodies and rhythms and their distinctive characteristics. As scholars in the nascent field of ethnomusicology (at this time known as comparative musicology) would demonstrate as they learned from anthropology to see music as culture, an analysis of musical sound is only the first step in understanding what music means to a particular society. Instinctively Dvořák understood the importance of exploring what lay beneath the surface of the music.

Camille Zeckwer's response in the Philadelphia Orchestra program notes confirmed the truth of Burleigh's remarks. Zeckwer recalled that while Dvořák was writing the symphony in spring 1893, he had "talked freely with his composition students about 'what he was doing and what he thought they ought to do.' Dvořák had played through the entire score for Zeckwer and had repeatedly spoken of his intention to use African American melodies as his inspiration for the Symphony."[28] As Harry Rowe Shelley recalled, "He did not know that morning that he was going to write it, he just did." And like the world's creator, in biblical terms that Dvořák would have appreciated, Shelley said, "When he saw it he knew that it was good, and rejoiced therein."[29]

*　*　*

In April 1894 Washington, D.C., black music critic Walt B. Hayson responded to the controversy stirred by Dvořák's advocacy of an American school of music based on Negro music. Dvořák's statements, he said, were "a recognition of and a compliment to the musical nature of the Negro-American." For white Americans, this was "too much. They therefore hastened to discover that these Negro melodies were not *Negro* melodies after all." One example of the backlash, an article on Negro melodies by G. Wilford Pearse, had recently been published in the New York *Sun*. Pearse contended that "there is not a jubilee or Negro minstrel song known in [the South] that was not written by northern or European whites." Even some African Americans "in ignorant belief or thoughtless credulity, [had joined] the ranks of the whites against Negro melodies as such." One was Rev. Dr. J. W. Bowen, who in speaking to the Bethel Literary and Historical Society of Washington made the "extravagant assertion [that] 'the Negro has not made one original piece of music in all his life. . . . His claims to originality in American music cannot be substantiated.'" Hayson countered that the truth was the reverse: surely in the future, those white Americans who were "humanized, civilized, Christianized about prejudice" would doubt that "the white American, who stole away everything else from the slave, actually stopped at his songs and tunes." Hayson wasn't sure that it was the intrinsic artistic value of "the melodies themselves" that made them worth preserving, but they were invaluable because, "like our folk-tales of 'Brer Rabbit' and 'Brer Fox,' . . . they make up our folk-lore, the only intellectual inheritance our enslaved forefathers have left us."[30]

Especially after 1917 when Burleigh's arrangements of spirituals and those by other composers began to appear frequently on recital or choral programs, it was not unusual to find a Dvořák piece on the program. Often it was an arrangement of the Largo theme, sometimes his "Humoresque." At St. George's Episcopal Church an organ prelude based on the Largo melody frequently opened the Annual Vesper Service of Negro Spirituals or it might be played as a violin solo. The Largo also appeared occasionally in the regular Sunday services, always reminding the congregation of their baritone soloist's connection to the composer. In nearly every public presentation, speech, or news article about Burleigh's years at St. George's Episcopal Church, his close acquaintance with Antonín Dvořák resurfaced as confirmation of Burleigh's importance as a singer and composer. It was not only at St. George's that Dvořák's name was associated with Burleigh and with Negro spirituals. A study of recitals and concerts of spirituals throughout the United States in the past century would reveal a persistent pattern of association between spirituals and Dvořák's music, most often represented by the Largo theme.

It is even more striking to note how consistently black writers and musicians have referred to Dvořák's words and his music as validation of the artistic worth of their folk music heritage. True, American composers before Dvořák's arrival had drawn on Negro melodies as compositional flavoring. But the vivid contrast between the contemporaneous demeaning descriptions of black music and Dvořák's forthright assertion that it was an indispensable element of American musical culture startled them, invigorating a new sense of pride in many African Americans. The success of Burleigh's career (as of any prominent "race leader" of public note within and beyond the black community) inspired others, and the wide reception of his pioneering arrangements of spirituals confirmed Dvořák's initial insights. That Dvořák moderated his views during his three years in the United

States, broadening his definition of American folk music to include folk traditions rooted in the music of Europe and the British Isles, was noted by the musicians for whom the nationalism debate was important. But for many Americans, and particularly for African Americans, it was his earliest statements of May 1893, that in the music that was their deepest heritage, he found "all that was needed for a national school of American music" that continued to resonate.

One can scarcely overestimate the profound impact of Dvořák's initial public statements on black musicians and composers. Dvořák's pronouncements presented a sharp contrast to the prevailing social, political, and cultural attitudes in American society at the time. Post-Reconstruction racism was sweeping away the hard-won social, political, and economic gains of African Americans. Lynching proliferated, and the doctrine of African American racial inferiority was being "scientifically" established. Popular culture glorified the "good old plantation life," and minstrel songs and the more degrading "coon" songs demeaned African American culture and character even while they drew their most engaging musical elements from the culture they caricatured. Against this background Dvořák's assertion was revolutionary, giving impetus to the work of Harry T. Burleigh, Will Marion Cook, Samuel Coleridge-Taylor, William Dawson, William Grant Still, Florence Price, Margaret Bonds, Undine Smith Moore, and generations of African American composers after them.[31]

8. Foremost Musician and Engaged Citizen

"The celebrated western baritone"

One might be tempted to assume that from 1894 when Burleigh was hired as baritone soloist at St. George's Protestant Episcopal Church on Stuyvesant Square, his life revolved primarily around his contacts there, among the wealthy and influential Gilded Age elite in whose homes he sang, and eventually within the white music establishment of publishers, singers, and composers where he made his primary living. But such a perspective would fail to comprehend his prominence and his persistent leadership in the social, educational, and artistic life of New York City's black community and its ripples into the cultural life of black communities throughout the United States. Burleigh's public success as singer and composer was a source of pride and encouragement to all African Americans, as were the achievements of any who were seen to defy racial barriers and whose lives gave the lie to persistent racial stereotypes and prejudices. In addition to the merit of his personal success, Burleigh remained an active participant in the life of the black community in New York and other cities on the eastern seaboard, lending the weight of his renown to benefit numerous social and educational causes.

Burleigh's singing and his training at the National Conservatory carved out a place for him in both the black and the white music arenas. He soon connected with the social and political leaders of the metropolitan black communities along the east coast. His early New York activities, detailed by Cleveland *Gazette* editor H. C. Smith, reveal a milieu very different from what most accounts of Burleigh's early New York years have described. Through Smith's reports we glimpse Burleigh's extracurricular life and the opportunities available in the 1890s for a young man of his ability and ambition.

His immediate family remained for a time in Erie, Pennsylvania, but some members of his extended family were in the New York City area. Burleigh's second cousin, Rev. W. F. Johnson, was director of the Howard school for orphans in Brooklyn, an institution known for its fine academic and music program. Though blind, he had been Elizabeth Taylor Greenfield's agent,[1] and he was well known as a lecturer. Sometime guests in the Johnson home included novelist Francis Ellen Watkins Harper and T. Thomas Fortune, editor of the New York *Age*, among other luminaries.[2] Burleigh's aunt Louisa and his sister Eva Grace visited them from time to time, and on at least one occasion Burleigh sang in a concert to benefit the orphanage.[3]

For black musicians not interested in the vaudeville scene, the most promising career path was through the church, and Burleigh was quick to connect with New York's black church community.[4] St. James A.M.E. Church in Erie had sister congregations in New York City, but Burleigh gravitated to the black Episcopal congregations where he would be most likely to find choral traditions similar to those he had enjoyed at Erie's Episcopal Cathedral of St. Paul. Eventually he joined the Men and Boys' Choir at historic St. Philip's Episcopal Church (not yet in Harlem), but he reached St. Philip's by way of smaller black Episcopal congregations. After a visit to New York, H. C. Smith described enthusiastically (if somewhat hyperbolically) Burleigh's activities in New York City and his connections to a group of influential young black men.[5] Several of Burleigh's friends were musicians who performed with him. Two with significant connections to the New York state legislature invited Burleigh three years later to join them in a day of radical political activism. And one, George W. Broome, the first black filmmaker,[6] also established the first black recording company, precursor to the better-known Black Swan Record Company. In 1919 Broome produced the only known commercial recording of Burleigh's voice.

Smith visited Burleigh at the National Conservatory, assuring himself that Burleigh was achieving success in that cosmopolitan center of European and American music. In Erie, Burleigh's skill as a singer had taken him into social settings that would not otherwise have been open to one of his economic background and to the top of the roster of classical musicians, most of whom were white. But the black community in Erie was relatively small, and its upper echelon less isolated from working-class African Americans than in the urban centers of New York, Boston, and Washington, D.C. As is true today, the audience for classical music was drawn primarily from the middle and upper classes. The black press of the period often listed names of those occupying the boxes or the preferred seating area at music events as evidence of their advanced social standing and their enlightened taste, and as examples to others. Like other well-educated African Americans, Burleigh assumed the responsibility to demonstrate a life style and a standard of achievement that was exemplary. The constant need to prove one's essential humanity and innate potential for intellectual and artistic refinement to white Americans had its corollary in the need to assist in the process of racial uplift.[7]

Smith wanted "his many friends here in Cleveland and at his home in Erie, Pa." to know of Burleigh's early New York success and in what distinguished circles he moved. "Our people in New York City and Brooklyn appreciate Mr. Burleigh, too,"

Smith wrote, "and show him every attention, social and otherwise." Burleigh was "in constant demand" for concerts and recitals.[8] On his first day in the city, Smith accompanied Burleigh to a charade at the Brooklyn home of a Mrs. White, the widow of a successful drugstore owner. She was hosting a benefit for a "charitable race institution" in her "magnificent and spacious home." Burleigh sang two solos that were encored. Other vocal and piano selections, dramatic readings, and a tableau rounded out the program. The event was "a financial and artistic success," and certainly a fine place to be seen and heard.[9]

Smith's political involvement may have led to an invitation to an intimate dinner, with Burleigh, at the home of Mr. and Mrs. Isaac B. Joseph, "a very successful real estate and insurance broker and quite a republican leader in his district." Smith did not disclose whether he and Burleigh escorted the two single women, Mrs. Estelle L. Jarvis, "a charming young widow," and Miss Lillian Matthews, both of whom had also attended the charade at the White home, to the dinner.[10]

On Sunday morning, Smith attended St. Paul's Episcopal Church, where Burleigh sang. Smith expressed surprise at the advanced nature of the church service and was especially impressed by the large choir of boys' voices, "augmented by carefully selected gentlemen voices," and directed by a white organist, "an advanced student of the National Conservatory of Music."[11] This may have been one of the choirs Burleigh helped to train.[12]

On the social front, Smith extolled the two exclusive black men's clubs in the city. The first was the Sons of New York, who had sponsored a benefit concert in June by soprano Sissieretta Jones that raised $1,100 for the Free Bread Fund "for the African American poor of New York city." Though not eligible for membership (as he was not born in New York City), Burleigh was a featured singer on this program.[13]

Burleigh was a member of the year-old Toussaint L'Ouverture Club. He introduced his friend to its officers and to the "three-story commodious brick building" rented and "beautifully furnished from roof to cellar" by the club.[14] For black men who could not join the white social clubs of the city or dine at the better restaurants in the area and were sometimes denied even the facilities of a YMCA, the club served a practical purpose as well as a social and beneficial one. The building featured a parlor and reading and card rooms on the first floor. Perhaps Burleigh accompanied himself as he did in some of his early solo recitals on the piano in the parlor as he sang for the club members. The chairman of the house committee was "sweet tenor-voiced Richard Stovall."[15]

Exactly when Burleigh joined the Men and Boys' Choir at St. Philip's Episcopal Church has not been established. St. Philip's was the financial and social pinnacle of black Episcopalianism in New York City, and characteristically Burleigh rose to the ecclesiastical and musical *crème de la crème* of the city's black community. Described as "perhaps the wealthiest congregation of Negroes in the country," the congregation at this time was located in the Tenderloin District at 161 West

Twenty-Fifth Street, just over a mile from Dvořák's home and the National Conservatory. A decade and a half later the historic building designed by the black architectural firm Tandy and Foster was built at 212 West 135th Street in Harlem, covering the block from 133rd to 134th Street, where the congregation anchored the emerging black community. Though the Twenty-Fifth Street building where Burleigh sang was less elaborate, one indication of the financial status of its members was the gold chalice, "richly studded with rubies, pearls and diamonds and other precious stones," used in the sacrament of communion.[16] Counting many of the city's financial, social, and political black elite among its members, the congregation had a rich legacy of civil-rights activism and community outreach. St. Philip's built and later purchased apartment buildings "to ensure fair and safe housing for African Americans," a Young Men's Guild, and "aid and insurance" to the sick among its social programs.[17] The first floor of the clubhouse at 127 West Thirteenth Street provided the Young Men's Guild "a billiard table, a library well stocked with books," and tables "for innocent games."[18] Like the Toussaint Club, the recreational facilities provided by the church were important to young people who were barred from the better class of public recreational facilities. Joining the St. Philip's vested male choir gave Burleigh expanded entrée to the social groups that could support his ambitions as a classical singer. From his first months in New York City, Burleigh's connections with the city's black social elite established his place among the network of artists who performed in the urban communities of the Mid-Atlantic and Northeast.

The sober, dignified persona suggested in later portraits of Burleigh and in Smith's portrayal of the socially aspiring young singer disguise his more private, informal character. Among his close friends, Burleigh revealed a robust, witty, even boisterous humor, sometimes bordering on the ribald. This side of Burleigh's personality emerges in a scene described by his vaudevillian friend Bert Williams, in a venue ostensibly far removed from the exalted social circles Smith described. The group of black theater performers who gathered in Williams's apartment on Fifty-Third Street—Burleigh, Will Accoo, Bob Cole, Bob Johnson, and Jessie Shipp—would "sit around in their shirtsleeves and talk, drink, and play endless hands of a poker game called 'smut.'" The loser of each hand would have to smear on his face "a daub of the soot" they collected on a plate smoked over an oil lamp. "Then," Williams recalled, "we kids would sit around and howl at the grotesque appearance."[19]

However distant from the Manhattan and Brooklyn salons and parlors this may seem, the world of New York City's black vaudeville and musical theater and the homes of the social elite overlapped at many points, especially in the years when such performers as Bert Williams and George Walker drew the highest pay in the business. The next generations of black performers would reap far greater financial rewards, but these pioneering black artists and members of the intelligentsia spent their weekends and vacations in the same seaside cottages and resort areas as "the best sets." Another hint of Burleigh's livelier persona appears in an 1894 account that recalls Burleigh the Erie dancing master to mind: "Harry Burleigh is one of the few artists who are able to combine their love for art with a liking for social diversions."[20] He had not yet cracked the shell insulating Boston's elite black society, but he was "a social light of some distinction in the society circle of New York City and Brooklyn" and was "well known in the best sets of Philadelphia, Washington and other eastern cities."[21] And no doubt there was room even among "the best sets" for robust if private jocularity.

Burleigh's audiences in these venues were among the first to hear his early song compositions. Four years before his first art songs were published, "his work in musical composition" attracted "considerable attention."[22] So modest about his songs that he had to be urged by friends to submit them for publication, singing—and testing—his songs in the friendly parlors of Brooklyn, Manhattan, and Washington, D.C. was a first step. He was not ready to submit his songs for publication and distribution—to say nothing of critical evaluation—by the white music establishment, but that would come soon, as his career progressed.

*   *   *

In 1895, some of Burleigh's associates at the Toussaint L'Ouverture Club, knowing him to be committed to the cause of social justice, invited him to join in a sophisticated but radical act of civil-rights protest. This was fully in character for the son of Henry Thacker Burley and the stepson of John Edgar Elmendorf. On Monday, July 18, 1895, three black men, as the New York *Tribune* reported, "cool in spotless linen and suave, with true Chesterfieldian elegance," gathered at Sixth Avenue and Twenty-Third Street in New York City, preparing to enter O'Neil's Restaurant, as well as the nearby Shanley's Restaurant, the Bartoldi Hotel, the Brunswick, Delmonico's, and the Continental Hotel. They presented themselves to be served along with the usual clientele of these establishments, in effect, to integrate the restaurants.[23] They were testing a new law, "an act to protect all citizens in their civil and legal rights,"[24] which had been passed by the New York legislature and signed into law the previous Saturday by Governor Levi Morton. The three men were Charles W. Anderson, private secretary to the state treasurer, Charles Colvin; Richard E. Stovall, president of the Kenmore Club (the sweet-voiced tenor of the Toussaint Club); and H. T. Burleigh.

Anderson chose his associates carefully. As framer of the law, he said, "it becomes my bounden duty to see to its enforcement. The colored citizens of this city and state do not propose to abuse their privileges—that we will prove by our deportment today—but we propose to stand by our rights, confident of the support of every fair-minded white man."[25] He was careful also to secure press coverage of this quiet but determined civil-rights action.

In some of the restaurants they entered, the three men were studiously ignored, in others they were met with threats that their steaks would be laced with rat poison or loaded with pepper. In the restaurant where they were actually served, they dined deliberately, then took out their cigars and enjoyed a leisurely after-dinner cheroot. One can imagine the quiet satisfaction with which Burleigh and his colleagues relished every bite of their dinner. If some of the restaurant's regular customers were offended, others enjoyed the quiet drama these elegantly dressed young men created in their midst.[26]

After moving about the district, "dining and stretching landlords upon the rack of mental anguish," the three men proceeded from the "swell" restaurants on their list in the Tenderloin District to several Turkish bathhouses in the area—Lafayette Place, Everard's, and Murray Hill. In one bathhouse after another they were informed, in the echoing silence of the empty buildings, that there was no space available to them. Only one proprietor agreed to let them use his facilities. But he pointed out that if they did so, they would ruin his business. Thanking him for his support and acknowledging the validity of his claim, they respectfully declined. They had made their point.[27]

In summing up the day's adventure, Charles Anderson promised that this was only the first volley of the campaign. "I will employ counsel—the best that money can command—and the restaurant men and Turkish bath proprietors who have declined to serve us today shall be prosecuted, civilly and criminally. There will be no lack of funds to press this campaign." Burleigh and Stovall would continue the direct action while Anderson returned to Albany, "assisted by a corps of volunteers," and Anderson would return to New York City two days later to continue the campaign.[28]

This scenario may seem surreal to those who believe civil-rights agitation began in the 1950s and 1960s, but Reconstruction died more slowly in New England and the urban centers of the East than in the South. In Massachusetts, eastern New York state, and Washington, D.C., it was not unusual at this time for African Americans to hold political office. In the light of his family background, it is easy to see why twenty-nine-year-old Burleigh would be glad to join in such a direct civil-rights demonstration, especially one conducted with such grace. But one wonders whether he fully anticipated the effect this public action might have on his career. He had sung his first solo at St. George's, "The Palms," on Palm Sunday a few months earlier, a performance that would become a fifty-two-year tradition. J. P. Morgan had supported his hiring, and St. George's progressive rector Rev. William S. Rainsford was no stranger to social action. But how they received the news of this public demonstration by the soloist they had so recently shielded against his detractors we can only guess. To reconcile our understanding of the Harry Burleigh we thought we knew with this young civil-rights demonstrator raises questions to which we have only tentative answers.

Three months later, Tuskegee Institute founder Booker T. Washington delivered the landmark address at the opening of the Atlanta Exposition that would echo across the country, setting a tone for racial interaction far different from that of

Frederick Douglass, who had died a few months before. Douglass had wielded his pen and his powerful oratory to challenge injustice directly, speaking and working primarily in the North and gathering international support in his trips to England. Washington, living in Alabama, building Tuskegee Institute surrounded by stricken southern whites determined not to lose their political and financial power to the former slaves who in many areas of the South outnumbered them, found it expedient to work for the progress of his people by focusing on fostering friendly relations between the races.

In what became known as his Atlanta Compromise speech, he reassured white Southerners that his goal was not social equality, but progress in "agriculture, mechanics, in commerce, in domestic service, and [last] in the professions."[29] Washington worked quietly behind the scenes to challenge unjust laws and persuaded northern industrialists to hire black workers who had been trained at Tuskegee and other southern industrial schools. But his wily and powerful opposition to W. E. B. Du Bois and others who were prepared to demand full and immediate equality and franchise earned him the title of accommodationist and even traitor to the best interests of his people.

In a few years Burleigh would be closely associated with Washington, traveling with him to the New England hotels and resorts where Washington raised the funds to sustain his industrial school. Burleigh remained largely apolitical, but his later public statements suggest that in time he consciously chose a different means of bringing social change than participating in civil rights demonstrations. Like the early leaders of the Harlem Renaissance, he believed that demonstrating excellence in the musical, literary, and visual arts was more effective than direct political action to bridge the gap between the races and to bring social change and justice for African Americans.[30] His fifteen-year association with Booker T. Washington, from 1900 to 1915 (the year of Washington's death), traveling with him on his fundraising tours along the eastern seaboard and through New England resort areas, suggests he developed a conservative view of political action.

Throughout his career Burleigh persisted in working for change in less confrontational ways within the communities in which he moved. He did not hesitate to insist, always with great self-possession and dignity, on his personal right to participate fully in his chosen sphere of work and worship.[31] But as he moved farther in and higher up in the white music establishment, he never forgot that he acted, spoke, composed, and sang, as the representative of his race, an advocate for full social, political, and musical equality.

* * *

We do not know exactly when Burleigh first met Booker T. Washington, but by 1897 he felt free to enlist Washington's help for a charitable benefit. He wrote the Tuskegee principal introducing his friend George W. Broome of New York City and Dr. L. A. Scruggs, the manager of the Pickford Sanitarium for Consumptive

Negroes in Raleigh, North Carolina, who were planning a Carnegie Hall concert to benefit the sanitarium. Washington's presence would strengthen their appeal if he would grant his "approval and assistance to what seems without a doubt a needful and worthy cause" by speaking on the program.[32] Washington's first allegiance was to Tuskegee Institute, but he was generous in fund-raising efforts for his alma mater, Hampton Institute, and other black institutions to benefit the needy. On April 27, 1898, Burleigh was one of several musicians whose performance at the Carnegie Chamber Music Hall supported Washington's appeal to benefit the New York Free Kindergarten for Colored Children.[33]

One might assume with some cynicism that Burleigh cultivated his relationship with Washington primarily to further his own career. It was certainly to his benefit to be introduced to the hotel proprietors and wealthy clients who might invite him to perform. In August 1902 Burleigh wrote that he had been congratulated "for the privilege of being associated with you for two or three weeks—all of which I appreciate greatly."[34] But there was more than simple self-interest at work in Burleigh's association with Booker T. Washington. Washington had grown up with the music of the slaves singing in his ears, and he intended his school to be active in collecting and preserving that heritage. Doing so required music teachers who understood and valued their folk music. On more than one occasion he asked Burleigh's help in finding a music teacher who would share his vision.[35]

Washington's commitment to preserving African American folk music was not casual or superficial. In his letters, he detailed his concern for the careful preservation and documentation of folk music and instruction in the music that should be used at Tuskegee. Students would sing Moody and Sankey hymns (gospel hymns popularized by the evangelistic team Dwight L. Moody and Ira B. Sankey) and "the classical selections students learned as part of their formal education," but he insisted that they "regularly sing the songs they brought from their home areas." Their teachers should assign them "to collect and preserve" these songs. In 1894 Washington wrote music teacher Robert Hannibal Hamilton that he was also to collect songs, not as generic Negro folksongs, but document the specific localities from which they came and the traditional social and cultural contexts that produced them. Even more specifically, "I wish you would try to get hold of some of the peculiar songs that are sung in Louisiana while the people are boiling syrup; also some of the rice plantation songs of South Carolina as well as of the Mississippi bottom songs. A few of the Mississippi steamboat songs will do well." New students brought with them invaluable gifts in the songs from their home traditions, so Hamilton should make "a constant effort among the new students," to gather such songs.[36] The Washington-Burleigh correspondence contains little discussion of folksongs, but Burleigh's interest in preserving this music as well as his baritone voice likely made him Washington's choice to assist him in fundraising. Their fifteen-year association gave Burleigh many opportunities to develop and test his art song arrangements of spirituals in the genteel milieux of the hotel and resort drawing rooms where they appeared together.[37]

The July 11, 1903, *Outlook* magazine carried a review of W. E. B. Du Bois's book *The Souls of Black Folk*. Immediately on reading the review, which defended Washington against Du Bois's critique of his leadership, Burleigh wrote Washington, "It is so strong and true an article that I can [not] refrain from writing you because it states your position so clearly that a blind man can see that Du Bois's work is purely personal while your work is general. You are for the masses while he pleads for the classes. It is obvious who has the greater and higher field. The article is a truthful justification of your methods and is timely, for many others of the (highly educated and cultivated class)? [sic] may be influenced by what Du Bois says."[38] Had Burleigh read *The Souls of Black Folk*, he would have been moved to see that each chapter was headed by the words of a Negro spiritual, followed by the opening phrase of music. And had he read the final chapter, "Of the Sorrow Songs," he would have understood that he, Du Bois, and Washington shared a deep appreciation for the sacred folksongs or spirituals Burleigh would do so much to preserve and promote.

In chapter 3 of *The Souls of Black Folk*, "Of Mr. Booker T. Washington and Others," Du Bois offered carefully worded criticism of Washington's leadership, but he also placed Washington's work in the social and historical context that made his approach so effective. Though thoughtful and balanced, Du Bois's critique was a clear challenge to Washington's influence.[39] Burleigh's letter assured Washington that he could count on his favorite singer to stand by him in the swirling controversy that was building to a public confrontation.

Burleigh displayed his loyalty to Washington less than two weeks later, when he was summoned to Boston by telegraph: "You are expected to sing tonight where I speak, Zion colored church Columbus Avenue Boston. Do not fail to be present."[40] That evening, July 30, 1903, at Boston's Zion A.M.E. Church, the militant William Monroe Trotter (son of James Monroe Trotter, the first African American music historian) publicly challenged Washington's accommodationist stance, inciting a disturbance that became riotous. Burleigh "arose and opportunely sang 'King of Kings.' The song had a quieting effect."[41] Trotter was arrested and sentenced to thirty days in jail (the daughter who carried a hatpin to use as a defensive weapon escaped official notice). Burleigh wrote Washington, "Of course you've heard the news about Trotter. He better serve his 30 days—because the higher court might double it."[42]

Two weeks after the Boston appearance, Burleigh and his wife combined a vacation jaunt with a fundraising date at Lake Mohonk, one of Washington's most lucrative venues. The Burleighs planned to "take the Hudson River boat at 8:40 tomorrow morning and go to [Poughkeepsie] by water; then—trolley to New Paltz where [Louise] may spend a few days. This route is much cheaper and pleasanter and gets you into Lake Mohonk about 4 o'clock. Can't you both go with us up the

Hudson?" In a postscript he invited the Washingtons to join him and his wife for dinner that evening.[43]

* * *

Burleigh's relationship with Afro-British composer Samuel Coleridge-Taylor demonstrated and solidified his status as the race's premiere baritone, and Booker T. Washington's relationship with the two of them created intriguing complications. Coleridge-Taylor's cantata *Hiawatha's Wedding Feast,* based on Henry Wadsworth Longfellow's long poem *The Song of Hiawatha,* was performed by white choral societies in the United States soon after its 1898 publication. Burleigh sent a copy of the score to Mrs. Andrew F. Hilyer, a Washington, D.C., pianist and singer who with her husband was planning a trip to London. The Hilyers visited the young composer at his home and, on their return to the States, helped establish the S. Coleridge Taylor Choral Society.

After months of intense rehearsal, on April 23, 1903, the society gave its first performance of *Hiawatha's Wedding Feast* at the Metropolitan A.M.E. Church in Washington, D.C. The all-black choir of one hundred sixty voices was prepared by public school music teacher John T. Layton. Baritone Burleigh, tenor Sidney Woodward, and soprano Kittie Skeene-Mitchell were the soloists. The poorly prepared white orchestra that had been engaged was dismissed and replaced by two pianos and a vocalion played by black musicians (one of them pianist Mary L. Europe, sister to bandleader James Reese Europe) more than equal to the task.

Children were not forgotten; for "the small fee of ten cents admission," children of the District were invited to hear the dress rehearsals to give them "great inspiration from listening to this grand creation so beautifully sung." The newly established *Negro Music Journal* gave voice to the palpable sense of validation in the success of this concert. The performance was "one of the most notable events in the musical history of the colored race."[44]

The production was an artistic and financial success. "The large auditorium of Metropolitan Church was filled to overflow with representative people of our race, . . . listening with discriminating judgement to the production of a masterpiece composed by a colored composer and musician." The *Negro Music Journal* urged that musicians from other cities should "band together for the musical elevation of the race. We will never learn to know, love and appreciate the best music unless we hear it often well performed. Those musicians of ability, who are asleep, need to awaken and gather available forces together for the study and production of the larger musical forms—the cantata, oratorio and symphony."[45] To this end, soon after the triumph of the S. Coleridge-Taylor Choral Society, the Burleigh Choral Society was organized "to devote its time and energy to the study and production of choruses from the leading oratorios and cantatas."[46]

When Mrs. Hilyer wrote Coleridge-Taylor reporting on the success of the occasion, he replied, "I have heard a great deal about Mr. Burleigh from people I have met here. . . . Everyone agrees that he is a splendid singer and also—more rare—a splendid musician."[47]

Burleigh played a more substantial role the following year when the Coleridge-Taylor Choral Society brought the composer to the States to conduct a second performance of *Hiawatha's Wedding Feast.* Coleridge-Taylor wrote Booker T. Washington asking his advice in planning his stateside tour. He preferred to avoid using agents. Washington presented the pros and cons of engaging an agent to handle publicity. While "the intelligent colored people of this country" were familiar with the composer's name, it would be best to "find a perfectly reliable, unselfish businesslike colored man in the large centers of Negro population and depend upon that individual to arrange the details" of his appearances. Coleridge-Taylor should include Boston, New York, Brooklyn, Newport, Philadelphia, Washington, and Chicago in his itinerary. If he wanted to tour the South, the larger institutions such as Fisk University in Nashville, Atlanta University in Atlanta, and, of course, Tuskegee would welcome him. Indeed, he should make Tuskegee his headquarters in the South. Washington expected to see Burleigh a few days later, and he would "lay the whole matter before" him. "Mr. Burleigh's judgment is sound," Washington assured him, "and he is a man on whose word you can depend."[48]

Burleigh wrote Coleridge-Taylor, who hastened to correct Washington's grandiose expectations. "I am afraid I have made you misunderstand my purpose in coming over, which is not to pose as a 'star' or 'drawing-power' (Heaven forbid!) but simply to conduct the Society at Washington and incidentally to see one or two of your American towns." If any other engagements "*could* be done," such as a recital in New York, he would be "much gratified." Burleigh might recommend an agent, but "Of course, I would wish you to sing for me." He added mischievously, "Mrs. Coleridge-Taylor is not coming with me so I shall be prepared for anything!"[49]

In writing Washington, Coleridge-Taylor was diplomatic: "You have a most ardent admirer in me as you may imagine!" But in a "strictly private" addendum to his letter to Burleigh he expressed his wariness of Washington's power. "Washington did offer a Correspondence with me but I heard such fearful things about him from *Every* musician I meet here who had had any connection with him that I closed all negotiations as far as he was concerned."[50] The "strictly private" portion of the letter further explained that Williams Arms Fisher, an editor at Boston's Oliver Ditson music publishing company, had commissioned a volume of piano pieces based on Negro melodies, the *Twenty-Four Negro Melodies* that would be published in 1905, before Coleridge-Taylor's second United States tour. Burleigh certainly knew how easily Washington's word could make or break the career of any aspiring black musician, and it may have been on his advice that Coleridge-Taylor asked Washington to write the foreword to the volume. Washington's imprimatur would lend cachet to the first publication of piano pieces based on African and African American melodies, and neither Burleigh nor Coleridge-Taylor could afford to forfeit his good will.

A few months later Washington wrote Burleigh, "I am preparing a preface for a very important publication of Mr. S. Coleridge Taylor's compositions by a Boston firm." He asked Burleigh's help: "In fact anything that you will let me have in print or over your own signature covering Mr. Taylor's accomplishments, and the esteem in which he is held by the musical world will be gratefully received by me."[51] Without disclosing that Coleridge-Taylor had written him of the "very important publication," Burleigh responded immediately. He suggested that Washington comment on "the growing tendency to neglect the old plantation songs for more modern kinds of music; forgetting that as folk songs of a people they should never be slighted or forgotten." Any "well-defined effort to chronicle and thereby perpetuate these old tunes" should be encouraged, as they were "rapidly passing away."[52]

Burleigh drew on Thomas P. Fenner's Preface to Hampton Institute's *Cabin and Plantation Songs*: "At present, the freedmen have an unfortunate inclination to despise this music as a vestige of slavery; those who learned it in the old time when it was the natural outpouring of their sorrows and longings are dying off, and if efforts are not made for its preservation, the country will soon have lost this wonderful music of bondage." Fenner hoped that "this people which has developed such a wonderful musical sense while in bondage" would "in its maturity produce a composer who will bring a music of the future out of the music of the past." Burleigh suggested that Coleridge-Taylor, though not a descendant of slaves, could help birth "the music of the future": "I believe Mr. Taylor will, in arranging the old tunes for the piano, preserve the real melody," developing it "in a musicianly manner." His arrangements might "popularize the melodies without running any danger of their descending to the level of the so called 'ragtime' and more reprehensible 'coon' songs." Musicians and music lovers would welcome such a collection, so Washington "ought to very gladly attach [his] name, even in a casual way," to the volume. These old melodies "not only possess vital and inherent charm of their own," but also, as Coleridge-Taylor was "the most cultivated musician of the race thus far," his work was "bound to shed illumination on all the previous efforts to arrange these melodies."[53]

Through the years Burleigh needed to remind Washington on a number of occasions that he could not neglect his commitments to St. George's Church and Temple Emanu-El on Friday, Saturday, and Sunday in order to assist him. But he would give Washington first choice of dates when he could, especially during August, the optimal fundraising period, when he was on vacation. Washington's often imperious demands strained their relationship at times, especially in the last years of Washington's life, but Burleigh continued to support the Tuskegee cause.[54]

The late 1905 and early 1906 correspondence about plans to celebrate the 25th anniversary of Tuskegee's founding reveals the importunity with which Washington often demanded Burleigh's services and the shrewd diplomacy Burleigh might employ when he felt it necessary to decline. Washington urged Burleigh to spend two months at Tuskegee preparing the student body to sing plantation songs at the anniversary celebration. The festivities, scheduled for April 16–18, 1906, would force Burleigh to be absent from his positions at St. George's Episcopal Church and Temple Emanu-El during March and April (over Palm Sunday and Easter and the Jewish holidays of Purim and Pesach).[55] Burleigh wrote that he was attempting to secure the consent of the music committees to "accept a substitute to sing" in his place so that he could go to Tuskegee to drill the students. He was flattered to be asked, adding, "I think I shall enjoy drilling your students and improving their rendition of the good old stirring tunes of our people."[56]

He would leave the terms of his payment to Washington, but to the founder of the National Negro Business League he laid out his expenses in a businesslike way: "Of course I shall have to pay my substitute at St. George's and the Temple, which amounts to $150.00 a month; and to keep up my regular affairs here during my absence which might, with what you feel disposed to give me for my work with the students, make the whole thing look rather expensive; but I trust you realize how much I have at stake and how much I lose in professional engagements by going away for any length of time." If he could afford to "look solely on the artistic or racial side of the question," he would "crave the privilege" of donating his services; but unfortunately he was "forced to approach the question in a business way—for I would be compelled to give up all professional engagements that would come in for my singing, and that form the greatest source of revenue, of my income." If he worked "all of March and April up to the date of the anniversary," he was sure he would have "ample time to get good results from the school." As one suspects Burleigh fully anticipated, after reading this letter, Washington replied that the Tuskegee Executive Council felt "compelled . . . to arrange otherwise" than to underwrite Burleigh's two-month absence from his significant sources of income.[57]

In 1915, when Washington could not meet the Mohonk House appointment, Burleigh went alone. By this time he was a favorite with the Mohonk audiences. He reported that the house was crowded, "so the parlor was filled." He sang for an hour and a half, then George Smiley, the Mohonk House proprietor, "made an appeal which was very sincere and direct." Washington assured Burleigh that the collection was "quite satisfactory" and thanked him for his "generous support" in covering for him.[58] Two months later, Washington was dead.

Burleigh was happy to support Tuskegee and other black schools in the South by singing for their benefit in northern venues, but he never visited Tuskegee even when he was free of other commitments. His grandson, Dr. Harry T. Burleigh II, reported that Burleigh had never been further south than Petersburg, Virginia,[59] but in fact, he sang at Nashville, Tennessee, on at least two occasions; he came to Atlanta, Georgia, to accept an honorary degree from Atlanta University; and in the 1920s spent a period of time at the Burge Plantation south of Atlanta working with Dorothy Bolton on the *Old Songs Hymnal*. But these southward journeys were few, and he declined to travel to the Deep South—Alabama, Mississippi, and Louisiana—where he knew he would be subjected to the most degrading humiliations of entrenched segregation.

* * *

On the other side of the political divide, Burleigh worked with Du Bois on numerous occasions. Burleigh's grandson commented that Burleigh respected Du Bois but was uncomfortable with his political views.[60] He was surely among the Talented Tenth whom Du Bois argued should be nurtured to lead the race. He sent his son to a private school in England rather than to an industrial school such as Tuskegee or Hampton Institute. He has been described as "a patrician,"[61] but like many of the black social elite, Burleigh kept his finger on the pulse of what was happening to those around him who were less fortunate.

In October 1906, Burleigh sang at the ninth annual convention of the Afro-American Council Meeting, whose delegates from twenty states included Booker T. Washington's assistant Emmett J. Scott; Mary Church Terrell of Washington, D.C.; Oswald Garrison Villard, editor of the New York *Evening Post*; and ex-Governor P. B. S. Pinchback of Washington, D.C. This group constituted a conservative contingent supporting Washington's approach to racial progress.[62] Understandably, Burleigh was not invited to the Niagara Convention organized by W. E. B. Du Bois and William Monroe Trotter the following week. Their movement led to the founding of the National Association for the Advancement of Colored People (NAACP) in 1910. Burleigh appeared with Du Bois from time to time on public programs, and he was often a featured soloist and occasionally a speaker at regional or national NAACP meetings.[63]

* * *

While Burleigh's career was rising, he was keenly aware of the lynchings and race riots in various parts of the country. In the first decade of the twentieth century, race riots broke out in the North as well as in the South. As one writer pointed out, black mass migrations were always in consequence of racial turmoil,[64] and the Burleighs were in the vanguard of one such migration. New York City's 1900 race riot was triggered in the Tenderloin District when a policeman in civilian clothes who made unwelcome advances to a black woman was stabbed by her lover. Hundreds of white people poured into the streets, indiscriminately attacking any black person they met, sacking and burning their homes and their places of employment. Vaudeville stars Ernest Hogan, Bert Williams, and George Walker were not protected by their fame; their celebrity made them special targets. The black community demanded a police investigation but found the result to be "a sham and whitewash," and their leaders in the press and pulpits issued militant warnings: "Have your houses made ready . . . to afford protection against the fury of white mobs. Carry a revolver. Don't get caught again."[65] Eventually tempers cooled and the immediate danger passed. But this unrest, along with Burleigh's increasingly generous financial resources, may have prompted the Burleighs' first move to more privileged surroundings.

Early in their marriage the Burleighs lived in Black Bohemia, nestled between the Tenderloin District and San Juan Hill. Here they were near their friends Bert Williams, George Walker, and Bob Cole on 53rd Street and the Marshall Hotel, where the black intelligentsia gathered for tasty food, stimulating conversation, and lively entertainment. In a deposition at the time of his mother's death, the Burleighs' son Alston reported that he was born in an apartment on 33rd Street and Seventh Avenue. But by 1902 they had moved east and north, to 449 Park Avenue—not far in walking distance, but perhaps far enough removed from the potential focus of racist turmoil. Park Avenue was the Burleigh residence at least through 1906, but by 1910 they and their friends Bert and Lottie Williams, and Charles L. Reason (son of mathematician and teacher Charles Lewis Reason), leaders in "the black aristocracy," had broken the path into "the elegant green pastures of Harlem."[66] First on the top floor of the Alberta Apartments at West 136th and Lenox Avenue, then at 210 West 133rd Street, the Burleigh apartment and those of their friends were "scenes for many gay parties and gatherings among the theatrical personalities from the Lafayette Theater." By 1912 the Burleighs lived at West 166th Street in the Bronx. Burleigh remained active in the cultural life of Harlem throughout his career, though he lived at this Bronx address until he was moved to a nursing home in 1947.[67]

Several years before the Burleighs and the Williamses led the way to Harlem, Burleigh demonstrated his awareness and concern for continuing racial tensions. One source of agitation was a trilogy of racist novels by North Carolina writer Thomas Dixon Jr. that "under the guise of dramatic romance, drew a ghastly picture of the Negro as a maniacal beast" who threatened the inviolability of white women and the supremacy of the white South. After reading "The White South Sunk in Mediocrity," a 1905 letter from Archibald Grimke to the New York *Age*,[68] Burleigh sent the author a letter of appreciation. Grimke, a North Carolina native, argued that contrary to public opinion, the black population of the South was making greater strides in education, business, and social progress than Southern whites. Burleigh found Grimke's letter to be "truthful and therefore powerful." He extended congratulations "for such really vital efforts to show the world the actual state of conditions in the South." As for Dixon's novels, "Such articles not only put Dixon and all his kind in their real places as demagogues—but show *us* in our true light, which is of very great help and cannot be too gladly welcomed." In a postscript Burleigh added, "I wish I could feel sure that Thomas Dixon would see this article."[69]

For the next decade the black press vigorously protested Dixon's novels and led efforts to ban stage productions based on the books. But despite their efforts, in 1915 D. W. Griffin directed the "landmark and notorious film" *The Birth of a*

Nation, still praised today for its "cinematic innovations." The film brought images of Negro bestiality and raving cruelty into movie theaters throughout the country, fixing "a blind fear of every Negro man, a fear that persisted long after the novels themselves were forgotten."[70] The NAACP monthly journal *Crisis,* edited by Du Bois, led the protests against the film, along with black newspapers and journals across the country.

Crisis magazine also listed reports and statistics of lynchings and other atrocities alongside items documenting the achievements of African Americans in all areas of endeavor. Expressive of Du Bois's understanding of the central importance of the arts, the lead section of each issue was the "Music and the Arts" department, followed by his trenchant editorials and news items detailing the challenges faced and the progress and achievements won by African Americans across the country. Burleigh's friend Daisy Tapley edited the "Music and the Arts" pages, which frequently reported his accomplishments as a singer and composer along with those of the growing number of his colleagues and protégés.[71]

* * *

The list of Burleigh's many recitals benefiting organizations that provided social services to the black community is long and varied, even including a May 1916 concert for the Colored Working Girls and St. John's Club for Boys, a concert at Delmonico's, the upscale restaurant he and his colleagues had attempted to integrate more than twenty years earlier. He continued giving such benefit recitals into the 1940s.[72]

In addition to his solo work, Burleigh's activities demonstrated his concern for education, music education in particular. From late 1909 to April 1910 the New York *Age* carried a series of advertisements announcing a new music school, the Marion School of Vocal Music, located on West Thirty-Seventh Street. Will Marion Cook was the director, and Burleigh the vocal instructor. The advertisement sought "young men and women of pleasing appearance," who were to be given "thorough instruction in concert, dramatic and ensemble singing." Cook's lessons in sight singing, choral singing, and "first principles in harmony" were offered free of charge. Burleigh's "advanced vocal training in Voice Placing, Coaching and Repertoire" were available "for moderate fee if deemed necessary." The contact address was the Gotham-Attucks Music Publishing Company, with which Cook was affiliated, but as no additional information about the school is available, we can only assume that, like so many of Cook's ventures, this one could not be sustained.[73]

A more successful institution was the Music School Settlement for Colored People, founded in the 1911–12 season. Cook was only marginally affiliated with this school in its first years, but Burleigh and his music were involved from its beginning. The school's founder was violinist David Mannes, brother-in-law to Frank and Walter Damrosch, all of them leaders in the New York white music establishment and interested supporters of their black colleagues. Mannes had founded the Music School Settlement on the Lower East Side some years earlier "to cultivate the musical talent of [white] children." As he credited a black violinist, John T. Douglas, with giving his "first legitimate musical instruction," setting him on the road to a distinguished career, the Music School Settlement for Colored People in Harlem was his tribute to Douglas, "the disappointed genius" to whom he owed his musical life.[74]

Burleigh served on the original Board of Directors of the Music School Settlement for Colored People, with Natalie Curtis, W. E. B. Du Bois, Mannes and his wife, Lyman Beecher Stowe, and others. When James Reese Europe's Clef Club engaged Carnegie Hall in April 1912 for the first of several annual concerts to benefit the school, an advertisement in the New York *Age* listed Burleigh, "New York's favorite baritone," as one of the artists who would sing several songs.[75] In fact, Burleigh did not appear on the program, but contralto Elizabeth Payne sang his 1903 song "Jean."[76] The second annual concert at Carnegie Hall was held on Lincoln's Birthday, and the Clef Club Orchestra played an arrangement of Burleigh's "On Bended Knee," one of his suite of piano sketches in *From the Southland*. Two weeks later, Burleigh and Du Bois shared a lecture and recital on African American folksongs at the Ethical Culture Meeting House under the auspices of the Music School Settlement for Colored People.[77]

In 1914 Burleigh and Will Marion Cook were persuaded to establish a choral society affiliated with the school. They "enthusiastically entered upon their duties," and the choral society made its debut in the third annual concert at Carnegie Hall. Previous efforts to organize a choral society in New York City had failed. It seemed "the average colored person" was not interested because it was assumed that the repertoire would be limited to "ragtime or primitive spirituals, better known as jubilee songs." Much of the music taught at the school and performed by guest artists was standard classical repertoire, and perhaps some believed "that to give attention to Negro music you must necessarily stop singing the best things in musical literature." Cook, always insistent that African Americans did not sufficiently value their own musical heritage, found such attitudes discouraging. Perhaps, he sniffed, they would not "wake up to the great possibilities of our music and legends offer for development until white Americans publicly and unreservedly voice their appreciation." Cook's solution was choral societies in black communities that would show African Americans and the communities that surrounded them what was distinctive about their own heritage. "When we possess more race consciousness we shall have more Negro choral societies and other distinctive racial organizations." The choral society Burleigh and Cook were organizing would be "a permanent affiliate of the Music School Settlement for Colored People," providing a model.[78]

At the third annual concert benefitting the Music School Settlement at Carnegie Hall in March 1914, Burleigh conducted the new eighty-voice chorus in singing his choral arrangements of "Deep River" and "Dig My Grave," presented a month later by Kurt Schindler's Schola Cantorum. He also sang three spirituals, "You May

Bury Me in de Eas,'" "Weepin' Mary," and "I Don't Feel No-Ways Tired." Abbie
Mitchell and J. Rosamond Johnson sang and James Reese Europe's Negro Symphony
Orchestra played "two fine arrangements of Mr. Burleigh's (fine enough for our Philharmonic or Symphony Orchestras to perform)," in the view of *Musical America*'s
A. Walter Kramer. But Burleigh's performance of Alex Rogers's "Why Adam Sinned,"
always an audience favorite, earned him severe criticism from Kramer, ever the
apostle of high art. For Burleigh, "excellent musician that he is, after distinguishing
himself by singing his spirituals," to sing this popular ditty "spoiled his contribution to the musical excellence of the program."[79] This program also featured Cook's
Afro-American Folk Singers in several of his 1912 songs that are among his most
enduring: "Rain Song," "Swing Along," and "Exhortation, a Negro Sermon."[80]

That Cook's goal was realized in part is suggested by the New York *Times* review:
"Perhaps [the concert's] most significant feature was a demonstration of what
may be expected of negro composers trained in the modern techniques, as they
are affected by their racial traits in music. The fact that the programme consisted
largely of plantation melodies and spirituals, which were in each case 'harmonized,'
'arranged,' or 'developed,' showed that these composers are beginning to form an art
of their own on the basis of their folk material."[81] The fourth annual Carnegie Hall
concert in 1915 again featured music by Burleigh, but his busy life as an art song
composer and singer and his editorial duties at the G. Ricordi Music Publishing
Company prevented him from as much personal involvement in the school in the
years that followed.

* * *

In addition to his role in adult education projects in Harlem, Burleigh was also
active in efforts to improve the health and general welfare of African Americans.
In 1926 when the Health Circle for Colored People launched a national health campaign, Burleigh served on the national committee with attorney Paul D. Cravath
(son of the longtime president of Fisk University), novelist Edna Ferber, publisher
Alfred A. Knopf, Tuskegee president Dr. Robert R. Moton, Atlanta race leader
Reverend Henry Hugh Proctor, former president Theodore Roosevelt, and Emmett
J. Scott (now at Howard University), among others. The Health Circle, formerly
the Circle for Negro War Relief during World War I, had sent supplies to thousands of soldiers and supported many on their return home while they looked for
work. The executive secretary, Belle Davis, top singer and dancer in 1890s black
musical theater, focused her considerable energy on surveying the health needs of
the residents of Harlem and the surrounding areas as well as in the South and on
assisting the training of health workers. In a related effort in 1934, Harlem leaders
were active on an advisory committee to help the Welfare Bureau "to assist in the
administration of relief in the city." Burleigh was the only black member from the
Bronx.[82]

In May 1927 Burleigh lectured at the 135th Street branch of the New York Public Library on the value of spirituals. The Chicago *Defender* commented that Burleigh had "probably done more to create among the races a respect for the cultural value of Race music than any other musician. For 30 years he has been arranging and singing these songs, and his name is known to musicians and music lovers throughout the world."[83] The following year Burleigh chaired the program committee for Harlem Music Week, with a stellar list of musicians and community leaders. A special feature of the week was a Canadian Folksong Festival and Handicraft Festival, directed by Sigmund Spaeth.[84]

In 1930 Burleigh was general chairman of an interracial committee that brought together musicians involved with classical spirituals—with Langston Hughes as cochair and members Melville Charlton, Hall Johnson, William Grant Still, J. Rosamond Johnson, and James P. Johnson—and those involved with popular music—with Duke Ellington and Andy Razaf as cochairs and members Noble Sissle, C. Lucketh Robert, and W. C. Handy.[85] This may have been the advance planning committee for the pageant "O Sing a New Song," organized by Noble Sissle, for the 1933–34 Chicago World's Fair. In accordance with the fair's theme, "A Century of Progress," the pageant featured an ambitious program showcasing the contributions to American culture in all styles of African American music.[86]

Burleigh served again in 1932 on the Harlem Committee on Adult Education, centering at the 135th Street library with Mrs. William Pickens and Arthur A. Schomberg. They were joined by Alain LeRoy Locke, Mr. and Mrs. George Schuyler, and others. The choral society organized by Burleigh and Cook in 1914 was no longer active in 1932. Now, with the assistance of Minnie Brown and Charlotte Wallace Murray, two of his younger protégés, Burleigh spearheaded the organization of a Manhattan Negro Chorus that would rehearse at the library. There would be no auditions; "every one who would like to join this chorus, or who thinks it will be a good thing for Harlem" was invited to be involved.[87]

Most of Burleigh's public work in Harlem was promoting musical events, but his support was not limited to the musical arts. In 1935 he joined Alain Locke and Countee Cullen as patrons of an exhibit of the work of pupils of sculptor Augusta Savage at the Harlem YMCA.[88] He also kept an eye on the theatrical success of his younger colleagues in the theater, sending a congratulatory telegram to Rose McClendon in January 1932: "Wish it were possible to witness what I hope will be the greatest triumph of your enviable career."[89]

* * *

Burleigh was deeply affected by the entrance of the United States into the Great War, the War to End All Wars, World War I. Despite controversy over whether African Americans should help "bring democracy" to Europe when they were in greater need of democracy at home, patriotism won out, and many young black soldiers volunteered to serve. Madam C. J. Walker's biographer describes the mood in Harlem: "Protest and patriotism vied for headlines in the New York *Age* during the summer of 1917 as African American troops trained for the war abroad and Harlem leaders challenged mob violence at home." Black New Yorkers

> were captivated by the military drills their khaki-clad sons, husbands and friends practiced outside the 132nd Street armory. That James Reese Europe—now a sergeant in the Harlem-based 15th Infantry Regiment of the NY Guard—had signed on to lead the regimental band only boosted their pride. With Noble Sissle strutting as his drum major, and a dozen handpicked Puerto Rican enlistees filling his reed section, Jim Europe's impromptu street parades did more for recruitment than any ten Selective Service offices.[90]

Intensely patriotic and proud of his son Alston's military service, Burleigh wrote six art songs inspired by the war, and he participated in events to honor the soldiers and to raise money for their relief and that of their families. In early November 1917, he appeared on a program to honor the men who had left for Camp Upton, Yaphank, Long Island, and several weeks later he appeared with Bert Williams, Abbie Mitchell, J. Rosamond Johnson, famous white actor John Barrymore, and others at a Mammoth Rally concert under the auspices of the Circle for Negro War Relief. In February and May 1918 Burleigh participated in benefits at the Lexington Opera House for the 367th Infantry (earlier known as the 15th Infantry), attached to the Fourth French Army. A year later, in February 1919, this company would celebrate the war's end, marching proudly up Fifth Avenue to the irresistible beat of James Reese Europe's "Hell-Fighter's" band.[91]

* * *

Burleigh's special relationship to Cheyney State Teachers College reflected his friendship with Leslie Pinckney Hill. With his Harvard bachelor's and master's degrees, Hill headed Cheyney Training Institute for Teachers from 1913 until 1932, when it became Cheyney State Teachers College, and was president until 1951.[92]

Over the years Hill invited Burleigh on a number of occasions to sing and to speak to the students about the value of their music heritage. In October 1922, Burleigh was guest soloist and speaker at Cheyney Day.[93] At the 1924 commencement, he spoke on "the extraordinary development of the Negro in music since the Civil War."[94] He gave the 1927 Commencement Address and, as always, sang. In fall 1928 the new men's dormitory was named Burleigh Hall in his honor. Principal Hill said the designation was "not only because [Burleigh] is probably the foremost Negro citizen in Pennsylvania, but especially because of his creative genius, by which he has given to Negro music a world significance." A Connecticut newspaper commented, "Burleigh has achieved a high place in music, so Cheyney and Pennsylvania laud him as a man who has brought honor not only to himself, but by his creative genius he has brought honor to his race, Pennsylvania and the world."[95] In 1932 when Cheyney was granted status as a Pennsylvania state teachers college, Burleigh led the graduation procession, followed by Hill and commencement speaker W. E. B. Du Bois. In his remarks, Burleigh "urged the development of state teachers' colleges as a great center of music here in Pennsylvania, placing special emphasis upon the inherent talent and beauty and originality to be found in the race and the wealth of material right there on the campus."[96]

*   *   *

Until Paul Robeson's deep, majestic bass voice became widely known in the mid-1920s, Burleigh was commonly called "the foremost baritone of the race." Even after that title slipped away, Burleigh was called on to sing at signal events in the black community, many of them funerals. After Samuel Coleridge-Taylor's death in 1912 at the age of thirty-seven, a memorial concert was held at Jordan Hall in Boston in January 1913. Burleigh and the young tenor Roland Hayes were accompanied by Melville Charlton; Boston baritone William H. Richardson was accompanied by Maud Cuney Hare. As a mark of the respect for Coleridge-Taylor shared by musicians across the color line, two string players from the Boston Symphony Orchestra and an organist also played. The memorial address was given by W. E. B. Du Bois.[97]

In May 1919 Harlem grieved the loss of three of its citizens: first the shocking death of James Reese Europe, stabbed by an unstable young member of his band in whom he had taken special interest. Harlem, so recently giddy with the thrill of Europe's band leading the 367th Infantry up Fifth Avenue, was stunned at this terrible, senseless loss. Burleigh, with whom Europe had studied music theory, brought the funeral service to a close singing "Now Take Thy Rest." Three days later, accompanied by Melville Charlton, Burleigh sang at the funeral of Mrs. Walter F. Craig. Charlton and Burleigh had often performed with Walter Craig's orchestra and on occasion with Craig as soloist violinist. Two weeks later, grooming and hair culture entrepreneur and philanthropist Madam C. J. Walker, whose terminal illness was exacerbated by grief at losing her neighbor and friend James Reese Europe, was mourned by a thousand friends and relatives in the spacious rooms of Villa Lewaro, her mansion on the Hudson. Burleigh sang Madame Walker's special favorite, "Safe in the Arms of Jesus," and "One Sweetly Solemn Thought."[98]

Several years later he served as honorary pallbearer for the funeral of tenor Sidney Woodward in 1924. When Florence Mills, who had become the sweetheart of the nation, died unexpectedly in 1927 in the prime of her stage career as a singer and dancer, Burleigh, Abbie Mitchell, and Hall Johnson led the gathered mourners in singing spirituals. A few months later, on a visit to his hometown, Burleigh spoke of his sense of loss at her death: "A brightness and an electric something that cannot be replaced has gone."[99] Burleigh was also an honorary pallbearer at the

1939 funeral of Dora Cole Norman, sister of Bob Cole, for whom Burleigh wrote his setting of "O Perfect Love"; his friend Melville Charlton was at the organ, and contralto Charlotte Wallace Murray sang.[100]

But it was not only occasions of mourning to which Burleigh lent his voice. In November 1920 when St. Philip's celebrated its centennial, Burleigh was a featured soloist on one of the programs of the weeklong events. And when Tuskegee scientist George Washington Carver spoke at the Marble Collegiate Church to the Women's Board of Domestic Missions of the Reformed Church of America in November 1924, it was Burleigh who sang.[101]

*　*　*

Burleigh and his wife often spent weekends at one of the black-owned cottages at Asbury Park, New Jersey, where they socialized with their affluent friends, and he continued to spend occasional weekends at the Jersey shore in the years that followed. But after their separation in 1915, Burleigh spent his summer vacations in Oak Bluffs on Martha's Vineyard, an island retreat first claimed by Boston's black elite. Charles and Henrietta Shearer of Everett, Massachusetts, opened Shearer Cottage in 1912, a summer home that welcomed African American guests who could not find lodging at other Martha's Vineyard hotels and inns. As novelist Dorothy West recounted, Burleigh was "the first to bring back glad tidings of the Island's fair land to his New York friends."[102] For thirty years he was a regular guest at Shearer Cottage. There he shared delicious family-style meals and spirited conversations with other guests such as Adam Clayton Powell Sr., pastor of Abyssinian Baptist Church in Harlem; actor-singer Ethel Waters; actor-singer-activist Paul Robeson and his wife Eslanda; attorney William H. Lewis, President Woodrow Wilson's assistant attorney general; Henry Robbins, court reporter for the Sacco-Vanzetti case; and many others. Often fifty or sixty guests filled the dining room, and the pies were legendary.[103]

In addition to the woodsy, rustic environment and the easy access to the East Chop Beach Club, Burleigh found Oak Bluffs conducive to composition. His studio-bedroom "overlooked the lush green countryside."[104] When he needed a quiet place with a piano, he set up his composer's studio in a Sunday school room at the Grace Episcopal Church in Vineyard Haven. He told an interviewer in 1938 that many of the pieces sung by the St. George's choir in New York City were born in Oak Bluffs, where he found "peace and quiet."[105]

The adults who came to Oak Bluffs provided stimulating activities and friend-ship, and Burleigh took special interest in the children of his friends. Everyone knew "H.T.," who "always dressed in a white suit, hat, shoes, shirt, and tie."[106]

The children loved to walk to town with him, and as Barbara Townes remembers, if it was bad weather during the day, "we found Burleigh. He would give us money to go to the movies and do the things we wanted to do, and there was quite a gang of us, there must have been ten kids."[107] Dorothy West, too, had fond memories of

Burleigh at the beach with Melville Charlton, Oak Bluffs. (Courtesy of the Burleigh Family)

Burleigh's kindness to her and the other children. "He gave us money every time he saw us. . . . He rented cars and took us on tours of the Island. He told us about his trips abroad. To be with him was a learning experience."[108]

Jill Nelson in her book reflects on what Oak Bluffs has meant to generations of African Americans. In this village, on this island, security was not an issue. "The litany of what to watch out for that was a constant of life off-island was essentially unnecessary here in this place," where doors were left unlocked. But more important, here privileged, well-known black Americans could relax in a way that was rare in their busy public lives. "Here we were not the only one, or one of very few, as was so often the case where we lived, worked, and went to school." Oak Bluffs was an integrated community with "a significant number of black families. A community largely composed of people who were college educated, many of them professionals, all of them hardworking. There was no need to be the exemplary Negro here, or to show white people that we were as good as or better than they were, to conduct ourselves as ambassadors for integration and racial harmony. For the months of summer the weight of being race representative—and all the political, emotional, and psychic burdens that come with demanding that an individual represent a nonexistent monolith—was lifted."[109] For Burleigh, as for Oak Bluffs

Burleigh at the beach
with friends, Oak Bluffs.
(Courtesy of the Burleigh
Family)

visitors today, this was a rare space of respite and retreat. And as photographs in
the Burleigh Family Papers show, it was a place where even H.T. could lay aside
his dignity and frolic in the sun and sand.

* * *

One measure of Burleigh's stature in the black community is the awards by
which he was honored. On May 16, 1917, at the height of his renown as an art song
composer and the year his solo arrangements of spirituals became standard recital
fare, the NAACP awarded him its highest honor, the Spingarn medal. The Spingarn
was given annually "to the colored American achieving the greatest success among
the lines of uplift."[110] The Cincinnati *Union* commented, "The achievements . . .
which won Mr. Burleigh the Spingarn medal are but the mature fruitage of a long
life of consecrated labor."[111]

Two weeks later Atlanta University awarded Burleigh and J. Rosamond Johnson
honorary master of arts degrees. In his remarks, former Atlanta University president Rev. Horace Bumstead described Burleigh as "a composer and interpreter of
music, a broad-minded, congenial man, welcome in the homes of wealth and in
the humblest cottages, attacking the fastnesses of prejudice by the winsome power

of song and good will."[112] Howard University conferred the doctor of music degree on Burleigh in 1920.

In 1927 Burleigh was one of the three Harmon Award music judges. He, with his colleagues Clarence Dickinson, organist and director of music for Union Theological Seminary in New York, and composer Preston Orem Ware declined to give a Harmon award for music, as in their estimation, of the twenty-eight submissions no "original creative work was submitted of such outstanding importance as to merit the William E. Harmon Award." The fund for the award would be held in trust for the future, "when productions worthy of the awards are submitted."[113] Three years later, Burleigh was given the Harmon gold medal and $400. Opera composer Henry Lawrence Freeman was given the $100 award, and pianist-composer Carl Diton received honorable mention.[114]

In November 1937 the Chicago *Defender* reported on plans for the 1940 New York Exposition. A young African American sculptor had been commissioned to sculpt three busts, of "well known figures in church, music and science." They were Rev. A. Clayton Powell Sr., Harry T. Burleigh, and George Washington Carver. Burleigh was chosen for the distinction "of having contributed more to the music world than any other New Yorker."[115]

* * *

Though Burleigh was not known as "a race man," one who insisted on confronting the powers of mainstream American society, directly challenging prejudice and discrimination, he was often cited in the black press as a leader whose accomplishments were a credit to the race. As early as 1912 the Chicago *Defender* listed him in its "Summary of Great Negroes." In the Pittsburgh *Courier*'s 1927 column "How Much Do You Know about Your Own Race?" the question of the week was "Who Is Harry T. Burleigh?" In the March 31, 1930, Philadelphia *Tribune* "Junior-Kiddie Page Features," the challenge was "Harry T. Burleigh! Recognize the name? Leading Figure in World of Music." In April 1932 the Chicago *Defender* called Burleigh "one of the greatest living musicians, who put voice back of feeling." The item continued, "Put Hayes, Burleigh, Robeson and Abbie Mitchell in the Metropolitan Opera House and the horse shoe circle would stop talking and listen." An unidentified 1933 clipping in the Burleigh papers challenged young people by detailing Burleigh's life story: "Think YOU'RE handicapped?" The column ended "In spite of his severe handicaps, his full, rich voice overcame all prejudice. He was the first colored man to win world fame as a composer."[116]

Burleigh's renown as singer and composer inspired numerous societies that bore his name. The Burleigh Choral Society founded in Washington, D.C., in 1903 was the earliest of at least two dozen Burleigh music societies formed in the 1920s and 1930s from Portland, Oregon, to Atlanta, Georgia; from New Bedford, Massachusetts, to Fort Worth, Texas; from Saginaw, Michigan, to Clarksville, Tennessee;

and from South Bend, Indiana, to Darlington, South Carolina. Some were choral groups or glee clubs, and some were study groups, whose goal was to learn more about music by black composers. Musicians in Terre Haute, Indiana, formed the Harry T. Burleigh Orchestra.[117] Young people in Darlington, South Carolina, formed the H.B.M.B.—the Harry Burleigh Music Bunch.[118] And the Davis sisters of New Rochelle, New York, soprano Ella Belle and her pianist sister Marie, established the Burleighettes, later known as the Junior Burleigh Glee Club.[119] One suspects that Burleigh considered the second title more appropriate to his dignified status.

* * *

The importance of Burleigh's achievements as a singer, composer, arranger, and music editor for African Americans may be better understood by pondering T. R. Poston's New York *Amsterdam News* report of Caterina Jarboro's performance of the title role in Verdi's *Aïda* at the Hippodrome in July 1933. To say that Black Manhattan turned out for this event was an understatement. "Hours before the doors were opened . . . Black Manhattan began its trek to the Hippodrome. From Striver's Row in limousines, from Sugar Hill in taxicabs, from Seventh avenue in motorbuses, from Lenox and upper Fifth on the I.R.T. and from San Juan Hill on trudging feet, the descendants of Verdi's Ethiopian princess converged on the world-famous theatre." At least twenty-three hundred were turned away, as tickets were exhausted two hours before the curtain, but at 8:53, when Caterina Jarboro began to sing, "fully 1,800 dark faces turned imploring eyes" on her. The opera record books might critique her singing. "But the real drama of the situation was encompassed in a split minute—the thirty seconds which elapsed between the cessation of the spontaneous applause which greeted Miss Jarboro's entrance" and her first note. "In that thirty seconds, as has been the case in every story of racial achievement since 1861, the Black Man's Burden rested heavily on the brown shoulders of a freedman's descendant who dared aspire to higher things. And eighteen hundred souls, representing 12 million others whose hopes and dreams are frustrated daily because of that burden, looked imploringly at the soprano and vainly tried to share her load."[120]

Poston listed some of Harlem's celebrities in the house, including Harry T. Burleigh, "whose beautiful arrangements of spirituals had been rendered by the soprano when her dreams of grand opera were far from realization." Jarboro could not escape awareness of the weight on her shoulders; the 300 telegrams plastering the walls of her dressing room both blessed and challenged her. In the end, whether hers was an immortal performance was not the ultimate question. "The untrained ears of a mere newspaper reporter could not tell. But the trained eyes of this same reporter could watch the faces of perfect strangers as they passed each other during the intermissions and smiled a smile which seemed to say: 'Another milestone, Lord!'"

Burleigh's voice would never echo across the cavernous space of the Hippodrome, though John McCormack often sang Burleigh's songs to thousands there. But Burleigh's achievements, like those of Caterina Jarboro, represented a succession of milestones, marking hopeful paths for those who followed. His lifelong presence among them, offering his voice and his actions to public health, education, and music demonstrated that however far his career carried him into the world of New York's mainstream elite and the white music establishment, he never forgot his roots in the black community, and all that he accomplished was ultimately for the benefit of the race.

9. Burleigh's Singing Career

"An art of astonishing versatility"

When Burleigh auditioned for admission to the Artist's Course at the National Conservatory of Music, his goal was to become a classical concert singer. Like soprano Sissieretta Jones, he wanted to sing arias and art songs in recital, as he had begun to do in his home town of Erie, Pennsylvania. Unlike Sissieretta Jones and a number of other black singers, Burleigh never attempted a tour of the West Indies, Australia, South Africa, or India, though he sang in London, and perhaps in Italy. He did fulfill his goal to become a classical performer, and he extended the role of the black classical singer from guest appearances on a varied program of singers, instrumentalists, and elocutionists or dramatic readers to full recitals that featured German lieder, Italian and French opera arias, American art songs, plantation songs and spirituals, and songs from black musical theater.

Like other well-known black singers, Burleigh sang for audiences in African American venues throughout the East and Midwest, as well as for mixed audiences, and on many occasions he sang for audiences that were primarily white. In some cases, these appearances were arranged by an agent. As he became known nationwide as "the premiere baritone of the race"[1] and as the leading black composer in the early twentieth century, he was often invited to present full recitals, to represent African Americans as part of a program of American music, or to give a lecture-recital on spirituals.

Black classical singers at this time usually appeared in Star Concerts or benefit concerts. The Star Concert, developed by white impresario John G. Bergen, featured one or more well-known artists supported by local talent. Bergen managed black singers such as Florence Batson (whom he married), Sissieretta Jones, and Marie Selika.[2] In a format that may have originated in black vaudeville and other touring companies, the star artist sang one or two numbers on programs that featured several other singers, usually local singers of less renown, sometimes instrumentalists and nearly always an elocutionist or dramatic reader. In that generation, only Anita Patti Brown seems to have been able to sustain a career giving full recitals.[3] But like Brown, Burleigh gave full solo recitals, a model that his friend Sissieretta Jones was able to sustain only briefly; the next generation of singers, such as Roland Hayes, Marian Anderson, and Paul Robeson, would make them commonplace.[4]

* * *

It is important to see Burleigh as inheritor of a tradition of African American art musicians, a legacy to which he contributed significantly. He was a member of a small but important company of vocal artists whose careers still demand serious attention. Repeatedly throughout the last half of the nineteenth century and well into the twentieth, classically trained African American singers attempted to build an operatic or recital career but found themselves forced to return to or create a role for themselves in minstrel, vaudeville, or jubilee troupes.

Burleigh would not have heard Elizabeth Taylor Greenfield sing, though he surely knew of her. As we have seen, he did hear the Hyers sisters (see chapter 3), who were "greatly admired in Erie," when they appeared with the Callender Minstrels.[5] Nellie Brown-Mitchell sang primarily in New England churches, but she also appeared in New York, Chicago, Baltimore, and Washington, D.C. She sang "polite ballads and parlor songs," a repertoire that displayed her "smooth, sweet, and exceptionally well-controlled voice."[6] Burleigh's colleague, tenor Sidney Woodward, was a protégé of Brown-Mitchell. Brown-Mitchell's contemporary, Marie Selika, became known as the "Queen of Staccato," and occasionally as "the Brown Patti," a reference to the Spanish soprano Adelina Patti. Like the Hyers sisters, she drew her primary repertoire from the operas of Donizetti, Bellini, Meyerbeer and Verdi.[7] With the perennial consciousness of the effect any African American in the public eye might have on the attitudes of white citizens, a Columbus, Ohio, reviewer called her "a pride to the race."[8] Florence Batson-Bergen was praised for the sweetness of her voice, her clear articulation, her extensive range, and her "unostentatious and childlike naturalness."[9] Her repertoire consisted largely of sentimental ballads, and occasionally, opera arias. Sometimes styled "the Colored Jenny Lind," but more often "the Queen of Song," she sang primarily in black churches and sometimes in rented halls, often to overflow audiences.[10]

Coloratura soprano Anita Patti Brown, who gave her debut recital in Chicago in 1903, toured extensively in the United States, Europe, the West Indies, and South America, earning the title "our globe-trotting prima donna" and sometimes "the Bronze Tetrazzini," after Italian coloratura soprano Luisa Tetrazzini. She studied voice in Europe and was one of the first black artists to make recordings, though they were never released.[11] She built a successful career as a solo recitalist for a number of years, appearing often in Chicago and throughout the country, primarily for events sponsored in black communities. She collaborated with many of the professional black musicians of Burleigh's time.

By the time Burleigh arrived in New York City in January 1892, he would have known the names of all these singers, whose itineraries and performances were reported in detail in the black press, whether or not he had heard them sing. Upon moving to New York City, they became personal acquaintances, and he soon appeared with them in concerts. While Burleigh's singing never achieved the international renown of Anita Patti Brown or Sissieretta Jones, his carefully programmed recitals provided a model for younger singers. His recital career enriched the nineteenth-century lineage, linking it to the next generation of singers: tenor Roland W. Hayes, contralto Marian Anderson, soprano Florence Cole-Talbert, bass-baritone Paul Robeson, and their contemporaries Jules Bledsoe, Ruby Elzy, Abbie Mitchell, and others, whose careers were more varied, including acting and musical theater as well as song recitals.

* * *

Burleigh's reputation as a fine baritone preceded his arrival in New York City in January 1892. Within a few short months, reports in the black press and several surviving programs document his immediate recognition as a gifted singer. In April 1892 he appeared at the Carnegie Recital Hall with his Buffalo friend Thad Talbert,[12] and in May he joined Talbert in Newark, New Jersey, for a second recital that featured contralto Deseria Plato, violinist Walter F. Craig, and pianist Blanche Washington, all of whom would appear with Burleigh in later concerts.[13] Burleigh's second Carnegie Recital Hall appearance signaled his ascension into the top echelon of black concert singers. On June 15, the Sons of New York, a prominent African American fraternal organization, featured Sissieretta Jones. Now the most famous and highly paid black singer, Jones was appearing before diverse audiences sometimes numbering in the thousands. She was the obvious choice to draw a paying audience to benefit the Free Bread Fund for poor African Americans in New York City. Jones was the drawing card, and the Sons of New York honored her with a solid gold medal and their best wishes for a successful European tour. But Burleigh's admirers also greeted him with great enthusiasm. "The audience at the next number went wild as Mr. H. T. Burleigh came upon the stage. Mr. Burleigh being a prime favorite, as well as one of the best baritones this city has known since [Marie Selika's husband] Sampson Williams left these shores." Burleigh's rendition of Schumann's "Die Beiden Grenadier" needed "no commendation, as Mr. Burleigh [was] well known to patrons of concert in this city." The audience responded generously, raising $1,100 for the Free Bread Fund.[14]

By this time Sissieretta Jones (born Matilda Sissieretta Joyner) was the veteran of two concert tours to the West Indies and one to Europe, as well as many appearances in the United States and Canada. "While her earliest concerts were given in African American venues, as word of her superior singing abilities spread beyond the black community, she was increasingly sought after to appear before diverse audiences. As one of the first black women to associate professionally with white musicians and entertain predominantly white audiences," Jones was forging new paths that Burleigh intended to follow.[15] And like Burleigh, she hoped to establish a career as a solo recitalist or to study opera in Europe, a goal beyond Burleigh's ambition. Ironically, after 1896, she was best known as the star of her own company, the Black Patti's Troubadours, in which she appeared "only as part of an elegant operatic finale following the comic playlets and vaudeville specialties of her all-black company." Burleigh joined her troupe for a brief tour in 1896.[16]

His connection with Sissieretta Jones introduced Burleigh to a broader audience. She had recently signed a one-year contract with Major James B. Pond (also agent for Charles Dickens, George Washington Cable, John Greenleaf Whittier, Mark Twain, and Paul Laurence Dunbar).[17] She had sung for President Benjamin Harrison in February of that year, the first of the four United States presidents for whom she would sing.[18] At the Pittsburgh Exposition in late September 1892 she

Sissieretta Jones. (The Granger Collection, New York)

appeared before 15,000 with Italo Campanini, the Italian tenor whom Burleigh had heard in Erie from his hiding place in the balcony of the Park Opera House. Major Pond secured $2,000 for this appearance, "the highest salary ever paid a colored artist."[19] In Burleigh's appearance with Jones and Selika in early September at the Grand Encampment in Washington, D.C., he sang for thousands, likely his largest audience yet.[20] He also sang with Jones at the Metropolitan A.M.E. Church in Washington, D.C., with tenor Sidney Woodward and violinist Joseph Douglass, grandson of Frederick Douglass. Just as his appearances with Sissieretta Jones advanced Burleigh's singing career, Burleigh's connection with the National Conservatory of Music introduced Jones into the distinguished circle of musicians who taught there, where she especially captured the attention of its director, Antonín Dvořák.[21]

* * *

The sparse records of the National Conservatory of Music reveal some of Burleigh's accomplishments in that milieu. A scrapbook in the Burleigh papers holds clippings documenting early recitals, often undated and from papers not fully identified. Some feature extensive reviews of his repertoire and detailed comments on his voice and his interpretation of the variety of songs he presented. The Booker T. Washington correspondence also reveals performance venues and some repertoire from 1900, when he began to tour New England with the Tuskegee founder, until 1915, the year of Washington's death. News of St. George's Protestant Episcopal Church appeared weekly in the New York *Times*, often announcing oratorios and other special music with solos by Burleigh. By the mid-1910s, as Burleigh achieved recognition as an art song composer, the mainstream journal *Musical America* reviewed his song compositions and carried reviews of his solo appearances in addition to reporting performances of his songs by nationally and internationally known singers in New York City and throughout the country. From these sources and from letters to younger singers, it is clear that Burleigh's singing career, particularly his full recitals, provided a model for younger singers, just as Sissieretta Jones had demonstrated that with the right management black singers could reach white as well as black audiences.

In the 1890s Burleigh's performances consisted primarily of singing several opera arias or art songs as a supporting artist on a Star Concert or singing in private homes for the black and the white elite, though he occasionally presented solo recitals. By 1894 he was "well known in the best sets of Philadelphia, Washington and other eastern cities."[22] Sometimes he appeared in the mansions of New York's Gilded Age as one of several distinguished entertainers such as violinist David Mannes or baritone David Bispham, but on other occasions he was the sole artist, presenting a full recital.[23]

When Antonín Dvořák heard Sissieretta Jones, he joined the thousands who were captivated by her singing. Burleigh later commented that Dvořák was "mad about her voice."[24] In January 1894, just two months after the premiere of Dvořák's Symphony No. 9 in E Minor, "From the New World," Burleigh and Jones were featured soloists under Dvořák's direction. The 1893 recession had hit hard, and the New York *Herald* proposed a benefit concert for its Free Clothing Fund. Sissieretta Jones was the only musician in the concert not directly associated with the National Conservatory; her fame added luster to the event. Burleigh and Jones sang the baritone and soprano solos in Rossini's *Stabat Mater* with the male choir of St. Philip's Episcopal Church, whose organist and choirmaster Edward H. Kinney was a composition student of Dvořák. Maurice Arnold, another Dvořák composition student (who had accompanied Burleigh at the Chicago World's Fair), conducted his own *Plantation Dances* in their premiere orchestral performance. Another feature of the program was Dvořák's arrangement of Stephen C. Foster's "Old Folks at Home," more commonly known as "Swanee River." Dvořák's arrangement featured solo parts for Jones and Burleigh, and at the end of the performance, he gave his copy of the score to Burleigh: "Here, Barley," as he called his assistant, "This is for you."[25]

* * *

By 1900 Burleigh was touring as a recitalist throughout the Northeast and Midwest, and began to accompany Booker T. Washington on his fundraising tours. Burleigh started the new year with two recitals in Albany, New York, in the afternoon and evening of January 23. Before an evening recital at the home of Mrs. John Clinton Gray,[26] Burleigh was the featured singer at an afternoon reception for the Albany newsboys' home at the residence of Governor Theodore Roosevelt. A number of newsboys from New York City were among the 350 guests. In her diary entry for the day, Edith Roosevelt commented that Burleigh sang Rudyard Kipling's verse "The Absent-Minded Beggar," written for the Soldier's Fund, "to his own very spirited setting."[27] Among his selections were "The Bedouin Love Song," and "some pathetic negro melodies."[28] After the reception, when Governor Roosevelt learned that Burleigh was unable to find lodging in Albany hotels, he invited him to spend the night as his guest. So seventy years after Burleigh's grandmother, Lucinda Duncanson, worked as a servant for New York Governor Enos Throop, her grandson was honored as a singer and a guest in New York Governor Theodore Roosevelt's mansion—a year before President Theodore Roosevelt would excite fierce criticism for inviting Booker T. Washington to lunch at the White House.[29]

Prominent white musicians such as New York Symphony conductor Walter Damrosch and his brother Frank Damrosch, a leader in public music education, engaged Burleigh on occasion. In March 1900 he was baritone soloist at a concert of Frank Damrosch's Cooper Union Advanced People's Singing Class with a 300-voice choir conducted by Edward G. Marquard.[30] Ten years later he was a soloist in Gabriel Pierne's Christmas oratorio *The Children at Bethlehem* with the New York Symphony at Carnegie Music Hall under Walter Damrosch's baton. This event was chronicled in "Notes on Racial Progress" in the New York *Age*. His solos, "An Ox" and "A Herdsman" were small parts, but he "got a real ovation" from the audience.[31]

In April 1900 Burleigh appeared with Booker T. Washington at a benefit for the Kindergarten for Colored Children, held at the Madison Square Garden Concert Hall. The event drew a distinguished audience, including Columbia University President Seth Low (a St. George's parishioner) and Fanny Garrison Villard, only daughter of fiery abolitionist William Lloyd Garrison. W. E. B. Du Bois, now a professor at Atlanta University, who would soon challenge Washington's leadership, also participated, reading his story "When John Comes Home." Burleigh's first group of songs after Washington's address was encored repeatedly, and he closed the program with "The Absent-Minded Beggar" and several other selections.[32]

In a letter to Washington assistant Fred Moore several days before the event, Burleigh, just back from a concert tour "as far west as Niagara Falls," laid out his tentative program: "If I am to play for my own singing (and I often do) I should prefer a baby grand piano—not high pitch—so that I can see some of the audience; but if I am to have an accompanist an upright piano will do." He would be willing to sing two or three times, but invited to sing his own compositions at the main event, he demurred: "I must ask you to excuse me from singing any of my own songs—I cannot do them well." Always concerned about excellence, he chose to perform for the public only works that he could do with distinction. This was not to be a full recital, but its format was suggestive: leading off with the Beethoven hymn "The Heavens Declare" ("Die ehres Gottes aus der Natur") and "A Red, Red Rose" by Frank S. Hastings; a group of plantation songs in the second group (Geibel's "Kentucky Babe" and Noll's "Doan You Cry Ma Honey"); and despite his earlier refusal, his unpublished song, "The Absent-Minded Beggar."[33]

After the program, Washington and his entourage were guests of Mrs. Villard at Thorwood, her home in Dobbs Ferry, New York, and Burleigh sang there as well. A fine pianist, Mrs. Villard enjoyed holding concerts in her gold and white music room, "the center of Thorwood activity," according to her son Oswald Garrison Villard.[34] Burleigh agreed to sing "one or two from my own pen—as it will be more confidential and less presumpt[uous]."[35]

* * *

The year 1900 also brought Burleigh his second long-term singing position. Max Spicker, with whom Burleigh had studied counterpoint at the National Conservatory of Music, was the music director at Temple Emanu-El, the largest and wealthiest of the city's Reformed Jewish synagogues, then at Forty-Third Street and Fifth Avenue. Formerly director of the Brooklyn Conservatory of Music and an editor at the G. Schirmer music publishing house, Spicker hired Burleigh for his choir, a position he held for twenty-five years. Burleigh's years of singing at the Jewish Reform Synagogue in Erie had prepared him well, and his determined scholarship at the National Conservatory continued to open doors that enhanced his career.[36]

There has been some confusion over whether Burleigh was a soloist at Temple Emanu-El. In 1924, immediately after the celebration of Burleigh's thirtieth anniversary at St. George's and the initiation of the Annual Vesper Service of Negro Spirituals, the New York *Times* carried a telling correction. An article the previous week had referred to Burleigh as Temple Emanu-El's baritone soloist. The April 1 article, "Burleigh Not Temple Soloist," firmly refuted this: "Mr. Burleigh is a member of the choir at Temple Emanu-El. The choir numbers twenty and he is one of the two members who sing baritone. The other is Carl Schlegel, who is the baritone soloist."[37] According to the temple archivist, the small choir did not always have a designated soloist, and though Burleigh probably did sing solos on occasion, at least in 1924 he was not so designated.[38]

Burleigh retired from Temple Emanu-El in 1925. His grandson, Dr. Harry T. Burleigh II, reported that a copyright disagreement was a factor in his leaving the position, but no documentation of this has been found.[39] The disagreement may have caused Simon Schlager, the cantor throughout Burleigh's tenure, to be concerned that Burleigh be given appropriate recognition on his retirement, and he appealed to the temple controller to see that "something big . . . be done to honor him. This honor will honor us," he wrote. "It is needless for me to state to you his abilities as a musician, singer, composer, and his reputation in the United States, as well as in other countries." Having observed Burleigh through the twenty-five years, Schlager considered it "an honor and joy to count him as a member." In his view Burleigh had been "the most faithful" member of the choir. "I know," he told the controller, "that you love real men who work with heart and soul, and I know that Harry Burleigh is of such a caliber." Indeed, "such a man helps us in our music which stands high in the world." He asked the controller to help him "see to it that Congregation Emanu-El appreciates faithful service of a quarter of a century."[40]

Schlager's urging was effective; the May 8, 1925, press release quoted a letter from the president and the secretary of Emanu-El congregation. It extended "warmest greetings" to Burleigh. During all his twenty-five years at Temple Emanu-El, it continued, "nothing has marred the harmony of our mutual relations. They have been marked by reciprocal friendship, esteem and confidence. You have contributed much to the maintenance of the high standard of excellence for which we have striven in the musical portion of our service. Your melodious voice and your artistic compositions have added greatly to the devotional attitude of the worshipers within our sanctuary." The testimonial was "inscribed on parchment and bound in gold-tooled morocco leather.[41]

The reference to Burleigh's compositions suggests that the choir sang some of his choral works or perhaps he sang some of his solo arrangements of spirituals. He arranged the music of the spiritual "Deep River" for the "May the Words," the "Silent Prayer," sung in every service in the Jewish liturgy, but no copies of Burleigh's arrangement have been found in the temple's choir library, and it is not among the arrangements of that prayer currently sung by the choir.[42] No record of other Burleigh compositions or arrangements that were used during that quarter century have been located. In May 1935, however, the service music featured music "from the pen of outstanding musicians who played a prominent part in old Temple Emanu-El's musical life." Burleigh's "Silent Prayer" was featured, along with three compositions by Max Spicker and a former organist.[43] In the 1930s Temple Emanu-El music director Lazare Saminsky held a series of annual choral festivals in which he lectured on the history of Jewish sacred music that typically included music by Burleigh. The 1936 lecture was entitled "From the Old Biblical Chant to the American Folksong." Saminsky held that one origin of Negro spirituals was Hebrew chant, a view Burleigh sometimes expressed. Burleigh's "Deep River" was sung by the choir and soloists.[44]

* * *

Burleigh opened his full-length recitals with standard recital repertoire: Beethoven, Schubert, Schumann, Franz, Grieg, Leoncavallo, Bizet, or Massenet, followed by American art songs, often by composers he knew personally. He always included songs that reflected his African American cultural heritage: plantation songs, songs written by his friends who were producing the vibrant and trendsetting black musical theater on and off Broadway, and the spirituals that would become his trademark. Many of his spiritual arrangements appeared on his recitals more than a decade before they were published. Since he always accompanied himself at the piano when singing spirituals, these renditions were doubtless improvisatory, but with no recordings to compare with his published arrangements, we cannot trace their development in style. In some instances, he also performed his art songs before publication, and he performed a number of songs and spiritual arrangements that were never published. Some arrangements were written for specific singers such as Marian Anderson and Lillian Evanti.

Burleigh's reviewers stressed the skillfully sequenced variety in his recitals and, in addition to applauding his rich vocal quality, praised his sensitive and effective interpretation of each song. An undated clipping in the Burleigh papers documents a Rochester, New York, recital on Thursday, December 14 (1899 or 1905), for the Tuesday Musicale at the YMCA hall. Except for one by Cécille Chaminade, this program featured songs by American composers. Three Edward MacDowell songs headed the list: "Thy Beaming Eyes," "Long Ago," and "The Sea," all of which he sang frequently in his first decade of recitals. The second set consisted of three plantation songs—Adam Geibel's "Kentucky Babe"; his own "My Merlindy Brown," from his 1901 collection *Plantation Melodies Old and New*; and Albert Noll's "Don't You Cry Ma' Honey"—after which Burleigh "was obliged to add two more to satisfy encores." Victor Herbert's "Gypsy Love Song" led the third set, followed by George Nevin's "Twilight," the Chaminade "Song of Faith," an unidentified song by Samuel Coleridge-Taylor, and by request, his own "Absent-Minded Beggar." The fourth and final group combined art songs and plantation songs. Two were by William

Arms Fisher: "Under the Rose" and "My Coursers Are Fed with the Lightning" (lyrics by Percy Bysshe Shelley). After Edwin S. Brill's "My Lady Lu," Will Marion Cook's "Who Dat Say Chicken in Dis Crowd?" and his own "Negro Serenade" (from *Plantation Melodies*), Burleigh ended the recital with Walter Damrosch's setting of Kipling's "Danny Deever" as a finale.[45]

Of his singing, the reviewer said, "Mr. Burleigh has a baritone voice of wide range and good quality, which he uses well." Possibly for financial reasons, Burleigh played his own accompaniments for some of his early recitals, including this one. Though he was a fine pianist, the reviewer thought it "a pity, for in spite of the fact that he plays them extremely well, he is obviously hampered by them and his tone at times suffers in consequence. . . . His voice is of such a delightful quality that one cannot but wish to hear it under the most favorable circumstances." MacDowell's "Thy Beaming Eyes" was "perhaps the best known and was feelingly sung." Burleigh's "Malindy Brown" was "very characteristic and was heartily applauded." The term "characteristic" usually appears in comments by white reviewers and indicates the special authenticity or African American quality they heard or assumed to be in Burleigh's singing.[46]

In the third group, Nevin's "Twilight" and the Chaminade "Song of Faith" "were in complete contrast to each other," and despite their difficult accompaniments Burleigh sang and played them skillfully. Of the requested "Absent-Minded Beggar," the reviewer thought the tune "a striking one, and it was much enjoyed by the audience." Fisher's "My Coursers Are Fed with the Lightning" was "a very dramatic song . . . brilliantly sung and played." The finale was "a most dramatic and finely given rendering of 'Danny Deever,' in which the reviewer felt Mr. Burleigh was "at his best," singing "with great abandon as well as with complete authority."[47]

In May 1903 Burleigh gave an "unassisted" recital for the Women's Institute in Yonkers, New York, reviewed by Indianist composer and author Frederick R. Burton. As Burleigh included four of Burton's Ojibway harmonizations in the program of "30 distinct compositions," he cannot be regarded as a disinterested listener, but his comments are worth considering. The publicity brochure, probably written by Burton, who was the program manager, called Burleigh "one of the most successful entertainers in New York," whose work "ranges from the severely classical to the delicately humorous." Like most white listeners, Burton considered Burleigh's specialty to be "his own compositions in the style of plantation songs. . . . He has raised the 'coon song' to the level of high art, and several examples of this class of compositions will be on his programme."[48] The term "coon song" refers to the popular ragtime songs that often promoted the worst of racist imagery and stereotyping, but it is clear here that the term was also applied more broadly to plantation songs and popular songs by black songwriters. Similarly, the term "ragtime" was often used to refer to any "characteristic" black music, not just to the specific rhythmic style of turn-of-the-century piano and ragtime songs as they are currently designated.

A newspaper notice predicted that this would be "one of the best" of the entertainments of the season, though the less musically sophisticated might be deterred by the term "song recital": "A song recital is often looked upon as rather severe for all but the few who are versed in the art, but Mr. Burleigh's recital need frighten nobody. His plan is always to mingle the humorous with the classic, and he does his humorous things in such a delicately clever way that even the most advanced music lovers are delighted." Burleigh was "the first if not the only Negro to make the 'coon song' a work of genuine art in which the catchy character of the darky melody is enhanced by the most subtle harmonies and elaborate accompaniments." Further, the audience could rest assured that their attendance put them in the company of the best of society: "Entertainments similar to the one in the Institute have been given this season by Mr. Burleigh at the house of Mrs. H. B. Hollins, for the Duke and Duchess of Manchester, at the houses of J. Borden Harriman, William Jay, James Speyer, Hermann Oelrichs, William C. Whitney, and at the Union League Club."[49] Besides the four Ojibway songs harmonized by Burton, this recital of songs featured ten by five of his white composer colleagues. Burleigh sang eight of his own songs and his arrangements of two by J. Rosamond Johnson. His final encore was an audience favorite: "The Creation."

Burton's review said the audience was "large and enthusiastic," partly because Burleigh's performance of the bass solos in *Hiawatha* the previous season had "made a deep impression," so "the mere announcement that he would sing in the Institute was sufficient to bring out the music lovers."[50] This was likely Burton's *Hiawatha* cantata rather than one of the cantatas by Samuel Coleridge-Taylor. The long Yonkers recital, "a notable achievement for the most veteran" singer, expressed nearly "every conceivable phase of human sentiment"—"idyllic love, tragedy, pathos, mystery, religious fervor, parental love, philosophic reflection, rollicking humor." Each of the thirty songs (including encores) appealed "to the heart and understanding, and to the interpretation of these varying sentiments the singer brought an art of astonishing versatility." His voice could be only inadequately described as "rich, mellow, pure," but he seemed "to have a special tone color for every emotion." He achieved the variety in his interpretations "not merely by gradations of volume or changes in tempo, but by tone quality," a skill that placed Burleigh "among the very few great artists of the day." Having heard "substantially all of the famous artists who have been in vogue during the past twenty years," Burton placed Burleigh "solidly among the best of them."[51]

Burton praised Burleigh's own art songs, especially "Thy Heart," with lyrics translated from the Sanskrit by A. V. Williams of Yonkers. But the "real climax" of the recital came in the "Racial" songs, especially the plantation songs, in which Burleigh had "a field in which he can have no rivals." It was the plantation songs that moved the audience "alternately to tears and laughter. The singer played upon the emotions of his hearers with as much skill as he touched the keys of the pianoforte." Burton did not feel Burleigh was limited by playing his own accompaniments, as they were "models of clearness of pianistic expression and perfect adaptability to the occasion." While today it might seem that some of his plantation repertoire pandered to white nostalgia for the antebellum South, Burleigh's deft interpretations could tweak the racial consciousness of his audience. As Burton explained, "The Creation," his final encore, riffed on the contentious color line that ensnared both black and white: "In the stress of bringing order out of chaos, causing light and making human life to appear, there was one thing that 'De Lord done forgot,' and that was to 'turn de black folks white!'" Burton concluded, "In view of the delightful entertainment provided by this representative of the forgotten, it was the general feeling that the Lord's mistake was eminently pardonable."[52] Burleigh, though lighter-skinned than many African Americans, never forgot that he was a representative of his race, and one can imagine the twinkle in his eye as he evoked the audience's laughter.

Two of Burleigh's early performances in the homes of New York's white elite set off ripples that buoyed his later career. Philanthropist Mrs. James Speyer, the wife of an international banker, counted many singers and theater people among her friends. When she invited Burleigh to her home to sing for Ignace Paderewski, the great Polish pianist accompanied him in singing one of his Polish songs. Burleigh sang some of his own songs for Paderewski, eliciting a testimonial that graced Burleigh's 1908 publicity brochure: "The songs you have composed show a genuine and artistic temperament, and it has given me great pleasure to hear them rendered by yourself."[53] It may be that Burleigh's first commercial success, his 1903 song "Jean," was dedicated to Mrs. Speyer in gratitude for this opportunity to sing for Paderewski. And in April 1901 when he sang for French comedian M. Constant Coquelin at the studio of George A. Glaenzer, banjoists Brooks and Denton and violinist David Mannes were among the featured artists.[54] By 1907 Brooks and Denton were Burleigh's publicity agents.

Burleigh's singing in the homes of the Gilded Age elite provided an important source of income. "But," as Lester Walton commented in 1924, "the singing of Burleigh is not enjoyed exclusively by the rich and influential. Many poor people on the east side have been charmed and comforted by the baritone while on one of his missions of good cheer."[55]

* * *

Burleigh clearly enjoyed serving as his own accompanist, but when he sang in New York City or the immediate area, his friend Melville Charlton often accompanied him. Burleigh also sometimes sang in Charlton's organ recitals. In a recital with Charlton at Thorne Memorial Hall in Millbrook, New York, in October 1901, Burleigh led with his favorite Schumann song and followed with four by Euro-American composers, as well as one each by J. Rosamond Johnson and Will Marion Cook and his own arrangement of a plantation song. He ended the program with Italian songwriter Paolo Tosti's "Good Bye."[56]

Burleigh planned to go to London in the summer of 1902; Booker T. Washington had written some of his letters of introduction. But the coronation of King Edward VII made such a tour inadvisable at that time. Instead, he scheduled the first two weeks in August for recitals at Greenacre-on-the-Piscataqua in Eliot, Maine. Greenacre, founded by Sarah J. Farmer, was a school for the study of comparative religions and world unity.[57] No programs have been found documenting Burleigh's recitals at Greenacre, but on his way to join Washington at Waumbek House in Jefferson during his second week at Greenacre, he carried a letter from Miss Farmer introducing him to the manager of the nearby Young's Hotel. She suggested that Burleigh, accompanied by Greenacre's music director, be allowed to sing for the hotel guests "and receive a collection[,] whatever the guests might like to give." This young singer, who had sung for Paderewski and Prince Henry of Russia, had "a most beautiful voice." Like many of Burleigh's listeners who focused more on his "characteristic negro melodies" than on his German lieder or American art songs, Miss Farmer wrote, "I think I am safe in saying that your guests have never heard such an interpreter of negro melodies."[58]

* * *

One of Burleigh's favorite accompanists was pianist R. Augustus Lawson. A native of Shelbyville, Kentucky, Lawson heard Paderewski play while studying for his music degree in piano and theory at Fisk University and vowed to follow in the great Polish pianist's footsteps. Shortly after his graduation in 1895, Lawson played his debut recital in Hartford, Connecticut at the Memnon Club, assisted by Burleigh. Susan Lee Warner, wife of the novelist and publisher Charles Dudley Warner, herself a pianist, was so impressed with Lawson's playing at the recital that she funded a four-year scholarship for him at the Hartford Conservatory.[59] Burleigh returned to Hartford several times to share recitals with Lawson.

A review from December 1902 illustrates the delight their Hartford audience felt at the excellence of Lawson and Burleigh's musicianship and their satisfaction at the role the Memnon Club played in helping Lawson develop his career as a pianist. "Pleasure, surprise, delight were the emotions which found expression in the faces of the audience at Unity Hall last evening." Burleigh and Lawson were all too familiar with the surprise white listeners expressed at hearing professional black musicians demonstrate the level of artistry they had achieved. "The Memnon Club can congratulate itself that it has the credit of bringing before the Hartford public two such finished artists as A. R. Lawson and H. T. Burleigh, the New York baritone. Both are colored men. All who have been connected with the musical education of these two young men congratulate themselves that they should have so developed their talents and ability that they can give such an entirely satisfactory concert as that of last evening."[60]

Lawson opened the diverse program with Beethoven's Variations in C Minor, in which the reviewer praised "the vigor and delicacy of his touch" and the "sympathetic feeling" in his interpretation. Burleigh's first selection, Edward German's robust "My Song Is of the Sturdy North," was "strong, vigorous and forceful, well calculated to display marked characteristics of his voice and method." Burleigh used his "high baritone voice of wide range" in "a dramatic manner, with full expression and without effort." In contrast, William Arms Fisher's "Under the Rose" and Stanley Avery's "Songs of Jenny" were love songs that "gave opportunity for a contrast" and were "an agreeable prelude to Kipling's "patriotic Recessional" in a setting by Reginald DeKoven. For his encore Burleigh sang a piece by H. L. Brainard."[61]

"Pleasure and surprise had impressed the audience and then came the delight," the reviewer reported, "the singing of four 'coon' songs by Mr. Burleigh." Lawson accompanied Burleigh in the classical selections, but Burleigh accompanied himself in the popular songs. "With voice modulated to the most delicate shade, rising at intervals to tones of deepest force," Burleigh sang Noll's "Doan You Cry Ma Honey," J. Rosamond Johnson's "Li'l Gal," and his own "Sleep Li'l Chile" and "You'll Git Dar in de Mornin'," "all to the great delight of his auditors." Encores included two more songs of a similar character, "My Castle on the Nile" and "Under the Bamboo Tree," both songs by Bob Cole and J. Rosamond Johnson. "All were exquisitely rendered in voice and manner."[62] Five years later Burleigh returned to Hartford for another shared recital under the auspices of the Memnon Club, garnering similarly enthusiastic reviews.

Lawson made his career as a piano teacher in Hartford. His studio produced many fine piano students, primarily from the white population. Burleigh followed Lawson's career with great interest, often congratulating him and telling others about his fine interpretation of particular compositions. In a letter dated April 3, 1910, he wrote, "I am sorry you could not do the Ravel in Wash. because I had told them so much about it (Couldn't you have done it as an encore?). However, they enjoyed your playing immensely. My wife's sister [Ray Farley]—(and by-the-way, isn't she an attractive girl) was charmed by your work. She writes me 'Words are inadequate to express my appreciation and admiration of Mr. Lawson's playing. He is certainly a great artist. Mama [Mrs. Rachel Farley] and Alston were just as entranced as I was.' This is great praise old boy, and I know you deserve it. Love to all. Yours, Harry."[63]

* * *

The mutual recognition Burleigh was earning among American song composers can be seen in his frequent use of their songs and in their collaboration with him in various ways. Some composers he may have met through their mutual publishers. Occasionally, Burleigh's accompanist was the composer of songs he sang, or he might appear on a program with one or more of them. In November 1902 Burleigh and M. L. Brainard, whose "Music, When Soft Voices Die" he often sang, performed in an entertainment arranged by the wife of Ethelbert Nevin. Several of Nevin's songs were also in Burleigh's recital repertoire.[64]

On September 9, 1903, he was accompanied in a recital by Willis Alling, one of whose songs he sang on the program. The first group and the first three numbers in the second group were by Beethoven (the "Hymn to Nature" that he often used as a recital opener), Schubert, Schumann, Franz, Grieg, and Sinding, followed by MacDowell's "The Sea" and Percy Atherton's "When All the World Is Young, Lad." The third group, the "characteristic negro melodies," included Alex Rogers's "I'm a Jonah Man," a song Bert Williams made his own; and Johnson and Cole's "Under de Bamboo Tree." The fourth and last group featured Alling's "When Love Is Done," and "Bedelia," by Jean Schwartz. Burleigh closed the recital with Gus Edwards's patriotic "My Own United States."[65]

* * *

Burleigh's friendship with Samuel Coleridge-Taylor was cemented by his singing the baritone solos in the historic performance of *Hiawatha's Wedding Feast* in Washington, D.C., in 1903 and his tours with the composer in 1904, 1906, and 1910. Several of Coleridge-Taylor's songs became standards on Burleigh's recitals: "Beat, Beat, Drums," "The Corn Song," "She Rested by the Broken Brook," and "Unmindful of the Roses." The signed photograph of the composer on the mantel in Burleigh's Bronx apartment titled Burleigh "My true friend and greatest singer of my songs."[66]

Despite his initial hesitation to sing his own songs, in 1903 Burleigh performed twenty-three of them, including his arrangement of "Under the Bamboo Tree." The art songs were "Life," one of his first three published songs; "Mammy's Little Baby," a setting of verse by his wife Louise; "Myrra"; the pathetic plantation ballad "Sleep, Li'l Chile"; "I Lo'e My Jean," an arrangement of the Robert Burns folksong; "Thy Heart"; and "Song ob de Watcher," published in *Everybody's Magazine*; and the unpublished "Look Ahead." Of the rest, four were spirituals and plantation songs from his *Plantation Melodies Old and New*, four were spirituals published much later, and two, "King of Kings" and "Gwine to Ride Up in de Chariot," were never published.

Burleigh appeared in Niagara Falls at a music teacher's association meeting in June 1904 with Americanist composer Arthur Farwell. A reviewer commented that Burleigh's paper "was one of [the most] concise, artistic and understandable of the whole convention." He "played several delightful melodies in which a touch of rare musical quality was heard. Also illustrative were the songs which sung unaccompanied gave an opportunity to hear a voice of natural beauty and excellent training. An attentive and appreciative audience gave hearty applause to the talented lecturer musician who has done so much for the music of his race."[67] This was more than a decade before Burleigh began to publish the solo and choral arrangements of spirituals for which we now remember him.

That same month Burleigh presented a recital in Lake Forest, Illinois, at the home of Lake Forest College President Richard Harlan. The review, written by a professor who was among the friends at President Harlan's home, called it "one of the most remarkable and delightful musical Programs ever given in Lake Forest."

Burleigh sang "German ballads of the classical type; American ballads; Hungarian folksongs; negro melodies, partially written or at least harmonized by himself; Indian chants—all were given with a sympathy and understanding that seemed to make each race group claim as to the manner born." As for the German lieder, "No product of centuries of Teutonic blood and culture could have given a more genuinely classical interpretation to the four or five German ballads which Mr. Burleigh sang."[68] Burleigh was invited to return in October of that year for a full recital at the Moraine Hotel.

Percy Lee Atherton, an American song composer, two of whose songs Burleigh sang in these early years, wrote a letter to the Boston *Transcript* before Burleigh's first full recital in Boston early in 1905. This was a benefit for Fernside, the Working Girls Vacation Home in Princeton, Massachusetts. Atherton wrote that Burleigh "gives something distinctively his own, a reading of the melodious folksongs of his own people in the light of their whole pathetic history. . . . Mr. Burleigh's accompaniments, characterized by invariable judgment and good taste, form an important feature of his work." Again the emphasis was on the songs Burleigh was seen to be uniquely qualified to interpret—the songs of "his own people."[69]

Burleigh returned to Boston in February 1905 for a benefit recital for Atlanta University and the Calhoun Colored School in Calhoun County, Georgia. This was a joint recital with contralto Mattie Allan McAdoo, wife of Orpheus McAdoo, who with his company, the McAdoo Jubilee Singers, had toured Britain, South Africa, and Australia. Potter Hall "was filled to overflowing and many persons had to stand." On this occasion Burleigh's selections were his own or were by Coleridge-Taylor. One of his many encores was Alex Rogers's "Why Adam Sinned," a play on the sentimental nostalgia for the black mammy: the fall of Adam was inevitable; he had no mammy! This never failed to amuse his audience, whether black or white, though likely for somewhat different reasons.[70]

Later in February 1905, Burleigh was a featured soloist on the Pre-Lenten Recital and Assembly at Palm Garden on West Fifty-Second Street, organized and promoted by violinist Walter F. Craig. This was a much anticipated annual event, and reports of the evening noted the social luminaries who filled the boxes. On this occasion Burleigh was joined by organist and pianist Melville Charlton, prima donna soprano E. Azalia Hackley, a harpist, and a reciter. Burleigh sang Tchaikovsky's "Don Juan Serenade" and Coleridge-Taylor's "Beat, Beat, Drums," a setting of a Walt Whitman poem.[71]

It was also in 1905 that the first report appeared of a series of recitals in which Burleigh assisted a younger musician, lending the weight of his prestige and singing several "classic selections with his usual feeling." This March event was a piano recital by Nellie Moore of Richmond Hill on Long Island, a pupil of Ralph Dayton Hausrath of the New York College of Music. In the following years Burleigh appeared several more times with Miss Moore in recitals she gave with her piano students.[72]

In 1906, when Burleigh toured with Samuel Coleridge-Taylor, he sang seven art songs by Coleridge-Taylor in addition to the baritone solos in *The Atonement,* "Quadroon Girl," and two of his solos from *Hiawatha's Wedding Feast.*[73] Six European composers and six American composers filled out his repertoire for the year. From 1906 to 1908, Burleigh used fifteen of his own songs and arrangements, the majority of them spirituals and other African American folksongs or music theater songs. He continued to sing a fairly consistent group of German lieder by Anton Rubinstein, Franz Schubert, Robert Schumann, Robert Franz, and Edvard Grieg, with Beethoven's "Die ehres Gottes aus der Natur" as an opening selection. Italian songwriters Denza and Tosti were represented, along with the Toreador Song from Bizet's opera *Carmen,* the Prologue from Leoncavello's *I Pagliacci,* and "Don Juan's Serenade" by Tchaikovsky. Songs by his American colleagues filled out the varied repertoire. In 1909 and 1910, the documentation is sparse. Except for St. George's Church and an appearance with Walter Damrosch's New York Symphony Orchestra, most of them were in African American venues.

Burleigh could count on a large turnout and rave reviews when he returned to Erie, Pennsylvania. In May 1908, as he and his wife Louise were preparing for their first trip to England, he made "his annual appearance in his home town." He gave a full recital at St. Paul's Parish House; this program doubtless consisted of the repertoire he would perform in London for the royal and noble patrons with whom J. P. Morgan, Booker T. Washington, and others had connected him.[74]

* * *

When the Burleighs arrived in London, his telegram to the New York *Age* assured his friends that they "had a fine trip over. Fooled the fish after all."[75] Their London arrangements were made by U.S. ambassador Whitelaw Reid, who knew Burleigh in New York City. Burleigh sang for King Edward VII and the Queen at the home of the Earl of Londale, at Stafford House for the Duke and Duchess of Sutherland and the Crown Princess of Sweden, the King's niece, who was visiting her parents, the Duke and Duchess of Connaught. The Burleighs attended a tea hosted by the Persian embassy. At a tea at the home of Lady Maude Warrender, Signor F. Paolo Tosti, whose song "Good-Bye" Burleigh sang, was present, as were "many prominent musicians." Pleased with Burleigh's success, Ambassador Reid hosted a tea "at which many distinguished persons were present." It was announced that "arrangements have been completed whereby he is to return to England next summer and appear in a big public recital." Approval by English royalty would ensure a "flattering success" in his public appearances.[76] Burleigh's agents made good use of reports from his London sojourn in their 1908 publicity brochure.[77]

Burleigh and his wife returned to New York on the *Lusitania* in time for him to join Booker T. Washington at Lake Mohonk, New York, on August 11, only four days before a devastating four-day race riot in Springfield, Illinois, the town of Abraham Lincoln in his early adulthood. This catastrophe would lead to The Call, a summons to civil-rights activists, black and white, to form "an organization that

PROGRAM *Song Recital*

By HARRY T. BURLEIGH, (Baritone)
of New York City
AT ST. PAUL'S PARISH HOUSE, ERIE, PA., MAY FOURTEENTH.
UNDER AUSPICES OF BROTHERHOOD OF ST.
ANDREW OF TRINITY EPISCOPAL CHURCH.

GROUP No. 1.

"The Wanderer" (Schmidt) · Schubert
"Serenade"
"Ich Grolle Nicht" (Heine) · Schumann
"Verrath" (Lemcke) · Brahms
"Du Bist Wie Eine Blume" (Heine) · Rubenstein
"Ich Liebe Dich" · Greig
"Don Juan's Serenade" (Tolstoi) · Tschaikowsky

GROUP No. 2.

"De Danville Chariot"
"Josua Fit the Battle ob Jericho"
"Moanin' Dove"
"I Don't Feel No Ways Tired" — Plantation Songs

GROUP No. 3.

"All the World Awakes To-Day" (Boulton) · Ed. G......
"O, For a Day of Spring" (Blunt) · Andrews
"May Morning" (Weatherly) · Denza
"The Years at the Spring" (Browning) · Beach

GROUP No. 4.

"Mighty Lak a Rose" (Stanton) · Nevin
"Li'l Gal" (Dunbar) · Johnson
"A-Singinan' A-Singin" (Stanton) · Neidlinger
"Dreamland" (Louise Burleigh)
"Keep a Good Grip on the Hoe" (Howard Weedon) — Burleigh

GROUP No. 5.

"A Corn Song" (Dunbar)
"Beat, Beat Drums" (Whitman) — Coleridge-Taylor
"The Deserted Plantation" (Dunbar)
"Mandalay" (Kipling) — Damrosch

HUMBLE PRINT, 631 WEST 11TH ST.

Erie program, May 1908. (Courtesy of the Burleigh Family)

would fight for black civil and political rights and an end to racial discrimination." In February 1909 this multiracial group would establish the National Association for the Advancement of Colored People (NAACP), the organization most successful in challenging Washington's leadership, largely because of the efforts of Du Bois and his editing of the NAACP monthly journal, *Crisis*.[78] Among the sixty founders whom Burleigh knew well were Ida B. Wells-Barnett, W. E. B. Du Bois, Oswald Garrison Villard, and Mary Church Terrell.

* * *

As his first decade of recitals drew to a close, the record suggests that a larger proportion of Burleigh's appearances were in African American settings, though the audiences were often mixed. One of the rare occasions when Burleigh ventured south of the Mason-Dixon Line was his July 1910 appearance as guest soloist at Rev. Henry Hugh Proctor's Atlanta Colored Music Festival held at the Municipal Auditorium-Armory, said to be the largest auditorium in the South. When Proctor learned that some of his women parishioners were prepared to "don uniforms and pose as maids in order to hear the performances of the Metropolitan Opera Company" on its annual tour to Atlanta, he formed the Atlanta Colored Music Festival to bring "the best musical talent of the race" to the city. The goals of the festival were to "instill race pride, to present struggling black musicians to the public, and to further appreciation of the black musical heritage."[79] This first festival featured Burleigh, violinist Joseph Douglass, the world-renowned Fisk Jubilee Singers, and a local chorus of one hundred voices.

"Enthusiastic appreciation and approval of the efforts of those responsible for the venture was forthcoming not only for those who composed the audience but from the large gathering of white people who were also present." Burleigh's recital apparently included some art songs that earned him a mixed review: "H. T. Burleigh, of New York, sang well, though one could not help regretting that simpler songs had not been chosen. His own composition, 'You Ask Me If I Love You,' was a very pretty little song."[80] Burleigh returned for the third festival in August 1912, with coloratura soprano Anita Patti Brown, Howard University contralto Lulu Vere Childers, organist Roy W. Tibbs (who later headed the Howard University keyboard department), and the Fisk Jubilee Singers.[81] As the yearly festivals showcased the works of black composers, Burleigh's music was a staple of the repertoire in the later festivals, even in his absence.

* * *

Through the next five years Burleigh continued to be called on to grace many events with his singing, such as Mrs. Charles W. Anderson's Whist Club;[82] the graduation exercises of the Lincoln Hospital Training School for Nurses;[83] a performance of Massenet's oratorio *Mary Magdelene* with Gerald Tyler's Choral Society of Kansas City, Missouri;[84] and an NAACP meeting at which, as Charles W. Anderson reported to Booker T. Washington, the attendance was small but he suspected "that as many of these were drawn thither because Mr. Burleigh was expected to sing as for any other reason."[85] The largely apolitical Burleigh often sang at NAACP events, and his achievements were reported regularly in *Crisis* magazine.

Burleigh was the Elijah of choice for performances of Mendelssohn's oratorio *Elijah* by black choral groups in the eastern part of the country. Among these were the April 1915 performance in Boston, with soprano Minnie Brown, contralto Daisy Tapley, and the young tenor Roland Hayes completing the solo quartet.[86] Not long after, Burleigh and Hayes reprised their roles in an *Elijah* performance at Fisk

University in Nashville. Two years later, at another *Elijah* performance in Boston, Burleigh and Hayes were joined by Cleveland soprano Rachel Walker-Taylor and "the girl contralto," Marian Anderson of Philadelphia.[87]

On occasion, Burleigh shared recitals with his wife Louise, who recited her dialect verse. Despite his reluctance to travel in the South, he sang at Fisk University in Nashville in May 1913, and a year later at Hampton Institute in Hampton, Virginia, where R. Nathaniel Dett was building an outstanding choral program. He continued to give full or shared recitals with his preferred format through the early 1910s. He often shared recitals with other black musicians, such as those already noted, and violinist Clarence Cameron White, pianist Melville Charlton, and organist Roy W. Tibbs and his wife, soprano Lillian Evans (later known as Lillian Evanti). From 1911 his time for concertizing and for teaching individual music students was curtailed by the editorial responsibilities he assumed for his publisher, William Maxwell, and even more by his assuming a position as staff editor in the New York office of the G. Ricordi Music Publishing Company in 1913.

The New York *Age* reported that many of the "anxious music lovers" who thronged a concert of the Music School Settlement for Colored People in October 1914 could not be admitted. For those present, Burleigh's singing "two Negro songs composed by himself" was a "rare treat." Burleigh had his audience with him "from the beginning, because the general personality of this rare genius is wont to impress itself favorably from the first. His resonant baritone gave satisfaction in each of his numbers, particularly, however, in 'Don't Let Dis Harvest Pass,' in which his wonderful lingual facility and exceptional breath control was marked."[88]

Two years later, Lucien H. White, who had replaced Lester A. Walton as music and theater critic for the New York *Age*, expressed regret that Burleigh did not sing his own compositions at a concert in Brooklyn. "Mr. Burleigh sang with consummate art and gave great pleasure to the vast audience." Burleigh's solo appearances in the city were rare at this time, and White acknowledged that his musicianship had carried him beyond racial boundaries. "It is not often that Mr. Burleigh can be secured for a metropolitan appearance of race music lovers, but that is not because of selfishness on his part, or from any lack of interest. It is simply that he has developed as an artist and composer to such a degree that he is unable to respond to all the demands for his artistic services. As a matter of fact, in the world of musical achievement, Burleigh has gone beyond any mere racial lines; it is not essentially the work of a Negro musician, although racial sympathy and affinity has given him a peculiarly attractive ability of expression."[89]

In fact, this "racial sympathy and affinity" were about to take Burleigh's singing career in a new direction. Despite the firm grounding of his recitals in the European art song tradition, his distinctive rendition of songs arising from his African American cultural heritage were always especially relished by his audiences, black and white. With the publication in the 1916–17 season of his first art song arrangements of spirituals and their immediate adoption by many of the famous singers who had been using his secular art songs and ballads, Burleigh's solo appearances now shifted primarily to lecture-recitals on the spirituals.

He continued to appear with younger musicians whom he mentored, and his solos at St. George's Episcopal Church would draw growing numbers to the church on Stuyvesant Square. By 1927 Burleigh had stopped giving solo recitals, with one notable exception. In January 1930 he appeared with one of his protégés, pianist and organist Carlette C. Thomas, at Asbury Methodist Episcopal Church in Tarrytown, New York. This program resembled many of his earlier recitals, beginning with his usual Beethoven, Schubert, and Schumann pieces and his own "Ethiopia Saluting the Colors," followed by six spirituals. But from 1917 on, Burleigh's fame as the pioneer arranger of solo and choral arrangements of spirituals, and his effective singing of spirituals, eclipsed his reputation as a distinguished interpreter of European and American art songs and ballads.[90]

* * *

Two media technologies that were finding their way into the homes of Americans in the first decades of the twentieth century helped to carry Burleigh's voice farther than his personal appearances could reach. In 1919 Burleigh's friend George Broome established the first black recording phonograph recording company, and he prevailed on Burleigh to lead the list. He sang his own arrangement of "Go Down, Moses," most likely to his own accompaniment, for this, his only commercial recording. Tim Brooks in his invaluable account of African Americans in the recording industry describes it as "splendidly recorded."[91] But Burleigh was not pleased with the sound of his recorded voice. It is likely that his usual engaging performance was inhibited by the crude technology of the nascent recording industry.

Later Burleigh was present in the studio when Edward H. Boatner, a younger baritone and a protégé of Roland Hayes, recorded "Sometimes I Feel Like a Motherless Child" and "I Don't Feel No-ways Tired" (both Burleigh arrangements), and it is likely that Burleigh accompanied him. Additional Burleigh recordings were planned, but Burleigh did not sing for Broome's records again. He did accompany at least one other singer, baritone J. C. H. Beaumont, on a 1921 private recording of his sacred song "His Word Is Love." Brooks comments, "Burleigh's accompaniment was fine: the recording revealed him to be an excellent, sensitive accompanist," though the baritone's rendition was "somewhat unsteady." Brooks also reports that Burleigh made "at least one piano roll for QRS in 1921 or 1922," with "short versions" of "I Want to Be Ready" and "Go Down, Moses."[92]

For years, Dr. Harry T. Burleigh II, knowing of his grandfather's discomfort with the Broome recording, told interviewers that there was no recording of Burleigh's voice. Always intent on excellence, Burleigh did not want this recording to be the enduring record of his singing. Ironically for him and sadly for those of us who have come after him, it remains the only aural record we have, as he never consented to another commercial recording. Dr. Burleigh said that he had never heard a recording of his grandfather that sounded like his voice.[93]

There was a recording of his fiftieth anniversary celebration at St. George's that was made available to members of the congregation and the choir, but these 1944 recordings of Burleigh at age seventy-eight would preserve even less of the warmth and richness of the voice for which Burleigh was known.[94] The Broome recordings did not reach a wide audience, but another new technology would soon carry Burleigh's voice and his inimitable interpretations of spirituals throughout the country.

* * *

With the advent of radio in the early 1920s, Burleigh's voice could be heard far beyond his usual New York and eastern United States performance venues. His radio debut was the broadcasting in 1924 of the first Vesper Service of Negro Spirituals in celebration of his thirtieth anniversary as baritone soloist at St. George's. The St. George's 4:00 p.m. vesper services were held from November to May, and in 1925 "St. George's became the first church in the [New York City] area to have its vesper services broadcast weekly over a major network." These broadcasts over the next four years, often featuring solos by Burleigh, became an effective outreach of the congregation, drawing many new parishioners to the church.[95]

Burleigh's radio broadcasts were not confined to those from St. George's Church. In May 1924 the Pittsburgh *Courier* reported that he had broadcast on station WUP from Philadelphia. The *Courier* exulted in the "wonderful sendoff to one of America's greatest composers and singers in the person of our own Harry T. Burleigh. He sang with his usual poise and tenderness, winning the hearts of the thousand radio fans who listened so intently."[96]

Two years later, the *Courier* reported on another broadcast featuring Burleigh and spirituals. The New York City reviewer wrote, "Once in a while something happens in radio music that makes up for many sins. Something exciting happened last night. Out of the flood of jazz—which is invariably good jazz—. . . came the Negro spirituals of Harry T. Burleigh." The New York Edison hour broadcast over WRNY featured the "colored baritone of St. George's" singing five spirituals, "and each one came clearly through the air, perfectly sung," with a "powerful, exotic emotion which is new and enriching to American music." Burleigh explained that in his arrangement of the spiritual "I Stood on the River ob Jerdon," his use of the word "Jerdon" rather than "Jordan" reflected its origin in Virginia.[97] Burleigh appeared again on the Edison Hour in March 1927.[98]

In February 1928, Burleigh, "a specialist in negro spirituals," was featured on WEAF and twenty-nine NBC networked stations with the Hall Johnson Singers, a concert band conducted by Edwin Franko Goldman, and a symphony orchestra conducted by Roderic Graham, on the General Motors Frigidaire family party. The reach of this hour-long broadcast is confirmed by a letter from tenor Charles

W. Hatcher, a member of the Harry T. Burleigh Harmony Club of Fort Worth, Texas. Hatcher said he could have heard the program on several stations, but the clearest of them was "WGN of the Chicago Tribune." Hatcher had invited a large party to hear Burleigh sing. "I haven't words to express how much we enjoyed the entire program," he wrote, "and your numbers were more than delightful to us." One activity of Burleigh Harmony Club was to take spirituals into the schools in the area; the previous week they had sung Burleigh choral arrangements before fourteen hundred high school students.[99]

* * *

Burleigh's lecture-recitals and his singing of spirituals at St. George's Episcopal Church and in other churches made it possible to extend his public singing career well beyond the late 1920s when he ended his solo recitals. By this time Roland Hayes and Paul Robeson were emerging as superlative interpreters of spirituals, and Leopold Stokowski was programming spirituals for Marian Anderson to sing. But even after his voice had lost its early luster, his informative lectures and his moving interpretation of the spirituals continued to make a place for him as the legendary pioneer arranger and singer of Negro spirituals.

10. Music Mentor and Colleague

"He always had time for us"

An important part of Burleigh's legacy is his mentoring of younger musicians, especially singers and composers. The list is long, and among the singers are some of the most distinguished African American recital and musical theater performers of the early to mid-twentieth century. In 1934 a black newspaper commented that Burleigh "was always ready to show a helping hand by way of advice to some struggling artist" such as Abbie Mitchell. "Countless others whom he has helped will rise up and pay honor to him."[1] Burleigh's support and encouragement of younger musicians enabled their careers in very practical ways. He collaborated with instrumentalists as well, and though his standards of excellence were high, he was generous in his support of musicians whose talent and professionalism he respected.

Abbie Mitchell was among the first of the long line of singers Burleigh helped set on the path to success. In her handwritten autobiography Mitchell tells of her first meeting in 1896 with Paul Laurence Dunbar, "tall, black, homely, but with kindly eyes and gentle expression"; her future husband Will Marion Cook, "tall, slender, with great burning eyes, a little mustache, hat on the side of his head"; and Harry T. Burleigh, "not so tall as Cook nor so thin, with gray eyes and brown mustache."[2] She found them on the stage of the Casino Theatre Roof Garden, where they were preparing the hit show *Clorindy, or The Origin of the Cakewalk*. On the advice of Billy English, who had heard her singing on the fire escape outside the apartment she shared with her Aunt Josephine, she had come to audition for a part in the show.[3]

Completely unaware of the fame of the three men, twelve-year-old Abbie was sure of her voice: only the Black Patti (Sissieretta Jones) was her superior. She informed Cook that she did not know any Negro songs: "I'm a nice girl. I only sing classics." When he brushed her off with "You have a glorious voice, plenty of fire, but you can't sing a damn thing!" it was Burleigh who "spoke in a reassuring voice: 'Come here, little girl, sing a scale for me." Mitchell recalled, "As long as I live, I shall never forget that man—the kindly quality of his voice and face." At the time, she could not have guessed how significant a role he was to play in her life. "Was I honored by Mr. Burleigh? No, who was he in my young life?" The audition that began so inauspiciously earned her a place in the *Clorindy* cast at $35 a week; it was not long before she was the leading lady at $75 a week.[4]

After the aborted *Senegambian Carnival* tour, Abbie eventually joined Cook's touring company, bore his first child at barely fourteen years of age, and in October 1900 married "Mr. Cook," as she called him, "in the New York Music Building with Harry T. Burleigh and his wife as witnesses."[5] The friendship with Burleigh was a constant throughout Mitchell's long career as a singer, actress, and teacher.

Together Burleigh and Cook gave young Abbie an immersion course in music. They took her to the Metropolitan Opera House, where a memorial concert for the late Wagnerian conductor Anton Seidl featured nine acts from nine operas sung by the greatest voices of the time: Emma Eames, Jean and Eduard de Reszke, Pol Plançon, Emma Calvé, Marcella Sembrich, Nellie Melba, Lilli Lehman, Ernestine Schumann-Heink, and Louise Homer. "The thrill of that night has lived with me through the years," she wrote. "Several times during different acts my enthusiasm overwhelmed me—I jumped up—remained standing until either Mr. Cook pulled my hands with the whispered [']Sit down Abbie['] or Mr. Burleigh would take my hand and pull me down most quietly. He knew I didn't know the etiquette of behavior at the opera." Chastened and humbled, Abbie began to understand how limited her understanding of singing had been and how much she had to learn.[6]

When Cook's company performed in Europe, he arranged for Mitchell to study with Jean de Reszke in Paris. On their return, she searched for a teacher who could help her with voice placement and other basic vocal issues. Finally she asked Burleigh for help; he was too busy to teach her himself, but he arranged an audition with Emilia Serrano, a distinguished Italian voice teacher.[7] Mitchell's versatility as a singer, moving easily from art songs and opera arias to musical theater to the dramatic stage was enhanced by her lifelong pursuit of vocal excellence, a standard instilled in her by Cook and her mentor, Harry T. Burleigh.

Because of the racial restrictions of the time, Mitchell's primary career was in black musical theater and the dramatic stage, but her gifts as a classical singer were recognized by her colleagues and critics. "She sang recitals at concert halls in Chicago, New York, Atlanta, and San Francisco, winning special praise in those cities, as in Europe, for her [lieder] interpretations. Her programs also highlighted operatic arias in addition to songs by Burleigh, Will Marion Cook, Florence Price, and Margaret Bonds."[8] After hearing Mitchell in a 1923 recital, Burleigh wrote her accompanist, Melville Charlton, a letter that was published in the New York *Age*. He noted her "progress from musical comedy, through the exacting demands of spoken drama on to the dizzy heights of opera." He applauded her programming of eighteen art songs and praised her musicality in terms similar to those in reviews of his own early recitals: She had a "special tone color for every emotion," a capacity he felt she had learned through her study of drama.[9]

Even after their divorce, Mitchell was Cook's preferred singer of many of his songs. When he formed the Afro-American Folk Singers in 1912, she and Burleigh anchored the group. In 1927, Cook wrote a letter to Carl Van Vechten protesting the promotion and exploitation of "unready" African American "poets, musicians and actors" during the Harlem Renaissance. Though their talent was great, they needed to be held to the supreme test of mastery. In his opinion, "only Harry Burleigh, Roland Hayes, and Abbie Mitchell of American Negro [musical] artists" were ready."[10]

In 1926 Mitchell costarred with her Lafayette Theatre colleagues Rose McClendon and Jules Bledsoe in the Pulitzer Prize–winning play *In Abraham's Bosom,* and the following year she appeared with Helen Hayes in *Coquette.* In 1935, in her last major dramatic singing appearance, she created the role of Clara in Gershwin's *Porgy and Bess.* Josephine Harreld Love recalled hearing "that wonderful soaring sound of her voice singing 'Summertime'" from backstage in a Boston pre-Broadway performance.[11]

In his 1929 article "The American Negro in Music," pianist-composer Carl Diton called Mitchell "one of the most gifted interpreters of art songs to be found probably in any race."[12] Forty years later, pianist William Allen Duncan recalled accompanying Mitchell and Lillian Evanti. "Undoubtedly both Abbie Mitchell and Lillian Evanti would have sung at the Metropolitan had the doors been open 30 years ago," he wrote.[13]

* * *

Georgia-born tenor Roland Hayes, another of Burleigh's early protégés, came to Boston with the Fisk Jubilee Singers in 1911. His goal was to become a successful concert tenor. Because Boston, "the Athens of America,"[14] offered opportunities for the best in musical training, when the Fisk ensemble returned to Nashville, he remained behind in Boston to study with Arthur J. Hubbard. Soon he was appearing in recital with Boston's finest black concert artists, among them violinist Clarence Cameron White, pianist Maud Cuney Hare, baritone William R. Richardson, and Howard University keyboard professor Roy W. Tibbs.[15]

In January 1913 Hayes was the featured soloist at Walter F. Craig's Pre-Lenten Recital and Assembly at Palm Garden in New York City, where he sang "Onaway, Awake, Beloved," from Coleridge-Taylor's *Hiawatha's Wedding Feast,* "La Donna è mobile" from Verdi's *Rigoletto,* and Burleigh's "Just Because."[16]

Recitals with prominent African American musicians continued, and in 1914 Booker T. Washington's assistant Emmett J. Scott invited the young tenor to join Burleigh and Washington on a fundraising lecture tour, singing duets with Burleigh. "I was pleased when he chose me to travel in that distinguished company," Hayes wrote. He had not met Dr. Washington, but he knew the story of Burleigh's performance of "Swing Low, Sweet Chariot" for Antonín Dvořák and its brief quotation in Symphony No. 9 in E Minor, "From the New World." Traveling with Burleigh, Hayes "felt close to the inspired sources of our native music.[17]

Hayes recalled that one night after a lecture in Attleboro, Massachusetts, Washington suggested that the three of them "walk part of the way over a dusty back-country road. At every railroad crossing we learned that we had missed the last train to the city. We had walked many a mile, and Dr. Washington was limping, when we tottered into the outskirts of Quincy, where we hoped at last to pick up a haul." With characteristic good humor, Burleigh said, "Take my arm, Dr. Washington. I guess this is one time when you've had enough of the soil."[18]

Burleigh and Hayes were the ideal male vocalists for performances of Mendelssohn's *Elijah*. From 1913 to 1916, they sang these roles in Philadelphia and Boston with soprano Minnie Brown and contralto Daisy Tapley; in Boston with soprano Rachel Walker-Taylor and the contralto Marian Anderson; and at Fisk with soprano Henrietta Lovelace and contralto Mrs. John W. Work II.[19]

The Fisk *Elijah* performance had special personal significance for Hayes. When news of his public appearances with "such great men as Booker T. Washington and Harry Burleigh filtered back" to Fisk in Nashville, Hayes received a letter of congratulations from Jennie Asenath Robinson, the director of the music department at Fisk. Though she had given him a sound musical foundation, Robinson, who "couldn't abide Negro music,"[20] had not been happy with Hayes's preoccupation with the Fisk Jubilee Singers. She often treated him with hostility, and it was only after she had him expelled from the university at the end of his fourth year that he learned it was she who had gathered the funds for his tuition and room and board. Her disapproval troubled him, but he moved on with his studies and recital appearances. Now that he was gaining some distinction as a classical singer, Robinson suggested that it was time for them to "bury the hatchet." He replied that he "would be glad if she would bury hers," but for himself, he had "never carried one."[21] Returning to Fisk in May 1915 to sing the tenor solos in the Mozart Society's performance of *Elijah* was his gesture to prove his desire for reconciliation. The performance was directed by Professor John W. Work, and Burleigh sang the title role.[22]

In his recitals Hayes programmed at least fifteen of Burleigh's art songs, and beginning in 1917 when they were first published, at least fourteen of his art song arrangements of spirituals. On a number of occasions before Hayes went to London in 1920, Burleigh joined him in recital, accompanying his own spiritual arrangements. Hayes continued to sing and to record Burleigh arrangements along with those of other arrangers throughout his career. Eventually he performed his own arrangements reflecting the Georgia oral tradition in which he grew up.[23]

In addition to performing with Hayes, Burleigh referred him to concert managers and event planners with whom he had worked, and he followed Hayes's career closely. Seven years after Burleigh was awarded the prestigious National

Burleigh, Roland Hayes, and Jennie Asenath Robinson at Fisk University, 1915 *Elijah*
performance. (Courtesy of the Burleigh Family)

Association for the Advancement of Colored People's (NAACP's) Spingarn Award,
in 1924, Hayes was awarded the Spingarn in absentia while he was in Europe. The
following April, as Hayes was leaving for another European tour, Walter Damrosch
presented the award on board the Cunard Trans-Atlantic liner *Aquitania*. Burleigh
was among the "enthusiastic audience of about 100 friends" gathered around and
was one of the speakers.[24]

When Hayes returned from Europe in 1925, Burleigh wrote him, welcoming
him back "to your homeland and our people and the race for whom you've done
so much." He hoped that the upcoming season's concerts would "deepen and
strengthen the ties that bind you to our hearts and convert countless new friends
who have not had the privilege of hearing you before." Burleigh knew Hayes "had
lots to tell" him, and he was especially eager to hear about his time in Austria. He
closed the letter "with sincere assurance of [his] abiding friendship."[25]

* * *

Another singer inspired by Burleigh's success was soprano Minnie Brown. "About
a year before I left my home in Spokane, Wash.," she wrote, "I was told by a white
musician . . . of the baritone soloist of St. George's Episcopal Church; a man who
had a wonderful voice, was considered to be one of the finest of New York's artists,
and a Negro! My imagination of musical opportunity, financial returns and ideal
musical association was fired by the achievement of this man and I decided more
firmly to go to New York."[26]

The following year, the Williams and Walker company "fresh from London
triumphs," came to Spokane. In the company were contralto Daisy Tapley and

her husband Green Tapley. "Almost my first question of Mrs. Tapley was 'do you know Mr. Harry T. Burleigh?' and when she answered in the affirmative I became awe-stricken that she knew so well this man whom I had already begun to idealize and idolize." Determined to get to New York City, Brown prevailed on her parents, who were friends of the Tapleys, to allow her to join the Williams and Walker company.[27]

Soon after arriving in New York City, Daisy Tapley took Brown to St. George's "to hear and meet Mr. Burleigh. I soon realized the great respect he had for Mrs. Tapley's musicianship and that they had so much in common—musically and mentally." After questioning Brown about her ambitions, Burleigh invited the two of them to his home on Park Avenue. "Such a glorious afternoon! Mr. Burleigh was at that time reveling in MacDowell, and he and Mrs. Tapley took turns playing MacDowell's compositions. Then he brought forth manuscripts of his own songs; some about to be published; some not finished. We three discussed music, literature and art. And from that day I have enjoyed the privilege of his friendship and have had a keen interest in the development of his wonderful career."[28]

Minnie Brown, Daisy Tapley's lifelong companion after the Tapleys' divorce, often appeared as a soprano soloist with Burleigh. In addition to the *Elijah* performances, Brown, Tapley, Hayes and Burleigh sang in the June 1917 and 1921 songfests at the Lexington Avenue branch of the YWCA in Brooklyn, accompanied by Melville Charlton. In 1918 after Tapley "angrily canceled a recital at the YMCA when she learned that the organization would not allow a mixed-race audience," she and Minnie Brown established a series of monthly educational recitals "featuring the best black concert talents of the day." Among the artists they presented were soprano Florence Cole-Talbert, Roland Hayes, violinist Clarence Cameron White, Burleigh, and lecturer W. E. B. Du Bois. Ultimately the series was a financial loss, but Tapley continued "because of her desire to increase the artistic appreciation of the colored race."[29] Both Brown and Tapley were active in the New York chapter of the National Association of Negro Musicians, founded in 1919. In 1920 Brown was vice president and Tapley was treasurer, and in 1929 Minnie Brown served as president.[30]

In 1924 Daisy Tapley was diagnosed with cancer, and she died on February 5, 1925.[31] Her funeral drew a large crowd of musicians of both races. One newspaper reported, "the procession was a lengthy one, and the streets were choked for some time with cars containing actresses from the Broadway theater districts and colored artists from Harlem." Among the many tributes in the black press, one called her "one of the most prominent colored women in the country [with] a wide reputation as a contralto singer and pianist."[32]

The "much-loved" Minnie Brown continued her active leadership in Harlem's music scene, as a soloist, lecturer on Negro music, organizer of music events and choral director. In 1929 Cleveland Allen, in his column, "Music," in the Chicago *Defender,* commented, "Miss Brown is known throughout the country in musical circles. She has a voice of fine quality and though she has been singing for many years, her voice still retains its power and beautiful tones."[33] The *Defender* again praised her in its review of the 1932 Manhattan Chorus Festival, which she, Burleigh, and Charlotte Wallace Murray organized. "The chorus was directed by Minnie Brown, one of the most able directors in the field of music."[34]

Writing out of her personal friendship with Burleigh, Brown honored him on several occasions with detailed reports of the Vesper Services of Negro Spirituals at St. George's Episcopal Church, held on the anniversaries of his hiring as baritone soloist. In her 1932 article (his thirty-eighth anniversary at St. George's) she wrote, "Through the years he has maintained the position with dignity, adding musical honors to himself, which in turn is an asset to the church where he sings." She described "a group of little Negro girls, the ages ranging seemingly from 7 to 12," who attended the service. "What a pretty sight and what a tribute to Mr. Burleigh and what a privilege for them to see and hear this great artist of their own race." At the service's end, "I filed out into the late afternoon, spiritually refreshed, racially proud and truly grateful to God for having given us such a splendid representative as Harry T. Burleigh."[35]

* * *

Burleigh delighted in the career of contralto Marian Anderson, and he was a trusted advisor in matters relating to her professional life. From her earliest appearances with him in April 1916, he was an ardent supporter and a close friend of her mother and her sister, Alyce. Shortly after Roland Hayes and the young Anderson, then a sophomore in high school, sang the tenor and contralto solos in a performance of Handel's *Messiah* at Musical Fund Hall in Philadelphia, Hayes, Anderson's most important early mentor, recommended her as contralto soloist for the rendition of Mendelssohn's *Elijah* in Boston, with Burleigh as Elijah.[36]

When he could, Burleigh attended her performances. The Philadelphia black music magazine *Master Musician* reviewed a concert featuring Minnie Brown and Marian Anderson accompanied by Melville Charlton: "Philadelphia was honored on this occasion by the presence of 'Our Composer,' Harry T. Burleigh, as it is seldom that Mr. Burleigh finds time to attend affairs of this kind."[37] He sent Anderson letters, notes, and telegrams of congratulations and encouragement such as the telegram at her 1927 departure on the *Ile de France*: "One thousand welcomes to America[,] two thousand regrets for leaving it [,] three thousand hopes for your triumphant return."[38] He was frequently among the friends and family who greeted her at the ship's pier when she returned from her tours abroad.[39]

In 1933, after Caterina Jarboro's debut as *Aïda* at the Hippodrome in New York City, Burleigh wrote Anderson, "I looked for your attractively alluring face but in all that immense audience I fear it was not possible to recognize many individual ones." He wanted to introduce her to Maestro Salmaggi, the conductor, who had "displayed such unusual and encouraging broadmindedness in hearing and employing our singers." He suggested that Frank LaForge, with whom she was studying, might arrange an audition. "There is no telling where this all may lead to. I have visions of a Negro Grand Opera Company under Maestro Salmaggi's Direction. Wouldn't that be a novelty and an achievement!"[40] Neither Anderson's opera career nor Burleigh's Negro Grand Opera Company were realized, but Burleigh stood by her with professional advice.

When the famed impresario Sol Hurok assumed Anderson's management after her 1934 success in Paris, he engaged her for an American tour in the 1935–36 season. Her accompanist in the United States had been African American pianist William (Billy) King, a Philadelphia native. During her several years' sojourn in Europe, her Scandinavian audiences had been especially responsive, and beginning in 1930 she was accompanied by Finnish pianist Kosti Vehanen. Hurok intended to engage Vehanen to accompany her American tour. Billy King mounted a strong offense, writing to a number of prominent black musicians—Burleigh and Atlanta string professor Kemper Harreld among them—arguing his case and asking help to persuade Anderson to continue working with him. King was joined in this effort by Anderson's mother, who wrote her that because of the racial prejudice in the United States, appearing with a white accompanist would hinder her success. Further, in an appeal to her characteristic modesty and sensitivity to her African American community, "some of our group might think that [she] had grown too big."[41]

Greatly troubled, Anderson wrote Burleigh a long letter (first painstakingly crafting a rough draft) describing the situation in detail: "Please forgive me for writing the kind of letter this must be, but I am in a rather difficult situation . . . and know of no-one whose opinion I value as yours." She wanted "above all things to please" her mother. But Hurok was "waiting for the success of the New York recital to determine how big the other engagements should be," and it was critical that she take no "unnecessary chances." She knew that Billy King was "very much upset," but continued, "I am not the least bit interested in presenting Kosti Vehanen nor Marian Anderson as individuals but rather that we should be a medium thru which the composer's messages are best transmitted." She also knew that she would do her best singing with Vehanen's accompaniment.[42]

Burleigh's response first spoke of his joy at her European success: "Every time I heard of you—London, Paris, Vienna, and then Salzburg—I got an extra thrill, deeper and more ecstatic." The review of her Vienna concerts was written by Herbie Peyser, his good friend. "I have the greatest regard for his critical ability. When he used the term 'A Black Lilli Lehman' in referring to you, it was the highest praise for I doubt if there has ever been a greater artist than she." Another friend wrote him that her Salzburg recital "was the best one of the season. . . . It was a superlative achievement, and she remains unspoiled by it all." There was no need to worry that she "had grown too big." Burleigh continued, "I just want you to know that I am prouder of you than ever,—and you know you were always very highly prized by me. It is not a recent development."[43]

Billy King had written him, but as always, excellence was Burleigh's primary concern. "Billy doesn't know that I heartily approve of Hurok's plans. I never felt that King was a good accompanist. He lacked poetry and imagination and technique too; and now, since you have such an extended repertoire he would be quite impossible."[44] Soon the black newspapers were commenting on the controversy, frankly quoting Burleigh's lack of confidence in King's ability as Anderson's accompanist.

In her letter, Anderson asked whether Burleigh had some new spiritual arrangements for her to use. He did not respond to her directly, but closed his letter saying, "Have a 'dandy' new song for you too. Langston Hughes' words. '*Lovely, dark and lonely one.* Thought of you and your voice when I wrote it." This was Burleigh's last published art song and one of the most enduring.[45]

The Baltimore *Afro-American* reported that Anderson had received "numerous letters" from friends and family, "advising her not to bring a white accompanist." The reporter telephoned Burleigh, who "insisted that no issue should be made of the matter," that "the point of view to be taken was that of racial co-operation in the music world." Vehanen "accompanied her so perfectly" that it was only "justice to her that he play for her American tour. He deplored efforts to make the race subject an issue and said it should be ignored."[46]

The Atlanta *Daily World* commented that "If Margaret Matzenauer, great Russian contralto, should bring a Negro accompanist to do her playing and white people objected, the Negro would send up a loud howl and perhaps attempt to secure the N.A.A.C.P., to take up the fight." The article concluded, "White and colored concert-goers in southern cities where she may appear will bring about no unpleasant or provocative situations. Who will get busy and bring these two artists to Atlanta?"[47]

After their exchange of letters, Anderson expected Burleigh to greet her after her Town Hall recital in New York City. When she did not see him, she sent a note: "Disappointed not to have spoken with you after recital." She wondered whether he could meet her in Philadelphia, as she planned to sing a group of his spiritual arrangements in a Carnegie Hall recital and wanted him to accompany her.[48]

Burleigh's response shows a characteristic emotional response to beauty in music and the depth of his personal connection with Anderson:

Marian dear:—I am very pleased to know that you noticed my absence from the hosts that crowded to greet you after your Town Hall concert.

The truth is—my beautiful Marian—that your great art had moved me so deeply that I was loathe to risk losing any of the exaltation I felt by mingling in the general company of congratulating devotees.

Had I gone back stage I should no doubt have fallen on my knees before you or (preferably) on your neck in adoration of your transcendent art.

Sincerely—you gave us all a clear, generous look into your great soul and I, for one, found the beautiful things that I've always believed existed there; this which yielded not only aesthetic pleasure of the deepest sort, but a measure of incredulous delight, that linger in my memory like the strains of beautiful music.—HTB[49]

The following year Burleigh again supported Anderson in insisting on the need for a professional singer to be treated professionally. This time it was not Sol Hurok but "an ambitious trio of newspaper folk" from Harlem who "decided they could cash in on" her "good fortune and fame." They would present her in concert at the Salem Church on Seventh Avenue and the money would roll in. They agreed to pay Anderson $300 (she had been receiving $3,000), and "the two young men and girl involved, strove diligently to make the concert a success. They put out tickets to well meaning friends—to pay for later—and they advertised as well as their limited means permitted." On the day of the concert Anderson and her accompanist "arrived on time and as usual, retired to the anteroom to await her formal appearance." But the crowd did not appear and "the sponsors didn't have the guaranteed $300, nothing like it, nor could they scrape it up." Bolstered by "her good friend and advisor, Harry T. Burleigh," Anderson declined to sing without the promised fee. Burleigh had had similar experiences, and as he explained, "Once you start singing on promises to pay, you'll always be singing on promises." A contract was a contract; no money, no concert. Burleigh's was "the voice of experience and it paid off for Miss Anderson although that trio of young folk found it rather embarrassing to be seen around Harlem afterward."[50]

Like many of Burleigh's friends, Anderson visited St. George's Church on occasion. Choir member Dorothy Drummond Hauser recalled, "To me, the most outstanding service was the day Marian Anderson and Bill (Bojangles) Robinson came out to hear us sing 'Swing Low, Sweet Chariot.' Never shall I forget that moment, during the processional, while singing the magnificent hymn, 'Be Still My Soul,' when, from her place in the congregation, Miss Anderson's glorious molten-rich voice rolled out in waves of glory. Never had music poured more joyously from every throat, so inspired was each by the majesty of this gifted woman."[51]

Marian Anderson showed her esteem for her mentor in 1939 when she, like Burleigh and Roland Hayes before her, was awarded the NAACP's Spingarn medal. The award was presented by Eleanor Roosevelt, who several months earlier, when the Daughters of the American Revolution prevented Anderson from singing at Constitution Hall in Washington, D.C., arranged for her to sing on the steps of the Lincoln Memorial. Reporting on the climax of the NAACP convention, the Baltimore *Afro-American* carried a full-page photo of the crowd of 5,000, with an inset of Burleigh beside Miss Anderson. It was an emotion-charged moment. At her request, Burleigh "led the audience in singing 'We Are Climbing Jacob's Ladder.' Tears streamed as he waved to crowds." The ceremony was broadcast nationally; on the platform with them were Mary McLeod Bethune, NAACP secretary Walter White, Daisy Lampkin, and Mrs. Roosevelt.[52]

In 1942 Marian Anderson established her foundation to support the training of talented young singers. Burleigh, her later accompanist Franz Rupp, and Mary Saunders Patterson, her first teacher, were the primary judges who heard the auditions and chose the scholarship winners. Among the first winners were Camilla

Williams, "one of the first black singers to appear with the New York City Opera," and Mattiwilda Dobbs, who soon after Anderson and baritone Robert McFerrin broke the color bar at the Metropolitan Opera, sang the role of Gilda in Verdi's *Rigoletto*.[53]

Anderson sang and recorded many of Burleigh's spiritual arrangements. Few of his art songs appear on her programs, though "The Grey Wolf" and "In the Wood of Finvara," as well as the roustabout song "Oh! Rock Me, Julie," were in her repertoire.[54] There is no evidence that she sang "Lovely Dark and Lonely One," which Burleigh wrote with Anderson's voice in mind. Langston Hughes's lyrics speak Burleigh's encouragement that she "beat with tireless hands" at the walls of prejudice:

> Lovely dark and lonely one,
> Bear your bosom to the golden sun.
> Do not be afraid of light,
> You who are the child of right.
>
> Open wide your arms to life,
> Whirl in the wind of pain and strife.
> Face the wall with the dark closed gate.
> Beat with tireless hands—
> And wait.[55]

There is no known recording of Marian Anderson singing this song. Anderson, who always preferred to confront discrimination with quiet dignity,[56] may have found this too aggressive a statement, but it is a tribute to the singer whose regal bearing, rich, distinctive voice and consummate artistry fulfilled Burleigh's ideal of the musical artist, while her life and career indelibly affected the course and climate of race relations in America.

* * *

The third of the triumvirate of black singers—Roland Hayes, Marian Anderson, and Paul Robeson—to earn worldwide recognition in the early to mid-twentieth century was the extravagantly gifted bass-baritone Paul Robeson. As his career developed, the All-American football player, attorney, stage and film actor, civil-rights and labor activist and singer, moved easily across cultures, immersing himself in the language and culture of the peoples he met, ultimately focusing his uniquely memorable singing voice and his charismatic personal appearances on building connections with ordinary working people and confronting injustice wherever he found it.

Burleigh was an early mentor, coaching and advising Robeson in his presentation of Negro spirituals and urging him to prepare for a classical career as a singer of art songs. Robeson shared Burleigh's commitment to preserving and disseminating Negro spirituals and to helping both black and white audiences to understand their

intrinsic value as the folk music of a people and as America's folk music. Growing
up in New Jersey, where his father pastored a black congregation, most of whose
members were from the South, he knew the sound, the rhythm, and the deep
meaning of these songs. Robeson respected Burleigh's role in bringing spirituals to
the concert stage as solo songs and choral songs, arranged as art music. Burleigh
had brought the spirituals to a wider public, but Robeson felt his role was to sing
them in a presentation closer to the oral tradition he knew rather than through
the filter of the European art song.[57]

Like Burleigh, Robeson was criticized by the black elite for singing spirituals
to white audiences; Robeson found that many still did not understand their value
as art. Robeson's son writes: "It seemed as if Negro spirituals were not in vogue
among either the black or white elites. However, when he performed professionally
in black churches and at benefits for civil rights organizations such as the NAACP,
he liked to sing the familiar songs from his childhood. Spirituals were at the core
of the program."[58]

Burleigh coached Robeson in his preparation for his earliest solo recitals. Advised
by Burleigh, Robeson gave "small concerts throughout most of 1924 with a regular accompanist named Hooper, who was apparently a friend of Burleigh's." Paul
Robeson Jr.'s comment suggests that by this time Burleigh had come to expect his
protégés to take his advice without question: "A baritone, Burleigh had long enjoyed
being in the Manhattan spotlight and could help his protégé gain respect." Though
these concerts "elevated Paul's visibility," it was ultimately his performance as Rufus
Jones in Eugene O'Neill's play *The Emperor Jones* that interested a Boston socialite,
Mrs. Guy Currier, "in presenting Paul in concert at the Copley Plaza in Boston"
on November 1, 1924. As before, Burleigh coached him for this "first appearance
as a professional concert-hall soloist."[59] It was a decisive experience for Robeson.

Burleigh had coached him well, he had prepared, the house was packed, the
applause was generous, and the critics were kind. "Paul had confirmed that he had a
potential concert career." However, Robeson was not satisfied with his performance.
"The decidedly classical European concert style, favored by Burleigh and used so
successfully by Roland Hayes, didn't suit Paul. Its formal constraints and vocal style
inhibited the natural warmth of his delivery and attenuated the unique richness of
his tones. He decided to look for a voice coach who understood his unconventional
needs, and to seek out an accompanist-arranger who was steeped in the purity
of the original slave songs from the South. He continued to work diligently with
Hooper, but after that performance he distanced himself from Burleigh."[60]

Robeson first met the man who would be his accompanist in London at the
home of John Payne, a singer who made his home there after appearing with a
popular male quartet.[61] Lawrence Brown, then accompanying Roland Hayes, was
also staying with Payne, and each was impressed with the other: Brown with the
beauty of Robeson's voice, and Robeson "with Brown's authentic arrangements of
Negro spirituals." Three years later, when he was no longer working with Roland

Hayes, Brown returned to New York. Walking in Harlem one day, he met Robeson. Brown had sent Robeson a volume of his spiritual arrangements that he liked, and he wanted Brown's accompaniment. Robeson invited Brown to go with him to dinner with Jimmy Lightfoot (his director in Eugene O'Neill's plays), in Greenwich Village. When Robeson sang "Ev'ry Time I Feel the Spirit" for Lightfoot, Brown joined in spontaneously, harmonizing with Robeson's voice. Excited by their collaboration, Lightfoot exclaimed, "Why don't you fellows give a concert?" And that, Brown explained, is how the historic April 19, 1925, Greenwich Village recital, the first public recital composed entirely of Negro spirituals and secular folksongs, came about.[62]

This time it was not Burleigh who coached Robeson; it was Lawrence Brown, a native of Jacksonville, Florida, who like Robeson knew spirituals as a deeply personal heritage. Within a week a concert date was announced, "Larry Brown made up a program and coached Robeson 'as if,' in Paul's words, 'we were children he was teaching' (and, he added, 'we slept like children all week, not to catch a cold')." In the three weeks before the concert white critic Carl Van Vechten and Walter White of the NAACP took on the publicity, and the day before the recital, 'Heywood Broun devoted his column in the New York *World* to touting it."[63]

The tickets were sold out the day before the recital, "and at 8:15, when the theatre doors opened, the lobby, sidewalk and vicinity were packed" with an elite audience of both races, and "hundreds were turned away." Despite the performers' nervousness, they were greeted with thunderous applause when they appeared and after every song, and they "got curtain call after call."[64]

The New York *Times* critic "raved. The Negro songs, he said, 'voiced the sorrow and hopes of a people,' and Paul's spirituals had the ring of the revivalist, they hold in them a world of religious experience; it is this cry from the depths, this universal humanism, that touches the heart.'" For Paul, a note from one of his Sigma Theta Sigma fraternity brothers meant more than the public triumph. "Frankly," it read, "I didn't know that an evening of Spirituals could afford so much pleasure. Unfortunately, I am in the same position with the majority of Northern Negroes educated in these schools. I do not know my own music." He found the performance "wonderful, exhilarating, altogether ineffable." Perhaps even more than his white audiences, Robeson wanted to reach the privileged African Americans who refused to claim the music of their ancestral heritage, and this note assured him that he was on the right path.[65]

Each voice in its own way—Burleigh's voice, Roland Hayes's voice, and Marian Anderson's voice—reached its respective audience of varied backgrounds and won many to a greater understanding and appreciation of the spirituals. Robeson's voice would reach even farther, to a broadly international audience and well beyond the middle- and upper-class elite who formed the typical classical concert audience.

Studying Robeson's recital repertoire, one sees that Burleigh's arrangements were nearly always represented, especially at the beginning of the program. The program

does not reveal that along with completing the program with his own arrangements, Lawrence Brown took the liberty of modifying Burleigh's arrangements to
reflect his and Robeson's sense of something "more authentic."[66] When Burleigh,
music critics, and some of his audiences, including middle-class and upper-class
blacks, "urged him to sing the classical concert repertoire," as did Roland Hayes
and Marian Anderson, he replied that "they didn't suit his culture, his voice, or his
musical preferences."[67]

Despite his divergence with Burleigh on the presentation and accompaniment
of the spirituals and his resistance to any pressure to focus on standard European
art song repertoire, his public statements about the importance of the spirituals,
their artistic, spiritual and cultural value, were very similar to Burleigh's. Negro
music, Robeson said, "portrays the hopes of our people who faced the hardships
of slavery. They suffered. They fled to God through their songs. They sang to forget
their chains and misery. Even in darkness they looked to their songs to work out
their destiny and carve their way to the promised land." Despite their suffering,
"There is no expression of hate or revenge in their music. That a race which had
suffered and toiled as the Negro had did not express bitterness but expressed love
is strong evidence of the influence of Christianity." Throughout his multifaceted
career, Robeson asserted the invaluable worth of the slave songs. "I am not ashamed
of the Spirituals. They represent the soul of my people. White and colored people
react alike to the song. Differences are forgotten and prejudices vanish when mixed
audiences meet at the concerts. Humanity is helped and lifted to higher levels."[68]

As his career as a recitalist specializing in Negro spirituals and the folksongs of
people of other nations progressed, Robeson did not rely on Burleigh as a vocal
coach. But he took Burleigh's name and his (somewhat modified) spiritual arrangements wherever he sang. In October 1927 Robeson and Brown "charmed Paris with
the first-ever European concert made up entirely of Negro spirituals and folk song."
In the standing-room-only audience was Roland Hayes, who had captured Paris a
few years earlier, and blues singer Alberta Hunter. Robeson was pleased to share
news of his European success with his former mentor. In March 1929 he wrote
Burleigh from London describing "the great honor done him by members of the
British law-making bodies, when they dined him last week in the house of parliament." Members of Parliament and their families were "almost steady patrons" of
the musical *Show Boat,* in which Robeson starred. They showed their respect by
giving the Robesons a testimonial dinner, "preceded by all the highest and most
respectful preliminaries usually given royalty on such occasions."[69]

Throughout his career, Robeson sang and recorded a significant number of
Burleigh's spiritual arrangements, and he honored Burleigh publicly on many occa-
sions. Like Burleigh, he believed that at least in the short term, "artistic recogni-
tion was . . . the most effective means of advancing the civil rights cause."[70] When
Robeson was awarded the Spingarn Medal in October 1945, Burleigh and Marian
Anderson were among those at the speaker's table. Robeson paid tribute to Burleigh

and other previous recipients of the award, saying, "I am proud to be part of the work they represent."[71]

Two years after Burleigh's death, Robeson again paid him tribute. In a speech at the opening session of the Conference for Equal Rights for Negroes in the Arts, Sciences, and Professions, Robeson said, "I think of Larry Brown who went abroad, heard Moussorgsky, heard the great folk music of other lands and dedicated himself, as did Harry Burleigh before him, to showing that this was a great music, not just 'plantation songs.'"[72]

Despite their differences in approach, each was representative of his or her own time in the process of bringing African American music to the attention and greater understanding of the public, both in their own communities and in the larger world. Burleigh's pioneering work freed Paul Robeson and Lawrence Brown to reclaim the spirituals in versions closer to their folk origins, even while they presented them in solo arrangements on the classic European concert stage rather than in the improvisational, communal, congregational tradition in which they were created.

* * *

Another of the younger musicians Burleigh affirmed was contralto Lulu Vere Childers. As a student at Oberlin Conservatory of Music, she appeared as alto soloist in their 1895 rendition of Handel's *Messiah,* the only African American in the solo quartet and the chorus. Ten years later, when Childers was choral director at Knoxville College, she directed a performance of Mendelssohn's *Elijah,* with Burleigh as Elijah. Burleigh's praise of her work with the chorus was detailed and specific: "The work of the chorus under Miss Childers' skillful direction was magnificent from start to finish. Their tone, shading, phrasing, precision and response to every movement of the director's baton was a lesson in choral singing. Their climaxes were well approached and often thrilling." Childers could not be praised too much "for the really beautiful results she has by patient, diligent and resourceful efforts been able to accomplish in teaching a practically amateur chorus the most dramatic and difficult of all the older oratorios, and possibly no greater praise can be given her than to say that the work of the chorus reflected great credit upon her."[73]

Childers later assumed the position of choral director at Howard University and earned great respect for her gifts as conductor, contralto soloist, and vocal teacher. When Burleigh was a featured artist at the third annual music festival of the Atlanta Colored Music Festival Association in 1912, Childers was also featured as director of the choral performances, contributing "much to the success of the festival."[74] In his 1912 article "The American Negro in Music," former president of the National Association of Negro Musicians Carl Diton listed Childers with pianists R. Augustus Lawson and Roy Tibbs as outstanding African American music teachers.[75]

* * *

In the 1920s soprano Ella Belle Davis and her pianist sister Marie of New Rochelle, New York, gave a number of recitals featuring art songs and spiritual arrangements by Burleigh. Ella Belle consulted with Burleigh on her choice of a voice teacher and he met with her to advise her on her choice of recital repertoire. On several occasions Burleigh appeared with her and her sister in recital. In November 1927 he shared a recital with them, accompanying himself singing ten spirituals and speaking eloquently about them.[76]

When, in preparation for a 1930 recital, she sent the list of songs she planned to sing, Burleigh offered suggestions on the choice of songs and the organization of the program. He noted that on a previous recital she had grouped songs "that were unrelated in style." This, he wrote, "is not the way to get variety." He enclosed a program by German soprano Frieda Hempel to show the importance of keeping "the various styles of composition in their chronological order" and referred to Marian Anderson's programming as another example.

Burleigh also counseled Davis against exaggerated claims in her publicity: "I hope the word 'Grand' will be eliminated from the printed program. It is old style and over-worked." He cautioned her against misleading advertising. "I hope the arrangement will not lead people to imagine that I am giving the recital whereas I am only speaking at the end." The program "ought to read:—

Ella Bell Davis

soprano

Marie P. Davis

pianiste

assisted by

Harry T. Burleigh

in a short lecture on

Negro Folk Songs

"That," he concluded, "is honest and informing," and wished her and her sister "Good luck."[77]

Marie Davis accompanied her sister in her solo appearances with the 300-voice Westchester Negro Singers at the annual Westchester Music Festival in 1934 and 1935, with Burleigh's son Alston and Sandor Harmati conducting, respectively. In 1935 the junior Burleigh Glee Club, "trained and conducted by Ella Belle Davis," also participated. Ella Belle Davis went on to become a leading black concert singer in the 1940s, appearing in New York City's Town Hall in 1942. "In 1946 she made her operatic debut as Aida at the Opera Nacionale in Mexico City, and she sang the role again in 1949 at La Scala in Milan, Italy. In 1947 the League of Composers singled Davis out as the outstanding American singer of the 1946–1947 season and commissioned Lukas Foss to write a work especially for her. The composition, a cantata *The Song of Songs,* was performed by the Boston Symphony with Davis as soloist."[78]

* * *

Juilliard-trained soprano Ruby Elzy was among the singers Burleigh encouraged who might have gone on to a distinguished solo career had she lived beyond her thirties. In 1932 Elzy wrote friends that she had sung for Burleigh, "who was quite effusive in his praise for my work."[79] When she gave a full recital shortly before her graduation from Juilliard, Elzy was awarded the Certificate of Maturity, "a special diploma conferred only to those Juilliard students deemed ready to embark on a professional career." A few days later, she and several other African American Juilliard students, including soprano Anne Brown and pianist Josephine Harreld, presented a program entitled "The Negro in Music." Burleigh was "the presiding host," and Ruby sang "Cabin Boy" and "City Called Heaven." As a finale, a trio composed of Elzy Ruby, Anne Wiggins Brown, and mezzo soprano Carmen Shepperd sang Burleigh's arrangements of "Were You There?" and "Sinner, Please Doan Let Dis Harves' Pass." Both Elzy and Brown joined the brief run of the Aeolian Opera Company, founded by Peter Creatore in an effort "to prove to white audiences and critics that blacks had the voices to sing the great works of opera."[80]

Elzy went on to work with the Rosamond Johnson Choir in DuBose Heyward's film production of *The Emperor Jones* (1933), playing the role of Brutus Jones's girlfriend Dolly. When Charles L. Marshall founded the Manhattan Artists Bureau in 1937, Elzy and Burleigh were among the first singers to join his agency. Elzy starred in Gershwin's *Porgy and Bess* and Hall Johnson's *Run, Little Chillun,* and played unbilled minor roles in several films and the lead in a 1939 revival of Noble Sissle and Eubie Blake's musical revue *Shuffle Along.*[81] In the last year of her life Elzy toured with *Porgy and Bess,* supporting soprano Etta Moten as Bess. But her promising career was cut short on June 26, 1943, when after surgery at Parkside Hospital in Detroit, Michigan, to remove a benign tumor, she died at the age of thirty-five.[82]

* * *

Burleigh was especially proud of organist Carlette Thomas, his student in theory and harmony. She had three years of study at the Chautauqua School of Music and a course in choir training with Hugh Ross. Presenting Burleigh in his last full solo recital in 1930 was doubtless an expression of appreciation for his support.

At the reception following a 1932 organ recital by Dr. Melville Charlton at St. Philip's Episcopal Church in Harlem, Burleigh sang three spirituals and Thomas played "a beautiful interpretation" of the first movement of Schumann's Sonata in G minor. Two years later in an interview at Oak Bluffs where he spent his summers, Burleigh spoke enthusiastically of Thomas, who had received a "hard to earn" fellowship in the American Guild of Organists.[83] It was likely Burleigh's recommendation that earned her a place on the American Bible Society Day program at the 1939 New York World's Fair, where she played an organ prelude, "Fantasy on a Welsh Tune" by T. Tertius Noble (with whom she had studied organ, counterpoint, and orchestration), and for the postlude, the Finale from Charles-Marie Widor's Second Symphony.[84] In April 1943, Burleigh was the featured soloist with Thomas

at a concert at Ebenezer Baptist Church in New Brunswick, New Jersey. By this
time Thomas was a composer of choral works and had served as assistant director
and organist for the choirs of Grace Episcopal Church in the Bronx.[85]

Burleigh's standards were high, but his generosity toward musicians who proved
themselves serious and gifted was lavish. In 1944 Nora Douglas Holt wrote, "His
moments of joy are the hours spent with young artists who merit encouragement,
and he pulls no punches in his criticisms." She went with him to a church where
Carlette Thomas was preparing for a recital. "After noting the tempo, phrasing,
gradations, he made suggestions and we left." He commented, "Nora, that young
woman is a fine organist, and above all, she has musicianship."[86]

An indication of the respect Burleigh earned among choir directors and vocal
musicians is that John Finley Williamson, director of the Westminster Choir,
engaged Burleigh to coach tenor L. D. Higgins of his choir "to study voice culture
for two months," in preparation for their 1929 European tour.[87] Many of Burleigh's
mentees never won fame but if they were serious artists, he appeared in recitals
with them, knowing that his presence would encourage them and validate their
work for their audiences.

* * *

Young composers as well as singers sought Burleigh's advice in their work. Composer, arranger, and choral director Jester Hairston spoke warmly of Burleigh's
support of younger composers. He and others would stop in to see Burleigh in his
office at the G. Ricordi Music Publishing Company, bringing their compositions
with them for his suggestions. "He always had time for us," Hairston reported.[88]
Indeed, he was happy to "give them the benefit of his own rich experience. And
usually they went away with textbooks or music that he had paid for out of his
own pocket."[89]

Though supportive, Burleigh was very direct in his critiques, as in a March 1921
letter to William L. Dawson, just completing his studies at Tuskegee Institute. Dawson had sent Burleigh a song for his comments, and Burleigh found "many weak
spots" in the composition. In very specific detail, Burleigh criticized his "frequent
use of 6/4 chords (sometimes on the first beat of the measure) and the doubling of
3rds and 7ths." As "six-four chords always suggest a cadence," Dawson's use of them
in the middle of the song indicated "the hand of an amateur in the use of harmony."
Also, in the second part of the song, each verse was "*two bars short* for correct form
and the accent of the words." Burleigh noted "the alteration necessary to correct
this fault," hoping Dawson would "see the benefit of it." Ultimately, the song as
submitted to Burleigh had "no commercial value," though it had "many effective
points." Burleigh signed his letter "with kindest regards and all good wishes."[90]

Dawson, who went on to serious study in composition and orchestration in
Topeka and Kansas City, Kansas, and a master's in composition at the American
Conservatory of Music in Chicago, clearly took Burleigh's criticism to heart. Ten

years later he organized the School of Music at his alma mater Tuskegee Institute (now University), building a choral program at Tuskegee that earned international renown and compiling a catalog of choral arrangements of spirituals that are regarded among the best. Dawson's *Negro Folk Symphony* was premiered by the Philadelphia Orchestra under the direction of Leopold Stokowski in November 1934. In January 1933, shortly after Dawson completed the symphony, Burleigh autographed his 1931 photo to "W. L. Dawson as an evidence of the regard and esteem of his friend HTBurleigh."[91] Burleigh attended the premiere of the *Negro Folk Symphony,* and a letter to Dawson from Mrs. James A. Myers of Fisk University reported, "We are prouder of you than you can ever know. I could hardly stay in my seat and Harry Burleigh couldn't and didn't."[92]

* * *

Burleigh was as supportive of women composers such as Undine Smith Moore, Florence Price, and Margaret Bonds as he was of his male composer colleagues. In Moore's personal papers, in an envelope marked "Very Valuable," is a manuscript of her song "Once Again," in what may be Burleigh's hand. Except for a Christmas greeting from her in the Burleigh papers, no other documentary evidence has been found, but these tidbits indicate a warm personal connection.[93]

Margaret Bonds wrote warmly of the influence of Burleigh's music on her art song compositions. In her late teens she worked closely with Abbie Mitchell, who introduced her to Burleigh's "Ethiopia Saluting the Colors" and the *Saracen Songs.* "Ethiopia" especially impressed her. "I myself had never suffered any feelings of inferiority because I am a Negro, and I had always felt a strong identification with Africa, but now here was a poem which said so many different things I had known and was not able to verbally express." Burleigh's "Ethiopia Saluting the Colors" became Margaret Bonds's "The Negro Speaks of Rivers." She reported that "In my teens and highly impressionable, I began unconsciously to copy Harry T. Burleigh." She later studied with Florence Price and William Dawson, both of whom Burleigh mentored, so the lineage of influence continued.[94]

Florence Price's biographer Rae Linda Brown believes Burleigh met Price in Chicago at the August 25, 1934, Century of Progress Exhibition "presented by the Negroes of America at Soldier Field."[95] These pageants "were like plays with pre-composed unrelated music," usually featuring Chicago's African American artists, but the 1934 pageant brought "many of the most prominent black composers and performers in all of America." It was conceived as a retrospective of the transformation of the African to the African American. Burleigh presented an "Ode to Ethiopia," most likely an orchestration of his 1915 song "Ethiopia Saluting the Colors." Price's Piano Concerto in One Movement followed, possibly with Price conducting.[96]

In addition to her piano and orchestral compositions, Price wrote more than seventy art songs and fourteen spiritual arrangements, as well as thirteen popular

or commercial songs.[97] Burleigh was very supportive of Price's career, both by singing her songs and by attempting to have his publisher issue some of them. When
she sent him several songs in 1943, he wrote her warmly but with regret: "My dear
Mrs. Price—Thank you so much for sending me your delightful songs; and the
beautiful photograph—which I shall cherish *always*. I looked over the songs with
genuine interest," and presented them to the editors at G. Ricordi, knowing "that
they would give your songs careful attention and every possible consideration."
The editors had commented "*very* favorably" on them, but they regretted "that at
this time the market for songs is not one that warrants such publications," as they
"cannot sell any songs at all." The market for octavo or choral pieces was strong,
but the market for art songs, so advantageous to Burleigh in the 1910s and 1920s,
had seriously diminished. Burleigh considered her setting of the Paul Laurence
Dunbar poem "Sympathy," or "I Know Why the Caged Bird Sings," "a great setting of those words and melodically effective and dramatic," though "in one or
two spots" it appeared "too chromatic (perhaps the second verse—and even there
it is in the look of the accidentals, rather than the sound."[98] This song was never
published during Price's lifetime, but Rae Linda Brown traces Burleigh's influence
in Price's song "The Heart of a Woman," with lyrics by Georgia Douglas Johnson.
She also finds Price's spiritual arrangements to be strongly influenced by Burleigh's
approach to text setting and accompaniment.[99]

* * *

Composer William Grant Still garnered numerous firsts in the course of his
career, among them "the first time in history that a major American symphony
orchestra had played a symphonic work written by a black composer": Still's *Afro-
American Symphony* was premiered in 1931 by Howard Hanson, conducting the
Rochester Philharmonic Orchestra.[100]

Still wrote numerous instrumental works, including his six symphonies, but
his favorite genre was opera. Of his six completed operas, three were performed
during his lifetime. Still asked Burleigh's help "in calling one of his early operas to
the attention of the Metropolitan Opera House people." Burleigh was kind in his
response but he explained "that Still should submit his manuscript directly to the
Met." Still was hurt at the unexpected rebuff from one of his heroes; he assumed
Burleigh's influence was such that "he would have only to say a word and all the
doors would open." Later when Still received similar requests from young composers, he understood that Burleigh did not have such influence. More important,
any composer must "succeed on the merits of his music first, not through friends
or influence."[101] Burleigh followed Still's career with keen interest, often going to
concerts where Still's works were played and then sending programs and clippings
with his own account of how the music was received. In an undated letter Burleigh
commented on a radio broadcast of one of Still's works: "My dear Still, Notwith-
standing enclosed newspaper criticism, friends of mine who heard the broadcast

assure me the piece made a profound impression."[102] When Pierre Monteux conducted a performance of Still's *Old California,* Burleigh wrote across the program "'Twas a triumph!"[103]

* * *

Nora Douglas Holt commented in 1944 that Burleigh "fledged and mature in the fullness of his art" was "benign and generous but permit[ed] no pretense to enter the domains of music." He "holds a high standard to which the traveler must comply, no matter which sphere in art he elects to pursue. Finesse, meticulous detail, technique, ready knowledge, and above all, the aura of that indefinable thing, talent or genius."[104]

There are reports of Burleigh's impatience with younger musicians who were sometimes ungrateful for his critiques. Choral conductor and spiritual arranger Eva Jessye wrote Burleigh's first biographer, "He was cordial to me, though considered cool and almost a snob. . . . He was very critical and impatient, but explained that he found most people ungrateful, but supposed one should assist anyone who aspired." She said "people kept their distance; some were in awe of him, some thought he wanted to disclaim his heritage."[105] In conversations with the author, two musicians who knew Jessye commented that she herself could be very critical and somewhat cranky; one chuckled, "Oh, that was just Miss Jessye being Miss Jessye." Burleigh was fond of Jessye and respected her musicianship. In the late 1920s and early 1930s her arrangement of "March Down to Jerdon" became part of his repertoire, and his 1930 arrangement of "Who Is Dat Yondah?" was from her collection. But, as Jessye indicated, in his later years, Burleigh was seen by some younger musicians as a man whose time had passed, and mutual distrust tarnished the earlier wholehearted admiration he had enjoyed. Those who thought he "wanted to disclaim his heritage" were very much mistaken, but that sentiment seems to have emerged in the late Harlem Renaissance, when the reclaiming of black folk traditions without "development" was seen to be important.

Comments by William Grant Still in a 1950 Pittsburgh *Courier* article, "Fifty Years of Progress in Music," show his regard for Burleigh as a mentor to younger musicians and his understanding of the criteria of excellence Burleigh expected from those he assisted. After commenting in detail on Burleigh as one of "our most important pioneers," he wrote, "Finally, Dr. Burleigh was a generous man as concerned other aspiring musicians, even other composers. Not everyone, for he was impatient with mediocrity. But when something proved to be worthy, he was never sparing with his praise. We need more like him to day—not to encourage tawdry work just because it is by one of our own group, but to hold standards high, so that all will aim for the best and bring honor to the group."[106]

11. Family Matters: Fame and Its Discontents

"The tranquility of happy companionship"

Harry T. Burleigh more than fulfilled his mother's fondest dreams for him. His success and his fame increased steadily into the 1920s. Even when the flowering of the Harlem Renaissance to some extent overshadowed his reputation and he was no longer the most renowned African American musician, Burleigh was still regarded as one of the "grand old men" of black art music. But the fame of one member of a family is often a mixed blessing for the favored one's siblings and offspring, and perhaps especially to his or her spouse.

Burleigh's success drew his sister Eva and his half-brother Elzie Elmendorf to New York City after him, and both to some extent shared the social benefits associated with his fame and eventual affluence.[1] His older brother Reginald could not hope to realize such status, even had he wished to do so; his interest lay in following the horses.[2] Their half-sister Bessie Duncanson Elmendorf remained in Erie, though her story is also tinged with sadness. She shared her mother's sometimes precarious emotional balance, and though she married Richard Marshall in Erie, she died soon after their son Duncan was born.[3]

The more intimate cost was to Burleigh's own family: the marriage he entered with such elation and hope disintegrated painfully but with no real closure, and Alston, the son born to that marriage, though he shared many of his father's artistic gifts, struggled with alcoholism, leaving Burleigh a deeply disappointed father.[4] Burleigh's grandson, veterinarian Dr. Harry T. Burleigh II, seeing his father struggle to cope with the family's dysfunction, chose to raise his family quietly in Clarksburg, West Virginia, away from the conflicting expectations imposed on a family whose name "everyone" knew.[5]

Erie remained the family home until the early 1920s. Burleigh's mother Lizzie Elmendorf and his stepfather John Elmendorf remained in Erie, anchoring the family during their lifetimes. After his mother died in 1903, his stepfather kept the home and his boarding stable for horses until about 1915. Various family members boarded at the family home on East Third Street until his death in 1919.[6]

By the time he completed his studies at the National Conservatory of Music in 1896, Harry T. Burleigh's career in New York City was flourishing. He was a frequent soloist in New York City and in Philadelphia, Boston, and Washington, D.C. His engagements were not limited to African American venues; he sang in the homes of the Morgans, the Astors, and the Vanderbilts and gave music lessons to the children of some of New York City's wealthiest families. He was also active in New York's black musical theater crowd, joining the aspiring young literary, music, and theater professionals who gathered at Marshall's Hotel on West Fifty-Third Street. This area, "Black Bohemia," with two black-owned hotels, the Marshall and the Maceo, offering living space, good food, and fine musical entertainment, drew the artists, musicians, actors, and other black professionals who in a score of years would move uptown to Harlem, where they, the "New Negroes," as Alain Locke termed them, would spearhead the New Negro (Harlem) Renaissance. At the Marshall Hotel and in these small apartments, vigorous late-night discussions debated the future of black artistic culture and how musicians, actors, artists, and writers could advance the process of racial uplift while making room for their unique contributions in or alongside the white-dominated establishments. These conversations spawned new visions of the power of the arts to bring social change.[7]

Just as his contacts among the leaders of the white music establishment at the National Conservatory and among the wealthy financial and social elite radiating from the Morgans and others at St. George's Episcopal Church on Stuyvesant Square opened doors for Burleigh that would otherwise have been barred, so his friendships on Fifty-Third Street drew him into the yeasty, ebullient world of black musical theater. The dignified though engaging performer of lower Manhattan could relax in these circles, releasing his jocular, sometimes bawdy sense of humor. His closest friends called him "Burly Harry," a sardonic reference to the "burly negro" who often appeared in crime reports.

* * *

Louise Alston, Burleigh's future wife, grew up in Brookland, an outlying neighborhood of Washington, D.C. (near Catholic University), now part of the city. She was said to be "a promising young artiste, who has made considerable reputation in local circles as a violist and writer of verse." She was "industrious and enthusiastic," with "a natural adaptability for stage work. Her friends predict bright things for her."[8] Exactly how or in what circumstances they met is not known, but Burleigh often sang in D.C. and moved easily among the various strata of Washington's middle- and upper-middle-class black society. Louise joined the Williams and Walker company in September 1898,[9] and their courtship developed while Burleigh conducted the orchestra. This was a momentous year, reported to be the year of

Louise Alston Burleigh. (Courtesy
of the Burleigh Family)

his marriage, though the wedding actually took place in 1899. We can infer from
his first set of three art songs, published by G. Schirmer in 1898, that this was the
year Burleigh lost his heart to Louise, an attractive, dark-eyed girl in her late teens.

One detects autobiographical motifs in the lyrics of the tender melody "If You
But Knew," and in Christina Rossetti's poem "A Birthday" which Burleigh titled
"A Birthday Song": "My heart is like a singing bird . . . because my love has come
to me."[10] Louise toured with Williams and Walker's *Senegambian Carnival* in the
fall of 1898, and she and Burleigh became lovers during his stint as conductor for
the show in its fall run in Washington, D.C., and New York City.

The Senegambian Carnival grew out of *Clorindy, or The Origin of the Cakewalk,*
the first Broadway production written, orchestrated, conducted, and performed
by African Americans.[11] *Clorindy*, produced by George Lederer and described as
"a forty-five-minute musical sketch" with music by Will Marion Cook and lyrics
by Paul Laurence Dunbar, opened with startling success at the Casino Theatre
Roof Garden on July 5, 1898.[12] Piano and vocal ragtime were all the rage, but
Cook's production brought new energy to the style, with a full Broadway orchestra
"playing an entire score of syncopated music." Up to that time, singers sang and
dancers danced, but *Clorindy*'s twenty-six-member chorus sang the syncopated
rhythms while dancing the cakewalk.[13] Cook, always short of funds, had assumed
the conductor's podium in an outfit contributed by several of his friends, none of
whom matched his physique; Burleigh, who was much shorter than Cook, provided

his vest.[14] A triumphant Cook recalled, "My chorus sang like Russians, dancing meanwhile like Negroes, and cakewalking like angels, black angels! When the last note sounded the audience stood and cheered for at least ten minutes."[15]

Cook exulted, "Negroes were at last on Broadway, and there to stay. Gone was the uff-dah of the minstrel. Gone the Massa Linkum stuff! We had the world on a string tied to a runnin' red-geared wagon on a down-hill pull. Nothing could stop us, and nothing did for a decade."[16] In the emerging black musical theater of Cook and his colleagues, they could finally begin to shape the black stage persona to their own purposes, trimming away the demeaning stereotypes that were staples of white-dominated minstrel shows or using them satirically in complex, multilayered performances.

Cook wrote *Clorindy* to star Bert Williams and George Walker, but because the comedy duo had a prior commitment during *Clorindy*'s run on the Casino Theatre's Roof Garden, the production starred comedian-singer-songwriter Ernest Hogan.[17] To follow up on *Clorindy*'s summer's success, George Lederer expanded the company to a touring group of more than sixty performers, with Williams and Walker in the starring roles originally intended for them. The revised production, essentially grafting Williams and Walker's vaudeville act onto *Clorindy,*[18] was called *The Senegambian Carnival.* The tour opened in Boston on September 5.[19]

The fate of the *Senegambian Carnival* tour illustrates theatrical success on one hand and its precarious tenure on the other, especially for black performers. According to the New York *Dramatic Mirror,* the first performances of the proposed twelve-week tour of "prominent Eastern houses" (to be followed by a visit to London) failed to draw the enthusiastic crowds that had made the summer's Roof Garden run so exciting. To salvage the production, Cook took a smaller company on a tour of the Midwest, while a company of forty, headed by Williams and Walker, returned to New York City, where they were featured at Koster and Bial's Music Hall.[20]

A different account was reported by a cast member in the Indianapolis *Freeman,* the black newspaper that most prominently featured news of the black stage in the 1890s. According to the company's magician, Black Carl, and contrary to the "official" report in the *Mirror,* the production drew large crowds in Boston, Philadelphia, Cincinnati, and Washington, D.C., in September and early October, but Lederer's partner W. A. McConnell left the company stranded in Washington, D.C., in mid-October. When Lederer attempted to seize the personal property of cast members in addition to the stage properties, Williams and Walker led the company in making it clear that they were prepared to defend their rights, by whip, if necessary. Lederer withdrew, and the following week, on October 23, the company appeared at Koster and Bial's Music Hall in New York City.[21] Clearly both Lederer and the cast members had an interest in spinning the public reports to their respective advantages, so the truth may lie somewhere between the two accounts. At any rate, the stage was now set for Burleigh's entrance.

Burleigh's singing career was developing in several worlds away from Broadway, but he was no stranger to the vaudeville-musical theater world. In 1896 he had toured briefly with Sissieretta Jones's company, Black Patti's Troubadours.[22] And the loan of his vest to Will Marion Cook for the premiere performance of *Clorindy* was not made at arm's length; he was on the Casino Garden Roof stage with Cook and Paul Laurence Dunbar as they planned and refined the production.[23] When critics pointed out that Williams and Walker's *Senegambian Carnival* needed fine-tuning with new songs and a tighter, crisper script, Burleigh was on hand to help. Eventually he took the conductor's baton, a role he relished as a diversion, though he was not inclined to leave his stable position at St. George's for the theatrical circuit. However he might deplore ragtime in newspaper or radio interviews, at Koster and Bial's the versatile Burleigh "led the rag-time music with great success."[24]

Years later, Burleigh regaled interviewer Nora Douglas Holt with a hilarious account of his version of "the show must go on," even if the conductor himself must ascend to the stage to carry it. One of the actors (Bert Williams) had over-indulged, and suffering "an attack of the spirits," failed to appear on cue for his big song. Burleigh vamped through several orchestral introductions; then left the orchestra pit; went backstage, where he hastily snatched his tall friend's costume accessories and, cane and hat in hand, sang "Who Dat Say Chicken in dis Crowd?" with appropriate improvised dance steps. Williams's later Ziegfeld Follies audiences might never have accepted Burleigh as his stand-in, but on this occasion, Burleigh saved the day—or the night.[25]

Burleigh's stint in the orchestra pit was so successful that Williams and Walker offered him a more permanent position for Williams and Walker's Own Company.[26] The immediate financial rewards must have been tempting, and he accepted their offer briefly, but he decided against leaving St. George's and the singing career he was developing in the mansions of the robber barons of New York City's Gilded Age. Such a move would also have interrupted his promising career as an art song composer.[27]

* * *

Louise Alston stayed in New York City with the Williams and Walker troupe. On December 16, 1898, just as Williams and Walker's *Senegambian Carnival* ended its successful run in New York City, thirty-one-year-old Burleigh wrote his prospective mother-in-law, Rachel Turner Farley, in Washington, D.C., asking permission to marry her nineteen-year-old daughter Louise. His letter breathes Victorian elegance and charm, but it is also disarmingly self-revealing. This was not the public persona speaking; in this letter Burleigh presented himself at his most vulnerable, though confident that his request would be favorably received.[28]

He described the gradual progress of his friendship with Louise: "We were but good friends and little did we think when glancing at each other across a crowded room with eyes so full of mutual intelligence, of the precious feeling that would soon proceed from this new and quite external stimulus. . . . From exchanging glances we advanced to acts of kindness, and courtesy—then to ardent devotion and plighting troth; one crowning step remains to be taken and we trust it will soon be reached and realized." His acquaintance with Mrs. Farley and her daughter had begun earlier. "You know something of me," he writes; he could have made his request in person when the troupe was in Washington, "had the proper opportunity come." But as one of Burleigh's generation expected to make this particular petition only once in a lifetime, he found himself hesitant—not undecided, but resolved to "approach the question properly."[29]

Known as dangerously charming to young ladies, Burleigh's reference to earlier attachments confirms that Louise was not his first flirtation; the term *sport* probably applied to him before his marriage as well as after his eventual separation from Louise: "I may have loved before in my life—I know not and care less—but I do know that the sum total of all former infatuations or affections would not begin to equal the depth and sincerity of the feeling I have for her. *Then* I loved (?) because I knew no better:—now I love because I see the soul of my life and inspiration is in her keeping" [Burleigh's punctuation].[30]

The rising young singer-composer had not achieved wealth, but he was able to support a wife. He had never shrunk from physical labor, and even now he could resort to that if necessary: "My mind and arms are strong and (without being over confident) I feel that they can work sufficiently;—so that together with [God's] grace and her love I shall be able to cope with the realities of life and the added responsibility marriage brings." He describes himself as a man of good habits, though "born with a passionate and excitable temperament." As his ready ascent into the upper echelons of black society on the eastern seaboard demonstrated, he was "keenly susceptible to the pleasures of society." But Mrs. Farley need not worry that his attachments were transitory. "My heart and mind were, even from childhood, prone to the most tender feelings of affection." To Burleigh love was "a 'light which illumines, not a flame that burns.'"[31]

Reading this letter with the knowledge of how utterly Burleigh's marriage failed, one senses that even at this stage he saw the potential for problems in their relationship. She was "in many ways a beautiful girl," he writes, but he knew her faults; they were few, "and they are completely lost sight of in the superabundance of her good qualities." In an allusion to Shakespeare's *Julius Caesar*, Burleigh said he would not flatter her, but being a proper Victorian gentleman and knowing "her likes and desires," he was confident he could make his young bride's life happier, "keep her heart warm and good and lead her to the higher and more influential life of Christian womanhood."[32]

One wonders whether Burleigh and Louise, more than a decade apart in age, shared a common definition of Christian womanhood. Burleigh's entreaty is couched in religious terms: "I am truly thankful that God saw fit to so turn my steps that they led me to your daughter's side; that He has given us both the proper fear and reverence of His name, and made us keenly sensible of the great obligations that rest upon every child of His." Louise's later correspondence with her son Alston reveals a woman of very different character than Burleigh saw at this stage of their relationship. Perhaps he was an unconscious Pygmalion hoping to shape Louise into the supportive wife he needed. Or he may have frustrated her ambitions unintentionally, leaving no room on the stage of their too-public lives for her lesser talents to flourish.[33]

Burleigh's friends were not concerned about Louise's fate; they were more worried that Louise would limit the full range of Burleigh's artistry. Or perhaps they saw Louise more clearly. Some friends expressed concern that marriage might distract him from his artistic vocation: "Lots of people think that I should not marry: that a man who is so much in love with music—so romantic[,] so fanciful and imaginative[,] should be wed to his art and let no other attachment encroach upon this union!" Burleigh regarded this caution as "high words from an empty stomach." Such advice came from those who did not know his inner nature, "how dual it is—how dependent upon the sympathy and interest of someone else." Far from the marriage distracting him, he asserted, "My art will be greater when my love is knit to its object because *I* will be greater." Burleigh was sure that Louise, whom he loved "with all the nobility of [his] heart," would also inspire him "to truer work" than he could do alone.[34]

Ultimately, except in their early years together, "the tranquility of happy companionship" that he anticipated would elude them, but Burleigh foresaw a life of shared artistic creativity, even if unconsciously he assumed that she would enhance his career rather than that he would enable hers. These words would echo hollowly through the long years of their estrangement, but that disillusionment was for a later decade. Now Burleigh "deeply—hopefully—prayerfully" considered it his duty and a privilege to ask Mrs. Farley for her daughter's hand, wishing for her "warmest blessing" on their life together.[35]

Posting this letter just at the triumphant close of the New York run of *The Senegambian Carnival* in mid-December, Burleigh managed to juggle his singing at St. George's Episcopal Church throughout the busy Christmas season with serving as musical director for Williams and Walker's Own Company, now in rehearsal for appearances in Philadelphia and Brooklyn in January 1899. But by January 21 Burleigh, "the accomplished musical director," had resigned the position, leaving Williams and Walker to search for a replacement. They chose Charles F. Alexander, who would fill it "in a dignified, painstaking manner," a description that would have applied equally to Burleigh's tenure.[36]

In the meantime, Mrs. Farley gave her consent, and Harry and Louise were married on February 9, 1899, in Brookland, in the Farley home.[37] The Burleigh family Bible lists their marriage date as February 1898, but that would have been ten months before Burleigh's December 1898 letter. Their son Alston Waters Burleigh was born seven months after their marriage, on August 18, 1899, so it appears the date in the family Bible was adjusted to conceal an indiscreet intimacy during their engagement. Other discrepancies show that the family Bible is not an infallible record, and Alston may simply have arrived a bit early. But propriety and protecting one's public persona were important, and this was not the only disjuncture between the public record and the private reality.[38]

* * *

In his early years their son Alston spent a great deal of time with his grandmother, Mrs. Rachel Turner Farley, in Washington, D.C., though he traveled with his parents in the summer.[39] Burleigh was increasingly busy and his wife began to carve her niche among the amateur stage performers and the dialect poets and dramatic readers often featured on concerts or recitals and in variety shows. Their friends Paul and Alice Dunbar had married a year before the Burleighs and were residing in Washington, D.C., where Dunbar worked in the Library of Congress Reading Room until he was able to make his living by his writing and public readings.[40] Dunbar's dialect poetry had made his a household name after William Dean Howells, editor of the *Atlantic Monthly* "discovered" his first book of poems, *Oak and Ivy,* which Dunbar distributed from the Haiti Pavilion at the 1893 Chicago World's Fair.[41]

At first the Burleighs' creative partnership showed promise. He set five of Louise's poems to music, songs issued by William Maxwell. The first, "Mammy's Li'l

Rachel Farley, Louise and Alston Burleigh. (Courtesy of the Burleigh Family)

Baby" (1903), dedicated to and sung by Madame Ernestine Schumann-Heink, also attracted Isabelle Bouton, a Metropolitan mezzo-soprano.[42] The published version, a sentimental lullaby, is not in dialect like the version in Louise's handwritten notebook, but the words place it squarely in the plantation cabin tradition. Other differences raise a question: Who did the editing to make the song more credible to Schumann-Heink's audience, Louise or her husband—or an editor at the William Maxwell publishing house? It is impossible to say, but Burleigh would have had a much surer sense than Louise of what a singer like Schumann-Heink could present.

Louise's handwritten version	*Published song lyrics*
Mammy's dark brown baby,	Mammy's little baby,
Sleepin' on ma bres'	Lay your curly head
Seems to me de angels	On this snow white pillow,
Crooned a song of res'	In your trundle bed
Mammy's dark brown baby	Mammy's little baby,
Cheeks so sof' an new	Dropping just a tear
Like de zephyr breezes	Mammy's got you honey
In de spring time true	In this cabin here
	Mammy's got you honey
	Don't you have a fear![43]

Revisions to Louise's poems published in black journals such as Boston's *Colored American* or Hampton Institute's *Southern Workman* suggest that her editors in these journals assisted her before publication. Most of Louise's public readings were of her dialect poems, but her published verse was in standard English.

Louise's two cradle songs, "Mammy's Little Baby" (1903) and "Dream Land" (1905), suggest that she enjoyed caring for her son. But even at this time Burleigh often felt that he must sacrifice family gatherings in favor of his professional responsibilities. During his mother's final illness in December 1903, Burleigh arranged for Louise and four-year-old Alston to take the train to Erie to see her. In a letter to his mother-in-law, he thanked her for being "willing to have Louise go" in his stead. "My heart is much lighter to-night to know that Louise and my mother are together once more. It will be the last time she will see Alston, I fear, and I know it will do her lots of good."[44]

Burleigh would also be unable to join the family in Washington, D.C., for Christmas. "I'm sorry it looks like I cannot get away even for a day. This is my busy time you know." As his Christmas Eve and Christmas Day engagements included singing at J. P. Morgan's home, one can understand why they took priority.[45] Church singers and other musicians must often defer their Christmas celebrations to fulfill their professional duties. But Burleigh seems not to have managed to compensate his family in other ways for his frequent absences.

The Burleighs' social life revolved around music and other social events (names of prominent attendees were listed in reviews), weekends at several of the black-owned cottages in Asbury Park, New Jersey, and Burleigh's ever-widening circle of recitals and entertainments in wealthy homes, black and white. Louise and her sister Ray Farley's names often appear in the social notes, along with his sister Eva Grace Burleigh and his half-brother Elzie Elmendorf. Burleigh was also beginning his fifteen-year association with Booker T. Washington and was on call to sing at Washington's fund-raising appearances throughout New England.[46]

Until 1908, Louise was not listed in the black newspapers as a performer; though Alston spent much of his early years with his grandmother in Washington, D.C., Louise laid the foundation for a relationship that despite its long silences seems to have been genuinely affectionate. She also continued writing verse. Two of her pieces, "People Will Talk" and "Look Pleasant," are indebted to Paul Laurence Dunbar's "We Wear the Mask." "People Will Talk" reflects her experience of the less convenient side of the renown she sought and shared as Burleigh's wife. Verses two and three of the six-verse poem suggest the social price exacted of a woman of independent mind: "If quiet and modest, you'll hear it presumed / That your humble position is only assumed / You're a wolf in sheep's clothing or else you're a fool /But don't get exited Keep perfectly cool / For people—will talk." "And then if you show the least boldness of heart / Or a slight inclination to take your own part / They will call you an upstart, conceited and vain / But keep straight ahead don't stop to explain / For people—will talk."[47]

Louise's verse brought her recognition for a time, but she was not in the same poetic league as Paul Laurence Dunbar or in her husband's league as a vocal artist. However, some insight into the relationship between Burleigh and his wife may be gleaned from the lyrics he chose to set to music. Autobiographical analysis of either Louise's verse or other lyrics Burleigh set to music must be approached with caution but may be suggestive in the absence of other primary materials. A timeline from a 1959 legal deposition given by their son Alston can be supplemented with press notes, primarily from the New York *Age,* providing a framework for such analysis.

In Burleigh's five settings of poems by Louise one can infer something of the joy and the deterioration of their relationship in the early years of their marriage. In every instance, Burleigh's musical setting adds a memorable grace to Louise's lyrics, which sound trite to a twenty-first-century ear. "Mammy's Little Baby" (1903) and "Dream Land" (1905) are both sentimental cradle songs, published when Alston was a young boy. "Just My Love and I" (1904) and "Love's Dawning" (1906) are love lyrics. The first, a boat song, Burleigh sets in typical rocking barcarolle style. The second verse expresses the contentment of a trusted if romanticized love: "Over the waves we gently glide / Simply afloat with the breeze our guide / Ever content to be side by side / Just my love and I! / Just my love and I!" This song arises out of the optimism and promise of their early life together.

The Burleighs, who hoped to be in England in summer 1902, did not make it to London until summer 1908, but in the meantime, 1904 brought England to them, in the person of Afro-British composer Samuel Coleridge-Taylor. "Just My Love and I" portrays the relationship Samuel Coleridge-Taylor observed when he was with Burleigh and his wife during his 1904 visit to the United States. He writes from Philadelphia, "Please tell Mrs. Burleigh how much I enjoyed her company yesterday, though I am sorry she came back on my account—if that were true—I'm inclined to think she had other reasons!" He continued, "After Mrs. Coleridge-Taylor she is the sweetest woman I have ever met—how proud you must be of her![48] Coleridge-Taylor also set several of Louise's poems to music, and his observations of their marriage were very positive, as one would expect from a guest in their home. But other lyrics her husband chose may be more revealing.

Burleigh dedicated a 1904 song, "If Life Be a Dream," to his wife. The lyrics by Frank L. Stanton acknowledge life's challenges but affirm the certainty of hope: "This, when no star in the dim sky is beaming; / If life be a dream, it is well worth the dreaming; / If thorns will grow along the way Life goes / It still looks to God for the gift of a rose!" Refrain: "Take heart in the trouble, Stem the swift stream, / If Life be a dream, dear, We'll live out the dream!"

"Love's Dawning," one of two 1906 settings of Louise's verse, portrays a woman, alone through the evening, awaiting the return of her lover who slips into bed beside her after she is asleep: "The gentle breeze is softly sighing, at the evening's close; / The robin's song is slowly dying, Like the first spring rose; / The crimson sun is sinking, sinking, 'Neath the far off hill / While of you, dear, I am thinking As the night grows still; / And I long for love's full morning Till you enter here—/ Though asleep, I'll know it's dawning By your presence dear!" If their love is dying, like the song of the robin, the spring rose, and the daylight, his presence is still the light of her life. Despite the wistfulness of the waiting lover, his coming in the night brings her the hope of love's dawning again in his return to her.

"Perhaps," the last of Louise's poems that Burleigh set to music, also in 1906 (and published in 1919 by *Etude* magazine), portrays the waning of love:

> "Not long ago 'mid the birds and flow'rs, / Where lovers spend many quiet hours / You touched my lips and taught me dear / To love you more as the days flew by: / My heart was gay, all the world was singing / As soul to soul we were ever clinging / But now you've gone and I am lonely / And still I sing to you ev'ry day: / Perhaps you may remember! / Perhaps you may forget, / My heart is ever constant / And says I love you yet / The years can never change me / Nor take from me your kiss / Perhaps you may remember this / Perhaps you may forget!"[49]

This lyric expresses a sense of love diminished or strained, but it also suggests a shared regret for the loss. This verse, along with "The Wounded Heart," published in the same year in Boston's *Colored American* magazine, suggests that the marriage is, to say the least, troubled.[50] But several years passed before the strain led to a complete break. On February 9, 1908, Louise wrote a short verse entitled "Dear One" commemorating their ninth wedding anniversary. Labeled "To Dad," as she referred to her husband, in a corner of the page, the lines suggest that his financial success meant less to her than his love: "Dear one, if all the world were yours to give / Would you gladly give it,—me / And all the Kingdoms far and near / As great as great can be? / If you would gladly give me these / Without them, have no dread / For I will cast the world aside / And take your heart, instead."[51]

During these years, Burleigh's achievements as a singer and composer earned him increasing recognition: In 1903 he was the baritone soloist for performances in Washington, D.C. of Afro-British composer Samuel Coleridge-Taylor's *Hiawatha's Wedding Feast*; he toured with the composer in 1904 and 1906; Burleigh Choral Societies were being formed in several cities; he was in demand to sing the title role of Mendelssohn's *Elijah*; he sang before visiting royalty who were guests of the Morgans and other wealthy New Yorkers; in 1905 his 1903 song "Jean" was issued on a piano roll, and in 1906 tenor Evan Williams recorded it for Victor Seal Records.[52] In 1910 Burleigh appeared at Carnegie Hall with Walter Damrosch's New York Symphony Orchestra.

How could Louise find her place as a performer in such rarified company? For a time, writing and giving public readings of her dialect verse seemed promising. Paul Laurence Dunbar had soared to fame and financial success in just a few short years. Perhaps she could do the same. In 1906 Dunbar died of tuberculosis complicated by heavy drinking, and the prolific outpouring of poems, essays, plays, and novels of a mere decade and a half came to an abrupt end; his marriage to Alice Ruth Moore had ruptured hopelessly four years earlier.[53] Burleigh published several settings of Dunbar's works, in addition to unpublished settings mentioned in his papers. A handwritten verse in Dunbar's handwriting is also among the Burleigh papers, apparently never published.[54] The Burleighs would have been deeply affected by his death. Predictably, Louise memorialized Dunbar in verse.

To Louise Alston Burleigh, Dunbar's fame and financial success in the few short years of his public career suggested one route for her own approach to fame. If she could not make it as a vaudeville headliner (an ambition she confessed in a letter to Alston after Burleigh's death),[55] perhaps she could take up Dunbar's torch. Several years would pass before Louise began public readings of her own dialect poems, but there is no doubt that Dunbar's death strengthened her resolve to follow his example. For the following two years, 1906–08, Louise's name appeared in the public record simply as the wife of the distinguished baritone singer, spending weekends at Whitehead House or Wigfall Cottage in Asbury Park, New Jersey, or visiting family and friends in Washington, D.C.

In April 1908 Louise was mentioned in less than flattering terms in a review of an amateur minstrel show put on in Brooklyn's Saengerbund Hall to benefit the Willing Workers' Circle of the Kings Daughters.[56] Her name did not appear in the advertised cast list before the show, but she was one of the circle of "picnickers," the Bedford Singers ("who lived up to their reputation as the 'Badford'" Singers, according to critic Lester A. Walton) in the garden party "of the Darktown Society at

Lakewood" in the minstrel first part of the program. John Nail and his sister Grace (later the wife of James Weldon Johnson) were among those with more prominent parts who were roasted in Walton's review, and the mocking tone of the entire piece requires close attention to sort serious panning from grudging respect. But in the second part of the program, Louise and her husband both came in for some ribbing: "The writer knows that Harry Burleigh never bothers about coon songs, but Mrs. Louise Burleigh tried herself as a 'coon shouter' when she sang 'I've Got Good Common Sense.' As a matter of fact her rendition was above the ordinary. However someone near me remarked when she was dancing that her feet hurt her. Of course we won't touch that—it's a live wire."[57] Perhaps the sting of the last two sentences were soothed by his comment that her singing was "above the ordinary," but she did not appear publicly as a singer again, at least in New York City. She turned her attention to a medium in which she did not need to compete with her husband: writing and reading her own verse, specifically, her dialect verse.

Actors of the rising generation would perform onstage in both musicals and drama. In the first decade of the twentieth century, however, while black musical theater for a time burst out on Broadway, the theatrical stage doors were still closed for black actors, unless, like Ira Aldridge, they could make their careers in Great Britain and Europe. So those with dramatic gifts were featured as elocutionists and dramatic readers on music programs or in solo recitals, or perhaps in vaudeville companies, reading or dramatizing—sometimes in costume—parts of plays, passages from Shakespeare, or more rarely, their own verse. This was for Louise Alston Burleigh the most easily accessible route to an independent stage career. She could appear in recitals with her husband, or perhaps she could build an independent career as a poet and dramatic reader. Less than two months after her dubious debut as a coon shouter, Louise Alston Burleigh accompanied her husband on his first singing tour in England.

A number of the young women in their circle of performers were making headlines in the first decade of the twentieth century, at least in the black press, and some of them in the New York *Dramatic Mirror*. Having tasted the performer's life and as the wife of a man whose burgeoning career as a singer and composer made his time in their home sporadic and unpredictable at best, Louise must increasingly have felt pushed to the all-too-quiet margins of his busy life. In fact, in this first decade of the twentieth century, the three African Americans best known to many Americans were Paul Laurence Dunbar, poet; Booker T. Washington, educator; and Harry T. Burleigh, singer-composer. Louise was to some extent intimately connected with all three, but she herself was known only by her reflection in the light of their public acclaim. It would not be easy for a woman with ambition for public recognition to create an independent identity at this time and in these circumstances.

12. Wife and Family of the "Eminent Baritone"

"You were too busy being Mr. Burleigh!"

Burleigh's success in singing for the English royal and noble families led not only to his returning to perform in England the following summer, but also to his wife's determination to strike out in a new direction in a setting where she could create an identity distinct from her role as the wife of "the eminent baritone." In fall 1909 she took their son Alston to England, where she placed him at Malden College for Boys just outside London.[1]

Then, assuming the stage name of Princess Redfeather, she "played in her own Indian Act in London music halls."[2] Hoping to build her own identity, she did not reckon on meeting a young Indian woman who charged her with stealing *her* identity: At one of her later performances in the United States, the "real" Princess Redfeather, Princess Tsianina Redfeather who often performed with Indianist song composer Charles Wakefield Cadman, appeared and demanded that Louise must find another stage name.[3] From that point on, Rachel Louise Alston Burleigh would be known in her American Indian presentations as Ojibway Princess Nadonis, and later as Princess Nadonis Shawa. Eventually she assumed that identity permanently and went to great lengths to disassociate herself from her African American roots and family, except to demand financial support from her husband, and later, from her son.

One can only speculate about the negotiations between Burleigh and his wife from 1909 to 1915, when they separated. But in 1909 Burleigh and his wife were still officially a married couple, spending weekends at Asbury Park, often accompanied by her younger sister, Ray Farley.

For a number of years early in the twentieth century Asbury Park was the town on the New Jersey shore most open to elite black Americans seeking a weekend or a holiday at the ocean. The New York *Age* reported weekly the roster of distinguished guests at Whitehead House and several surrounding cottages, and the grand hops, teas, baseball games, surf bathing, and "continuous round of pleasure and mirth"

Alston and friend at Malden
College for Boys. (Courtesy of the
Burleigh Family)

that entertained the exquisitely gowned and bejeweled guests, Burleigh and his
family among them. In September 1906 the *Age* reported "fewer restrictions on
account of color [in Asbury Park] . . . this season than during any past season and
a movement is on foot among the property owners to remove every vestige of
discrimination on account of color."[4] But this freedom was always under threat,
and in July 1911, black vacationers were suddenly barred from the section of the
beachfront that had been reserved for them. Negotiations eventually reversed the
prohibition, but many of the black music and theater set found other places, such
as New Rochelle, New York, and Seabrook on Long Island, to enjoy their summer
weekends.

In September 1910, the first notice of Louise's readings appeared in the report of
the music program presented as a testimonial to the proprietors of the Eldorado
Cottage at New Rochelle, New York, as they closed the summer season.[5] In October Louise's career as a writer and dramatic reader of Southern dialect poems was
given a boost by her appearance on a recital at the American Academy of Music in
Philadelphia. E. Azalia Hackley, a prominent African American soprano and choral
director, gave her farewell solo recital, as she was retiring from recital performance
to devote her time to "developing young musicians."[6] This time it was Mrs. Louise

Alston Burleigh (not Mrs. Harry T. Burleigh) who appeared with Hackley, the violinist Clarence Cameron White, pianist Mayme White, and baritone Walter Nicholson. The "immense audience" responded with "much enthusiasm" to the favorite selections Louise read "from her own book of poems. Those reflecting childhood days reveal[ed] the genius of the author in a happy vein."[7] A second reviewer commented that specific mention should be made of Louise's recitation of "Marie Brown," a selection featuring a young black man boasting of how cleverly he pursues the most beautiful light-skinned girl in town. Her reading "was received with uproarious applause."[8] A third clipping identified her as "the wife of the great singer" but reported that to the "discriminating and appreciative audience, made up of the best element of Philadelphians," she was "a decided novelty. She gave an original dialect poem with a Southland flavor and won a positive encore. . . . She has a pleasing stage presence, and her personality was as effective as her art." For this occasion such notables as the elderly star soprano Marie Selika and her husband and New York *Age* editor T. Thomas Fortune could be seen in the parquet circle boxes.[9]

November and December 1910 and January 1911 brought more opportunities for Louise to read her dialect poems in Manhattan, Boston, and Brooklyn. As Boston and Brooklyn were among the most sophisticated black communities, success in these appearances counted for a great deal. The review of the December 14 Benefit Concert in Brooklyn for the Woman's American Baptist Home Mission Society listed the specific pieces she dramatized: "Popping the Question," about a lovesick but shy young man who tries valiantly to ask his love to marry him but in the end dashes off, promising to ask her the next evening; "A Study in Colors," an ironic commentary on the black-white color line; "Sandy Andy Mindy Mo" (usually titled "Sandy Andy Lindy Mo"), about a mother who wants to be sure she gives her baby a long enough name; and "Lemme Love You," a young man teasing his "dark brown honey," until she puckers up and lets him kiss her.[10] On the January 25 program in Boston, where she was featured with a young tenor making his debut at Court Hall, Louise made her Boston debut as a dramatic reader. She added "Possom Pie," a paean to Granny Jones's cooking skill, especially her possum pie; and "Back Home," a nostalgic tribute to the pull of "Mammy's lil cabin / Over yondah, 'hin' de hill," even on one who has traveled the world.[11]

The transcriptions of these verses in Louise's handwritten notebooks show inconsistencies in the dialect as well as careless punctuation. But from all reports, her delivery was effective, delighting her audiences, except on one occasion when the hall was too large for her voice to carry effectively without amplification. Her lively presentation carried her generalized version of rural Southern speech effectively enough to please her audiences, many of whom had roots in the South.

In 1911 Louise and her husband presented several joint recitals in which he sang and she read her dialect verse. In March they appeared at Boston's Steinert Hall to benefit St. Monica's Home for Sick Colored Women. The "large and appreciative audience" was racially mixed but primarily white. Burleigh gave his usual varied program, though in this case, the first group of songs rather than the last consisted of "plantation spirituals," and, perhaps to create the setting for Louise's dialect poems, included more secular plantation songs (by white writers and composers) than usual. His second group featured the German lieder that usually headed his solo recitals, along with a song by Samuel Coleridge-Taylor and a plantation song by white American composer Sidney Homer. After Louise's second set of "original dialect poems," he concluded the recital with "Hush-a-by, oh Baby," by A. Stuart Pigott; "Mighty Lak a Rose," by Ethelbert Nevin (a Pennsylvania composer), and his setting of Louise's cradle song "Dream Land."[12]

Her April reading at a benefit concert presented by Helen Eugenia Hagan, one of the premiere African American pianists of the time, and contralto Beatrice Rheinhardt again put Louise in the company of the top echelon of black musicians whose repertoire was primarily classical. A review "by Duval" gave Louise the hoped-for imprimatur: "Mrs. Burleigh in her readings gives promise of succeeding Paul Laurence Dunbar in carrying on the songs of the Negro. Her poems are true to nature and give evidence of much thought as well as genuine talent" and provided an example that "others should rightfully follow."[13] Again her effective stage presence was mentioned: Her "interpretation of her words [is] beyond criticism as she has set her own standard for them." After a lively change of musical pace by an instrumental trio that created "an atmosphere of 'get you ready for to swing our partners to the Virginia reel,'" she was joined by R. Henri Strange, one of the most gifted black dramatic readers, for "a creditable rendition" of a scene from *Ingomar,* a drama in which she played the part of the Greek woman Parthenia.[14]

In addition to joint recitals with her husband, Louise was gaining a reputation of "Distinction as a Poet at Fashionable Summer Resorts," both with Booker T. Washington and as a solo performer. In August she appeared at Greenacre-on-the-Piscataqua in Eliot, Maine, where "college professors from Harvard, Cornell and Yale" were in the audience, and in early September she appeared with Burleigh at Lake Mohonk House before "a very exclusive audience." A "titled lady" from Scotland who heard Louise said she would bring her to Scotland the following year.[15]

These joint appearances may have been an attempt to recover their dream of a creative partnership. Louise was at the apex of her New York career as a dialect poet and dramatic reader. She was planning to publish her first book, *Echoes from the Southland*, and she was to tour the South in the winter, "reciting and singing the old Negro spirituals."[16] She was said to have several European engagements for spring 1912, and a New York *Age* review of her recital at Hampton Institute in Hampton, Virginia, in December 1911 said, "Mrs. Burleigh has taken the every-day life of the Negro and given it a poetic expression, which appeals to white and colored people. She has added dignity to the common things of life and has won the respect of all classes."[17]

After a visit to the family in Erie in February 1912, Louise left for a tour of Florida, where she appeared at Palm Beach, Sea Breeze, St. Augustine, and Jacksonville. In a program in the Octagonal Ball Room of the Palm Beach Royal Poinciana Hotel, she claimed her own name: "Mrs. Louise Alston Burleigh, the celebrated authoress and reader of negro dialect," was assisted by the Poinciana Quintette, and New York soprano Abbie Mitchell (no longer Mrs. Will Marion Cook, but still a star in black musical theater). The review of the Jacksonville recital at Bethel Baptist Church was especially gratifying: "She is of an agreeable personality, full of soul, and reads with a spirit that wins her audience." She explained how she began writing dialect verse, attributing her first inspiration to "the late Paul [Laurence] Dunbar, who was an acknowledged authority in that class of literature." Her southern audience found her poems to be "rigidly true to the mass of traditions from which they spring."[18] Not only were her press reviews gratifyingly positive, but an undated clipping in her scrapbook contains a thirteen-verse poetic tribute to her by C. A. Whitfield, professor of literature at Edward Waters College, placing her in the classic line of Negro poets: "Thou, a second Phillis Wheatley, / Sparkle with poetic flame, / You control the Muse completely, / Muses bow before your name."[19]

The last verse offered a benediction Louise would sorely need in the several years following the success of her Florida tour: "I pray heaven's benedictions / Be upon thee, and His grace / Fill thy soul without restrictions, / Thou true poet of the race." But for now, she had become Louise Alston Burleigh of New York City, "the Queen of Dialect Writers," whom "many high-class critics" claimed to be a reader without equal.[20]

Louise disappeared from public notice in the black newspapers in 1913, just as her husband assumed a career-long position as staff editor at the New York branch of the Ricordi Music Publishing Company, the publishing house based in Milan, Italy.[21] This position gave Burleigh unprecedented access to publication of his songs and allowed him to assist his black composer colleagues in publishing their work. Burleigh was receiving a kind of recognition Louise could only dream of, despite the heady praise she had earned in Florida. And even Florida was not far enough away from New York to free her completely from her identity as the wife of "the eminent baritone."

No documentation is available to reveal the private drama behind the public façade, but a song published in 1907, "You Ask Me If I Love You," may be a response to the poems by Louise he had published in 1906: "You ask me if I love you? / Is this love? / To want to see no other face, / To want to hear no other voice / To want to feel no other touch, / To want you only, you know how much, / In all the earth or heav'n above / To want no other living soul to love: / You ask me if I love you? Is this love?" The second verse ends more emphatically: "To feel no fear in life or death / To know no joy apart from you / To feel that for all time you will be true: / If all this be love, Then I love you!"[22]

This song, one of Burleigh's more popular 1907 publications,[23] builds with each phrase to a climax as the verse ends. The emphasis at the close of the second verse is created by textual repetition and with careful shaping of the singer's tempo and volume. If this is a tender plea to his wife, it seems to have helped only temporarily, if at all.

In 1913 Burleigh's first choral arrangements of spirituals were published and performed the following year by Kurt Schindler's Schola Cantorum. The significance of these arrangements becomes clearer in the light of the emergence of his solo and choral arrangements of spirituals three years later (after Burleigh and his wife had separated). An indication that 1913 was a critical year in the marriage is Burleigh's song "He Sent Me You!" published by Ricordi in 1915, the year of the separation. Dedicated "To A____ [not identified] remembering June 27th 1913," the lyrics are suggestive: "My days were shadow'd with dark despair, / Never God's sun the clouds broke through; / Till in response to my wordless prayer, / He sent me you!"[24]

The Burleighs placed their son Alston in a private school after they brought him home from England in 1914 at the beginning of World War I, but when they separated in 1915, they sent him to live with the matriarch of Louise's family, his grandmother, Rachel Farley, in Washington, D.C.[25]

Louise stayed in New York City until early 1918, but there is little documentation of her activity except the report in December 1917 of a Red Cross benefit concert at the Hudson Theatre on Broadway to aid the horses and other animals at risk in the war. She was listed on a poster as Ojibway Princess Nadonis (Silver Fox).[26] Burleigh's first solo arrangements of spirituals were published the preceding season. They were performed by an impressive roster of distinguished singers, most of whom had been singing his secular art songs. Burleigh was at the height of his fame as a song composer, and now he had brought before the public a new repertoire that ultimately would secure his place in American music, nationally and internationally.

* * *

In 1918 Louise Alston Burleigh left the New York concert, recital, and vaudeville stage, with all its social expectations and conventions, completely and entirely to her husband—she saw no room for her beside him. The world of art music, which was his native air, could not sustain her. Skilled as she might be in less formal presentations, she could never compete or even effectively complement her husband's work. There was another American folk culture to be exploited. Like many African Americans, Louise Alston claimed Native Americans among her ancestors. For years the Burleigh family doubted that Louise's assuming the role of a Native American princess had any basis in fact. But in the early 1990s David Peterson, a faculty member at the University of Wisconsin at Madison, found references to her work, and intrigued by her connection to the distinguished singer-composer, decided to explore her Wisconsin career and her possible Indian ancestry. He came to believe that her father, Philip C. Alston, probably did have some Indian ancestry and that he may have talked with her about it when she visited him at the Veteran's Hospital in Hampton, Virginia, in the early 1890s, during his final illness.[27]

Alston, a Civil War veteran who served in the Rhode Island Colored Artillery Company, was born in Raleigh, North Carolina, about 1840. According to census records, his parents lived in Warren and Wake Counties, North Carolina, during his youth. North Carolina's policy toward its Indian population was either to drive them out (e.g., the Cherokee Nation) or to officially deny their existence by listing them as "mulatto" in the census records. As there was a substantial Indian population in Wake and Warren Counties, and as he and his parents were listed as mulattos in the 1840, 1850, and 1860 censuses, it is quite possible that there was Indian heritage in the family.[28]

Exploring this part of her ancestry, Louise made connections with the Native American community in New York City. Sometime between 1914 and 1917 she began to perform with Albert Lowe, a Winnebago from Black River Falls, Wisconsin, who the Burleigh family believe worked on the New York City subway. His stage persona was Chief Konoka White Eagle.[29] Louise had grown up in the highly stratified middle- and upper-class black community of Washington, D.C., and, having married a prominent black musician, had until this point affirmed that identity. But now her Native American heritage, however tenuous, offered an escape from the frustrations of her life on the shadowy margins of her husband's

Louise as Princess Nadonis. (Courtesy of the Burleigh Family)

fame. North Carolina was not the land of the Ojibway nation, but anyone might recognize the Ojibway people as a major American Indian nation, so Louise Alston Burleigh began to construct an autobiography to support her claim to be of American Indian royalty.

In July 1917, Albert Lowe enlisted in the U.S. Army; he served in Europe from June 1918 until July 1919. Not long after performing in the wartime benefit in late 1917, Louise left New York City for Wisconsin, her primary residence for the remaining forty years of her life.[30] When Lowe returned from military service in 1919, he joined her in Wisconsin. In 1920 she purchased a small cottage (which she referred to as a log cabin) on Mirror Lake near the Wisconsin Dells, where she and Lowe spent their summers for the next ten years. Their company, the Princess Nadonis Indians, was headed by "Ojibway Princess Nadonis" and "Winnebago Chief Konoka White Eagle," with two young women of different tribes, singer Wahetah Fawn (an Oneida) and pianist Richenda Wanikpiwega (nation unspecified). For some years the group performed for chautauquas and on lyceum programs around the country.[31]

A poster in her personal papers advertising their chautauqua performances shows Chief White Eagle with a drum, leading the three women in a dance. Close-ups of the princess and the chief show why the princess was able to sustain the illusion of her Indian identity. Her olive complexion, along with her dark eyes and hair, hanging in braids over her shoulders, make her a convincing partner to the chief. In the text (obviously written by the princess), she asserts with unconscious irony that "Wahetah Fawn's musical ability has been developed under the best vocal teachers of America, and when she sings to you, the primitive note of the wilderness seems to hover over her song."[32] As one of the persistent criticisms of singers who have been trained "by the best vocal teachers" is that they quickly lose "the primitive note of the wilderness" or of the plantation, this claim is open to question. But white audiences failed to see or hear that irony.

Her description of Chief White Eagle is more credible: "Study the features of Chief Konoka White Eagle. A typical Indian face—a face you associate with the 'story-book' type of Indians, with Tepees, tomahawks, Braves and wampum. From the lodge of the Winnebagos comes Chief White Eagle, attired in his tribal costume. He will give a short, instructive talk and his very manner of speech will make it decidedly interesting."[33] A handwritten copy in her papers attests that the princess likely wrote the chief's "short, instructive talk."[34]

The company performed in Washington, D.C., in 1920, and a family photograph shows Louise in Indian garb, her mother wrapped in a blanket, holding the little papoose, her grandson, Harry T. Burleigh II. The princess and her chief could not marry legally because her devout Episcopalian husband would not divorce her, and at this time few women without independent financial resources could obtain a divorce without their husband's consent. This complication also prevented Louise and Albert from formally adopting two young Indian girls, Carol and Della, whom

Poster—Princess Nadonis Indians. (Courtesy of the Burleigh Family)

they took into their home. During the school year, the two girls were sent to the Tomah Indian School, while their foster parents pursued their performing career on the lyceum circuits throughout the eastern United States. In the late 1920s Louise and Albert Lowe maintained a home in Chicago, where Lowe worked for the Elevated Railroad Company.[35] During their summers at Mirror Lake, Lowe, as Chief Konoka White Eagle, worked as a tourist guide, and Princess Nadonis occasionally performed in resorts.

Sometime in the mid-1920s, Nadonis added "Shawa" to her name, possibly because in her contacts with Ottawa Indians in Michigan she learned that the short form of the name one of the Ottawa bands call the northern part of Michigan's lower peninsula is "Shawa." This lent credibility to her claim to have been born of Indian parents in Michigan, as was stated in a handwritten "deposition," allegedly by a judge (but in Louise's hand), who averred that he "of [his] own knowledge" could attest to the veracity of her claim. In this document her Indian father's first name is Philip, and her Indian mother's name is Rachel. Louise's fictional world often drew significant details from her former life or that of her husband.[36]

Unfortunately for Louise, Albert Lowe left her about 1930 and married an Indian woman. This betrayal could not be accommodated in Louise's carefully constructed world; to the end of her life she maintained that he had been "stolen" from her by his Winnebago relatives, even though it was common knowledge that he and his wife often spent the summers only a few miles from her home in the Indian village adjacent to the Stand Rock Ceremonial site.[37] She looked for help through her studies of theosophy and the occult to bring Lowe back to her.

But as a performer, the princess was undeterred. She went on to a solo career as "Princess Nadonis Shawa, American Indian Entertainer," who had "entertained Royalty and received distinguished patronage on both continents." She was featured on an International Lyceum Association tour with Carolina Assemblies, presenting her original "drama, poetry, and history," in schools and colleges.[38] Her fringed costume now was lent dignity by the addition of a war bonnet. If Indian women did not traditionally sport war bonnets, none of her audiences were inclined to quibble.

Even in her late sixties, her success on tours in the southeastern United States and California and on the lyceum circuits brought enthusiastic testimonials from sponsors and booking agents showing that Louise Alston Burleigh, in her chosen identity as Princess Nadonis Shawa could satisfy her audiences' expectations. Much of her success must be attributed to her audiences' ignorance of the realities of Native American life; she was perpetuating an idealized mythology, while claiming to authenticate it. But one must also acknowledge that a charismatic presence, informed by her partial immersion in a culture not fully her own, gave her performances an ersatz credibility, just as impersonating rural Southerners had charmed the African American audiences hearing her dialect verse readings.[39]

Princess Nadonis Shawa in war bonnet. (Courtesy of the Burleigh Family)

What of her husband in New York City and her son living in Washington, D.C., when he was not in military service or touring as an actor? The only time one can be sure that Louise and Burleigh met after 1918 was in 1919, when her sister Ray Farley died in New York City as the result of a skating accident at Rockefeller Center. One surmises from the poem Louise wrote memorializing Ray that she came from Wisconsin to attend the funeral in Washington, D.C. "In the Great Somewhere," the song Burleigh wrote for Ray, expresses strong affection for his sister-in-law and a deep sense of loss. That J. P. Morgan offered his private railroad coach to transport Ray's body to Washington, D.C.,[40] suggests that Burleigh could count on Morgan's assistance to resolve difficult situations in addition to making important connections to further his career, though he politely declined Morgan's direct financial assistance.

In the years following their separation, Burleigh sent Louise occasional financial assistance at her request, in what his grandson referred to as "poison pen letters." When newspaper reporters asked Burleigh about his wife, his standard response was that she was "doing Indian work in Wisconsin."[41] However painful their estrangement may have been, Burleigh found solace in his work and in his small apartment in the Bronx. This was a haven where he could work in quiet

Ray Farley. (Courtesy of the Burleigh Family)

Burleigh at work in
his Bronx apartment.
(Courtesy of the
Burleigh Family)

solitude, except for the assistance of his housekeeper Thelma Hall and the quiet admiration of her young son James, Burleigh's godson.[42]

The princess attended Alston's graduation from Dunbar High School in 1917 and visited him in Washington, D.C., in 1920 when her company performed in the city; she visited him and his new wife Erma again in 1922. She was living in Chicago in 1929 when Alston appeared there with the touring company of *Harlem*. She met him with one of her foster daughters and took him home with her to Mirror Lake for the night and then to Eau Claire, Wisconsin, to rejoin his company for their performance there. She visited him and his family in Washington, D.C., in 1926, 1936, and 1945.[43]

* * *

In 1917, the year that Burleigh's arrangements brought the Negro spiritual into concert repertoire just as his wife Louise was preparing to leave New York City, and against the turbulent background of the U.S. armed forces entry into the Great War (World War I), lynchings, and race riots, Burleigh suffered another personal loss in the sudden death of his sister Eva Grace Burleigh. After her teaching career in Erie and Lawrenceville, Virginia, Eva involved herself in social service in New York City. She would often meet incoming vessels at the seaport to find girls who arrived alone and were not met by friends or family. Having grown up on the shores of Lake Erie, where passengers and crews of lake steamers and cargo ships brought a constant influx of travelers and transient residents, she understood the needs of young women traveling unattended. She also helped raise funds for Sojourner Truth House, a home for delinquent girls where for a time she served as an administrator, and she worked with the Urban League.[44] But her life in education and social service was to end all too soon.

She stopped by her brother's apartment on his fiftieth birthday, December 2, 1916, and finding him out, left her card: "Dear Harry: Many, many more returns of this anniversary—50—eh? Some day. Eva. Hope you are better."[45] Her message indicates that they were in fairly close touch, though his busy schedule may not have allowed them to meet often except at musical and social functions. A question about her own health would have been more to the point.

Less than a year later, on November 6, 1917, Eva died suddenly, just as her father had. Two days earlier, on Sunday, she had appeared to be in good health at "an entertainment" at Mother Zion Church, though it was known that she suffered from heart trouble. But on Tuesday, a pedestrian found her unconscious on 133rd Street in Harlem between Lenox and Seventh Avenues, a scenario hauntingly similar to her father's death in Chicago forty-four years earlier. She died a few hours later at Harlem Hospital at the age of forty-seven."[46] After her funeral at St. Philip's Protestant Episcopal Church on West 134th Street, her body was sent to Erie for burial near her mother and grandparents. The passing of Eva, the sister who shared his life and music interests most deeply, was a sharp personal loss for Burleigh.

Now he would lean more heavily than ever on his half-brother, Elzie Elmendorf. Within two years of his arrival in New York City in 1903, Elzie's name began to

Elzie Elmendorf. (Courtesy of the Burleigh Family)

appear with those of Eva and Harry and his wife in the society columns of the New York *Age,* attending or serving as an usher at various music events and enjoying weekends at Wigfall Cottage and Baker Cottage in Asbury Park.[47]

By 1913 Elzie was serving as assistant secretary of the Manhattan YMCA. He helped run the building fund campaign for the YWCA and YMCA. He soon carried more than his share of responsibility for the programming, as occasional illness or short trips to Erie for a rest indicate. In 1915 he resigned from the YMCA to go into the ice cream business in New Rochelle, New York, with Charles Franklin, "a junior member" of his father's Franklin Ice Cream Company in Erie. Four years later, on August 23, 1919, Elzie married Priscilla Hamilton in nearby Poughkeepsie, New York. He eventually returned to the YMCA.[48]

Elzie was the family business man, and as his half-brother Harry was too busy with his music profession to worry about his own business affairs, Elzie served as Burleigh's financial manager. One wonders whether Elzie approved of one business decision Burleigh made: when J. P. Morgan offered him the gift of some stock, Burleigh declined the offer, saying he did not have time to tend to a stock portfolio. This may have occurred after Elzie's death; on the other hand, Burleigh may simply have preferred not to be indebted to his wealthy friends. He had learned from his parents long before how to relate with integrity to the wealthy and powerful, helping him to sustain his long career among the some of the nation's wealthiest families.[49]

In 1921, when Burleigh's older brother Reginald died, Elzie and his wife came to Erie to close the family home. While there, Elzie's only child, christened Elizabeth Waters Grace Florence Elmendorf (Blackwell), was born, the last of Burleigh's relatives to be born in Erie.

Elzie died in March 1939, at the age of sixty-one. His daughter Grace Blackwell believes that his work at the YMCA contributed to his early death; the young man who had learned "to do a common thing in an uncommon way"[50] took his work responsibilities seriously, often to his own detriment. The family member closest to Burleigh in the last decade of his life, Grace describes the relationship between her father and her Uncle Harry as closer than most full-blood brothers. But Elzie did not hesitate to call his famous half-brother to account, a trait Burleigh appreciated. Grace could confront her Uncle Harry frankly, too, when she felt he allowed his professional duties to interfere with family responsibilities.[51]

Grace Blackwell's memories of her Uncle Harry are precious to her, despite his thwarting of her most precious dream, that of becoming a jazz singer. She knew she had a good voice, and though Uncle Harry was little interested in the jazz scene, she and a friend persuaded him to go with them to a jazz performance. They were amused to see that he could not resist moving his foot to the beat. But when a friend arranged for her audition with Jimmy Lunceford's band, he put that foot down, emphatically. Hearing of the upcoming audition, Harry T. Burleigh declared, his hand on his hip, "No niece of mine is going to sing jazz!"[52] As an alternative to a career as a jazz singer, Uncle Harry sent her to secretarial school at the Harlem Y, where she worked for many years. There she became acquainted with the celebrities who roomed there from time to time, though she could not join them on stage. She mourned the loss of that opportunity for many years but insists that she never resented her uncle for his interference.[53]

Though he was not personally involved in the popular music and jazz scene, he maintained friendships with singers he respected, Ethel Waters among them. When Grace and her friends went to see Waters in a stage production, he told her to be sure to go backstage after the show and tell them that her Uncle Harry sent them. "Dear Harry Burleigh!" Waters exclaimed, when they introduced themselves. But his niece was not to follow Ethel Waters' career path.[54]

A stark example of the personal price Burleigh sometimes paid in maintaining his professional career occurred when Elzie died in 1939. Because his funeral was held on Sunday, Burleigh felt compelled to sing at St. George's rather than attend the service. He came to see the family the next day, but Grace could not easily forgive his absence. During a dinner together sometime later she saw that he was in tears. When he said, "I miss Elzie. He was like my right arm," she retorted, "Yes, you missed him so much that you couldn't even come to his funeral. You were too busy being Mr. Burleigh!" Far from being offended, Burleigh said fondly, "That's why I love you, Grace; you're just like your father." In her nineties Grace (Blackwell)

Grace Elmendorf Blackwell, 2004.
(Photo by Jean E. Snyder)

still shows the frank, vigorous spirit Burleigh admired; "When I have something on my mind, I say it!" she declares.[55]

* * *

For his part, Alston felt responsible to help his mother financially, and after he graduated from college he sent her money regularly from his military pay and his teacher's salary. His commitment to his distant mother may have been strengthened by a sense of estrangement from his father. To some degree, Burleigh's wife and son suffered similarly in being unable to live up to the public and private expectations of the family of Harry T. Burleigh.

Though Burleigh failed in some measure as a father, he supported Alston financially through college, and he took great pride in his son's military service and in his stage career. While sending one's children to private schools in England and New England was a long tradition among families who could afford it, in Alston's case

Burleigh and Alston in Europe, 1925. (Courtesy of the Burleigh Family)

it was part of the pattern that Burleigh's grandson Harry T. Burleigh II described: "My grandfather gave him money, but he didn't give him himself."[56]

In summer 1925, Alston accompanied his father to Europe, where he studied with Nadia Boulanger, the famous mentor to American composers. Burleigh's influence might make such a connection possible, but it could not compensate for his absence from Alston's life during his formative years. Nor could such privileged educational sojourns help Alston move successfully beyond the shadow cast by his father's renown. Like many sons of famous fathers, Alston could not satisfy his father's expectations or live comfortably in his father's artistic domain. But he made his own contributions as an actor, a choral director, and a composer, and in his last years as a teacher in Washington, D.C., helped the students in his drama club understand the challenge and joy of the theater.[57]

Alston's son, Harry T. Burleigh II, had fond memories of being with his grandfather in New York City. But he and his wife left New York City, Washington, D.C., and Petersburg, Virginia, to raise their family in Clarksburg, West Virginia, out of the limelight. His wife Mary also grew up in a prominent African American family, and she understood the pressures such connections could exert on the children; her father, Luther Foster, was president of Virginia State College in Petersburg, Virginia, and her brother was president of Tuskegee. They chose to live far enough away from the centers of black institutions that the family simply blended into the community around them. Their three children, Anne, Marie, and Harry III, were known in Clarksburg simply as veterinarian "Doc Burleigh's kids," free to explore and claim their heritage as descendants of the distinguished singer-composer-arranger Harry T. Burleigh in their own time and by their own choice.[58]

13. St. George's Becomes Mr. Burleigh's Church

"A man of grace, gentleness, courtesy, humor and loyalty"

When twenty-seven-year-old Harry T. Burleigh stood for the second most important vocal audition of his life in 1894, he could not have guessed (and certainly the audition committee would not have dreamed) that his successful competition against the fifty-nine other baritone candidates would launch a national and, indeed, an international career as a singer, song composer, and arranger of Negro spirituals.

The drama around Burleigh's hiring as baritone soloist for the wealthy St. George's Protestant Episcopal congregation where financier J. P. Morgan was chief warden is legendary. When National Conservatory founder Jeannette Thurber heard of the vacancy for a baritone soloist, she recommended Burleigh to the rector, Rev. William S. Rainsford. Both knew that including Burleigh in the audition pool would be controversial. A sister congregation, the aristocratic St. Thomas Episcopal Church at Fifth Avenue and Fifty-Third Street, had recently dismissed "a well-known lady" who had sung there for years when members of the congregation discovered "she had Negro blood."[1]

But not all Episcopal parishes, rectors, or choirmasters were of that mind. Four years earlier the chancel choir of Christ Episcopal Church in Trenton, New Jersey, had brought in a young African American boy with "a peculiarly fine voice" who was "an able and accurate singer." When the other boys in the choir threatened to strike, the choir director earned Bishop Scarboro's commendation for refusing to remove him. The bishop promised that the church would protect the young black singer, even if he remained the only singer in the choir. Eventually the other boys "straggled" back and the choir regained its full strength.[2]

On the Sunday when Burleigh walked the two blocks and around the corner from the National Conservatory to St. George's Church in hopes of talking with Dr. Rainsford about the baritone solo position, an usher suggested he stay to see the rector after the service. "I remember my anxiety as I approached the man whose words, heard but a few moments before, had seemed so helpful and sincere. I summoned courage and handed Dr. Rainsford my card. Reading it, he grasped my hand warmly and told me he would tell his organist of my application. Something in his tone and simple manner set me completely at ease. I left the church full of hope that a man who could be so big and yet so simple would not allow my color to prejudice him, but would give me a chance."[3]

Anticipating objections to Burleigh's application, Rev. Rainsford and the choir-master wisely arranged for the applicants to audition behind a screen.[4] Indeed, the committee was aghast to discover that the voice they had chosen among the sixty singers issued from a handsome young Negro singer who was studying at the nearby National Conservatory of Music. Intending to correct their "error," they proposed rescinding their choice, but Rev. Rainsford pronounced their decision final; Harry T. Burleigh was their new soloist. Chief Warden J. P. Morgan cast the deciding vote, saying, "He's my man!"[5]

A brouhaha similar to that in Bishop Scarboro's diocese ensued at St. George's. When the rector announced to the choir that their new baritone soloist was Harry Burleigh, a Negro, "division, consternation, confusion and protest reigned for a time." Rev. Rainsford preferred not to know who supported and who objected to his decision. "Nothing like it had ever been known in the church's musical history. The thing was arranged and I gave no opportunity for its discussion."[6] A choir member who joined the group later reported that seeing Burleigh in the choir "so scandalized the congregation that it rose as a body and left the service."[7] Burleigh was prepared to withdraw quietly, but William Chester, the choirmaster, who had worked hard to make the choir a circle of friendship, reassured him: "You are now a member of this group, and your place is here with us."[8]

Burleigh in St. George's Choir Robes, 1894. (Courtesy of the Burleigh Family)

Some parishioners were not easily mollified. When one huffed that "if the church was to become a minstrel house," he would resign, Dr. Rainsford dismissed his complaint: "Yes, I have heard that you prefer burlesque."[9] When others threatened to withdraw their pledges, in a gesture typically generous to those he cared about (and he cared deeply about St. George's), J. P. Morgan told the rector not to worry; he would cover the missing pledges. Reflecting on this time years later, Burleigh told his grandson he had been amazed at Rev. Rainsford's staunch support. The conservatory faculty assisted him in many ways, but Rainsford "did more for him than anyone else had since he had come to New York."[10] Burleigh soon learned that Rainsford was not inclined to sail with the prevailing winds; arriving at a decision he believed was right, he would risk the loss of friendship, parishioners, or financial support to carry it out. Rainsford's support and that of J. P. Morgan and other wealthy parishioners had far-reaching effects on Burleigh's New York career, eventually reaching from New York to London and other parts of Europe.

With such strong allies, Burleigh found his place in the St. George's choir loft, a position that provided a secure career foundation and spiritual home nearly to the end of his long life. The benefit flowed in both directions. St. George's gave Burleigh financial security and public affirmation, but it must also be said that this congregation with its diverse membership—from the upper-class carriage trade to the middle class to the struggling workers from the Lower East Side tenement neighborhoods—gained greater credibility for its social activism from Burleigh's public renown as its baritone soloist. Led by a succession of distinguished rectors convinced that social reform lay at the heart of the Christian gospel, St. George's evolved into a much more diverse and open congregation than has often been understood.

The New York *Times* was one of the city newspapers that carried weekly announcements of church events, and St. George's was among the congregations that regularly published details of their worship services and special events. From 1894, his first year in the choir, Burleigh's name often appeared in the press announcing his solos in oratorios and on other special occasions. They reported his singing of Jean Baptiste Fauré's "The Palms" on every Palm Sunday from 1895 until his retirement in 1946, and from 1924 on, announcements of the Annual Vesper Service of Negro Spirituals, which continued at least until 1955, six years after his death. Many people looked forward to these occasions and the audiences grew with each succeeding year until his retirement in 1946.[11]

Today we may observe that it would be another twenty years before St. George's hired other African American singers such as contralto soloist Carol Brice. Rev. Elmore McKee, St. George's rector in Burleigh's later years, commented that the congregation "took unwarranted satisfaction in the greater diversity in the choir. How superficial we whites were to have taken any special pride in these crumbs sprinkled along the path of social justice."[12] But organizations and institutions, as well as individuals, incorporate change by degrees, and often with marked inconsistencies. This was true at St. George's and for Burleigh as well. Eventually Burleigh's presence drew many African Americans to St. George's, a welcoming church for them to attend in the long years before legal segregation ended. They came to hear him sing, frequently and in large numbers.

* * *

The Rev. Dr. William S. Rainsford came to Midtown St. George's Protestant Episcopal Church from Toronto, Ontario, in 1883, just over a decade before Burleigh joined the choir. Rainsford had thought carefully about how to build a strong inner-city congregation, and he found St. George's in desperate need. The brownstone houses surrounding Stuyvesant Park had originally been occupied by affluent families who could afford single-family dwellings on the East Side of Midtown Manhattan. But in the years following the Civil War, many of these families moved uptown toward Central Park. The migration left only a handful of the original families, most of whom thought the church should follow her former members Uptown, abandoning the building on the land that George Stuyvesant had provided for the church. Now many of the brownstones had been taken over by multiple families, and some of New York's most desperate tenement houses, inhabited by recent immigrants, were not far away. A few wealthy families remained in the area, and Burleigh supported himself partly by washing dishes in these brownstone homes.[13] But this was a changed and changing community, and St. George's was deep in debt. Even the Roman Catholics declined to take over the building as a mission.[14]

William Rainsford believed that rather than follow its affluent families to more pleasant surroundings, the church should learn to meet the needs of its new community. Like his good friend Theodore Roosevelt, Rainsford was an enthusiastic hunter (especially of grizzlies) and a skilled fisherman, and like Christ, he drew a fisherman's metaphor to explain his reasoning: "The Church ought to be able to fit herself to new conditions. She is like a fisherman accustomed to earn his bread at catching herrings; presently the run of herrings goes away from that section of the sea; in their place comes a tremendous run of smelts. If the fisherman could change his net, he would be a richer man than before, because smelts are better fish; but he starves because he cannot change the size of the meshes."[15]

St. George's had been a pew church; members paid a yearly fee to claim a specific pew as their place in the sanctuary. The first of Rainsford's three conditions for his coming to St. George's was to make it a free church, open to anyone, with no one owning "a piece of real estate in the floor" of the church.[16] Several more of the wealthier families left rather than give back their pews; in Rainsford's view that left fewer "old families" to resist the changes he felt were necessary. Now their middle-class, working-class, and impoverished neighbors would be welcomed as warmly as the wealthy, and some of the wealthiest men, notably J. P. Morgan and William J. Schieffelin, stood at the front door beside the rector before every Sunday service to greet all who entered.[17]

Believing that the best way to build a community church was to start with the children and youth, Rainsford established a Sunday school and a mission to the young men of the neighborhood. Confronted with gangs of recalcitrant street toughs, the towering, athletic rector on one occasion found it necessary to use his fists, only to find that by knocking down a belligerent youth, he gained an ally who would help him soon after in "a scrimmage outside the Sunday-school room."[18] Rainsford's friend, photographer Jacob Riis, who documented in his famous images the stark reality of life in the New York City tenements, found one of the subjects he would immortalize as "Tony" "pasting the ugly old stained-glass windows of St. George's . . . with mud." Rainsford reflected, "If we had things to teach Tony, Tony certainly had much to teach us." Tony became one of Rainsford's boys, a representative of many who joined the St. George's Battalion and went on to fight in the Great War.[19]

As the young men in the area had no facilities for recreation, Rainsford had a fine gymnasium built in the parish house behind the church; space in the dark church basement became a bowling alley; he held dances in the parish house to keep "his girls" from attending "bad dances"; and to expose the young people to good drama, he formed a theater group. Cooking and sewing classes for women were established, along with medical and dental clinics to serve the physical needs of the extended parish family. Rainsford's muscular Christianity, his carefully trained group of clergy assistants to help in visitation and administrative tasks, his determination to serve the most practical physical and social needs of his community, and his democratic methods of enabling leadership among these new constituents brought marked change to St. George's neighborhood and to the congregation.[20]

By 1894 when Burleigh was hired, many of the first Sunday school children had become young adults and were being trained to participate fully in the congregational life. Church attendance, which was sparse in the early months of Rainsford's tenure (he closed the galleries to bring the small congregation closer together),[21] gradually increased. In 1899, five years after Burleigh joined the choir and sixteen years after Rainsford arrived, the number of communicants had increased twentyfold, and of the more than seven thousand members and attendants, nearly six thousand were tenement or boarding-house dwellers. Only forty-nine families owned single-family homes.[22]

This historic church had found its mission at its doors, and throwing open those doors, had come to vigorous new life. Now the church was filled to capacity. A visiting newspaper reporter noted one Sunday that even J. P. Morgan had difficulty finding a seat. After the service he asked an usher, "How do the old St. George's people, like Mr. Morgan there, stand this sort of thing?" "Oh," the usher replied, "most of the old stand-bys have gone away long ago, and those that remain will stand anything."[23]

Central to Rainsford's vision of the great city church was its music. "What we want is to have the most beautiful churches in the crowded districts, and the best music. Where life is sordid, you want beauty; where life is crowded, you want the big church; where there is discord, you want the most beautiful music."[24] One of his innovations was to replace the professional solo quartet or octet with a volunteer choir brought to the front of the church, the young Sunday-school boys in the front row, with the women behind them and the men at the back. Their robes gave singers with diverse financial resources a uniformly dignified appearance, and from their position at the front of the sanctuary the choir could lead the congregation in singing the hymns and liturgical responses. His insistence on these changes cost Rainsford one of his wealthiest parishioners and delayed the building of his beloved parish house. When the man offered him $200,000 to build a parish house if he would hand the choir over to him, Rainsford refused. "Then I won't come to your church any more."[25] Rainsford stood his ground, and a year or two later J. P. Morgan quietly underwrote the building of the parish house (also known as Memorial House), which still serves the congregation more than a century later.[26]

Morgan's immediate approval of Burleigh as baritone soloist reflected his own forthright character. In his tribute to Morgan after his death, Rainsford commented that Morgan was attracted to "a man in whom he saw possibilities of action," and "having made up his mind that the man chosen was at least the best instrument to be found, that none others available could do the thing that had to be done better," he placed full trust in and "exacted a great deal" from him.[27] Though Burleigh would never assume social equality with Morgan, his personal integrity nurtured a profound mutual respect. Morgan loved to hear Burleigh sing at church and in his home. He sang in the Morgan home every Christmas, and at their specific request, Burleigh sang the solos in the hymn "Calvary" at the funeral of both J. P. Morgan and his son J. P. Morgan Jr. The Morgan Library holds a handwritten manuscript of "Deep River," Burleigh's most famous spiritual arrangement, penned for J. P. Morgan Jr., in 1926.[28]

Burleigh's initial salary was $40 per month but rose to $800 per year and eventually to $1,500 annually.[29]

* * *

Except for press notices of his singing, records of Burleigh's early years at St. George's are sparse. But before the end of his first year, he was participating in entertainments put on by the St. George's Men's Club. In November the Athletic Club put on a program at the Central Opera House filled with friends of Men's Club members. Original songs by members were performed, among them one by "H. Burleigh."[30]

In 1898 the St. George's Choir was said to be "one of the largest vested choirs in New York," still with William Chester as director. The male choir consisted of fifty-five voices, with an auxiliary choir of twenty women. There were two soloists, Burleigh and a boy soprano, Charles Meehan, who had toured a number of

European cities and had sung for French composer Jules Massenet and for the French soprano Emma Calvé and the Polish de Reszkes.[31]

The congregation at St. George's brought Burleigh into contact with some of New York's wealthiest citizens, presenting opportunities for him to perform on social occasions in their homes. It was no doubt Rev. Rainsford's friendship with Theodore Roosevelt that led to Burleigh's engagement in January 1900 to entertain New York governor Roosevelt and 350 guests in the governor's mansion.

Burleigh's St. George's connections sometimes drew him more directly into the political arena. An eminent member was Seth Low, president of Columbia University from 1890 to 1901, delegate to the first Hague Peace Conference in 1899 and two-term mayor of New York City. When Low campaigned against the Tammany Hall machine on a reform platform in 1901, Harry T. Burleigh led a gathering of black voters in a rousing campaign battle song to the tune of "Rally Round the Flag": "Union forever, three cheers for Seth Low! / Down with the "grafters," ring rule must go! / For we're marching to the polls, boys, . . . / Three hundred thousand strong, / Shouting the battle cry of freedom." The black voters of the East Side were enthusiastic about Low's candidacy and likely played a significant role in his election.[32] Low's political views coincided with those of his rector, and he was active in the church's outreach in the community. Low told Rev. Rainsford that he found the men's Bible study he taught at St. George's for many years to be more satisfying than his many public offices.[33]

William J. Schieffelin was a member of Booker T. Washington's Tuskegee Institute Board of Trustees and an active supporter of the Hampton Institute in Virginia. In March 1902 the Schieffelins hosted the Thursday Evening Club and "a large number of special guests" in their home on Sixty-Sixth Street. The evening's program featured a chorus of thirty Hampton singers, including Native American singers and dancers, and a number of solos by H. T. Burleigh. The extensive guest list included Mr. and Mrs. Henry Cabot, Mr. and Mrs. Walter Damrosch, Mr. and Mrs. Cornelius Vanderbilt, Mrs. Astor, George Foster Peabody, and many others whom the Schieffelins likely hoped to interest in supporting the Hampton and Tuskegee Institutes.[34] Burleigh's performances at such social occasions led to increasingly frequent engagements at the homes of New York's Gilded Age aristocracy such as Mrs. Vanderbilt, who offered him $300 to sing at her home in 1903.[35] As William Schieffelin, George Foster Peabody and others were also among Booker T. Washington's supporters, these contacts interfaced with Burleigh's appearances on Washington's fundraising tours. Burleigh was quick to take advantage of these opportunities. Later in 1902 Burleigh requested Washington's approval of his asking Schieffelin to arrange for singing engagements in the cottages of Bar Harbor, Maine, where the Schieffelins, the Damrosches, and many other New York society folks spent the summer, and where Morgan's yacht *The Corsair* often docked. Washington was scheduled to speak in Bar Harbor that summer, accompanied by the Hampton Singers, and Burleigh, who frequently appeared with the Hampton students, hoped to join them.[36]

* * *

Several years before Burleigh's appearance at the Schieffelin residence, Schieffelin and Rev. Rainsford explored the possibility of having Burleigh sent South to Tuskegee or Hampton to address problems not clearly identified. On April 8, 1899, Victoria Earle Matthews, "a journalist, author, lecturer, clubwoman, social worker and missionary,"[37] active in promoting the rights and welfare of African American women, wrote Booker T. Washington to describe a conversation she had had with Schieffelin and Rev. Rainsford. Washington had referred them to her, and she was reporting what she had told them. The letter in Matthews's handwriting is barely legible, so it is difficult to be sure exactly what problem or potential problem they were addressing. Two issues are suggested: Burleigh's somewhat problematic relationship with young women, and a possible drinking problem. Rainsford and Schieffelin's conversation with Matthews began with their confirming that she had said she would not object to introducing Burleigh to "the young lady in your charge but you did not care to have him c[illegible]." Is the word "call" or "court"? It is not clear. The two St. George's emissaries acknowledged Burleigh's gifts but felt he needed mentoring; with the "influence of Mr. Washington the good in him might be developed sufficiently strong to over balance his [illegible]." In the "sheltered environment of the Tuskegee Community" Burleigh would be prevented from indulging in drink. If not Tuskegee, perhaps Hampton Institute. Burleigh's musical work need not be limited to New York City; "it might be a Christian brother's act to place him where his best qualities will be called into action and where his influences racially could affect permanent good."[38] This letter is in sharp contrast to the usual references to Burleigh's fifty-two-year tenure at St. George's, which came to be a near-beatification.

Burleigh's ability to charm women was well known, though this letter was dated just two months after his marriage to Louise Alston. But this research has found no other reference to Burleigh's drinking to excess.[39] The letter raises puzzling questions: Was Burleigh's presence in the choir problematic because of the mutual attraction he elicited among young—or not so young—white women in the congregation? Many years later Burleigh shared with Josephine Harreld [Love], who as a young piano student at Juilliard often served this lonely elderly man as his confidant, that he knew there were women at St. George's who would gladly engage him in a sexual affair.[40] Or was his tendency to involve himself in civil-rights actions too public and forthright for this socially active congregation? With the lack of other evidence of a drinking problem throughout Burleigh's career, was this a cover for some other, perhaps racially sensitive, issue that Rainsford and Schieffelin were unwilling to address directly? The timing is intriguing, as it comes just months before Burleigh began his fifteen-year association with Booker T. Washington.

Washington may well have intervened to reassure Rainsford and Schieffelin that Burleigh did not need to leave New York City; he would advise the young man and monitor his behavior to make such a move unnecessary. There is no evidence that Burleigh knew of this correspondence. More likely, Washington advised him appropriately and helped him resolve whatever problem troubled St. George's leadership. Men such as J. P. Morgan, William J. Schieffelin, and Rev. William Rainsford were skilled at covert action to resolve problems in a manner that left no paper trail. If Burleigh did learn of this unsuccessful effort to send him south, it would certainly explain why he declined invitations to enter the rector's residence through all the years of his association with St. George's, as Rev. Edward O. Miller reported after his death. But his warm appreciation for Rainsford's support makes it unlikely that he was ever told of the clandestine effort that would have dramatically changed the course of his career.[41]

* * *

The St. George's Men's Club, founded by Rev. Rainsford in 1888, gave Burleigh a congenial place to spend leisure time and fostered a degree of social intimacy with men of the congregation. The club's large reading room was in the parish house, and its activities centered on "the intellectual and social side of the parish life," providing "concerts, plays, 'socials,' and 'smokers,'" supplementing the work of the assistant clergy by providing wholesome recreation for the men of the congregation. During Rainsford's tenure as rector, membership was limited to members of St. George's Church, but in later years it welcomed any man of Protestant faith.[42] The club rooms were open from 8:00 a.m. to 11:00 p.m. every day except Sunday, when it opened at 1:00 p.m.

In addition to the quiet reading room with its library of books and subscriptions to the major daily papers and the gymnasium (largely patronized by the younger men), the club eventually offered shower facilities and billiard rooms. It also afforded "a place for entertainment and social development within the environment of the Church and within the financial reach of those in all walks of life."[43] Among the entertainments was an occasional Gilbert and Sullivan operetta, such as the 1914 staging of *H.M.S. Pinafore,* which Burleigh helped to produce. The nominal membership fee was easily within Burleigh's budget. Photographs in the annual reports show well-dressed men seated at tables or in comfortable chairs enjoying their reading. Burleigh would have found the club a stimulating complement to the lively gatherings at the Marshall Hotel. He often used St. George's Men's Club stationery for his correspondence, and he quickly became a valued member of the organization.[44]

* * *

The most startling aspect of Burleigh's participation in the St. George's Men's Club is his role in producing a series of minstrel shows, beginning in 1906 (the year after Rev. Rainsford left St. George's, though no indication has been found of his approval or disapproval of this activity). In a sense, St. George's did become a "minstrel house," facilitated, in fact, by Harry T. Burleigh, the Negro baritone soloist. The St. George's Men's Club Minstrel Shows continued into the mid-1920s, even after the Annual Vesper Service of Negro Spirituals had been instituted, but Burleigh's involvement as music director ended after a decade.

Minstrel shows, America's most popular entertainment during the nineteenth century, had dwindled with the rise of vaudeville at the beginning of the twentieth century, but amateur productions continued for many years, even in the black community. Many of the most distinguished black stage performers of the early twentieth century had their start in minstrelsy. African Americans in both the North and the South enjoyed seeing talented black performers on stage. It was not unusual even into the late 1910s to see announcements in the New York *Age* and other black newspapers of minstrel shows produced by and for black audiences. As late as 1921 the New York *Amsterdam News* featured an article by a long-time minstrel performer who found his transient life in minstrel shows demanding but fully satisfying.[45]

As Eric Lott observes in *Love and Theft,* minstrelsy demonstrated the persistent fascination of white America with black culture.[46] But one ponders with a certain bemusement the complex resonances echoing from a stage filled with black-faced white men under the direction of a prominent black musician such as Harry T. Burleigh. Certainly the intent of Burleigh's friends in the St. George's Men's Club was not to demean him or his cultural heritage; this is a complicated example of the "love" of well-meaning white people for black culture, however deeply rooted in cultural theft and misappropriation, to say nothing of a lack of cross-cultural sensitivity that is shocking to twenty-first-century sensibilities. But in Burleigh they apparently saw one who could make their minstrel productions "authentic," however incongruous that seems. A full treatment of the many levels of irony this aspect of Burleigh's St. George's career represents is beyond the scope of this study, but Burleigh's decade as musical director illustrates the complex and contradictory set of expectations black performers of Burleigh's generation faced.

Burleigh served as musical director of the first minstrel show, in 1906, held at Palm Garden on February 21. The "crowning social success of the season," the minstrel show and reception drew an audience that crowded the hall despite stormy weather. The profits enabled the club to make some improvements, including a new billiard table to replace the eighteen-year-old one.[47] The performers were drawn entirely from the club's 525 members, a source of continuing pride as the minstrel show became a widely anticipated annual event. St. George's was not the only church to produce minstrel shows; the Protestant Episcopal Church of the Redeemer, "noted also for its broadness of view," was known to present minstrel shows as well as other dramatic productions.[48]

The program for the 1907 minstrel show reported that the committee in charge of the previous year's show "were obliged by lack of previous experience to feel their way 'step by step' in their efforts to make that entertainment a success." Gratified by their initial triumph, they found that their first task in preparation for the second annual minstrel show was to find a larger hall. Burleigh was warmly credited for his able direction: "It is the continued good fortune of the Club to have for our leader Mr. Harry T. Burleigh, whose musical ability and personal popularity is so well known to every member, that his earnest efforts on behalf of the Club [are] always a guarantee of success." In addition to his duties as director Burleigh appeared in the minstrel "circle as a featured soloist and led a quartette that promised 'a musical treat.'"[49]

The 1907 program reveals an important benefit of these performances for Burleigh. In part one of the program another circle performer sang Burleigh's "Just Because," published in 1906. Burleigh's solo, "I Want What I Want," appeared in part two, and the St. George Quartette, with Burleigh as baritone, ended the Olio with the final flourish. In addition to showcasing a Burleigh song in the stage performance, page fifteen of the printed program featured a half-page photo of Burleigh, "Our Musical Director and Leader," courtesy of Brooks & Denton, his

Burleigh as Musical Director of St. George's Men's Club Minstrel Show, 1907. (Program, 1907 St. George's Men's Club Minstrel Show, courtesy of Karen James)

Our Musical Director and Leader

By Courtesy of Brooks & Denton

MR. H. T.
BURLEIGH
Baritone Soloist -- St. George's Church

agents. A half-page ad on the back cover listed twenty of his "New Songs and Ballads" available at his publishers, the William Maxwell Company. So the St. George's Men's Club Minstrel Shows offered Burleigh a prime opportunity to publicize his growing list of song publications.[50] The shows turned out to be excellent fundraisers. Profits from the second minstrel show were sufficient to purchase a new piano for the club room and contribute $100 to help equip the girls' gymnasium.[51]

A study of the 1907 program repertoire suggests that the music was quite different from the stereotypical mid-nineteenth-century minstrel show fare, though the format was the classic minstrel show with a first part, an olio, and a second part. Most minstrel shows at this time were really variety shows, only loosely organized in the minstrel tradition. The olio was usually omitted and the caricatures focused on the Irish, the Germans, the Italians, and other recent immigrant arrivals rather than primarily on African Americans. Only one song in the 1907 show is unmistakably of the popular ragtime "coon song" genre: "If the Man in the Moon Were a Coon" (1905), written (but not credited in the program) by Fred Fisher. All were popular songs of 1905 and 1906, except for "Down in the Depths," a 1902 song deploring the hard lot of coal miners. The printed program, of course, gives no indication of the stage business, the jokes, or the cavorting and clowning of the face-blackened performers, and one can only speculate on Burleigh's role in the staging.[52]

It is difficult to reconcile Burleigh's role in producing minstrel shows in this setting with his well-documented efforts to counteract the racist stereotypes of minstrelsy and ragtime. Granted, he was well acquainted with the black musical theater produced by his friends Bert Williams and George Walker, Will Marion Cook, and others. Cook and Dunbar's *In Dahomey* had played under Broadway's white lights in 1903 and gone on to great success in England, delighting King Edward VII and his son in a command performance at Buckingham Palace. Perhaps inevitably at the time, minstrelsy was at the heart of most black popular music and musical theater. The Johnson brothers from Jacksonville, Florida, James Weldon and J. Rosamond, along with Bob Cole and others, were writing songs that today sound uncomfortably close to the minstrel tradition. But on careful examination it becomes apparent that these composers and performers used the minstrel tradition in ways that often mocked its conventions while seeming to perpetuate them. Black performers entertaining black audiences or ethnically mixed audiences could give multilayered presentations that subverted the demeaning caricatures for those who could read the cues.

Though their ability to "authenticate" African American culture and music provided stage careers for gifted black performers like Burleigh, these artists were caught between their efforts to win acknowledgment of their creative gifts, their commitment to racial uplift, and the demands of their audiences to lend authenticity to the performance traditions rooted in a pretense of racial representation. During the years Burleigh was musical director of minstrel shows for the St. George's Men's Club, he was enjoying weekends at Asbury Park with Bert and

Lottie Williams, George and Aida Overton Walker, and other performing artists in the black theater. Surely their conversations included discussions of their theatrical work and the strong ambiguities and tensions with which they struggled in preserving a public integrity.

Throughout the years when his friends were working their way through the thickets of performative representation, Burleigh was helping to produce the increasingly successful minstrel shows for the St. George's Men's Club. We have no documented record of his personal comfort or discomfort with his role in these performances. But it is significant that Burleigh never referred to this chapter of his St. George's story in later years; that silence thunders in our minds. We can only speculate about Burleigh's inner response to the dilemma this task presented him. Like his black colleagues in the performing arts, his public career and his financial survival to a certain extent depended on his collaboration and collusion with a performance tradition that seems entirely antithetical to nearly every other part of his life as a musician.

The Men's Club section of the 1911 *St. George's Annual Report* featured a large photograph of the 1910 St. George's Men's Club Minstrel Show personnel. The club suffered a decrease in membership during the 1910–11 season, with a resulting loss of income from membership dues, and the more elaborate stage setting and costumes for the 1910 show reduced the profit from the performance. But the annual report asserted that "the Minstrel Show, as ever, was the most important social

1910 minstrel show. (Courtesy of Episcopal Disocesan Archives, New York City)

event of the year."[53] The photograph shows a stage full of performers in blackface, with only four in the center of the picture appearing in their natural complexions. Burleigh stands among them, directly in the middle below a floral arrangement, darkened only by the pigmentation that was his birthright.

Burleigh's primary role was musical director, and in 1913 the minstrel show committee hired an experienced minstrel performance coach to work with him. The performance coach was re-engaged for the 1914 show. The Sunday bulletin reported, "We will have six end men, at least four soloists and a chorus of seventy-five all in costume, coached by Mr. Doyle and under the direction of Mr. Burleigh."[54] The 1915 annual report said that the production, which brought a profit of $557.67, "was as successful as ever and served to more firmly establish the reputation of the club for its achievements along that line of theatricals."[55]

In February 1917, just as Burleigh's first solo arrangements of spirituals were bursting on the New York City recital scene, the St. George's Evening Trade School produced an "African Minstrel Show." The Sunday bulletin urged, "Do not miss it! It's never been equaled even on the banks of the Congo!"[56] But in late April of the same year another program offered an antidote to the minstrel show caricatures of black musical life, to be presented at the St. George's parish house: "The American Church Institute for Negroes" would give a "FREE Presentation of 'Progress,' A NEGRO PLAY BY NEGRO ACTORS—Followed by Negro Songs and Melodies."[57] There was no mention in the Sunday bulletin of who would be in the cast or what part Burleigh might have played in bringing this performance to St. George's. But surely at a time when his national renown as a leading composer of American art song was reaching its peak and he was about to introduce Negro spirituals into concert repertoire, he must have wished to establish a more truly representative view of his heritage in music. By 1922 the minstrel shows seem to have run their course as fundraisers for the church, and for Burleigh a new day for his public recognition as baritone soloist at St. George's Church was about to dawn.

* * *

The young Rev. Hugh Birckhead, who assumed the position of rector when Rev. William Rainsford resigned, had served for four years as one of Rainsford's assistants at St. George's. Like his predecessor, he was tall and athletic, and though his New England background "had better fitted him for aristocratic life than for pastoral calls to crowded tenements," Dr. Rainsford had trained and inspired him.[58] Birckhead was committed to leading the same socially active congregation as his mentor. Though the foundation for recognition surely was laid during Rainsford's tenure, in the second year of Birckhead's term the Paris Exposition Internationale awarded St. George's the Grand Prix for "socialized work."[59] But the community surrounding St. George's continued to change, and by 1908 only a third of the congregation lived in the immediate area. Members living at a distance tended to be less directly involved in congregational life, and in 1909 Henry Ford's new mass-produced Model T motorcar created a new Sunday diversion: driving out of town on the weekend. Adult attendance declined, though the Sunday schools continued to grow.

Birckhead believed that philanthropy and providing social services were necessary expressions of Christian service, but he understood the need to go further than "patching up" social conditions. Like Rainsford, he believed that systemic injustice also must be addressed: "The whole scheme of philanthropy, necessary as it is," was not sufficient. "It is part of our good-natured kindness that we would rather bind up the broken arm than correct the machinery which inflicted the fracture." In 1912 Birckhead resigned to accept a call to Emmanuel Church in Baltimore. As the community that surrounded St. George's was now increasingly diverse, religiously as well as ethnically, he felt he lacked the skills to meet the challenge. "It is going to take a new man with a new method to see the situation clearly and to administer it for those at our doors who need most what we have to give them in the way of uplift."[60]

In April 1912 Rev. Karl Reiland began his twenty-four-year tenure as St. George's rector. When he arrived, J. P. Morgan summoned him to the marble library on Madison Avenue that housed and displayed his "magnificent collection of books and manuscripts." In typically abrupt fashion he laid out his guidelines for the new rector. Rev. Reiland should understand three cardinal rules. "The pulpit of St. George's is free. I know you are a liberal. Say what you want and we'll stand by you. Never answer a newspaper. And when you want to raise money, put me down for half."[61]

A year later, Reiland officiated at Morgan's funeral, along with the bishop of New York, the bishop of Massachusetts, and the bishop of Connecticut. In accordance with Morgan's wishes, the simple service included no eulogy. The congregation sang three hymns selected by Morgan, and the choir, with Burleigh as soloist, sang Paul Rodney's "Calvary."[62]

Like Rainsford, the Rev. Karl Reiland would affect Harry T. Burleigh's role in the St. George's choir and congregation in important ways. Reiland greatly admired his predecessor Rainsford, who he felt "had created the spirit of St. George's, a spirit that was inspirational, liberal, and institutional."[63] A choir boy for nine years and a leader of his college glee club, Reiland shared Rainsford's belief in the central importance of music in the life of the congregation. During Reiland's second year as rector, Charles Louis Safford began his ten-year position as organist and choir director, coming from the Madison Avenue Presbyterian Church where Dr. Henry Sloane Coffin was pastor. Safford had also been director of music at the New York High School and at the Brooklyn Polytechnical School.

Building on his experience in music education, Safford expanded the choir program. By 1919 there were four choirs: the Main Choir sang for the Sunday services, the Chapel Choir sang for Wednesday night services; the Chancel Choir of young girls and the Junior Choir of boys sang at weekday Lenten Services and for the children's service on Sunday afternoons. The Chancel Choir also sang simple anthems at services in the summer, when adult members were on vacation. A series of 4:00 p.m. vesper services were added to the calendar from November to April, and all the choirs, each with its distinctive vestments, participated in these events. The busy schedule of rehearsals and services required careful planning on Safford's part and loyal commitment on the part of choir members. Safford made it clear that other church organization meetings were to be considered a lower priority: "Choir rehearsals necessarily conflict with other organization meetings, and there can be no remedy. The rule, however, is that choir rehearsals take precedence, and each person must make a choice between things which are in conflict. Regularity at choir rehearsals is of the first importance. This should be understood to be the invariable rule."[64]

In addition to these extensive weekly choir duties, Burleigh was on call to sing at funerals, weddings, and other special events at St. George's. Rev. Rainsford had opened the church to funerals for those in the community who could not afford expensive funeral arrangements or had no other church home. As a professional musician, Burleigh was available when most of the adult choir members were busy at their daily work, so he could serve at funerals during the work week and was also free to sing for parishioners who were confined to their homes. A 1928 letter written by William Seaman Bainbridge on the death of his mother shows how much Burleigh was loved for this music ministry. At her request, Mrs. Bainbridge's funeral was held in her home. "Mr. Harry T. Burleigh, the well known baritone, who gave Mother such joy on her eightieth and eighty-sixth birthdays by coming to our home and singing some old time melodies, was present on this, her Eternal Birthday. His heart went into his singing 'How Firm a Foundation,' 'The King of Love My Shepherd is,' and 'The Strife Is O'er, the Battle Won.'"[65]

Just as Burleigh's singing ministered to members of the congregation, the St. George's sanctuary and all that the congregation represented were for him a spiritual refuge, a retreat. Reverend Edward O. Miller wrote biographer Anne Key Simpson, "I remember this dignified gentleman, with balding white hair and finely-trimmed mustache, sitting alone in the church every Sunday at least a half hour before choir rehearsal. As he said to me, 'I have to get the feel of the place before I sing.'"[66]

* * *

The extensive music program at St. George's was enriched by frequent participation of artists who resided in the city or who performed there on occasion. Rev. Reiland and choirmaster Charles Safford drew on their wide circle of acquaintances in the arts, and on Burleigh's contacts as well, to engage these guest artists. The 4 o'clock Sunday afternoon vesper services often featured special music by a soloist from another church, an opera singer or instrumentalist, or a well-known actor to read the scriptures. Among these were tenor Reed Miller, with whom Burleigh sang in Norfolk, Connecticut, during Samuel Coleridge-Taylor's second American visit in 1906;[67] David Bispham, who sang Burleigh songs in London as early as 1901;[68] David Mannes, who established the Music School Settlement for Colored People in 1912;[69] and contralto Mary Jordan, soloist at Temple Emanu-El, to whom Burleigh dedicated his 1916 "Deep River" arrangement.[70]

Burleigh's earliest known music publication was his 1895 "Christmas Bells," a simple hymn for junior choir. He wrote a number of other hymns and anthems for the St. George's choir and several sacred solo songs. Notable among these are the anthem "St. Patrick's Breastplate," a setting of "While Shepherds Watched Their Flocks," and a lovely setting of the Lord's Prayer. As Burleigh's reputation as a composer grew, Charles Safford occasionally programmed his work. These instances increased after 1917, when Burleigh's pioneering solo and choral arrangements of Negro spirituals established him as a leading exponent of African American sacred song.[71]

* * *

In 1923 George W. Kemmer assumed the position of choir director and organist at St. George's. Rev. Karl Reiland recognized Kemmer's artistic temperament as a boy soloist at Grace Church,[72] and Kemmer remembered Burleigh from his days as boy chorister. In 1924, his second year at St. George's, Kemmer established the Annual Vesper Service of Negro Spirituals, honoring Burleigh's work as an arranger of spirituals and recognizing his thirty years as baritone soloist at St. George's. During Kemmer's tenure, the choir sang Negro spirituals with some frequency, primarily but not exclusively those arranged by Burleigh. Sometimes the spirituals were featured in the regular Sunday morning services, but more often they were a part of the afternoon vesper services held from November to May. The special Annual Vesper Service of Negro Spirituals became a tradition that drew large audiences to the church and increasing public recognition both to Burleigh and to St. George's liberal and inclusive role in New York City's church and music community.[73]

The cover of the program for the 1924 Vesper Service of Negro Spirituals featured photos of the twenty-eight-year-old Burleigh in 1894, when he was first hired as baritone soloist, and of the fifty-seven-year-old Burleigh at his thirtieth anniversary. In many ways the first Vesper Service of Negro Spirituals in March 1924 marked the apex of Burleigh's public career. The celebration of his thirtieth anniversary as baritone soloist at St. George's Protestant Episcopal Church on Stuyvesant Square acknowledged and extended Burleigh's renown as the premiere singer and arranger of spirituals. At the close of the morning service, the vestry presented Burleigh with a gold-filled purse. The afternoon vesper service drew crowds that required police assistance to "keep the streets open for traffic" and filled all seats and standing room a half-hour before the service began. For the hundreds who could not be admitted to the March 30 vesper service, it was repeated at 4 o'clock on April 27, "with some additional Negro spirituals never used in public before."[74]

Burleigh's reputation as a singer and composer of art songs had been well established since the second decade of the century. When his solo arrangements of Negro spirituals "hit the charts" in the 1916–1917 season, his focus shifted to preserving and disseminating them through his polished arrangements. The solo arrangements immediately began to appear in recitals by many of the artists who had used his art songs. By 1924, spirituals were being arranged and performed by composers and singers of every ethnic and national background. Indeed, the following year saw the publication of several anthologies of Negro spirituals, a "vogue," in James Weldon Johnson's term.[75]

The gratification and pride of the St. George's congregation in Burleigh's accomplishments was more than matched by its significance to the black community, in and far beyond New York City. Evidence of the impact can be seen in reports of another service of spirituals by the St. George's choir, this time in Harlem, near the end of May 1924, a month after the repeated Vesper Service of Negro Spirituals. The Mother A.M.E. Zion congregation had recently moved into their new building on West 137th Street, and the people of Harlem paid "a wonderful tribute" to "Dr. Harry T. Burleigh, the race's most distinguished musician," packing "the spacious auditorium," to welcome Burleigh and "his fellow-members of the choir of aristocratic St. George's Protestant Episcopal Church," with their rector, Dr. Karl Reiland, and the organist-choirmaster, George W. Kemmer. "This was the first time a choir from one of the large, wealthy and prominent white churches in New York City had paid a visit to a Harlem colored church and the tremendous audience which assembled seemed to sense the fact that they were taking part in a history-making event."[76]

George Kemmer's recognition of Burleigh's work as singer, composer and arranger in this special vesper service affirmed and capitalized on Burleigh's fame. Now in addition to the yearly press notices of his Palm Sunday rendition of Fauré's "The Palms" and the frequent mention of his solos in anthems and oratorios, the major New York newspapers carried feature articles announcing the Annual Vesper Service of Negro Spirituals and often a review after the service. The reports of the first Vesper Service of Negro Spirituals in 1924 reveal how profound was Burleigh's impact on the St. George's congregation, New York City's diverse music community, and on the social and cultural elite of the city.[77]

Several papers described the emotional response of many in the March 30 vesper service crowd. Hundreds of those who were turned away stayed, hoping to greet Burleigh "after the service. People well known in exclusive social and business circles sat in the same pew, or stood side by side, with people of Burleigh's race."[78] The service began with a choir processional, Burleigh's new "O Brothers, Lift Your Voices." "The pageant of the church led by the flag with its red cross glowing on a white ground, proceeded solemnly from end to [end] of the thronged nave," Burleigh's voice sounding "above the whole choir when he marched in the procession."[79]

After a brief address, rector Dr. Karl Reiland called Burleigh, his "faithful co-worker, devoted friend and inspiring companion," to join him. "Out of the choir strode the musician, a small man, gray haired, not very dark, but distinctly Negro, wearing insignia of the degree of doctor of music over his white surplice."[80] "There was no applause, of course, but an audible murmur swept through the crowd, as the white-haired negro, garbed in snowy vestments, stood beside the rector, and bowed several times." At the John Pierpont Morgan memorial pulpit, Burleigh and Dr. Reiland stood a moment "with hands clasped." As Burleigh left the pulpit, "the choir began the singing of one of his best known compositions:

> "An' I couldn't hear nobody pray;
> An' I couldn't hear nobody pray;
>> O 'way down yonder by myself,
>> O Lord, I couldn't near nobody pray.

"Then came the real Burleigh. Singing without accompaniment, the choir did his settings of several Southern Negro spirituals."[81]

Another description reflected the persistent ambiguity of perception some white listeners brought to their encounters with black music. "Strange music from a choir that has sung the noble old anthems of the masters; music with a barbaric richness of color that gripped the congregation. Sometimes it would be hummed, sometimes there was a humming accompaniment to the words. When the last chord of 'Deep River' shaded into silence more than one handkerchief mopped wet eyes."[82] More aptly, Dr. Reiland described the Negro's contribution to music as a "wondrous, limpid, delicate, spiritual song."[83] Reflecting on Burleigh's thirty years with the choir, he continued: "Thirty years ago we took into the choir a good man with a fine voice. . . . We did not know that he would become, as he is now, the leading creative genius of his race in music, as a composer and as an interpreter."[84]

In addition to solo renditions of "Nobody Knows de Trouble I've Seen" and "Weepin' Mary," the choir sang "My Lord, What a Morning," and as the processional, "Let Us Cheer the Weary Traveler." Burleigh also wrote "I Hope My Mother Will Be There" for the occasion, and movements 2 and 3 of his violin-piano suite *Southland Sketches* were played.

Some African Americans in the audience might a decade earlier have been critical of Burleigh's singing of the spirituals, especially for white audiences. But by 1924, Burleigh's singing and his artful arrangements had generated a sea-change, awakening pride in these songs of which some had been ashamed or believed should be sung only by those whose ancestors had created them.

This first Vesper Service of Negro Spirituals was broadcast over radio station WJZ, and in 1925 St. George's was "the first church in the area to have its vesper services broadcast weekly over a major network." These broadcasts made Burleigh's voice familiar to a wide radio audience and "brought many to St. George's who had not previously been interested in religion." St. George's historian summed up the impact: "Karl Reiland's sermons—like Rainsford's legacy, Burleigh's music, and the legend of J. P. Morgan's generosity—helped to characterize St. George's."[85]

In December 1924 St. George's choir sold out a Town Hall concert to raise money for the choir rooms. Among the choral pieces were works by Schubert, Ethelbert Nevin, Brahms, and Elgar, and then Burleigh sang "a group of his own works to his own accompaniment and received a double encore." The choir sang Burleigh's arrangements of "Steal Away" and "I'm a-Rolling," and "Were You There?" and closed the concert with Samuel Coleridge-Taylor's "Viking Song."[86] New York audiences could always count on the fine musicianship of St. George's choir, but their baritone soloist and his arrangements of Negro spirituals enhanced the programs they presented from 1924 on.

In the 1924 Vesper Service of Negro Spirituals and for the following several years, all the spiritual arrangements were by Burleigh. Later, arrangements by other composers began to appear on the programs. Most of the arrangers were Burleigh's friends and colleagues and several were younger artists he mentored. Violin arrangements by his friend Clarence Cameron White were played in 1926 and in 1932. In the 1930s arrangements by Hall Johnson, Natalie Curtis Burlin, Nathaniel Dett, Carl Diton, and Carlette Thomas were featured. From 1937 on, arrangements by choirmaster George Kemmer were programmed with increasing frequency. Also in 1937 the arrangement of "Great Day, the Righteous Marching" by Burleigh's son Alston Waters Burleigh became a program standard, and Alston was sometimes interviewed by the press along with his father. In 1939 the choir sang a Kemmer arrangement dedicated to Burleigh, "Cert'n'y Lord," which became a standard selection. That year the Hampton Institute Quartet were the featured guest soloists. Arrangements by William Dawson and Florence Price were featured in 1948, two years after Burleigh's retirement from St. George's.[87]

In addition to the increasing variety of arrangers, the programs presented an engaging variety of performing forces, from solos to the adult choir of mixed voices to the junior choir, sometimes in combination with the adult choir, and often a choral arrangement featured a soloist. Burleigh was the featured soloist during the early years, but other St. George soloists also appeared. Burleigh frequently sang "Go Down, Moses," but in later years, two of his favorite solos were "I Know the Lord Has Laid His Hand on Me," and "I Don't Feel No-ways Tired." Toward the end of his fifty-two years as soloist at St. George's, these two spirituals challenged any who might think his best years of service had passed.

Most of Burleigh's choral arrangements were meant to be sung a cappella, and their complex harmonies demanded a trained choir for effective performance, a challenge which St. George's choirs were well prepared to meet. In the sixteen years for which programs were available for analysis, four of the vesper services featured Burleigh arrangements for theremin, and on one occasion the theremin accompanied the violin in one of his violin sketches. In all, at least forty-three Burleigh arrangements of spirituals were used during the years from 1924 to 1955, along with eighteen by George Kemmer, and seven by Hall Johnson. As might be expected by those familiar with Burleigh's work, one could count on "Deep River" as the most common element on the program. The choir sang Burleigh's 1913 choral arrangement of "Deep River" every year but one of those examined, reflecting the view that "Deep River" was his most masterly arrangement, for both choir and solo voice.[88]

The Annual Vesper Services of Negro Spirituals continued to draw large crowds even when it was clear that Burleigh's "indestructible baritone"[89] was showing signs of wear. Rev. William S. Rainsford recalled that "Harry Burleigh's sweet baritone voice [was] worn a little," though "it still leads the choir which he entered against much protest . . . and St. George's is proud of him, proud of what he has accomplished as a musician, and loves and honours him for what he has proved himself to be as a Christian man."[90]

In addition to the yearly Vesper Service of Negro Spirituals, special celebrations marked Burleigh's fortieth anniversary in 1934, and his forty-fifth in 1939. The disparity between public statements about Burleigh's singing in his last years and the loving but frank descriptions of those who knew him best is striking. Newspaper reports of interviews and reviews of his Palm Sunday singing and the Vesper Services of Negro Spirituals in these later years gave no hint of his declining vocal power. But St. George's had become for Burleigh a lifeline that he could not easily relinquish.

Whatever a coldly objective critic might have heard, Burleigh's voice still evoked strong emotions in his audience. In 1942 the Pittsburgh *Courier* reviewed Burleigh's Palm Sunday singing: "His moving rendition of 'The Palms' by Faure brought tears to the eyes of many in the congregation, which was sprinkled with Harlem friends of the composer." A white parishioner who had been ten years old on the Palm Sunday when she first heard Burleigh sing "The Palms" expressed pride that she "had not missed the rendition a single year, and on Sunday was able to bring along her grandchild to hear Mr. Burleigh sing it."[91]

As for retiring, Burleigh told the *Courier* reporter that he had "tried to retire years ago, but the congregation would not allow him." This view was publicly supported by the choirmaster, George W. Kemmer, and S. Lewis Elmer, registrar of the American Guild of Organists. They agreed that "the only effect of advanced age on Burleigh's voice was to make it more rich and resonant." Kemmer went further: "That man is remarkable. Every year I think he does a better job than before."[92]

* * *

For his fiftieth anniversary in 1944, St. George's went all out to commemorate their most famous choir member and soloist. The rector at this time was Rev. Dr. Elmore M. McKee, for whom Burleigh named his hymn "In Christ There Is No East or West," based on a spiritual. A year earlier Chief Warden C. C. Burlingham had suggested to Columbia University president Nicholas Murray Butler that the university grant Burleigh an honorary doctor of music degree. When Butler did not follow through, Burlingham wrote Bishop Manning suggesting that "a word from you to N.M.B. would be weighty."[93] But Burleigh's star was setting, and Columbia University did not respond. Rev. McKee hoped for editorials from the major newspapers, as the event was "of community interest, national interest and international interest."[94] The newspapers as usual ran feature articles, but the governor declined a request to sponsor the event.

By this time, the younger members of the choir may have begun to tire of the attention given the elderly baritone soloist. In a letter to Burlingham, Rev. McKee reported that "Kemmer feels strongly that the impression should not get abroad that HTB is the only member of the choir." He admitted, "I haven't done this part a bit well." McKee urged Burlingham to make the formal presentation, possibly entitling his remarks, "From One First Citizen to Another." The rector insisted, "I want this good."[95]

Rev. McKee's own remarks at the fiftieth anniversary reception highlighted the drama of Burleigh's background: "As a lad he would not take no for an answer. Grandson of a blind slave, lamplighter in the city of Erie, determined to sing, he borrowed money, came to New York and won.

"A man of grace, gentleness, courtesy, humor and loyalty.

"A man who, as a composer, singer and interpreter, has given to multitudes a lift along life's steep ascent.

"A representative of a race which having suffered much at the hands of its brothers, has chosen to express its suffering not in retaliation, but in song.

"A man of faith who took his religion seriously and counted it a high privilege to pray much, to serve humbly and to sing for half a century to the glory of God in St. George's, New York."[96]

Burleigh was presented with a purse of $1,500.[97]

An undated newspaper report of the occasion reported, "His resonant voice and buoyant spirit were indications to his friends that he would sing 'The Palms' by Faure for the fiftieth consecutive time at St. George's next Easter, April 9." And when the president of the Erie Club of New York presented him with a cane, Burleigh joked, "That's right, I'm getting old. I'll need one of these pretty soon."[98]

Burleigh's place at St. George's and what it meant to him and to the congregation is aptly summarized by Tim Brooks in his compendium of the history of African Americans in the recording industry: "His long tenure at St. George's was his anchor. . . . At age seventy-seven, this voice was obviously not the deep, rich instrument it once had been, but the parishioners did not seem to care. He was by now an icon, a living legend. He dressed the part, too, dapper in his suit and vest. *Cue* described him as a 'chunky, voluble little man . . . incredibly nimble. Neatly groomed, he carries a cane and wears spats.'"[99]

Dapper Mr. Burleigh, early
1940s. (Courtesy of the
Burleigh family)

Burleigh's place in the St. George's congregation was still significant. The shadow
of World War II lay over New York City in 1944. Just before Christmas of that
year members gathered for Church Decoration Night, a tradition started in 1888
by Rev. Rainsford to bring the parish together. That night in 1944 "the church was
crammed with visiting British seamen, the usual St. George's parishioners, and
people who, despite gas rationing, had returned from afar to share this traditional
reunion of friends. The choir was in street clothes and everyone sang 'We Three
Kings of Orient Are' as the star rose slowly, high in the chancel arch." But just as
the service drew to a close, the rector was alerted that the city was going into a
blackout. The congregation would need to stay in the church for the duration of
the blackout. In the darkness, "everyone sang more carols. Harry Burleigh spoke
from the pulpit about the origin of Church Decoration Night in Rainsford's time.
. . . George Kemmer played more Christmas music and more carols were sung
until the 'all clear' sounded and at last the people could go home." It was a night
no one would forget.[100]

Rev. McKee's anniversary tribute to Burleigh was sincere, but he also knew Burleigh's struggles to reconcile generations of effort by African Americans, including

his own family and himself, to win equality and respect from the majority of Americans with the reality of the mid-twentieth century. Racial segregation and the persistent denial of civil rights for African Americans still kept many from the accomplishments that he had achieved. Burleigh had benefited in many ways from his half-century of service at St. George's, but racial discrimination and prejudice persisted. Burleigh shared with Rev. McKee his frustration. How could white Americans, especially those who professed to be Christians, perpetuate such injustice?[101]

McKee wrote to Burleigh's grandson Harry T. Burleigh II in May 1949, enclosing his sermon on May 4, the morning before the last Vesper Service of Negro Spirituals before Burleigh's death: "My rectorship coincided with the last 10 years of your grandfather's 52 at St. George's. Almost nothing has pleased me more than to have him put my name on his arrangement for 'In Christ There Is No East or West' which is increasingly popular and is in most hymn books. I have a Yale friend in California who writes me about twice a year to say 'We sang the Burleigh hymn today.'"[102]

Burleigh's influence on the St. George's congregation continued long after his death, and in 1980 former rector Elmore M. McKee participated in a Burleigh Day to which former choir members and parishioners who knew Burleigh gathered. In a letter to Rev. Edward O. Miller, who succeeded McKee as rector, he reported, "The 'Burleigh Day' proved rewarding, I think. His life, his music, his mission were so significant! . . . Some 20 of the Junior choirs of Burleigh's time returned with some other old timers." One former soloist flew in from California.[103]

Rev. Edward O. Miller, who took over as rector a few months after Burleigh's retirement, shared some of the most revealing observations of Burleigh's last years in a letter to Burleigh's first biographer, Anne Key Simpson. Miller served as assistant to the St. George's rector from 1938 to 1941, and he came to know Burleigh well during that time. "He seemed to enjoy taking me as a very young man, under his tutelage." Just as Rev. McKee reported, Rev. Miller found that St. George's was known by many who were not part of the parish as "Mr. Burleigh's Church," "When, in 1946, my wife and I arrived in Pennsylvania Station to take up our new church duties, I told the cab driver to take us to St. George's Church. 'Where's that?' 'On Stuyvesant Square, on the East Side.' 'O, you mean Mr. Burleigh's church.'"[104]

But Miller reflected with sadness on the social distance that Burleigh felt it necessary to maintain throughout his long years of service at St. George's with most of the parishioners. "Though the parish worshipped him, he remained aloof. Mr. Morgan might invite him to his home, but always as a performer. The Rectory (residence of the rector) was located between the church and the parish house; Mr. Burleigh had to walk past it twice a week for fifty-two years, yet never would he accept the most cordial invitation to come inside."[105]

Burleigh's closest relationships were with choir members and with choir director-organist George W. Kemmer. But even among choir members, Burleigh knew who could be trusted. Dorothy Drummond Hauser was among the younger members of the choir who shared many Sunday afternoon lunches at a restaurant near St. George's, where Burleigh would regale his younger colleagues with tales of his childhood, even telling them that he had "married an American Indian princess." "I can see him now," she mused, "sitting, at our insistence, at the head of the long table. Pappa's Greek Restaurant on Third Avenue, although not of Waldorf reputation, had a genteel shabbiness about it, was clean, and the food hot. It was in this setting that we listened, spellbound, to Harry's life story."[106]

Rev. McKee reflected on Burleigh's loneliness and his inability to leave his post as soloist when he was no longer capable of upholding the standard of excellence that had been his hallmark. "He was a very private person. Long before his retirement, his voice began to falter, embarrassingly so at the end. Yet he would not retire. Estranged from his son, who had deep personal problems, he bottled up his personal life, especially so toward the end, when his mind was not sharp."[107]

Even when his voice had lost its strength, the consummate performer could deliver. Josephine Harreld Love remembered his last rendition of "The Palms" in 1946. Little of the fabled voice remained, but "he was a man who could put a song across,"[108] and many still found their way to the church to honor him. This Palm Sunday the New York *Times* quoted him: "I can't say how much longer I'll be here. They won't let me retire, and I'm willing to go on singing until they tell me not to."[109]

When he retired in November 1946, Dorothy Drummond Hauser described the contrast between the Burleigh she knew in her first years in the choir and the Burleigh at the time of his retirement: "I still see Harry in his Easter finery, impresario that he was. Approaching 80, his grooming was meticulous—top hat, morning coat, striped trousers, gray spats, silver-headed cane, and always a fresh gardenia in his button-hole. Yet, sadly, time had caught up with him. . . . It was plain to see, as well as hear, that Harry was growing weary. All the old vitality had drained from him. His step was not as firm. His hands shook [perceptibly]. His rich round baritone was ready to be stored away as memory."[110]

Rev. Edward O. Miller's memory of Burleigh's retirement strengthened his conviction that "the Lord has a sense of humor." At Miller's first vestry meeting as rector at St. George's, the entire session was spent discussing what kind of pension they should give Burleigh. "The Vestry of St. George's consisted of twelve aristocratic gentlemen who met once a month in dinner jackets." These "leaders in the fields of law and finance" reflected that Burleigh had meant a great deal to St. George's through the half century of his tenure, so he should be given "a generous pension for the rest of his life." They spoke condescendingly of "the financial needs of an elderly musician who was also black. Finally, they voted the munificent sum of $60 per month." Rev. Miller continued, "After his death it was found that his estate was estimated at $300,000, and that royalties from his 300 songs amounted to $15,000 annually!" In fact, Burleigh's estate was considerably less than $300,000, though his royalties were as Miller reported.[111] But the vestry J. P. Morgan had once led with such alacrity was now composed of men who knew Burleigh primarily in his later years, and they understood little of who he really was and had been.

The ironies continued after Burleigh's death in December 1949. An Erie funeral director telegrammed the rector demanding that Burleigh be buried next to his mother in the Erie Cemetery. Burleigh's widow Louise (now Princess Nadonis Shawa in Wisconsin), his housekeeper Thelma Hall in the Bronx, and his son Alston expressed their wishes emphatically. Rev. Miller negotiated an agreement that Burleigh should be buried in New York, only to discover that "none of the well-known cemeteries in the New York area would bury a black man." Disgusted and angry that "a man good enough to sing twice for King Edward VII, and every Christmas in Mr. Morgan's home!" should be barred a proper burial, Rev. Miller called prominent members of the cemetery boards, without success. He finally persuaded Mt. Hope Cemetery in Hastings-on-Hudson, New York, to sell a lot to the church.[112]

Rev. Miller described Burleigh's funeral: "The service at St. George's was over-whelming, the church packed, and the congregational singing raised the roof. A large number drove in the cortege to the cemetery. As I was conducting the service, suddenly it came over me that I was hallucinating, for louder and louder came the strains of 'Swing Low, Sweet Chariot.' Someone had placed a loud speaker beneath the blanket of flowers that covered his grave, and the music of Harry Burleigh was engulfing us, even beyond his death."[113] The speaker had been placed there by the funeral director, who arranged with ASCAP (the Association of Singers, Composers and Publishers, of which Burleigh was a charter member) to send Burleigh's music pealing from his grave. One who attended the funeral and the burial reported that "it was a most unusual and beautiful service."[114]

Burleigh's long tenure at St. George's was not just an individual triumph. "[T]he connection . . . afforded him unusual opportunities for breaking down race and color prejudice, and for opening doors for other colored singers and musicians never opened before." Burleigh's modesty and unassuming personality endeared him to "his thousands of friends," and though "his splendid and unusual gifts brought him great honor and distinction," his "sweet and modest nature . . . kept him simple and unaffected and so he is warmly enshrined in the hearts of his people."[115]

PART III

Art Song Composer, Music Editor,
and Pioneer Arranger of Spirituals

14. A Singer-Composer Learns His Craft

"Passionate sincerity and harmonic richness"

Burleigh's two-hundred-plus vocal and instrumental works brought him national and international renown in the first half of the twentieth century, and a study of his songs reveals the strength of his contribution to American song literature.[1] Burleigh's songs reflected his thorough knowledge of the prevailing forms and musical idioms of the European and American art song, both as a singer and as a composer.[2] All his songs were written for the recital or concert stage, and they compare favorably with the output of his European American songwriter colleagues. Often they set the same lyrics, and it was not unusual for Burleigh himself to appear in concert or recital with other song composers. This chapter focuses on the songs published from 1896 to 1913, the first two of the three compositional periods identified by Roland Allison: the first, 1896–1903, and the second, 1904–13.[3] An examination of Burleigh's compositional output demonstrates their artistic and historical value for musicians in the twenty-first century and offers insight into the world of the neo-Romantic American art song of the first half of the twentieth century.[4]

In his 1903 work *The Souls of Black Folk*, W. E. B. Du Bois introduced the image of "the veil" through which African Americans must view themselves and their world. Frequent references to "the veil" in the spoken and written rhetoric of African Americans confirm the continuing aptness of the metaphor. The veil denotes a double consciousness, an awareness of the surrounding American culture as "a world which . . . only lets him see himself . . . through the eyes of others." Though on the one hand, to be born "with a veil" or a caul, in an African view, is a gift, the favor of being "born with second sight," the benefit is also burden. "One ever feels his twoness,—an American, a Negro; two souls, two thoughts, two unreconciled strivings; two warring ideals in one dark body, whose dogged strength alone keeps it from being torn asunder."[5] But that second sight, that double consciousness, also grants the creative artist who can appropriate and integrate the cultural resources from within and without the veil a unique endowment from which to enrich the whole.

In his essay "Interpreting Classical Music," composer Olly Wilson cites Burleigh along with Philadelphia bandleader Francis Johnson and ragtime composer Scott Joplin as composers of music "that was successful within both a written and [an] oral tradition." He references Du Bois's image of the veil to describe how these composers demonstrated bimusicality, drawing on and integrating their unique cultural heritage with the music traditions of the majority culture. Each was thoroughly familiar with (indeed, was first educated in) American and European music traditions and each made a significant contribution to American music by bringing to these traditions aspects of their own cultural heritage: "The new musical paradigms established by these composers did not occur within a cultural vacuum. While working within a written music tradition, they reveled in musical concepts that were intrinsic to Black oral music practice." As composers, "they possessed those elusive sensibilities that characterize the extraordinary creative musical mind. They also thoroughly internalized musical concepts both within and without the veil that allowed them to make that leap of creativity that resulted in a new ordering of traditional concepts."[6]

These composers also, particularly Joplin and Burleigh, worked at a time when a sacralization of art music, primarily music written by European and European-trained composers, was in progress. The music of ordinary people, the music of "the folk," and even more specifically, commercially produced popular music, was seen by the arbiters of taste to be qualitatively inferior in artistic terms, less valuable than music written and performed by classically trained musicians. Wilson argues that in addition to their involvement with both oral and written music traditions, Johnson, Joplin, and Burleigh successfully "traverse[d] . . . the perceived divide between the high-brow and low-brow, cultivated and vernacular, religious and secular" in music, a transaction or transformation that he identifies as "an important contribution of African American music that helped to define a new paradigm for American music."[7] This observation is particularly helpful in considering the variety in Burleigh's songs.

The art song, a musical setting of poetic lyrics for a trained singer usually accompanied by piano, can be traced to the late Baroque period and found alongside the better-known instrumental and vocal works of Classical composers.[8] But with the increasing importance of the piano and settings of verse by Goethe, Heine, and other nineteenth-century poets by their contemporaries Schubert, Schumann, Grieg, Wolf, and other composers, the art song emerged as a major genre for both professional and amateur musicians. As the nineteenth century drew to a close, the influence of German Romanticism replaced the florid melodic line typical of English, Italian, and French song with "more emphasis upon syllabic rather than melismatic writing"; greater use of nondiatonic tones, chromatically altered harmonies, and harmonic, contrapuntal and rhythmic interest in the accompaniment; a preference for modified-strophic and through-composed forms rather than simple strophic settings; a "more subtle union" between music and the text, and "finally, an increased awareness of the importance of craftsmanship."[9]

One can see in the development of Burleigh's compositional style his own movement from strophic (every verse set to the same music) to modified strophic to through-composed settings (the music evolves throughout the song, to express the changing meaning of the words). His grounding in German Romanticism is evident in both his recital programs and his compositions. As his style developed, his exploration of late Romantic and Impressionist harmonic practices became more pervasive. But even in his earliest songs his artistry is shown in his harmonic language and in the increasing intensity as a song moves toward its climax. Except for a few of the plantation songs, Burleigh rarely created a simple strophic setting; shifts in melodic contour and accompaniment style, and, increasingly, in harmonic modulations, mark textual and musical sections. Even his earliest songs exhibit a variety of accompaniment techniques that reinforce structure.

Burleigh's secular art songs do not fit stereotypical expectations of a black composer, and some singers who programmed his songs were unaware of his African American identity. Not only were the texts universal in theme, but in some of the early songs such as "Love's Garden" and "Thy Heart" (both 1902 publications) the beloved is fair, golden-haired, blue-eyed, and lily-white (though the "nut-brown maid," and the "dark-eyed maid of beauty rare, With midnight shadows in [her] hair" soon follow). Of the two songs just mentioned, the lyrics of "Thy Heart" are stronger, and the ironic twist of the last line forms an effective contrast to the sensuous description in the preceding lines. This song, with lyrics from the Sanskrit, is tinged with the orientalism that Burleigh, like many of his contemporaries, found attractive: "Thy face a lovely lily, / Thine eyes, the lotus blue, Thy teeth are jasmine blossoms, / Thy lips, the rosebud's hue. The velvet touch of the champak / Thy tender skin doth own, How comes it, that the Creator / Hath made thy heart a stone?"

Love lyrics predominate in his art songs, but Burleigh was also fond of dramatic narrative, even the semioperatic scena, and a rousing drinking song such as "Heigh-Ho!" (1904) or a humorous novelty song such as "He Met Her in the Meadow" appeared from time to time. He frequently set lyrics by black writers, but except for those with Southern plantation themes, the content usually reflected universal human concerns such as the joy of love, the pain of unrequited or lost love, or the beauty of nature rather than those unique to former African slaves.

The idiomatic vocalism of Burleigh's art songs reflects his competence as a singer. An accomplished pianist despite the congenital shortening of the fourth finger on both hands, he sometimes accompanied himself in his early art song recitals, as he also did later in performing his spiritual arrangements, as we have seen in chapter nine. His accompaniments enhance the vocal line but do not overwhelm it, and their level of difficulty is well within the capability of most amateur musicians.

However, as his mature songs increased in harmonic complexity, more expertise on the part of both singer and accompanist was required.[10]

Burleigh's compositions include sacred choral anthems and solos; secular art songs and light classical ballads; plantation songs, both of folk origin and settings of dialect verse; arrangements of folk melodies from several countries; arrangements of songs by other composers; novelty songs; the solo and choral arrangements of Negro spirituals for which he is now best known; and several orchestral arrangements of spirituals. There are also two sets of instrumental sketches: six piano sketches, *From the Southland* (1904, 1907, 1910); and the four-movement *Southland Sketches* (1916), for piano and violin (a 1901 set of six violin sketches has not been located). As their titles indicate, these instrumental pieces draw on the African American oral traditions of folksongs and spirituals and even the rhythmic energy of ragtime.

It is tempting to treat any discussion of Burleigh's songs by creating categories of style, based partly on the lyrics and partly on the degree to which the songs display specific black musical characteristics. It is impossible to discuss Burleigh's varied song output without reference to categories of style, but examining the songs chronologically, as they were published, shows how both his recital programs and his song publications brought these various styles together, treating the texts as equally worthy of artistic presentation.

Burleigh was an astute music craftsman, and he knew his market. The choice of musical and lyrical content in his songs might be in response to a request by the author of a set of lyrics, might be a tribute or gift to a friend or benefactor, might reflect his life experience at a particular time, might represent his persistent advocacy of the artistic worth of African American folk and popular music, or might reflect a publisher's desire to capitalize on popular demand for black-inflected music. Publishers knew Burleigh could be relied on to produce well-crafted songs that would sell. He might publicize them in his own recitals and solo appearances, but increasingly, his songs were in demand by an extensive international roster of opera and recital singers. The dedications on many of his solo and choral songs reflect his wide acquaintance with church and choral conductors as well as concert and recital singers. Dedications are not an infallible guide; they may simply signal the hope that a famous singer might help to popularize the song by singing it. But Burleigh's contacts were increasingly widespread, even international in scope, and comments by performers, critics, and other American song composers indicate that in the first quarter of the twentieth century, Burleigh was regarded as one of the most accomplished American art song composers, well before his arrangements of Negro spirituals secured his place in music history.[11]

Burleigh's first set of three art songs was published in 1898, but three years earlier, "Christmas Bells," a simple unison Christmas song for the Sunday school at St. George's Episcopal Church, was published by Luckhart and Belder. This strophic arrangement from the Sunday school hymnal features bell-like chords in the four-measure introduction and in the accompaniment.[12]

From 1896 to 1913 secular art songs and ballads predominate. But looking at Burleigh's compositions chronologically, one is struck by how consistently he advocated the artistic worth of black music of various kinds by setting folk melodies and dialect or plantation songs. The nineteen songs published from 1896 through 1903 include one sacred song; ten plantation songs; and eight secular art songs, including "Mammy's Li'l Baby" and "Sleep, Li'l Chile," which transcend the plantation song category though their lyrics suggest that identity.

A telling example is his "When de Angels Call," a 1901 setting of verse by (Maria) Howard Weeden, one of three written especially for *Everybody's Magazine* in that year. This is a "mammy song," a genre that has a distasteful resonance as a relic of the sentimental nostalgia for the benevolent maternal presence of the servant women who nurtured generations of white children. But the editor's comments emphasize Burleigh's purposeful presentation of music rooted in African American heritage as works of art. Burleigh gives this three-strophe verse a simple melodic setting for solo voice, enhanced by a harmonic accompaniment that complements the visual imagery that surrounds it. This mammy, as pictured in the accompanying sketch, is an individual, not a caricature; it is one of Weeden's sensitive portraits of black Americans in the South, and both the imagery and the lyrics are sentimental and nostalgic. Burleigh's musical setting gives it an ingenuous artistry that confirms the editor's remarks: "Mr. Burleigh, well known as a baritone at St. George's Church, New York, and as a composer, has long been working to show that the true negro music is really worthy of serious attention, and is by no means adequately represented by the cheap 'coon songs' that have so much vogue."[13] Like Burleigh's musical settings, Weeden's portraits reveal the inherent dignity and strength of character in her subjects, and Burleigh's choice of lyrics by Weeden shows the care with which he selected the texts for his plantation song settings. Weeden's lyrics were published under the name Howard Weeden; like other women writers, she found it expedient to use a masculine pseudonym to give her work greater credibility. "When de Angels Call" is one of three songs with lyrics by Weeden published in *Everybody's Magazine* in 1901: "Hush" appeared in April 1901, and "The Song of the Watcher" in August 1901. Each of the three songs carried the editor's comments quoted above and featured a character portrait by Weeden.[14]

Post-Reconstruction nostalgia for the "good old South" created a demand for songs extolling romanticized aspects of antebellum Southern culture. The Southern plantation ballad (in this case settings of dialect verse rather than arrangements of orally transmitted folksongs) had roots in antebellum song traditions as well as in the emotional need to evoke a mythical time and place. Many black Americans shared the fondness for these songs, including some of Stephen Foster's songs. Though Burleigh never commented on this, it may be that for those like himself

"When de Angels Call," *Everybody's Magazine,* June 1901, 588. (Library of Congress)

who had never lived in the South, identification with Southern culture was a way to affirm their African American identity and heritage. Despite the horrors of slavery on Southern plantations, a genuine love of the South can be seen in such writings as the James Weldon Johnson poem "O Southland" that Burleigh set in 1914.[15]

"When de Angels Call" appeared less than ten years after Burleigh's arrival in New York City and less than seven years after his hiring as baritone soloist at St.

George's. Except for a few recital programs, we have little documentation of how and in what venues Burleigh presented his case for black music in these early years. But it is clear that more than a decade before "Deep River" made Burleigh's name famous as a pioneer arranger of spirituals, he was speaking and singing his assertion of the artistic worth of a wide variety of black music, or music that portrayed some aspect of African American life, as well as demonstrating it through his musical settings. While we may find his choice of texts problematic in some cases, he and his colleagues—Will Marion Cook, Bert Williams, Bob Cole, J. Rosamond, and James Weldon Johnson, and others—relished their cultural heritage and exploited it in various ways. Of necessity, in their songs they gave their (often white) audiences what they expected—at least superficially—but they clothed it in accessible, artistic, and sometimes satirical musical garb.

As we have seen in Burleigh's recital programs, his compositions included settings of plantation lyrics by white writers such as "Atlanta's poet," Frank L. Stanton, as well as verse by black colleagues such as James E. Campbell and Paul Laurence Dunbar as representative of black culture and in contrast to the reprehensible "coon songs" and minstrel songs that perpetuated demeaning racial stereotypes. White composers such as W. H. Neidlinger, Sidney Homer, and others were setting the same or similar verse.[16] While to a twenty-first-century sensibility these lyrics may sound condescending, even racist, one must always consider the background against which they were chosen. The prevailing public image of African Americans was dominated by the shuffling watermelon-loving, chicken-stealing darky or the razor-wielding citified dandy; some of these images even appear in several Burleigh plantation settings, for example, James E. Campbell's "Ring, My Bawnjer, Ring": "Moon come up, de sun go down, / Sing, my bawnjer, sing! De niggah's am all come f'um town, / Ring, my bawnjer, ring! Den it's roun' de hill an' froo de fiel,' / Look out, niggah, dar, doan' you steal! De milyuns on dem vines am green, / De moon am bright, O you'll be seen, Ring, my bawnjer, ring! / Oh! Ring, my bawnjer, ring!" But Campbell is writing from "within the veil," and one can imagine how in performance the singer can mock the stereotype while delighting in the southern cultural references.[17]

Plantation Melodies Old and New, an anthology of seven songs published by G. Schirmer, also in 1901, spread his message of the worth of black folk music far more widely than "When de Angels Call" and the other two songs published in *Everybody's Magazine.* This collection featured settings of dialect verse by three lyricists—R. E. Phillips, James Edward Campbell, and Paul Laurence Dunbar. According to the publisher, the music was "composed, or transcribed and adapted" by Burleigh. Five of the seven songs feature folk tunes arranged by Burleigh: "I Doan' Want fu' t' Stay Hyeah No Longah" ("Danville Chariot"), "My Lawd's a-Writin' Down Time" ("He Sees All You Do, An' Hyeahs All You See"), "When de Debble Comes 'Round" ("You Shall Have er New Hidin'-Place Dat Day"), "De Blackbird an' de Crow" ("We Will Go er-Pickin' Up Cohn"), and "An Ante-Bellum Sermon" ("Joshua Fit de Battl'

"Negro Lullaby," mm. 25–36.

ob Jerico"). Each folk tune is listed under the title. Burleigh wrote the music for the remaining two, "My Merlindy Brown," a Negro serenade, and "Negro Lullaby," both texts by James E. Campbell. The excerpt from "Negro Lullaby" illustrates the basic simplicity of these settings as well as the kind of harmonic flourish Burleigh often added (mm. 25–36).

Each of Burleigh's strophic settings begins with a piano introduction. He enhances the folk texts and melodies with harmonic accompaniment that demonstrates his intention to elevate the folk tradition through artistic presentation. Burleigh knew James Campbell and Paul Laurence Dunbar and may have known R. E. Phillips (of whom no information has been found); in using their lyrics, he was also supporting and disseminating their work. Burleigh later set two additional songs by James Campbell: the just-mentioned "Ring, My Bawnjer, Ring," a plantation song (1902); and the Highland drinking song, "Heigh-Ho!" (1904). He wrote several additional settings of verse by Dunbar, not all of which were published.[18]

Schirmer publicity materials claimed that Burleigh transcribed the "old" melodies from memory, "arranging and harmonizing the melodies so as best to present and preserve their characteristic features." The final sentence of the description unconsciously portrayed the prevailing attitude toward unadorned folk music: "The *value* of it all is greatly *enhanced* [italics added] by the discreet, characteristic and always artistic accompaniment that Mr. Burleigh has provided." Burleigh's two original settings of verse by James Campbell were composed "in the spirit of negro melody, of which no one is in fuller possession than he."[19] African Americans born and raised in the South may have questioned his "full possession" of this spirit, but to most northern white critics in New York and New England in these early years of Burleigh's career, he was the prime creator or promoter of "characteristic" Negro song as art music.

The New York *Tribune* reviewer (possibly Henry E. Krehbiel) "applauded the effort" in *Plantation Melodies* but expressed some reservation as to the outcome: "Readers of The Tribune will scarcely need to be told that essays like that made by Mr. Burleigh in this case are viewed with sincere delight by this journal. There is a large artistic treasure in the folksongs of those who once were slaves in America, and it must be fulfilled sooner or later. Every *dignified* [italics added] effort to make them known to music lovers is therefore commendable." While Burleigh had achieved "notable results," his setting of "Danville Chariot," "the most striking tune" in the collection, was, according to this reviewer, marred by his "strained harmonization"; not every attempt to elevate by harmonization was equally successful.[20]

The lyrics of two of these *Plantation Melodies* illustrate a sly humor that recalls the African trickster tradition. "When de Debble Comes 'Round" riffs on the chicken-stealing stereotype: When the Devil comes, don't let him catch you "totin' er bag wiv three chickens in / Dat de Lawd only made fu' two!" And in "De Blackbird an' de Crow" the blackbird advises the crow not to be "erskeer'd ob ol' black Joe" hoeing in the cornfield: "We steal cohn, an' what does he care? / Saves him hoe'n

ef de cohn ain't dere!" The real danger is the "massah": "Black crows bettah drap
dere cohn, than ahgue wiv massah's gun!"

Lest one think that these songs simply reinforced negative stereotypes, the "Ante-
Bellum Sermon" combines the oral tradition of the black sermon with the spiritual
"Joshua fit de Battle ob Jerico" and the tumbling-down walls, a classic image of
freedom from oppression: "I'se a judgin' Bible people by deir ac's; / I's a givein' you
de Scriptuah, I'se a handin' you de fac's. / Case ole Phar'oh b'lieved in slav'ry, But
de Lawd he let him see / Dat de people he put bref in, Evah motha's son was free."

Plantation Melodies Old and New was welcomed as an example of Burleigh's
unique ability to make black folksongs accessible to white singers in elevated form.
All the songs employed the "characteristic" syncopation often mistakenly termed
the "Scotch snap," but only two of the melodies strictly adhere to the expected
pentatonic scale, and two are in the minor mode. While the accompaniments are
sparse and primarily chordal, Burleigh used a variety of accompaniment patterns
to clarify the structure and provide variation.[21]

Philadelphia baritone David Bispham (a Quaker), who on occasion appeared
at the same evening entertainments in wealthy homes as Burleigh, sang several
of these songs in London shortly after their publication. A reviewer commented,
"Why, when the originals are so priceless, should anyone be at pains to produce
imitations which have no merit?"[22] Purists would argue that the songs in this collection hardly represented "the originals," but for Burleigh, and apparently for the
majority of his audiences, the occasional highlighting of a phrase or a cadence
with deceptive cadences and unusual harmonic progressions was the essence of
the enhancement that made these songs appropriate for recital performance.[23] The
comment suggests that Burleigh's treatment of the songs was distinctive, especially
in contrast to the ragtime coon songs and minstrel songs so popular at the time.
Burleigh himself often used songs from this collection in his own recitals and solo
appearances, and as early as 1903 (the year of W. E. B. Du Bois's essay "The Sorrow
Songs" in *The Souls of Black Folk*) his solo repertoire also featured spirituals that
were published in solo or choral arrangements years or even decades later.[24]

* * *

Burleigh considered himself primarily a singer rather than a composer, essentially subscribing to the view that composers of songs who did not also create longer
works such as symphonies or operas were less entitled to recognition as composers.
By this measure, the first "real" African American composers were Henry Lawrence
Freeman (1869–1954), William Levi Dawson (1899–1990), and William Grant Still
(1895–1978). Though H. Lawrence Freeman composed a number of operas and a
symphonic poem, his work never achieved the broad public exposure that either
Burleigh's or Still's work earned. Scott Joplin (1868–1917), who consulted Freeman
on the writing of his opera *Treemonisha,* also hoped for success as an opera composer, but he died before attaining that elusive goal. And the classical compositions

of Gussie Davis (1863–1899), whose prolific output included a great many serious pieces, including longer instrumental and choral compositions in addition to the sentimental songs for which he was well known, still await examination by scholars and performers; they remain obscure today, just as their performance was scarce and little remarked upon outside the black community during his lifetime.[25]

Burleigh argued that he himself should be called "a composer of songs," rather than a composer, because he earned his living by singing, not by composing. However, when A. Walter Kramer, song reviewer for *Musical America,* asked how he would occupy himself if he could choose, Burleigh admitted that he would choose to compose.[26] Despite his modesty, he took his role as composer seriously. "I sometimes think," he told an interviewer in 1938 "that those who simply love music for the enjoyment, the pleasant experience it gives them in hearing, have more than we who create it. We are constantly listening for effects, noting construction as we hear a composition—we seldom just sit back and enjoy."[27]

Burleigh's success in composing art songs and ballads that were performed by many professional singers of national and international eminence was unprecedented for black composers and has seldom been exceeded, in volume if not in enduring fame. Just as his teachers at the National Conservatory of Music recognized his ability, his thorough training and expertise as a song composer were recognized by editors at the G. Schirmer music publishing company, who published all but one of his songs from 1898 to 1902. It is possible that Max Spicker, Burleigh's counterpoint teacher at the National Conservatory and the music director who hired him to sing at Temple Emanu-El, was the G. Schirmer editor who facilitated the publication of Burleigh's early work.[28]

With the publication of "Love's Garden" in 1902, George and William Maxwell replaced G. Schirmer as Burleigh's primary publishers and became the most important facilitators of Burleigh's long career as a song composer. George Maxwell was managing director of Boosey and Hawkes Company and the New York representative of G. Ricordi and Company of Milan, Italy. He believed in Burleigh and "aided him, perhaps more than any other individual in America, in striving for his ideals in composition."[29] His brother William, owner of the William Maxwell Music Company, published all of Burleigh's songs from 1903 to 1911. William Maxwell also offered practical support by loaning him an upright piano to facilitate his composing. With the establishment of the New York office of G. Ricordi and Company, George Maxwell became Burleigh's publisher and within a year he hired Burleigh as an editor, thus securing him extraordinary access to publication.[30] G. Ricordi & Company was one of Europe's foremost opera publishers, counting Giuseppe Verdi and Giacomo Puccini among their many composers.

* * *

One might assume that as an active soloist and recitalist, Burleigh wrote his early songs for himself to perform. However, his first set of three songs, for baritone or mezzo-soprano, was dedicated to A. M. Perry, and though "If You But Knew," the first of the three, and the third, "A Birthday Song," would seem to be inspired by his growing love for Louise Alston, it was the second, "Life," that he performed on a number of occasions. Except for plantation songs and the spirituals mentioned earlier, in his early years as a published composer he seldom sang his own art songs. In 1900 when he was to appear with Booker T. Washington and then go with him to the home of Fanny Garrison Villard, he demurred: "I must ask you to excuse me from singing any of my own songs—I cannot do them well; perhaps at Mrs. Villard's . . . I may be allowed to sing one or two from my own pen—as it will be more confidential and less presumptious [sic]—though I thank you very much for considering my efforts in this line."[31] It was not until three years later that his own art songs began to appear on his recital programs. The majority of his compositions featured in his public performances were plantation songs and spirituals that were published years later, and some, such as "March Down to Jerdon," "Moanin' Dove," and "Singin' with a Sword in Ma Hand," among others, were never published.

Of his early compositions, he often sang "The Absent-Minded Beggar," a setting of a Rudyard Kipling poem that he was not able to attain permission to publish, so he could use it only in his own performances. Kipling's verse portrayed the problems created for the family of an indigent English soldier recruited to fight the Boers in South Africa. Sir Arthur Sullivan's setting publicized the verse in England, but when Burleigh sang his version in Erie in 1899, a reviewer commented that Sullivan's music was "in a rather light vein," and Burleigh had given the narrative "a new musical garb" that displayed "the deep underlying sentiment" of the poem.[32] Another reviewer described the "wonderfully dramatic musical recitative and chorus" that "when given in Mr. Burleigh's magnificent voice produces a most impressive effect."[33] The introduction and first phrase demonstrate the irresistible vigor of Burleigh's setting (mm. 1–7).

* * *

Boston pianist and African American music historian Maud Cuney-Hare called Burleigh's earliest songs "more than the trial of unused wings." They were "more than pleasant and singable"; they "displayed a fine command of the principles of harmony and the gift of poetic imagination."[34] A survey of the eight secular art songs or ballads published from 1898 to 1903 reveals compositional patterns that became Burleigh trademarks: singable, expressive melody; careful attention to the wedding of text and tune, sometimes resulting in word painting; a strong sense of structure and the movement through musical climax and resolution, the form often clarified by changes in melodic contour, rhythmic flow, harmony, and accompaniment pattern; active harmonic rhythm and increasingly bold harmonic exploration; expressive use of the lowered third and seventh step of the scale; and an inventive craftsmanship that brings an unconventional touch to even the most predictable of his settings. More of these songs were strophic or modified strophic

"The Absent-Minded Beggar," mm. 1–7. (Courtesy of the Burleigh Family)

than the later songs, and the tone was lighter, in a style often referred to as the ballad or light classical operetta style.[35]

The term *ballad* was often set in opposition to *art song* by reviewers of Burleigh's songs to indicate a less serious artistic effort, drawing a distinction between high and low culture. This use of the term *ballad* had its roots in the parlor song tradition, referring not to a narrative text but to "a short simple song of natural construction, . . . any unvaried simple song," usually in strophic form rather than through-composed.[36] A number of Burleigh's songs were in this lighter semiclassical style. Charles Hamm describes the operetta style of Reginald DeKoven and Victor Herbert: "The vocal line rises to small climaxes in each phrase with the final large climax—the point to which the entire song has been moving—reserved for the end of the last phrase, where the singer has a fortissimo high note supported by a thickened accompaniment and a crashing dynamic level."[37] This style was ideal for encores, and a number of Burleigh's ballads were used as encores by concert singers. His songs were not part of the Tin Pan Alley popular music genre that was flourishing at the time, but A. Walter Kramer in particular, while very supportive of Burleigh's work, pressed him to move away from writing ballads to focus his gifts on writing serious art songs: "Mr. Burleigh is capable of more distinguished music than this and should devote himself to songs of a serious nature."[38]

Burleigh's 1902 song "Thy Heart" earned praise from Percy Lee Atherton, another American songwriter, two of whose songs Burleigh performed in recital. Atherton wrote that the song "ranks, in its passionate sincerity and harmonic richness, with the most notable of American songs." He regarded Burleigh's accompaniment as "characterized by invariable judgment and good taste," "an important feature of his work."[39]

The plantation lullaby "Sleep, Li'l Chile, Go Sleep!" (1902), is an especially moving lullaby for a child whose father "doan come home no more," because he has either died or been sold away. Ann Sears cites this as an example of Burleigh's sensitive wedding of text and tune: "After the first verse text, "An' do he hear yo' Mammy moan?' Burleigh adds a hummed measure that he calls a 'croon' (m. 17), effectively expressing the mother's feelings. Melodically echoing the text that just ended, this added measure and the subsequent added measures of repeated text, 'Sleep li'l chile' (mm. 18–20), create a phrase pattern" that slows the rhythm, "convey[ing] the text's sadness and resignation."[40] Burleigh later arranged this song for mixed

"Sleep, L'il Chile," mm. 1–7.

"Southern Lullaby," mm. 8–10.

voices and soprano solo for the Burleigh Club of New Bedford, Massachusetts, published under the title "Southern Lullaby" (1920). As can be seen in the first line of the soprano solo, Burleigh sharpened the distinctive rhythmic and melodic patterns of the soprano solo in his choral arrangement, bringing it closer to the black oral tradition (mm. 8–10).[41]

* * *

Burleigh's first commercial success was his 1903 song "Jean." As he recalled later, it immediately "caught on." Penman Lovinggood wrote in his 1921 *Famous Modern Negro Musicians* that "Jean" was "just a little thing done between his exacting duties, as Church and Concert Singer." But Burleigh's public heard more, "something new; an element that was more than just the ballad type."[42] It was one of Burleigh's first contributions to the American art song. Lucien H. White, theater and music reviewer for the New York *Age,* mentioned "Jean" several times in his column, calling it "one of the most popular songs ever heard from the concert stage," a song that "age has not withered, nor custom staled."[43] And Ellsworth Janifer, in his review of Burleigh's work ten years after his death, wrote of its "grave, classic beauty," calling it "a first-rate example of early twentieth-century American song literature."[44] Roland Allison observed that the "languishing melodic line is typical of the works of many popular American composers of the early twentieth century, such as Victor Herbert, W. H. Neidlinger, Reginald DeKoven, and Harry Rowe Shelley."[45] As has been mentioned in an earlier chapter, Burleigh may have dedicated this song to Mrs. James Speyer in gratitude for her inviting him to hear and sing for the Polish pianist Ignacy Paderewski at her home. Its success made it an especially apt gift.

Burleigh himself sang "Jean" for Prince Louis of Battenberg in November 1905, and several reviewers wrote of "its common use in parlor performances and in voice studios."[46] By 1905 "Jean" could be heard on a piano roll. Welsh tenor Evan Williams recorded it in England in 1906 and in the United States in 1912 "for the prestigious Victor Red Seal label." The Victor supplement publicizing the release said that "this effective song" was "one of Mr. Williams's favorite concert numbers, its rather pathetic tone affording the tenor a fine opportunity for some expressive singing." Sales figures are not available, but it remained in the Victor catalogue for ten years. In 1915 Columbia announced a recording of "Jean" by baritone Albert

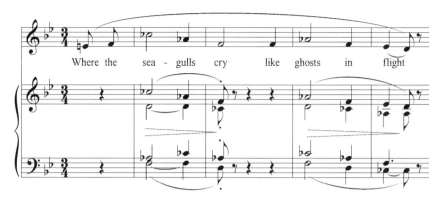

"Seagulls cry like ghosts in flight," mm. 36–40.

Wiederhold: "Everyone knows 'Jean.' Everyone should hear Albert Wiederhold's interpretation of this song." In 1918 tenor Paul Althouse recorded it on Pathé and in 1920 Edith MacDonald recorded it on Edison.[47] In all, seven recordings were made in these early years by professional singers, including Australian soprano Nellie Melba.[48] "Jean" is written in classic ABA song form and demonstrates Burleigh's ability to create elegant, expressive melody. The accompaniment is relatively spare, allowing the vocal line to predominate. After an introductory phrase . . . it unfolds through sixty-four measures without interludes or coda. The lowered sixth and third of the scale are used expressively in measures sixteen and twenty-two of the first A section, and in the corresponding measures of the return of A.[49]

Burleigh sets the B section (mm. 25–44) apart by inverting the melodic movement and introducing an arpeggiated accompaniment. A melodic sequence of diminished chords introduced by a melodic tritone (mm. 36–40) paints the sound of the seagulls that "cry like ghosts in flight" (mm. 36–40).[50]

In the last phrase of the section, "And the dark falls lone and drear," the only movement is in the descending line of the accompaniment, while the singer, after the pickup, sings the last three measures *ritardando*. In "Jean" we see Burleigh's gift for achieving profound effect through simplicity, giving his lyrical melody unobtrusive harmonic support and using chromaticism expressively but with restraint.[51]

Burleigh's first published setting of verse by his wife Louise Alston Burleigh was also the first of his songs dedicated to specific famous singers. "Mammy's Li'l Baby" (1903), a cradle song, was "specially composed for and sung by Mme. Schumann-Heink." As mentioned in chapter eleven, the version in Louise's papers is a dialect song, but the text was standardized for the German soprano. Schumann-Heink included this in her farewell concert before beginning "her operatic starring tour at the head of her own opera company," in a group of songs by Wagner, Franz, Strauss, Wolf, and Becker. A reviewer described Burleigh as "a new American composer" who "has shown promise in his song 'Lullaby.'"[52]

* * *

Burleigh's second developmental period began in 1904. It is possible that the success of his song "Jean" and Madame Schumann-Heink's performance of "Mammy's Li'l Baby" in 1903 convinced William Maxwell to release the fifteen songs published in 1904. No doubt Burleigh had been writing songs all along, and now his publisher brought a more extensive assortment before the public. The songs published from 1904 to 1908 are notable in number, in variety, and in the striking intensity of several that move from the light classical ballad into the art song category. The 1904 songs include James E. Campbell's robust drinking song "Heigh-Ho!" as well as Burleigh's attractive arrangement of the Robert Burns folksong "I Lo'e My Jean," both of Scottish flavor (like his unpublished solo setting of "Ho-ro! My Nut-brown Maiden," later arranged for male voices and published in 1930); his very useful setting of the wedding hymn "O Perfect Love"; three additional sacred songs, including his setting of the Christmas carol "While Shepherds Watched Their Flocks"; a male chorus setting of James Weldon Johnson's poem "O Southland"; and "Waiting," a brief gem with lyrics by Martha Gilbert Dickinson, the niece and literary executor of Amherst poet Emily Dickinson.[53] Allison describes the songs of this middle period as "more complex, displaying much chromaticism, high tessituras, long phrases, wide intervallic skips, [and] rhythmic complexities."[54] Even the lighter ballad-style songs show great melodic and harmonic facility, often ending with a climactic flourish that made them ideal encore material. Few of the songs published in these years were as widely performed as his later art songs, but they included a number of songs of a more intense character that tended to be through-composed rather than strophic, with great care for text-tune relationships and frequent text painting. The harmonic exploration characteristic of his mature work begins to appear.[55]

Burleigh's setting of the Robert Burns Scottish folksong "I Lo'e My Jean" is an early example of his approach to arranging folksongs from several countries. These settings are closer in style to his light classical ballads than to his more intense through-composed art songs and foreshadow his approach to arranging spirituals. Here, as in all of his folk-song settings, he preserved the melodic simplicity but provided a sophisticated harmonic treatment. In this case the only change to the melody is in the last phrase, where he intensifies the nostalgic mood by lowering the third and the sixth of the scale on the final phrase "But minds me o' my Jean" (mm. 31–37). The harmony and shifts in register and the rhythmic motion in the accompaniment create a delicate elegance that enhances but does not overwhelm the melody.[56]

"But minds me o' my Jean," mm. 31–37.

Burleigh dedicated his setting of the Frank L. Stanton verse "If Life Be a Dream" to his wife, Louise Alston Burleigh. This is a modified strophic ballad that shifts from the 4/4 meter of the first four lines to 3/4 for the refrain: "Take heart in the trouble, / Stem the swift stream, If Life be a dream, dear, / We'll dream out the dream!" He uses modulations in key as a type of word painting. The song begins in D major, reflecting the phrase "If Life be a dream, it is well worth the dreaming!" but the second verse moves to D minor on "Tho' the road be rough, and though the night be long, / We are here for sorrow as well as for song!" then to A major beginning with the words "But a rainbow in it whisper'd: All is well!" Rather than a rousing flourish at the end, the climax comes on the repeated phrase "If Life be a dream, dear," and the song ends quietly, pianissimo, on a descending affirmation, "We'll dream out the dream."

A two-measure mandolin-like introduction opens Burleigh's second setting of lyrics by his wife, "Just My Love and I." The rocking 6/8 motion in both the melody and the accompaniment of this boat song or barcarole, is repeated in verse two, with variations in the accompaniment pattern that increase in complexity. The fresh noonday of verse one moves to "crimson light" that "tells of the coming night" in verse three. In a pattern that Burleigh often used to provide contrast, he inverts the melodic movement of the third verse, shifting the key from D major to D minor, adding chromatic variation to the descending line that ends in F major, preparing for the return of D major and the rocking ascent of the melody in verse four, as "the sun is gone behind the hill" and "the dancing waves are calm and still." The accompaniment thickens and ends climactically with the repeat of the recurring final phrase, "Just my love and I!" This is a singable, expressive ballad that reflects the romantic warmth of the Burleighs' early marriage. It also provides an example of lyrics in which the progress of time through a day symbolizes an emotional experience or journey, the clarification of lyric structure through key modulation and melodic contour, and the principle of increasing complexity as the song moves to a climax, particularly in the accompaniment. Like the rollicking "Way o' the World," dedicated to Rosamond Johnson, another Frank Stanton setting, "Just My Love and I" shows the facility with which Burleigh could turn out a tuneful ballad, always competent, seldom predictable, often memorable.

One of Burleigh's most successful sacred songs is his 1904 setting of the wedding hymn "O Perfect Love." It is dedicated to Bob Cole's sister—dancer, actress, and schoolteacher Dora J. Cole [Norman], of Philadelphia and later of Staten Island. His 1914 choral setting for male voices of James Weldon Johnson's poem "O Southland" highlights his choice of texts that emphasize the importance of the southern heritage for African Americans. Author James Weldon Johnson and his musician brother J. Rosamond were sons of a Baptist minister in Jacksonville, Florida, and this poem expresses a native's love for the South: "O Southland, Dear land so far away / We dream of thee by night, We long for thee by day." The years of labor by generations of African Americans felled its forests and "brought forth All rich treasures" of its soil. The beauty of the South, "its rocks, forest streams and flowers," belong to those who once were slaves; it is theirs "by right of toil, by right of birth, by right of love."[57] Burleigh's *a cappella* setting was written for the Williams and Walker Glee Club, a male chorus established by W. C. Elkins to provide summer employment to members of the Williams and Walker company during George Walker's final illness, when the future of the company was in doubt. In contrast to the comic and popular songs of their professional season, the glee club sang a classical repertoire; "O Southland" would be a strong addition to any male chorus program.[58]

"One Day" and "Waiting" are examples of Burleigh's early exploration of a more intense art song style of composition. The twenty-nine measures of "One Day" move from the dawn of love, accompanied by "a bird's sweet voice in a tree," to "the glory of love" at noonday. But sunset "darkens the sky above" and the bird's voice in the tree is hushed. The dramatic climax is abrupt: "In my heart is a crucified love," and after the crescendo molto, the final phrase, diminishes to a *ppp* in the accompaniment, the voice motionless on "A death in life for me!" intoned on middle C, the fifth of the scale.

"Waiting" (lyrics by Martha Gilbert Dickinson) is another short, intense song that challenges both singer and pianist with rhythmic and tonal ambiguity, portraying the anxiety of a lover awaiting the return of the beloved. The time signature is 3/4, but in the first verse, the vocal melody is set against a 6/8 pattern in the piano: "Hills that miss you, / Pines that whisper you, Days that dawn in vain; / Brooks that mourn you, Paths hard worn for you, / Beaten by lonely rain." This pattern shifts briefly into a 6/8 meter just as the key shifts from B minor to B major, on the words "Birds that call you, / Buds that fall for you, Stars that seek and wave," with the accompaniment trilling bird calls under the cuckoolike vocal pattern, before the 3/4–6/8 restlessness returns on "Hands that need you, / Hearts that plead for you," closing with a quiet entreaty, "Pray for your coming again!" over motionless chords, followed by a soft sequence of bird calls, then three chords ending *pianissississimo*. Both of these early art songs demonstrate Burleigh's careful attention to the setting of text by creative melodic, harmonic, and structural expression.

Burleigh's Christmas anthem, "While Shepherds Watched Their Flocks," provides an example of his approach to sacred choral music. The words are certainly familiar to choir and hymn singers, but this setting is not for the untrained church choir. After a decade as baritone soloist for the St. George's Protestant Episcopal Church choir, Burleigh was accustomed to a level of choral singing that required good sight-reading skills and careful pitch tuning. Many of his choral pieces are for unaccompanied choir, but "While Shepherds Watched Their Flocks" has an organ accompaniment that provides an introduction and several brief interludes and supports the voices in chromatic passages and a wide pitch range. After the seraph speaks in alto/bass duet, the sopranos and tenors carry the phrase "Of angels praising God who thus address'd their joyful song." Though this is primarily an SATB setting, the soprano line splits at several points, taking the first sopranos up to a high A several times and up to a high B-flat on the climactic phrase "Good will hence forth from Heav'n to men." Both the alto and bass parts divide at the end, calling for low contralto and bass voices in the final cadence. This anthem robes a familiar Christmas carol in new expressive garb, a welcome challenge to the experienced church chorister.

* * *

Burleigh's piano sketches, *From the Southland,* have been variously dated 1904, 1907, and 1910. He dedicated the suite "To my friend S. Coleridge-Taylor, Esq. London, England." Joseph Smith, whose sensitive interpretation of this "tenderly nostalgic suite" can be heard on his 1995 recording *From the Southland,* edited them for publication by G. Schirmer, in an anthology of piano sketches by black composers and also as a separate publication. Confirming 1904 as the original publication date, Smith observes that Burleigh was working on these pieces at the same time that Coleridge-Taylor was composing his *Twenty-four Negro Melodies,* so "Who influenced whom?"[59] Coleridge-Taylor headed each of his pieces with a few measures of the original melody, "as a motto," then, as he says in his foreword, uses it as the theme for "Tema con Variazioni," or Theme with Variations. Burleigh also uses some traditional themes, though his treatment of the themes is freer than Coleridge-Taylor's. The most striking difference between Burleigh's piano pieces and those of Coleridge-Taylor, however, is Burleigh's use of syncopated rhythms that are clearly influenced by ragtime.[60]

The suite has six movements, each prefaced by a few lines of verse signed with Louise Alston Burleigh's initials, though some lines are from spirituals, and the first verse of the preface to "The Frolic" is partially taken from James E. Campbell's "Ring, My Bawnjer, Ring." In the first three sketches, Burleigh followed Dvořák's principle of creating melodies similar to traditional African American melodies rather than quoting specific melodies. The suite opens quietly with the expressive "Through Moanin' Pines," in a mood similar to Edward MacDowell's 1896 "Woodland Sketches." The second piece, "The Frolic," is a ragtime-flavored dance, full of syncopated patterns and clever key changes framing "a pensive middle section."[61] "In de Col' Moonlight," returns to a somber mood, this one more challenging to the amateur performer, with its reaches of tenths in the left hand. The three last movements call for increased technical facility in the pianist. Each features two contrasting themes, including snatches of familiar melodies. "A Jubilee" returns to the ragtime idiom, then moves to a playful reference to the phrase "Way Down upon the Suwanee River" from Stephen Foster's "Old Folks at Home." "On Bended Knees," marked *Andante con gran espressione,* draws on the melody of the spiritual "Nobody Knows the Trouble I've Seen."

Burleigh's most interesting use of two contrasting themes is in the culminating sketch, "A New Hiding-Place," portraying the Last Judgment. The first theme is "My Lord, What a Morning," which Burleigh arranged for solo voice in 1918 and for a cappella choir in 1924. As Smith observes, Burleigh moves from a simple hymnlike harmonization of this introspective melody to the more assertive title song, "A New Hiding-Place," which Burleigh had arranged for his 1901 *Plantation Melodies Old and New.* He treats the second melody developmentally, first with a countermelody in the left hand that is elaborated into a bridge leading to a maestoso return of "My Lord, What a Morning." Burleigh then combines the two themes, using one as a countermelody to the other. His treatment of these themes creates a climactic finale to the suite, which progresses from melodies written in the spirit of African American folksong to an increasingly complex treatment of traditional melodies.[62]

As Burleigh frequently disparaged ragtime as "the old plantation melody caricatured and debased," his use of ragtime rhythmic procedures in these pieces is intriguing. We know from his stint as conductor for *The Senegambian Carnival* that he was no stranger to ragtime.[63] The apparent contradiction is resolved if we consider the distinction between "ragging" classics and the use of syncopated rhythms in instrumental rags and ragtime songs. Burleigh was adamant that "ragging" or "jazzing" traditional melodies, spirituals in particular, was offensive and degrading. But in these pieces written for parlor performance, he made effective use of ragtime rhythms.[64]

Smith comments that composers who are not pianists often are "unable to gauge sonorities in solo piano music," but Burleigh proved "a happy exception."[65] These are salon pieces, comparable in style to his many light classical ballads. Anne Simpson believed this suite was neglected by performers, as it did not appear in its entirety on recital programs. She suggested that if Burleigh had performed it as frequently on his recitals as R. Nathaniel Dett played his *In the Bottoms* suite, *From the Southland* might have found its place in the piano repertoire.[66] However, the first five of these pieces did appear individually from time to time on recital and concert programs. Boston pianist Maud Cuney-Hare performed "In de Col' Moonlight" and "Through Moanin' Pines" in 1911, and Melville Charlton, Burleigh's close friend and frequent accompanist, adapted these two pieces for organ, performing them in recital in 1920 and 1925. The Clef Club Orchestra brought "The Frolic," "A Jubilee," and "On Bended Knees" to a much wider audience; they programmed "A Jubilee" and "On Bended Knees" on a 1911 concert, and both pieces were featured occasionally on later Clef Club programs.[67]

In 1905 William Maxwell published another eleven songs, again representing a variety of styles and intentions. They included four short, intense art song explorations, all settings of lyrics by Frances Bacon Paine: "Achievement," "And as the Gulls Soar!" "Apart," and "Tide." The most successful may be the shortest, the sixteen-measure through-composed song "And as the Gulls Soar!" "Tide" is the most accessible; some might consider it a ballad, its climactic flourish a suitable encore. There are also two ballads—a cradle song, "Dream Land," by Louise Alston Burleigh, and "O Love of a Day," dedicated to Mrs. Florence Le Baron Emanuel. Two sacred solos provide alternative settings to familiar hymns: C. F. Alexander's Christmas carol "Once in Royal David's City" and Adelaide Proctor's "Through Peace to Light." Two plantation songs, "I'll Be Dar to Meet Yo'" and "Keep a Good Grip on de Hoe" (the second another Maria Howard Weeden lyric) were published separately this year and as a set in 1907.

Not least is Burleigh's first setting in 1905 of a lyric by Laurence Hope. Laurence Hope was the pseudonym of Adele Florence Nicolson Corey, whose "exotic Orientalist" love lyrics were immensely popular in the early twentieth century, even after her death by suicide in 1904. Born in 1865, at age sixteen she joined her father in India, where she spent most of her adult life. Her first volume of poetry, *The Garden of Káma, and Other Love Lyrics from India,* was published in 1901, and the last, *Indian Love,* was published posthumously in 1905.[68]

Hope's lyrics are prime examples of the sensuous imagery that so fascinated Americans and Europeans, a cultural phenomenon that had many literary, musical, and societal expressions. To some extent this fascination was kindled on the Midway Plaisance of the 1893 Chicago World's Fair, where the Egyptian bellydancers titillated Victorian fairgoers. Concurrent with the success of Laurence Hope's poems was the 1905 premiere of Richard Strauss's controversial opera *Salome,* with its "Dance of the Seven Veils" and the shocking final scene where Salome embraces the head of John the Baptist. Some commentators attribute heightened fascination with Far Eastern and Middle Eastern themes to *Salome* and its popular reincarnations on stage and in literary productions.[69] Orientalist-themed plays, operas, masquerades, and tableaux abounded, and songwriters, both of Tin Pan Alley and of concert hall renown, drew extensively on the freer and more explicit sexual imagery that characterized orientalist expression. In his book *Contemporary American Composers*, published in 1900, Rupert Hughes discussed twenty-nine American composers whose song output included orientalist songs.[70] Laurence Hope's "Request" illustrates the type or stereotype: "Give me yourself one hour; / Give me yourself. / I do not crave any love or even thought of me: / Come, as a Sultan may caress a slave / And then forget forever, utterly. / Come! As west winds, that passing, cool and wet, / O'er desert places leave them fields in flower; / And all my life, for I shall not forget, / Will keep the fragrance of that perfect hour! Give me yourself, / And I shall not forget!"

Burleigh was not alone in his preference for orientalist, particularly Middle Eastern, themes, but his choice of lyrics and, to a limited extent, of orientalist tonal and harmonic procedures in a significant number of his songs is striking in even his earliest work. As his 1915 song cycle, *Five Songs of Laurence Hope,* is considered by some to be the best of his art songs, this first Hope setting is an important anticipation of the later songs. His second Hope setting was the 1906 "Malay Boat Song."

* * *

Burleigh's publications in 1904 and 1905 illustrate the variety of styles that characterized Burleigh's work. His 1906 ballad "Just A-Wearyin' for You,"[71] is another Frank Stanton lyric, a pleasant but unremarkable effort. The 1901 setting by Carrie Jacobs-Bond was more successful and is better-remembered today.[72] "Perhaps," another 1906 release, was republished in 1919 in *Etude* magazine, as were a number of Burleigh's earlier songs.[73]

Burleigh's 1907 setting of "Since Molly Went Away," also a Frank Stanton lyric, is a lilting Irish melody. When it was recorded in 1916 by Italian baritone Emilio de Gogorza, the Victor announcement made it clear that despite his renown, Burleigh was regarded as "being in a special class, a black composer writing 'white' art music." "We all know how things change when 'Molly' goes away. On this tender theme H. T. Burleigh has spun a touching thread of melody which De Gogorza sings with becoming sympathy. H. T. Burleigh has the fine tunefulness and rhythmic feeling so frequently met with among the best of the Negro composers."[74]

Another 1907 ballad, "You Ask Me If I Love You," was among Burleigh's more popular songs, occasionally used as a wedding song. In 1934, when Juilliard students

Josephine Harreld (Love), Anne Wiggins Brown, and Ruby Elzy presented a recital of songs by Burleigh, Anne Wiggins Brown sang "Tide" and "You Ask Me If I Love You." Burleigh delighted his audience by insisting (in a somewhat sardonic reference to his failed marriage) that he had written the latter song "when he was a love-sick boy and knew no better."[75]

Burleigh's compositional output decreased markedly from 1908 to 1913. His 1908 setting of the Alfred, Lord Tennyson, poem "Now Sleeps the Crimson Petal," is one of his strongest pieces from this period. Joseph Smith's description is apt: "As Tennyson's lovers 'fold' into one another, so do the voice and piano in this early lied-like song."[76] "Yours Alone" (1909), one of two Burleigh settings of lyrics by Edward Oxenford, also reflects the influence of the German art song on Burleigh's approach to songwriting. As Simpson describes it, "The accompaniment uses a right-hand counter melody over a left-hand after-beat figure, independent of the vocal line. The middle and ending sections give way to typically Schubertian triplets."[77]

Burleigh's most remarkable, if somewhat puzzling, 1909 publication is the G. Schirmer anthology, *Negro Minstrel Melodies.* Burleigh had proved to be adept at presenting "characteristic" Negro songs; it seems that the Schirmer publishing house wanted to cash in on the popularity of America's most persistent popular song genre, the minstrel song, and Burleigh could be counted on to fashion harmonizations that would elevate these songs, giving them greater elegance or polish for salon or recital performance. A comparison of Burleigh's harmonic treatment with the original minstrel song publications bears this out. However, as he did not include these songs on his recital programs, it is unlikely that this publication was initiated by Burleigh. He sang Henry Clay Work's "Wake Nicodemus" for a meeting of the railway workers in Erie in 1891, shortly before he left for New York City;[78] he sang the baritone solo part in Dvořák's arrangement of "Old Folks at Home" in 1894;[79] and he sang "Old Black Joe" in Erie, as an encore, by request, in 1908.[80] With these exceptions, none of the twenty-one songs in this collection has been found on a Burleigh recital program. However, an advertisement for this anthology was carried in the NAACP's *Crisis* magazine for a number of years, suggesting that both black and white purchasers found it interesting—or that the publisher hoped to increase sales among the readers of *Crisis* magazine.[81]

In his long preface to the anthology, W. J. Henderson, music critic at the New York *Sun,* acknowledged that the era of Negro minstrelsy was past but argued for the preservation of the songs that "were the delight of an earlier generation." They have "a value both historical and sentimental. All of us take a certain pleasure in contemplating the amusements of our fathers, and among them there was none which was more specifically American than the negro minstrel performance."[82] Though *Negro Minstrel Melodies* was published during the time that Burleigh was musical director for the St. George's Men's Club annual minstrel shows, as we have seen, their programs featured current popular songs, not the nineteenth-century minstrel songs that make up this collection.

* * *

Theodore Presser purchased the William Maxwell catalog in 1914, and from 1915 to 1919 Presser's *Etude* magazine published seven of Burleigh's early songs, to which Presser now owned the copyright:[83] "Just Because" (1906)—June 1915, p. 450; "Jean" (1903)—September 1915, p. 664; "Dream Land" (1905)—February 1916, p. 128; "Since Molly Went Away" (1907)—April 1916, p. 292; "Mammy's Little Baby" (1903)—May 1917, p. 334; "Keep a Good Grip on Your Hoe" (1905)—April 1919, p. 237; and "Perhaps" (1906)—December 1919, pp. 802–3. In 1925, "A Jubilee," one of the piano sketches in *From the Southland,* appeared. Though all the *Etude* publications were featured when Burleigh's later songs were being sung by John McCormack and other distinguished singers, these early ballads could be used by voice and piano teachers to prepare their students for Burleigh's more challenging compositions.

Two songs published in 1913, this time by G. Schirmer, were harbingers of an important new development in Burleigh's compositional output: two choral arrangements of spirituals—"Deep River" and "Dig My Grave"—written for Kurt Schindler's Schola Cantorum. Schindler, who emigrated to the United States from Germany in 1905 to serve as a staff conductor at the Metropolitan Opera House, was "a reader, editor and critic" for the G. Schirmer publishing house. In 1913 he became choir director at Temple Emanu-El, where Burleigh sang. He founded the Schola Cantorum (first called the MacDowell Chorus) in 1909.[84] Schindler was interested in folksongs of many countries, and he took a particular interest in African American folksong. Five years later, in their April 1918 concert at Carnegie Hall, the Schola Cantorum sang Negro folksongs "newly collected" by Natalie Curtis Burlin (the reviews comparing her arrangements to Burleigh's will be discussed in Chapter 17). Burleigh's 1913 arrangements are historic not only because they were the first of Burleigh's pioneering choral arrangements of spirituals for concert use but also because they remained in the active G. Schirmer catalog from 1913 for many years.[85]

The sparseness of Burleigh's output from 1910 to 1913 may be accounted for in a number of ways. In addition to the demands on his time by his growing recital schedule and his responsibilities at St. George's Episcopal Church and Temple Emanu-El, and perhaps the strains in his marriage, he was likely aware that George Maxwell would soon be establishing the New York office of G. Ricordi and would take over the publication of his songs. Even more important, Victor Herbert and George Maxwell were preparing to establish the American Society of Composers, Authors, and Publishers, which would protect the copyright of his songs and substantially increase his income. Very likely he was busy composing the song cycles and the other masterful compositions that were to burst upon the music scene in 1914, to be published by one of the most respected music publishers in Europe. From then on his songs and his income from their publication would be protected as had not been possible before. ASCAP was to usher in a new day for African American musical and literary artists, and Burleigh, a charter member of the organization, would be one of its earliest beneficiaries.[86]

15. "Composer by Divine Right"

"The American Coleridge-Taylor"

Harry T. Burleigh's best-known art songs were published by G. Ricordi for more than three and a half decades. They include his three song cycles—*Saracen Songs, Five Songs of Laurence Hope,* and *Passionale*—some eighty individual songs in a variety of styles similar to his earlier work, a set of four violin sketches, and the solo and choral arrangements of spirituals that had become his signature compositions. The spiritual arrangements will be discussed in chapters sixteen and seventeen. This chapter examines a selection of the art songs that won Burleigh renown through their performance by an impressive roster of American and European opera and recital singers, making him one of the most respected American art song composers of the first quarter of the twentieth century.[1]

The first five years of publications by G. Ricordi and Company (1914–19) represent the majority of the strongest, most memorable, and most enduring of his art song oeuvre: the three song cycles in 1914 and 1915, thirty-four secular art songs (two of which were also arranged for choral ensembles), two songs for male chorus, the violin-piano *Southland Sketches*, one sacred solo song, and one dialect song ("Promis' Lan'" [1917]). In the 1920s in addition to a dozen or so art songs, more sacred songs appeared, especially from 1924, the year of the first Vesper Service of Negro Spirituals at St. George's Episcopal Church. There were several songs written for historically black colleges (Talladega College, Cheyney College, and North Carolina College), several novelty songs, and a number of arrangements of folksongs and operatic choruses for choral ensembles. Two songs are especially notable: "Lovely Dark and Lonely One" (1935), his setting of a Langston Hughes poem, Burleigh's last published art song and arguably one of his best; and "In Christ There Is No East or West" (1940), a hymn setting based on a spiritual that has become a standard in Protestant hymnals and continues to be the Burleigh composition most often republished.[2]

It is important to remember that Burleigh was not "trying to be white" in his work as a singer, composer, arranger, or music editor. He was an American who inherited all of American culture, including the wide range of American and European art music. His early formal music training was in European and American classical music, in addition to his distinctive inheritance of African American music, both orally transmitted in his family and community and transcribed or composed.

By 1914 the success of Burleigh's work as a song composer was assured by its increasingly positive reception in two influential circles: singers and music critics. Irish tenor and matinee idol John McCormack was a personal friend, and he introduced Burleigh's songs to the thousands who thronged to his recitals. He performed at least seventeen of Burleigh's art songs in addition to *Five Songs of Laurence Hope* and *Passionale,* and he often premiered them. It was common for Burleigh sheet music to be headed "Sung by Mr. John McCormack."[3] In the 1916–17 recital season, McCormack picked seventy-eight American songs of about six hundred songs that were sent to him. That several Burleigh songs were among the seventy-eight songs he picked indicates McCormack's high regard for Burleigh's music.[4] In a February 1917 ad that featured the programs for four of McCormack's February concerts, three of the four included a Burleigh song: "One Year (1914–1915)," "Deep River," and "Till I Wake," from the cycle *Five Songs of Laurence Hope.*[5]

McCormack was only the foremost of a long list of renowned opera and recital singers who sang Burleigh's art songs, some of whom listed them among their "Ten Favorite Songs by American Composers." In June 1915 *Musical America* began featuring "Some Compositions by Americans Who Are Worthy of Recognition." The first list included Burleigh's "Jean" (1903) and the *Saracen Songs* (1914). Following issues listed "Ethiopia Saluting the Colors," "He Sent Me You," "Just You" and "The Glory of the Day Was in Her Face" (*Passionale*), all published in 1915.[6]

The October 16, 1915, issue featured twenty-seven "Noted Concert Artists" who listed "Their Ten Favorite American Songs."[7] Six singers listed songs by Burleigh: Contraltos Eleanora de Cisneros and Mary Jordan listed "The Grey Wolf" (1915); tenors John McCormack, Dan Beddoes, and Paul Althouse, "Her Eyes Twin Pools" (*Passionale,* 1915), "The Hour Glass" (1914), and "Just You" (1915), respectively; and bass Herbert Witherspoon, "Ethiopia Saluting the Colors" (1915). Of the other twenty-one singers, at least ten others performed Burleigh songs at various times, and two of them appeared on a list of ten singers who programmed at least one Burleigh song during 1915.[8] When Zabetta Brenska, a contralto who often performed with her husband, tenor Paul Althouse, was asked in February 1916 to name her favorite American song, she found it difficult to choose only one. "But if I had to narrow my choice down to one composer I should select Harry Burleigh's songs."[9] In a group of thirteen Boston singers naming their "Ten Favorite American Songs" the following month, tenor George Rasely chose "Ahmed's Song of Farewell" (*Saracen*

Songs).[10] Arthur Hackett, another Boston tenor, programmed Burleigh's spiritual arrangements in later years.[11]

Burleigh's New York career began at a time when New York City's music establishment was led by a distinguished trio of music critics, each of whom knew and respected him first as a singer, then as a composer of songs: Henry E. Krehbiel, James Gibbons Huneker, and W. J. Henderson. Krehbiel, music critic for the New York *Tribune* from 1880 until his death in 1923 and acknowledged "dean" of the New York critics, has been described as "a daunting figure, caustic and pontifical, and of vast and varied learning."[12] Friend and influential supporter of Antonín Dvořák and of his search for a distinctive American musical voice, Krehbiel was a wide-ranging and serious scholar of the folk music of the United States and far beyond, who often reviewed Burleigh's song publications. He provided the Prefatory Note for Burleigh's highly regarded cycle *Five Songs of Laurence Hope* (1915). W. J. Henderson, music critic first for the New York *Times and* then for the New York *Sun,* "nearly always agreed" with Krehbiel,[13] and like Krehbiel, he received Burleigh's work with interest. He wrote the Preface to Burleigh's 1909 anthology *Negro Minstrel Melodies* and the Prefatory Note for his first song cycle, *Saracen Songs* (1914). James Gibbons Huneker, who served as Jeanette Thurber's publicist for the National Conservatory of Music, knew Burleigh from his earliest days in the city. His inaccurate report that Burleigh was a composition student of Dvořák speaks to his view of Burleigh as a well-qualified musician.

Of the Boston critics, Philip Hale of the Boston *Globe* was seldom in agreement with Krehbiel, especially on Dvořák and his view of American music, though his reviews of Burleigh's singing and later of tenor Roland Hayes's recitals were largely positive. And Boston *Evening Transcript* music critic Hiram K. Moderwell wrote insightful and appreciative reviews of Burleigh's songs.

As for music journals, the *Musical Courier* was slow to acknowledge Burleigh's work, but A. Walter Kramer of *Musical America* paid close attention to his publications and wrote some of the most consistently favorable, sometimes hyperbolic, reviews. His evaluations proclaimed the gospel of high culture, calling Burleigh to ascend its heights rather than waste his talent catering to the inferior tastes of the low.

We have seen that Burleigh's thorough grounding as a singer in European and American art song provided a firm foundation for his own compositions. He contributed significantly to American art song as both performer and composer. His training at the National Conservatory of Music brought him into a circle of some of the most dedicated American Wagnerians among New York City's musical luminaries either at or in constellations near the conservatory, and his later harmonic procedures incorporated a Wagnerian loosening of the dominance of a tonic key. Some of Burleigh's songs reflect his appreciation for the operas of Puccini, and his love of musical drama was expressed in some of his most successful art songs. In criticizing the work of some African American colleagues, he referred to Brahms and Debussy as models.[14] We know that Dvořák revered Beethoven and Schubert, and Burleigh's recital programs demonstrated his preference for the songs of Beethoven, Schubert, Schumann, and Grieg. His interest in orientalist-flavored lyrics and musical practices was completely in accordance with the prevailing interest of the era in musical exoticism. In his career-long efforts to counteract the negative presentation of black exoticism, and to bring African American musical traditions into the mainstream of American musical culture, he played a complex and persuasive role as a pioneer black composer.

In a 1916 interview with Burleigh, A. Walter Kramer commented on a change in Burleigh's compositional intention: Though "the splendid quality of his work" had been known "for a great many years," about two years earlier (the year Kramer scolded Burleigh for writing ballads rather than focusing on the art songs of which he was surely capable), Burleigh had "entered upon a new epoch in his work." He "set himself the task of studying [the art song]," so as to make art song composition his primary goal.[15] He continued to write some lighter ballad-style songs, but many of the songs published by G. Ricordi and Company feature a thicker, orchestral-like accompaniment. The majority of the later songs are through-composed, with the accompaniment more contrapuntal, more independent from the vocal line, often weaving countermelodies against the voice. The vocal range remained fairly consistent, but the melodic movement tended to be less conjunct, with wider, less predictable intervallic leaps.[16]

Though the atonality explored by some early-twentieth-century composers seems not to have interested Burleigh, he made greater use of tonal ambiguity in his later songs. He frequently employed secondary dominants and deceptive cadences, and from 1914 on, ninth and eleventh chords and augmented chords that weaken the tonal center appeared more frequently.[17] Pungent nonharmonic minor seconds are not uncommon. The tonic seventh chord begins to appear on final cadences and sometimes at the opening of a song, and he makes occasional use of the whole-tone scale or a chord of the fourth. As before, the ballads tend to be more predictable harmonically, with chromaticism filling a primarily decorative function, in neighboring tones, passing tones, or ascending or descending chromatic lines, rather than in the abrupt or bold harmonic modulations that characterize some of the more serious art songs. In the best of his later songs all of these elements are wedded, creating songs of memorable intensity and elegant melodic and harmonic expression.[18] Darryl Taylor, founder of the African American Art Song Alliance, has called Burleigh's compositions "balanced and tasteful," and his songs "models of sincerity and sensitivity to text."[19]

* * *

As is evident from his earliest publications, Burleigh was drawn to lyrics described at the time as orientalist. This term has been discredited both for its racist presumptions and, in the writings of Edward Said and others, shown to reflect the power relationships of European and American imperialism over their colonies: France in North Africa, northern sub-Saharan Africa, and Southeast Asia; England in India and sub-Saharan Africa; and the United States in Japan (though Japan was never colonized as were the British and French colonial territories, it became a source of cultural exoticism in the American imagination).[20]

Burleigh's interest in lyrics and musical procedures that were described as orientalist arose partly from his interest in folk music and distinctive musical identities such as Irish, English, and Swedish in addition to the pseudo-Persian and East Indian lyrics that inspired his *Saracen Songs* and the *Five Songs of Laurence Hope.* We do not know how often he visited the Midway Plaisance at the 1893 World's Fair in Chicago, but it is not surprising that he was infected by the early-twentieth-century fascination with the ultimate "Other," the "East" as represented in song, story, and drama. From September 30 to October 4, 1913, Liza Lehmann's "In a Persian Garden," a staged presentation of texts from Omar Khayyam's "Rubai-yat" played to capacity audiences at New York City's Wanamaker Auditorium.[21] At least twenty-nine of Burleigh's contemporaries wrote one or more orientalist songs before 1900, and the trend continued.[22] In this environment, an enthusiastic reception of Burleigh's settings of the Eastern-flavored verse of Fred Bowles and Laurence Hope could be expected.

Burleigh and his American contemporaries who created orientalist songs may have found that the bolder sensuality of such texts freed them from the Victorian sexual inhibitions that overlaid the surface of polite society. But Burleigh did not rely only on exotic texts for sensuality; James Weldon Johnson's lyrics in the second song cycle, *Passionale*, were frankly sensual, as were lyrics by other writers, including other black writers such as Georgia Douglas Johnson and Jessie Faucet.[23]

Frederick G. Bowles was an English poet, many of whose religious and secular poems were set to music by Burleigh and other American song composers.[24] Bowles worked in Milan, Italy, as the English representative for *Teatro Libero;* his Middle East–flavored verse included the *Saracen Songs, Songs from Cairo,* and *In the Wake of the Sun,* but there is no indication that he personally spent time in the Middle East.[25] The seven poems of his 1912 *Saracen Songs* suggest a narrative that may have been familiar to Burleigh and Bowles and their contemporaries, but there is no commentary in the slender volume, and its original sources have yet to be discovered. Almona, "Queen of the Desert," is awakened to love by Hassan (1, "Almona"; 2, "O, Night of Dream and Wonder"), then finds fulfillment in the love of Yussouf (3, "His Helmet's Blaze"; 4, "I Hear His Footsteps, Music Sweet"; 5, "Thou Art Weary"; 6, "This Is Nirvana"). But Ahmed's love for Almona is unrequited, and he leaves her, devastated and desolate (7, "Ahmed's Song of Farewell: Mark How a Saracen Fell!"). These songs present a tale of love among Bedouin tent-dwellers in a desert setting, where warrior horsemen court a beautiful young woman, who, contrary to the stereotypes, has control over her relationships with her suitors and is free to decline the advances of one whom she does not love. The sensuality is restrained: the joys of love are described metaphorically, first as sunrise, consuming fire, flame, and torch, and later as tenderness, surrender, beauty, "peace after war, calm after strife," and ultimately, Nirvana. One may wonder how the Buddhist Nirvana finds its way into Islamic cosmology, but neither Burleigh nor any of his critics commented on this syncretic anomaly. Islamist Vika Gardner suggests that the *Saracen Songs* narrative may originate in South Asia, where Islam was very syncretic.[26]

Musically, this first song cycle was seen to represent "a new and higher standard of vocal music" in Burleigh's development as a composer and more generally "of vocal music to English text."[27] W. J. Henderson's Prefatory Note to *Saracen Songs* signaled a recognition of Burleigh's increasing importance as a composer of art songs; it was also a deft marketing move for Ricordi. A note in the *Musical Courier* commented, "Many a musician longs for a place in the Sun, and the particular spot is William J. Henderson's column."[28] This was Henderson's second significant public affirmation of Burleigh's work: his praise of the American minstrel song in his long preface to Burleigh's 1909 *Negro Minstrel Melodies* may have set ambiguous reverberations ringing in some African American readers' ears, but it doubtless enhanced distribution statistics while it also responded to the long perseverance of Negro minstrelsy. Henderson's commendation of *Saracen Songs* represented an even more significant imprimatur, proclaiming Burleigh's increasing competence as a composer.

Henderson termed *Saracen Songs* "without question Mr. Burleigh's most ambitious and successful achievement." Like the reviewer for the London *Musical Opinion and Music Trade Review* who found that "the thoroughly Oriental character of the cycle" could be "discerned on every page,"[29] Henderson wrote that the "rich Orientalism" of the texts had so "warmed the composer's imagination" that it "found eloquent and captivating musical" expression in Burleigh's musical setting.

Henderson observed that Burleigh's harmonic treatment in the first song, "Almona (Song of Hassan)" was "moderate," allowing for "increasing wealth and poignancy in chord combinations" as the cycle developed. He characterized the habanera rhythm in the accompaniment of this first (primarily pentatonic) song as "a fine embodiment of the passionate and sensuous fancy of the East." For listeners today the habanera rhythm is more likely to evoke Cuba or sub-Saharan Africa than the Middle East, but it can also be heard as the first echo of the hoof-beats of the horses that bring Almona's suitors to her tent. "O, Night of Dream and Wonder (Almona's Song)," the second in the cycle, expresses Almona's rapture at the dawning of love: "My tent no more a prison, / All fear and waiting past; / Love's sun hath truly risen, / For Love, for Love hath come at last!" Almona's exaltation is expressed in a breathless sequence of six short disjunct phrases (with slight

"O Night of Dream and Wonder," mm. 11–22.

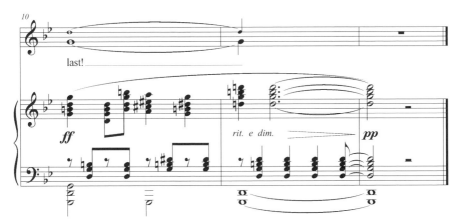

"O Night of Dream and Wonder," mm. 11–22 *(continued)*.

variations) featuring a drop of a fourth then a return to the first pitch, followed by a repeat of the pattern a minor or a major second lower. The final two phrases build to the climactic conclusion: "For Love has come at last!" (mm. 11–22).

Her excitement intensifies in "His Helmet's Blaze (Almona's Song of Yussouf to Hassan)," which one reviewer called "thirty seconds of ferocity and brilliance."[30] These twenty-one measures, marked allegro agitato, pass almost too quickly to be fully absorbed by the listener. Built on augmented chords and melodic tritones (the tritone or augmented fourth was considered a signal element of orientalism), the song communicates an oriental aesthetic not with pentatonicism but with its intensity of passion.[31] The triplet pattern in the introduction brings the horseman closer as Almona eagerly demands that Hassan help her see who gallops toward her over the shimmering desert. In her melody, a pair of chromatic descents of a third, underlaid by the syncopated figures in the accompaniment, is followed by three rising tritones—"His horse's tread, His helmet's blaze, His lifted head"—that convey her thrill of recognition, culminating in the climactic "Ah," on F, an octave drop, then another tritone ascent to "day of days," over the accelerating hoofbeat pattern in the accompaniment (mm. 10–21). The "almost fiery utterance"[32]—Henderson's words—"of the helmet song," demonstrates Burleigh's ability to bring the text alive through his music.

Songs 4, 5, and 6 suggest years of a fulfilling love relationship between Almona and Hassan, but the last song, "Ahmed's Song of Farewell," brings the cycle to a sad, even tragic, end. Ahmed, deprived of Almona's love, bids farewell not only to her but to all, the desert, life, and love. Burleigh adds a remarkable touch in the middle section, using the melody of the spiritual "Somebody's knocking at your door" for Ahmed's mournful remembrance of Almona's beauty: "Never so stately a star / Rode the fair mansions of Heav'n." Other melodic quotations in Burleigh's songs have

"His Helmet's Blaze," mm. 10–21.

symbolic meaning, but in this case, it seems that he uses the melody simply for its solemn beauty. In the next two melodic phrases, he varies the melody sequentially: "God's gather'd beauties afar, / Mine at her dark eyes were given" (mm. 17–26). He recalls her perfection: "Matchless in beauty and grace, / Perfect in body and soul." The solemn melody returns on "Deserts shall dream of her face, / Long as the ages shall roll," before the dramatic outburst, "Here in the heart of the hills, / Mark

"Ahmed's Song of Farewell," mm. 17–26.

how a Saracen fell! Love! How it stifles and kills, Ah, my Almona, Farewell!" The music climaxes with an affretando fortissimo on "Mark how a Saracen fell!" After a quieter farewell to Almona, the song swells to a forte in the voice, supported by sforzando and fortissimo in the closing chords in the piano.

The Middle Eastern character of the *Saracen Songs* was emphasized by the cover art, with a stylized helmet; a stringed instrument resting on a tapestry or carpet

Cover of *Saracen Songs.*
(Courtesy of the Carnegie
Library of Pittsburgh.)

that might be found in a desert tent, golden yellow against a tan background, with contrasting blue accents; a sword; and blue and gold gems set into the brown title typeface.

The dedication "al Tito Ricordi" appeared on the cover. This first Burleigh cycle published by Ricordi was designed to draw the attention of singers, teachers, and critics to the publisher's new composer whose songs would constitute a significant portion of their American vocal catalog for years to come. An undated Ricordi Vocal Catalog in the Erie County Public Library Burleigh Collection lists seventy-five art songs for solo voice, including eight songs reflecting some aspect of African American life; the three song cycles, most published in at least two keys; and forty-six solo arrangements of Negro spirituals.[33]

Less concerned with their oriental flavor, A. Walter Kramer commended the consistently high quality of the *Saracen Songs,* each of which could stand alone. "Mr. Burleigh," he observed, "has not lagged behind in the onward race toward harmonic freedom"; he "feels in the modern way."[34] This cycle has had intermittent but significant use in voice studios and recitals, and several recent recordings and vocal dissertations indicate that it continues to interest twenty-first-century vocalists, both as a cycle and, as Kramer predicted, as individual songs. For George Shirley, retired Metropolitan tenor, "Almona," the first song of the cycle, became "almost a signature song."[35]

Cover of *Five Songs of Laurence
Hope.* (Courtesy of Sibley
Library, Eastman School
of Music.)

Kramer was pleased to note that Burleigh's second orientalist song cycle, *Five Songs by Laurence Hope* (1915), demonstrated the composer's continuing exploration of modern harmony. The Hope songs were "far more modern than anything else Mr. Burleigh has given us," and there was "nothing of the ballad" in them. They were art songs, "finely sensitive to the meaning" of the lyrics.[36] This cycle was received at the time of its publication as Burleigh's best work, and it continues to appeal to singers. Hiram K. Moderwell of the Boston *Transcript* described them in some detail: "Here are haunting melodies, accompaniments rich in detail, yet not overwritten, striking bits of delineation, and much skill in the wedding of music to words." They exhibited "sheer emotional effectiveness," and the composer "shows much cleverness in the weaving of brief thematic snatches into the harmonic framework." The songs were written in "a melodic rather than a declamatory idiom," and the accompaniments displayed an "easy chromatic flow."[37] Their introduction to the public by John McCormack, who premiered them to an overflow crowd at New York City's Carnegie Hall (with 600 seated on the stage), helped to assure their reception. "One can easily understand," Moderwell wrote, "that the melting tones of John McCormack's voice have made thousands applaud them. But it is not so evident, until one comes to study them, how much musicianship and taste has gone into their construction."[38]

Like the *Saracen Songs,* the *Five Songs of Laurence Hope* was given an attractive cover with subtle pastel coloring, featuring an olive-skinned young woman partially draped in a sarilike garment, seated among the requisite lotus blooms, her left arm raised to her right shoulder in an implied passionate but arrested response.

The copyright page carries stylized decoration, and the text of each song is printed with the specific volume of Laurence Hope poems from which it is taken under each title. This cycle is also to be taken seriously by performers, teachers, and critics for the composer's skill as for the orientalism that pervades the lyrics and musical setting. Orchestral accompaniments by German composer Alfred Brüggemann were available from the publisher.

This cycle was also given weight by the Prefatory Note, this time by the redoubtable Henry Krehbiel. He had recently called on Burleigh for sixteen of the arrangements in his 1914 study, *Afro-American Folksongs,* and he routinely reviewed Burleigh's compositions. He praised the "artistic distinction" of Hope's lyrics. Burleigh's settings, "without being out of the convenient reach of amateurs" were "artists' songs, in which singer and pianist are paired in a lovely union." Like Kramer, Krehbiel described these songs as "far removed" from "the commonplace melodic phrase" heard in "the bulk of English sentimental ballads," as well as "the bathos and affected harmonic phrase" of the contemporary German lied and French *melodie.* The music springs "naturally and unconstrainedly from the poetic word," and "the instrumental voice has an independent development" that increases the emotional intensity, carrying it along "as on a flood." Finally, "We have had occasion to learn how adept Mr. Burleigh is in imbuing music with his own national voice, and it is a pleasure to observe that the idiom of the East is also at his command."[39]

When McCormack sang three of the Hope songs at Symphony Hall in Boston soon after the New York premiere, the Boston *Transcript* review was written by Horatio T. Parker and reprinted in the *Musical Courier.* Parker commented that he was "scarcely known to Mr. McCormack's manifold public and too little known" in general except to those who studied American music closely. "Mr. Burleigh has a vein of fresh melody that is individually fragrant and without a hint of the commonness and triteness that beset most songs from American pens. He uses no cheap or hackneyed devices to catch the expectant ear; he has sensibility, humor, and even imagination; he shuns our molasses-like sentimentality as though it were the plague upon our songs that it really is."[40]

In his review Hiram K. Moderwell praised the Laurence Hope cycle as "well-made songs which contain some rich and appropriate coloring and generally fitting expression" for the orientalism of the texts. But he criticized Burleigh's inconsistent use of musical orientalism. "Most of the middle sections of the songs, especially, employ harmonization and melodic line, and the devices of form in sequence and 'working-over' that are not suggestive of Oriental music." Burleigh may have done this deliberately, "with the idea of furnishing contrast," but though "the work of a practiced hand and a taste that is above mediocrity" Moderwell felt this departure from consistency in orientalist musical markers diminished the songs, relegating them to less than "the highest class."[41]

The reviewer for the *Musical Standard* found "Worth While," the first song in the cycle, to be "just a little labored . . . mind-born rather than heart-born," but the second, "The Jungle Flower," was "a really beautiful song, replete with deeply-felt emotion."[42] Moderwell praised "The Jungle Flower" for the appropriately oriental "exotic pulsating syncopation that throbs beneath."[43]

Moderwell considered the third, "Kashmiri Song," "the best achieved" of the five songs, "the moody sentiment of the words . . . heightened into something approaching tragic pathos."[44] These lyrics had been popularized in a setting by Amy Woodforde-Finden titled "Pale Hands I Loved," but the *Musical Standard* reviewer assured readers that Burleigh's setting had "nothing to fear by comparison."[45] Kramer "remarked that those who knew the Woodforde-Finden setting would praise Mr. Burleigh for having done them in an entirely different way."[46]

In "Among the Fuchsias," Moderwell acknowledged that Burleigh had "caught admirably that 'oriental' exoticism which is none the less charming because it happens to be fashionable in present-day song literature." He termed the final song, "Till I Wake"—which McCormack's audience had demanded be repeated at its premiere—"a lyric of real distinction."[47] A more recent reviewer recommends the *Five Songs of Laurence Hope* as "a big, expansive, lush set on Eastern (Indian) themes, from which *Kashmiri Song* is especially recommended."[48] This cycle also has been the subject of several recent dissertations and recordings.[49]

The *Five Songs of Laurence Hope* were the last of Burleigh's songs in orientalist style. Another common type of musical exoticism explored by his contemporaries was the "Indianist" movement. In his 1903 and 1904 recitals he sang a group of Ojibway songs by Frederick Burton, but Burleigh published no Indianist songs. In a 1914 performance at Hampton Institute he was reported to have sung "his own arrangements of" Indian melodies, but no copies of such arrangements have been found.[50] It is likely that his wife's stage presentations as an Ojibway princess and the tensions that resulted in her leaving him to assume a lifelong identity as "Princess Nadonis Shawa" made this a less attractive part of his repertoire and deterred him from publishing his own attempts in this genre. Very likely Burleigh's reputation as the most authentic and skilled presenter of black music and themes persuaded him to focus on mining the distinctive resources of his own heritage.

Passionale, Burleigh's third song cycle, also published in 1915, set four lyrics by James Weldon Johnson to music. Each song was dedicated to a tenor who had performed Burleigh songs and could be counted on to sing the new publications: "Her Eyes, Twin Pools," dedicated to John McCormack; "Your Lips Are Wine" to Evan Williams; "Your Eyes So Deep" to Ben Davies; and "The Glory of the Day Was in Her Face" to George Hamlin. The second song, "Your Lips Are Wine," with lyrics slightly revised, was a new setting of Burleigh's 1914 song "Elysium," damned with faint praise by A. Walter Kramer as "written in a comparatively simple lyric mood and vocally happy," but not the "distinguished music" of which Burleigh was capable.[51] "Your Lips Are Wine," with minor text revisions in Johnson's hand, was now given a serious setting, transforming it into an art song.

Though *Passionale* was presented less elaborately by the publisher, it too had a decorative cover, with leaves framing the title. Critical reception of this cycle was positive if less fervent than for *Saracen Songs* and *Five Songs of Laurence Hope*. A. Walter Kramer wrote that "The merit of these songs is unquestionable, yet in 'Passionale' he has once more outdone himself. He stands, more firmly than ever, a musician who can reflect in his music the spirit of the poem he is working on." The James Weldon Johnson lyrics "are fine examples of impassioned verse," and Burleigh's music "in all four songs is vital." Despite Kramer's caveat that "at times he lapses into a somewhat less distinctive speech," the cycle demonstrated Burleigh's "really individual manner . . . employ[ing] harmonies with rare skill and appropriateness."[52]

Moderwell wrote that the songs offered "grateful material to the accomplished tenor,"[53] a view Roland Allison shared: "In them, Burleigh seems to have brought to the fore all the drama, musical mastery, emphasis, and intensity at his command." Like many of Burleigh's later songs, they featured "wide intervallic skips, frequent chromaticism, and high tessitura," the last "to be expected in a group of songs for a quartet of such gifted tenors. They also demand a wider than usual range, reaching to an eleventh, but fully in the capability of the singers for whom they were created."[54]

The reviews of Burleigh's songs, especially those by A. Walter Kramer, demonstrated the tension between high and low culture as conceived in the early twentieth century. Burleigh's lighter ballads sold well and appeared frequently on programs by opera singers and recitalists, but his own inclination and the sometimes condescending evaluation by even his most supportive critics created challenges for him. Fortunately, he was skilled at satisfying the demands of his diverse audiences, as we see in the exceptional variety of his compositions.

Ellsworth Janifer, in his retrospective of the songs ten years after Burleigh's death, commented that though the *Passionale* songs "lack the delicacy of 'Lovely Dark and Lonely One,' the dramatic strength of 'The Young Warrior,' and the grave, classic beauty of 'Jean,' they are melodious, finely constructed and, above all, easy to sing. . . . In this instance particularly, [Burleigh] understood the essence of the poem and was able to blend text and music into an aesthetically satisfying whole."[55] The last of the four songs, "The Glory of the Day Was in Her Face," has been regarded as the strongest in the cycle and is the one most often performed.[56]

Passionale was not performed as often in its entirety during Burleigh's lifetime as was the *Saracen Songs*, and it has found less favor among current singers than *Five Songs of Laurence Hope* as well. Tenor Darryl Taylor commends it to twenty-first-century singers. The songs are "characterized by lyrical melodies in the voice undergirded by mostly homophonic piano accompaniment." He comments on the vocal range, difficulty, and dynamic range for the benefit of singers and voice

teachers. "Harmonically lush, with chromaticism layered on a firmly diatonic structure," *Passionale* is "a fine period cycle."[57]

* * *

The cataclysmic effect of World War I on Europe and the United States can
scarcely be overstated. Though the United States did not enter the conflict until
1917, the reverberations across the Atlantic were profound. In February 1915 the Clef
Club Orchestra and Wanamaker's Colored Jubilee Club, which Burleigh helped
train, gave a series of concerts on Ellis Island, "where large numbers of immigrants
[were] detained on account of the war."[58] The first of six songs Burleigh wrote in
response to the Great War was his 1915 setting of James Weldon Johnson's poem
"The Young Warrior," a soldier's farewell to his mother. Johnson, prominent African
American poet and diplomat who served as U.S. consul to Venezuela and Nicaragua
under President Theodore Roosevelt (1906–13), wrote the lyric shortly after the war
began in Europe in 1914. Even before its premiere in New York City, the song was
translated into Italian by Eduardo Petri and orchestrated by Richard Zandonai, who
dedicated his orchestration to Burleigh. Distributed in Italy (Ricordi was based in
Milan, with offices in Rome, Palermo, and Naples), "Il Giovane Guerriero" "swept
Italy like a flash. Italian soldiers sang it on the battlefield and their people sang
it at home."[59] Operatic baritone Pasquale Amato presented the American debut
of "The Young Warrior" in February 1916 at an Italian war benefit concert at the
Biltmore Hotel, sponsored by the Italian ambassador and Countess Delores de
Allere, "through patronage of the Queen of Italy."[60]

An immediate hit, the song was reviewed in numerous American newspapers
and journals, often commenting on the "high honor" the song's international appeal
conferred on "a negro-boy from Erie, Pa."[61] According to *Current Opinion*, it was
"not to be classed with 'Tipperary,' which is of a pretty cheap order,"[62] but like other
Burleigh songs critics preferred to more popular settings, "The Young Warrior"
never achieved the broad popular recognition of its lesser contemporary. A black
newspaper commented, "It is of general interest to the Afro-American people that
one of their number had achieved such a high distinction in the land of music
and song, for such Italy is. What Italy stamps as poetry and music the world usually accepts."[63] *Musical America* agreed: "What a triumph for an American Negro
musician to write the marching song for the most musical nation in this war!" The
United States had not yet entered the conflict, but "after all, we are doing our bit
with our music."[64]

In "The Young Warrior," Burleigh used a drum roll and an ostinatolike descending octaval bass line as a martial motif that unifies the through-composed setting.
The song also exhibits other aspects of Burleigh's later style of accompaniment. He
builds it on a one-measure motif (mm. 1–8). He uses key modulation expressively,
beginning at the end of the first verse. The primary key is A-flat. After a brief toni-
cization in B-flat, he moves to C, briefly leaving the martial motif for a hymnlike

passage on the phrase "But bless me with thy word," ending with a plagal cadence that emphasizes the hymnlike effect (mm. 10–12). The marching pattern returns, with additional modulations back to the tonic key in measure seventeen. Another prayerlike phrase in the key of C sets the words "Still pray not to defend from harm, Nor danger to dispel." "But rather that with steadfast arm I fight the battle well" moves to E major. The tonic key returns with the fourth verse as does the opening melodic phrase, on the words "Mother! oh Mother! Pray, I keep through

"Young Warrior" motif, mm. 1–8.

all the days, / My heart and purpose strong, / My sword unsullied, and always / Unsheath'd against the wrong."[65] African American tenor Roland Hayes and baritones C. Sumner Wormley and Garfield Warren Tarrant performed "The Young Warrior," as did Euro-tenors Paul Althouse, Dan Beddoe, and Reinald Werrenrath, and Italian tenors Luca Botta and Luigi Simonetta during the war years.[66]

Burleigh's setting of "One Year 1914–1915" and of Rupert Brooke's poem "The Soldier" were published in 1916. Brooke, one of England's beloved poet soldiers, died shortly after this sonnet was published. The *Musical Courier* commented favorably on "The Soldier" but expressed reservations about Burleigh's quotation of snatches of the popular patriotic songs "Rule Britannia," the "British Grenadiers," and "God Save the Queen." The reviewer regarded Burleigh's original "brief theme of four notes" to be more effective than the borrowed motifs.[67] But A. Walter Kramer could be counted on to come through for him: "I think that this Burleigh setting of Rupert Brooke's inspired lines will be among the important art products of the Great War, when the record is made. It is a composition that will stir deeply those who hear it; and best of all, it is vital, because it is not a contribution to a cause but a spontaneous musical reflection of Brooke's sublime sentiment."[68]

In her analysis of Burleigh's careful setting of this patriotic text, "If I should die, think only this of me: That there's some corner of a foreign field that is forever England!" Ann Sears points out that "Burleigh sets the words 'die' and 'me' to long notes at the ends of two short phrases and then ends a long phrase with 'forever,' further lengthening the notes with a ritard as the phrase ends with 'England!'" thus "inextricably" associating the words 'die,' 'me,' 'forever,' and 'England!'"[69]

The body of the song "turns to reminiscences of English life in an earlier, happier time," but the emphasis is on the patriotic message. "In the last phrase, 'under an English heav'n,' crashing chords, a quickening tempo, and the critical placement of the highest note of the piece on 'heav'n' provide the song's final majestic moment. . . . The heroic phrases that open and close the song are military in character, using a minor key and with thick chords and dotted rhythms that Burleigh indicates should be played 'quasi una Marcia funebre.'" Reminiscences of a happier England are

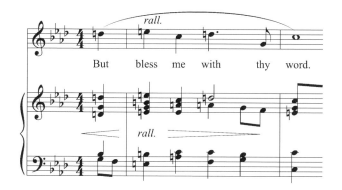

Hymnlike pattern, mm. 10–12.

portrayed by "more lyrical melodies, more chromatic harmony, smoother rhythmic patterns, slower tempos, and considerable *rubato*. This ability to paint a variety of moods with musically and emotionally successful transitions makes Burleigh's longer songs a singer's delight. Burleigh the singer must have enjoyed the storytelling element in performing texted works, for he consistently composed songs that demand great skill in communicating the story line and feelings of the poetry."[70]

"One Year 1914–1915" traces in stark terms the devastation of war and this war in particular. Verse one, 1914: Lovers framed by "Dark pines 'gainst the blue; Clean winds, a wide view;" snatch "One moment of bliss" before they are parted, bereft of all but this memory. Verse two, 1915: "Battle birds in the sky; Shriek of guns as they die; Crash and roar, bloody drench; Black death in the trench." An interlude includes a four-measure chordal quotation of the German chorale "Praise to the Lord" / "Lobe den Herrn" before the final despairing exclamation: "[F]orever to miss! /Ah My God! her kiss / and *this!*" John McCormack premiered it on April 9, 1916. Kramer called it "colossal. Singers will grip their audiences mightily with it. . . . It is one of those cases of true simplicity of style wherein greatness is to be found; vital in every sense in this war essay!'"[71]

Baritone Reinald Werrenrath, tenors Reed Miller and Pasquale Amato, who premiered "The Young Warrior," and John McCormack sang "One Year" and "The Young Warrior" during the war years. After the U.S. entered the war in 1917, both "One Year" and "The Soldier" appeared more frequently. A reviewer of a McCormack performance commented, "Mr. McCormack was wise in introducing Burleigh's stirring "One Year," an epitome of the personal tragedies resulting from the war."[72] Only a singer deeply moved by the slaughter in the trenches could do justice to this dramatic setting.

"Under a Blazing Star" (1918) evokes a similar situation. An asterisk in the title alerts the singer that the "Blazing Star" is a star shell, two of which can be seen descending through the dark sky in the cover art, and in the lower left corner a third exploding in a landscape of trees battle-blasted, denuded. Also sung by John McCormack, this song voices the wistful hope of a soldier too long entrenched:

Blow, wind, blow,	Sing, wind, sing,
From the mountains or the sea;	Till I only hear your song;
And banish the mist that veils my eyes,	And never a sound of battle roar
Send my dreams to me!	Through the night so long, so long.
Blow, wind, blow!	Sing, wind, sing!

"Under a Blazing Star" was performed by operatic contralto Sophie Braslau in December of 1918,[73] by John McCormack and Charles Harrison, and by baritone Judson House, accompanied by Burleigh.[74]

Burleigh's last two World War I songs, "The Victor" and "Down by the Sea," both published in 1919, the year the surviving soldiers returned from the war, set lyrics by George F. O'Connell to music. These two poems and "Love Watches"

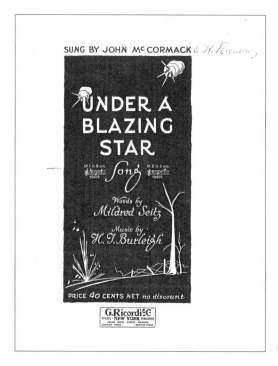

Cover of "Under a Blazing Star."

appeared in O'Connell's 1920 collection *Memory*; Burleigh may have had access to the verses in manuscript. Dedicated "to all those who gave their lives for the Right: 'REQUIESCAT IN PACE,'" "The Victor" is a requiem for the troops who did not return from the war. A reviewer commented that Burleigh "has written a song that in the hands of an artist of lesser capabilities would have been maudlin; and at the close he has introduced the taps of our army as a postlude, accompanied by a series of perfect and augmented fifths, powerful and affecting because it is done with so much repression."[75]

While the success of "The Young Warrior" may have been a factor in Burleigh's choosing to compose an additional five songs during the war years, these settings demonstrate Burleigh's personal response to the war. At the start of the war in 1914, it was necessary to bring his son Alston back to the United States from his private school in England. He was too young to serve in Europe, but four years later Alston enlisted in the Students' Army Training Corps and was sent to Camp Pike for Officer's Training Camp in Little Rock, Arkansas. He served in Europe in World War II, and Burleigh took great pride in his son's and his grandson's military service. Through his songs, he, too, "did his bit" for the war effort.[76]

* * *

Some of Burleigh's songs that were highly regarded during his lifetime by both critics and singers have not fared so well in the following years. One example of this is "Little Mother of Mine," a frankly sentimental song reflecting a stereotypically Victorian mother–son relationship. Like Burleigh's homage to his own mother, several of his songs are in this vein: "Mother o' Mine" (Kipling, 1914), "The Young Warrior" (1915), "Little Mother of Mine" (1917), "Don't You Weep When I'm Gone," (1919), and "I Hope My Mother Will Be There" (1924).

From the premiere by John McCormack, "Little Mother of Mine" was among the most popular of Burleigh's songs, as shown by reports of performances and by its publication in a variety of voicings. In one performance at the Hippodrome before a capacity audience (1,000 were seated on the stage), the audience responded with a standing ovation. McCormack turned to Burleigh, seated near him on the stage, to insist that he join him to acknowledge the applause. Burleigh modestly declined, saying later, "I couldn't. I couldn't. But he sang it wonderfully."[77] Ricordi responded to the demand for sheet music by issuing it in four keys for solo voice rather than the usual two or three. Choral arrangements for mixed voices, three-part women's voices, four-part male voices, and two-part male voices also were published. Only his signature spiritual arrangement of "Deep River" comes close to this variety of published versions.

"Little Mother of Mine," mm. 8–16.

Late-twentieth-century reviewers have been less kind: "sentimental" is the mild-est of adjectives used, but "treacly" is closer to the modern judgment (despite Hora-tio Parker's statement that "he shuns our molasses-like sentimentality as though it were the plague upon our songs that it really is"). Retired conductor James Sample commented that Burleigh's era "was a time of tenderness, sentimentality, and he seems to have found that lovely ridge in a dangerous area between sentimentality and sentiment."[78]

However one views the sentimentality of "Little Mother of Mine," there are musical reasons for its success beyond its accordance with a late Victorian mind-set. Ann Sears points out that Burleigh transcended popular style through his fine craftsmanship. In songs "that shared the sentimental melodies and nostalgic texts of the parlor-song tradition," he avoided "the predictability of most parlor-song repertoire." The expressive devices that characterize his art songs, "the sevenths, non-chord tones, and chromatic melodic notes" help to make this setting memo-rable as well. He uses half steps to underscore the words "evening" and "twilight" and "their metaphorical allusions to the past." Half steps in the piano counter-melody in measures 19 and 20 "are anticipated by the half steps in the melody in measures 10, 14, and 18 around the poetically significant words 'evening,' 'west' and 'twilight.' . . . The final chromatic, expressive half step in the first verse occurs . . . at the word 'sometimes' in measure 34." Through this subtle strategy Burleigh creates "an effective mood" (mm. 8–16).[79]

This is a strophic song, but as usual, Burleigh creates contrast in the verses "by altering the vocal rhythm to fit the text of the verse, as well as adding simple yet memorable countermelodies and richer chordal textures in the second-verse accompaniment. Burleigh's use of countermelody is particularly obvious" in this song. "The piano doubles the vocal melody in the first verse" but features "dotted half notes, and half-note-quarter-note patterns above the vocal line in the second verse, along with richer chords in the left hand of the accompaniment."[80]

McCormack's recording of "Little Mother of Mine" was featured in the July 1918 Victor supplement, with a photograph emphasizing McCormack's personal con-nection to the lyrics. "Alongside a full-page picture of McCormack, his wife, and their two small children in a homey family scene, the florid copy tied the song to the singer's own childhood. 'Perhaps John McCormack was thinking of the little home in Athlone [Ireland], where his childhood days were spent, when he made this record. . . . and as the last high note sinks softly into silence one cannot help feeling that the song is a genuine tribute, a genuine expression of the man's own secret thoughts. The song is worthy of John McCormack.'"[81]

Tim Brooks is among the contemporary reviewers who describes "Little Mother of Mine" as "treacly," though he acknowledges the power of McCormack's perfor-mance: "McCormack excelled at this kind of sentimentality. His pure tenor glided effortlessly between tender reverie and powerful crescendos, and his rendition is affecting even today. A full orchestra, complete with harp, provided a very classy accompaniment. It is no wonder that he brought the house down with the song in encores, and his recording of it must have produced more than a few moist eyes in parlors across America."[82] Initially credited to Walter H. Brown in the sheet music and first pressings of John McCormack's recordings, the lyrics were actually written by George Swift Brengle; later pressings and publications corrected the error.[83]

* * *

Burleigh was a confirmed Anglophile; he was drawn to verse by British poets, especially to texts with an Irish flavor. Eight songs published between 1915 and 1921 were settings of Arthur Symons texts written between 1894 and 1900. Three were from "Days and Nights" (1899): "Before Meeting" (1921); "I Remember All" or "Remembrance" (1919), dedicated to Sophie Braslau; and "Memory" (1915). The other five appeared in Symons's *Images of Good and Evil* (1899), in a group entitled "In Ireland": "By the Pool at the Third Rosses" (1916), "The Grey Wolf" (1915), "In the Wood of Finvara" (1916), "On Inishmaan: Isles of Aran" (1916), and "The Prayer" (1915). The first four of these Irish settings were highly regarded by critics and often performed by prominent singers. As might be expected, John McCormack was among them. "By the Pool at the Third Rosses" was dedicated to him, and he sang the premiere in manuscript at Carnegie Hall on January 16, 1916.[84] Three of the Symons songs were dedicated to and sung by contraltos. "On Inishmaan: Isles of Aran" was dedicated to Pittsburgh contralto Christine Miller (Clemson), who premiered it in October 1916 before its 1917 publication. "The Grey Wolf," a dramatic scena representing evil in *Images of Good and Evil*, and "In the Wood of Finvara" were dedicated to Mary Jordan, the contralto soloist at Temple Emanu-El who often performed Burleigh art songs and spiritual arrangements. Christine Miller also sang "The Grey Wolf" on a number of occasions, as did Burleigh's friend Daisy Tapley.

In his review Hiram K. Moderwell classed "By the Pool at the Third Rosses" among "the conventional type of 'light concert pieces,' which are beloved of singers for the latter part of their programs," though "notably successful," revealing "invention and musicianship well above the average." He regarded "By the Pool" as an especially fine example of the type.[85]

Most of the published reviews of Burleigh's work appeared in mainstream publications, and it seems that until the mid-1910s his songs were performed more frequently by white singers than black. Burleigh was not known as "a race man" in the sense that term was applied to leaders such as W. E. B. Du Bois, but in his May 18, 1916, column, Lucien H. White conferred on him an analogous title: "A Race Musician." White, who succeeded Lester A. Walton as music reviewer of the New York *Age,* commented on a number of occasions on the importance of Burleigh's work as a composer. Having "passed beyond the prejudicial bounds set by racial limitations," he "has long enjoyed a reputation as one of the leading singers of the country, without regard to color." He had also "long held a high place" as a composer. His songs such as "Jean" held "a place in the repertoire of many of the most successful singers in the country." White also commented on the shift toward art song compositions: "[A] study of its beauties tempted him and he has made its creation his task of love," resulting in an outpouring of significant publications from 1914 to 1916.[86]

White expressed his wish that in an upcoming recital at the Fleet Street Memorial A.M.E. Zion Church, "an event in the musical life of Brooklyn," Burleigh would "confine his numbers entirely to the songs of his own composing." His most recent songs were "all of an unusual character. Their degree of difficulty places them out of the scope of most of the amateur singers of the race" and because the majority "of the people of the race" heard only amateur black singers, they seldom had "an opportunity to hear the compositions of this man who in the realm of music is no longer a mediocrity." White especially wished to hear Burleigh sing "The Young Warrior" and songs from his three song cycles. Burleigh "would be doing some splendid educative work if he were to give his audience a chance to hear" his own compositions.[87] Burleigh, by the way, did not oblige.

Years later, in June 1941, White again lamented that Burleigh's art songs were so little known by aspiring black singers. Other outstanding composers, such as R. Nathaniel Dett, William L. Dawson, and William Grant Still, had "made rapid strides" in the two recent decades. But in White's opinion, "the man to whom [was] due the most credit" for African American song forms was Burleigh. He had "inspired all of the lesser lights who have attempted to compose with his arrangements of spirituals and his masterful art songs." Burleigh's songs "should be sung in preference to many of the songs which have been done to death by Negro singers" such as "Trees," "Mandalay," "Sylvia," Malotte's "The Lord's Prayer," "At Dawning" by Cadman, and even "Vesti la Guibba" from *Pagliacci* and Verdi's "Celeste Aïda," "as though every half-way sophisticated concert-goer were not heartily tired of them." White recommended Burleigh's art songs "not because they are by one of our race, but because they are meritorious in themselves." He listed sixteen songs in addition to the *Saracen Songs* and *Passionale* cycles."[88]

By this time professional black singers such as Roland Hayes, Daisy Tapley, William Richardson, Maud Cuney-Hare, Minnie Brown, Lillian Evanti, Charlotte Wallace Murray, Anne Wiggins Brown, Florence Cole Talbert, Ruby Elzy, Jules Bledsoe, and others were featuring Burleigh's art songs as well as his spiritual arrangements in their performances. But as White urged, it was time for younger black singers to follow the example of the many white opera and recital singers who had made Burleigh's songs a significant part of their repertoire.

* * *

Burleigh wrote a number of songs that demonstrated his skill in bringing a dramatic narrative to life. The most enduring of these is his 1915 setting of Walt Whitman's poem "Ethiopia Saluting the Colors." A journalist rather than a soldier, Whitman spent many months nursing wounded soldiers in the makeshift hospitals around the nation's capital, listening to their stories. In "Ethiopia" Whitman portrays a young Union soldier whose view of the war and of his world is transformed when, on the march through the Carolinas in General Sherman's army, he comes upon an aged slave woman "who gives a human face and a life story to 'Ethiopia,' the anonymous race of Africans in America whose humanity he has not confronted before." Going off to war, with its "flourishes of fifes and drums" has been an adventure, "an initiation into manhood." But when he asks, "Who are you, dusky woman?" she shares her memories of being captured a century earlier "as a savage beast is caught," and he begins to understand the monumental import of the historic drama in which he is an actor.[89]

Burleigh's music "enhances the emotional depth in Whitman's portrayal of the profound effect" this meeting has on both the soldier and the slave woman. He creates an operatic vignette, "weaving a series of motives that enrich the dramatic texture." Snatches of Henry Clay Work's "Marching through Georgia" over the hypnotic marching chord ostinato contrast with "the harmonically unstable setting" that prepares for the soldier's epiphany: "Thou Ethiopia com'st to me, as under doughty Sherman I march tow'rd the sea." As the woman tells of "being wrenched from her parents' home, harmonic modulations reflect the disruption in her world." Ominous rolled chords underlie her account of the horrific slave ship passage and "as the soldier takes in the grim reality of her story, the 'Marching Through Georgia' motive, now in the minor mode, becomes progressively more subdued." As he muses on "the things so strange and marvelous" that she has seen, he sees her not as "hardly human," but as a queenly presence surveying "the guidons moving by."[90]

Bass Herbert Witherspoon, to whom "Ethiopia" was dedicated, listed it as one of his "Ten Favorite American Songs." The New York *Times* review of his premiere performance at Carnegie Hall called it "artistically conceived and skillfully executed—the work of a true musician deeply felt—and it has impressiveness, as the poem has. It was natural that Mr. Witherspoon should devote much care to Mr. Burleigh's fine composition, and he sang it with a pathos that rang through with a poignant intensity."[91] Hiram K. Moderwell praised Burleigh's choice of texts; "the robust spirit that dictated 'Ethiopia' . . . is one that is much needed to lift American song-literature from the deadly average of mediocrity which now holds it fast."[92] "Ethiopia" can be heard on several recent recordings, most notable among them by baritone Thomas Hampson, who sings it in recital, has recorded it, and includes it in his online and broadcast series *Song of America*.[93]

* * *

Brief mention must be made of another theme in Burleigh songs. Having grown up along the shore of Lake Erie and having spent summers working on the lake steamers, he set several seaside lyrics to music. The most dramatic, "The Sailor's Wife" (1917), dedicated to Christine Miller and a favorite of her audiences, is the cry of a woman longing for her lover to come home from sea, a scene Burleigh must have witnessed as a young man in Erie. Perhaps the loveliest is "Have You Been to Lons?" (1920), a folksonglike modified strophic setting of lyrics by Gordon

Johnstone. Lons is a mythic shore, where one might "meet the man with a strange, sad smile and a voice like music's fall" who "knows the sea, every mile on mile, Like a sailorman knows his yawl." Burleigh sets the first verse in the major mode but shifts to minor for the first half of the second verse: "Have you been to Lons, on a clear salt day, / Where the road runs down to the lea, / Where the wild gulls ride on the cold white spray? / Where they seem to talk with thee?" The last lines build to a climax, again in the major mode, describing the encounter with "a man with a Godlike face," a scene recalling Jesus greeting his fisherman disciples on the Galilean shore: "Did he send his love to me? / For he meets my soul in that star-hung space / Where I'll walk with God o'er the sea."

* * *

Burleigh is said to have written two sets of violin sketches, but the first, *Six Plantation Melodies for Violin and Piano,* written or published about 1901, has not been found.[94] Ricordi published *Southland Sketches,* his second set of violin and piano sketches, in 1916. Like the piano sketches, the violin sketches are parlor pieces. Burleigh weaves snatches of folk melodies into his instrumental sketches, though the violin pieces feature fewer quotations than his piano sketches. In both suites he treats the melodies developmentally rather than simply creating a setting for them. The four violin movements are marked andante, adagio ma non troppo, allegretto grazioso, and allegro. Moderwell wrote that they were "based on negro themes. Yet they are in no sense an attempt to set in relief the Negroid musical characteristics. Rather, they are aimed and well fashioned for practical effectiveness in the authorized manner." The andante is "a wistful and ingratiating piece" that "preserves just a trace of the rhythmic sparkle of the negro tune." The third movement, allegretto grazioso, which briefly quotes and plays with Stephen Foster's "Swanee River," is "altogether charming" and calls Dvořák's "Humoresque" to mind. Moderwell found the allegro to be "brimming with high spirits."[95] Each movement is progressively more lively, making the suite a delightful recital piece. These are excellent teaching pieces for a young violinist.

In 1918 Richard Keys Biggs issued a book of organ transcriptions that included the second movement, adagio ma non troppo, and the same year, violinists Cyril Towbin and Clarence Cameron White performed the entire suite in recital. Each of the four movements was featured at some point in the annual Vesper Service of Negro Spirituals at St. George's Episcopal Church, often played by Eugene Ideler. The second movement, adagio ma non troppo, was performed most often and on several occasions was performed by violin and theremin.[96]

Commenting on his relatively few instrumental compositions, Burleigh acknowledged he felt himself limited by the realities of the marketplace. The myth that real composers write regardless of whether, how, and by whom their creations may be performed often casts a dubious shadow on the work of composers whose output has in some obvious way been affected by its reception. But Burleigh was working in a real world, where the precariousness of his position was frankly affected by the interactions of publishers who published songs, singers who sang them, teachers who taught them, and sheet music vendors who sold them—and by critics who reviewed them. He commented on the stifling effect on composition of the prospect of little or no performance of his work: "I started a string quartet. I would like to do work in different fields, but . . . songs are the only things it pays publishers to issue. A chamber music piece may be played once and forgotten. You can't get it published. You get a little discouraged and you go back to writing songs." But it was not simply an economic choice; Burleigh said, "You see, I have a mission; I must make my music known."[97] As A. Walter Kramer wrote, Burleigh "is a thinker, a man who writes music not because he wants to see his name on a program but because he feels it deeply, profoundly in the language of tone. He is contributing to American art song examples of creative music that deserve world-wide attention and respect."[98]

* * *

On several occasions Burleigh commented on how he chose the lyrics for his songs. He told A. Walter Kramer that "The text determines the character of the music," and his sensitive text setting is one of the strengths of his songs. Burleigh's choice of texts reflected core values: Composers should "look for poems in which the spiritual forces of mercy, justice, truth, play a part. . . . [A] poem must have more than just an ordinary sentimental reference before I can set it." He added that he read "hundreds of perfectly good poems" in order to find the few that he would set to music.[99]

He also wrote for specific voicings and for specific singers. In a draft of an undated letter (probably the late 1930s or early 1940s) to Mrs. N. W. Maise of Spelman College in Atlanta, Georgia, Burleigh commented on how the performance by certain singers affected the success of his songs. He also spoke of the reduced demand for his art songs and the degree to which his compositional choices were determined by the singers who would perform them. Many of his earlier songs were "no longer in demand," so his publishers did "not feel justified in reprinting them. At that time the great Irish tenor John McCormack, George Hamlin, Oscar Seagle, Lawrence Tibbett, and Roland Hayes were singing my songs at many of their concerts, and the contraltos Mary Jordan and Sophie Braslau were also using [them]. . . . These recitalists created a certain vogue for the type of songs I was writing."[100]

Writing for specific singers called for compositional sensitivity in range and melodic contour. "That is why many of my songs are more suitable for tenor and contralto voices than for sopranos. I cannot imagine a soprano voice doing as good a job with 'Oh, My Love,' as a tenor voice would do. I do not refer to the sentiment of the words but rather to the general tessitura of the composition."[101]

His style of accompaniment was also affected by performance. While the orchestral texture of many of Burleigh's later songs was far from Straussian, there is a discernible thickening of texture in a number of the songs from 1914 on. As some of the singers who introduced them to the public sang and recorded them with orchestras, Burleigh tended to write in a style that was adaptable to that medium and that took into account an orchestra's tonal resources.

* * *

Burleigh's last published art song, "Lovely Dark and Lonely One" is in important ways a culmination of his art song catalog. The Langston Hughes poem published in *The Dream Keeper* (1932) is without question an expression of black pride. Burleigh wrote Marian Anderson that in writing this "dandy new song," he had her voice in mind.[102] Though he set numerous lyrics written by black writers to music, "Lovely Dark and Lonely One" is the first that speaks so clearly of the beauty of being black and the frustration of "the dream deferred."[103] Throughout his long career as singer and songwriter, Burleigh's persistent intent was to demonstrate that African Americans could participate as equals (but with a unique perspective and contribution) in American art music, as creators and performers. As a singer he presented black folksongs and songs related to the black experience with artistry and dignity—and wit—programmed with German lieder and art songs of his American songwriter colleagues. He brought these songs into concert repertoire, with his ballads and art songs as well as his art song spiritual arrangements.[104]

Lawrence Schenbeck has traced in his book *Racial Uplift and American Music, 1878–1943,* the often stated and deeply committed intent of African American leaders—and of black citizens at every economic and social level, but especially the elite and middle class—to bend every effort to improvement of their personal situations and to assist others in the struggle for upward mobility. "Lifting as we climb," the motto of the National Association of Colored Women, voiced the ideal, "so much a part of the *Zeitgeist* that leaders as disparate in their philosophies and followers as Marcus Garvey, Booker T. Washington, and W. E. B. Du Bois all made use of the [word *uplift*] to describe hopes for their people." Their profound differences in strategy bred deeply partisan controversy, but racial uplift was always the ultimate goal.[105] Burleigh, the grandson, son, and stepson of civil-rights activists, chose the art of music as his keenest weapon for this lifelong crusade.

The poet Langston Hughes was of the second generation of Harlem Renaissance leaders, an outspoken advocate of unapologetic, even pugnacious assertion of racial pride. His 1926 article "The Negro Artist and the Racial Mountain," published in *The Nation,* abandoned the traditional uplift posture of humility and modesty (two terms often used to describe Burleigh's public posture, at least in his relations within the white musical and social establishments in which he worked), demanding a black aesthetic that was not dependent on the approval of white consumers and critics—or that of the black elite.[106]

One might assume that Burleigh and Hughes would be at odds, but Burleigh always respected and supported excellence. He and Hughes worked together on various cultural projects, and he followed the progress of his younger colleagues with satisfaction and delight. At the October 24, 1935, opening of Hughes's play *Mulatto* at the Vanderbilt Theatre on Broadway, Burleigh's telegram said, "Congratulations may you achieve the honor you richly merit tonight."[107] The following summer Burleigh sent Hughes a postcard featuring Florence, Italy, and he wrote Hughes from Oak Bluffs about the manuscripts of songs by a young Chicago woman submitted to Ricordi for publication, apparently with Hughes's sponsorship. Ricordi had not chosen to publish the songs, but Burleigh wanted to communicate to her his interest in her "pronounced talent"; he felt her songs were "well written, sensitively felt and deeply expressive of the texts."[108] These few items document that at least by the mid-1930s Hughes and Burleigh recognized that they shared similar goals, however different their strategies may have been. Burleigh's choice of Hughes's "Lovely Dark and Lonely One" to conclude his career as an art song composer suggests that by this time, he understood that his own choice of weapons, perhaps unduly influenced by Booker T. Washington's accommodationist stance, had failed to win many battles, and had certainly lost the war against racial discrimination.

* * *

Most of Burleigh's sacred choral anthems were written for the St. George's Episcopal Church choir. "Christ Be with Me," a particularly fine setting of words selected from the Celtic prayer "St. Patrick's Breastplate," was published for mixed voices in 1929, though it may also have been published for solo voice in 1906. His valuable setting of "The Lord's Prayer," published for both solo and mixed voices has not been well known (the SATB version seems to have existed only in manuscript in the United States but may have been published in England). It should receive due attention now that it has been edited by Atlanta choral directors Uzee Brown and James Abbington and published by GIA Publications (2010). Several others of Burleigh's sacred anthems will be welcome additions to contemporary choral repertoire when they have been reissued.

Burleigh's last publication, the hymn "In Christ There Is No East or West," is an adaptation of a spiritual set to John Oxenham's text. Burleigh named the tune "McKee" in honor of Rev. Elmore McKee, one of the rectors of St. George's Episcopal Church. In this song he declares his belief in the equal worth and familial relationship of universal humanity, based in his Christian faith, a belief that was tested throughout his life. Burleigh seldom commented on his experience of discrimination resulting from his identity as an African American, but his last two published works are evidence that in spite of the recognition and love that sustained him at St. George's, he never forgot that he represented a people whose lives had been and continued to be limited by the power structures created by persons of wealth and influence like many of those who sat in the pews of his congregation at St. George's. In a 1980 sermon, Rev. Elmore McKee spoke of this reality. Despite Burleigh's reticence to share the details of his personal life, Rev. McKee believed

"Burleigh struggled with the relationship of his faith to injustice to the end of his life." In his last publication, "In Christ There Is No East or West," Burleigh left his last will and testament of faith. "Burleigh would have agreed that no moral principle in the Constitution or religious principle in the Bible, nor both together, could be powerful enough to bring about the changes needed in the souls of men." McKee believed Burleigh continued "wrestling with this matter of atonement by whites long after he left the choir" in 1946.[109] It is fitting that this final declaration of Harry T. Burleigh's faith continues to find use in church hymnals of many denominations:

> In Christ there is no East or West, in Him no South or North,
> But one great fellowship of love throughout the whole wide earth.
> In Him shall true hearts everywhere their high communion find.
> His service is the golden cord close binding all mankind.
> Join hands then, brothers of the faith, whate'er your race may be!
> Who serves my Father as a son is surely kin to me.
> In Christ now meet both East and West, in Him meet South and North.
> All Christly souls are one in Him throughout the whole wide earth.

* * *

Burleigh would not have accepted A. Walter Kramer's title, "the American Coleridge-Taylor." According to Burleigh's definition of a composer, Coleridge-Taylor's many instrumental works in addition to his art songs qualified him for that honor, but as one whose compositions consisted almost entirely of songs, Burleigh modestly declined the title. Others disagreed; critic F. J. McIsaac called Burleigh a "worthy contemporary of Cadman, Carpenter, and MacDowell. . . . It is erroneous to assume that he rose to fame because of his spiritual arrangements since those songs only climaxed a career already eminently successful. The art songs are set to fine poems whose essence he understood, and he was able to blend text and music into an aesthetically satisfying whole."[110]

Burleigh's position within the white art music establishment enabled him to foster appreciation and acceptance of African American folk music as a creative force in American music even before Ricordi began to publish the solo and choral arrangements of spirituals for which he is now best known. While recognition does not always correspond to enduring artistic merit, the recognition of merit cannot occur without the serious consideration of one's work by the arbiters of taste. Burleigh's stature as a composer of songs for well-known concert and recital singers guaranteed that the solo and choral arrangements of spirituals that began to appear during the 1916–17 concert season would be performed and seriously evaluated by critics. Their inherent artistic merit would ensure them a permanent place in American song literature.[111]

16. Bringing Spirituals to the Concert Stage

"A music of the future out of the music of the past"

To those who gathered to congratulate Burleigh after the ninth Annual Vesper Service of Negro Spirituals in 1933, Burleigh's son Alston commented on his father's lifelong appreciation for the spirituals. Burleigh had been singing spirituals "for the pure pleasure of it ever since he was a boy in Erie," joining his father and mother, who "hummed them at their work." He began arranging them while he was studying at the National Conservatory of Music, but he first sang them in public from 1900 to 1915 when he toured with Booker T. Washington, helping to raise money for Tuskegee Institute.[1]

His earliest published adaptations of spiritual melodies (though he did not use that term) were in the 1901 collection *Plantation Melodies, Old and New.* But from the 1916–17 concert season, when Burleigh's solo arrangement of "Deep River" became the hit of the recital season, Burleigh's role as pioneer arranger and interpreter of spirituals began to eclipse his role as recital singer and art song composer. He had won his place among U.S. composers of secular art songs, and singers and critics were prepared to welcome his art song spirituals with enthusiastic appreciation. A complex of personal, social, and historical factors brought Burleigh to the point where he was ready to publish the spiritual arrangements he had been performing for more than a decade. His public was also being prepared to welcome his solo and choral spiritual arrangements as an important genre of American song that would take its indispensable place in the music of America and the world.

Just as the background of blackface minstrelsy, vaudeville, ragtime, and coon songs stirred Burleigh to insist that African American folk music be developed and presented with dignity and excellence, so the recurring controversy over the origins of black music made Burleigh a spokesman for the uniquely expressive gifts of African Americans who, he argued, had created America's first genuine folk music.

Musicians who had never heard African Americans sing in traditional, characteristic fashion studied transcriptions made by white collectors and built an elaborate theory that denied to the originators of the music an independent creative ability. The controversy touched Burleigh in that he interacted with persons on both sides of the argument and collaborated with one of the major contenders. He also outlined his own position on several occasions. In 1893, the same year Antonín Dvořák's Symphony No. 9 in E Minor, "From the New World," was first performed, a year when Burleigh's pride in the music of his slave ancestors was strengthened in the evenings he spent in Dvořák's home, a German scholar, Richard Wallaschek, published his *Primitive Music: An Inquiry into the Origin and Development of Music, Songs, Instruments, Dances, and Pantomimes of Savage Races.* Wallaschek presented this as a scholarly study of "primitive" music, in which category he included Chinese, Jewish, and gypsy as well as African American music. Wallaschek had not visited China, Africa, or the United States, and he had never heard performances of the music he described. But examining the transcriptions of the 1867 collection *Slave Songs of the United States*—which he assumed to be totally accurate despite the editors' qualifying statements—and *Plantation Melodies,* a collection of minstrel songs by Edwin P. Christy, he concluded that "these negro-songs [were] very much overrated." They were "mere imitations of European compositions which the negroes [had] picked up, and served up again with slight variations." He charged further that the spirituals were "unmistakably 'arranged'—not to say ignorantly borrowed—from the national songs of all nations, from military signals, well-known marches, German student-songs, etc."[2]

Musicians aghast at Dvořák's contention that American composers could find "all that is needed for a great and noble school of music" from African American melodies seized on Wallaschek's statement to bolster their objections. If black music consisted of poor imitations of white music, Dvořák's theory was clearly untenable.

W. J. Henderson, music editor of the New York *Sun,* who wrote the preface to Burleigh's 1909 collection of *Negro Minstrel Melodies,* accepted Wallaschek's conclusions. Citing Wallaschek, he said, "the negroes have received a great deal of glory to which they are not entitled."[3] No doubt Henderson's preface helped sell Burleigh's collection of minstrel melodies, but it is unlikely that Burleigh gave "tacit consent" to Henderson's views, as has been assumed.[4] In 1909 Burleigh would not have been in a position to argue with Henderson or his publishers about the content of the preface. But several years later Burleigh collaborated with Henry E. Krehbiel on a study that forcefully repudiated Wallaschek's arguments,[5] and his later public statements made his views very clear. Burleigh did not accept all of Krehbiel's conclusions, but he often cited Krehbiel's work in his comments about African American folk music, and he used some of Krehbiel's arguments to refute Wallaschek's and Henderson's claims.

Long before *Afro-American Folksongs* was published in 1914, Krehbiel wrote provocatively on the origin of African American music. In 1906, three years before the publication of *Negro Minstrel Melodies,* he sharply refuted a New York *Sun* article (probably by Henderson) that characterized the attempt to trace African origins in Louisiana Creole as making "a silk purse out of a sow's ear." Krehbiel responded in a letter to the editor of *The Musician.* After rebutting the *Sun* article in detail, Krehbiel concluded, "Better not to know so much than to know so much that isn't so."[6]

From the time he first heard the Fisk Jubilee Singers in the 1870s, Krehbiel had studied the characteristics of African American song and attempted to trace correspondences with African music. He heard the music at the Dahomeyan Village on the Midway Plaisance at the 1893 Columbian Exposition as an opportunity for fieldwork, listening, transcribing, and analyzing what he saw and heard from these West African singers and dancers. He also gathered materials from many other collectors.

Early in the 1900s Krehbiel published a series of articles in the New York *Tribune* on the use of folksongs in national music that he hoped would spur the systematic study of African American folk music. Though the study of folklore developed in the first decade of the century and emotional responses to Dvořák's views resurfaced from time to time, the serious study of black music was still neglected. Krehbiel intended his 1914 book, *Afro-American Folksongs,* to bring this music "into the field of scientific observation" and to present it "as fit material for artistic treatment."[7] Burleigh wrote the arrangements for sixteen of the forty-one songs Krehbiel used as musical examples, and his public statements in lectures and articles throughout the remainder of his career suggest that he was more than peripherally involved in the project.[8]

Though Krehbiel used published transcriptions for much of his analysis, he understood the problems with transcriptions. He based his arguments on 527 songs from six collections, including the 1867 *Slave Songs of the United States*, the 1880 edition of the Fisk Jubilee collection, the 1909 edition of the Hampton Jubilee collections, Charles L. Edwards's *Bahama Songs and Stories* (1895), Emily Hallowell's 1901 and 1907 editions of *Calhoun Plantation Songs,* and his own private collection.[9] He argued that the objections to Dvořák's advocacy of incorporating African American folk music into American music arose from a "want of intelligent discrimination" and an "ungenerous and illiberal attitude" toward African Americans. But his purpose was not to argue for an American school of music. Rather, he intended to establish that the oral tradition of black music fulfilled the scientific definition of folksong as defined by philosopher Herbert Spencer, to demonstrate that it was American music, and "by comparative analysis to discover the distinctive idioms of that music, trace their origins and discuss their correspondences with characteristic elements of other folk-melodies [most notably African], and also their differences." He would do so by examining the music itself, as transcribed by the collectors whose qualifications as musicians he felt offered the greatest likelihood of accurate transcription.[10]

Krehbiel systematically refuted Wallaschek's arguments against the originality of black music. Not only had Wallaschek never heard performances of the songs, he had not examined the context from which the songs came: "It is plain that [unlike Dvořák] Dr. Wallaschek never took the trouble to acquaint himself with the environment of the black slaves in the United States." Anyone familiar with African American oral performance practice would know how inadequate the transcriptions must be. Finally, Krehbiel charged that Wallaschek's underlying condescension toward Americans in general had led him to disastrous misconceptions. "The truth is that, like many another complacent German savant, Dr. Wallaschek thinks Americans are barbarians. He is welcome to his opinion, which can harm no one but himself."[11]

Krehbiel concluded that African American folksongs were "original and native products." They contained idioms that "were transplanted hither from Africa, but as songs they are the product of American institutions," as nowhere "save on the plantations of the South could the emotional life which is essential to the development of true folksong be developed." White Americans had never "been in the state of cultural ingenuousness" that was necessary to produce folksong, and as "the finest, the truest, the most intimate, folk-music is that provoked by suffering," black slaves were uniquely equipped to give to America its only true folk music.[12] It could be argued that Native Americans had also suffered greatly, but despite attempts by collectors and composers to preserve and arrange American Indian songs, their influence on the American public was less pervasive.[13]

Krehbiel acknowledged that to add accompaniments to the African American melodies he included in his book diminished the "scientific purity" of their presentation, but to "make their peculiar beauty and usefulness known to a wide circle of amateurs" he presented them "in arrangements suitable for performance under artistic conditions."[14] He supplied some of the arrangements; Burleigh supplied the greatest number (sixteen); and three white composers, Arthur Mees (who had previously published arrangements for male voices), Henry Holden Huss, and John A. Van Broekhoven, provided the rest. Burleigh's later statements on African American folk music in general, and on spirituals in particular, show that he knew Krehbiel's book thoroughly.[15] When Krehbiel died in 1923, Burleigh presented a eulogy entitled "Mr. Krehbiel as I Knew Him," at a joint memorial service for him and Natalie Curtis Burlin at the Harlem branch of the New York Public Library (now the Schomberg Center for Research in Black Culture). Burleigh mentioned correspondence that "shed an illuminating insight" into Krehbiel's character.[16]

Burleigh later published arrangements of eight songs from Krehbiel's book. G. Schirmer published his choral arrangements of "Dig My Grave" in 1913 and "Father Abraham" in 1916. G. Ricordi published "Nobody Knows the Trouble I've Seen," "Weepin' Mary," and "You May Bury Me in de Eas'" in 1917; "Hard Trials" in 1919;

the roustabout song "Oh! Rock Me, Julie" in 1921; and a mixed-voice arrangement of the Louisiana Creole song "Mister Banjo" in 1934.

* * *

Edward MacDowell would seem an unlikely influence on Burleigh's movement toward arranging spirituals as art songs, given his persistent and often biting rejection of Dvořák's statements urging American composers to draw on African American and Native American music to create a national school of American music. In an 1897 letter he commented, "In spite of Dr. Dvořák's desire to clothe American music in darkey costume I hold that such foreign artificiality should have no place in our art if it is to be worthy of our free country."[17] But when Mac-Dowell heard Burleigh sing a traditional version of "Swing Low, Sweet Chariot," he issued a challenge: "Burleigh, why not give that melody a setting that will make it available to all musicians and music lovers—to the Caucasian interpreter as to the Negro creator?" Burleigh said he showed MacDowell an early sketch of his setting of this spiritual, and the composer helped him "increase the sophistication" of his arrangement.[18]

In a less direct way, A. Walter Kramer's praise and criticism of Burleigh's work affected the reception of Burleigh's art songs and spiritual arrangements. In his sharp critique of Burleigh and his colleagues' performances on the third Carnegie Hall concert for the benefit of the Music School Settlement for Colored People on March 11, 1914, Kramer criticized the "vaudeville character" of much of the program. Even Burleigh, "excellent musician that he is," had "spoiled his contribution to the musical excellence of the program by singing the popular 'Why Adam Sinned,'" after he had sung his (as yet unpublished) fine harmonizations of "You May Bury Me," "Weepin' Mary," and "I Don't Feel No-Ways Tired." Rather than waste their time with popular music, Burleigh and his colleagues should devote themselves to the preservation and performance of spirituals. "The northern negro has neither the love for nor the knowledge of what the old spirituals mean; and he does not sing them with warmth. This is negro music however and it should be preserved!"[19]

Burleigh did not need Kramer to teach him the value of the spirituals. He had been performing them for years, and at this time frequently accompanied chanteuse Kitty Cheatham in performance of his arrangements.[20] But Kramer's was an influential voice. His support helped create a climate of receptivity for Burleigh's spiritual arrangements and may have influenced him to begin publishing the solo arrangements he had been performing for nearly fifteen years.

Many white Americans were fascinated by black music and borrowed extensively from it, but most of their presentation of black music in minstrel shows was a caricature, intended to elicit hilarity rather than respect. Dr. Robert R. Moton, principal of Tuskegee Institute after Booker T. Washington's death, described how attending a white minstrel show performed in blackface had affected him: "I felt that these white men were making fun, not only of our color and of our songs, but also of our religion. It took three years' training at Hampton Institute to bring me to the point of being willing to sing Negro songs in the presence of white people. White minstrels with black faces have done more than any other single agency to lower the tone of Negro music and cause the Negro to despise their own songs."[21]

Even after the Fisk Jubilee Singers and other jubilee ensembles introduced the world to somewhat refined versions of spirituals, white minstrel and vaudeville performers created parodies of spirituals for comic effect. Sandra Graham has traced the many transformations of spirituals from the Fisk Jubilee Singers' tours in the 1870s to the early twentieth century.[22]

Despite the prevailing negative attitudes, articles and books published from the 1860s to the 1920s that discussed African American music showed an increasing awareness and respect for black music in general and spirituals in particular. Burleigh found support for his advocacy of black music in this growth in interest. In addition to popular and scholarly publications about spirituals, composers from the mid-nineteenth century onward made occasional use of African American themes. By the second decade of the twentieth century, compositions that drew on African American folklore for programmatic inspiration or that made use of the rhythmic and thematic resources of black folk music appeared frequently in the United States and in Europe.[23]

Each chapter of sociologist W. E. B. Du Bois's eloquent 1903 collection of essays, *The Souls of Black Folk*, was headed by a musical quotation from a spiritual. The final chapter from "within the Veil" of African American life, "Of the Sorrow Songs," was immediately recognized as a definitive tribute to this repertoire, and the term "Sorrow Songs" was adopted by other writers on the spirituals. Du Bois's essay and the publication two years later of Coleridge-Taylor's *Twenty-four Negro Melodies Transcribed for Piano*, brought many black Americans a new sense of pride in their music. Despite his initial criticism of Du Bois's book, Burleigh began to include spirituals in his recitals in 1903, the year *The Souls of Black Folk* was published.[24]

From 1911 to 1916 when Burleigh published his first solo arrangement of spirituals, the tide of interest in African American folk music, especially spirituals, was building toward its mid-1920s crest. At least nineteen white American composers joined the stream. Black composers also produced compositions reflecting their folk heritage during these years. Organist Melville Charlton wrote *Poème Érotique* (1911); pianist Carl Diton brought out several sets of spiritual arrangements for mixed voices (1912, 1914, 1915, 1916); violinist Clarence Cameron White published *Berceuse* (1912), *Cradle Song* (1915), and *Negro Chant* (1915) for violin and piano; pianist and vocal coach Montague Ring (pseudonym of Amanda Aldridge, daughter of actor Ira Aldridge) published *Three African Dances* for piano (1913); Chicago composer and conductor James A. Mundy published *Ethiopia* (1913); R. Nathaniel Dett performed and published several piano suites—*In the Bottoms* and *Magnolia Suites I* and *II* (1913)—and Will Marion Cook published *A Collection of Negro Songs*

(1912), which included some of his finest songs—"Exhortation: A Negro Song," "Rain Song," and "Swing Along."[25]

Though Burleigh is usually referred to as the first composer to arrange spirituals as art songs, two white composers brought out solo settings of spirituals during this period. In 1905 Arthur Farwell, who wrote many art song settings of Native American songs, published solo arrangements of "De Rocks a-Renderin'" and "Moanin'," through his Wa-Wan Press. And in 1916 David W. Guion's first collections of *Darkey Spirituals* also appeared.[26]

Burleigh's reputation within the white music establishment as a singer and music editor and the regard for his work as an art song composer partly account for the acclaim with which critics, singers, choral directors, and publishers greeted Burleigh's arrangements. But the near-unanimity of their praise indicates that Burleigh's arrangements were perceived to be significantly different from those by other composers. Burleigh's "Deep River" and his other 1917 solo arrangements stood out as masterful presentations of an invaluable American song tradition. A. Walter Kramer's review of three spirituals for four-part chorus is typical: "No one can examine . . . 'Didn't My Lord Deliver Daniel?' . . . without feeling grateful that we have an H. T. Burleigh who can harmonize these tunes as no one else living."[27]

Adding to the general climate of fascination with black music as a resource for composition were articles, folksong collections, and performances by musicians who regarded the preservation and study of African American folk music to be an important priority. Burleigh was in touch with a significant cluster of these musicians and other interested persons, black and white, during the years when he began to publish his spiritual arrangements. The Music School Settlement for Colored People provided the locus around which some of this interaction can be documented.

When J. Rosamond Johnson replaced David Martin as director of the Music School Settlement for Colored People in Harlem in 1914, he strengthened the school's classical music program and broadened its curriculum to include compositions by African American composers and lectures on the folk music of other cultures. Musician and folklorist Natalie Curtis (later Burlin) managed the weekly lectures and recitals.[28] Among the speakers and performers in 1914 and 1915 were Curtis herself, who lectured on Native American music; Kurt Schindler, founder and conductor of the Schola Cantorum, whose interest in world music was reflected in the Cantorum's programs; W. E. B. Du Bois; Henry E. Krehbiel; Percy Grainger, the Australian pianist and composer whose writings on fieldwork and the music of oral cultures posed perspectives that became standard among ethnomusicologists only in the latter part of the twentieth century;[29] French-Canadian mezzo-soprano Eva Gauthier, "the first white woman" to learn ancient Javanese folksongs, which she performed in Javanese royal dress; and Kitty Cheatham, storyteller-singer who performed some of Burleigh's spiritual arrangements before their publication.[30]

Burleigh was not involved in the day-to-day operation of the school, but he served on the board of directors and he supported the program by singing on the annual benefit concerts at Carnegie Hall and on programs at the school, occasionally assisting speakers such as Krehbiel and Du Bois in their lectures on black music. Here Burleigh interacted with a network of people who would have encouraged and supported his decision to bring his arrangements of spirituals before a broader public than he could reach though his own singing.[31]

* * *

No other explanation may be necessary for the immediate and profound effect of Burleigh's 1917 solo arrangements on concert repertoire than the beauty of their melodies, the fundamental spirituality of their texts, and the artistry of his settings. But the entry of the United States into the Great War that had been raging in Europe for several years also created a climate that made Americans particularly receptive to the spirituals that Burleigh's solo arrangements brought into home parlors, churches, and recital halls. The product of intense suffering, these songs embodied a triumphant faith in the face of insuperable odds. They entered the repertoire of white and black musicians throughout the United States, not just in New York City. The white press and music journals such as *Musical America* reported the use of Burleigh's spiritual arrangements in recitals around the country.[32]

In the trenches of World War I, Europe and the United States were witnessing the destruction of human life on a scale never before experienced in Western Europe. The optimism engendered by late-nineteenth-century social evolutionism was being obliterated. A generation of young men was being slaughtered for little apparent reason except official mismanagement and ineptitude. The foundations of human civilization seemed to be crumbling in the face of the catastrophe. The race of the oppressors now stood in need of such comfort as they might gain from the songs of former slaves.

The October 1918 *Musical Courier* reported that "Negro spirituals" ranked first on a list of "Songs the Soldiers Like," compiled by American baritone Francis Rogers.[33] It seems that on the battlefield the spirituals addressed a universal human need. A month later the *Southern Workman* carried an article by a YMCA worker entitled "Negro Spirituals in France" that commented, "Some of the refrains of the Negro songs are so appropriate to the world situation and to France under present conditions, that when I first heard them they startled me with their universality of emotional expression." The soldiers sang an apt refrain to "The Old-Time Religion." "It is good for a world in trouble. . . . And it's good enough for me." The writer continued, "Somehow you feel that the Negro in his folk-song has sung what is in all of our hearts. 'The old-time religion' is about the only thing that we have found that will cure the poor old war-worn, war-torn, war-wounded world." The songs the soldiers sang expressed nostalgia for home and their lives before the war; the spirituals spoke to a particular aspect of that nostalgia. They were a vehicle of faith and hope for "a world in trouble," and, as the writer concluded, "If ever the poor old, crippled, bleeding world was in trouble it is certainly now."[34]

When Frank Damrosch included two of Natalie Curtis Burlin's spiritual arrangements on the program of the first concert of the Musical Art Society after the war ended, she commented on the "lasting offering to our National culture" the spirituals represented. This music "forms a bridge of sympathy that makes a greater friendship for the black man instinctive and natural." Damrosch's inclusion of spirituals on his first program after the war ended had "a certain human significance, a prophecy of true democracy." Well aware of the racial tumult that followed the return of black soldiers, Burlin felt Damrosch's inclusion of spirituals promised "that greater justice which should be accorded those black men who fought in Europe for the rights of oppressed races and are asked to accept peaceably oppression at home. Those of us who have seen the bravery of the Negro's efforts towards self-development and self-respecting economic independence, cannot but rejoice that on so significant a program as this of the Musical Art Society, the music of the Negro is accorded so prominent a place."[35]

* * *

In 1916 Burleigh arranged "Deep River" for Mary Jordan, a recitalist and opera singer, the contralto soloist at Temple Emanu-El where Burleigh also sang. Known as an "ardent champion of American musical independence," Jordan had been performing Burleigh's art songs, especially "The Grey Wolf" (1915).[36] Occasionally Burleigh accompanied her in performance. In February 1916 she premiered "In the Wood of Finvara," which was dedicated to her, with Kurt Schindler as accompanist.[37]

The success of Burleigh's "Deep River" was a phenomenon much discussed in the music press, and Burleigh's name came to be permanently linked with this setting. Several G. Ricordi advertisements in *Musical America* listed professional singers who were using Burleigh's songs in the 1916–17 concert season, and one listed fourteen who were singing "Deep River."[38] On November 24, 1916, the New York *Tribune* reported that "Deep River" had been "on a majority of programs of song recitalists" in the preceding three weeks.[39] Walter Kramer called it "the most conspicuous success of the song recitalist's offerings,"[40] and Hiram K. Moderwell reported that in Boston "those who have heard concerts during the present season have probably noticed on the programs one song more than any other. This is 'Deep River,' credited to Harry T. Burleigh."[41]

In addition to several Ricordi ads in *Musical America* that listed singers performing Burleigh art songs and spiritual arrangements in the 1916–17 season,[42] the cover of one 1917 edition listed the names of twenty-one singers who were singing it—Frances Alda, Zabetta Brenska, Pauline Donalda, Alma Gluck, Louise Homer, Mary Jordan, Christine Miller, Alice Nielson, Anita Rio, Emma Roberts, Marcella Sembrich, Paul Althouse, Dan Beddoe, Charles Norman Granville, George Hamlin, Percy Hemus, Arthur Herschmann, Redferne Hollinshead, Francis Rogers, Edgar

Schofield, and William Wheeler."[43] President Woodrow Wilson's daughter Margaret sang it; composer Dudley Buck's voice students sang it; African American tenors Roland Hayes and Sidney Woodward sang it. Hiram K. Moderwell commented that the recognition Burleigh was receiving for this arrangement was overdue: "It has justly brought him into a prominence which he has long deserved."[44] Reviews of these performances often commented that audiences found them "of particular interest," and "deeply impressive."[45]

Burleigh said he intended to preserve the traditional melodies of the spirituals and simply add harmony rather than change or "develop" the melodies, but in his "Deep River" arrangement he made several changes to the original melody as it was transcribed in the Fisk collection, which was likely one of his sources. "Deep River" did not appear in the 1867 collection *Slave Songs of the United States*. But in the various editions of *The Story of the Fisk Jubilee Singers,* "Deep River" was song number 77.[46]

The three repetitions of the final phrase, "I want to cross over into camp-ground," the last of which ends on the C# minor tonic rather than the E major tonic, provide closure to the chorus and accentuate the minor mode.

The first art music arrangement of "Deep River" appeared in Samuel Coleridge-Taylor's *Twenty-four Negro Melodies Transcribed for Piano,* published more than a decade earlier (mm. 1–5). This arrangement became well known through the violin and piano transcription by Maud Powell, one of the most highly regarded American violinists of the time. Coleridge-Taylor substituted his own theme for the verse, "Oh, don't you want to go to that gospel feast?" (mm. 7–10) and used the

Samuel Coleridge-Taylor, "Deep River," mm. 1–5.

repetition of "I want to cross over into camp-ground" as a developmental motif rather than quoting it exactly, creating an ABA song structure.[47]

Burleigh published three versions of "Deep River," two in 1916 and a final version in 1917.[48] To a large extent Burleigh based the harmony of his first section on the Coleridge-Taylor harmony. The four rolled opening chords became a trademark introduction for this piece; even J. Rosamond Johnson used this motif in his introduction to "Deep River" in *The Book of American Negro Spirituals* in 1925. Burleigh shifted to an augmented chord on the third beat of the word "Deep" (m. 3), and created more harmonic movement at the cadence of the first phrase, but most of the harmony would have been familiar to those who knew the Coleridge-Taylor and the Powell arrangements. The distinctive gesture Burleigh added was a counter-melody above the voice on the final phrase of the first chorus, "I want to cross over into camp-ground" (m. 9).

In Burleigh's repetition of the chorus the accompaniment becomes more pianistic (mm. 11–18). Though the beginning of his theme for the B or verse section, "O don't you want to go to that gospel feast?" resembles Coleridge-Taylor's version, Burleigh makes the B section his own. Hiram K. Moderwell said the climax in Burleigh's setting of "That promis'd land where all is peace" was "hardly surpassed in emotional intensity in many a renowned song."[49] In his first version Burleigh ended on the subdued phrase "deep river," with no repetitions of the "I want to cross over into camp-ground" motif. In the second 1916 version he created a more satisfying ending by adding a countermelody above the final "deep river" (mm. 27–28) and one repetition of the phrase "I want to cross over into camp-ground" (mm. 29–30).

Though both Marian Anderson and Paul Robeson recorded the second 1916 version, Burleigh's third version of "Deep River" (1917) is the one best known today. A. Walter Kramer found no fault with Burleigh's earlier settings, but the new version was "more in the spirit of folksong." The accompaniment was simpler, and the harmony more in tune with the pentatonicism of the melody (e.g., m. 3), with greater use of thirds and sixths, which Kramer considered a characteristic of traditional harmony.[50] Burleigh also expanded his use of countermelodies in the accompaniment, providing elegant counterpoint to the melody of the spiritual, a trademark of his solo arrangements.

The progression in Burleigh's treatment of this, his most famous solo arrangement of a spiritual, is instructive. His art songs at this time were often quite complex harmonically, with abrupt, explorative harmonic modulations. His spiritual arrangements, while crisp, harmonically interesting, and often witty, are deliberately restrained in their harmonic structure. He created more satisfying closure in the second and third versions of "Deep River," and he moved toward harmonic simplicity more nearly reflective of oral traditions.[51]

The reception of "Deep River" set a new standard of success for Burleigh's songs. A number of other composers issued arrangements of "Deep River." William Arms Fisher of the Oliver Ditson Company (a composition student of Dvořák) published a version based on the Coleridge-Taylor setting, even including the motto of the original melody below the title. In his review of this arrangement, A. Walter Kramer implied that Burleigh's version was truer to the spirit of the original song: "Fine as [Coleridge-Taylor's] arrangements of these melodies were they leaned often on the European, for the late Anglo-African composer knew little of American negro folk-song. Mr. Fisher has followed the Coleridge-Taylor harmonization closely and so his version is also at times European; it is in those places where he had been free and given his own fancy rein that his harmonization of the melody is most happy."[52] A few weeks later *Musical America* carried an advertisement for a violin arrangement of "Deep River" by Eddy Brown, and in April the John Franklin Music Company advertised a special arrangement of "Deep River," "the famous old American Negro spiritual," by Christopher O'Hare, in three keys.[53] Several instrumental transcriptions of Burleigh's arrangement appeared as well. A. Walter Kramer wrote a violin transcription and a string quartet transcription that was played by the Zoellner Quartet during the 1917 season; Richard Keys Biggs wrote an organ transcription that he performed at St. Luke's Church in Brooklyn on March 1, 1917; and Mischa Elman wrote and performed a violin transcription.[54]

* * *

Until baritone Oscar Seagle's March 1917 concert in Brooklyn, few white performers sang spirituals in recital. But Seagle's recital, in which he used five Burleigh spiritual arrangements as his closing group, marked a turning point. When the audience insisted that the group be repeated, Seagle added "Deep River" as well. One reviewer wrote that this was the first time that "fitting expression" had been given the spirituals.[55] The reviewer did not specify, but it was likely both Burleigh's arrangement and Seagle's interpretation that created the "fitting expression." Seagle's extensive performance of Burleigh's arrangements in the 1917 concert season, including a concert as far south as Little Rock, Arkansas,[56] helped establish them in concert repertoire. He knew the oral performance tradition from personal experience in the South. A native of Tennessee, Seagle had often traveled with his lay-preacher father on his preaching circuits in the mountains. He heard the singing and preaching at revival services in congregations where spirituals often "broke out" spontaneously during the sermon. His familiarity with the oral tradition prepared him to sing the spirituals with greater understanding than most white performers, but he attributed the success of his performance to Burleigh's arrangements. Much as he had wanted to sing spirituals in his recitals before this, no composer before Burleigh had written arrangements that he felt were suitable. "Of course arrangements have been made from time to time, but invariably they have been too crude or else over-sophisticated. Those of the latter class distorted the spiritual's underlying the folk melody and hence could not help but convey to my audience an erroneous idea of the song." Burleigh's arrangements, however, were "just what I had been seeking for so long a time."[57]

Seagle explained how he prepared himself to sing spirituals. African Americans sang "because of the necessity for expression for the pure joy of singing," so he tried to enter that same mood. "I let myself get right into the spirit, relying on my memory of the old revivals and striving for the same frame of mind as was the negro preacher's."[58] Burleigh, who was present at the March 1917 Brooklyn recital, felt Seagle succeeded. He remarked to the reviewer seated beside him, "Just like a negro preacher. No one could do them better," a comment Seagle regarded as high praise.[59]

Other white singers followed Seagle's lead in using Burleigh's arrangements as a group to end their recitals. Ironically, some refused to use them when they realized that the arranger was an African American, "even though they had been much impressed by their musicianship." Seagle commented, "The prejudice against the black race dies hard and even in matters of art it still exists."[60] However, the practice of ending a recital with a group of spirituals, sometimes mixed with other folksongs, became a convention among concert singers.[61]

Prejudice did not diminish the market for spiritual arrangements; other composers immediately brought out arrangements of spirituals for solo voice. At William Arms Fisher's suggestion, black composer J. Rosamond Johnson wrote two arrangements, "Walk Together, Children" and "Nobody Knows the Trouble I've Seen," that Oliver Ditson published in 1917. Among white composers, James H. Rogers published a solo version of "Swing Low, Sweet Chariot" (1917). The following year, Pittsburgh composer Harvey B. Gaul, who had been encouraged by Samuel Coleridge-Taylor in London to go home and listen to what was around him, published a collection of *Nine Negro Spirituals*.[62] The same year (1918) Carrie Jacobs-Bond published a collection of *Old Melodies of the South;* David Guion brought out a second collection of *Darkey Spirituals;* G. Schirmer published Mitchell Humphrey's version of "Stay in the Field, Warrior" and John Alden Carpenter's song, "The Lawd Is Smilin' Thro' the Do'" also appeared.[63]

Among black composers, Carl Diton published his arrangement of "Swing Low, Sweet Chariot" for organ (1916); Clarence Cameron White's *Bandana Sketches,* arrangements of four spirituals for violin and piano, were published by Carl Fischer (1918); J. Rosamond Johnson wrote the orchestral accompaniment for the Roland Hayes recording of "Steal Away to Jesus" (1918); and E. Aldama Jackson published "Don't Be Weary" and "Go Down, Moses" (1919). The flood of arrangements by both white and black arrangers increased each year until the mid-1920s, when, as James Weldon Johnson wrote, the spirituals had "a vogue."[64] From 1917 to 1925 G. Ricordi published forty Burleigh arrangements, mostly spirituals, but also several secular folksongs such as "Oh! Rock Me, Julie" and "Scandalize My Name" (both in 1921, and labeled "Negro Folk Songs, Not Spirituals"). Burleigh also arranged many of these pieces for mixed voices and for men's or women's ensembles, usually to be performed without accompaniment.

The programming of Burleigh's choral arrangements by such conductors as Frank Damrosch on the twenty-fifth anniversary concert of the Musical Art Society at

Carnegie Hall in December 1917 demonstrated that as choral literature the spirituals were of worth equal to that of ancient and modern classics. The reviewer for the New York *Sun* commented, "The Negro spiritual has climbed to a seat beside [the] a capella motet of musical antiquity. Three of them, one being "Deep River" (of course arranged by Harry T. Burleigh), were on the program of the . . . Musical Art Society at Carnegie Hall last night. A remarkable concert it was, too, for it put the spirituals right beside Elgar's 'Death on the Hills' and Berlioz's 'Sara in Baigneuse.'"[65]

At first Burleigh's arrangements were used more extensively by white than by black singers, but the enthusiastic reception of his arrangements was noted within the black community. The 1917 Spingarn Award acknowledged his contribution in bringing spirituals to the attention of distinguished audiences nationwide and in Europe. Later honors, such as the honorary master of arts degree from Atlanta University in 1918 and the honorary doctor of music degree from Howard University in 1920, also recognized his contribution in helping African Americans reclaim spirituals as an artistic heritage, rescuing them from their association with minstrelsy and vaudeville, and making them accessible to singers and music lovers of every cultural background.[66]

Comments in the white press were almost uniformly laudatory. One of the most eloquent was the H. L. Mencken review in November 1917: "I know of no later-day series of songs with more of interest in them, or more of the fine skill than Burleigh's versions of some of the famous jubilee spirituals." He praised the "fine harmonic ingenuity" in Burleigh's arrangement of "Swing Low, Sweet Chariot." It embodied "so accurate a feeling for the inner spirit of the old hymn, that the result is a song of quite unusual charm. . . . And above all, it is restrained, dignified, honest in atmosphere." In contrast to later critiques, Mencken said Burleigh was "a highly sophisticated tone-poet," but when he arranged a plantation song, "he always keeps in mind that it is a plantation song and not a Russian ballet, and so he keeps the thing on its proper plane." African Americans had created "these incomparable songs to begin with; now they have a composer to do for them what Silcher did for the German folksong."[67] A few years later critic Henry Finck remarked that China needed a Harry Burleigh to help newly educated young Chinese people to respect their Chinese music heritage by transforming it into [Western-style] art music![68]

In the mid-1920s both black and white writers reviewed specific Burleigh arrangements and commented on the importance of his leadership in arranging spirituals. In 1924 a reviewer for Hampton Institute's *Southern Workman* (probably R. Nathaniel Dett) wrote: "Great as has been the satisfaction and pleasure Mr. Burleigh has given through his singing to thousands who have heard him, more important still is his work as a composer and musician. . . . Doubtless his greatest gift to the world is in his unexcelled arrangements of Negro spirituals, which have universal appreciation." Burleigh's approach to arranging was appropriate: "Mr. Burleigh's own deep love for the songs of his people, together with his gifted musicianship, has led him to handle these in such a way as to preserve their original appeal and simple beauty." These songs had brought "comfort and inspiration" to thousands of admirers.[69] The following year James Weldon Johnson commented that while earlier the public heard spirituals only through the jubilee quartets from black colleges, "today the public buys the spirituals, takes them home and plays and sings them." He gave Burleigh principal credit as the pioneer who had widened their appeal and extended their use to singers and the general public. A number of other black composers, choral directors, and singers had joined the effort, but Burleigh had led the way.[70]

In 1926 the *New Yorker* commented on the "array of new talent" among composers who were arranging spirituals. Fine as their work was, it partly obscured Burleigh's work, "whose arrangements of spirituals and other negro songs have not been surpassed and are not likely to be." Burleigh was undoubtedly gratified at the "genius interest" that characterized the work of his colleagues, but the reviewer felt Burleigh had "not had complete justice" from commentators. "To expound this theme would embarrass Mr. Burleigh, who is a singularly modest musician; therefore, we content ourselves with suggesting that if anybody is going to do more for negro songs than Harry T. Burleigh has done, it will be Harry T. Burleigh."[71]

The 1928 Symposium on American Music confirmed that the general public had taken Burleigh's arrangements to heart. In a survey of the ten most popular folksongs, Stephen Foster's "Old Folks at Home" ranked first, and Burleigh's arrangements of "Deep River" and "Swing Low, Sweet Chariot" came second and third respectively. In the Class Three choral group, his arrangement of "Were You There?" placed second.[72] As the popularity of his spiritual arrangements increased, churches, music clubs, and other organizations in both the white and black communities began to call on Burleigh to lecture on the spirituals. Few instances of his performing secular art songs are found after 1917, but he sang spirituals and spoke about their history, their value, and how they should be used in many settings. He worked with soloists, quartets, and choirs, sometimes accompanying the soloists or directing the choirs, and when he sang, he accompanied himself.[73]

Burleigh stated his views of how the spirituals should be performed in newspaper interviews, letters, articles, and speeches. His reputation as spokesman for the spirituals spread after 1917, but he expressed the central themes more than a decade earlier. In 1904, the year of Dvořák's death and a decade before Krehbiel's study and the surge in interest in spirituals, Burleigh argued the worth of African American songs, both as the repository of musical identity for black Americans and for their inherent musical value. Spirituals offered a unique corpus of song to the world of art music, and their treatment should be on the basis of thoughtful, "well-defined effort," so as to treat them "in a musicianly manner." These phrases from Burleigh's 1904 letter to Booker T. Washington outlined the perspective that was to inform all of Burleigh's work with spirituals.[74]

Burleigh's arrangements were crafted "in a musicianly manner," the work of his maturity as a composer. For more than a decade, Burleigh had been developing an art song style of presentation, preserving the melodies with their distinctive modal and rhythmic characteristics but giving them harmonizations appropriate to art music. "My desire was to preserve them in harmonies that belong to modern methods of tonal progression without robbing the melodies of their racial flavor."[75] His later criticism of other composers and performers arose out of his convictions about the appropriate treatment of spirituals as art music.

* * *

An examination of several of Burleigh's spiritual arrangements illustrates the harmonic sophistication, the contrapuntal ingenuity, and transformation that drew such warm praise from his supporters and that some of his critics found inappropriate. "Go Down, Moses," which Burleigh himself recorded in 1919, was one of his most widely used and frequently recorded arrangements (mm. 1–8).[76]

The opening four bars in the piano introduce the contrapuntal figure in the inner voice of the accompaniment that gives this setting its distinctive flavor. This

"Go Down, Moses," mm. 1–8.

pattern underlies all but the last statement of the words "let my people go" in each verse. In combination with the syncopated pattern of pedal fifths in the left hand, this rhythmic motif lends a propulsive urgency to the command for release of the captives. Paul Robeson and Lawrence Brown recorded this arrangement at a considerably faster tempo than the lento marked, bringing a triumphant inevitability to fulfillment of the dream.[77] Burleigh himself recorded it at the more solemn pace he indicated in the score. The accompaniment weaves countermelodies around the vocal line in the verse section but supports the voice in the chorus, over a syncopated chordal pattern in the inner voices and an octaval chromatic descent in the bass. In this setting the interest is in the contrapuntal voices and the rhythmic energy rather than in venturesome harmonization.

In "By an' By," also frequently recorded, Burleigh used contrasting accompaniment styles to set off the two halves of each melodic and textual phrase (mm. 1–6). The first half of the phrase, sung by the leader in the call-response style of its communal origin, is given a lighter texture, using the primary melodic motif (mm. 1–4) or broken chords in the bass line. The second half of each phrase, "I'm goin' to lay down dis heavy load," the group response, he sets with thickened chords and

"By an' By," mm. 1–6.

more active harmonic progressions, in a variety of configurations. This setting uses diminished, seventh, and ninth chords (mm. 5, 8, 9, e.g.), but Burleigh preserves the pentatonicism by avoiding the dominant chord at cadences, using it only in passing progressions on the weak beat (e.g., mm. 9, 13).

"Swing Low, Sweet Chariot" (1917) is one of the more venturesome harmonic treatments in a Burleigh spiritual arrangement. Burleigh said Edward MacDowell helped him "increase the sophistication" of this arrangement, though he did not specify what MacDowell's suggestions were.[78] But Burleigh's setting reflects his acquaintance with MacDowell's late Romantic harmonic exploration. He creates an impressionistic modality through a bitonal accompaniment. In the first statement of the chorus, a gong-like ostinato pattern in F major in the left hand (in the low-voice version) underlies D minor tonic and dominant seventh chords in the right hand. In the interlude before the second statement of the chorus, D minor seventh and ninth chords introduce a brief melodic excursion into the minor key, with a lowered third (mm. 13–14). In this setting Burleigh was clearly more interested in exploiting modern tonal resources than in creating an "authentic"

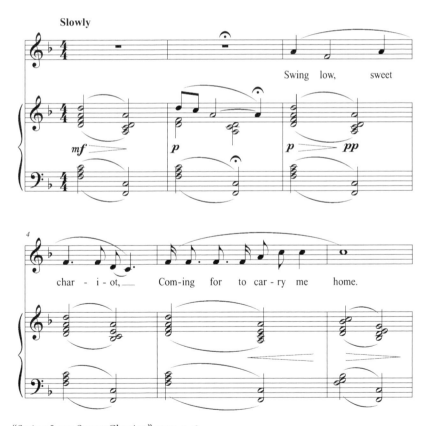

"Swing Low, Sweet Chariot," mm. 1–6.

concert version of a spiritual. In the verse section the accompaniment emphasizes the vocal melody, first in the bass, with rolled chords in the right hand, then in the soprano line, with left-hand rolled chords.

Until the 1920s few collectors or arrangers attempted to preserve the harmonic practice of the oral performance of spirituals. The essence of the music was assumed to be in "the airs," as Lucy McKim called them, or the melodies. As Thomas Fenner wrote in 1874, "There are evidently, I think, two legitimate methods of treating this music: either to render it in its absolute, rude simplicity, or to develop it without destroying its original characteristics, the only proper field for such development being in harmony."[79] The principle of "absolute, rude simplicity" did not fit Burleigh's standard of artistic presentation; he retained a version of the traditional melody and applied harmonic principles he had mastered in his art song composition, within certain limits that he considered appropriate to the folk material.

* * *

As to the origins of African American songs, Burleigh agreed with Henry E. Krehbiel that they were "the only songs in America that conform[ed] to the scientific definition of folk songs," as outlined by philosopher Herbert Spencer, therefore they constituted "our one, priceless contribution to the vast musical product of the United States."[80] They were valuable in themselves and as a source of ethnic identity. They must be preserved, and the best way to preserve them was to use them in creating art music. "Some say these melodies are not American, but they are indigenous to the soil. They are the experience in song of the people, who were in America, when Balboa discovered the Pacific Ocean. If the Negro is not American, I do not know who is."[81]

The controversy over the origin of black music continued to resurface. In January 1924, Lucien H. White, music reviewer for the New York *Age,* strongly refuted arguments by a white reviewer in Virginia that Negroes could not be credited for their music. In the 1930s the controversy assumed new proportions, with the work of a new generation of white scholars. In 1930 Guy Benton Johnson of the University of North Carolina published his book, *Folk Culture on St. Helena Island, South Carolina,* one chapter of which was devoted to a comparison of recent transcriptions of African American songs with earlier transcriptions. While Johnson studied the material more carefully than Wallaschek had and even made use of phonograph recordings, he still based his argument on transcriptions rather than on performance style.[82] In 1932 George Pullen Jackson, who became the primary advocate claiming white origins for the spirituals, published his first article on the subject, "The Genesis of the Negro Spiritual," in *American Mercury.*[83] The following year he published *White Spirituals in the Southern Uplands,* the first of several books presenting this view.[84]

In the face of these new arguments, in 1934 Burleigh made his most direct statement on the question. He rejected the notion that African Americans simply imitated the music of white people. "I differ with some musicians who think it a form of the German chorale, and also with others who feel that the spirituals are derived entirely from the hymns the Negro heard in the religious services of the white people." He acknowledged, as did Krehbiel, that some black music bore traces of white influence, but he disassociated himself from the view of Johnson and Jackson and their predecessors that the spirituals were simply imitations.[85]

Burleigh was adamant that spirituals could only have been created in America, by African Americans. In a radio interview, "The Story of the Song," broadcast on station WABC on March 29, 1939, he reiterated the point: "The spirituals—in my opinion—were born of the geographical, communal, and emotional life that the Negroes met with in the United States . . . and no other influences whatever had an important effect on their development."[86] The phrase "no other influences whatever" bears on the part of Krehbiel's study with which Burleigh could not agree: his tracing of African lineage for certain musical elements of the songs. In his own first edition of Krehbiel's book, he underlined a passage in the preface: "Does it follow that, because the American negroes have forgotten the language of their savage ancestors, they have also forgotten all of their music? May relics of that music not remain in a subconscious memory?"[87] But many African Americans of his time and social class perceived Africa as primitive and in need of redemption. Like Frederick Douglass, Burleigh seems to have considered the barbaric music and dancing at the Dahomeyan Village at the 1893 Chicago World's Fair to be proof that Africans and their cultural expressions represented a lower rung on the evolutionary ladder.[88] The mockery and condescension black Americans endured as "children of a savage race" was too pervasive; the insights of Melville Herskovits and other anthropologists and ethnomusicologists that in the 1930s began to break down the stereotypes had not filtered into popular consciousness.[89]

In his address to the NAACP in July 1924, Burleigh said, "The race came to the United States laden with gifts—gifts of the spirit, gifts of the kind that we need to cultivate and nurture," a statement (echoing Natalie Curtis Burlin) that seems to contradict his rejection of African origin.[90] But in an article a decade later, "The Negro and His Song," and a radio interview, he followed his dismissal of the white imitation theory by arguing for Hebrew influence rather than African. This soloist in Hebrew synagogues, first in Erie, then for twenty-five years in New York City, held a higher opinion of Hebrew song than of African song. If spirituals were "at all African," he wrote, they "resemble more the exalted beauty of the songs of the Israelites than the barbaric yells and rhythms of the Negroes of Africa, the latter probably the result of structural peculiarities of African languages."[91]

Burleigh's speculation on the relationship of African languages and the rhythmic flow of music was apt, but his tracing of cultural diffusion was as strained as Henderson's had been: "Who can tell, a beautiful melody sung by the Hebrews in those far-off days recorded in the Old Testament may have come, by being overheard by African negroes and carried through centuries of trials and countless mutations, to flower on American soil!"[92] This view was not unusual for the time; historian John Tasker Howard reported, "One writer claimed that "Go Down, Moses" so resembles an old Jewish chant "Cain and Abel" that Hebrews think the Negro song is theirs, and that Negroes claim the Jewish song. This has led to the theory that there was an ancient relation between Negro and Semitic races on the African continent."[93] Burleigh repeated his rejection of an African origin in the 1939 radio interview: "I don't at all agree with the critics and historians who hold that the songs of the American negro derive from the musical traditions of Africa."[94]

Burleigh's stance is particularly striking in light of the scholars and performers of his acquaintance, black and white, who argued persuasively for the strength of the African musical heritage. When Roland Hayes went to London in 1921, he spoke freely of his intention to proceed from England to West Africa, where he would collect African songs and trace the relationship. Even in his command performance for King George and his family (after he had sung several Burleigh arrangements of spirituals), Hayes described his plans to "visit Africa and make a collection of native melodies at their source" in order to compare them "with the songs of the American Negro, which are believed to be an inheritance of the slave from his African forebears."[95]

Natalie Curtis Burlin, who dedicated her fourth collection of African American folksongs to Burleigh, also explored the African roots of black music. She spent several summers in the South, recording with an Edison phonograph so as to transcribe as accurately as possible the music she heard. Before she attempted the transcription, she wanted to study the background of the music. To "reach back . . . to the very well-springs of Negro song," she spent a year working with two African students at Hampton Institute. Like Krehbiel, she concluded that "the characteristics which give [Negro] music an interest worthy of particular study are precisely those which differentiate Negro songs from the songs of the neighboring white man"; they are "racial traits, and the black man brought them from [Africa]."[96]

The strongest evidence corroborating the African roots of black music at this time was the work of Nicholas George Julius Ballanta-Taylor, a scholar-composer from Sierra Leone. He studied composition at the Institute for Musical Art, headed by Frank Damrosch.[97] He spent time on St. Helena Island, recording and transcribing spirituals at Penn School. His collection of ninety-five songs was published in mid-1925, shortly after his return to Sierra Leone. Unlike most previous collectors, Ballanta-Taylor recorded the harmonies in oral performance as well as the melodies.[98] Some white musicians who knew his work judged Ballanta-Taylor to have greater potential than Samuel Coleridge-Taylor, also of Sierra Leonean descent, who had died in 1912.

R. Nathaniel Dett summarized Ballanta-Taylor's contribution to the debate on the origins of black music: "Here, in an excellent literary style which is quite his own," he explains "the peculiarities of Negro music as evidenced in its melody, its rhythm, and its harmony. Taking advantage of his lineage (it should be remembered that the author is of pure African stock) he goes further and traces the origin of the songs to an African stem, then as a climax to his argument he explains why this is as it is and why it could not be otherwise, due to the characteristic psychological reactions of the African mind."[99] No evidence of Burleigh's personal acquaintance with Ballanta-Taylor has been found, but the number of their mutual acquaintances and the interest both had in the study of spirituals make it hard to imagine that they would not have met during Ballanta-Taylor's time in New York City.[100]

In the face of such evidence, that Burleigh could argue against the African roots of black music is puzzling. One answer must lie in the ambivalence of persons of his social class toward the primitive music that he worked so hard to present in dignified, artistic transformation. The vehemence with which Burleigh criticized what he considered the mistreatment of spirituals by other arrangers may also have arisen partly out of this rejection of his African heritage. Though Burleigh could not appreciate the vitality and complexity of African music, he spoke eloquently of the musical gifts of African Americans. His belief in the innate creative ability of black Americans was implicit in nearly every statement he made about spirituals or about black music in general. Had he been acquainted with the variety and wealth of African music, he would have understood that many of the characteristics of his musical heritage that he most admired were also elements of African music aesthetic and practice and were surely African in origin.

* * *

In addition to his concern that the spirituals be preserved and that they be treated "in a musicianly manner," other themes emerge in Burleigh's speeches and writing on spirituals that underlie and support these values. Spirituals must be preserved because they represented "the deepest aesthetic endowment of the race." In his lecture-recitals he demonstrated specific examples of this artistry. The "expressive" texts often revealed "a fertile imagination," as in "Swing Low, Sweet Chariot," "Father Abraham," and "I Stood on de Ribber of Jerdon."[101] He explained how he attempted to bring out these descriptive qualities in his arrangements. After commenting briefly on their history, he would turn to the piano and sing, "playing his own accompaniments, making running comments as to his effort to correlate his harmonic arrangements with the spirit of the original melodies [so] as to accentuate the marvelous imagery and descriptive beauty of the race concep-tion."[102] He particularly enjoyed showing skillful wedding of text and tune. In a 1935 lecture "he illustrated the ability of the Negro to coalesce true word painting with music by singing portions of songs." "The negro can express his religious experience adeptly, forcefully and spontaneously," he said. But because in their original form spirituals could be understood and performed only by the carriers of the tradition, they needed to be made "intelligible" and usable through their transformation into art music. "In the old form the spirituals were just simple tunes. Only the Negroes could sing them because they understood, instinctively, the rhythms. They could harmonize them with their voices and produce some of the strangest, most subtle effects. They had no accompaniments. There was nothing in the tune to guide the singers. No one else could understand them. They were really hidden from the world. You know that they have been in print for years, but it is only since they were arranged that they have become widely known."[103]

Burleigh intended his arrangements to facilitate their use by any singer, regardless of race or ethnic background, but two pitfalls awaited the white singer, or the black singer who was out of touch with traditional African American performance styles. The singer might approach the song with too technical a concern for voice quality and miss the spirit of the songs, or a singer somewhat familiar with African American performance but not native to it might fall into unintentional parody in the attempt to imitate that style. Intentional parody was distressingly prevalent in minstrel and vaudeville performance of parodies of spirituals, but even the best intentions might betray a singer into mannerisms that would detract from effective performance.

To ensure appropriate performance practice, beginning in 1918, the Burleigh arrangements and collections of arrangements published by G. Ricordi carried on the inside front cover Burleigh's statement of how the spirituals should be performed.[104] After a brief history (taken partly from Thomas Seward's preface to the Fisk Jubilee song collections), Burleigh addressed the first issue: "Success in singing these Folk Songs is primarily dependent upon deep spiritual feeling. The voice is not nearly so important as the spirit; and then rhythm, for the Negro's soul is linked with rhythm." In addressing the opposite problem Burleigh recommended presentation appropriate for the salon or recital hall: "It is a serious misconception of their meaning and value to treat them as 'minstrel' songs, or to try to make them funny by a too literal attempt to imitate the manner of the Negro in singing them, by swaying the body, clapping the hands, or striving to make the peculiar inflections of the voice that are natural with colored people." In words reminiscent of Du Bois's description, he called for a dignified approach that would highlight their message of hope for freedom and human brotherhood. "Their worth is weakened unless they are done impressively, for through all these songs there breathes a hope, a faith in the ultimate justice and brotherhood of man. The cadences of sorrow invariably turn to joy, and the message is ever manifest that eventually deliverance from all that hinders and oppresses the soul will come, and man—every man—will be free." Burleigh believed that presenting the spirituals with appropriate dignity would foster greater understanding among people of different races and cultures and help bring the time when "the ultimate justice and brotherhood of man" was a reality.

Though the musical score was inadequate to communicate the spirit in which spirituals should be sung, to Burleigh it was sensitivity and understanding that made effective performance of spirituals possible, not racial or ethnic background. In the late 1920s, when black singers were using his arrangements in recital, Burleigh made it clear that in his view race neither ensured nor precluded sensitive performance. In a 1928 interview he and his son Alston discussed how black and white singers performed them. In the oral tradition black singers "intoned" the spiritual "with exaltation, suppressed ecstasy and abandon which the white people who sing it try to copy." The two agreed that black singers often sang spirituals the way they thought white people expected them to, rather than giving them their own interpretation. "It does not necessarily follow that just because a person is colored he can sing spirituals. I know some who haven't the faintest conception of how they should be handled."[105] Burleigh's primary concern was that spirituals be sung with understanding and respect, and that their performance inspire the same response in the hearers, whoever the singer might be.

Burleigh's view of spirituals as a profoundly religious expression was as basic to his aesthetic as artistic excellence, and it intensified his concern for excellence. Their musical treatment and performance must reflect their spiritual quality. "They were inspired by the conditions of slavery and the longing of the Negro people for freedom. Spirituals have a plaintive, tender quality but they are not sad—rather they are inspirational in character. For their intrinsic beauty and artistic worth, for the remarkable story they tell of the triumphant progress of a gifted race through an estate of bondage and servitude to a place on the heights of creative art, they stand today a permanent evidence of the race's spiritual ascendancy over oppression and humiliation."[106]

In his 1924 letter to the St. George's choir at the celebration of his 30th anniversary, he wrote, "In honoring me so significantly, you also honored and exalted my race—from whose sorrowful hearts came these matchless prayer and praise songs—in which the Negro voices a religious security as old as creation, older than hope, deeper than grief, more tender than tears; the utterance of a race unshaken in faith."[107] In Natalie Curtis Burlin's words, these songs were "among the loveliest of chanted prayers"[108] and invaluable for use in worship services. They "always denote a personal relationship. It is 'my Saviour,' 'my sorrow,' 'my kingdom.' The personal note is ever present."[109] Furthermore, spirituals "are adaptable to any form of religious service. They provide the accent that is needed, a warm personal feeling which goes directly to the heart of people and which they don't have to go through any theology to understand."[110]

Burleigh did not object to singing spirituals in secular settings if the presentation was appropriate. His own performance demeanor in recital halls and salons sacralized them. He was described as singing with his eyes closed in reverence.[111] He also supported the artistic use of spirituals in dramatic productions. In 1928 he praised the use of "local" spirituals in Dorothy and Dubose Hayward's "superb dramatic version" of *Porgy*.[112] When Lawrence Tibbett created the controversial role of Rufus Jones in Louis Gruenberg's 1933 opera based on the Eugene O'Neill play *Emperor Jones*, which made powerful dramatic use of several spirituals, Burleigh wrote Tibbett an "enthusiastic letter" of appreciation. Tibbett replied, "I believe that of all the letters of praise I received, yours means most to me. You who stand so high in the esteem of the Colored race, as well as in the esteem of my own race.

You saw the inner significance of the work, and that was lacking in most everyone else's analysis. . . . Believe me, your appreciation for the philosophic as well as the dramatic significance of the work itself and my part in it, makes me very happy indeed.[113]

* * *

It was important to Burleigh to counteract what he felt were inadequate or misleading impressions of authentic African American music. In his view, minstrel songs, coon songs, ragtime, and jazz were all unworthy representations of black musical culture. He recognized the blues as "cousins" to the spirituals[114] and a valid expression arising from African American experience, but for him the spirituals represented the most valuable form of black music. The very success of minstrel songs had buried the spirituals. "People thought that the minstrel songs were Negro music. They are cheaper, more popular. They are gay and attractive. They have a certain rhythm, but they are not really music." He acknowledged that black performers had helped to perpetuate minstrel songs because of "economic pressure," but in the process, "everyone hummed the minstrel songs and forgot the spirituals." He intended to "rescue the spirituals" from this obscurity.[115]

Burleigh hoped his spiritual arrangements would also demonstrate that ragtime and jazz were distorted expressions of African American musical culture. Ragtime, in Burleigh's view (as in Krehbiel's), was "the old plantation melody caricatured and debased." No evidence has been found of any contact Burleigh might have had with Scott Joplin, who came to New York City in 1917; his comments were general, not differentiating Joplin's carefully constructed rags from the more improvisatory ragtime versions. He believed that some African Americans were ashamed of spirituals because they associated them with ragtime. Jazz was also a spurious form of black music, in his view. He was pleased at the recognition younger jazz artists like Duke Ellington won for themselves, but to him jazz was not "real music," nor was it Negro music. He seldom spoke of jazz; for the most part, he ignored it.[116] But, when jazz musicians used the melodies of spirituals for their improvisation, or when black musicians used spiritual melodies in popular songs that could be "jazzed up" in performance, Burleigh protested with fierce eloquence: "The preposterous jazz arrangements" were just a fad. Spirituals "will never live as jazz, but they will always be in the first rank of the world's folk music.[117]

In 1922 two young black musicians, Henry Creamer and J. Turner Layton, used a syncopated version of the "Deep River" melody for their song "Dear Old Southland," which immediately became a popular hit. Layton (the son of John T. Layton, under whose baton Burleigh had first sung the baritone solos in Coleridge-Taylor's *Hiawatha's Wedding Feast*), liked the song best of any he had written; he could not have anticipated the heated controversy it would arouse. It was a short step from the Broadway stage to the dance hall, and soon jazz bands were playing the tune. On July 8, 1922, Lucien H. White devoted his New York *Age* "In the Realm of Music"

column to a protest of this "Desecration of 'Deep River.'" The term "musical sacri-
lege" was seldom used, White said, but many musicians found it appropriate for this
misuse of the spiritual melody. Some dancers refused to dance while the number
was being played. And soprano Jessie Andrews Zachary, the first African American
woman booked to perform "classic, operatic and semi-classical numbers" in the Fox
Theaters in the greater New York area adamantly refused her employers' request
that she perform "Dear Old Southland" in her shows. When they persisted, she
explained the origin of the melody and sang Burleigh's arrangement for them. To
her amazement her employers were so moved by Burleigh's arrangement that they
asked her to substitute it in her repertoire for the popular "Dear Old Southland."[118]
White argued that black composers could find in secular folksongs "scope for the
fullest expression of their desire to transcribe race music into modern forms, even
into jazz, without having to transgress upon" the spirituals. Philanthropist George
Foster Peabody wrote a strong letter agreeing with White's position, and two weeks
later the annual convention of the National Association of Negro Musicians meeting in Columbus, Ohio, passed a resolution of support.[119]

In November of that year Burleigh wrote a protest letter to the NAACP that was
published in the New York *World* and a number of other newspapers. This 650-word
statement urged white and black Americans to join in "preserving from debase-
ment in Jazz the musical treasure of the Negro spirituals." To use these melodies
for "fox trots, dance numbers and semi-sentimental songs" was "a serious menace
to the artistic standing and development of the race."[120] "Delinquent musicians,"
he charged, "contemptuously disregard [this priceless mine of musical wealth] for
personal, commercial gain." He continued, "Their work is meretricious, sacrilegious
and wantonly destructive. It offends the aesthetic feelings of all true musicians—
white and black—and because some of us have endeavored never to sink the high
standard of our art nor commercialize the sacred heritage of our people's song, but
rather to revere and exalt it as a vital proof of the Negro's spiritual ascendancy over
oppression and humiliation, we feel, deeply, that the willful, persistent, superficial
distortion of our folk-songs is shockingly reprehensible." Most musicians could
"detect instantly the flagrant misappropriation, the amateurish perversion" of the
spirituals, but unskilled musicians and young people might be misled by this "per-
nicious musical trickery." The perpetrators did not seem to realize the seriousness
of their offense, and as folk music was in the public domain, the only protection
could be race pride. "Have these men sufficient race pride to forego the cheap
success and easy money? Have they sufficient racial pride to refuse to prostitute
the inherent religious beauty of our spirituals? Can we not convince them that it
is all in bad taste; that it is like polluting a great, free fountain of pure melody?"[121]

Burleigh's view of the spirituals as the primary artistic contribution of African
Americans may seem narrow by twenty-first-century standards, but seen in its
social context, the reasons for his staunch convictions become clear. His views
were shared by a number of the early leaders of the Harlem Renaissance.

17. Burleigh Spirituals and the Harlem Renaissance

"A dangerous tendency toward sophisticated over-elaboration"

A gradual change in the attitudes of African American artists toward their folk traditions can be traced from the midteens to the mid-1920s. The younger writers, visual artists, and musicians who were drawn to New York City during the twenties took the development of new forms of black music in directions not anticipated by the early leaders of the New Negro Renaissance, popularly known as the Harlem Renaissance. New voices began to call for black artists to formulate and affirm their own aesthetic values, and to draw on the language, oral literature, and music of "the folk" for their forms and aesthetic principles, not merely as raw material that needed to be transformed into "high art" to be worthy, or in Burleigh's term, "intelligible." His contemporary, Will Marion Cook, had been making similar arguments since the 1890s.[1] But the concept of a black aesthetic was most vigorously asserted in Langston Hughes's artistic credo published in *The Nation* in April 1926. Hughes called on black artists to "express our individual dark-skinned selves without fear or shame. If white people are pleased we are glad. If they are not, it doesn't matter. We know we are beautiful. And ugly too. The tom-tom cries and the tom-tom laughs. If colored people are pleased we are glad. If they are not, their displeasure doesn't matter either. We build temples for tomorrow, strong as we know how, and we stand on top of the mountain, free within ourselves."[2] A corollary to this in the treatment of spirituals was the movement toward simpler settings with harmonic treatment more closely reflecting oral performance, and the practice of singing spirituals with no instrumental accompaniment. Burleigh came to be the target of criticism from some of the most outspoken of the younger Harlem or New Negro Renaissance voices, and he did not hesitate to criticize his colleagues in return when he felt the movement was chauvinist and separatist, or sacrificed what he felt were basic artistic standards.

The music columns of the New York *Age* and other black journals and newspapers show how the reclamation of spirituals by African American singers evolved.

Before 1917 Burleigh's art songs and the few plantation songs he published were in more frequent use by white singers than black. The number of black artists who used Burleigh's compositions and arrangements increased after 1917. From 1921 through 1925 the *Age* listed recital programs nearly every week. In these years almost all recitals followed the pattern set by Burleigh's early recitals and those of Oscar Seagle and Roland Hayes: several groups of European and American art songs and operatic arias, often arranged in chronological order, with at least one group of spirituals. Most singers included at least one Burleigh arrangement, and often the entire group of spirituals were Burleigh's arrangements. By 1925 arrangements by Roland Hayes, Lawrence Brown, J. Rosamond Johnson, Major N. Clark Smith, and Gerald Tyler appeared more frequently, with an occasional arrangement by a white composer such as Harvey B. Gaul or William Arms Fisher.[3]

But even as the use of Burleigh's arrangements increased, a movement away from the more sophisticated transformations of these folksongs is evident. Occasional items indicated a growing interest in reclaiming spirituals unadorned by "artistic" settings, and from time to time singers offered a program that traced the development of African American music from Africa in several stages to its "modern" transformations.[4] As authentic African music was not easily accessible, it might be represented by one of Coleridge-Taylor's piano settings of an African melody from *Twenty-Four Negro Melodies* or a West African melody taught to Roland Hayes by West African friends he met in London.[5] More frequently a singer would perform one or more of the spirituals in "authentic" or "primitive" unaccompanied style. Several articles also discussed traditional practices such as "lining out" hymns and spirituals in "old Southern style," or expressed regret at the passing of "real [Negro] harmony such as "once existed over the entire South."[6]

This trend was influenced by singers who had close ties to the oral tradition. Roland Hayes and Paul Robeson each brought a new level of awareness of the spirituals to black and white audiences. Hayes sang Burleigh art songs as early as 1913. In 1917 he performed at least fourteen Burleigh songs, including five spirituals. He sang spirituals at Jordan Hall in Boston with Burleigh accompanying him in 1917 and 1919 before he went to London in 1921. But on his return from Europe, the white press hailed his concerts in New York and Boston in 1923 and 1924 as a revelation of the power of spirituals and Hayes as one of the finest singers of the time. Olin Downes's review of his November 16, 1923, appearance with the Boston Symphony said Hayes sang "Go Down, Moses" "with the tone and the manner of one who prophesies."[7] Heywood Broun wrote, "Roland Hayes sang of Jesus and it seemed to me that this was what religion ought to be. . . . I saw a miracle in the Town Hall. Half of the people who heard Hayes were black and half white, and while the mood of the song held they were all the same. They shared together the close silence. One emotion wrapped them. And at the end it was a single sob." While Hayes's sensitive interpretations of all of the spirituals moved his audiences, his unaccompanied singing of "The Crucifixion" drew special note. "'He never said a mumbling word,' sang Hayes, and we knew that he spoke of Christ, whose voice was clear enough to cross all the seas of water and blood."[8] In 1925, when Paul Robeson and Lawrence Brown presented what the white press called "the first solo concert ever presented in the United States consisting entirely of African-American folk songs," Robeson's singing gave a new sense of the power in simplicity of presentation.

Hayes and Robeson used Burleigh's arrangements throughout their singing careers, but they also began to use arrangements that were closer to traditional oral performance. More of Robeson's arrangements were by his accompanist Lawrence Brown. Hayes began to write his own arrangements, based on memories of his father's singing. Alain Locke described the care with which Hayes transcribed and performed spirituals in his 1925 essay "The Negro Spirituals." Locke felt that certain white composers, such as David Guion, were more careful than were some of their black colleagues in studying the oral tradition. "There is no more careful and expressive student of the spirituals than David Guion; as far as is possible from a technical and outside approach, he has bent his skill to catch the idiom of these songs." Locke showed with comparative musical examples how much more detailed were Hayes's transcriptions, with "the subtler rhythmic patterns, the closer phrase linkage, the dramatic recitative movement, and the rhapsodic voice glides and quavers. . . . It is more than a question of musicianship, it is a question of feeling instinctively qualities put there by instinct."[9] Burleigh relied on singers to learn how to interpret his score by familiarizing themselves with the oral tradition, but Guion and Hayes created descriptive arrangements, attempting to reproduce the performance practice of the oral tradition in their settings.

* * *

By the mid-1920s Burleigh was still regarded as the pioneer and by most as the master arranger of spirituals, but dissenting voices were heard among white commentators as well as black. Few white reviewers found fault with Burleigh's arrangements in 1917 and the first years following their publication and adoption by concert singers, though several commented that Burleigh's arrangements did not authentically reflect the oral tradition. Hiram K. Moderwell wrote that Burleigh's "Deep River" arrangement "makes no attempt at exotic or racial effect." In fact, "no one studying [his arrangements] would guess the composer's race. Some may wish that 'Deep River' had been arranged with a view to carrying out the [unspecified] negro elements of the melody, but none could ask for a more effective piece for the recital hall."[10] Moderwell's tone was objective rather than critical, but several white writers felt he carried the melodies too far from their original form.

Henry Krehbiel warned against oversophistication of African American folk music "by standardizing its form, making it conform to the standard of music of European conception." He implied criticism of Burleigh's settings in his review of Frank Damrosch's Musical Art Society concert in December 1919 featuring arrangements by Natalie Curtis Burlin. Burlin's arrangements were "a new experiment," in contrast to those featured two years earlier, "beautifully and reconditely arranged by Mr. Burleigh." In her settings, "Mrs. Burlin made a good and convincing demonstration of the proper treatment of folk-songs of this character." Another number, a "North Country" folksong setting, was an illustration of "how a good folk-song can be spoiled by too much sophistication."[11] American music historian John Tasker Howard concurred with Krehbiel's reservation. In his survey of American music, first published in 1929, he wrote, "Strange to say, though he was a Negro, [Burleigh's] harmonizations and treatment are often far from negroid. He brought to the melodies a sophistication of treatment, chromatic harmonies and the like, which sometimes lifts them from their native element."[12]

The most outspoken white writer on the arrangement and performance of spirituals was drama critic Carl Van Vechten. In his 1925 article "Folksongs of the American Negro," he traced the history of the interest in spirituals and the flood of transcriptions and performances then in vogue. He gave Burleigh credit for their popularity: "The progress of these spirituals into the repertory of most public singers is due, perhaps, more than to any other one man, to the indefatigable efforts of H. T. Burleigh. For nearly a decade, Mr. Burleigh, who is still occupied with the task, has been issuing his concert arrangements of these masterpieces of homely music." However, the very mission Burleigh assumed, to make spirituals available to white singers, earned Van Vechten's censure. "I cannot look upon all of Mr. Burleigh's arrangements with favor, principally because they have been instrumental in bringing these songs to the attention of white singers and I do not think white singers can sing spirituals." And, he continued, "Women, with few exceptions, should not attempt to sing them at all."[13] (Marian Anderson, whose career was in its early stages at this time, would surely be among the exceptions.)

It was the very artistic excellence to which Burleigh was committed and his skill as a song composer that Van Vechten felt made his arrangements problematic. "White singers have been attracted to Mr. Burleigh's arrangements, because they include many of the 'tricks' which make any song successful, while the accompaniments are often highly sophisticated." He then qualified his remarks, but did not specify which arrangements he excluded from criticism: "This is not true of all of Mr. Burleigh's arrangements and I think it may safely be stated that it is only true of any of them insofar as he failed to express the real love for this music that he indubitably feels." However, too many of the arrangements by Burleigh and his colleagues, white and black, gave "a false impression of the original Negro spirit of these songs," because in the arranging they were "adulterated with sophisticated modern French harmonies or disfigured by effective 'concert endings.'"[14] Van Vechten felt black singers took Burleigh's instructions on the dignified presentation of spirituals too seriously. "As a piece of advice directed to white singers this may be all very well, but I have already stated my conviction that it is being heeded by too many colored singers, who not only avoid the natural Negro inflections, but are inclined to avoid the dialect as well." Just as Caruso took care to sing his

Neapolitan folksongs in dialect "on the manner of the authentic interpretation," so black singers should maintain "the *original* manner in which they were sung."[15]

Van Vechten's critique must be evaluated in the context of the primitivism he and other white sponsors and patrons of African American artistic expression espoused. Van Vechten's promotion of black music, literature, and visual arts assisted many of the younger Harlem Renaissance artists, but his call for authentic expression was tainted by his enthusiasm for the primitive. Another strong voice for the primitive was the wealthy Charlotte Mason, financial patron of Langston Hughes, Zora Neale Hurston, and Alain Locke. She supported them generously, but her patronage came at a price. Eventually each of them found they could no longer play the role of primitive innocents she required them to be. Each found it necessary, in varying degrees, to assert independence, and in doing so sacrificed her financial patronage.[16] Van Vechten's patronage was less intrusive than Mason's, but both were motivated by their fascination with the primitive. Their promotion of the primitive in black artistic expression interacted in complicated ways with African American social class structure. Some black performers avoided Burleigh's arrangements precisely because of his occasional use of dialect. He explained that "the dialect softens the hardness of the Anglo-Saxon language. The trouble is that this dialect has become caricatured, but this is no reason for not using it."[17] Some of the Harlem Renaissance artists were reclaiming the distinctive use of language by African Americans as an important aspect of their culture, and Van Vechten was one of several white commentators who understood this to be more than an exercise in self-deprecating humor.[18]

Van Vechten argued that Harlem Renaissance musicians should base their work on the twentieth-century music of the South. He criticized Burleigh and his colleagues for relying on the Hampton and Fisk collections for most of their arrangements. If they really wanted to preserve the spirituals, they should go to the South and do their own fieldwork. "What is needed at present is original research. A trained musician—to no other than a Negro would the material be available— should scour the South, not only for new songs, but to make accurate records of harmonized performances of the old ones before it is too late. Any such seeker, it is evident, will find a mine of hitherto unearthed material."[19] As we shall see, Burleigh actually did this in a series of trips to rural Mansfield, Georgia, where he transcribed hundreds of spirituals sung by former slaves. But his venture into song collection in the South was little known and the resulting publication seems to have had little effect on public understanding and use of the spirituals.[20]

By this time black writers were also criticizing Burleigh's work. They prefaced their criticism with statements of gratitude for his "yeoman work" in helping to preserve the spirituals from extinction and restoring them to use by black performers as well as white. But now that the universal artistic value of the spirituals was established, a new generation could see the intrinsic value of the folksongs as they were continually recreated in improvisatory oral performance.[21] Burleigh's most astute, careful critic was his friend, philosopher and arts patron Alain Locke. For thirty years Locke's books and articles presented thoughtful analysis of the creative work of black musical, literary, and visual artists and its reception by white audiences, often within the perspective of a historical survey. Though their friendship was doubtless tested by Locke's critiques of Burleigh's work, their relationship was grounded in mutual respect.[22]

One of the first major essays in which he commented on Burleigh's work was "The Negro Spirituals" in his 1925 book *The New Negro*. He traced the natural process of rejection and reclamation of traditional folk culture in successive generations. "Folk art," Locke wrote, "is always despised and rejected at first; but generations after it flowers again and transcends the level of its origin." The spirituals, a folk art "uniquely expressive of the Negro," had survived, and their universality "looms more and more as they stand the test of time. They have outlived the particular generation and the peculiar conditions which produced them; they have survived in turn the contempt of the slave owners, the conventionalizations of formal religion, the repressions of Puritanism, the corruptions of sentimental balladry, and the neglect and disdain of second-generation respectability." Indirectly he credited Burleigh with the "vision and courage" that it took "to proclaim their ultimate value and possibilities" in the face of the second-generation "neglect and disdain." The Fisk Jubilee Singers and other jubilee troupes had taken these songs "to an alien atmosphere," thus causing "damage to the tradition" through "transplanting" them. Setting them for the concert stage, as Burleigh had done, had taken them "an inevitable step further from their original setting."[23]

Locke did not share Van Vechten's view that artists should perform them only as they had been originally sung. "In calling for the folk atmosphere, insisting upon the folk quality, we must be careful not to confine this wonderful potential music to the narrow confines of 'simple versions' and musically primitive molds. . . . So long as the peculiar quality of the Negro song is maintained, and the musical idiom is kept unadulterated, there is and can be no set limitation." In spite of "a dangerous tendency toward sophisticated over-elaboration," art song transformations of the spirituals were appropriate, and Locke felt that no artist had fully realized the potential for their artistic development. But he criticized the "somewhat hybrid treatment" of Burleigh and "the older school of musicians." He agreed with Van Vechten that Burleigh's arrangements "tincture the folk spirit with added concert furbelows and alien florid adornments." But "the predominance of solo treatment and the loss of the vital sustained background of accompanying voices" violated their essential character even more seriously. The spirituals were a choral form and "the proper idiom of Negro folk song calls for choral treatment."[24]

In 1934, the same year that Burleigh's essay "The Negro and His Music" appeared, Locke wrote an extended essay, "Toward a Critique of Negro Music," published in the November and December issues of *Opportunity* magazine. In the first article Locke denounced most commentaries on black music. "The platitudinous piffle, the repetitious bosh; the pounds of [indiscriminate] praise" were "if anything, more hurtful and damning than the ounces of disparagement." Having read through the "four to five thousand pages" that had been published, he felt that "four-fifths could be consigned to the flames to the everlasting benefit of the sound appraisal of Negro music and of constructive guidance of the Negro musician." In terms similar to Will Marion Cook's 1927 letter to Van Vechten, Locke continued: What "the state of Negro music" needed, and what "especially the state of mind of Negro musicians need[ed was] the bitter tonic of criticisms more than unctuous praise and the soothing syrups of flattery." Black musicians who were "in vital touch with the folk traditions of Negro music" were "in commercial slavery to Tin Pan Alley and subject to the corruption and tyranny of the ready cash of our dance halls and the vaudeville stage." On the other hand, musicians (like Burleigh), who had formal training, were in his opinion "divorced from the people and their vital inspiration by the cloister-walls of the conservatory and the taboos of musical respectability."[25]

The second article featured Burleigh's photograph, though the discussion gave him faint praise. Burleigh had "served well in his generation," but Locke argued that in his solo arrangements Burleigh had developed the spirituals "in a line false to their native choral nature." Hall Johnson was known for his insistence that performance of his arrangements be exactly as written, as they faithfully reflected the oral tradition. Locke felt that Johnson's versions of both spirituals and secular black folksongs pointed to "the promise of the future," in choral arrangements equal to the versions of Russian folk music by Russian choral composers.[26]

Zora Neale Hurston, whose novels and plays as well as her descriptive essays demonstrated keen observations of Southern folk culture, wrote in a similar vein. She did not single Burleigh out but named him among his contemporaries— J. Rosamond Johnson, Lawrence Brown, Nathaniel Dett, and John W. Work II—and she included Hall Johnson in her criticism: "There has never been a presentation of genuine Negro spirituals to any audience anywhere. What is being sung by the concert artists and glee clubs are the works of Negro composers or adaptors *based* on the spirituals. . . . All good work and beautiful, but *not* the spirituals. . . . With all the glee clubs and soloists, there has not been one genuine spiritual presented."[27]

The spirituals were "not solo or quartette material." But more importantly, the creative, interactive process of their continual recreation in traditional oral performance was of their essence, rather than incidental. To isolate the melody and supply alien harmony was only the worst of the violations of art song renditions. Even attempts to reproduce some version of authentic folk harmonies would violate the spirit of the songs by standardizing and smoothing out the characteristic elements. "The jagged harmony is what makes it, and it ceases to be what it was when this is absent." This harmony could not be taught. "Its truth dies under training like flowers under hot water. The harmony of the true spiritual is not regular. The dissonances are important and not to be ironed out by the trained musician. The various parts break in at any old time. Falsetto often takes the place of regular voices for short periods. Keys change. Moreover, each singing of the piece is a new creation. The congregation is bound by no rules. No two times singing is alike, so that we must consider the rendition of a song not as a final thing, but as a mood. It won't be the same thing next Sunday."[28] Hurston said she intended no condemnation of the "neo-spirituals," but one must be clear as to their relationship to "genuine Negro spirituals. The [neo-spirituals] are a valuable contribution to the music and literature of the world. But let no one imagine that they are the songs of the people, as sung by them."[29]

Hurston articulated the importance of the music event in African American culture, which could not be reproduced in art music transformations. And indeed Burleigh had taken the spirituals, which "derived from group performance in particular contexts and were the product of artistic procedures rooted in an African music aesthetic. European solo performance practices, like the ritualized protocol of the concert stage where the distance between performer and audience is preserved, violated that aesthetic."[30] But as Philip Miller commented in his notes accompanying the reissue of several Burleigh arrangements on the recording *When I Have Sung My Songs: The American Art Song 1900–1940,* "Purists have criticized Burleigh's arrangements as inappropriate for folk music. This misrepresents his intention. In his time the folklorists had barely begun their work. Burleigh gave us a kind of idealized spirituals, a transformation of the melodies into art songs very much in the manner of the Brahms Deutsche Volkslieder."[31] Burleigh would have appreciated the comparison, which acknowledged Brahms as one of his sources of inspiration, a connection no doubt strengthened by his friendship with Dvořák, whose own work had been championed by Brahms.[32]

It could be argued that in her novels Hurston essentially did with traditional African American narrative and other oral literary forms what Burleigh and others did in their spiritual arrangements: using literary forms not native to traditional black culture she brought an African American voice to the American novel, just as Burleigh had brought the voice of the spiritual into American art song repertoire. Drawing on Houston Baker's concept of the "mastery of form," and Locke's challenge to black artists to go beyond the "outer mastery of form and technique" to achieve "an inner mastery of mood and spirit," Jon Michael Spencer proposes a "two-tiered mastery," that Burleigh, Dett, Still, and other composers and arrangers exhibited. In *God's Trombones,* James Weldon Johnson brought the rich lyricism of the black sermon into American poetry, without duplicating any sermon by any black preacher, just as these other literary and musical artists drew on the treasury of African American artistic expression, creating new American song, poetry, and narrative literature.[33] But Locke's and Hurston's critiques demonstrate why, in the later years of the Harlem Renaissance, artists wished to reclaim the songs of the people "as sung by them," not merely as the raw material for creating art music. The process of reclamation that Burleigh had facilitated was moving into a phase that Burleigh found difficult to accept.

* * *

In 1925, the year a number of important collections of spiritual arrangements by other composers appeared, Burleigh published four arrangements, including "Wade in de Water" (mm. 1–4). Like the 1917 settings of "Go Down, Moses" and "By an' By," the piano introduction sets up a propulsive syncopated rhythmic pattern in the accompaniment. In the first verse (mm. 11–18) the upper accompaniment voice adds a countermelody obligato. In the final statement of the chorus Burleigh departs from the circular mode of the folk form to build a climax, with thicker chords and a rallentando e crescendo that prepares the melodic leap in the voice to the upper octave (mm. 39–40), before a quietly intense finale in measures forty through forty-six, with the syncopated drumbeat accompaniment pattern continuing in the bass two measures beyond the final cadence in the voice. As in his earlier arrangements, Burleigh presented the spiritual melody simply, but through the emphasis of characteristic rhythmic motifs, expressive use of chromaticism, countermelodies, and colorful, active harmonic progressions and the creation of formal climax and final cadence formulae, transformed it into a classic American art song.

In his analysis of Burleigh's spiritual arrangements, composer Olly Wilson gives us a twenty-first century perspective on Burleigh's achievement. What made his arrangements special "was his ability as a composer-arranger to retain the powerful expressive essence of the spiritual and simultaneously create a piano accompaniment that complemented the songs and singers without detracting from the spiritual's inner musical logic or poetic content." They "assumed the aesthetic values within the spiritual tradition, but reinterpreted the musical event using conventions associated with the concert stage." Wilson identifies several specific techniques. "First, Burleigh always gives hegemony to the original spiritual's vocal line in its relationship to the piano accompaniment. Accordingly, the piano line is often sparse, simple, and essentially supportive of the vocal line." This "encourages

"Wade in de Water," mm. 1–4.

the vocalist to take opportunities to add subtle timbral nuances and rhythmic variations in the performance of the song, a practice idiomatic with traditional performances."[34]

Second, Burleigh often incorporated the traditional antiphonal or call-and-response form in the accompaniment, "filling in the gaps at the ends of phrases with appropriate countermelodies as is often the case in communal vernacular spirituals. These accompaniment countermelodies and interjections often contain idiomatic extended syncopated rhythmic patterns characteristic of the religious style."[35] Third, Burleigh's harmonic choices are "guided by the use of chords that appropriately support the modal implications of the original spirituals." He used chromaticism "as a color device or melodic overlay (usually a descending chromatic scale fragment)," and his harmonic rhythm "tends to be slow" (particularly in comparison to his secular art songs). "Functional harmony tends to be clearly directed toward dominant-tonic and subdominant-tonic polarities," as can be heard in the oral tradition. "Burleigh's most refreshing harmonic choices work, even the chromatic ones, because they adhere to the modal implications of the melodic line while implying new relationships to the tonic center, often a third above or below the original tonic. Burleigh also carefully explores timbral nuances and registral variety to clearly distinguish the piano as an accompanying voice. Yet the text is brought into sharp relief." Through these means Burleigh creates "a new model of the spiritual, a model that consists of a clearly stylized spiritual endowed with new, carefully composed elements that shape the musical content of the spiritual to reflect its composer-arranger's unique artistic reinterpretation of the original. The musical result is different from the original vernacular spiritual, but, contrary to some thought of the period, it is not an 'elevation' of that tradition. The art song spiritual seeks to communicate to an audience the artistic statement of its composer-arranger as interpreted by its performer. It is an object of intrinsic perceptual interest."[36]

* * *

Burleigh's reaction to the 1925 publication of *The Book of American Negro Spirituals* by his friends James Weldon and J. Rosamond Johnson and Lawrence Brown demonstrates his refusal to relinquish the aesthetic standards that shaped his settings, even if it meant criticizing some of his closest associates. By 1925 forty of Burleigh's spiritual arrangements had been published in sheet music format. Several important anthologies of spirituals were published in 1925, perhaps the most influential being the Johnsons' anthology. They intended to make spirituals accessible to ordinary nonprofessional musicians. The dedication of the book obviously included Burleigh: "To those through whose efforts these songs have been collected, preserved and given to the world this book is lovingly dedicated."[37] The dedication of individual songs saluted a roster of black performers and composers who had worked to ensure the preservation of spirituals (e.g., E. Azalia Hackley, Paul and Eslanda Robeson, Samuel Coleridge-Taylor, W. E. B. Du Bois, and Burleigh) and of white musicians, artists, and philanthropists who had supported their efforts (e.g., Walter Damrosch, David Mannes, Otto Kuhn, Joel Spingarn, and Carl Van Vechten). James Weldon Johnson's forty-page preface traced the history of spirituals, discussed their musical and textual elements, and summarized some of the current discussion, including Van Vechten's recent article. Of the sixty-one songs included, five were arranged by Lawrence Brown and the rest by J. Rosamond Johnson.[38]

Johnson and Brown intentionally departed from the approach Burleigh and most other arrangers had taken in their harmonizations. Rather than lift the melody from its context, they attempted to capture in their harmonizations "the orchestrational timbre" of the spontaneous harmony created in oral performance, not of the slave plantation, but of contemporary black singing. They were arranged for solo voice, but the piano accompaniments were designed "to give the characteristic harmonies that would be used in spontaneous group singing. Of course," James Weldon Johnson's preface explained, "these harmonies are not fixed. A group or congregation singing spontaneously might never use precisely the same harmonies twice; however, Mr. Rosamond Johnson and Mr. Brown have shown great fidelity to what is characteristic. The ordinary four-part harmonies can, without difficulty, be picked out from the accompaniments to most of the songs, but what the arrangers had principally in mind was to have the instrumentation approach the effect of the singing group in action."[39]

Burleigh, who was regarded as the master arranger by most white critics and many black reviewers and performers, objected vehemently to the book. Carl Van Vechten reported in a letter to Eslanda (Mrs. Paul) Robeson that Burleigh "is in a frightful stew and does not hesitate to show it. Meeting Larry and Rosamond on the street he abused them roundly, saying that neither of them knew anything about spirituals or even music itself and that the book was a botch." In a comment that revealed his basic misunderstanding, or—more likely—his rejection, of the rationale for their harmonizations, Burleigh continued, "If you knew anything about Brahms and Debussy, your harmonizations would be far different." In his view Johnson and Brown had betrayed their responsibility to harmonize the spirituals according to the principles of musical excellence, as he defined excellence. In citing Brahms and Debussy as models, he identified two composers who represented the standard of Romantic and Impressionist style against which he measured his own work. So serious was Johnson and Brown's failure in Burleigh's estimation that "he threatened to talk to certain critics and promised them bad notices."[40]

Burleigh enjoyed positive relationships with some of the most powerful white music critics in New York City, but he had little success in influencing their response to *The Book of American Negro Spirituals,* if indeed he tried. Comments in both the black and the white press suggest that Burleigh's reaction smacked of someone attempting to protect artistic territory he unwisely assumed to be his own. Walter Damrosch wrote the editor of the New York *World,* in response to a favorable review of the book, "I certainly doff my hat to the writer of your beautiful editorial. It is a fine appreciation of a fine piece of work, and I wish to subscribe to every word of it. Those wonderful old Negro folk-songs have been used and also abused for many years, but at last Mr. Rosamond Johnson has given them an appropriate and at the same time a musicianly setting."[41]

As would be expected from his criticism of Burleigh's "sophisticated modern French harmonies," Carl Van Vechten found *The Book of American Negro Spirituals* free of such errors. Viking Press had chosen the ideal volume with which "to inaugurate their new publishing house," and they had "turned to the very best Negro talent available." Johnson's and Brown's arrangements had "reproduced, insofar as it is possible for a piano to do so, the harmonies that might be employed by a Negro chorus in the actual performance of spirituals under the conditions incident to their creation. They have done more than this; certain figures and arpeggios actually suggest the moans and groans, the startled 'Oh yesses!' of a congregation of mourners."[42]

The black press also welcomed the Johnson-Brown collection. The New York *World* agreed that "authentic harmonies," which Johnson and Brown had recaptured, were "as much a part of the complete effect as the melodies."[43] Lucien H. White of the New York *Age* commented on Burleigh's contribution to the work of Natalie Curtis Burlin and Henry E. Krehbiel but did not refer to his arrangements. White praised James Weldon Johnson's "learned treatise" on Negro music and commented at length on the arrangements themselves. In his musical settings, J. Rosamond Johnson had arranged "wisely and well. He has, in most cases, avoided the temptation to construct a sophisticated garment with which to clothe these primitive airs, but he has, at the same time, not been satisfied to give them a carelessly meretricious modern musical background. Maintaining a dignified poise at all times, he has entered into the spirit of each song, and the result is that a distinctive color and cadence is preserved, while at the same time the musically hypercritical can find no fault with the splendid musical structure which conforms always to the rigid requirements of the essence of musical theory and composition.[44]

White had announced the publication of *The Book of American Negro Spirituals* in his column of August 29. Both his extensive review and his reprinting of the favorable review from the New York *World* and Walter Damrosch's response appeared in late October after Burleigh's attack on Rosamond Johnson and Lawrence Brown. Though his columns often praised Burleigh's work, his reference to "the musically hypercritical" may well have been directed at Burleigh.

R. Nathaniel Dett at Hampton Institute shared Burleigh's discomfort with Rosamond Johnson's approach. His December 1925 review of *The Book of American Negro Spirituals* in *The Southern Workman* criticized some of the elements that must also have disappointed Burleigh. Dett found James Weldon Johnson's preface admirable in both content and style. He had termed the spirituals "noble": "All true spirituals possess dignity." From that perspective, Dett maintained, any "development" or "adaptation" of the music should "follow along the line of the natural tendency of the music" and should be "undertaken in . . . the spirit of reverence." Johnson's preface claimed that "the only development has been in harmonizations and these have been kept true in character." But Dett found numerous departures from this standard in the arrangements, such as "the use of jazz, the 'Charleston,' and other dance-like motives in the accompaniment [that threaten] seriously the spirit of nobility and dignity of which the Preface assures us." Despite the assurance that no changes had been made in song form, the very first song featured an "innovation" in form, and Dett listed other innovations and manipulations that "seem to go gaily on." After the claim in the preface, he saw no excuse for these changes of structure. Dett found only one song in the collection, "Stan' Still, Jordan," that was "well treated with an evident deep appreciation of the dominant mood" and whose setting "suggests the church rather than the theatre or concert hall."[45]

The program Burleigh and James Weldon Johnson gave together in Bridgeport, Connecticut, on April 15, 1926, suggests that Johnson, ever the diplomat, managed to mollify Burleigh, and Burleigh himself must have recognized the importance of restoring their friendship. The program, under the auspices of the YWCA, was held at the United Church. Burleigh sang ten of his spiritual arrangements, with "references, comments and explanations." Johnson spoke on the "Origin and Development of the Spirituals," and "The Making, Dialect, Poetry and Significance of the Spirituals." The Johnson brothers dedicated their *Second Book of Negro Spirituals* to "John W. Work and Natalie Curtis Burlin, Lovers of the spirituals and toilers for their preservation." James Weldon Johnson's fourteen-page preface did not mention Burleigh by name, though by implication it did mention his help in fostering the "leaping pride" that energized young black artists as they reclaimed their musical heritage in the spirituals.[46] And Rosamond Johnson dedicated his arrangement of "Po' Mourner's Got a Home at Las'" to Burleigh.

* * *

Like the Johnsons, Burleigh recognized the need to preserve the vast repertoire of spirituals in simpler versions accessible to untrained singers, as well as in art-style transformations for professional singers. But his approach to such a collection was very different from that of J. Rosamond Johnson. He collaborated with Dorothy G. Bolton, a white woman from Georgia, in compiling the *Old Songs Hymnal,* published in 1929. This featured 187 songs that Bolton remembered from hearing them in her childhood or collected from former slaves. Burleigh transcribed and arranged the music. Unlike the Johnson collections, in which the piano accompaniments sometimes added an overly popular flavor and often were not easy to sight-read, Burleigh arranged these songs in simple hymn-like four-part settings. In the foreword, Bolton and Burleigh described the traditional practicing of "lining out" these hymns: "Until now we have had to depend upon memory alone to sing them, and when the Minister could not 'line' them for us some old brother or sister would undertake to lead them." As the passing of the generation who knew these songs well enough to teach them to congregations threatened their survival, Bolton and Burleigh offered the collection in a form accessible to most church musicians. They addressed the problem of accessibility, and without mentioning the Johnson collections or others similar to them, implied that despite the stated intent, their work did not fill the need of untrained musicians for simple versions. "There are many beautiful collections of these songs, but all with accompaniments too difficult for the average person to play at sight, and so we present this volume as a hymnbook with the music as simple as possible, hoping that it will be used in church and home and school, preserving to us this precious heritage."[47]

Because in oral performance verses were often improvised, lines of text might be unequal in length. In the oral tradition the words of the verses were adjusted to the music "with the greatest freedom by the individual singer. The natural sense of rhythm of the old folk found no difficulty in doing this." Burleigh and Bolton set one line of text to the music, printing additional verses at the bottom of the page, with no attempt to align them to the music. Singers were then free to adapt them to the melody in the traditional fashion. Thus, the songs were presented so they could be used by congregations in a manner close to that of their origin. "We offer this book with the hope that in these songs the human heart will continue to find expression for its deepest emotions of joy, of sorrow, of inspiration and that exaltation of the soul which gave them the name—spirituals."[48]

Today the Johnson collections can be found in many public libraries, but few copies of the *Old Songs Hymnal* are extant, and no information has been found as to its use by congregations. The necessary silence surrounding the Bolton project may have been a factor in its lack of acceptance. For a well-to-do white woman to host a black man, however eminent a composer, in her home in rural Georgia might have made any public knowledge of their work scandalous, if not actually dangerous in the mid-1920s. For whatever reason, Burleigh's venture into ethnomusicological fieldwork and the hymnal he and Dorothy Bolton produced seems to have had little impact on either the course or the controversy surrounding the appropriate presentation of spirituals.

The *Old Songs Hymnal* represented one answer to Burleigh's critics. Another answer that demonstrated his continual commitment to presenting spirituals in art song transformation may be seen in his 1930 arrangement for Paul Robeson of "Dry Bones." This is not the "Dry Bones" of comic jubilee and barbershop quartet fame, though it is based on the same passage from Ezekiel 37. The texture of the setting is relatively spare, allowing the richness of Robeson's voice to predominate, but Burleigh creates a programmatic orchestration of the text through his dramatic use of chords. An early example of this technique is the progression accompanying the first statement of the phrase "dead men's bones; An' every bone was dry" (mm. 8–12). This series of chords paints the dry valley in vivid tonal strokes. In contrast, the E-flat seventh smorzando chord that concludes the phrase "Come togethuh an' rise an' shine" (mm. 47–50) brightens the harmonic landscape like a shaft of light. Burleigh demonstrates his love for highlighting the text painting that he saw to be characteristic of the spirituals throughout this arrangement, broadening the final phrase, "some o' dem bones is mine," by rhythmic augmentation and adding a raised sixth to a final G minor tonic chord. Robeson seems not to have recorded this arrangement, though he recorded at least fifteen other Burleigh arrangements, and no record has been found of his performing it.

Burleigh would not retreat from his position that the spirituals, while they needed to be preserved in unadorned versions accessible to untrained musicians, also deserved creative, artistic treatment in art music compositions. Burleigh's later arrangements such as "Dry Bones" also seem not to have found as ready acceptance as those that first created the demand for solo arrangements in the late 1910s and early 1920s, but they may have suffered the fate of his art songs, which, as he commented, were no longer in as great demand by singers and publishers.

"Dry Bones," mm. 8–12.

"Dry Bones," mm. 47–50.

The issues raised in the controversy between Burleigh and his colleagues and critics are still under debate, if stated in the variety of their presentation rather than in their vehemence. Those familiar with arrangements of spirituals by late twentieth-century and early twenty-first-century composers will recognize that the range of approaches to setting spirituals is far greater than in the 1920s. In addition to solo and choral arrangements in widely varying styles, black composers often make reference to spirituals as themes, even in their most avant-garde compositions. As in the rhetoric of black writers and orators, phrases from spirituals have become proverbial, so in compositions of many musical genres (including jazz), spirituals continue to provide an indispensable and efficient resource of meaning through musical reference and quotation.

Though the concept of a black aesthetic was emerging during the Harlem Renaissance, Burleigh would not have used or espoused such a term. To him the standards of artistic excellence were universal, and he consistently refused to participate in movements he considered separatist or chauvinistic. He acknowledged in 1924 that the struggle for full recognition of African American artistry was not won, even at a time when white and black Americans were applauding his work. He believed that a truly representative American music would "show the influence of the Negro spirituals." But that time had not yet come. Spirituals would not substantially affect American music "until America is willing to admit that Negroes can be artists."[49]

At the end of his life Burleigh expressed regret that his many art songs had fallen out of use, but he took satisfaction in the continuing popularity of his spiritual arrangements. He had helped to ensure that "this great free fountain of pure melody"[50] would continue to flow, that the spirituals, with their message of "hope," of "faith in the ultimate justice and brotherhood of man"[51] would continue to be sung. At the time of his death the creative frontiers of black music lay in directions Burleigh did not choose to explore. He could not reconcile his search for artistic excellence and human dignity with the improvisatory exuberance of jazz and gospel music. The search for human brotherhood and understanding was incomplete. But in the image he often used, his work had helped to unlock the hidden musical treasure, the "pure gold" of the African American spiritual.[52] He had helped to coin that treasure in universal currency. He had, as Antonín Dvořák urged, helped to "give those melodies to the world."[53]

PART IV

Burleigh's Legacy

18. The Impact of a Life

"I Know the Lord Has Laid His Hands on Me"

Burleigh's retirement in 1946 from his position as baritone soloist at St. George's Protestant Episcopal Church marked the end of an exceptional public career. The "indestructible baritone" voice had lost its resonance, and Burleigh's mind was faltering. He had always been generous, but as his mind failed, his housekeeper worried that he was an easy mark for women he met in restaurants and bars. It was reported that he was found wandering on the street, handing out money. Walking in Harlem with his niece Grace Elmendorf one day, he suddenly darted away from her, and she knew the time had come to get help for him. She alerted his son Alston, who placed him in the Oakes convalescent home in Amityville, Long Island.[1]

But Burleigh was not forgotten. A network broadcast on radio station WSB, originating in New York City, devoted fifteen minutes of their April 14, 1947, Monday morning program to tell the story of his life, featuring some of his most famous songs. "It was a pleasant tribute, effectively aired, and brought a feeling of pride to every Negro who heard it."[2]

In December one of his protégés, organist Carlette Thomas, with her mother and two other friends, brought a surprise party to celebrate Burleigh's eighty-first birthday. Burleigh delighted them by singing and playing three of his favorite spirituals on the portable organ they had brought: "Go Down, Moses," "Were You There?" and "I Know the Lord Has Laid His Hands on Me." In addition to this private party, conductor Fred Waring, "paid tribute to the beloved composer on his morning broadcast with his glee club singing Mr. Burleigh's spiritual 'Were You There?'" Many friends sent telegrams and letters congratulating him on his birthday.[3]

When it became apparent that he was not receiving proper care at the Oakes, Alston moved him to Stamford Hall, a private nursing home in Stamford, Connecticut, where he had a private cottage "with 24-hour nursing service and tranquil surroundings." Alston and his wife Erma visited him often and found him very contented there. He spent a great deal of time reading. They discouraged visits by all except "his more intimate friends," but he delighted in visits from them. Though he needed constant care, Alston reported that his father's health was excellent, and "when he converses on musical matters, he is exceedingly fresh and alert on dates, places and people."[4]

The following year, the Howard University Choir honored him on their tour of New England, presenting a concert for him and the more than three hundred residents at the nursing home. The director, Warner Lawson, son of his pianist friend R. Augustus Lawson, arranged with the administrator of the home for bedridden patients to hear the concert over the loudspeakers. The ambulatory guests gathered in the large hall for a program of choral works by Tchaikovsky and Brahms, spiritual settings by Nathaniel Dett, William Dawson, Roy Ringwald, Hall Johnson, and Warner Lawson and two of Burleigh's arrangements, "Were You There?" and "My Lord, What a Morning." They ended the program with several comical folksongs, "which gave the shut-ins a moment of laughter and joy."[5] Burleigh responded with "a glowing speech of thanks, quite in his own warm and learned manner." Even now he emphasized the importance of preserving their musical heritage. He reflected on "the days when he addressed young students all over the country and instilled in them not only the appreciation of good music, but a racial conscientiousness to preserve their musical heritage by sincere application to study and dignity in performance." He thanked Mr. Lawson "for remembering him at a season of the year when his voice had always been lifted in singing 'The Palms' at St. George's Episcopal Church every Palm Sunday morning for more than fifty years."[6]

In April 1949, several months before his death, Carlette Thomas and her mother visited him again, with contralto Charlotte Murray. In her letter to Alston, Murray reported that Burleigh's "mind was clear, his spirit radiant." They "chatted with him" about younger singers in whose careers he took great satisfaction: Roland Hayes, Marian Anderson, and others. They spent "a happy hour and left him smiling. . . . He looked fine in lovely suit, blue shirt, new tie and nice slippers."[7]

On September 6, 1949, the medical director of Stamford Hall wrote Alston informing him that his father had had an attack the day before "in which his breathing became labored and heart action was found to be poor." This was not the first such attack, though he had "always come through them and been comfortable afterward." The director wanted Alston to be prepared for the possibility of a "more critical attack of this nature."[8] A week later, on September 12, 1949, Burleigh died of cardiac failure.

Burleigh's body lay in state in St. George's Chapel of Peace the two days preceding his funeral. The Norfolk *Journal and Guide* reported the service in detail: "The millionaires of Wall Street mourned with the plain people of Harlem here last Thursday night while New York City paid its last respects to 82-year-old Harry T. Burleigh, master of the Negro spiritual, as he made his final journey across the 'Deep River' of which he loved to sing." Rector Emeritus Karl Reiland spoke of him as "a great man, a great artist and a great friend who has gone out from among us." Burleigh "had displayed 'a peculiar genius' which endeared him to everyone he met." The report continued: "In tribute to his artistry the musical portion of his final rites saw him surrounded by talented colored singers, many of whom he had helped in their [careers]." When the combined choirs sang "Deep River," "snowy white handkerchiefs appeared all through the audience as the rich and the poor fought back the tears which accompanied the memory of the man they all loved."[9]

Burleigh's passing was noted in obituaries in the black and the white press across the country. The New York *Times* and the New York *Herald Tribune*, which had reported regularly on his singing and his published songs, gave his passing significant notice. The *Herald*'s obituary said, "His warm, instinctive humanity, reflected in his voice, brought him friends of every class, race, and creed. His long life was as happy and triumphant as the spirituals he loved to sing."[10] Some black newspapers quoted from the New York City papers but added personal tributes: "Young people preparing for a life of service nowadays can find many fruitful examples to emulate in Mr. Burleigh's life. . . . The Negro public and the white public knew him well and appreciated his great works. This recital is intended as an inspiration for youth."[11] Another wrote, "Possessed of one of the truly great voices of his time, Harry T. Burleigh certainly was a melodist of distinction. He sang with natural power but with compelling artistry. . . . He was a bridge in effect between his own people and others. . . . His gifts of personal character, dignity and poise earned him the position [at St. George's Episcopal Church], yet it was not to human listeners so much as to the very essence of divinity that Mr. Burleigh addressed himself in his performance of religious themes. A visiting clergyman summed up his achievement when he remarked: 'I should be terribly handicapped in trying to preach to folk who had just heard you sing!'" referring to "the persuasive eloquence of Mr. Burleigh's delivery. . . . He was an outstanding American in every proper meaning of the term."[12]

* * *

All too soon after the flood of laudatory obituaries, the press got wind of the conflict over Burleigh's estate. He had written two wills, the first dated September 10, 1942. This will specifically excluded his wife Louise, "for the reason that she deserted and abandoned me without cause." The second will, dated four years later, June 28, 1946, left her $2,500, with the remainder to be divided among Burleigh's grandson, Harry T. Burleigh II; his niece, Elzie Elmendorf's daughter Grace; and his longtime housekeeper, Mrs. Thelma Hall, and her son James. Burleigh's son Alston, whose alcoholism had led to his estrangement from his father, was not named.[13] Louise, who had spent the previous thirty years hiding her identity as an African American and the wife of a prominent black musician, now found it expedient to reclaim her earlier identity. Correspondence between Louise and Alston indicates that they suspected Burleigh's housekeeper, whom he called "my devoted friend, whose friendship has contributed greatly to my happiness," of undue influence on Burleigh. They challenged both wills, charging that Burleigh had been declared mentally incompetent several years before his death.[14]

The six-day trial resulted in a hung jury. The attorneys quickly ascertained that his niece Grace Elmendorf had exerted no influence, though he had informed her of his intent when he made his second will. The attorneys and the judge negotiated a settlement among the parties that allotted Louise one-ninth of the estate. The other four heirs each received two ninths: his son, Alston Burleigh; his grandson, Harry T. Burleigh II; the heirs of his half-brother Elzie Elmendorf (Grace Elmendorf and her mother); and his housekeeper, Thelma Hall, and her son James. The wide range in the reported worth of his estate, from $10,000 to $400,000, likely represented the difference between the immediate financial worth of his assets and the continuing value of royalties from the sale of his music.[15] Burleigh's personal effects were placed with a storage company that unfortunately went out of business, and most of his personal belongings disappeared. Some personal effects, including manuscripts and sheet music, were in the possession of Thelma Hall and her son James. A number of manuscripts and sheet music that were in the possession of James Hall's daughter were recently deposited in the archives at Emory University in Atlanta.

* * *

The Burleigh Society was founded in Erie in 1991, and the Harry Thacker Burleigh Memorial Center at Mercyhurst College (now Mercyhurst University) in Erie, Pennsylvania, was inaugurated on February 11, 1991, by the late Rev. Charles Kennedy Jr., who was at that time teaching at Mercyhurst.[16] The founding program featured Burleigh biographer Anne Key Simpson, Ada Lawrence, Dr. Harry T. Burleigh II, Rev. Kennedy, and myself. Historian Dr. William Garvey, who was president of the college, was fully supportive of the society and hosted a luncheon for the Burleigh family and other guests. At that luncheon Burleigh's grandson, Dr. Harry T. Burleigh II, Dr. Garvey, and Burleigh Society board members began discussing the importance of bringing Burleigh's body back to his hometown, where his grave would be more accessible to those interested, rather than in the cemetery in Hastings-on-Hudson, where the unmarked grave attracted little notice. After several years of negotiation, arrangements were made for Burleigh's reinterment in the Erie Cemetery on May 28, 1994.

The weekend celebration opened at the gazebo in Perry Square, a few blocks from Burleigh's Erie home and still an important Erie landmark, with singing by a interdenominational choir, several speakers, and solos by tenor Rev. Charles Kennedy from Erie; bass-baritone Oral Moses from Kennesaw University, Marietta, Georgia; baritone Jonathan Overby from Madison, Wisconsin; and soprano Demareus Cooper from Pittsburgh. After the program, a horse-drawn carriage bearing Burleigh's casket led the procession the short distance from Perry Square to St. Paul's Episcopal Cathedral, where the memorial service was led by the Rt. Rev. Robert D. Rowley Jr., bishop of the Diocese of Northwestern Pennsylvania, and the Rt. Rev. Arthur B. Williams, bishop suffragan of the Diocese of Ohio. Ada Lawrence spoke of her memories of Burleigh's visits to her family home when he returned to sing in Erie. Then the cortège wound its way to the Erie Cemetery on Twenty-Sixth Street, where Burleigh's body was reinterred, with the Very Rev. John P. Downey, dean of the Cathedral of St. Paul, presiding.[17]

* * *

Horse-drawn carriage with Burleigh's remains at the re-interment, May 28, 1994. (Photo by Jean E. Snyder)

Dr. Harry T. Burleigh II being interviewed at the re-interment. (Photo by Jean E. Snyder)

Rev. Charles Kennedy Jr., who served as president of the Burleigh Society for a number of years, created a one-man show called *Deep River* that brought Burleigh to life for many audiences. In addition to performances and recordings of his reinterpretations of Burleigh spiritual arrangements, he presented programs for elementary and secondary students that made Burleigh's life relevant to their own experience. Local historian Karen James spent more than a decade digging out the history of the nineteenth-century black community in Erie from public records and other documents. Much of the information on the society's now-defunct website came from her research. Since Rev. Kennedy's death, Johnny Johnson, a retired teacher and charter member of the Burleigh Society, has continued the search for information about Erie's African American history. He has spearheaded a number of commemorations such as renaming Front Street, where Ada Lawrence's family lived, to Lawrence Way, and the 100 block of East Third Street, where Burleigh's family lived, to Harry T. Burleigh Way.

Burleigh's memory was revived on a number of occasions in the early 2000s, when a series of five Harry T. Burleigh Legacy weekends were sponsored by Edinboro University of Pennsylvania, including a national conference in April 2003, "The Heritage and Legacy of Harry T. Burleigh," which drew scholars and singers from across the country. These events featured gospel choir concerts and workshops in Erie's black churches, choral concerts, and recitals by the Edinboro University choirs; and performances by contralto Bessie Sewell-Hudson of Pittsburgh, Pennsylvania; bass-baritone Oral Moses of Kennesaw University, Marietta, Georgia; soprano Louise Toppin, now of the University of North Carolina, Chapel Hill; the late tenor William A. Brown, of Jacksonville, Florida; tenor Darryl Taylor, of University of California–Irvine; pianists Ann Sears of Wheaton College, Norton, Massachusetts, and Joseph Joubert, of New York, New York; the Morehouse Glee Club, of Morehouse College, Atlanta, Georgia; and composer-in-residence Nkeiru Okoye, now of SUNY New Palz, New Palz, New York. The participation of choirs from Erie's black congregations was coordinated by Mrs. McClaudia Nolley of Greater Calvary Full Gospel Baptist Church and Dr. Kahan Sablo of Edinboro University. The Burleigh family attended and warmly supported each of these events.[18]

* * *

The Harlem or New Negro Renaissance has been seen primarily as a literary movement, but the affirmation of the African American folk music heritage and its twentieth-century transformations was a generative and inseparable aspect of the movement that drew many gifted African Americans to Harlem in the 1920s. Burleigh was well established in New York City before the Harlem Renaissance was formally recognized by the press, and much of his work to preserve and promulgate spirituals and many of his statements presaged key themes articulated by the early intellectual leaders of the movement. The most active of these, "The Six" (identified by David Levering Lewis), were Jessie Redmond Fauset, Charles S. Johnson, Casper Holstein, Alain Locke, Walter White, and James Weldon Johnson.[19] Rawn Spearman adds W. E. B. Du Bois and George Schuyler to the list of "the old patron guards . . . whose primary aspirations included promoting and converting black folk materials to the level of 'high' culture."[20] These men were Burleigh's friends and associates, and he often participated in the discussions on the arts and the cultural development of the race at the Marshall Hotel and other New York settings where black artists and intelligentsia gathered.[21]

Burleigh believed artists had a serious responsibility to lead the race. In his lecture recital to Cheyney Institute students in October 1922, he "stressed the necessity of a racial aristocracy in the colored race and the cultivation of the aesthetic sense in order that the negro folk literature may live."[22] This "racial aristocracy" seems indistinguishable from Du Bois's promotion of the "Talented Tenth," which Burleigh critiqued in his letter to Booker T. Washington after reading a review of *The Souls of Black Folk* in 1903. Obviously nearly two decades later, Burleigh recognized the importance of a leadership class, of which he was a distinguished member. Two years later in an address to the NAACP, "The Negro in Music," he expanded on this theme. He distrusted political action to effect social change, but he articulated his belief that in their music African Americans had "one of the most potent weapons to secure those equal rights which seem to be our great desire." Artists, not politicians, would lead the way. "Artists, after all, represent, or they express, the highest mentality of any race. The men and women who give themselves to artistic endeavor are the true stars of any race. They are the true physicians who heal with melody the ills of mankind. They are the torch-bearers, beautifully illuminating the darkness. . . . They are the trail-blazers. They find new worlds."[23] African American artists would find their greatest resource in their folk heritage. In using it, they would make their greatest contribution to the universe of art; and at the same time they would create "human bonds of spiritual understanding" that would bring the races together more effectively than "ties of creed."[24] Burleigh's 1924 statement to the NAACP on the leadership role of the artist echoed some of his concluding remarks in the 1922 letter protesting the misuse of the spirituals in jazz:

> In the interest of millions of colored people who love and revere the spirituals and who believe these old melodies can be an essential factor in the cultural evolution of the race as well as a powerful stimulus to its higher artistic development—and in the interest of millions of white people who love and revere the spirituals and who believe that the 'Negro stands at the gates of human culture with hands laden full with musical gifts,' I earnestly solicit your help and cooperation in a determined effort to persuade our misguided friends to cease their desecrating work and join with us in honoring, and protecting from any secular or degenerate use the Negro spirituals.[25]

The concern for "the cultural evolution of the race," and the belief that artistic development was the most effective means "to secure economic, social and cultural equality with white citizens," were central to the thinking of the Harlem Renaissance. As Nathan Huggins writes in the introduction to his study of this period, "Most Harlem intellectuals aspired to *high* culture as opposed to that of the common man, which they hoped to mine for novels, poems, plays and symphonies. They saw art and letters as a bridge across the chasm between the races. Artists of both races, they thought, were more likely to be free of superstition, prejudice, and fear than ordinary men. They might meet on the common ground of shared beauty and artistic passion. . . . Despite a history that divided them, art and culture would re-form the brotherhood in a common humanity."[26]

Burleigh's use of the term *re-birth* in his 1924 address to the NAACP indicates that he shared the optimism and sense of renewed opportunity for African American creative artists that characterized the Harlem Renaissance: "To my mind the most distinctive growth that we have made is the re-birth of the spiritual. I say re-birth because it has been hidden, it has been disguised, it has been caricatured." In his closing remarks, Burleigh said, "A renaissance is coming and we are coming into our own." He went on to discuss the importance of the artistic transformation of the spirituals and to affirm their value: "So I want you to have a deeper reverence for them and feel that they are something no one can take away from us. Be ready to give a reason why they are priceless and precious to you, why you believe they represent the truest expression of the race artistically." And in a phrase he often quoted, "They do more than that—they are our greatest evidence of a spiritual ascendency over oppression and humiliation."[27]

In these remarks Burleigh allied himself with the early leaders of the Harlem Renaissance. In fact, in his preface to *The Second Book of Negro Spirituals,* published in 1926, James Weldon Johnson went so far as to say that Burleigh's work had been "the principal factor" in reclaiming the spiritual as a universally valuable artistic expression. This process had to a significant degree helped the literary artists of the Renaissance develop a black aesthetic. The emergence of these artists, "zealous to be racial, or to put it better, to be true to themselves, to look for their artistic material within rather than without, got its first impulse . . . from the new evaluation of the spiritual reached by the Negro himself. Almost suddenly the realization broke upon the Negro that in the spirituals the race had produced one of the finest examples of folk-art in the world. The result was a leaping pride, coupled with a consciousness of innate racial talents and powers, that gave a rise to a new school of Negro artists."[28] The "new vogue" that the spirituals enjoyed crowned "long and steady development in the recognition of their worth." But the accumulating interest and pride in the spirituals had finally released new levels of creativity among African American artists.[29]

Another significant tribute to Burleigh and his work was Natalie Curtis Burlin's dedication of her fourth book of *Negro Folk-Songs, The Hampton Series* (several phrases of which Burleigh sometimes quoted in his speeches and articles about spirituals). Burlin wrote, "Negro music in America has had as one of its prophets and standard-bearers a colored artist of great dignity, simplicity and worth: Henry T. Burleigh, singer and composer. . . . Nor did Burleigh's association with the best in art ever lead him away from the music of his race. On the contrary, it is he . . . who has steadily upheld the value and beauty of true Negro music. On his concert programs, along with the songs of great composers, he has always placed a group of the old Negro Spirituals, thus telling the world that this racial music of his people is worthy to be heard beside the great songs of Art. Nor has he ever shared that instinctive turning away from the old melodies that has characterized many modern colored people. For to him the Spirituals were not to be looked down on and

A 1931 photo of Burleigh inscribed to Alston. (Courtesy of the Burleigh Family)

willfully ignored as reminders of a condition of servitude, but rather to be revered . . . as living proof of a race's spiritual ascendancy over oppression and humiliation."[30]

"Never has Henry Burleigh sunk the high standard of his art or commercialized the sacred heritage of his people's song. Quietly, unassumingly, but with singular strength of purpose and conviction he has fought for and won a foremost place among the great artists of America, taking with him the Negro folk-song. As singer he is known on the concert platforms of our finest musical organizations, and as composer of songs and choruses his name is found on programs throughout the country."[31]

"The Negro race in America looks to Henry Burleigh with no greater respect than does the white race which acclaims him as one of the modest builders of a truly American art. . . . For the fact that better days are now dawning for Negro artists in America is due in no small degree to the example of Burleigh, and to the perseverance and devotion of all these pioneers who through sacrifice and struggle are trying to lift the standard of the Negro musician and to help dissolve the 'color-line' through Art."[32]

The Harlem Renaissance has been studied extensively as a literary and visual arts movement, but a number of scholars have pointed out the importance of music as more than peripheral, in fact, as having made the Harlem Renaissance possible. As Samuel A. Floyd Jr. writes, "It should be remembered . . . that although Harlem's literary movement 'began to be recognized in 1924 black *music* was in ascendancy much earlier." Indeed, it "had its beginnings, even before the turn of the century, in towns and cities all across the United States."[33] The many musicians who were Burleigh's contemporaries and immediate successors were producing and performing a wide range of music across the country and taking it to the Caribbean, South America, and Europe years before the official call went out to bring artists to Harlem. "The Harlem Renaissance has been treated primarily as a literary movement, with occasional asides, contributed as musical spice, about the jazz age and the performances of concert artists. But music's role was much more basic and important to the movement. In fact, the stance of the black leadership and scattered brief comments about music during the period suggest the primacy of music to Renaissance philosophy and practice." Indeed, "despite its obvious importance to the Renaissance, black music was taken for granted because it had always been a pathbreaker and a central part of black culture."[34] In his insightful book *The New Negroes and Their Music: The Success of the Harlem Renaissance,* Jon Michael Spencer quotes Martin Blum's analysis that "black music not only contributed to and benefited from the Renaissance but in fact spearheaded it by example."[35]

* * *

Burleigh's mastery in arranging African American spirituals is still recognized a century after they first entered American music art song repertoire. His art songs, much less well known, are earning new respect, as singers discover them in libraries and archives and publishers reissue them. The proliferation of recordings of his songs and spiritual arrangements continues. On programs and recordings of American song, his choral arrangements of spirituals are a mainstay, and his solo arrangements are a staple in anthologies of songs for singers in training. As his pathbreaking work as singer-recitalist, art song composer, mentor, and music editor is more fully understood, he will take his place as a significant figure in American musical culture.

Perhaps the most apt tribute comes from Burleigh's friend and frequent collaborator, Will Marion Cook. The first part of his statement about their time at the National Conservatory of Music (that Dvořák didn't like Cook, but Burleigh was his pet) has often been quoted, but the words that followed are of greater significance: "I know of no Negro (not even Coleridge-Taylor) during the last 50 years so respected, so loved—and who has done so much to lift his and my God forsaken Race out of the mire as has this grand old man—Harry T. Burleigh."[36]

Notes

Abbreviations

BTWP   Booker T. Washington Papers
CBMR   Center for Black Music Research
CHS   Connecticut Historical Society
ECHS   Erie County Historical Society
LOC   Library of Congress
MRSC   Moorland-Spingarn Research Center, Howard University

Chapter 1. Hamilton Waters and the Struggle for Freedom and Education

1. Copy of the manumission papers, ECHS, Harry Thacker Burleigh Collection, Coll. 3, Box 4, ff 74.

2. Karen James, interview, July 26, 2001, Erie, PA.

3. Somerset County Court (Certificates of Freedom), 1835 MSA C1744–2.

4. "The Harry T. Burleigh Family Chronology," Burleigh Society Website, www .burleighsociety.org.

5. New York *Colored American,* May 30, 1840, 1.

6. Henry Beckett, "A Mighty Voice at 77," New York *Post,* Apr. 24, 1944, n.p.

7. St. James A.M.E.Z. website, www.stjamesithaca.org/History.htm; thanks to Karen James for alerting me to this source.

8. Karen James, telephone conversation, June 3, 2005.

9. Items in the New York *Age,* e.g., Dec. 26, 1891.

10. *Christian Defender,* Oct. 28, 1865; courtesy of Karen James.

11. Anne Key Simpson, "The Amateur Historian at Work: Norman Tyler Sobel and Harry T. Burleigh." *Journal of Erie Studies,* 16 (Spring 1987): 63–69.

12. Burleigh Family Bible; John Claridge letter to John Marsh, Sept. 23, 1980, ECHS, Harry Thacker Burleigh Collection, Coll. 3, Box 5, ff 85. Information on Lansing, New York, was given Karen James by a relative of John Elmendorf, Burleigh's stepfather.

13. *Erie Business Directory, 1868–1869,* 7.

14. "Timeline," Burleigh Society Website; James interview; James, personal communication, July 13, 2002, and June 3, 2005.

15. S. B. Nelson, *Nelson's Biographical Dictionary and Historical Reference Book of Erie County* (Erie, PA: printed by author, 1896), 742.

16. Ibid.

17. Burleigh Family Bible.

18. Interview with Karen James, June 6, 2007.

19. James conversation, July 2002.

20. Erica Erwin, "A History of Erie's Bayfront" and "History: A Peek at Erie Waterfront's Past," Erie *Times News,* June 1, 2003, 1A, 8A.

21. Burleigh Society Website.

22. Eric Ledell Smith, "The End of Black Voting Rights in Pennsylvania: African Americans and the Pennsylvania Constitutional Convention of 1837–1838." *Pennsylvania History* 65, no. 3 (Summer 1998): 279–99.

23. Burleigh Society Website.

24. Ibid.

25. Charter of the United Benevolent Society, Erie County Courthouse, Room 121, Deed Book 10, p. 310.

26. William Himrod Jr. remarks made at the thirty-seventh anniversary of the Himrod Mission, 1876, Himrod Collection, ECHS, Historical Museum and Planetarium Archives, Reference Files, "Himrod Mission—Methodist," Box 15, ff 1.

27. Ibid.

28. John Diehl, "Harry Burleigh, Tenor [*sic*], Is Son [*sic*] of Former Slave," Erie *Daily Herald,* Apr. 10, 1931, 25.

29. Records of the Himrod School, ECHS, Himrod Collection, ECHS, Historical Museum and Planetarium Archives, Reference Files, "Himrod Mission—Methodist"; "Half a Century," Erie *Morning Dispatch,* Dec. 18, 1889.

30. Himrod Collection, ECHS.

31. Karen James, *Timeline,* 2001, unpublished.

32. Ibid.

33. Sarah S. Thompson, *Journey from Jerusalem: An Illustrated Introduction to Erie's African American History, 1795–1995* (Erie, PA: Erie County Historical Society, 1996), 19, 20.

34. Ibid., 20.

35. Ibid., 20.

36. James, *Timeline*; James interview, 2001.

37. *Nelson's Biographical Dictionary,* 742.

38. Erie *Observer,* Oct. 12, 1850, 2.

39. *Erie City Directory, 1859–1860,* 37–38.

40. John Miller, *A Twentieth Century History of Erie County, Pennsylvania. A Narrative Account of its Historical Progress, Its People, and Its Principal Interests*), vol. 1 (Chicago: Lewis, 1909), 315, 319.

41. Frank Severance, "Underground Trails," *Old Trails on the Niagara Frontier* (Buffalo: printed by author, 1899), 255.

42. James conversations, 2001 and 2005.

43. Miller, *Twentieth Century History,* vol. 1, 871.

44. Ibid., 871–72.

45. Ibid., 872.

46. *1853–1854 Erie City Directory,* 66; *Nelson's Biographical Dictionary,* 742.

47. Miller, *Twentieth-Century History,* vol. 1, 129.

48. *Nelson's Biographical Dictionary,* 742.

49. Ibid.

50. James, 2001 interview.

51. Saul Sack, *History of Education in Pennsylvania,* vol. 1 (Harrisburg: Pennsylvania Historical and Museum Commission, 1963), 167.

52. See, for example, the 1895 eighth-grade graduation examination from Salinas, Kansas, on Snopes.com, http://www.snopes.com/language/document/1895exam.asp.

53. Conversations with my husband, John G. Burt, who has lectured frequently on abolition in western Pennsylvania as a member of the Pennsylvania Commonwealth Speaker's Bureau and for other events.

54. John G. Burt, "Poet of the Iron City: Charles P. Shiras (1824–1854)," *Carnegie Magazine* 67 (Jan.–Feb. 1987), 20–22, 25.

55. John Greenleaf Whittier to Julius LeMoyne and Charles Francis Adams to Julius LeMoyne, Correspondence of Dr. Julius LeMoyne, Washington County Historical Society, Washington, Pennsylvania.

56. Burt, "Poet of the Iron City," 20, 25.

57. Sack, *History of Education in Pennsylvania,* vol. 1, 167; Erasmus Wilson, *Standard History of Pittsburg* [*sic*], *Pennsylvania* (Chicago: H. R. Cornell, 1898), 518.

58. Pittsburgh *Gazette,* Jan. 23, 1850.

59. Greater Pittsburgh Convention and Visitors Bureau, *Visit Pittsburgh* (n.d.), http://www.visitpittsburgh.com/about-pittsburgh/. See esp. "Pittsburgh History," "Underground Railroad," "Demolished Sites," "Allegheny Institute and Mission Church."

60. Sack, *History of Education in Pennsylvania,* vol. 1, 168.

61. "Twin City News," "Avery College to Be Made an Industrial School," Cleveland *Gazette,* Dec, 10, 1887, 1; "Allegheny City News," Cleveland *Gazette,* Sept. 8, 1888.

62. Alexander L. Murray, "*The Provincial Freeman:* A New Source for the History of the Negro in Canada and the United States," *Journal of Negro History* 44 (1959), 133; Victor Uhlman, *Martin R. Delany: The Beginnings of Black Nationalism* (Boston: Beacon Press, 1971), 187.

63. Pittsburgh *Gazette,* Jan. 23, 1850.

64. Norman Sobel notes, ECHS, Harry Thacker Burleigh Collection, Coll. 3, Box 1, ff 13; Charlotte W. Murray, "The Story of Harry T. Burleigh," *The Hymn,* vol. 17 (Oct. 1966), 101–2.

65. Burt, "Poet of the Iron City," 22; Ed Yates, "'Underground Rail Road' Exists in Northside," Pittsburgh *Post-Gazette,* Jan. 12, 1957.

66. Pittsburgh *Gazette,* July 12, 1855, 1.

67. "Local Paragraphs," Erie *Weekly Gazette,* July 19, 1855, 2.

68. Lester A. Walton, "Harry T. Burleigh Honored To-Day at St. George's," New York *World,* Mar. 30, 1924. Reprinted in *The Black Perspective in Music* 2 (Spr. 1974): 81.

69. She is listed as "Lizzie Burley, janitress" in the 1874–1875 *Erie City Directory,* 161.

70. Bessie is listed as a teacher in P.S. 1 in the 1901 *Erie City Directory,* 542; the 1903 *Erie City Directory,* 29; and the 1904 *Erie City Directory,* 511; James conversation.

Chapter 2. The Family and Community That Shaped Burleigh's Youth

1. Sarah S. Thompson, *Journey from Jerusalem: An Illustrated Introduction to Erie's African American History, 1795–1995* (Erie, PA: Erie County Historical Society, 1996), 27.

2. "Timeline," Burleigh Society Website.

3. "The President's Response to Horace Greeley," Erie *Weekly Dispatch,* Aug. 28, 1862, 2.

4. James M. McPherson, *Battle Cry of Freedom: The Civil War Era* (New York: Oxford University Press, 1988), 557–63; Stephen A. Wynalda, *365 Days in Abraham Lincoln's Presidency: The Private, Political, and Military Decisions of America's Greatest President* (New York: Skyhorse, 2010), 179–80; 197–98; 237–38.

5. Burley's leadership in the Colored School, Karen James, July 26, 2001, interview; the marriage and this child's birth and death, Burleigh Family Bible (in the custody of Burleigh's great-nephew, John Marshall).

6. Thompson, *Journey from Jerusalem,* 27.

7. Burleigh Society Website; *Erie Business Directory, 1868–1869,* 160.

8. Burleigh Society Website.

9. Cleveland *Gazette,* Nov. 24, 1883, 3; "Erie's News," Cleveland *Gazette,* Oct. 1, 1887, 3; Nora Douglas Holt, "St. George's Fete Harry Burleigh, Soloist at Church for 50 Years"; "Tribute to His Mother," New York *Amsterdam News,* Feb. 5, 1944, 1A.

10. John Miller, *A Twentieth Century History of Erie County, Pennsylvania* (Chicago: Lewis, 1909), 1:310; founding of St. Paul's, "notes from memory of an address by Dean Blodgett in memory of C. H. Strong," n.d., St. Paul's Parish files, Parish Office.

11. Text of presentation by Sarah Reed, Mar. 15, 1927, St. Paul's Parish files, Parish Office.

12. St. Paul's Parish files, Parish Office.

13. "Harry Burleigh, Singer-Composer and Churchman," *Forth* (Apr. 1944): 18–19.

14. Minutes of the Women's Friendly Society, St. Paul's Parish files, Parish Office.

15. T. W. Shacklett, "History of Saint Paul's—Erie, Pa., Read at the Centennial of That Parish, March 15, 1927," Erie *Herald,* Mar. 20, 1927, 10 C.

16. "Another Sudden Death," Erie *Weekly Gazette,* Feb. 27, 1873, 3.

17. Cleveland *Gazette,* July 1, 1893; Cleveland *Gazette,* Oct. 7, 1893; "Mr. Albert Vosburg Dead," Cleveland *Gazette,* Jan. 9, 1897, 2.

18. Erie *Weekly Gazette,* Mar. 9, 1871, 3.

19. Thompson, *Journey from Jerusalem,* 27; Burleigh Society Website.

20. Burleigh Society Website; conversation with Karen James.

21. *Southern Michigan Railroad,* "Our History," http://southernmichiganrailroad.com/about/our-history.html; Erie *Dispatch,* Feb. 25, 1873.

22. "Sudden Death: Harry T. Burleigh, of This City, Falls Dead—Heart Disease," Erie *Morning Dispatch,* Feb 25, 1873, 4; Erie *Observer,* Feb. 27, 1873; "Another Sudden Death," Erie *Weekly Gazette,* Feb. 27, 1873, 3.

23. Burleigh Society Website.

24. *1873–1874 Erie City Directory,* 97; *1874–1875 Erie City Directory,* 161.

25. Cleveland *Gazette,* May 3, 1863; Thompson, *Journey from Jerusalem,* 27; "He Should Receive the Appointment," Cleveland *Gazette,* Apr. 29, 1889.

26. *1871–1872 Erie City Directory,* 84; *1873–1874 Erie City Directory,* 110.

27. Burleigh Society Website.

28. Lester A. Walton, "Harry T. Burleigh Honored To-Day at St. George's," New York *World,* Mar. 30, 1924. Reprinted in *Black Perspective in Music* 2 (Spr. 1974): 81.

29. Photograph, Burleigh Family Papers.

30. Holt, "St. George's Fete Harry Burleigh." On the importance of Aunt Louisa's encouragement, see "How Harry T. Burleigh Rose to Fame and Fortune," *New Deal*, n.d., 1930s, 9, Burleigh folder, Vertical File, Erie County Public Library.

31. "Died: Waters," Obituaries, Erie *Morning Dispatch*, Feb. 7, 1877, 4; *Christian Recorder*, July 17, 1877.

32. "'The Palms' Sung by Burleigh for 41st Year at St. George's," New York *Herald*, Apr. 15, 1935.

33. Interview with Grace Elmendorf Blackwell, Mar. 25, 2000, Newark, New Jersey.

34. Telephone interview with Grace Blackwell, Dec. 14, 2008; untitled note, Cleveland *Gazette*, Oct. 10, 1890.

35. Karen James, personal communication; photograph, Burleigh Family Papers.

36. Erie *Morning Dispatch*, Mar. 29, 1886, 4; Erie *Morning Dispatch*, Dec. 20, 1886.

37. "Literary Entertainment," Cleveland *Gazette*, Oct. 29, 1885.

38. "Washington's Birthday Celebrated at the People's College," Erie *Morning Dispatch*, Feb. 20, 1886, 3.

39. See, for example, "Special Concert Engagement," Erie *Morning Dispatch*, Jan. 17, 1887, 4; "Clark's College Opening," Erie *Morning Dispatch*, Sept. 2, 1884, 4; "The Debate Last Night," Erie *Morning Dispatch*, May 23, 1885, 4.

40. "At Clark's College," Erie *Morning Dispatch*, Feb. 20, 1886, 3.

41. Erie *Morning Dispatch*, Aug. 20, 1886; "Brief Mention," Erie *Morning Dispatch*, Nov. 28, 1885, 4.

42. "Students Well Entertained," Erie *Morning Dispatch*, Apr. 15, 1889, 4.

43. "Y.M.C.A. Convention," Erie *Morning Dispatch*, Jan. 23, 1886, 4.

44. "Literary Meeting," Erie *Morning Dispatch*, Jan. 22, 1886; "Young Men's Debating Society," Erie *Morning Dispatch*, June 23, 1887; "The Y.M.C.A. Reception," Erie *Morning Dispatch*, Jan. 2, 1888; "Y.M.C.A. Notes," Erie *Morning Dispatch*, Apr. 15, 1889, 4.

45. "Commencement Day," Erie *Morning Dispatch*, June 24, 1887.

46. Ibid.

47. Ibid.

48. "He Should Receive the Appointment," Cleveland *Gazette*, May 29, 1889; "'Republican' Treatment," Cleveland *Gazette*, Dec. 21, 1889.

49. Unidentified Erie paper, May 25, 1889, reprinted in Cleveland *Gazette*; "He Should Receive the Appointment," Cleveland *Gazette*, May 29, 1889.

50. "He Should Receive the Appointment," Cleveland *Gazette*, May 29, 1889.

51. "'Republican' Treatment," Cleveland *Gazette*, Dec. 21, 1889.

52. Ibid.

53. Karen James, personal communication.

54. "News of Greater New York," New York *Age*, June 24, 1915, 8.

55. James, 2001 Timeline.

56. "Ho! For the Head," Erie *Morning Dispatch*, May 26, 1885, 4.

57. "Mr. Hicks Adds a New Store," Erie *Morning Dispatch*, Dec. 20, 1889, 8.

58. "Later Local Briefs," Erie *Morning Dispatch*, Aug. 17, 1887, 4.

59. *New Deal*, ca. 1930, 9.

60. S. B. Nelson, *Nelson's Biographical Dictionary and Historical Reference Book of Erie County* (Erie, PA: S. B. Nelson, 1896), 742; "Grace Mission Entertainment," Erie *Morning*

Dispatch, June 10, 1881, 3; "Erie Notes," Cleveland *Gazette,* Sept. 10, 1887; "Concert and Social," Erie *Morning Dispatch,* Nov. 2, 1890.

61. *New Deal,* 9.

62. "A Grand Success," Cleveland *Gazette,* Aug. 15, 1891.

63. "Erie Notes," Cleveland *Gazette,* Dec. 6, 1890; New York *Age,* Sept. 5, 1891; "Erie Notes," Cleveland *Gazette,* Oct. 8, 1892; Marriage to F. E. Williamson, St. Paul's Parish Records, Parish Office; Burleigh Family Bible; Burleigh's financial assistance to her, Karen James, 2001.

64. St. Paul's Records, Parish Office.

65. Identified by Karen James; F. J. Bassett Glassplate Negative Collection, Neg. No. 3464, ECHS.

66. Resolution on "the death of our beloved member, Mrs. Elmendorf," Minutes of the Women's Friendly Society, St. Paul's Parish Office.

67. Erie *Morning Dispatch,* July 9, 1899.

68. Monica Marshall Wilson, the daughter of Bessie's grandson John Marshall, reports that Elizabeth was the first psychiatric patient at Hamot Hospital, personal communication, Oct. 2, 1996.

69. Adrienne Rush, then a child, tried to call attention to the importance of this house, but was not taken seriously; personal communication, Feb. 22 and Mar. 16, 2014.

70. Cleveland *Gazette,* Mar. 12, 1892, from Erie *Daily Times,* June 18, 1892.

71. For example, "A.M.E. Picnic," Erie *Morning Dispatch,* Sept. 1, 1881; "Necktie Social," Erie *Morning Dispatch,* Jan. 24, 1884, 3; "Late Local Briefs," Erie *Morning Dispatch,* Aug. 14, 1889, 4; "Erie Notes," Cleveland *Gazette,* Sept. 22, 1883.

72. Burleigh Society Website; "Erie Notes," Cleveland *Gazette,* Sept. 22, 1883; "Erie Notes," Cleveland *Gazette,* May 6, 1893; "Erie Notes," Cleveland *Gazette,* Sept. 2, 1893.

73. "Erie Notes," Cleveland *Gazette,* Nov. 28, 1891.

74. "Don't Approve Dancing," Cleveland *Gazette,* Dec. 12, 1891.

75. Cleveland *Gazette,* Aug. 11, 1894.

76. On the continuity between secret societies in African culture and the importance of the Black Masons, see Samuel A. Floyd Jr., *The Power of Black Music: Interpreting Its History from Africa to the United States* (New York: Oxford University Press, 1995), 82.

77. Erie *Daily Times,* Dec. 11, 1891, 4.

78. "A Prominent Colored Society," Erie *Morning Dispatch,* Mar. 13, 1891, 7; Cleveland *Gazette,* Apr. 11, 1891; Re Upper Ten, Cleveland *Gazette,* Feb. 2, 1892.

79. Cleveland *Gazette,* Oct. 17, 1891.

80. Cleveland *Gazette,* July 4, 1891; "A Grand Success," Cleveland *Gazette,* Aug. 15, 1891.

81. "Cleveland Notes," Cleveland *Gazette,* June 22, 1895.

82. Kenneth Kusmer, *A Ghetto Takes Shape: Black Cleveland, 1870–1930* (Urbana: University of Illinois Press, 1976), 132.

Chapter 3. Burleigh's Music Experience and Training in Erie

1. Henry Lee, "Swing Low, Sweet Chariot," *Coronet* 22 (July 1947): 55.

2. John G. Carney, *Tales of Old Erie* (Erie, PA: printed by author, 1958), 235–37.

3. Ibid., 227.

4. Ibid., 230, 236–37.

5. Ibid., 236–37.

6. Lester A. Walton, "Harry T. Burleigh Honored To-Day at St. George's," New York *World*, May 30, 1924. Reprinted in *The Black Perspective in Music* 2 (Spr. 1974): 81.

7. Letter from Fannie Moorhead to Anne Key Simpson, Jan. 1, 1986. ECHS, Harry Thacker Burleigh Collection, Coll. 3, Box 5, ff 87.

8. Walton, "Harry T. Burleigh Honored To-Day," 81.

9. Letter from ECHS archivist Helen Andrews to Norman Sobel, Dec. 29, 1976. ECHS, Harry Thacker Burleigh Collection, Coll. 3, Box 1, ff 1.

10. Marien Dieterman, "Great Revival of Music," Erie *Daily Herald,* June 9, 1944, 1.

11. Alain Locke, *The Negro and His Music* (Washington, DC: Associates in Negro Folk Education, 1936), 18–19; Willard Gatewood, *Aristocrats of Color: The Black Elite, 1880–1920* (Bloomington: Indiana University Press, 1990), 113–14.

12. Robert Stevenson, "America's First Black Music Historian," *Journal of the American Musicological Society* 22 (Fall 1973): 396.

13. Daniel Payne, *Recollections of Seventy Years* (1888; repr., New York: Arno Press and the New York Times, 1969), 93 and 233–38; and Daniel Payne, *History of the African Methodist Episcopal Church,* vol. 1, (Nashville, TN: Publishing House of the A.M.E. Sunday-School Union, 1891), 452–59.

14. Barbara Hawley, "Harry Burleigh Observes 40th Palm Sunday," Erie *Daily Herald,* Apr. 1, 1934, 1; "Harry Burleigh, Tenor [*sic*] Is Son [*sic*] of Former Slave," Erie *Dispatch Herald,* Apr. 10, 1931, n.p.

15. Erie *Morning Dispatch*, Aug. 20, 1886.

16. Advertisement and feature article, "The Hampton Singers Tonight," Erie *Morning Dispatch,* Apr. 20, 1875, 4.

17. Karen James, 2002, and June 12, 2007.

18. "The Hyers Sisters," Erie *Morning Dispatch,* Dec. 31, 1881; "The Callender Minstrels," Erie *Morning Dispatch*, Mar. 27, 1884, 1; "Brief Mention," Erie *Morning Dispatch,* March 20, 1884; "The Minstrels," Erie *Morning Dispatch,* March 25, 1884, 3.

19. Lynne Abbot and Doug Seroff, *Out of Sight: The Rise of African American Popular Music, 1889–1895* (Jackson: University Press of Mississippi, 2002), xi, 44.

20. Eileen Southern, "Black Musicians and Early Ethiopian Minstrelsy," in *Inside the Minstrel Mask: Readings in Nineteenth-Century Blackface Minstrelsy,* ed. Annemarie Bean, James V. Hatch, and Brooks McNamara (Hanover, NH: Wesleyan University Press, 1996), 43.

21. Eugene Levy, *James Weldon Johnson: Black Leader, Black Voice* (Chicago: University of Chicago Press, 1973), 81, 89, 91–93.

22. "The Tennesseans," Erie *Morning Dispatch,* Jan. 15 1884; "The Callender Minstrels," Erie *Morning Dispatch,* Mar. 27, 1884; "Wallace King, the Tenor," Cleveland *Gazette,* May 1, 1886; "Music and the Stage," "Negro on the Stage," New York *Age,* Nov. 24, 1910, 6; John Graziano, "The Early Life and Career of the 'Black Patti': The Odyssey of an African American Singer in the Late Nineteenth Century," *Journal of the American Musicological Society* (Fall 2000), 543–96.

23. "Amusements: The Tennesseean Singers," Erie *Morning Dispatch,* Jan. 12, 1884, 3.

24. "The Tennesseans," Erie *Morning Dispatch,* Jan. 15, 1884, 3.

25. "The Callender Minstrels," Erie *Morning Dispatch,* Mar. 27, 1884, 1.

26. Eileen Southern, "An Early Black Concert Company: The Hyers Sisters Combination," In *A Celebration of American Music: Words and Music in Honor of H. Wiley Hitchcock,* ed. Richard Crawford, R. Allen Lott, and Carol J. Oja (Ann Arbor: University of Michigan Press, 1990), 25, 31.

27. Grace Overmyer, "Harry Thacker Burleigh," *Famous American Composers* (New York: Thomas Y. Crowell, 1944), 130; Sarah Ball letter, Aug. 12, 1956, ECHS, Harry Thacker Burleigh Collection, Coll. 3, Box 2, ff. 57, ECHS.

28. Bill Campbell, "Harry T. Burleigh Contributed Much," Erie *News,* Aug. 12, 1961. Burleigh Folder, Vertical File, Erie County Public Library. (This date, written in ink on the clipping, is inaccurate. The correct date has not been found.)

29. "Local Department: Grace Mission Entertainment," Erie *Morning Dispatch,* June 10, 1881, 3.

30. Cleveland *Gazette,* Nov. 24, 1883, 3.

31. Frank S. Anderson, *A History of the School District of the City of Erie, Pennsylvania, 1795–1970* (Erie, PA: School District of Erie, 1976), 52.

32. "His Little Hatchet," Erie *Morning Dispatch*, Feb. 17, 1885, 4.

33. From a survey of church bulletins from February to August 1899, seven years after Burleigh left Erie, but the music was directed by the same organist and choir director, St. Paul's Parish Office.

34. "Musical Taste," *St. Paul's Parish Guide,* Apr. 1873, 30, St. Paul's Parish Office.

35. Burleigh Society Website.

36. "Longfellow Day," Erie *Morning Dispatch,* Mar. 25, 1885, 4.

37. Ibid.

38. "Y.M.C.A. Quarterly Meeting," Erie *Morning Dispatch,* Feb. 29, 1888.

39. ECHS, Harry Thacker Burleigh Collection, Coll. 3, Box 5, ff 95; Maurice Peress, *Dvorak to Duke Ellington: A Conductor Explores America's Music and Its African American Roots* (New York: Oxford University Press, 2004), 22.

40. Anne Key Simpson, *Hard Trials: The Life and Music of Harry T. Burleigh* (Metuchen, NJ: Scarecrow Press, 1990), 20.

41. Erie *Observer,* Jan. 3, 1884; "Parochial Society Entertainment," Erie *Morning Dispatch,* Feb. 18, 1884, 3; Nov. 1, 1884.

42. Carney, *Old Erie,* 225.

43. "To-Morrow's Concert: The Orpheus Programme for Tuesday's Entertainment," Erie *Morning Dispatch*, Dec. 8, 1884, 3; "A Singing Class," Erie *Morning Dispatch,* Jan. 5, 1885, 4; "Personal," Erie *Morning Dispatch*, Jan. 12, 1885, 3.

44. Cleveland *Gazette,* Oct. 1, 1887.

45. For example, "Madame Rivé-King," Erie *Morning Dispatch,* June 5, 1886; "The Sternberg Concert," Erie *Morning Dispatch,* Nov. 1, 1886; "The Scherzo Society," Erie *Morning Dispatch,* Nov. 16, 1886; "The Maas Recital," Erie *Morning Dispatch,* Mar. 5, 1887, 4.

46. "This, That and the Other," Erie *Morning Dispatch,* Feb. 18, 1882, 4.

47. "The Joseffy Recital," Erie *Morning Dispatch,* Apr. 27, 1886, 4.

48. A. Walter Kramer, "H. T. Burleigh, Composer by Divine Right," *Musical America,* Apr. 29, 1916, 25.

49. Ibid.

50. "Brief Mention," Erie *Morning Dispatch,* May 7, 1885, 4. A careful survey of the Erie *Morning Dispatch* reveals some discrepancies in Burleigh's account. Joseffy's first musicale

in the Russell home took place on Easter Monday evening, April 26, 1886; the temperature that evening was 48° Fahrenheit, considerably warmer than Burleigh described. Also, Teresa Carreño's first musicale performance in the Russell home was a year earlier, in May 1885. But this narrative, which Burleigh told thirty years later, with its sequel in Mrs. Frances MacDowell's assistance to him when he auditioned at the National Conservatory of Music in January of 1892, played a defining role in the Burleigh legend.

51. "A Regal Reception," Erie *Morning Dispatch*, Jan. 21, 1881, 4.

52. "Harry Burleigh, Tenor [*sic*], Is Son [*sic*] of Former Slave," Erie *Daily Herald*, Apr. 10, 1931, 25.

53. "A Fine Programme at the Tabernacle This Evening," Erie *Morning Dispatch*, June 5, 1890, 7.

54. "At the Grace Mission," Erie *Morning Dispatch*, Aug. 11, 1886.

55. "Last Night's Concert," Erie *Morning Dispatch*, Apr. 23, 1887, 4.

56. "The Ladies Receive," Erie *Morning Dispatch*, Jan. 4, 4; "C.L.S.C.," Erie *Morning Dispatch*, Jan. 17, 1887.

57. "Public Meeting," Erie *Morning Dispatch*, June 25, 1887, 4.

58. Untitled, Erie *Morning Dispatch*, Oct. 13, 1887, 4.

59. "The Jubilee Singers' Concert," Erie *Morning Dispatch*, May 10, 1888, 4.

60. Ibid.

61. Abbott and Seroff, *Out of Sight*, 42–44, 51, 87, 184, 187–88, 196, 224, 338; Doug Abbott, "'Do Thyself a' No Harm': The 'Only Original New Orleans University Singers,'" *American Music Research Center Journal* 6 (Jan. 1996): 1–47.

62. "Sandusky, O.," Cleveland *Gazette*, Oct. 29, 1887; "Galion, O.," Cleveland *Gazette*, Jan. 28, 1888; "Painesville, O.," Cleveland *Gazette*, Apr. 28, 1888; "Williamsport, Pa.," Cleveland *Gazette*, Oct. 27, 1888; Erie *Morning Dispatch*, Dec. 4, 1888, 8.

63. Advertisement for Fisk Jubilee Singers, Erie *Morning Dispatch*, Dec. 8, 1888, 5.

64. "The Jubilee Concert," Erie *Morning Dispatch*, Dec. 15, 1888.

65. Abbott and Seroff, *Out of Sight*, 3.

66. Ibid.; "Loudin's Fisk Jubilee Singers," Cleveland *Gazette*, Nov. 1, 1890; "Local Department," Cleveland *Gazette*, Apr. 18, 1891, 3; "Cleveland Notes," Cleveland *Gazette*, Feb. 28, 1891, 3; "Cleveland Notes," Cleveland *Gazette*, Apr. 4, 1891, 3; Cleveland *Gazette*, July 27, 1895, 3.

67. "Local Briefs," Erie *Evening Herald*, Sept. 22, 1891, 7.

68. "Local Briefs," Erie *Evening Herald*, Oct. 7, 1891, 2; "Cleveland Notes," Cleveland *Gazette*, Oct. 3, 1891, 3; "Erie, Pa.," Cleveland *Gazette*, Oct. 10, 1891; "Local Department," Cleveland *Gazette*, Sept. 26, 1891, 3.

69. Cleveland *Gazette*, June 7, 1890.

70. "The Year in Retrospect," Erie *Morning Dispatch*, Jan. 1, 1891, 2; "A Pleasant Surprise," Erie *Morning Dispatch*, Jan. 1, 1891. 4.

71. Ibid.

72. "Last of the Season," Erie *Morning Dispatch*, June 12, 1889, 6; "Musical Soiree," Erie *Morning Dispatch*, May 25, 1889, 8; "Thursday's Concert," Erie *Morning Dispatch*, June 10, 1889, 5.

73. "Last of the Season," Erie *Morning Dispatch*, June 12, 1889, 6.

74. "City Items," "Fine Concert," Erie *Morning Dispatch*, Oct. 7, 1889, 8.

75. Cleveland *Gazette*, Oct. 5, 1889, quoting Erie *Daily Times*, Sept. 23, 1889.

76. "Greatest Musicians Living," Erie *Morning Dispatch,* Sept. 11, 1989, 7; "Companini in Opera," Erie *Morning Dispatch,* Sept. 25, 1989, 6; "Park Opera House: The Great Operatic Event," Erie *Morning Dispatch,* Sept. 26, 1889, 6; "Park Opera House: The Evening's Great Concert," Erie *Morning Dispatch,* Sept. 30, 1989, 5; "Park Opera House: Last Evening's Great Musical Entertainment," Erie *Morning Dispatch,* Oct. 1, 1889, 4; Walton, "Burleigh Honored To-Day," 81.

77. "A Good Entertainment," Erie *Morning Dispatch,* Feb. 8, 1890, 8.

78. "The Veterans Rejoice," Erie *Morning Dispatch,* Apr. 11, 1890, 6.

79. Ibid.; "A Fine Programme at the Tabernacle This Evening," Erie *Morning Dispatch,* June 5, 1890, 7; "Half a Century," Erie *Morning Dispatch,* Dec. 19, 1889, 7.

80. Erie *Morning Dispatch,* Feb. 8, 1890; "Late Local Briefs," Erie *Morning Dispatch,* Mar. 10, 1890, 8; "Interesting Services at St. Paul's," Erie *Morning Dispatch,* Mar. 22, 1890, 6; "A Grand Success," Erie *Morning Dispatch,* Mar. 29, 1890, 8; "The Veterans Rejoice," Erie *Morning Dispatch,* Apr. 11, 1890, 6; "Madrigal Club at the Tabernacle," Erie *Morning Dispatch,* Oct. 22, 1890, 7; "Christian Church Entertainment," Erie *Morning Dispatch,* Nov. 7, 1890, 5; "The First Fair," Erie *Morning Dispatch,* Nov. 12, 1890, 8; "Concert and Social," Erie *Morning Dispatch,* Nov. 20, 1890, 5.

81. "Local Department," Cleveland *Gazette,* Apr. 18, 1891, 3; "Buffalo," Cleveland *Gazette,* May 30, 1891.

82. "A Crayon Artist," Cleveland *Gazette,* May 9, 1891, 2.

83. "The Late Mrs. Jos. Johnson," Erie *Evening Herald,* Oct. 19, 1891, 2.

84. "An Obituary Notice," Cleveland *Gazette,* Oct. 31, 1891, 2.

85. Erie *Daily Times,* Dec. 11, 1891, 4.

86. "Cleveland Notes," Cleveland *Gazette,* Aug. 10, 1889; "Cleveland Notes," Cleveland *Gazette,* Jan. 4, 1890; "Cleveland Notes," Cleveland *Gazette,* May 24, 1890; "Cleveland Notes," Cleveland *Gazette,* July, 12, 1890.

87. "The Stage," Indianapolis *Freeman,* Apr. 30, 1892; "The Excelsior's Concert," Cleveland *Gazette,* May 17, 1884.

88. "Cleveland Notes," Cleveland *Gazette,* Aug. 23, 1890, 3; "Cleveland Notes," Cleveland *Gazette,* Sept. 20, 1890, 3; "Cleveland Notes," Cleveland *Gazette,* Feb. 20, 1886, 3.

89. "Buffalo," Cleveland *Gazette,* May 30, 1891.

90. "A Wealthy Resident," Cleveland *Gazette,* Dec. 24, 1892.

91. "A Phenomenal Pianist," Cleveland *Gazette,* May 14, 1887.

92. "Cleveland Notes," Cleveland *Gazette,* Feb. 21, 1891, 3.

93. "Wedding Surprises," "Buffalo," Cleveland *Gazette,* Sept. 5, 1891.

94. Priscilla A. Schechter, *Ida B. Wells-Barnett and American Reform* (Chapel Hill: University of North Carolina Press, 2000), 231, 232, 248.

95. "Cleveland Notes," Cleveland *Gazette,* Feb. 21, 1891, 3; "Cleveland Notes," Cleveland *Gazette,* Sept. 12, 1891, 3.

96. Cleveland *Gazette,* Dec. 16, 1891.

97. "Concert at the Cathedral," Erie *Morning Dispatch,* Dec. 14, 1891, 5.

98. "A Brilliant Success," Erie *Evening Herald,* Dec. 16, 1891, 2; "A Brilliant Success," Erie *Morning Dispatch,* Dec. 16, 1891, 5; "The Cathedral Concert," Erie *Daily Times,* 1.

99. "A Brilliant Success," Erie *Morning Dispatch,* 5.

100. "The Cathedral Concert," Erie *Daily Times,* 1.

101. "A Brilliant Success," Erie *Evening Herald,* Dec. 16, 1891, 2.

102. "A Brilliant Success," Erie *Morning Dispatch,* Dec. 16, 1891, 5.

103. "Gloria in Excelsis," Erie *Evening Herald,* Dec. 24, 1891, 2.

104. "Cleveland Notes," Cleveland *Gazette,* Jan. 9, 1892, 3.

105. "Erie, Pa., Topics," Cleveland *Gazette*, Jan. 9, 1892.

106. Erie *Evening Herald,* Jan. 15, 1892, 5; Abbott and Seroff, *Out of Sight,* 222.

107. "Table Talk," Erie *Evening Herald,* Jan. 15, 1892, 5.

108. "From Bystander," Erie *Evening Herald,* Jan. 16, 1892, 7; "From Bystander," Erie *Evening Herald*, Jan. 23, 1892, 7.

109. "Not Time Enough for a Benefit," Erie *Evening Herald,* Jan. 18, 1892, 7.

110. Erie *Evening Herald,* Jan. 20, 1892, 7; "Table Talk," Erie *Evening Herald*, Jan. 22, 1892, 5; "The Burleigh Subscription," Erie *Morning Dispatch,* Jan. 21, 1892, 3.

111. "City Chit-Chat," Erie *Morning Dispatch,* Jan. 19, 1892, 7.

112. ECHS, Harry Thacker Burleigh Collection, Coll. 3, Box 5, ff 95.

113. "Table Talk," Erie *Evening Herald,* Jan. 15, 1892, 5.

Chapter 4. Burleigh at the National Conservatory of Music

1. "A National School of Opera," Erie *Morning Dispatch,* May 22, 1885.

2. Emanuel Rubin, "Dvořák at the National Conservatory," in *Dvořák in America, 1892–1895*, ed. John C. Tibbets (Portland, OR: Amadeus Press, 1993), 54.

3. Merton Robert Aborn, "The Influence on American Musical Culture of Dvořák's Sojourn in America," Ph.D. diss., Indiana University, 1965, 58.

4. Ezra Schabas, *Theodore Thomas: America's Conductor and Builder of Orchestras, 1835–1905* (Urbana: University of Illinois Press, 1989), 165; Nicolas Slonimsky, "Plush Era in American Concert Life," in *One Hundred Years of Music in America,* ed. Paul Henry Lang (New York: G. Schirmer, 1961), 113; Edward N. Waters, *Victor Herbert: A Life in Music* (New York: Macmillan, 1955), 53.

5. Waters, *Victor Herbert,* 53; Claire L. Purdy, *Victor Herbert: American Music-Master* (New York: Julian Messner, 1962), 150.

6. Rubin, "Dvořák at the National Conservatory," 59.

7. "The National Conservatory of Music of America," *Harper's Weekly,* Dec. 13, 1890, 969.

8. Ibid.

9. Ibid.

10. Ibid.; Rubin, "Dvořák at the National Conservatory," 59, 61–62.

11. "National Conservatory," 969.

12. Ibid.

13. Rubin, "Dvořák at the National Conservatory," 58.

14. "National Conservatory," 969.

15. Ibid., 969, 970.

16. Rubin, "Dvořák at the National Conservatory," 62.

17. Slonimsky, "Plush Era," 114.

18. Ibid.

19. Rubin, "Dvořák at the National Conservatory," 62, 63.

20. Slonimsky, "Plush Era," 112–14; see Louis C. Elson's dismissive discussion in his 1904 *History of American Music* (New York: Macmillan), 119–20.

21. Rubin, "Dvořák at the National Conservatory," 63–64.

22. Ibid., 53, 67–68, 72.

23. "Free Scholarship," Indianapolis *Freeman,* Jan. 30, 1892. Quoted in Abbott and Seroff, 222.

24. Lester A. Walton, "Harry T. Burleigh Honored To-Day at St. George's," New York *World,* Mar. 30, 1924, reprinted in *The Black Perspective in Music* 2, no. 1 (Spring 1974): 82.

25. Ibid., 83.

26. Henry Lee, "Swing Low, Sweet Chariot," *Cornet* 22 (July 1947): 56.

27. Ibid.

28. Maurice Peress, *Dvorak to Duke Ellington: A Conductor Explores America's Music and Its African American Roots* (New York: Oxford University Press, 2004), 22.

29. Anne Key Simpson, *Hard Trials: The Life and Music of Harry T. Burleigh* (Metuchen, NJ: Scarecrow Press, 1990), 10.

30. Henry Beckett, "A Mighty Voice at 77," New York *Post,* Apr. 24, 1944; Lee, "Swing Low," n.p.

31. Charlotte Wallace Murray, "The Story of Harry T. Burleigh," *The Hymn* 17 (Oct. 1966): 104.

32. Rubin, "Dvořák at the National Conservatory," 77, n. 15.

33. Lucien H. White, "In the Realms of Music," New York *Age,* Mar. 31, 1934, 6.

34. Walton, "Harry T. Burleigh Honored," 82.

35. Burleigh Family Papers.

36. Henry T. Finck, *My Adventures in the Golden Age of Music* (New York: Funk and Wagnalls, 1926; repr., New York: Da Capo Press, 1971), 279.

37. *Temple Emanu-El,* "Composers," http://www.emanuelnyc.org/composers.php.

38. Simpson, *Hard Trials,* 61.

39. William K. Kearns, *Horatio Parker, 1863–1919: His Life, Music, and Ideas* (Metuchen, NJ: Scarecrow Press, 1990), 14.

40. "National Conservatory," 969.

41. H. F. P., "Advice on Composition from Rubin Goldmark," "Dvorak as a Teacher," *Musical America,* May 16, 1914, 6.

42. Cleveland *Gazette,* Mar. 19, 1892.

43. "Buffalo," Cleveland *Gazette,* Feb. 21, 1891, 3.

44. Peress, *Dvořák to Duke Ellington,* 204, n. 11.

45. John Graziano, "The Early Life and Career of the 'Black Patti': The Odyssey of an African American Singer in the Late Nineteenth Century," *Journal of the American Musicological Society* (Fall 2000), 571.

46. Simpson, *Hard Trials,* 12.

47. "Honor Burleigh on 39th Year as Church Soloist," Chicago *Defender,* June 3, 1933, 4.

48. For example, Walton, "Harry T. Burleigh Honored To-day," 83.

49. Cleveland *Gazette,* July 30, 1892.

50. Graziano, 570.

51. Ibid.

52. Ibid., 571.

53. Indianapolis *Freeman,* Oct. 15, 1892.

54. Cleveland *Gazette,* Aug. 13, 1892.

55. "Southern Outrages," Cleveland *Gazette,* June 4, 1892.

Chapter 5. Introducing Antonín Dvořák to African American Music

1. "Doings of the Race," Cleveland *Gazette*, Oct. 1, 1892, 1.

2. Graham Melville-Mason, "From London to New York: Dvořák's Introduction to America," in *Dvořák in America, 1892–1895*, ed. John C. Tibbetts (Portland, OR: Amadeus Press, 1993), 30.

3. Emanuel Rubin, "Dvořák at the National Conservatory," in *Dvořák in America*, 55.

4. Nicholas E. Tawa, "Why American Music First Arrived in New England," in *Music and Culture in America, 1861–1918*, ed. Michael Saffle and James R. Heintze (London, England: Routledge, 1998), 147.

5. Claire L. Purdy, *Victor Herbert: American Music-Master* (New York: Julian Messner, 1962), 13.

6. Ibid., 14.

7. John Clapham, *Antonin Dvořák, Musician and Craftsman* (New York: St. Martin's Press, 1966), 3–4.

8. Ibid., 5.

9. Ibid., 6.

10. Ibid., 7.

11. John C. Tibbetts, "The Missing Title Page: Dvořák and the American National Song," in *Music and Culture*, ed. Saffle and Heintze, 347.

12. W. E. B. Du Bois, *The Souls of Black Folk* [1903], ed. Henry Louis Gates and Terri Hume Oliver (New York: W. W. Norton, 1999), 11.

13. Rubin, "Dvořák at the National Conservatory," 67; Joseph Horowitz, *Dvořák in America* (Chicago: Cricket, 2003), 21.

14. John C. Tibbetts, "Dvořák's New York: An American Street Scene," in Tibbetts, ed., *Dvořák in America*, 34.

15. Tibbetts, "A Dvořák American Chronology," in Tibbetts, ed., *Dvořák in America*, 15.

16. Joe Chiffriller, "The Life and Times of Antonin Dvořák," *Town and Village*, Dec. 15, 1983, 16; quoted in Tibbetts, "Dvořák's New York," 35.

17. Maurice Peress, *Dvořák to Duke Ellington: A Conductor Explores America's Music and Its African American Roots* (New York: Oxford University Press, 2004), 204, n. 11; James Huneker, *Steeplejack*, v. 2 (New York: C. Scribner's Sons, 1920), 67–68.

18. "Music and Musicians," Washington *Post*, Jan. 14, 1889, 6.

19. Edward M. Waters, *Victor Herbert: A Life in Music* (New York: Macmillan, 1955), 87.

20. Ibid., 88.

21. Johann Tonsor, "Appendix: Negro Music," in Michael B. Beckerman, *New Worlds of Dvořák: Searching in America for the Composer's Inner Life*, (New York: W. W. Norton, 2003), 229–32.

22. Beckerman, *New Worlds*, 81–82.

23. John Clapham, "Dvořák and the Impact of America," *Music Review* 15, no. 3 (1954): 209.

24. "In New York City—The Rounder—Mr. Harry T. Burleigh and the Toussaint L'Ouverture Club Both Credits to the Race," Cleveland *Gazette*, Nov. 19, 1892.

25. Horowitz, *Dvořák in America*, 33.

26. Milos Šafránek, quoted in Beckerman, *New Worlds*, 130.

27. "'Sweet Chariot' Inspired Anton Dvořák," New York *World Telegram,* Sept. 12, 1941; Hazel Kinscella, *Music on the Air* (New York: Viking, 1934), 205.

28. David Beveridge, "Sophisticated Primitivism: The Significance of Pentatonicism in Dvořák's 'American' Quartet," *Current Musicology* 24 (1977): 25–35.

29. Waters, *Victor Herbert*, 88.

30. Henry T. Finck, *My Adventures in the Golden Age of Music* (New York: Funk and Wagnalls, 1926), 278.

31. Merton Robert Aborn, "The Influence on American Musical Culture of Dvořák's Sojourn in America," Ph.D. diss., Indiana University, 1965, 112.

32. A. Walter Kramer, "H. T. Burleigh: Composer by Divine Right and 'The American Coleridge-Taylor,'" *Musical America,* Apr. 12, 1916, 25.

33. New York *Herald,* May 28, 1893, quoted in Peress, *Dvořák to Duke Ellington*, 204, n. 9.

34. Waters, *Victor Herbert*, 88.

35. Ibid., 87.

36. Charlotte Wallace Murray, "The Story of Harry T. Burleigh," *The Hymn* 17 (Oct. 1966): 103.

37. Peress, *Dvořák to Duke Ellington,* 22.

38. Ibid.

39. "'Sweet Chariot.'"

40. Tibbetts, "A Dvořák American Chronology," in *Dvořák in America*, 18.

41. Murray, 104.

42. Paul Stefan, *Antonin Dvořák*, trans. Y. W. Vance (1941; repr., New York: Da Capo, 1971), 31.

43. Camille Zeckwer, "Dvořák as I Knew Him," *Etude,* Nov. 1919, quoted in Peress, *Dvořák to Duke Ellington,* 23.

44. "'Sweet Chariot.'"

45. Tibbetts, "Missing Title Page," 343.

46. Zeckwer, "Dvořák as I Knew Him," 694.

47. Edward N. Waters, *Victor Herbert: A Life in Music* (New York: Macmillan, 1955), 88.

48. Stefan, *Antonin Dvořák*, 207; Beckerman, *New Worlds,* 25–39.

49. Beckerman, *New Worlds,* 33.

50. Stefan, *Antonin Dvořák*, 213.

51. "The Real Value of Negro Melodies," Tibbetts, "Appendix A: Newspaper and Magazine Articles," *Dvořák in America*, 355–56.

52. Beckerman, *New Worlds,* 99–103.

53. Tibbetts, "Appendix A: Newspaper and Magazine Articles," *Dvořák in America*, 358.

54. Ibid.

55. Peress, *Dvořák to Duke Ellington,* 22.

56. "Dvořák on Negro Melodies," New York *Herald*, May 28, 1893; "Direct Testimony: Items from January to June, 1893," *From the New World: A Celebrated Composer's American Odyssey*, Robert Winter and Peter Bogdanoff, DVD, ArtsInteractive.org, 2010.

57. Peress, *Dvořák to Duke Ellington,* 24.

58. Marva Carter, *Swing Along: The Musical Life of Will Marion Cook* (New York: Oxford University Press, 2008), 19.

59. Peress, *Dvořák to Duke Ellington*, 25.

60. Ibid., 15 and 16.

61. *Southern Workman* 22 (Nov. 1893): 174.

62. Ibid.

63. Ibid.

64. Ibid.

65. Tibbetts, "Appendix A: Newspaper and Magazine Articles," *Dvořák in America,* 359.

66. Ibid., 360.

67. Peress, *Dvořák to Duke Ellington,* 24.

68. Tibbetts, *Dvořák in America,* 17.

69. Ibid., 84.

70. Ibid., 88–89.

71. "From Bell Stand to Throne Room," *Etude,* Feb. 1934, 79–80.

72. "In the Opera 'Faust,'" Cleveland *Gazette,* Feb. 11, 1893.

73. "Erie Notes," Cleveland *Gazette,* Apr. 22, 1893.

74. "Woman's World," Indianapolis *Freeman,* Apr. 22, 1893; "Doings of the Race," Cleveland *Gazette,* June 2, 1894, 1; Ida B. Wells-Barnett, *Crusade for Justice: The Autobiography of Ida B. Wells,* ed. Alfreda M. Duster (Chicago: University of Chicago Press, 1970), 115.

75. "A Young Afro-American Honored," Cleveland *Gazette,* June 3, 1893.

76. Cleveland *Gazette,* May 27, 1893.

77. "Personal Pencillings," Erie *Morning Dispatch,* June 8, 1893.

78. "Children's Day Services," Erie *Morning Dispatch,* June 12, 1893.

79. "The Cathedral Concert," Erie *Morning Dispatch,* July 12, 1893.

80. "The Benefit Concert," Erie *Morning Dispatch,* July 17, 1893.

81. "A Pleasing Concert," Erie *Morning Dispatch,* July 18, 1893.

82. "Sunday Services," Erie *Morning Dispatch*, July 29, 1893; Cleveland *Gazette,* Aug. 5, 1893.

83. "Bishop Mullen's Jubilee," Erie *Morning Dispatch*, July 29, 1893.

84. "Erie," Cleveland *Gazette,* Aug. 5, 1893; "Cleveland Notes," Cleveland *Gazette,* Aug. 12, 1893, 3; "The National Conservatory of Music of America," Cleveland *Gazette,* Sept. 23, 1893; "Personal Pencillings," Erie *Morning Dispatch*, Aug. 9, 1893; "Will Sing at Chicago," Erie *Morning Dispatch,* Aug. 21, 1893; "Erie," Cleveland *Gazette,* Sept. 9, 1893.

Chapter 6. The Columbian Exposition—The Chicago World's Fair

1. Mark Bussler, *EXPO: Magic of the White City,* DVD (Pittsburgh, PA: Inecom Entertainment, 2005), ch. 1.

2. "Chicago," *Poetry, 1914,* Jan. 3, 2014, http://www.poetryfoundation.org/poetrymagazine/poem/2043.

3. Bussler, *EXPO,* ch. 1.

4. Joseph Horowitz, *Moral Fire: Musical Portraits from America's Fin de Siècle* (Berkeley: University of California Press, 2012), 75–76. See also "World's Columbian Exposition," *Encyclopedia of Chicago,* www.encyclopedia.chicagohistory.org/pages/1386.html; Denton J. Snider, "The Plaisance in General," *World's Fair Studies,* 255–57.

5. William S. McFeely, *Frederick Douglass* (New York: W. W. Norton, 1991), 364.

6. Bussler, *EXPO,* ch. 20.

7. Burton Benedict, "Rituals of Representation: Ethnic Stereotypes and Colonized Peoples at World's Fairs," In *Fair Representations: World's Fairs and the Modern World,* ed. Robert W. Rydell and Nancy Gwinn (Amsterdam: VU University Press, 1994), 39.

8. "Appeal of Douglass," *Chicago Daily Tribune,* Aug. 26, 1893, 3.

9. Paul Laurence Dunbar, "Negro Music," In *In His Own Voice: The Dramatic and Other Uncollected Works of Paul Laurence Dunbar,* ed. Herbert Woodward Martin and Ronald Primeau (Athens: Ohio University Press, 2002), 183–84.

10. "At the World's Fair," Indianapolis *Freeman,* Feb. 25, 1893.

11. "No 'Nigger Day' Wanted," Indianapolis *Freeman,* Feb. 25, 1893.

12. "That 'Jubilee Day,'" Indianapolis *Freeman,* Mar. 18, 1893.

13. "White South Sunk in Mediocrity," New York *Age,* July 6, 1905, 1; Burleigh letter to Archibald Grimke, July 8, 1905, "Part I: Personal Correspondence, 1880–1916," Box 8, Reel 7, Booker T. Washington Papers, Library of Congress.

14. Eugene Levy, *James Weldon Johnson: Black Leader, Black Voice* (Chicago: University of Chicago Press, 1973), 41.

15. Levy, *James Weldon Johnson,* 37–39; Arna Bontemps and Jack Conroy, *Anyplace but Here* (New York: Hill and Wang, 1966), 92–93.

16. John H. Cook, "Secretary John H. Cook, Chicago, Writes *The Freeman* to Deny Certain Rumors," Indianapolis *Freeman,* Aug. 12, 1893.

17. "A World's Fair Outfit," Washington *Bee,* June 24, 1893.

18. "The Jubilee Day Folly," Indianapolis *Freeman,* Aug. 12, 1893.

19. Benedict, "Rituals of Representation," 53.

20. "Another Letter from Mr. Douglass," Indianapolis *Freeman,* Apr. 15, 1893.

21. Ibid.

22. Cook, "To Deny Certain Rumors."

23. New York *Age,* Nov. 30, 1889.

24. Doris McGinty, "Aspects of Musical Activities in the Black Communities of Baltimore and Washington, D.C., 1840–the Early 1920s," *Black Music Research Center Bulletin* 11, no. 2 (Fall 1989): 11.

25. Henry Louis Gates, "Harriet Beecher Stowe," *The Annotated Uncle Tom's Cabin* (New York: W. W. Norton, 2007), xlvii.

26. Ibid., xxxi.

27. "A Great Scheme—If It Can Be Carried Through Successfully," Cleveland *Gazette,* Jan. 21, 1893.

28. Ibid.; "An Opera by Colored People," New York *Times,* Jan. 7, 1893; for Burleigh's Simon Legree role, see "Will Sing at Chicago," Erie *Morning Dispatch,* Aug. 21, 1893.

29. Cook, "To Deny Certain Rumors."

30. Ibid.

31. Ibid.

32. "At the World's Fair—The Race's Best Musical Talent Will Appear in a Musical," Indianapolis *Freeman,* Feb. 11, 1893.

33. "The 'Dispatch' Party," Erie *Morning Dispatch,* July 3, 1893.

34. "A Special Train Secured," Erie *Morning Dispatch,* July 4, 1893.

35. Cleveland *Gazette,* July 29, 1893.

36. Maurice Peress, *Dvořák to Duke Ellington: A Conductor Explores America's Music and Its African American Roots* (New York: Oxford University Press, 2004), 207, n. 1.

37. Ibid., 31.

38. Ibid., 31–32.

39. Ibid., 32.

40. "Colored American's Day," *Daily Columbian,* Aug. 23, 1893, 1

41. Peress, 33.

42. Ibid.

43. Ibid.; John Graziano, "The Early Life and Career of the 'Black Patti,'" *Journal of the American Musicological Society* (Fall 2000): 577–78.

44. Advance program, Frederick Grant Gleason scrapbook, Midwest MS Gleason Series 1, vol. 10, Box 44, folder 457, Newberry Library, Chicago.

45. Peress, 30, 37–39.

46. Ibid., 37–38.

47. Ibid., 30.

48. McFeely, *Frederick Douglass,* 371.

49. Robert W. Rydell, ed., *The Reason Why the Colored American Is Not in the World's Columbian Exposition* (Urbana: University of Illinois Press, 1999), xxxi.

50. Ibid.

51. Ibid.

52. Virginia Cunningham, *Paul Laurence Dunbar and His Song* (New York: Biblio and Tannen, 1969), 103.

53. McFeely, *Frederick Douglass*, 171.

54. "The World in Miniature," Indianapolis *Freeman,* Sept. 2, 1893, 1.

55. Ibid.; Graziano, "Early Life," 578.

56. Bontemps and Conroy, *Any Place But Here,* 93.

57. Marva Griffin Carter, *Swing Along: The Musical Life of Will Marion Cook* (New York: Oxford University Press, 2008), 26.

58. McFeely, *Frederick Douglass,* 370.

59. "Woman's World," Indianapolis *Freeman,* Apr. 22, 1893.

60. "The World in Miniature," Indianapolis *Freeman,* Sept. 2, 1893, 1.

61. Ibid.

62. Rydell, *Why the Colored American,* xxxiii.

63. Ida B. Wells, *Crusade for Justice: The Autobiography of Ida B. Wells,* ed. Alfreda M. Duster (Chicago: University of Chicago Press, 1970), 117.

64. Graziano, "Early Life," 577.

65. "Boston: The Hub's Leading Tenor," Cleveland *Gazette*, Nov. 26, 1892.

66. "World's Fair Music," Cleveland *Gazette*, Oct. 21, 1893.

67. Ibid.

68. Rydell, *Why the Colored American*, xxxiii, xxxvii.

Chapter 7. The Symphony "From the New World"

1. Marva Carter, *Swing Along: The Musical Life of Will Marion Cook* (New York: Oxford University Press, 2008), 31.

2. Ibid., 37.

3. Ibid.

4. "Composer Shelley Recalls Dvořák as 'Kindly Martinet' in Theory Class," *Musical America*, Aug. 16, 1913, 22.

5. Carter, *Swing Along*, 31.

6. "Music and the Stage: Will Marion Cook," New York *Age,* May 7, 1908, 6.

7. "Cincinnati," Cleveland *Gazette*, June 2, 1894.

8. H. C. Smith, "The Rounder's Chat," Cleveland *Gazette*, Dec. 3, 1893.

9. Marva Carter, telephone conversation, June 22, 2006.

10. John C. Tibbetts, "A Dvořák American Chronology," in *Dvořák in America, 1892–1895,* ed. Tibbetts (Portland, OR: Amadeus Press, 1993), 17–18.

11. Ibid., 18.

12. Tibbetts, "Letters and Memoirs of Dvořák," in *Dvořák in America*, 400.

13. A. Walter Kramer, "H. T. Burleigh: Composer by Divine Right and 'The American Coleridge-Taylor,'" *Musical America,* Apr. 29, 1916, 25.

14. Dvořák letter to Fritz Simrock in Berlin, Dec. 20, 1893, "Direct Testimony: Items from July–December 1893," *From the New World: A Celebrated Composer's American Odyssey* [DVD], Robert Winter and Peter Bogdanoff (ArtsInteractive.org, 2010).

15. Henry E. Krehbiel letter to Dvořák, "Dec. 12, 1893: 'Direct Testimony.'"

16. Henry E. Krehbiel, "Dr. Dvořák's American Symphony," New York *Daily Tribune*; "Dec. 15, 1893: 'Direct Testimony.'"

17. Ibid.

18. Ibid.

19. Ibid.

20. Jean E. Snyder, "'A Great and Noble School of Music': Dvořák, Harry T. Burleigh, and the African American Spiritual," in *Dvořák in America, 1892–1895*, ed. John C. Tibbetts (Portland, OR: Amadeus Press, 1993), 133.

21. Krehbiel, "Dr. Dvořák's American Symphony."

22. John C. Tibbetts, "The Missing Title Page: Dvořák and the American National Song," in *Music and Culture, 1861–1918*, ed. Michael Saffle and James R. Heintze (London, England: Routledge, 1998), 360.

23. John Clapham, "The Evolution of Dvořák's Symphony 'From the New World,'" *Musical Quarterly,* Apr. 1958, 170–71; Michael Beckerman, *New Worlds of Dvořák: Searching in America for the Composer's Inner Life* (New York: W. W. Norton, 2003), 132.

24. Krehbiel, "Dr. Dvořák's American Symphony."

25. Snyder, "A Great and Noble School," 135.

26. Ibid., 134.

27. Ibid.

28. Ibid., 133.

29. Harry Rowe Shelley, "Dvořák as I Knew Him," *Etude,* Nov. 1919, 694. "Newspaper and Magazine Articles," in *Dvořák in America,* ed. Tibbetts, 383.

30. Walt B. Hayson, "Negro Melodies," Cleveland *Gazette*, Apr. 21, 1894, 1.

31. Snyder, "A Great and Noble School," 130.

Chapter 8. Foremost Musician and Engaged Citizen

1. Arthur LaBrew, *The Black Swan: Elizabeth Taylor Greenfield, Songstress* [1969/1984], (Detroit: printed by author, 2005), 2:106.

2. Cleveland *Gazette,* Dec. 16, 1891; "Mrs. W. F. Johnson's Dinner," New York *Age,* Nov. 14, 1891.

3. Cleveland *Gazette,* Oct. 8 and 29, 1892; Sept. 9 and 23, 1893; "The Empire State: East New York News," Chicago *Defender,* Nov. 25, 1916, 6.

4. Charlotte W. Murray, "The Story of Harry T. Burleigh," *The Hymn* (Oct. 1966): 104.

5. H. C. Smith, "In New York City: The Rounder: Mr. Harry T. Burleigh and the Toussaint L'Ouverture Club Both Credits to the Race," Cleveland *Gazette,* Nov. 19, 1892.

6. Tim Brooks, *Lost Sounds: Blacks and the Birth of the Recording Industry 1890–1919* (Urbana: University of Illinois Press, 2004), 464–65.

7. Jean E. Snyder, "Harry T. Burleigh and the Creative Expression of Bi-Musicality: A Study of an African-American Composer and the American Art Song," Ph.D. diss., University of Pittsburgh, 1992, 68.

8. Smith, "In New York City," Cleveland *Gazette,* Nov. 19, 1892.

9. Smith, "The Rounder's Chat," Cleveland *Gazette,* Nov. 26, 1892.

10. Ibid.

11. Ibid.

12. Murray, "Story of Harry T. Burleigh," 104.

13. John Graziano, "The Early Life and Career of the 'Black Patti': The Odyssey of an African American Singer in the Late Nineteenth Century," *Journal of the American Musicological Society* (Fall 2000): 570.

14. Smith, "In New York City," Cleveland *Gazette,* Nov. 19, 1892.

15. "A Christian (?) Association Discriminates," Cleveland *Gazette*, Mar. 26, 1887.

16. New York *Age,* Dec. 17, 1892.

17. "Our Glorious Beginnings," http://www.stphilipsharlem.diocesny.org/history.htm.

18. Cleveland *Gazette,* Dec. 21, 1895, 1.

19. Ann Charters, *Nobody: The Story of Bert Williams* (London, England: Macmillan, 1970), 35.

20. "Doings of the Race," Cleveland *Gazette,* Aug. 11, 1894, C-2.

21. Ibid.

22. Ibid.

23. "Our Harry Burleigh: Figures in a New York City Affair," Erie *Daily Times,* July 19, 1985, 5.

24. Ibid.

25. Ibid.

26. Ibid.

27. Ibid.

28. Ibid.

29. Brooks, *Lost Sounds*, 501.

30. "The Negro in Music," address to the NAACP, July 1, 1924, Burleigh Family Papers.

31. Anne Key Simpson, *Hard Trials: The Life and Music of Harry T. Burleigh* (Metuchen, NJ: Scarecrow Press, 1990), 200, 202; Barbara Hawley, "Burleigh—He Attributes His Success to Three Sources," Erie *Daily Herald,* Mar. 11, 1928, 6A; letter from Rev. Elmore M. McKee to Harry T. Burleigh II, 7, Burleigh Family Papers.

32. HTB to Booker T. Washington, Apr. 18, 1897, Part I: Personal Correspondence, 1880–1916, Box 8, Reel 7, Booker T. Washington Papers (hereafter, BTWP), Library of Congress (hereafter, LOC), Washington, DC.

33. "Society Notes," New York *Times,* April 28, 1898, 12.

34. HTB to Booker T. Washington, Aug. 2, 1902, BTWP, LOC.

35. HTB to Booker T. Washington, June 1, 1903, BTWP, LOC.

36. Louis R. Harlan, *The Booker T. Washington Papers* (Urbana: University of Illinois Press, 1974), 3:472.

37. "Honor Burleigh on 39th Year as Church Soloist," Chicago *Defender*, June 3, 1933, 4.

38. HTB to Booker T. Washington, July 18, 1903, BTWP, LOC.

39. W. E. B. Du Bois, *Souls of Black Folk* [1903], ed. Henry Louis Gates Jr. and Terri Hume Oliver (New York: W. W. Norton, 1999), 34–45.

40. Booker T. Washington to HTB, July 30, 1903, BTWP, LOC.

41. Boston *Globe,* Aug. 1, 1903; "Booker Washington Speaks under a Cordon of Police," Boston *Guardian,* Aug. 1, 1903, 11.

42. HTB note to Booker T. Washington, Aug. 9, 1903, BTWP, LOC. On a visit to the Schomberg Center I met the daughter who had carried the hatpin; she recounted the story with great relish.

43. HTB to Booker T. Washington, Aug. 25, 1903, BTWP, LOC.

44. *Negro Music Journal*, May 1903, 185.

45. Ibid.

46. Ibid.

47. Simpson, *Hard Trials,* 29.

48. Harlan, ed., *Booker T. Washington Papers*, 7:527–29; Coleridge-Taylor's letter, May 21, 1904, Burleigh Family Papers; Washington's reply, June 10, 1904, BTWP, LOC.

49. Coleridge-Taylor to HTB, June 20, 1904, Burleigh Family Papers.

50. Ibid.

51. Booker T. Washington to HTB, Oct. 17, 1904, BTWP, LOC.

52. HTB to Booker T. Washington, Oct. 22, 1904, BTWP, LOC.

53. Ibid.

54. HTB to Booker T. Washington, June 5, 1910, BTWP, LOC; Booker T. Washington to HTB, June 11, 1910, BTWP, LOC; HTB to Booker T. Washington, BTWP, LOC; Booker T. Washington to HTB, June 16, 1910, BTWP, LOC; HTB to Booker T. Washington, Sept. 13, 1912, BTWP, LOC.

55. My thanks to Deane Root for identifying the Jewish liturgical events that fell during these months in 1906.

56. HTB to Booker T. Washington, Jan. 6, 1906, BTWP, LOC.

57. Booker T. Washington to HTB, Nov. 28, 1905, BTWP, LOC; HTB to Booker T. Washington, Jan. 1, 1906, BTWP, LOC; Booker T. Washington to HTB, Jan. 9, 1906, BTWP, LOC.

58. *Mohonk Weekly Bulletin* 4/12 (July 31, 1915), 1, courtesy of Joan LaChance, Mohonk Archivist; HTB to Booker T. Washington, Aug. 2, 1915, BTWP, LOC; Booker T. Washington to HTB, Sept. 14, 1915, BTWP, LOC.

59. Harry T. Burleigh II conversations with the author, 1987, 1988, Pittsburgh, Pennsylvania.

60. Ibid.

61. Eileen Southern, personal communication, Apr. 4, 1987, Pittsburgh, PA; Josephine Harreld Love, telephone conversation with the author, Mar. 7, 1987.

62. New York *Age,* Oct. 11, 1906.

63. "To Help Colored School," New York *Times,* Apr. 4, 1900, 7; Brooks, *Lost Sounds,* 503; "To Be a Big Musical Event," New York *Age,* Apr, 25, 1912; "Music and Art," *Crisis,* Mar. 1913, 219; "Music and Art," *Crisis,* Apr. 1913, 272; Simpson, *Hard Trials,* 51.

64. Roi Ottley, "New World A-Coming," New York *Amsterdam News,* Apr. 8, 1944, 11A.

65. Roi Ottley, *New World A-Coming* (New York: Arno Press, 1968), 27.

66. Ibid., 27, 31.

67. Burleigh addresses are gleaned from his correspondence in the Burleigh Family Papers; Ottley, "New World," 31; "Hincty Harlem Spot," New York *Amsterdam News,* Apr. 23, 1966, E10; Cathy Aldridge, "What Is Negro Society?" New York *Amsterdam News*, Apr. 23, 1966, I28.

68. Archibald Grimke letter to the New York *Age,* July 6, 1905, 1.

69. HTB to Archibald Grimke, July 8, 1905, Burleigh Family Papers.

70. "Controversial History: Thomas Dixon and the Klan Trilogy," *Documenting the American South*, University Library, University of North Carolina at Chapel Hill, 2004, Jan. 13, 2010 http://docsouth.unc.edu/highlights/dixon.html.

71. A'lelia Bundles, *A Place of Her Own: The Life and Times of Madam C. J. Walker* (New York: Washington Square Press, 2002), 218.

72. "Music and Art," *Crisis,* July 1915, 115; for example, "Sunshine Mission's Benefit," New York *Times,* Nov. 28, 1902, 9; Benefit for Fernside, the Working Girls Vacation House, Princeton, Mass.; Simpson, *Hard Trials,* 28–29; "Notes of the Theatres," New York *Times,* May 5, 1904, 5; Benefit of Choir Fund, St. Luke's Parish House, Sea Cliff, LI, Aug. 31, 1911, Program, Burleigh Family Papers.

73. Thomas L. Morgan, "Gotham-Attucks," Jan. 31, 2010; http://jas.com/gattuck.html, 1997; Marva Carter, *Swing Along: The Musical Life of Will Marion Cook* (New York: Oxford University Press, 2008), 73.

74. "Negro Pointed the Way to David Mannes," *Musical America,* June 1, 1912, 26.

75. "Greatest Event of the Season," New York *Age,* Apr. 10, 1912, 6; New York *Age,* Apr. 18, 1912, 6.

76. Lester A. Walton, "Music and the Stage: Concert at Carnegie Hall," New York *Age,* May 9, 1912, 6.

77. Lucien H. White, "Clef Club Concert," New York *Age,* May 15, 1913, 6.

78. Lester A. Walton, New York *Age,* Jan. 1, 1914, 6.

79. A. Walter Kramer, "Negroes Perform Their Own Music," *Musical America,* Mar. 21, 1914, 37.

80. Ibid.

81. "Negroes Give a Concert," New York *Times,* Mar. 12, 1914, 3.

82. "Health Circle Starts Campaign," New York *Amsterdam News*, Dec. 22, 1926, 6; "Relief Board Numbers 500; Harlemites Listed on Committee to Help Bureau in Work," New York *Amsterdam News,* July 7, 1934, 2.

83. Cora Gary-Illidge, "Music and Drama: Harry T. Burleigh," Chicago *Defender,* May 14, 1927, 11.

84. "Arts and Leisure: Canadian Folksong Festival and Handicraft Festival Opens," New York *Times,* May 20, 1928, 107.

85. Langston Hughes Papers, James Weldon Johnson Collection in the Yale Collection of American Literature, Beinecke Rare Book and Manuscript Library, Yale University, JWJ MSS 26.

86. See "The World's Greatest Pilgrimage to the World's Greatest Events: A Century of Progress," Chicago *Defender,* June 16, 1934, 5.

87. "Music News: Announces Plan for New Chorus," New York *Amsterdam News*, May 4, 1932, 9.

88. "Drawings in Harlem Art Exhibit," Pittsburgh *Courier,* Feb. 23, 1935, 8.

89. HTB to Rose McClendon, Jan. 7, 1932, Rose McClendon Scrapbooks, Box 1, Vol. 2, Manuscripts, Archives and Rare Books Division, Schomberg Center for Research in Black Culture, New York Public Library.

90. A'lelia Bundles, *A Place of Her Own: The Life and Times of Madam C. J. Walker* (New York: Washington Square Press, 2002), 218.

91. Brooks, *Lost Sounds,* 278, 280.

92. "Leslie Pinckney Hill," *The Black Past,* http://www.blackpast.org/?q=aah/hill-leslie-pinckney-1880–1960.

93. Simpson, *Hard Trials,* 100.

94. Cheyney *Record,* June 11, 1924.

95. Ibid.

96. New York *Amsterdam News,* Oct. 10, 1928, 2; Bernice Dutreuille, "Cheyney Becomes State Teachers College as DuBois, Notables Speak," Pittsburgh *Courier,* June 11, 1932, A3.

97. "Music and Art," *Crisis,* Mar. 1913, 219.

98. "Mrs. W. F. Craig Dies after Long Illness," New York *Age,* May 24, 1919, 2; Bundles, *Place of Her Own,* 275; "Mme. Walker Is Laid to Rest," Chicago *Defender,* June 6, 1919, 1.

99. Hawley, "Burleigh—He Attributes His Success to Three Sources," 6A.

100. "Dora C. Norman in Burial Rites," New York *Amsterdam News,* Oct. 28, 1939, 7.

101. "Negro's Chemistry Astounds Audience," New York *Times,* Nov. 19, 1924, 5.

102. Dorothy West, *The Richer, the Poorer: Stories, Sketches, and Reminiscences* (New York: Doubleday, 1995), 174–75.

103. Jill Nelson, *Finding Martha's Vineyard: African Americans at Home on an Island* (New York: Doubleday, 2005), 30–31.

104. Simpson, *Hard Trials,* 75.

105. "Famous Baritone Soloist Creates Great Music in Vineyard Church," New Bedford *Standard Times,* Aug. 20, 1938, cited in Simpson, *Hard Trials,* 74–75.

106. Letter to Anne Key Simpson, Oct. 14, 1986, cited in Simpson, *Hard Trials,* 75.

107. Nelson, *Finding Martha's Vineyard,* 63, 116.

108. Simpson, *Hard Trials,* 74.

109. Nelson, *Finding Martha's Vineyard,* 4–5.

110. "Spingar[n] Medal Awarded to Harry T. Burleigh," Philadelphia *Tribune,* May 26, 1917, 1.

111. "Burleigh Wins Spingarn Medal," Cincinnati *Union,* May 19, 1917.

112. New York *Age,* June 7, 1917.

113. "Harmon Awards," *Messenger,* n.p.

114. "Radio," New York *Times,* 31.

115. "Plan Busts of 3 for New York Fair," Nov. 27, 1937, 6.

116. Burleigh Family Papers.

117. "Indiana News," Chicago *Defender,* Aug. 30, 1930, 20.

118. "Young People of Darlington Progressive—Organize Club to Study Race Characters," Chicago *Defender,* July 23, 1932, 7.

119. "Association to Have Burleigh for Guest," New York *Amsterdam News,* Mar. 2, 1935, 14; "Notes of Music and Musicians Here and Afield," New York *Times,* Apr. 28, 1935, X5.

120. "Harlem Goes to Opera and Acclaims Its Own," New York *Amsterdam News,* July 6, 1933, 1.

Chapter 9. Burleigh's Singing Career

1. "Notes for the Afro-Americans," Pittsburgh *Press,* Dec. 2, 1906, 40.

2. George C. Keck, "Promoting Black Music in Nineteenth-Century America: Some Aspects of Concert Management in New York and Boston," in *Feel the Spirit: Studies in Nineteenth-Century Afro-American Music,* ed. George R. Keck and Sherrill V. Martin, Contributions in Afro-American and African Studies, No. 119 (Westport, CT: Greenwood Press, 1988), 163.

3. Carl Diton, "The American Negro in Music: An Appraisal of the Outstanding Vocalists, Composers, Violinists, Organists, and Teachers Whose Work and Art Have Attracted Universal Attention Here and in Europe," New York *Amsterdam News,* Dec. 28, 1929, A6; Frankye A. Dixon, "Music," New York *Amsterdam News*, May 22, 1929, 11.

4. The long, successful careers of Roland Hayes, Marian Anderson, and Paul Robeson will be discussed in more detail in chapter 10.

5. Erie *Morning Dispatch,* Mar. 27, 1884.

6. Thomas Riis, "Concert Singers, Prima Donnas, and Entertainers: The Changing Status of Black Women Vocalists in Nineteenth-Century America," *Music and Culture in America, 1861–1918,* ed. Michael Saffle and James R. Heintze (London: Routledge, 1998), 59–60.

7. Ibid., 60.

8. "The Selika Concert," Cleveland *Gazette,* Mar. 5, 1887.

9. Ad, New York *Age,* Mar. 17, 1888.

10. Riis, "Concert Singers," 61.

11. Tim Brooks, *Lost Sounds: Blacks and the Birth of the Recording Industry, 1890–1919* (Urbana: University of Illinois Press, 2004), 504.

12. "Buffalo," Cleveland *Gazette,* Apr. 9, 1892; Cleveland *Gazette,* Apr. 30, 1892.

13. "Buffalo, NY," Cleveland *Gazette,* May 14, 1892.

14. John Graziano, "The Early Life and Career of the 'Black Patti': The Odyssey of an African American Singer in the Late Nineteenth Century," *Journal of the American Musicological Society* (Fall 2000), 570; Indianapolis *Freeman,* June 17, 1893.

15. Graziano, "The 'Black Patti,'" 545.

16. Riis, "Concert Singers," 61; Eileen Southern, "Harry T. Burleigh," *Biographical Dictionary of Afro-American and African Musicians* (Westport, CT: Greenwood Press, 1982).

17. Graziano, "The 'Black Patti,'" 569.

18. Ibid., 568, n. 40.

19. New York *Age,* Dec. 24, 1908, 9.

20. "Woman's World" and "Our Women," Indianapolis *Freeman*, Oct. 15, 1892.

21. Graziano, "The 'Black Patti,'"580.

22. "Doings of the Race," Cleveland *Gazette,* Aug. 11, 1894, 2.

23. Ibid.; Cleveland *Gazette,* Apr. 20, 1895, 3.

24. "'Sweet Chariot' Inspired Anton Dvorak to Immortalize Negro Spirituals." New York *World Telegram*, Sept. 12, 1941.

25. "Harry Burleigh, Singer-Composer and Churchman," *Forth,* Apr. 1944, 18.

26. "In Society," Albany *Times Union,* Jan. 24, 1900; "Dances," ibid.

27. Diary of Edith K. Roosevelt, Tuesday, Jan. 23, 1900, MS Am 2835 (295), Theodore Roosevelt Collection, Houghton Library, Harvard University, used by permission.

28. "In Society," Albany *Times Union,* Jan. 24, 1900.

29. The home of Governor Throop was no longer in use, so Burleigh was a guest in a newer residence; e-mail correspondence from Robert Moore, National Park Service, Apr. 25, 2007.

30. "People's Singing Class Concert," New York *Times,* Feb. 25, 1900, 14.

31. "Notes on Racial Progress," New York *Age,* Mar. 2, 1911, 5.

32. "To Help Colored School," New York *Times,* Apr. 4, 1900, 7.

33. HTB letter to Fred Moore, Apr. 18, 1897, Part I: Personal Correspondence, 1880–1916, Box 8, Reel 7, Booker T. Washington Papers (hereafter BTWP), Library of Congress (hereafter LOC).

34. Jean E. Snyder, "Harry T. Burleigh and the Creative Expression of Bi-Musicality: A Story of an African-American Composer and the American Art Song," Ph.D. diss., University of Pittsburgh, 1992, 79, n. 25.

35. HTB letter to Moore, Part I: Personal Correspondence, 1880–1916, Box 8, Reel 7, BTWP, LOC.

36. Anne Key Simpson, *Hard Trials: The Life and Music of Harry T. Burleigh* (Metuchen, NJ: Scarecrow Press, 1990), 25.

37. New York *Times,* Apr. 1, 1924, 3.

38. Email from Frances A. Hess, Emanu-El archivist, July 12, 2009.

39. Dr. Harry T. Burleigh II, personal communication, 1988, Pittsburgh, PA; the disagreement, according to Dr. Burleigh, was private and not to be acknowledged publicly.

40. Letter from Simon Schlager letter to Mr. C. Pollak, Mar. 13, 1925, Temple Emanu-El archives. Courtesy of archivist Frances A. Hess, July 12, 1909.

41. "Negro Composer Honored," New York *Times,* May 10, 1915.

42. E-mail, Frances A. Hess, July 17, 2009.

43. *The Bulletin,* May 1935, n.p., Temple Emanu-El, Temple Emanu-El archives. Courtesy of archivist Frances A. Hess, July 12, 1909.

44. "Programs of the Week: Drama." New York *Times,* Mar. 22, 1936, X6.

45. Unidentified clipping annotated Rochester, New York, Burleigh Family Papers.

46. Ibid.

47. Ibid.

48. Brochure, Burleigh Family Papers.

49. Clipping from unidentified Yonkers paper, Burleigh Family Papers.

50. Review from unidentified Yonkers paper, Burleigh Family Papers.

51. Ibid.

52. Ibid.

53. Brooks and Denton brochure, ca. 1908, Burleigh Family Papers.

54. New York *Herald,* Burleigh Family Papers.

55. Lester A. Walton, "Harry T. Burleigh Honored To-Day at St. George's," New York *World,* Mar. 30, 1924. Reprinted in *The Black Perspective in Music* 2, n. 1 (Spring 1974): 83.

56. Program, Burleigh Family Papers.

57. Anna Josephine Ingersoll, *Greenacre on the Piscataqua* (New York: Alliance, 1900), 3–4.

58. Letter from Sarah Farmer to the manager of the Young Hotel, Aug. 9, 1902, Burleigh Family Papers.

59. "Lawson-Putnam Scholarship," 1–2, Augustus Lawson Papers, CHS. Raymond Augustus Lawson Papers, Ms 83827, Box 2, folder 21.

60. "Lawson and Burleigh," Hartford *Observer,* Dec. 16, 1902, Burleigh Family Papers.

61. Ibid.

62. Ibid.

63. HTB letter to Lawson, Apr. 3, 1910, CHS, Lawson Papers, Box 1, folder 9. Used by permission.

64. "Sunshine Mission's Benefit," New York *Times,* Nov. 28, 1902, 9.

65. Program, Burleigh Family Papers.

66. Henry Beckett, "A Mighty Voice at 77," New York *Post,* Apr. 24, 1944.

67. Unidentified clipping, Burleigh Family Papers.

68. Publicity brochure for Oct. 5 recital, Burleigh Family Papers; *The Lake Forester,* July 2, 1904, Burleigh Family Papers.

69. Percy Lee Atherton, "An American Colored Composer's Career," Letter to the Editor, Boston *Transcript,* Jan. 4, 1905, Burleigh Family Papers.

70. R. C. DeW, "The Negro in Song," Feb. 15, 1905, Burleigh Family Papers.

71. New York *Age,* Feb. 2, 1905, 3.

72. "Young Artist Makes Debut," New York *Age,* Mar. 16, 1905, 1.

73. Simpson, *Hard Trials,* 37.

74. "Harry Burleigh Sings at the Home of His Birth," Erie *Morning Dispatch,* May 19, 1908; Program, Burleigh Family Papers.

75. New York *Age,* June 11, 1908, 6.

76. New York *Age,* July 16, 1908, 6.

77. Burleigh Family Papers.

78. "NAACP," "History," Oct. 15, 2009, http://www.naacp.org/about/history/index/htm.

79. Altona Trent Johns, "Henry Hugh Proctor," *The Black Perspective in Music* (Spring 1975): 26–27, 30.

80. "Atlanta Has Music Festival," New York *Age,* Aug. 11, 1910, 1.

81. "Music and Art," *Crisis,* Sept. 1912, 63.

82. "Mrs. Anderson Entertains Whist Club," New York *Age,* Jan. 21, 1909, 7.

83. New York *Age,* Jan. 14, 1909, 7.

84. "Musical Notes," New York *Age,* Apr. 15, 1909, 6.

85. Simpson, *Hard Trials,* 51.

86. Program, Burleigh Family Papers; *Crisis,* June 1915, 59.

87. "Musical and Dramatic," *Half-Century Magazine,* June 1917, 8.

88. R. G. Doggett, "Music School Opening," New York *Age,* Oct. 15, 1914, 6.

89. Lucien H. White, "Music Notes," Oct. 5, 1916, 6.

90. "Big Crowd Hears Burleigh Sing," Baltimore *Afro-American,* June 16, 1917; Simpson, *Hard Trials,* 100–101; "Harry T. Burleigh Gives Program of His Spirituals to Brooklyn Congregation," New York *Age,* July 7, 1923, 6.

91. Brooks, *Lost Sounds,* 467.

92. Ibid., 482, 467.

93. Dr. Harry T. Burleigh II, personal communication, Feb. 10, 1991, Pittsburgh, Pennsylvania.

94. Both George Kemmer and Burleigh were asked to sign a letter waiving their rights to any royalties from the sale of the recordings made at the fiftieth anniversary celebration. Burleigh's letter is dated Apr. 26, 1944. Burleigh Family Papers.

95. Elizabeth Moulton, *St. George's Church* (New York: The Rector, Church Wardens, and Vestrymen of St. George's Church in the City of New York, 1964), 116.

96. "Harry Burleigh Receives Hearty Welcome, When He Broadcasts in Philadelphia," Pittsburgh *Courier,* May 24, 1924, 14.

97. "Spirituals Put Spell on Radio," Pittsburgh *Courier*, May 15, 1926, 7.

98. Cora Gary Illidge, "Music and Drama," Chicago *Defender,* Mar. 19, 1927, 11.

99. Letter from Hatcher to HTB, Feb. 20, 1928, Burleigh Family Papers.

Chapter 10. Music Mentor and Colleague

1. "Burleigh Celebrates 40 Years as Soloist at St. George's," Philadelphia *Tribune,* May 24, 1934.

2. Abbie Mitchell, autobiographical notes, Mercer Cook Papers, MRSC, 157–7, folder 18, 28–36.

3. Marva Carter, *Swing Along: The Musical Life of Will Marion Cook* (New York: Oxford University Press, 2008), 47–48.

4. Ibid., 48, 49.

5. Carter, manuscript, *Swing Along,* 89.

6. Abbie Mitchell, autobiographical notes, 28–36.

7. Carter, *Swing Along,* 81–82.

8. Georgia Ryder biography, Mercer Cook Papers, MSRC, 157–8, folder 4.

9. Lucien H. White, "In the Realm of Music: Harry T. Burleigh Writes His Impressions on Classic Recital by Abbie Mitchell," New York *Age,* Oct. 20, 1923, 6.

10. "Noted Musician Assails White Authors [sic] Works," New York *News,* Oct. 29, 1927, CBMR 4941.

11. Letter from Josephine Harreld Love to Mercer Cook, Aug. 18, 1981, Mercer Cook Papers, MRSC, 157–2, folder 19.

12. Carl Diton, "The American Negro in Music," New York *Amsterdam News,* Dec. 18, 1929, A6.

13. "Calendar of Community Events," New York *Post,* Feb. 6, 1969, 14.

14. MacKinley Helm, *Angel Mo' and Her Son, Roland Hayes* (New York: Greenwood Press, 1942), 92.

15. For example, "Art," *Crisis,* Mar. 1912, 188; "Music and Art," *Crisis,* Jan. 1913, 116; "Music and Art," *Crisis,* Mar. 1913, 219.

16. "The Pre-Lenten Recital," New York *Age,* Feb. 6, 1913, 6.

17. Helm, *Angel Mo',* 106.

18. Ibid., 108.

19. Chicago *Defender,* May 9, 1915, 6.

20. "John Work, Martyr and Singer," *Crisis,* May 1926, 33.

21. Helm, *Angel Mo',* 108.

22. "Harry Burleigh and Roland Hayes at Fisk Concert," Chicago *Defender,* May 8, 1915, 6.

23. Lucien H. White, "Music Notes," New York *Age,* Oct. 12, 1916, 6; "General Race News," *Half-Century Magazine,* Apr. 1917, 8; "Music and Art," *Crisis,* Jan. 1918, 139; "General Race News," *Half-Century Magazine,* Apr. 1918; "Music and Art," *Crisis,* Aug. 1918, 188.

24. "Spingarn Medal Presented to Roland Hayes," Pittsburgh *Courier,* Apr. 28, 1925, 9.

25. HTB to Hayes, Nov. 9, 1925, Detroit Public Library, Hackley Collection, Roland W. Hayes Collection, Subseries A: General Correspondence, Box 1, folder 41.

26. "Among Noted Musicians," New York *Amsterdam News,* 8.

27. Ibid.

28. Ibid.

29. Tim Brooks, *Lost Sounds: Blacks and the Birth of the Recording Industry, 1890–1919* (Urbana: University of Illinois Press, 2004), 257.

30. Ibid.

31. Ibid.

32. Ibid.

33. Chicago *Defender,* June 15, 1929, 11.

34. "Manhattan Chorus Stages Festival," Chicago *Defender,* July 2, 1932, 11.

35. "'No Ways Tired' after 38 Years," New York *Amsterdam News*, May 18, 1932, 3.

36. "Music and Art," *Crisis,* Oct. 1916, 281; letter from Roland Hayes to Marian Anderson, Dec. 14, 1916, Marian Anderson Papers, Ms. Coll. 200, Kislak Center for Special Collections, Rare Book and Manuscripts, University of Pennsylvania, Box 39, folder 2434; "Musical and Dramatic," *Half-Century Magazine,* June 1917, 8.

37. *Master Musician,* Mar. 1920, 24.

38. HTB to Anderson, Mar. 14, 1927, Marian Anderson Papers, Box 13, folder 797.

39. For example, "Marian Anderson Back from England," New York *Amsterdam News,* 5; "Chatter and Chimes," New York *Amsterdam News,* Dec. 3, 1938, 8.

40. HTB to Anderson, July 25, 1933, Marian Anderson Papers.

41. Anderson to HTB, Sept 21, 1935, Marian Anderson Papers.

42. Ibid.

43. HTB to Anderson, Oct. 26, 1935, Marian Anderson Papers.

44. Ibid.

45. Ibid.; Anderson to HTB, Sept. 14, 1935, Marian Anderson Papers.

46. "Trouble Brews as Marian Heads Home—Noted Philadelphia Contralto Brings White Accompanist," Baltimore *Afro-American,* Dec. 14, 1935, 9.

47. "Themes and Variations," Atlanta *Daily World,* Dec. 16, 1935, 6.

48. Anderson note to HTB, after Town Hall recital, Dec. 30, 1935, Marian Anderson Papers.

49. HTB to Anderson, Jan. 11, 1936, Marian Anderson Papers.

50. Alvin White, "The Night She Cancelled Concert," New York *Amsterdam News*, Apr. 23, 1966, 8.

51. "A Man with a Glory," Newark *Sunday News,* Nov. 1, 1970.

52. "Five Thousand Sing 'We Are Climbing Jacob's Ladder,'" Baltimore *Afro-American,* July 8, 1930, 6.

53. Allan Keiler, *Marian Anderson: A Singer's Journey* (Urbana: University of Illinois Press, 2002), 271–72.

54. Ibid., 339, 351.

55. Langston Hughes, "Song," *The Dream Keeper and Other Poems: The Collected Poems of Langston Hughes,* ed. Arnold Rampersad and David Roessel (1932; repr., New York: Alfred A. Knopf, 1998), 45.

56. Keiler, *Marian Anderson,* 155, 203–4, for example.

57. Paul Robeson Jr., *The Undiscovered Paul Robeson: An Artist's Journey* (New York: Paul Wiley and Sons, 2001), 74, 139.

58. Robeson, *Undiscovered Paul Robeson,* 74.

59. Ibid., 83.

60. Ibid.

61. Keiler, *Marian Anderson,* 68, 69.

62. Robeson, *Undiscovered Robeson,* 86.

63. Martin Bauml Duberman, *Paul Robeson* (New York: Alfred A. Knopf, 1988), 79.

64. Robeson, *Undiscovered Robeson,* 86–87.

65. Ibid., 87.

66. Ibid., 140.

67. Ibid., 224.

68. Ibid., 140, 141.

69. "Paul Robeson Is Feted by English Parliament," Mar. 20, 1929, A3, Burleigh Family Papers.

70. Robeson, *Undiscovered Robeson,* 44.

71. Eric Foner, *America's Black Past: A Reader in Afro-American History* (New York: Harper and Row, 1970), 162.

72. Ibid., 211, 300.

73. "'Elijah' Sung at Knoxville," New York *Age,* July 6, 1905.

74. "Music and Art," *Crisis,* Sept. 1912, 63.

75. Carl Diton, "The American Negro in Music," New York *Amsterdam News,* Dec. 18, 1929, A6.

76. Lucien H. White, "In the Realm of Music: 'From Bach to Burleigh!' Is Gamut of Program of Music Rendered to Audience Filling Larchmont Church," New York *Age,* Nov. 12, 1927, 7.

77. HTB to Ella Belle Davis, Feb. 15, 1930, Personal Papers, Ella Belle Davis Papers, Manuscripts, Archives, and Rare Books Division, Schomberg Center for Research in Black Culture, New York Public Library.

78. Eileen Southern, *The Music of Black Americans: A History,* 3rd ed. (New York: W. W. Norton, 1983), 524.

79. David E. Weaver, *Black Diva of the Thirties: The Life of Ruby Elzy* (Jackson: University Press of Mississippi, 2004), 73.

80. Ibid., 78–79.

81. Ibid., 159.

82. Ibid., 184.

83. Alvin Hazzard, "Current Comments," Boston *Chronicle,* Sept. 8, 1934.

84. From the official program, Burleigh Family Papers.

85. New Brunswick *Sunday Times,* Apr. 11, 1943.

86. Nora Holt, "Music Notes: The Human Touch," New York *Amsterdam News,* Feb. 5, 1944.

87. "Harry Burleigh to Coach Tenor," Philadelphia *Tribune,* Jan. 31, 1929, 6.

88. Jester Hairston, personal communication, Jan. 1, 1991, Homestead, PA.

89. "WCBS Pays Tribute to Harry Burleigh," New York *Amsterdam News,* Sept. 24, 1949, 25.

90. HTB to Dawson, Mar. 17, 1921, Dawson Papers, MSS 892, Box 1, folder 5, Manuscript, Archives, and Rare Book Library, Emory University, Atlanta, GA.

91. Harry T. Burleigh photograph, Dawson Papers, MSS 892, Box 60, folder 46.

92. Mrs. James A. Myers to Dawson, Nov. 26, 1934, Dawson Papers, MSS 892, Box 2, folder 2. Thanks to Gwynne Kuhner Brown for alerting me to this letter.

93. Undine Smith Moore Papers, Manuscript, Archives, and Rare Book Library, Emory University, Atlanta, GA.

94. "A Reminiscence," *The Negro in Music and Art*, ed. Lindsay Patterson (New York: Publishers Company, 1967), 191–92.

95. Rae Linda Brown, "'I Know Why the Caged Bird Sings': Harry T. Burleigh's Influence on Florence B. Price," April 2003, unpublished, 4, courtesy of Rae Linda Brown.

96. Ibid., 4–5, 6–7.

97. Ibid., 12.

98. HTB to Price, Oct. 14, 1943, Florence Price Papers (MC 988), box 1, folder 1, item 29, Special Collections, University of Arkansas Libraries, Fayetteville. Thanks to Rae Linda Brown for sharing this with me.

99. Brown, "I Know Why," 20–23.

100. Southern, *The Music of Black Americans*, 432–33.

101. Verna Arvey, *In One Lifetime* (Fayetteville: University of Arkansas Press, 1984), 59–60.

102. HTB to Still, William Grant Still Papers, Burleigh Family Papers.

103. Arvey, *In One Lifetime*, 60.

104. Nora Holt, "Music Notes: The Human Touch," New York *Amsterdam News,* Feb. 5, 1944.

105. Anne Key Simpson, *Hard Trials: The Life and Music of Harry T. Burleigh* (Metuchen, NJ: Scarecrow Press, 1990), 107.

106. William Grant Still, "Fifty Years of Progress in Music," Pittsburgh *Courier*, Nov. 11, 1950, 15.

Chapter 11. Family Matters

1. "Erie," Cleveland *Gazette,* July 1, 1893; "Will Teach in Virginia," Cleveland *Gazette,* Oct. 7, 1893; "Drury's Opera," New York *Age*, Apr. 6, 1905; "Erie, Pa. Notes," Cleveland *Gazette*, Aug. 11, 1907.

2. Letter from Eva Burleigh to Mr. Talbot, June 26, 1908, Burleigh Family Papers.

3. Burleigh Family Papers.

4. Burleigh and his wife's separation in 1915, Alston Burleigh Deposition, 1959, Burleigh Family Papers; Anne Key Simpson, *Hard Trials: The Life and Music of Harry T. Burleigh* (Metuchen, NJ: Scarecrow Press, 1990), 173.

5. Marie Burleigh, banquet presentation at national conference, "The Heritage and Legacy of Harry T. Burleigh," Erie, Pennsylvania, Apr. 5, 2003.

6. Lizzie Elmendorf's death, "Died," Erie *Dispatch,* Mar. 11, 1903; "Mr. Elmendorf's New Departure," Cleveland *Gazette,* Mar. 12, 1892; Elmendorf's boarding stable, *Erie City Directories,* 1893–1907; John Elmendorf's death, Apr. 29, 1919, Burleigh Family Bible.

7. David A. Jasen and Gene Jones, *Spreadin' Rhythm Around: Black Popular Songwriters, 1880–1930* (New York: Schirmer, 1999), 47; James Weldon Johnson, *Along This Way: The Autobiography of James Weldon Johnson* (1933, repr., New York: DaCapo, 2000), 172–73, 175; James Weldon Johnson, *Black Manhattan,* 3rd ed. (New York: Atheneum, 1972), 118–20.

8. *Colored American*, Sept. 24, 1898; thanks to Peter Lefferts for sharing clippings confirming Louise's role in the cast of *The Senegambian Carnival* and the engagement and marriage.

9. Ibid.

10. Rossetti titled her poem "A Birthday"; my thanks to Laurie Matheson for alerting me to Burleigh's change in the title.

11. Johnson, *Black Manhattan*, 102–3.

12. Will Marion Cook in *Theatre Arts*, September 1947, 61–65; reprinted in Eileen Southern, *Readings in Black American Music*, 2nd ed. (New York: W. W. Norton, 1983), 217–23.

13. Jasen and Jones, *Spreadin' Rhythm Around*, 85.

14. Southern, *Readings*, 232.

15. Marva Carter, *Swing Along: The Musical Life of Will Marion Cook* (New York: Oxford University Press, 2008), 41.

16. Southern, *Readings*, 223.

17. Johnson, *Manhattan*, 102–3.

18. Jasen and Jones, *Spreadin' Rhythm Around*, 47–48.

19. New York *Dramatic Mirror*, Sept. 3, 1898, 18; Oct. 1, 1898, 20.

20. New York *Dramatic Mirror*, Oct. 29, 1898, 20; "Route," Indianapolis *Freeman*, Sept. 10, 1989, 5; "Stage," Indianapolis *Freeman*, Oct. 1, 1898, 5.

21. "The Stage," Indianapolis *Freeman*, Oct. 29, 1898, 5.

22. John Graziano, "The Early Life and Career of the 'Black Patti': The Odyssey of an African American Singer in the Late Nineteenth Century," *Journal of the American Musicological Society* (Fall 2000), 581.

23. Carter, *Swing Along*, 47–48.

24. New York *Dramatic Mirror*, Nov. 19, 1898, 18.

25. Nora Douglas Holt, "St. George's Fete Harry Burleigh, Soloist at Church for 50 Years," New York *Amsterdam News*, Feb. 5, 1944, 1A.

26. Indianapolis *Freeman*, Jan. 21, 1899, 5.

27. "Williams & Walker's Own Co.," Indianapolis *Freeman*, Jan. 21, 1899, 5; "The Stage: Route," Indianapolis *Freeman*, Jan. 28, 1899, 5.

28. HTB to Rachel Farley, Dec. 16, 1898, Burleigh Family Papers.

29. Ibid.

30. Burleigh's grandson often called him "a sport." Mrs. Mary Burleigh, July 15, 2008.

31. HTB to Rachel Farley, Dec. 16, 1898, Burleigh Family Papers.

32. Ibid. If Louise's mother should argue, like Caesar's friend Cassius, that "A friendly eye could never see such faults!" he would respond with Brutus, "A flatterer's would not—though they be/As huge as high Olympus!"

33. Letter from Louise to Alston, Jan. 15, 1950, Burleigh Family Papers.

34. HTB letter to Rachel Farley, Dec. 16, 1898.

35. Ibid.

36. Indianapolis *Freeman*, Jan. 27, 1899, 5.

37. *Colored American*, "New York and Columbia," Feb. 19, 1899, 5; marriage certificate, Burleigh Family Papers.

38. When I told Burleigh's niece, Grace Elmendorf Blackwell, what I had learned about the falsification of Burleigh's wedding date, she chuckled, "That doesn't surprise me."

39. Alston's handwritten autobiography, Oct. 8, 1915, Burleigh Family Papers.

40. Herbert Woodward Martin and Ronald Primeau, eds., "A Brief Dunbar Chronology," *In His Own Voice: The Dramatic and Other Collected Works of Paul Laurence Dunbar* (Athens: Ohio University Press, 2002), xxviii; Eleanor Alexander, *Lyrics of Sunshine and Shadow: The Courtship and Marriage of Paul Laurence Dunbar and Alice Ruth Moore* (New York: Penguin Group, 2004), 40.

41. Ida B. Wells, *Crusade for Justice: The Autobiography of Ida B. Wells,* ed. Alfreda M. Duster (Chicago: University of Chicago Press, 1971), 117.

42. Pittsburgh *Dispatch,* Dec. 6, 1906, 2.

43. Louise's handwritten version, Burleigh Family Papers; "Mammy's Li'l Baby" (William Maxwell Company, 1903).

44. HTB to "Mom Farley," Dec. 21, 1902, Burleigh Family Papers.

45. Frederick Allen Lewis, *The Great Pierpont Morgan* (New York: Harper, 1949), in Anne Key Simpson, *Hard Trials: The Life and Music of Harry T. Burleigh* (Metuchen, NJ: Scarecrow Press, 1990)*,* 20.

46. "Manhattan and Bronx," New York *Age,* July 12, 1906, 6; "Asbury Park Gayeties," New York *Age*; "Labor Day at Asbury Park—Annual Hop of Whitehead House Fine Affair—Many Guests." New York *Age*, Sept. 12, 1907.

47. Burleigh Family Papers.

48. Coleridge-Taylor to HTB, undated, 1904, Burleigh Family Papers.

49. "Perhaps," *Etude,* Dec. 1919, 802–3.

50. "Poor wounded Heart, / 'Tis faithful yet—/ All that is left is thine / And no regret. / "Poor wounded Heart, / The drops of blood that from it ooze / Are Nature's tears; / They pass away with the lonely night / And the empty years" (Louise Burleigh, "The Wounded Heart," *Colored American,* 1919).

51. Burleigh Family Papers.

52. This recording was first issued in England, and Victor issued it in the United States in 1912; Tim Brooks, *Lost Sounds: Blacks and the Birth of the Recording Industry* (Urbana: University of Illinois Press, 2004)*,* 476.

53. Alexander, *Sunshine and Shadow,* 124–25, 169.

54. Burleigh Family Papers. The first verse: "Sons and daughters, rise ye boldly—/ Children of the dusky brow./ Dark the past, but bright the future/ Rises o'er our pathway now./ Hate no more shall o'er us triumph,/ We will conquer ev'ry foe./ Ever striving, still contending,/ On and upward we shall go!" Dated October 21, 1893.

55. Louise Alston Burleigh to Alston, Jan. 15, 1950, Burleigh Family Papers.

56. "Music and the Stage: That Amateur Minstrel Show," New York *Age,* Apr. 30, 1908, 6.

57. Ibid.

Chapter 12. Wife and Family of the "Eminent Baritone"

1. Legal deposition by Alston Burleigh, February 1959, Burleigh Family Papers.

2. Ibid.

3. Anne Key Simpson, *Hard Trials: The Life and Music of Harry T. Burleigh* (Metuchen, NJ: Scarecrow Press, 1990), 23.

4. "Manhattan and Bronx," New York *Age,* Sept. 13, 1906, 6.

5. New York *Age,* Sept. 15, 1910, 2.

6. Unidentified Philadelphia clipping, Oct. 19, 1910, Burleigh Family Papers.

7. Ibid.

8. "Hackley Recital in 'Philly,'" New York *Age*, Oct. 27, 1910, 6.

9. Undated, unidentified Philadelphia review, Burleigh Family Papers.

10. Program, Burleigh Family Papers.

11. "Brilliant Boston Recital," New York *Age*, Feb. 2, 1911, 8.

12. "Boston Notes: Noted Singer and His Wife Appear at Steinert Hall," New York *Age*, Mar. 16, 1911, 3.

13. Duval, "Willing Workers' Recital," New York *Age*, Apr. 27, 1911, 6.

14. Ibid.

15. "Gives Successful Recitals," New York *Age*, Sept. 14, 1911, 6.

16. Ibid.

17. "News of Greater New York," New York *Age*, Dec. 28, 1911, 7.

18. Undated clipping, identified only as "Jacksonville, Florida," Burleigh Family Papers.

19. Undated clipping, identified only as "St. Augustine, Florida," Burleigh Family Papers.

20. Ibid.

21. Simpson, *Hard Trials*, 55–56.

22. "You Ask Me If I Love You" (William Maxwell Company, 1907).

23. Anne Key Simpson, *Hard Trials*, 221.

24. "He Sent Me You" (New York: G. Ricordi and Company, 1915).

25. Legal deposition by Alston Burleigh, February 1959, Burleigh Family Papers.

26. Poster courtesy of David Peterson.

27. Some information about Louise's relationship with Albert Lowe and her subsequent performing career as Princess Nadonis Shawa comes from Peterson, "The Life and Performing Career of Louise Alston Burleigh," unpublished manuscript, 1992. Peterson also shared newspaper clippings and legal documents that supplement materials from Louise's papers in the Burleigh family's possession. Burleigh's grandson, Dr. Harry T. Burleigh II, was greatly interested in the information Peterson gathered and accepted its credibility.

28. Peterson, "Life and Performing Career."

29. Peterson, "Life and Performing Career."

30. Alston Burleigh deposition, 1959, Burleigh Family Papers.

31. Poster, "The Princess Nadonis Indians: Four Original Americans." Burleigh Family Papers.

32. Ibid.

33. Ibid.

34. Handwritten speech, Burleigh Family Papers.

35. Peterson, "Life and Performing Career," 8.

36. Burleigh Family Papers.

37. Peterson, "Life and Performing Career," 9.

38. Burleigh Family Papers.

39. "Princess Nadonis at New Theatre," Dec. 23, 1921 [handwritten date], Burleigh Family Papers; "Fourth Lyceum Number—Princess Nadonis Indians Captivate Large Audience—A Complete Success," undated, unidentified clipping, Burleigh Family Papers; Testimonial, D. M. Morgan, Supt., Mineral Point Public Schools, Apr. 20, 1941, Burleigh Family Papers.

40. Dr. Harry T. Burleigh II, personal communication, April 11, 1992, Pittsburgh, Pennsylvania.

41. Henry Beckett, "A Mighty Voice at 77," New York *Post*, Apr. 24, 1944, n.p.

42. Simpson, *Hard Trials,* 189, 192.

43. Alston Burleigh, 1959 Deposition, Burleigh Family Papers.

44. "News of Greater New York: Sojourner Truth Home Meeting," New York *Age,* Nov. 27, 1913, 8; *Crisis,* Sept. 8, 1914, 243.

45. Greeting card, Burleigh Family Papers.

46. "Miss Eva Burleigh Dies of Heart Failure," New York *Age,* Nov. 8, 1917, 1.

47. "Drury's Opera," New York *Age,* Apr. 6, 1905, 1; "Asbury Park Gayeties," New York *Age,* Aug. 11, 1907, 6; "News of Greater New York: Many Attend Pre-Lenten—Large and Fashionable Audience—List of Boxholders," New York *Age,* Feb. 25, 1909, 7, for example.

48. "News of Greater New York," New York *Age,* June 24, 1915, 8; Elzie's marriage, Burleigh family Bible.

49. Grace Blackwell, personal communication about Elzie's care of Burleigh's business affairs, conversations with the author, March 25 and 26, 2000, Newark, NJ, and by telephone on other occasions. J. P. Morgan's stock offer, Harry T. Burleigh II, telephone conversations, between September 1989 and August 1992, Pittsburgh, PA.

50. HTB to BTW, Sept. 12, 1903, "Part I: Personal Correspondence, 1880–1916," Box 8, Reel 7, BTWP, Library of Congress, Washington, DC.

51. Grace Blackwell, telephone conversations, July 26, 2007, and Dec. 14, 2008.

52. Grace Blackwell, telephone conversation, Mar. 25, 2000, Newark, NJ.

53. Ibid.

54. Grace Blackwell, telephone conversation, July 26, 2007.

55. Ibid.

56. Dr. Harry T. Burleigh II, personal communication, 1988, Pittsburgh, PA.

57. "Still Loud in Praise of Virginia State Singers," *New Journal and Guide,* Mar. 19, 1932, 9; "East Praises Son of Harry T. Burleigh," Chicago *Defender,* Apr. 8, 1933; "Will Arrange 'Jezebel' Music," New York *Herald Tribune,* Sept. 1, 1933; Maurice Dancer, "Waters on Tour, New Plays Cast, Other Sepians." Pittsburgh *Courier,* Sept. 8, 1934, sec. 2, p. 9; letter to Alston from John D. Koontz, Mar. 23, 1960. Burleigh Family Papers.

58. Marie Burleigh, speaking at the "Heritage and Legacy of Harry T. Burleigh" Conference banquet, April 5, 2003.

Chapter 13. St. George's Becomes Mr. Burleigh's Church

1. Nora Douglas Holt, "Henry [Thacker] Burleigh," Chicago *Defender,* Mar. 27, 1920, 12.

2. "The Bishop and the Choir Boy—From the New York Sun," New York *Age,* Jan. 4, 1890.

3. Lester A. Walton, "Harry T. Burleigh Honored To-Day at St. George's," New York *World,* Mar. 30, 1924, reprinted in *The Black Perspective in Music* (Spring 1974): 82.

4. Dr. Harry T. Burleigh II, personal communication, Apr. 11, 1992, Pittsburgh, PA.

5. Rev. Elmore McKee, "Burleigh: The Man, His Music, His Message," Sermon, St. George's, May 4, 1980, Burleigh Family Papers.

6. William S. Rainsford, *A Preacher's Story of His Work* (New York: Outlook, 1904), 267.

7. Dorothy Drummond Hauser, "A Man with a Glory," *Newark Sunday News,* Nov. 1, 1978, 48.

8. Rainsford, *Preacher's Story,* 266.

9. Anne Key Simpson, *Hard Trials: The Life and Music of Harry T. Burleigh* (Metuchen, NJ: Scarecrow Press, 1990), 18.

10. Harry T. Burleigh II, personal communication, Apr. 11, 1992, Pittsburgh, PA.

11. "'Crucifixion' Sung at St. George's," New York *Times*, Mar. 23, 1896, 2; "Famous Choirs of New York," New York *Times* Illustrated Magazine Supplement, 5; "News Notes of the Musical World," New York *Times*, Drama X8; "Messages of Easter in Churches Today," New York *Times* Editorials, Apr. 4, 1926, E1; "Topics of Interest to the Churchgoer," New York *Times* Religion, 27; "Bishop Manning Will Act at Ceremonies in Two Churches," New York *Times* Religion, 23.

12. McKee, "Burleigh," 1.

13. Hauser, "A Man with a Glory," 48.

14. Rainsford, *Preacher's Story*, 118.

15. Ibid., 125.

16. Ibid., 131.

17. Ibid., 211, 213.

18. William S. Rainsford, *The Story of a Varied Life: An Autobiography* (Garden City, NY: Doubleday, Page, 1922), 132.

19. Ibid., 236.

20. Rainsford, *Preacher's Story*, 160–62, 165–67.

21. Ibid., 122–23.

22. Rainsford, *Varied Life*, 307.

23. Ibid., 225.

24. Rainsford, *Preacher's Story*, 170.

25. Ibid., 232–33.

26. Rainsford, *Varied Life*, 217.

27. William S. Rainsford, "Personal Recollections," Herbert Livingston Satterlee Papers, ARC 1219, Part 2: A4, Archives of the Pierpont Morgan Library, New York, NY, pp. 7–8.

28. Harry T. Burleigh, "Deep River," manuscript arrangement, Mary Flagler Cary Music Collection, Department of Music Manuscripts and Printed Music, Morgan Library and Museum, New York, NY.

29. The initial salary, unidentified clipping, Burleigh Collection, Hampton University archives, Hampton, Virginia.

30. "St. George's A. C. Reception," New York *Times*, Nov. 16, 1894, 6.

31. "Famous Choirs of New York," New York *Times* Illustrated Magazine Supplement, Oct. 23, 1898, 5.

32. "Lower East Side Again Welcomes Seth Low," New York *Times*, Nov. 1, 1911, 2.

33. Rainsford, *Varied Life*, 243.

34. "What Is Doing in Society," New York *Times*, Mar. 7, 1902, 7.

35. Telegram, Mrs. Borden Harriman to HTB, Dec. 5, 1903, Burleigh Family Papers.

36. HTB to Booker T. Washington, Aug. 14, 1902, "Part I: Personal Correspondence, 1880–1916," Box 8, Reel 7, Booker T. Washington Papers (hereafter, BTWP), Library of Congress (hereafter, LOC), Washington, DC.

37. "Victoria Earle Matthews," BlackPast.org. blackpast.org/view/vignettes.

38. Victoria Earle Matthews to Booker T. Washington, Apr. 8, 1899, General Correspondence, Box 155, folder M, Mar.–Apr. 1899, BTWP, LOC. Thanks to Steve Kramer for alerting me to this letter, and to Joseph Jackson, manuscript reference technician, Manuscript Division, Library of Congress, for sending me a copy.

39. In fact, his godson, James Hall Jr., reported that he remembered "no degree of drinking." Simpson, *Hard Trials*, 203.

40. Josephine Harreld Love, personal communication, Feb. 11, 1991, Erie, PA, and by telephone, Mar. 7, 1987.

41. Simpson, *Hard Trials,* 173.

42. Rainsford, *Varied Life,* 302.

43. "St. George's Men," *St. George's Bulletin*, Apr. 6, 1919, 4; "St George's Men's Club," 1912 Minstrel Show program, 12.

44. Examples of Burleigh's use of Men's Club stationery can be found in his correspondence with Booker T. Washington, BTWP, LOC.

45. "Movie and Stage," Chicago *Defender,* Aug. 27, 1921.

46. Eric Lott, *Blackface Minstrelsy and the American Working Class* (New York: Oxford University Press, 1993), 6.

47. St. George's *Yearbook,* Easter 1907, "Chairman's Report," 125.

48. "Angry at Action against a Church," New York *Times,* Feb. 17, 1907, 7.

49. Program, 1907 St. George's Men's Club Minstrel Show, "Greeting." The author's Burleigh collection, courtesy of Karen James.

50. Ibid.

51. "Chairman's Report," St. George's *Yearbook,* Easter 1907, 125.

52. Program, 1907 St. George's Men's Club Minstrel Show.

53. *St. George's Yearbook,* Easter 1911, 115.

54. Ibid., Oct. 18, 1914, 3.

55. *St. George's Annual Report,* Easter 1915, 16, 86.

56. St. George's church bulletin, Feb. 4, 1917, 4.

57. Ibid., Apr. 22, 1917, 3.

58. Elizabeth Moulton, *St. George's Church* (New York: The Rector, Church Wardens, and Vestrymen of St. George's Church, in the City of New York, 1964), 92.

59. Ibid., 93–94.

60. Ibid., 101.

61. Ibid., 105.

62. "Mr. Morgan Buried Just as He Wished," New York *Times,* Apr. 15, 1913.

63. Moulton, *St. George's Church,* 104.

64. St. George's church bulletin, Mar. 6, 1921, 3.

65. Letter from William Seaman Bainbridge, Nov. 21, 1928, St. George's Burleigh Papers.

66. Simpson, *Hard Trials,* 173.

67. "Church Services Tomorrow," New York *Times,* Feb. 16, 1919, 130.

68. "Four P.M. Service," *St. George's Bulletin,* Jan. 4, 1920, 3.

69. "Four P.M. Service," *St. George's Bulletin,* Jan. 11, 1920.

70. "Four P.M. Service," *St. George's Bulletin,* Jan. 25, 1920, 3.

71. For example, "Deep River" was the Introit Anthem, Jan. 28, 1917, *St. George's Bulletin,* 3; March 28, 1926, Vesper Service, "Were You There?"

72. Moulton, *St. George's Church,* 106.

73. For example, "Town Hall Meeting Honors Dr. Rainsford." New York *Times,* May 13, 1925, 2; *St. George's Bulletin,* Apr. 1, 1928.

74. Pittsburgh *Courier,* Apr. 5, 1924, 1; New York *World,* Apr. 26, 1924; New York *Times,* Apr. 27, 1924, E3.

75. James Weldon Johnson, *American Negro Spirituals* (New York: Viking Press, 1925), 48.

76. "Burleigh Honored," Boston *Chronicle*, May 26, 1924.

77. "Church to Honor Negro Composer," New York *Times*, E1 TR, Mar. 30, 1924; "Crowds at Church Honor Negro Singer," New York *Times*, Mar. 31, 1924; "A Negro Musician Honored," *Southern Workman*, Apr. 1924, 196; "Sang 30 Years, Never Missed a Sunday: Harry T. Burleigh, Composer and Singer, Honored by Fashionable N. Y. Church," Baltimore *Afro-American*, Apr. 4, 1924; "Signally Honored," Pittsburgh *Courier*, Apr. 5, 1924, 1, 3; "Negro Spirituals at St. George's," New York *World*, Apr. 16, 1924; "Negro to Sing Again in St. George's," New York *Times*, Apr. 27, 1924, E3.

78. "The World: Negro Baritone Is Paid Tribute in Old St. George's," Burleigh Collection, St. George's Episcopal Church, n.p.

79. Ibid.

80. "Crowds at Church Honor Negro Singer," New York *Times,* Mar. 31, 1924.

81. This description combines details from several newspaper reports. See note 77.

82. "The World: Negro Baritone Is Paid Tribute."

83. Ibid.

84. Ibid.

85. Moulton, *St. George's Church,* 116.

86. Olin Downes, "Amusements: Music: Choir Fills Town Hall," New York *Times*, Dec. 12, 1924, 28.

87. These details are gathered from the Vesper Service programs in the Burleigh Papers, St. George's Episcopal Church.

88. Ibid.

89. Henry Lee, "Swing Low, Sweet Chariot," *Coronet,* July 1947, 54.

90. Rainsford, *Varied Life,* 267.

91. "Charms Again at Palm Services," Pittsburgh *Courier*, Apr. 4, 1942, 20.

92. Ibid.

93. Rev. Elmore McKee to C. C. Burlingham, Jan. 24, 1944, Burleigh Papers, St. George's Episcopal Church, New York, NY.

94. Rev. Elmore McKee to C. C. Burlingham, Jan. 30, 1944, Burleigh Papers, St. George's Episcopal Church, New York, NY.

95. Rev. Elmore McKee to C. C. Burlingham, Jan. 24, 1944, Burleigh Papers, St. George's Episcopal Church, New York, NY.

96. Rev. Elmore McKee, remarks at the fiftieth anniversary reception, Burleigh Papers, St. George's Episcopal Church, New York, NY.

97. Simpson, *Hard Trials*, 145.

98. "Church Honors Harry Burleigh For 50 Years' Service in Choir," undated, unidentified clipping, Burleigh Family Papers.

99. Tim Brooks, *Lost Sounds: Blacks and the Birth of the Recording Industry, 1890–1919* (Urbana: University of Illinois Press, 2004), 484.

100. Moulton, *St. George's Church,* 134.

101. McKee, "Burleigh," 4.

102. McKee to HTBII, May 10, 1980, Burleigh Family Papers.

103. Rev. Elmore McKee to Rev. Edward O. Miller, May 10, 1980, Burleigh Papers, St. George's Episcopal Church, New York, NY.

104. Rev. Edward O. Miller to Anne Key Simpson, Mar. 15, 1988, Burleigh Family Papers.

105. Ibid.

106. Hauser, "A Man with a Glory," 48.

107. Simpson, *Hard Trials*, 173.

108. Josephine Harreld Love, telephone conversation, Mar. 14, 1990.

109. New York *Times,* Apr. 15, 1946.

110. Hauser, "A Man with a Glory," 49.

111. Simpson, *Hard Trials*, 173–74.

112. Rev. Elmore McKee to Anne Key Simpson, Mar. 15, 1988, Burleigh Family Papers.

113. Simpson, *Hard Trials*, 174.

114. Postcard from IEG (further unidentified) to Eileen Southern, Sept. 28, 1973. From the author's Burleigh collection, courtesy of Eileen Southern.

115. "Burleigh Honored," Boston *Chronicle*, May 26, 1924.

Chapter 14. A Singer-Composer Learns His Craft

1. This number does not include the 187 folksong and spiritual arrangements published in the *Old Songs Hymnal,* or the more than four hundred unpublished arrangements from Mansfield County, Georgia, that were not published in the *Old Songs Hymnal.* Though the organization of the discussion of Burleigh's songs is different, much of the analysis of songs in this chapter and the following two chapters is based on chapters three, four, and five of my dissertation, "Harry T. Burleigh and the Creative Expression of Bi-Musicality: A Study of an African-American Composer and the American Art Song," Ph.D. diss., University of Pittsburgh, 1992, and in some cases I have retained the wording from that source.

2. Snyder, "Harry T. Burleigh," 130.

3. Roland Allison, "Classification of the Vocal Works of Harry T. Burleigh (1866–1949) and Some Suggestions for Their Use in Teaching Diction in Singing," Ph.D. diss., Indiana University, 1965, 136, 140, 143, 147. This is the first dissertation to examine Burleigh's total compositional output, basing his research on primary sources, and it remains a valuable source of information on the songs.

4. Thirty-three of the songs mentioned in this chapter are available on the Library of Congress website. The Eastman School of Music has also digitized a number of Burleigh pieces, including *Southland Sketches,* which will be discussed in chapter 15.

5. W. E. B. Du Bois, *Souls of Black Folk* [1903], ed. Henry Louis Gates Jr. and Terri Hume Oliver (New York: W. W. Norton, 1999), 10–11.

6. Mellone V. Burnim and Portia K. Maultsby, eds., *African American Music: An Intro-duction* (New York: Routledge, 2006), 235.

7. Wilson, "Interpreting Classical Music," 235–36.

8. William H. Youngren, *C. P. E. Bach and the Rebirth of the Strophic Song* (Lanham, MD: Scarecrow Press, 2003), 2.

9. Leon Wilbur Gray, "The American Art Song: An Inquiry into Its Development from the Colonial Period to the Present," 2 vols. Ed.D. diss., Columbia University, 1967, 124.

10. Ibid., 133–34.

11. My website, *Friends of Harry T. Burleigh,* includes a list of nationally and internationally prominent singers who performed Burleigh's songs. Examples of dedications: "By the Pool at the Third Rosses," 1919, "Respectfully dedicated to Mr. John McCormack"; "A Corn Song," 1920, "To Royal Dadmun"; "I Couldn't Hear Nobody Pray," "To Nathaniel Dett, Hampton

Institute, Virginia"; "To the Chorus of The Schola Cantorum, New York—Kurt Schindler, Conductor."

12. Harry T. Burleigh, "Christmas Bells" (Luckhart and Belder, 1895).

13. *Everybody's Magazine,* June 1901, 588–89.

14. "Hush," April 1901, 378–80, and "Song of the Watcher," *Everybody's Magazine,* August 1901, 154–55.

15. "O Southland, O Southland, Dear land so far away / We dream of thee by night We long for thee by day. . . . / And so thy sun, thy soil, thy rocks, / Thy forests, streams and flow'rs / By right, by right of birth, By right of love are ours."

16. For example, Neidlinger's "Rockin' in de Wind" and Homer's "Mammy's Lullaby," "Uncle Rome," and "A Banjo Song."

17. James E. Campbell, "Ring, My Bawnjer, Ring" (New York: G. Schirmer, 1902).

18. Another Burleigh setting of lyrics by Dunbar is "A Corn Song."

19. Burleigh Family Papers.

20. New York *Tribune,* Mar. 31, 1901.

21. Snyder, "Harry T. Burleigh," 253–54.

22. London *Star,* July 1, 1901; Brooke and Denton publicity flyer, Burleigh Family Papers.

23. Snyder, "Harry T. Burleigh," 253–54.

24. For example, in 1903 he sang "Ride Up in de Chariot," unpublished; "Hard Trials," published in 1919; "I Don't Feel No-ways Tired," 1917; and "Swing Low, Sweet Chariot," 1917.

25. Gayle Murchison, "'Dean of Afro-American Composers' or 'Harlem Renaissance Man,'" *Arkansas Historical Quarterly* 53, no. 1 (1994), 42–74; Catherine Parsons Smith, *William Grant Still: A Study in Contradictions* (Los Angeles: University of California Press, 2000), 39–40; Thanks to Josephine Wright for her July 17, 2011, e-mail about the significance of Davis's concert music.

26. A. Walter Kramer, "H. T. Burleigh: Composer by Divine Right and 'the American Coleridge-Taylor,'" *Musical America,* Apr. 29, 1916, 25.

27. New Bedford (Mass.) *Standard Times,* Aug. 20, 1938, cited in Anne Key Simpson, *Hard Trials: The Life and Music of Harry T. Burleigh* (Metuchen, NJ: Scarecrow Press, 1990), 133.

28. Snyder, "Harry T. Burleigh," 62; *The Temple Emanu-El Bulletin,* May 1935, 194.

29. Kramer, "H. T. Burleigh," 25.

30. The information on George and William Maxwell and their support of Burleigh's work is gleaned from Allison, "Classification," 113–14. Allison was able to interview Mr. Leo Bernardone, who worked at G. Ricordi from 1932 through the transfer of ownership to Franco Columbo and knew Burleigh well; Bernardone verified the accuracy of Allison's account.

31. HTB to Fred Morse, Apr. 1, 1900, "Part I: Personal Correspondence, 1880–1916," Box 8, Reel 7, BTWP, Library of Congress (LOC), Washington, D.C.

32. Undated clipping from an unidentified Erie paper, Burleigh Family Papers.

33. Augusta da Bubna, "The Negro on the Stage," *Theatre Magazine,* April 1903, reprinted in *The Tuskegee Student,* n.d., Burleigh Family Papers.

34. Maud Cuney-Hare, *Negro Musicians and Their Music* (1936; repr., New York: Da Capo Press, 1974), 326.

35. Snyder, "Harry T. Burleigh," 133–34.

36. Nicholas E. Tawa, *Sweet Songs for Gentle Americans: The Parlor Song in America, 1790–1860* (Bowling Green, OH: Bowling Green University Popular Press, 1980), 8.

37. Charles Hamm, *Yesterdays: Popular Song in America* (New York: W. W. Norton, 1979), 321.

38. A. Walter Kramer, Review of Burleigh's 1914 setting of "Elysium," lyrics by James Weldon Johnson, "New Music—Vocal and Instrumental," *Musical America*, Apr. 25, 1915, 24.

39. Boston *Transcript,* Jan. 4, 1905, n.p.

40. "'A Certain Strangeness': Harry T. Burleigh's Art Songs and Spiritual Arrangements," *Black Music Research Journal,* Autumn 2004, 233–34.

41. Snyder, "Harry T. Burleigh," 268.

42. Penman Lovinggood, *Famous Modern Negro Musicians* (1921; repr., New York: Da Capo, 1978), 8.

43. Lucien H. White, "A Race Musician," New York *Age,* May 18, 1916, 6.

44. Ellsworth Janifer, "Harry T. Burleigh, Ten Years Later," *Phylon* 21, no. 2 (1960): 147.

45. Allison, "Classification," 140.

46. Kramer, "H. T. Burleigh," 25.

47. Tim Brooks, *Lost Sounds: Blacks and the Birth of the Recording Industry, 1890–1919* (Urbana: University of Illinois Press, 2004), 477.

48. Patricia Turner, *Dictionary of Afro-American Performers: 78 RPM and Cylinder Recordings of Opera, Choral Music, and Song, c. 1900–1949* (New York: Garland Press, 1990), 88–89.

49. Snyder, "Harry T. Burleigh," 139.

50. Ibid.

51. Ibid.

52. Undated, unidentified clipping, 1903, Burleigh Family Papers.

53. Thanks to Gilbert Dickinson scholar Marcy Tanter for alerting me to the relationship to Emily Dickinson.

54. Allison, "Classification," 140.

55. Snyder, "Harry T. Burleigh," 134.

56. Ibid., 152.

57. Ibid., 246.

58. Tom Fletcher, *100 Years of the Negro in Show Business: The Tom Fletcher Story* (New York: Burdge, 1954; repr., New York: Da Capo, 1984), 176.

59. Joseph Smith, liner notes, *From the Southland: Songs, Piano Sketches and Spirituals of Harry T. Burleigh* (Premier Recordings PRCD 1041), 1.

60. Snyder, "Harry T. Burleigh," 281.

61. Ibid., 283–84; Simpson, *Hard Trials,* 264.

62. Snyder, "Harry T. Burleigh," 283–84.

63. "Last Week's Bills: Koster and Bials," New York *Dramatic Mirror,* Nov. 19, 1898, 18.

64. "Eminent Musician Assails Mis-Use of Spirituals in Dance Tunes," New York *News,* Nov. 18, 1922.

65. Joseph Smith, "Practicing and Performing Burleigh's 'Hiding-Place,'" *Piano and Keyboard,* July–August 1998, 19.

66. Simpson, *Hard* Trials, 266.

67. R. Reid Badger, *James Reese Europe: A Life in Ragtime* (New York: Oxford University Press, 1995), 58.

68. http://www.gutenberg.org/8/1/9/8197.

69. Edward Said, "Introduction," in *Orientalism* (New York: Vintage, 1979), 1, 3; Jonathan Bellman, ed., "Introduction," in *The Exotic in Western Music* (Boston: Northeastern

University Press, 1998), xii; Ralph Locke, "Cutthroats and Casbah Dancers, Muezzins and Timeless Sands: Musical Images of the Middle East," in *The Exotic in Western Music,* ed. Jonathan Bellman (Boston: Northeastern University Press, 1998), 117–18.

70. *Contemporary American Composers* (Boston: L. C. Page, 1900).

71. The cover titles this song "Just a-Wearin' for You," but the first page and the lyrics list it as "Just a-Wearyin' for You."

72. Brooks, *Lost Sounds,* 476.

73. E. Douglas Bomberger, *An Index to Music Published in the Etude Magazine, 1883–1957,* (Lanham, MD: Scarecrow Press, 2004), 296.

74. Brooks, *Lost Sounds,* 477.

75. "Juilliard Student Club," *Juilliard Student Magazine,* May 10, 1934, 3.

76. Smith, "Practicing and Performing," 1.

77. Simpson, *Hard Trials,* 222.

78. Ibid., 10.

79. "Dvořák Leads for the Fund," New York *Herald,* Jan. 24, 1894.

80. "Harry Burleigh Sings at Home of His Birth," Erie *Morning Dispatch,* May 19, 1908.

81. Lawrence Schenbeck, *Racial Uplift and American Music 1878–1943* (Jackson: University Press of Mississippi, 2012), 269, n. 89.

82. *Negro Minstrel Melodies* (New York: William Maxwell Company, 1909), iii.

83. Bomberger, *Index to Music.*

84. "Biographical Sketch," Kurt Schindler Papers, 1882–1946, NYPL-LC JPB 93–1.

85. "Programs of the Week," New York *Times,* Apr. 7, 1918, 65.

86. Simpson, *Hard Trials,* 61.

Chapter 15. *"Composer by Divine Right"*

1. For a list of the singers who performed his songs during his lifetime, see my website, www.Friends of Harry T. Burleigh.com.

2. Mrs. Harry T. Burleigh II, who frequently receives requests for permission to publish the hymn, personal communication.

3. Anne Key Simpson, *Hard Trials: The Life and Music of Harry T. Burleigh* (New York: Scarecrow Press, 1990), 67; Tim Brooks, *Lost Sounds: Blacks and the Birth of the Recording Industry 1890–1919* (Urbana: University of Illinois Press, 2004), 478; "Music and Art," *Crisis,* July 1914, 111; "Harry Burleigh's Late Long Sung by John McCorm[ack]," Chicago *Defender,* Jan. 29, 1916.

4. "McCormack Picks 78 American Songs: That Number Chosen from 600 by Tenor," *Musical America,* Sept. 30, 1916, 13.

5. "One Man Festival of Song," *Musical America,* Mar. 17, 1917, 16.

6. Jean E. Snyder, "Harry T. Burleigh and the Creative Expression of Bi-Musicality: A Study of an African American Composer and the American Art Song," Ph.D. diss., University of Pittsburgh, 1992, 206–7.

7. "Their Ten Favorite American Songs," *Musical America,* Oct. 16, 1915, 3–5.

8. Simpson, *Hard Trials,* 73.

9. *Musical America,* Feb. 5, 1915, 13.

10. *Musical America,* Nov. 1915, 23.

11. M. B. Swaab, "Johnstown Chorus Has Hackett's Aid," *Musical America,* June 2, 1917, 41.

12. Joseph Horowitz, *Wagner Nights: An American History* (Berkeley: University of California Press, 1994), 4–5.

13. Ibid., 5.

14. Martin Bauml Dubermann, *Paul Robeson* (New York: Alfred A. Knopf, 1988), 594, n. 34.

15. "Harry T. Burleigh: Composer by Divine Right and 'The American Coleridge-Taylor,'" *Musical America,* Apr. 29, 1916, 25.

16. Snyder, "Harry T. Burleigh," 136–37.

17. Ibid., 137.

18. Ibid.

19. Darryl Taylor, "The Importance of Studying African-American Art Song: Song Cycles to Know," *Journal of Singing* 54, no. 3 (Jan 1998): 11.

20. Edward Said, *Orientalism* (New York: Vintage Books, 1979); Said, *Culture and Imperialism* (New York: Alfred A. Knopf, 1994); Jonathan Bellman, ed., *The Exotic in Western Music* (Boston: Northeastern University Press, 1998); Ralph P. Locke, *Musical Exoticism: Images and Reflections* (New York: Cambridge University Press, 2011).

21. Snyder, "Harry T. Burleigh," 180; "'Persian Garden' Transferred to Stage," *Musical America,* Oct. 25, 1913, 27.

22. Rupert Hughes, *Contemporary American Composers* (Boston: L. C. Page, 1900).

23. For example, "Fragments," lyrics by Jessie Fauset (1919), and "I Want to Die While You Love Me," lyrics by Georgia Douglas Johnson (1919).

24. Anne Key Simpson, *Hard Trials,* 225.

25. Ibid., 225–27.

26. Vika Gardner, personal communication, July 1, 2012, Meadville, PA.

27. Ricordi advertising flyer, Yale University Library, cited in Simpson, *Hard Trials,* 440n21.

28. *Musical Courier,* June 26, 1924, 34.

29. Ricordi flyer, Burleigh Family Papers.

30. James Sample, Apr. 10, 1991; personal communication with the author, Meadville, PA.

31. Snyder, "Harry T. Burleigh," 181.

32. Henderson, Prefatory Note to Harry T. Burleigh, *Saracen Songs* (New York: G. Ricordi, 1915).

33. Burleigh Collection, Vertical File, Erie County Public Library, Erie, PA.

34. "New Music Vocal and Instrumental," *Musical America*, Aug. 8, 1914, 24.

35. See Duana Demus, "A Composer by Divine Right: A Performance Guide to Harry Burleigh's Saracen Songs and Five Songs of Laurence Hope," D.M.A. thesis, UCLA, 2004. George Shirley, on singing "Almona," personal communication, Feb. 11, 1912, Irvine, CA.

36. A. Walter Kramer, "New Music—Vocal and Instrumental," *Musical America,* Mar. 13, 1915, 34.

37. Moderwell, "'Deep River' Popularizes a Composer," Boston *Evening Transcript*, Mar. 10, 1917.

38. Ibid.

39. Henry Krehbiel, Prefatory Note to Harry T. Burleigh, *Five Songs of Laurence Hope* (1915).

40. Simpson, *Hard Trials,* 72.

41. Moderwell, "'Deep River' Popularizes a Composer."

42. *Musical Standard,* Dec. 25, 1915.

43. Moderwell, "'Deep River' Popularizes a Composer."

44. Ibid.

45. *Musical Standard,* Dec. 25, 1915.

46. Kramer, *Musical America,* Mar. 13, 1915, 34.

47. Moderwell, "'Deep River' Popularizes a Composer."

48. Victoria Etnier Villamil, *A Singer's Guide to the American Art Song* (Metuchen, NJ: Scarecrow Press, 1993), 74; Villamil mistakes Brüggemann's orchestrations to be orchestral versions of the songs rather than orchestral accompaniments for singers.

49. See Philip Creech, *From the Southland: Songs, Piano Sketches and Spirituals of Harry T. Burleigh* (Premier Recordings PRCD 1041, 1995); Cynthia Haymon, *Where the Songs Come From: American Songs* (Argo 436–117–2ZH, 1992), which includes three of the five songs; Duana Demus, "A Composer by Divine Right: A Performance Guide to Harry Burleigh's 'Saracen Songs' and 'Five Songs of Laurence Hope,'" Ph.D. diss., University of California–Los Angeles, 2005.

50. "Entertainments," *Southern Workman,* July 1914, 420.

51. Kramer, "New Music—Vocal and Instrumental," *Musical America,* Apr. 5, 1914.

52. G. Ricordi ad, quoting Kramer's review in *Musical America,* Oct. 16, 1915.

53. Moderwell, "'Deep River' Popularizes a Composer."

54. Roland Allison, "Classification of the Vocal Works of Harry T. Burleigh (1866–1949) and Some Suggestions for Their Use in Teaching Diction in Singing," Ph.D. diss., Indiana University, 1965, 147.

55. Elsworth Janifer, "H. T. Burleigh, Ten Years Later," *Phylon* 21, no. 2 (1960): 147–48.

56. Moderwell, "'Deep River' Popularizes a Composer"; Snyder, "Harry T. Burleigh," 432, 434, 438, 439.

57. Taylor, "Importance of Studying African-American Art Song," 11.

58. "Music and Art," *Crisis,* Apr. 1914, 268.

59. Bangor (Maine) *Commercial,* Oct. 2, 1916, in Simpson, *Hard Trials,* 70.

60. Ibid.

61. "An American Negro Whose Music Stirs the Blood of Warring Italy," *Current Opinion,* Aug. 1916, 100–101.

62. Ibid.

63. Philadelphia *Tribune,* Oct. 7, 1916; quoted in Simpson, *Hard Trials,* 70.

64. *Musical America,* clipping fragment, Broughton Tall Manuscript Collection, Library of Congress (hereafter, LOC).

65. Snyder, "Harry T. Burleigh," 193.

66. Simpson, *Hard Trials,* 73, 87; "Schelling at Metropolitan," *Musical America,* Dec. 13, 1916, 42.

67. *Musical Courier,* Feb. 24, 1916, 50.

68. "'The Young Warrior,' by H. T. Burleigh, Causing Sensation," Chicago *Defender,* Aug. 16, 1916, 4.

69. Ann Sears, "'A Certain Strangeness': Harry T. Burleigh's Art Songs and Spiritual Arrangements," *Black Music Research Journal* 24, no. 2 (Autumn 2004): 244–45.

70. Ibid., 246–47.

71. Simpson, *Hard Trials*, 75.

72. K.S.C., "McCormack Offers Two Native Groups," *Musical America*, Feb. 27, 1917, 48.

73. "A Braslau Recital," New York *Evening Globe*, Dec. 30, 1918; A. Walter Kramer, "Braslau Displays Ripened Artistry," *Musical America,* Jan. 4, 1919, 5.

74. Lucien H. White, "Music Notes," New York *Age*, Nov. 2, 1916, 6.

75. Unpaged, undated *Musical America* clipping, Broughton Tall Manuscript Collection, LOC, n.d.

76. Alston Burleigh Deposition, 1959; "Alston Burleigh Elevated to Major in 366th Infantry," New York *Amsterdam News*, Aug. 23, 1941, 8; Bill Chase, "All Ears," New York *Amsterdam News*, Feb. 20, 1943, 8.

77. Anne Key Simpson, *Hard Trials*, 81.

78. James Sample, personal communication, Apr. 10, 1991, Meadville, PA.

79. Sears, "'A Certain Strangeness,'" 234–35.

80. Ibid., 235.

81. Brooks, *Lost Sounds,* 478–79.

82. Ibid., 479.

83. The mistaken identity came to light in an exchange of correspondence in the New York *Times* Book Review of Mar. 31, 1940, 99, and May 12, 1940, 31. In response to a letter from a reader correcting the March report, the New York *Times* contacted George Swift Brengle, who explained how the error came about. He gave contact information for Walter H. Brown and the former editor of the *Wesleyan Literary Monthly*, now Rev. Alfred D. Moore, for those wishing to confirm the truth of his account.

84. Simpson, *Hard Trials*, 75.

85. Moderwell, "'Deep River' Popularizes a Composer."

86. Lucien H. White, "Music Notes," New York *Age*, May 18, 1916, 6.

87. Lucien H. White, "Music Notes," New York *Age*, Sept. 14, 1916, 6.

88. Edward Boatner, "Negro Composers: Burleigh," New York *Age,* June 7, 1941, 10.

89. Snyder, "Harry T. Burleigh," "Ethiopia Saluting the Colors," *International Dictionary of Black Composers*, vol. 1 (Chicago: Fitzroy Dearborn, 1999), 189–90.

90. Ibid.; see also Sears, "'A Certain Strangeness,'" 247, and Thomas Hampson, "Ethiopia Saluting the Colors," The Library of Congress Song of America Project, Tour Song Highlights, www.loc.gov/item/ihas.200031151/.

91. "Mr. Witherspoon's Recital," New York *Times,* Nov. 24, 1915, 13.

92. Moderwell, "'Deep River' Popularizes a Composer."

93. *To the Soul—Thomas Hampson Sings the Poetry of Walt Whitman,* EMI Classics, 2005; *Song of America—Music from the Library of Congress,* Angel Records, 1997. Two 1995 recordings are by bass-baritone Oral Moses, *Deep River: Songs and Spirituals by Harry T. Burleigh,* reissued by Albany Records, Troy 4509; and mezzo-soprano Hilda Harris, *From the Southland: Songs, Piano Sketches and Spirituals of Harry T. Burleigh,* Premier Recordings PRCD 104.

94. Edward Mapp, *Directory of Blacks in the Performing Arts,* 2nd ed. (Metuchen, NJ: Scarecrow Press, 1990), 70.

95. Moderwell, "'Deep River' Popularizes a Composer."

96. "Music and Art," *Crisis*, July 1918, 136; the second movement, adagio, was played in 1924 and 1932 and on theremin and violin in 1934; the third movement was played in 1924.

97. "New York Church Pays Tribute to Burleigh," *Musical America*, Apr. 12, 1924, 27.

98. Charlotte W. Murray, "The Story of Harry T. Burleigh," *Hymn,* Oct. 1966, 107.

99. Ibid.

100. Draft of undated letter, HTB to Mrs. N. W. Maise of Spelman College in Atlanta, Georgia, Burleigh Family Papers.

101. Ibid.

102. HTB to Marian Anderson, Oct. 16, 1935, Marian Anderson Papers, Rare Book and Manuscript Library, University of Pennsylvania, Section 1, Box 2, Folder 797.

103. Langston Hughes, "Harlem [2]," in *Montage of a Dream Deferred: The Collected Poems of Langston Hughes,* ed. Arnold Rampersad and David Roessel (New York: Alfred A. Knopf, 1998), 426.

104. See chapter 9.

105. Lawrence Schenbeck, *Racial Uplift and American Music, 1878–1943* (Jackson: University Press of Mississippi, 2012), 4.

106. Langston Hughes, "The Negro Artist and the Racial Mountain," *The Nation,* June 23, 1926, 692–94.

107. HTB telegram to Langston Hughes, October 24, 1935, James Weldon Johnson manuscript collection, Box 33, Burleigh folder, Beinecke Library, Yale University.

108. Postcard, July 6, 1936; letter, July 6, 1936, James Weldon Johnson manuscript collection, Box 1063, Burleigh folder, Beinecke Library, Yale University.

109. Letter from Rev. Elmore M. McKee to Harry T. Burleigh II, May 10, 1980, 8, Burleigh Family Papers.

110. Charlotte W. Murray, "The Story of Harry T. Burleigh," *Hymn,* Oct. 1966, 107.

111. Snyder, "Harry T. Burleigh," 215.

Chapter 16. Bringing Spirituals to the Concert Stage

1. "Burleigh Celebrates 39th Anniversary as Choir Baritone," Chicago *Defender*, June 3, 1933, 63, 4.

2. Richard Wallaschek, *Primitive Music* (London: Longmans, Green, 1893); Dena Epstein, "A White Origin for the Black Spiritual? An Invalid Theory and How It Grew," *American Music*, 1/2 (1983): 55.

3. W. J. Henderson, "Preface," *Negro Minstrel Melodies* (New York: G. Schirmer, 1909), iv.

4. William W. Austin, "Susannah," "Jeanie," and "The Old Folks at Home," in *The Songs of Stephen C. Foster from His Time to Ours,* 2nd ed. (Urbana: University of Illinois Press, 1989), 297.

5. Henry E. Krehbiel, *Afro-American Folksongs* (New York: Frederick Ungar, 1914), 11–14.

6. *The Musician*, Nov. 1906, 544–45.

7. Krehbiel, *Afro-American Folksongs*, v, vi.

8. Harry T. Burleigh, "The Negro in Music," speech given to the NAACP, July 1, 1924.

9. Krehbiel, *Afro-American Folksongs*, vii, 13, 26, 43–43.

10. Ibid., vii, ix, viii, 35.

11. Ibid., 14.

12. Ibid., 4, 22.

13. Krehbiel, "Dr. Dvořák's American Symphony," New York *Daily Tribune*, Dec. 15, 1893.

14. Krehbiel, *Afro-American Folksongs*, x.

15. "Folk Songs Originated by Negroes," New York *Amsterdam News*, May 9, 1923, 1, 6; Harry T. Burleigh, "The Negro and His Song," in *Music on the Air*, ed. Hazel G. Kinscella (New York: Viking, 1934), 186–89.

16. Lucien H. White, "In the Realm of Music: The Krehbiel-Burlin Memorial Services," New York *Age*, May 5, 1923, 5. The Burleigh-Krehbiel correspondence has not been found.

17. Letter to an unidentified woman, Apr. 24, 1897, Edward and MacDowell collection, Box 29, folder 14, Music Division, Library of Congress.

18. Lucien H. White, "In the Realm of Music: 'From Bach to Burleigh!' Is Gamut of Program of Music Rendered to Audience Filling Larchmont Church," New York *Age*, Nov. 12, 1927, 7.

19. A. Walter Kramer, "Negroes Perform Their Own Music," *Musical America*, Mar. 21, 1914, 37.

20. See, for example, "Kitty Cheatham's Recital—H. T. Burleigh, Negro Composer, Joins Her in Singing Plantation Songs," New York *Times*, Apr. 18, 1911, 11; "Kitty Cheatham's Recital—American Singer Heard in Negro Songs and Stories," New York *Times*, Apr. 9, 1912, 22.

21. R. Nathaniel Dett, "The Emancipation of Negro Music," *Southern Workman*, Apr. 1918, 172.

22. Sandra Graham, "Reframing Spirituals in the Late Nineteenth Century," in *Music, American Made: Essays in Honor of John Graziano.*, ed. John Koegel (Sterling Heights, MI: Harmonie Park Press, 2011), 603–37.

23. Jean E. Snyder, "Harry T. Burleigh and the Creative Expression of Bi-Musicality: A Study of an African-American Composer and the American Art Song," Ph.D. diss., University of Pittsburgh, 1992, 309–11.

24. Burleigh's 1903 performances included seven spirituals, three of which were published more than a decade later: "Hard Trials," 1919; "I Don't Feel No-Ways Tired," 1917; "Swing Low, Sweet Chariot," 1917; and two that were not published: "Gwine to Ride Up in de Chariot," and "King of Kings." "I Doan Want Fu' t' Stay Hyeah No Longah" and "Joshua Fit de Battle ob Jericho" were published in *Plantation Melodies Old and New* (1901).

25. Snyder, "Harry T. Burleigh," 312.

26. Eileen Southern, *The Music of Black Americans: A History*, 2nd ed. (New York: W. W. Norton, 1983), 268.

27. "New Music—Vocal and Instrumental," *Musical America*, 1916, 20.

28. "Folk Song Recital," New York *Age*, Dec. 17, 1914, 6.

29. John Blacking, *A Commonsense View of All Music: Reflections on Percy Grainger's Contribution to Ethnomusicology and Music Education* (Cambridge, England: Cambridge University Press, 1987), 1.

30. "Kitty Cheatham's Recital—H. T. Burleigh Negro Composer, Joins Her."

31. Advertisement, New York *Age*, Apr. 25, 1912, 7; "Greatest Event of the Season," advertisement, New York *Age*, Apr. 18, 1912, 6; "To Be a Big Musical Event," New York *Age*, Apr. 25, 1912, 6; "Music and Art," *Crisis*, Apr. 1914, 267; "Concert of Negro Music," New York *Times*, Mar. 1, 1914, 13.

32. See, for example, "Alma Gluck Welcomed," New York *Times*, Feb. 10, 1918, 13; "Arts and Leisure: Brooklyn Music," New York *Times*, Apr. 14, 1918, X5; "Concerts of a Day,"

New York *Times*, Feb. 10, 1919, 11; "Royal Dadmun, Baritone, Returns," New York *Times,* "Amusements," Apr. 2, 1925, 24.

33. Francis Rogers, "Songs the Soldiers Like," *Musical Courier,* Oct. 3, 1918, cited in Anne Key Simpson, *Hard Trials: The Life and Music of Harry T. Burleigh* (Metuchen, NJ: Scarecrow Press, 1990), 93.

34. *Southern Workman,* Nov. 1918, 522; I am indebted to Sandra Graham who has examined the songsters the soldiers used.

35. "Recognition of Negro Music," *Southern Workman,* 49 (Jan. 1920): 6.

36. *Musical America,* July 24, 1914, 6.

37. Simpson, *Hard Trials,* 81.

38. Snyder, "Harry T. Burleigh," 320–21.

39. Quoted in Ricordi advertisement, *Musical America,* Jan. 6, 1917.

40. *Musical America,* Feb. 10, 1917.

41. Hiram K. Moderwell, "'Deep River' Popularizes a Composer," Boston *Evening Transcript,* Mar. 10, 1917, reprinted in *The Black Perspective in Music* 2 (Spring 1975): 75–79.

42. See, for example, *Musical America,* Mar. 31, 1917, 36.

43. Snyder, "Harry T. Burleigh," 322.

44. Moderwell, "'Deep River' Popularizes a Composer."

45. "Seagle Sings at Wells Graduation," *Musical America,* June 30, 1917, 37; "Christine Miller's Art Arouses Joy in Uniontown (Pa.) Concert," *Musical America,* Feb. 17, 1917, 21.

46. Lester A. Walton, "Negro Spiritual Rendition Stirs Up Big Composers War," New York *World,* reprinted in Pittsburgh *Courier,* Oct. 25, 1924, 11; William Francis Allen, Charles Pickard Ward, and Lucy McKim Garrison, *Slave Songs of the United States* (New York: A. Simpson, 1867); B. T. Marsh, *The Story of the Jubilee Singers* (Cleveland: The Cleveland Printing and Publishing Co., 1892), 230.

47. William Arms Fisher, *Seventy Negro Spirituals* (Boston: Oliver Ditson, 1926), xxv.

48. Thanks to Wayne Shirley, formerly of the Library of Congress, for alerting me to the second 1916 edition and for supplying copies of the three versions.

49. Moderwell, "'Deep River' Popularizes a Composer."

50. A. Walter Kramer, *Musical America,* Jan. 20, 1917, 34.

51. Wayne Shirley has studied the progression in "The Coming of 'Deep River,'" *American Music,* 15, no. 4 (Winter 1997): 493–534.

52. A. Walter Kramer, *Musical America,* Feb. 10, 1917, 40.

53. A. Walter Kramer, *Musical America,* Apr. 14, 1917, 30.

54. "Music and Art," *Crisis,* Dec. 1917, 85.

55. *Musical America,* Apr. 14, 1917.

56. Simpson, *Hard Trials,* 354.

57. Oscar Seagle, "The Negro Spiritual," *Musical Courier,* May 24, 1917, 36; quoted in Simpson, *Hard Trials,* 355.

58. Simpson, *Hard Trials,* 356.

59. M., *Musical America,* Apr. 14, 1917, 36; Seagle, "Negro Spiritual."

60. Seagle, "Negro Spiritual"; John Lovell Jr., *Black Song: The Forge and the Flame* (New York: Macmillan, 1972), 442.

61. Southern, *Music of Black Americans,* 271.

62. Fisher, *Seventy Negro Spirituals,* xxii, xxiii.

63. Carrie Jacobs-Bond, *Old Melodies of the South*; David Guion, *Darkey Spirituals*; Mitchell Humphrey, "Stay in the Field, Warrior" (New York: G. Schirmer, 1918); John Alden Carpenter, "The Lawd Is Smilin' Thro' the Do.'"

64. James Weldon Johnson, *The Book of American Negro Spirituals* (New York: Viking Press, 1925), 48.

65. "Burleigh Gets Ovation," New York *Age*, Dec. 22, 1917, 6.

66. Ellsworth Janifer, "Harry T. Burleigh, Ten Years Later," *Phylon,* 21, no. 2 (1960): 150.

67. H. L. Mencken, "The Hoe-Down Begins to Soar," unidentified newspaper, Nov. 1917, Burleigh Family Papers.

68. Lucien H. White, "In the Realm of Music: Henry T. Finck Says China Needs a Harry T. Burleigh," New York *Age,* July 30, 1921, 5.

69. "A Negro Musician Honored," *Southern Workman,* Apr. 1924, 197.

70. Johnson, *American Negro Spirituals*, 48.

71. R.A.S., "Music," *New Yorker,* Jan. 16, 1926, 21.

72. *Pittsburgh Musical Forecast,* Apr. 1929, 2; see also Philadelphia *Tribune,* Aug. 5, 1928.

73. "Programs of the Week," New York *Times,* Apr. 7, 1918, "Fashions," 65; "Harry T. Burleigh and C. Cameron White Appear in Concert," Philadelphia *Tribune,* June 15, 1918, 3; Olin Downes, "Music," New York *Times,* Dec. 12, 1914, "Amusements," 28; "Harry Burleigh to Sing at Town Hall," Pittsburgh *Courier,* Dec. 13, 1924, 10; Cora Gary Illidge, "Music and Drama," Chicago *Defender,* Mar. 19, 1927, 11; "Burleigh to Sing in Princeton," New York *Times,* Feb. 24, 1929, 26; "Harry T. Burleigh Heads Howard University Concert," *New Journal and Guide,* Jan. 26, 1932, 3; "Harry Burleigh Gives Address on Spirituals," Chicago *Defender,* May 20, 1933; *Vineyard Gazette,* Jan. 1, 1939, quoted in Simpson, *Hard Trials,* 133–34.

74. HTB letter to BTW, Oct. 22, 1904, Booker T. Washington Papers, "Part I: Personal Correspondence, 1880–1916," Box 8, Reel 7, LOC.

75. New York *World,* Oct. 24, 1924, quoted in Southern, *Music of Black Americans,* 268.

76. Patricia Turner, *Dictionary of Afro-American Performers: 78 RPM and Cylinder Recordings of Opera, Choral Music, and Song, c. 1900–1949* (New York: Garland Press, 1990), 91–102.

77. "Go Down, Moses," *Paul Robeson: The Complete EMI Sessions, 1928–1939,* EMI Classics, Disc 2.

78. Lucien H. White, "In the Realm of Music: 'From Bach to Burleigh!'" New York *Age,* Nov. 12, 1927, 6.

79. Thomas P. Fenner, "Preface to Music," in *Cabin and Plantation Songs; as Sung by the Hampton Students* (New York: G. P. Putnam's Sons, 1874).

80. H. T. Burleigh, letter to the NAACP, Nov. 10, 1922, Burleigh Family Papers.

81. "Big Crowd Hears Burleigh Sing," Baltimore *Afro-American,* June 16, 1917, Hampton Archives, Hampton University, Hampton, Virginia.

82. Lucien H. White, "In the Realm of Music: Negro Music A Distinctive Racial Emanation, Despite Objections of Prejudiced," New York *Age,* Jan. 1924, 6; Epstein, "White Origin," 57; Johnson, *Folk Culture* (Chapel Hill: University of North Carolina Press, 1930); George Pullen Jackson, "The Genesis of the Negro Spiritual," in *American Mercury,* 1932.

83. George Pullen Jackson, "Genesis," *American Mercury* 26 (June 1932): 243–49.

84. Epstein, "White Origin," 58–59.

85. Burleigh, "The Negro and His Song," 186.

86. Transcript in Burleigh Family Papers.

87. Krehbiel, *Afro-American Folksongs*, ix.

88. "Appeal of Douglass," Chicago *Daily Tribune*, Aug. 26, 1893; see ch. 6, p. 150.

89. Melville Herskovitz, *The Myth of The Negro Past* (Boston: Beacon Press, 1941).

90. Burleigh, "The Negro in Music."

91. Burleigh, "The Negro and His Song," 186; "Story of the Song" (Burleigh interview on WABC), Mar. 28, 1939, 1, Burleigh Family Papers.

92. Burleigh, "The Negro and His Song," 186.

93. John Tasker Howard, *Our American Music: Three Hundred Years of It*, 3rd ed. (New York: Thomas Y. Crowell, 1954), 625.

94. "Story of the Song," Radio Interview, WABC, Mar. 28, 1939. Transcript in Burleigh Family Papers.

95. Lucien H. White, "In the Realm of Music: American Tenor's Program as Sung before English Royalty," New York *Age,* May 21, 1921, 5.

96. Natalie Burlin, *Negro Folk-Songs: The Hampton Series, Books 1–4, Complete* (Mineola, NY: Dover, 2001), 42.

97. Lucien H. White, "In the Realm of Music: Full-Blooded African Is Talented Musician, with Great Gift for Composing," New York *Age*, Dec. 22, 1923, 6.

98. Nicholas Ballanta-Taylor, *St. Helena Island Spirituals, Recorded and Transcribed at Penn Normal, Industrial and Agricultural School, St. Helena Island, Beaufort County, South Carolina* (New York: Institute of Musical Art, 1924).

99. R. Nathaniel Dett, "Review of *St. Helena Island Spirituals*," *Southern Workman*, Nov. 1925, 527; see also Lucien H. White, "In the Realm of Music: Ballanta-Taylor, Young West African Student of Music, Returns Home," New York *Age*, Aug. 16, 1924, 7; Lucien H. White, "In the Realm of Music: Ballanta-Taylor Returns to Africa for Musical Research among Natives," New York *Age*, Sept. 13, 1924, 7.

100. Lucien H. White, "In the Realm of Music: Full-Blooded African," New York *Age*, Dec. 22, 1923, 6.

101. "Some Pertinent Points Concerning Negro Spirituals," *Music Journal* 2, no. 6 (Nov.–Dec. 1944), 2, 6.

102. Lucien H. White, "'From Bach to Burleigh!'" New York *Age,* Nov. 12, 1927, 7.

103. "'Sing Spirituals in the Church,' Burleigh Urges," *New York Herald Tribune*, June 12, 1935; *Musical America,* Apr. 12, 1924, 27.

104. A. Walter Kramer, "New Music Vocal and Instrumental," *Musical America*, Nov. 30, 1918, 24.

105. Joan Foster, "The Negro Spirituals—Fad or Folk Music?" *Musical Digest* (Apr. 1928): 16–17, 34.

106. Worcester *Daily Telegram*, Sept. 14, 1934.

107. "New York Church Pays Tribute to Burleigh," *Musical America*, Apr. 12, 1924, 21.

108. Burlin, *Negro Folk-Songs*, bk. 1, vii.

109. Lester A. Walton, "Harry T. Burleigh Honored To-Day at St. George's: In Retrospect," *Black Perspective in Music* 2, no. 1 (Spring 1974): 83.

110. "Harry Burleigh Gives Address on Spirituals," Chicago *Defender,* May 20, 1933; "Sing Spirituals in the Church," New York *Herald Tribune,* Mar. 30, 1924.

111. Marien Dieterman, "Great Revival of Music after War Seen by Harry T. Burleigh," Erie *Daily Herald,* June 9, 1944, 1.

112. Foster, "Negro Spirituals," 34.

113. Tibbetts, letter to HTB, Jan. 31, 1933, Burleigh Family Papers; see Lucien H. White, "Emperor Jones Is Not Racial But a Symbolic Study of Fear," New York *Age,* Nov. 25, 1922, 6.

114. W. C. Handy, *Father of the Blues: An Autobiography* (New York: Macmillan, 1941), 157.

115. Burleigh, "The Negro in Music," 3.

116. Harry T. Burleigh II, personal communication, Pittsburgh, PA, Mar. 23, 1991.

117. *Musical America,* Apr. 12, 1924, 27; Foster, "Negro Spirituals."

118. Lucien H. White, "In the Realm of Music," "Desecration of 'Deep River,'" New York *Age,* July 8, 1922, 5.

119. Lucien H. White, "In the Realm of Music: The Negro Spiritual's Place," New York *Age,* July 22, 1922, 5. Concern for the misuse of spirituals was often expressed in the black press: Lucien H. White, "An Unnecessary Desecration of Negro Spirituals by Men Singers at Colonial Theatre," New York *Age,* Nov. 15, 1924, 7; George A. Webb, "The Profanation of Negro Spirituals," *Opportunity,* June 1928, 182; and editorials by Elmer Anderson Carter, "The Misuse of Spirituals," *Opportunity,* Oct. 1929, 303.

120. Letter to the NAACP, Nov. 10, 1922, Burleigh Family Papers, 1.

121. Ibid.

Chapter 17. Burleigh Spirituals and the Harlem Renaissance

1. James Weldon Johnson, *Along This Way: The Autobiography of James Weldon Johnson* (1933; repr., New York: Viking Press, 1968), 173.

2. Langston Hughes, "The Negro Artist and the Racial Mountain," *The Nation,* June 23, 1926, 694.

3. Lucien H. White, "In the Realm of Music: Large Sunday Night Audience Greets New Amsterdam Players," New York *Age,* Feb. 12, 1921, 5; "Lloyd Hickman, Baritone, to Sing at Chickering Hall," New York *Age,* Feb. 21, 1925, 6; Lucien H. White, "In the Realm of Music: Program of Spirituals," New York *Age,* Nov. 21, 1925, 7.

4. Lucien H. White, "In the Realm of Music: Mrs. Hare's Folksong Lecture Recital," New York *Age,* Feb. 28, 1920, 6; Lucien H. White, "In the Realm of Music: 'Three Periods of Negro Music and Drama' at Town Hall Sunday," New York *Age,* Apr. 30, 1921, 5; Lucien H. White, "In the Realm of Music: Fine Tribute to Charm and Worth of Negro Spirituals," New York *Age,* Mar. 10, 1923, 6.

5. Jeffrey P. Green, "Roland Hayes in London, 1921," *The Black Perspective in Music* (Spring 1982): 33.

6. For example, "Negroes Gave a Rare Exhibition of Singing," New York *Age,* July 21, 1923, 6.

7. Olin Downes, "Roland Hayes Impresses Boston Symphony Audience with His Musicianship," Nov. 17, 1923, in *Olin Downes on Music: A Selection from His Writing during the Half-Century 1906 to 1955,* ed. Irene Downes (New York: Simon and Schuster, 1957), 75.

8. Quoted in R. Nathaniel Dett, "Hampton and Roland Hayes," *Southern Workman,* Feb. 1924, 55.

9. Alain Locke, *The New Negro: An Interpretation* (New York: Albert and Charles Boni, 1925), 207.

10. Hiram K. Moderwell, "'Deep River' Popularizes a Composer," Boston *Evening Transcript,* Mar. 10, 1917, reprinted in *The Black Perspective in Music,* Spring 1975, 77.

11. Krehbiel quoted in *Southern Workman,* Jan. 1920, 6.

12. John Tasker Howard, *Our American Music: Three Hundred Years of It,* 3rd ed. (New York: Thomas Y. Crowell, 1954), 587.

13. Carl Van Vechten, "Folksong of the American Negro," *Vanity Fair,* July 1925, as cited in *'Keep a-Inchin' Along'; Selected Writings of Carl Van Vechten,* ed. Bruce Kellner (Westport, CT: Greenwood Press, 1979), 38.

14. Ibid., 38, 39.

15. Ibid., 38.

16. David Levering Lewis, *When Harlem Was in Vogue* (New York: Oxford University Press, 1979), 151–55.

17. New York *Herald Tribune,* June 12, 1935.

18. Lewis, *When Harlem Was in Vogue,* 151–55.

19. Van Vechten, "Folksong of the American Negro," 39.

20. Brian Moon, "Harry Burleigh as Ethnomusicologist?" *Black Music Research Journal,* 24, no. 2 (Autumn 2004): 287.

21. Zora Neale Hurston, "Spirituals and Neo-Spirituals," in *Negro: An Anthology,* ed. Nancy Cunard (New York: Frederick Ungar, 1934), 224.

22. See Locke to William Grant Still, ca. Feb. 14, 1933, and Nov. 14, 1941; also HTB to Locke, June 24, 1908, Alain Locke Papers, Moorland-Spingarn Research Center, Box 19, folder 8.

23. Alain Locke, "The Negro Spirituals," 199, 201–2.

24. Ibid., 207–8.

25. Alain Locke, "Toward a Critique of Negro Music," *Opportunity,* 12, no. 12 (Nov.–Dec., 1934): 328.

26. Ibid., 366.

27. Hurston, "Spirituals and Neo-Spirituals," 224.

28. Ibid.

29. Ibid.

30. Jean E. Snyder, "'A Great and Noble School of Music': Dvořák, Harry T. Burleigh, and the African American Spiritual," in *Dvořák in America, 1892–1895,* ed. John C. Tibbetts (Portland, OR: Amadeus Press, 1993), 137.

31. New World Records 247, 1976.

32. Jean E. Snyder, "Harry T. Burleigh and the Creative Expression of Bi-Musicality: A Study of an African-American Composer and the American Art Song," Ph.D. diss., University of Pittsburgh, 1992, 409–10.

33. Jon Michael Spencer, *The New Negroes and Their Music: The Success of the Harlem Renaissance* (Knoxville: University of Tennessee Press, 1997), 23–25.

34. Olly Wilson, "Interpreting Classical Music," in *African American Music: An Introduction,* ed. Mellonee V. Burnim and Portia K. Maultsby (New York: Routledge, 2006), 236–37.

35. Ibid.

36. Ibid., 237.

37. James Weldon Johnson and J. Rosamond Johnson, *The Book of the American Negro Spirituals* (New York: Viking Press, 1925), 46.

38. Johnson and Johnson, *American Negro Spirituals.*

39. Ibid., 37.

40. Martin Bauml Duberman, *Paul Robeson* (New York: Alfred A. Knopf, 1988), 594, n. 34.

41. Reprinted in New York *Age,* Oct. 8, 1925, 7.

42. Van Vechten, "Folksong of the American Negro," 39.

43. Reprinted in New York *Age,* Oct. 24, 1925, 7.

44. Lucien H. White, "In the Realm of Music: Perpetuation of American Negro Music through Sympathetic Work of Qualified, Talented, Skilled Musicians of Race," New York *Age,* Oct. 24, 1925, 7.

45. R. Nathaniel Dett, "Review of *The Book of American Negro Spirituals,*" *Southern Workman* 54 (Dec. 1925): 563–65.

46. James Weldon Johnson, Preface to *The Second Book of Negro Spirituals,* ed. James Weldon Johnson, musical arrangements by J. Rosamond Johnson (New York: Viking Press, 1926), 19.

47. Dorothy G. Bolton, *Old Songs Hymnal: Words and Melodies from the State of Georgia,* collected by D. G. Bolton. Music Arranged by H. T. Burleigh. (New York: Century, 1929), v.

48. Ibid.

49. "New York Church Pays Tribute to Burleigh," *Musical America,* Apr. 12, 1924, 27.

50. HTB to the NAACP, November 10, 1922, Burleigh Family Papers.

51. Harry T. Burleigh, "The Negro and His Song," in *Music on the Air,* ed. Hazel Kinscella (New York: Viking Press, 1934), 187.

52. "Crowds at Church Honor Negro Singer," New York *Times,* Mar. 31, 1924.

53. "'Sweet Chariot' Inspired Anton Dvorak to Immortalize Negro Spirituals," New York *World Telegram,* Sept. 12, 1941.

Chapter 18. *The Impact of a Life*

1. Anne Key Simpson, *Hard Trials: The Life and Music of Harry T. Burleigh* (Metuchen, NJ: Scarecrow Press, 1990), 203; Grace Blackwell, telephone conversation, June 9, 2004, Jan. 1, 2011.

2. "Network Broadcast Honor Negro Song-Composer-Singer," Atlanta *Daily World,* Apr. 16, 1947, 2.

3. New York *Amsterdam News,* Dec. 21, 1947.

4. Nora Douglas Holt, "Music: Howard University Choir Gives Concert for Burleigh," New York *Amsterdam News,* Apr. 3, 1948.

5. Ibid.

6. Ibid.

7. Charlotte Murray, letter to Alston Burleigh, Apr. 8, 1949, Burleigh Family Papers.

8. Clifford D. Moore, M.D., medical director, Stamford Hall, Stamford, Conn., to Alston Burleigh, Sept. 8, 1949, Burleigh Family Papers.

9. James L. Hicks, "Millionaires, Plain People Mourn at Burleigh's Rites," Norfolk *Journal and Guide,* Sept. 24, 1949, 1, 2.

10. "Harry Thacker Burleigh," New York *Herald-Tribune,* Sept. 14, 1949.

11. Atlanta *Daily World,* Sept. 14, 1949.

12. Washington *Evening Star,* Sept. 15, 1949, A-18.

13. Anne Key Simpson, *Hard Trials: The Life and Music of Harry T. Burleigh* (Metuchen, NJ: Scarecrow Press, 1990), 153.

14. Louise Alston Burleigh letter to Alston Burleigh, Jan. 15, 1950; Alston Burleigh letter to Louise Alston Burleigh, Feb. 15, 1950; letter to P. N. [Princess Nadonis] Shawa [Louise Alston Burleigh] from Attorney James M. Vaughn, Aug. 9, 1950, Burleigh Family Papers.

15. "Burleigh Leaves $250,000 Estate," *Pittsburgh Courier*, Oct. 1, 1949, 1; "Family Contests Composer's Will," New York *Times*, Apr. 7, 1950; "H. T. Burleigh's Fight Dropped after 8 Hours," New York *Amsterdam News*, Apr. 15, 1950, 1.

16. Deborah Spilko, "The Harry T. Burleigh Memorial Center: Composing a Tribute to Erie's Own," Erie *Times News*, Feb. 10, 1991.

17. Victoria Fabrizio, "Famous Composer Returning Home to Erie," Erie *Daily Times*, May 5, 1994, 14A and B; Karen Carpenedo, "Burleigh Service Special for Ada Lawrence," Erie *Daily Times*, May 27, 1994, 2A and B.

18. Details of these events can be found on my website, *Friends of Harry T. Burleigh*.

19. David Levering Lewis, *When Harlem Was in Vogue* (New York: Alfred A. Knopf, 1891), 119ff.

20. Rawn Wardell Spearman Sr., "Vocal Music in the Harlem Renaissance," in *Black Music in the Harlem Renaissance*, ed. Samuel A. Floyd Jr. (Westport, CT: Greenwood Press, 1990), 43.

21. James Weldon Johnson, *Along This Way: The Autobiography of James Weldon Johnson* (1933; repr., New York: Viking, 1968), 172–75.

22. *The Cheyney Record,* Dec. 1922, 1, as cited in Simpson, *Hard Trials,* 291.

23. Harry T. Burleigh, "The Negro in Music," address to the NAACP at Philadelphia, NAACP, *Fifteenth Annual Report* (Baltimore, MD: Author, 1917), 45, http://mdhistory.net/naacp/1910_1927_annual_reports/pdf/msa_sc5458_000045_000517-0356.pdf, July 1, 1924, 1, Burleigh Family Papers.

24. Barbara Hawley, "Burleigh: He Attributes His Success to Three Sources," Erie *Daily Herald*, Mar. 11, 1928, 1.

25. Nov. 10, 1922, 2, Burleigh Family Papers.

26. Nathan Huggins, *Harlem Renaissance* (New York: Oxford University Press, 1971), 5.

27. Burleigh, "Negro in Music."

28. James Weldon Johnson, *The Second Book of Negro Spirituals* (1926), 19.

29. Johnson, *Second Book of Negro Spirituals*, 17.

30. Natalie Curtis Burlin, *Negro Folk-Songs, The Hampton Series, Books 1–4, Complete* (Mineola, NY: Dover, 2001), 127–28.

31. Ibid.

32. Ibid., 128.

33. Samuel A. Floyd Jr., ed. *Black Music in the Harlem Renaissance* (Knoxville: University of Tennessee Press, 1993), 3.

34. Ibid.

35. Jon Michael Spencer, *The New Negroes and Their Music: The Success of the Harlem Renaissance* (Knoxville: University of Tennessee Press, 1997), xix; Martin Blum, "Black Music: Pathbreaker of the Harlem Renaissance," *Missouri Journal of Research in Music Education,* 3, no. 3, 1974, 75.

36. Marva Carter, *Swing Along: The Musical Life of Will Marion Cook* (New York: Oxford University Press, 2008), 31.

Index

Ethnomusicologist JEAN E. SNYDER has taught in Kenya and Zambia, and at several colleges and universities in western Pennsylvania.

Music in American Life

One Woman in a Hundred: Edna Phillips and the Philadelphia Orchestra
    Mary Sue Welsh
The Great Orchestrator: Arthur Judson and American Arts Management
    James M. Doering
Charles Ives in the Mirror: American Histories of an Iconic Composer   *David C. Paul*
Southern Soul-Blues   *David Whiteis*
Sweet Air: Modernism, Regionalism, and American Popular Song
    Edward P. Comentale
Pretty Good for a Girl: Women in Bluegrass   *Murphy Hicks Henry*
Sweet Dreams: The World of Patsy Cline   *Warren R. Hofstra*
William Sidney Mount and the Creolization of American Culture   *Christopher J. Smith*
Bird: The Life and Music of Charlie Parker   *Chuck Haddix*
Making the March King: John Philip Sousa's Washington Years, 1854–1893
    Patrick Warfield
In It for the Long Run   *Jim Rooney*
Pioneers of the Blues Revival   *Steve Cushing*
Roots of the Revival: American and British Folk Music in the 1950s   *Ronald D. Cohen
    and Rachel Clare Donaldson*
Blues All Day Long: The Jimmy Rogers Story   *Wayne Everett Goins*
Yankee Twang: Country and Western Music in New England   *Clifford R. Murphy*
The Music of the Stanley Brothers   *Gary B. Reid*
Hawaiian Music in Motion: Mariners, Missionaries, and Minstrels   *James Revell Carr*
Sounds of the New Deal: The Federal Music Project in the West   *Peter Gough*
The Mormon Tabernacle Choir: A Biography   *Michael Hicks*
The Man That Got Away: The Life and Songs of Harold Arlen   *Walter Rimler*
A City Called Heaven: Chicago and the Birth of Gospel Music   *Robert M. Marovich*
Blues Unlimited: Essential Interviews from the Original Blues Magazine   *Edited by
    Bill Greensmith, Mike Rowe, and Mark Camarigg*
Hoedowns, Reels, and Frolics: Roots and Branches of Southern Appalachian Dance
    Phil Jamison
Fannie Bloomfield-Zeisler: The Life and Times of a Piano Virtuoso
    Beth Abelson Macleod
Cybersonic Arts: Adventures in American New Music   *Gordon Mumma, edited with
    commentary by Michelle Fillion*
The Magic of Beverly Sills   *Nancy Guy*
Waiting for Buddy Guy   *Alan Harper*
Harry T. Burleigh: From the Spiritual to the Harlem Renaissance   *Jean E. Snyder*

The University of Illinois Press
is a founding member of the
Association of American University Presses.

––

Composed in 10.5/13 Adobe Minion Pro
by Kirsten Dennison
at the University of Illinois Press
Manufactured by Sheridan Books, Inc.

University of Illinois Press
1325 South Oak Street
Champaign, IL 61820-6903
www.press.uillinois.edu